Myths and
Folktales from
Around the World

Myths and Folktales from Around the World

(Original title: *Supernatural Tales from Around the World*)

Edited by

Terri Hardin

BARNES
&NOBLE
BOOKS
NEW YORK

Originally published as *Supernatural Tales from Around the World*

Book design by Charles Ziga, Ziga Design

ISBN 0-7607-3463-1

Printed and bound in the United States of America

02 03 04 05 M 9 8 7 6 5 4 3 2 1

RRD-H

TO LEE SERVER

Contents

Part II   Tales from Africa & the Near East

Part III Tales from Asia & the Pacific

Introduction

When night falls, the creatures of darkness spread malignant wings over the imagination. Flying witches and harrowing demons hover in the upper air, and shadows conceal ghouls and goblins with deadly intentions — or so it seems. In the absence of light, how many of us have trembled, believing ourselves to be in the presence of the unseen and unknown?

Belief in the existence of the phantoms of the night — demons, ghosts, poltergeists, vampires, and witches — and in the efficacy of magic is practically universal. *Myths and Folktales from Around the World* brings together the most thrilling tales of demons and sorcery. On nearly every continent one finds blood-curdling accounts of ghouls who assume human or animal shape so they can prey on the unwitting; of ghosts who not only guard their own graveyards, but haunt the scenes of terrible passions; and of witches who change themselves into animal or spectral form so that they may conduct ancient, frightful rites with the help of their familiars.

Do we only imagine these terrifying creatures, or do they really exist? While some seem to be of supernatural power, others are definitely of human making. They are made by our fears, jealousies, and desires. For this reason, one should not seek wholesale explanations of these matters.

When seeking to solve the mysteries of the supernatural world, one should keep an open mind and try not to force explanations. Standard "solutions" for supernatural phenomena range from mass hysteria to ergot poisoning (a type of bread mold that is supposed to have a hallucinatory effect). Skeptics also point to diseases such as anemia and consumption to explain vampirism. Through these analyses can be found some, but not all, reasons for the phenomena presented in this book. Rationalizations such as these, glibly applied, can often be as unsatisfying as the mystery on which they purport to shed light.

While their actual existence may be disputed, most religions acknowledge a multitude of supernatural beings; and science, in the study of unexplained phenomena, has not been able to conclusively disprove their existence. There have also been enough eyewitness accounts of demonic possession and similar acts throughout the ages to admit or allow the probability of their having occurred.

Ghost sightings in particular are plentiful through the world. Ghosts provide a link between this life and the next, however that may be configured by various religions. Many superstitions are attached to graveyards and to the final containment of mortal remains, the violation of which is almost certain to bring on spectral visitation. Of special note, however, are hauntings inspired by guilty acts such as murder and other crimes. Passions such as hatred may also play a part, as in the story of Old Kate, the Bell Witch, where the spirit of a spiteful crone continued to plague a family long after her own death.

It is possible to be haunted by more than ghosts; demons and supernatural beings also torment. Banshees, those frightening Irish specters, will follow the fortunes of certain families, and announce a member's fate by piercing shrieks. In India, the sight of a "Bijli" demon is almost certain death. In Japan, the sighting of certain demons, called "female ghosts," is considered a baleful occurrence. Phantoms that appear in the form of animals also spell death. These "were-animals" seek to ensnare humans, whom they either kill or use for ghastly purposes. Were-animals are also common elsewhere, most notably in Europe in the form of the werewolf.

Vampires and other blood-sucking demons, tales of which fascinate the modern, popular imagination, have inspired terror and panic throughout history. The region that is home to Count Dracula, Eastern Europe, is rich in vampire lore; however, the normal run of vampire outbreaks, while frightening enough, have somewhat less cosmopolitan appeal than the legendary Count. Typical stories concern peasants who unaccountably turn into blood-thirsty ghouls, preying on their own families and fellow villagers until they are recognized for what they are and swiftly dispatched. In China and Japan, vampires appear as blood-sucking ghosts, rather than the half-dead ghouls traditional to European legend.

In the West, the Church has turned the common belief in devils and other malevolent beings to its own advantage. In medieval Europe, for example, images of demons and their woeful victims were carved into the stone portals of churches. It is likely that these sculptures, which were intended to awe the local congregation into righteous observation, also vicariously titillated. Sometimes they even had the effect of winning converts to Satan and his hellspawn. These followers would honor Satan in secret rites, finding the powers conferred by dark worship to be irresistible.

Historically, witchcraft has been both an abomination and a way of life. Sought for their skills and condemned for their rituals, practitioners of magic have at best endured an uneasy peace among the rest of society. Some of the great magicians of Europe, which include Nostradamus and Cagliostro, were frequently on call to royalty. Necromancers, like their spiritual cousins, the fortune-tellers and psychics, were often shunned in public, but nonetheless managed to endure and even thrive in private.

The most notorious form of magic is necromancy, or "black magic." Black magicians attempt to harness and command unseen forces for extreme personal gain or for vengeance. To these ends they are seemingly willing to make great sacrifices: they summon and pledge themselves to demons, they make themselves baleful by calling down curses, and they traffic in rites that set them apart from the rest of society. One might say that black magic is the physical, tangible expression of greed and envy. Since these are consuming passions, witchcraft has never failed to awaken the strongest emotions. Those suspected of wielding magical powers are either revered or mercilessly punished. There are many tales of powerful witches and their unholy acts, of which the account of Urbain Grandier is but one.

Another disturbing and scandalous story of witchcraft occurred in the New World, in Salem, Massachusetts. Most of us are familiar with the circumstances of the famous witch-hunt, where members of the tiny, struggling community of Puritans believed themselves to be personally challenged by Satan, and sought to harrow themselves by hanging several unfortunates who could not defend themselves against the charges of witchcraft. Reading the account of Bridget Bishop, one may grasp how real to the people of Salem the phantoms that plagued them were. Even so, not everybody, at the time or since, believed that there were witches in Salem. Some

believe that a form of hysteria carried the community away in an outbreak of bloodlust.

In fact, if one were to read all the accounts of witchcraft from all
over the world, one might be surprised how few actual blood-curdling tales there are, compared to the prosaic accounts having to do
with the destruction of private property. For example, many of the
stories that concern witchcraft have to do with the "witching" of livestock. A witch causes a cow to give curdled milk or a hen to cease laying. In some cases, witches accomplished these acts by taking the
form of a wolf or some other beast, and having been "caught" with
some evidence of this change upon them, are accused. When someone
gains an advantage over a neighbor, it may be attributed to witchcraft, and thus become a punishable offense. Thus, we may find
among the many accounts of witchcraft a common thread — accusations employed by neighbor against neighbor to settle grudges or to
weed out those considered "socially undesirable."

That does not mean that everyone accused of witchcraft is innocent.
Some are no doubt seeking the active destruction of their neighbors.
One of the most prevalent curses throughout the world is the "evil
eye." Practically every culture believes that harm can travel out of one
person's gaze and afflict the object of its attention. Some cultures, like
the Shilluks of the Near East, say that the evil eye may only be given
by those born to be witches; others say that anyone is capable of it.
Needless to say, there are many charms used to detect its presence
and ward off its evil power.

In fact, the making of charms, a form of magic, is the first line of
defense against magic. From the earliest times, people all over the
world have used charms and offerings, or have chanted verses to
guard themselves from the unseen world. Charmed objects might
make a West African feel safe from malicious spirits, while Christians
might uneasily finger a crucifix against the dreaded power of
demons. Charm making is a form of good, or "white magic." White
magic draws from a wealth of folk cures and — in the West — ancient,
pre-Christian beliefs. Like its infamous cousin, it seeks to influence
fate, but toward kindly ends, such as fair weather, fertility, or relief
from illness. Thus, white magic is generally considered benign.

Throughout most of the world, the monotheistic religions of
Judaism, Christianity, Islam, and Buddhism have supplanted the
beliefs that were native to each region, relegating local deities to mere

subordinate representations of good and evil. The good ones are considered "saints," or followers of the one God. As for the others, we of the West are most familiar with the fairy hosts of Celtic belief, the usual Christian "devils" transplanted from the Bible and its folklore, and the *djinns* or *genii* as are described in the *Thousand and One Nights*. Added to these are the hosts of deities which spring from the soil of the Americas, Africa, and Asia. Some people worship demons under the shadow of the new religion, because those spirits continue to be a part of their faith.

Examples of this hybrid of faith can be seen in three religions in the Caribbean, known as voodoo, Obeah, and Santeria. These religions appear to be an amalgam of the faiths of Europe, Africa, and the New World. Slave traders forcibly Christianized their human cargo, who in turn outwardly adopted the new religion while keeping their own beliefs and merging them with those of the New World natives. The combination resulted in powerful cults, which can be as terrifying and intriguing in reality as they are in legend.

Voodoo rites, some of which demand the shedding of animal blood, are conducted by a matriarch and patriarch, know as the Mamanloi and Papaloi. The secrecy, however, that was necessary for the religion's survival also provoked rumors of human sacrifice. The most famous, most terrifying type of black magic is that which calls for blood sacrifice. Belief in the efficacy of blood is one of the oldest and most widespread in the world. Because the blood of children is considered the most powerful, there are many repugnant stories concerning its quest. Stories of human sacrifice are revolting to modern sensibilities. Therefore, the claim that one of the tenets of Obeah or voodoo was the sacrifice of "the goat without horns," or child sacrifice, led to the denunciation of these religions and the call for their extinction. To this day, the taint of human sacrifice is attached to voodoo, despite passionate protests by voodoo followers.

Included with tales of powerful voodoo and Obeah deities of the Caribbean are stories about those people who claim demons as their servants and the Devil as their master. There are descriptions of how witchcraft was, and may still be, practiced on every continent—from England's lonely moors to the coasts of Africa, from the New World to the Far East. Also described are the many methods used throughout history to discover, catch, and punish witches.

Myths and Folktales is not a collection of fiction—all the stories found in this book should be considered true. In some cases, they are tenets of faith; in other cases, they are claimed as eyewitness accounts. As such, they belong to the realm of nonfiction. However, in many cases where material has been transcribed from lengthier texts, the stories in this volume have been edited for purposes of clarity and cohesiveness. It must fall to the individual reader to conclude what he or she will accept as the truth.

When Sir James Frazer, the celebrated author of *The Golden Bough*, wrote that demons were most real to the primitive mind, he chose, perhaps unconsciously, to ignore the increasing "civilized" enthusiasm for the supernatural, of which his famous work rode the crest. Whether they believe or not, readers will thrill to the stories found in *Myths and Legends from Around the World*. They may even make skeptics of the Devil and his dominion shudder on a moonless night!

—*Terri Hardin*

Part I

Tales from Europe

Demonic Possession of the Loudun Nuns

(France)

As regards the devils in the possessed, the church teaches us in its ritual that there are four principal signs by which it can be undoubtedly recognized. These signs are the speaking or understanding of a language unknown to the person possessed; the revelation of the future or events happening far away; the exhibition of strength beyond the years and the nature of the actor; and floating in the air for a few moments.

The church does not require, in order to have recourse to exorcisms, that all these marks should be found in the same subject; one alone, if well authenticated, is sufficient to demand public exorcism.

Now they are all to be found in the nuns of Loudun, and in such numbers that we can only mention the principal cases.

Acquaintance with unknown tongues first showed itself in the Mother Superior. At the beginning, she answered in Latin the questions of the ritual proposed to her in that language. Later, she and the others answered in any language they thought to be proper to question in.

M. de Launay de Razilli, who had lived in America, attested that, during a visit to Loudun, he had spoken to them in the language of a

From: Anon. [des Niau], *Collectanea Adamantaea.—xxi., The History of the Devils of Loudun, the Alleged Possession of the Ursuline Nuns, and Trials and Execution of Urbain Grandier, Told by an Eye-Witness* (trans. and ed. Edmund Goldsmith), 3 vols. (Edinburgh: privately printed, 1887).

certain savage tribe of that country and that they had answered quite correctly and had revealed to him events that had taken place there.

Some gentlemen of Normandy certified in writing that they had questioned Sister Clara de Sazilli in Turkish, Spanish, and Italian and that her answers were correct.

M. de Nismes, doctor of the Sorbonne, and one of the chaplains of the Cardinal de Lyon, having questioned them in Greek and German, was satisfied with their replies in both languages.

Father Vignier, Superior of the Oratory at La Rochelle, bears witness in his Latin narrative that, having questioned Sister Elizabeth a whole afternoon in Greek, she always replied correctly and obeyed in every particular.

The Bishop of Nîmes commanded Sister Clara in Greek to raise veil and kiss the railings at a certain spot; she obeyed and did many other things he ordered, which caused the prelate to exclaim that one must be an atheist or lunatic not to believe in "possession."

Some doctors questioned them also as to the meaning of some Greek technical terms, extremely difficult to explain and only known to the most learned men, and they clearly expressed the real signification of the words.

Lastly, Grandier himself being confronted with them, his Bishop invested him with the stole to exorcise the Mother Superior, who, he declared, knew Latin; but he did not dare to question her or the others in Greek, though they dared him to it, whereon he remained very embarrassed.

As to the revelation of hidden matters or of events passing afar off, proofs are still more abundant. We will only select a few of the most remarkable.

M. Morin, Prior of St. Jacques de Thouars, having requested M. de Morans, Commissioner appointed by the Bishop of Poitiers to watch over the possessed and to assist in the trial of Grandier, to allow some sign to be given proving actual infernal possession, whispered to M. de Morans that he wished one of the possessed to bring him five rose leaves. Sister Clara was then away in the refectory; M. de Morans ordered, in his thoughts, the demon who possessed her to obey the wish of M. Morin for the greater glory of God. Thereupon the nun left the refectory and went into the garden, whence she brought first a pansy and other plants and presented them with roars of laughter, saying to M. de Morans, "Is that what you wish, Father? I am not a devil, to guess your thoughts." To which he replied simply, *"Obedias"* (Obey). She then returned to the garden and, after several repetitions of the order, presented through the railings a little rose branch, on which were six leaves. The exorcist said to her, *"Obedias punctualiter sub paena maledictionis"* (Obey to the letter under penalty of malediction); she then plucked off one leaf and offered the branch, saying, "I see you will only have five; the other was one too many." The prior was so convinced by what he saw that he went out with tears in his eyes. An official report of the fact was drawn up.

Mme. de Laubardemontaise tried the same experiment in order to convince many skeptics who were present, and she was equally successful.

The Lieutenant-Criminel of Orleans, the President Tours, Lieutenant-General de S. Maixant, and myself also had our curiosity gratified. I desired that Sister Clara should bring me her beads and say an *Ave Maria*. She first brought a pin and then some aniseed; being urged to obey, she said, "I see you want something else," and then she brought me her beads and offered to say an *Ave Maria*.

M. Chiron, Prior of Maillezais, desiring to strengthen his belief in demoniacal possession, begged M. de Morans to allow him to whisper to a third party the sign he required; and he thereon whispered to M. de Fernaison, Canon and Provost of the same church, that he wished the nun to fetch a missal then lying near the door and to put her finger on the introit of the Mass of the Holy Virgin, beginning *"Salve, Sancta parens."* M. de Morans, who had heard nothing, ordered Sister Clara, who was likewise ignorant of what had been said, to obey the intentions of M. Chiron. This young girl then fell into strange convulsions, blaspheming, rolling on the ground, exposing her person in the most indecent manner, without a blush and with foul and lascivious expressions and actions, till she caused all who looked on to hide their eyes with shame. Though she had never seen the prior, she called him by his name and said he should be her lover. It was only after many repeated commands, and an hour's struggling, that she took up the missal, saying, "I will pray." Then, turning her eyes in another direction, she placed her finger on the capital *S* at the beginning of the introit aforesaid, of which reports were drawn up.

M. de Millière, a gentleman of Maine, certified that, being present at the exorcism of Sister Clara and on his knees, the devil asked him whether he was saying a *De Profundis* for his wife, which was the case.

The Marquis de la Mothé, son of M. de Parabel, Governor of Poitou, certified that Sister Louise de Nogeret had disclosed his most secret faults in the presence of Father Tranquille and Mme. de Neuillant, his aunt.

The same M. de la Mothé also asked an exorcist to make Sister Clara, who was in the convent, come out, kneel down, and say an *Ave Maria*; she came after repeated commands and obeyed.

Chevalier de Mère, who was present, asked the devil on what day he had last confessed. The devil answered Friday. The chevalier acknowledged this to be correct; whereupon Sister Clara withdrew. but as he wished to try the devil again, he begged the exorcist to make her return and whispered some words to the marquis and the monk for the nun to repeat. The exorcist refused, as the words were indecent. He changed them, therefore, into *Pater, et Filius et Spiritus Sanctus!* He whispered these words so low that the exorcist could hardly hear them. The nun, who was in another room, came at the command of the father and, addressing the chevalier, first said the indecent words the monk had refused and then repeated several times *Gloria patri et filio et Spiritui Sancto.* She was ordered to say the words exactly as she had been desired, but she said she would not.

The Bishop of Nîmes, being present at an exorcism by Father Surin, begged him to order something in difficult Latin; and the demon thereupon performed what was wanted.

A Jesuit, wishing to try what so many people stated they had experienced, gave an inward order to a demon who had been exorcised, and then immediately another. In the space of a second he gave five or six orders, which he countermanded one after another and thus tormented the devil, who was ordered to obey his intentions. The demon repeated his commands aloud, beginning by the first and adding, "But you won't," and when he had come to the last he said, "Now let's see whether we can do this."

"When it rained," says Father Surin, "the devil used to place the Mother Superior under the waterspout. As I knew this to be a habit of his, I commanded him mentally to bring her to me; whereupon she used to come and ask me, "What do you want?"

Another thing that struck the exorcist was the instantaneous answers they gave to the most difficult questions of theology, as to grace, the vision of God, angels, the incarnation, and similar subjects, always in the very terms used in the schools.

The corporeal effect of possession is a proof that strikes the coarsest minds. It has this other advantage, that an example convinces the whole assembly.

Now the nuns gave these proofs daily. When the exorcist gave some order to the devil, the nuns suddenly passed from a state of quiet into the most terrible convulsions and without the slightest increase of pulsation. They struck their chests and backs with their heads, as if they had had their necks broken and with inconceivable rapidity; they twisted their arms at the joints of the shoulder, elbow, and wrist two or three times around; lying on their stomachs, they joined the palms of their hands to the soles of their feet. Their faces became so frightful one could not bear to look at them; their eyes remained open without winking; their tongues issued suddenly from their mouths, horribly swollen, black, hard, and covered with pimples, and yet while in this state they spoke distinctly. They threw themselves back till their heads touched their feet, and they walked in this position with wonderful rapidity and for a long time. They uttered cries so horrible and so loud that nothing like it was ever heard before; they made use of expressions so indecent as to shame the most debauched of men, while their acts, both in exposing themselves and in inviting lewd behavior from those present, would have astonished the inmates of the lowest brothel in the country; they uttered maledictions against the three Divine Persons of the Trinity, oaths and blasphemous expressions to the execrable so unheard of that they could not have suggested themselves to the human mind. They used to watch without rest and fast five or six days at a time, or be tortured twice a day, as we have described, during several hours, without their health suffering; on the contrary, those that were somewhat delicate appeared healthier than before their possession.

The devil made them sometimes fall suddenly asleep: they fell to the ground and became so heavy that the strongest man had great trouble in even moving their heads. Within the body of Françoise Filestreau having her mouth closed, one could hear different voices speaking at the same time, quarreling and discussing who should make her speak.

Lastly, one often saw Elisabeth Blanchard, in her convulsions, with her feet in the air and her head on the ground, leaning against a chair or a windowsill without other support.

The Mother Superior from the beginning was carried off her feet and remained suspended in the air at the height of twenty-four inches.

A report of this was drawn up and sent to the Sorbonne, signed by a great number of witnesses, ecclesiastics, and doctors, and the judgment thereon of the Bishop of Poitiers, who was also a witness. The doctors of the Sorbonne were of the same opinion as the Bishop and declared that infernal possession was proved.

Both she and other nuns lying flat, without moving foot, hand, or body, were suddenly lifted to their feet like statues.

In another exorcism, the Mother Superior was suspended in air, only touching the ground with her elbow.

Others, when comatose, became supple like a thin piece of lead so that their bodies could be bent in every direction, forward, backward, or sideways, till their heads touched the ground; and they remained thus so long as their position was not altered by others.

At other times they passed their left feet over their shoulders to the cheek. They passed also their feet over their heads till the big toe touched the tip of the nose.

Others again were able to stretch their legs so far to the right and left that they sat on the ground without any space being visible between their bodies and the floor, their bodies erect and their hands joined.

One, the Mother Superior, stretched her legs to such an extraordinary extent that from toe to toe the distance was seven feet, though she herself was but four feet tall.

But sometime before the death of Grandier, this lady had a still stranger experience. In a few words this is what happened: In an exorcism the devil promised Father Lactance, as a sign of his exit, that he would make three wounds on the left side of the Mother Superior. He described their appearance and stated the day and hour when they would appear. He said he would come out from within, without affecting the nun's health, and forbade that any remedy should be applied, as the wounds would leave no mark.

On the day named, the exorcism took place; and as many doctors had come from the neighboring towns to be present at this event, M. de Laubardemont made them draw near and permitted them to examine the clothes of the nun, to uncover her side in the presence of the assembly, to look into all the folds of her dress, of her stays which were of whalebone, and of her chemise, to make sure there was no weapon; she had only about her her scissors, which were given over to another. M. de Laubardemont asked the doctors to tie her; but they begged him to let them first see the convulsions they had heard spoken of. He granted this, and during the convulsions the Mother Superior suddenly came to herself with a sigh, pressed her right hand to her left side, and withdrew it, covered with blood. She was again examined, and the doctors with the whole assembly saw three bloody wounds, of the size stated by the devil. The chemise, the stays, and the dress were pierced in three places, the largest hole looking as if a pistol bullet had passed through. The nun was therefore entirely stripped, but no instrument of any description was found upon her. A report was immediately drawn up, and monsieur, brother of the king, who witnessed the facts with all the nobles of his court, attested the document.

Father Lactance, the worthy monk who had assisted the possessed in their sufferings, was himself attacked some time after the death of the priest. Feeling the first symptoms, he determined to go to Notre Dame des Ardilliers, whose chapel served by the priests of the oratory is held in great veneration in Saumur and its neighborhood. M. de Canaye, who was going into the country, gave him a seat in his carriage. He had heard speak of his state and knew he was tormented by the devil, but he nevertheless joked about the matter, when all of a sudden, while rolling along a perfect level road, the carriage turned over in the air without anyone being in any way hurt. The next day, when they continued their voyage to Saumur, the carriage again turned over in the same way in the middle of the rue de Faubourg de Fenet, which is perfectly smooth and leads to the chapel of the Ardillier. This holy monk afterward experienced the greatest vexations from the demons, who at times deprived him of sight and at times of memory; they produced in him violent fits of nausea, dulled his intelligence, and worried him by so many evils, God called him to Him.

Five years later, Father Tranquille died of the same disease. He was a holy monk, a celebrated preacher, gifted with a judicious mind, great piety, and a profound humility. A laborious exorcist much feared by the devils, he had preferred that painful duty, generally little sought for, to the fame of preaching and had devoted himself to the service of the possessed of Loudun. The demons, irritated at his constancy, determined to possess his body. But God never allowed him to be entirely possessed. Nevertheless, his cruel enemies succeeded in attacking his senses to a certain extent. They cast him to the ground, they cursed and swore out of his mouth, they caused him to put out his tongue and hiss like a serpent, they filled his mind with darkness, seemed to crush out his heart, and overwhelmed him with a thousand other torments.

On the day of the Pentecost they attacked him more violently than ever. He was to have preached but was too ill to attempt it. But his confessor ordered the devil to leave him at liberty and commanded the father to ascend the pulpit. He did so, and he preached more eloquently than if he had prepared his sermon for weeks. This was his last sermon.

He performed mass for two or three days more and then took to his bed to rise no more. The demons caused him pains, the violence of which none knew but he; they shrieked and howled out of his mouth, but he remained clearheaded. The following morning the monks saw that God had given rein to the powers of hell and had determined to abandon to them the life of the monk; and he himself begged that extreme unction should be administered to him when they should see that he was passing away. About twelve o'clock a demon who was being exorcised declared that Father Tranquille was at his last gasp. They hastened to see if it were true. He was dying, so the sacrament was administered to him. He died and received the crown he had gained by combats with hell so courageously sustained.

The opinion of his holiness attracted an enormous crowd to his funeral. A Jesuit pronounced his funeral elegy, and a worthy epitaph was engraved on his tomb.

Another matter that should be mentioned is that, when extreme unction was administered to him, the devils, driven away by the sacrament, were forced to leave him. But they did not go far, for they entered the body of another excellent monk who was present and whom they possessed henceforward. They vexed him at first by violent contortions and horrible howlings, and at the moment of Tranquille's death they cried horribly, "He is dead," as if they would say, "It is all over, no more hope for this soul!" At the same time casting themselves on the other monk, they worked him so horribly that, in spite of the many that held him, he kept kicking in the most violent manner toward the deceased. He had to be carried away.

Father Surin, a Jesuit, had succeeded Father Lactance; he too had his trials.

The demons used to threaten him out of the mouth of the Mother Superior, who was under his care. Once, in the presence of the Bishop of Nîmes, the demon took up his position on the face of the nun. Suddenly he disappeared and attacked the father, made him grow pale, sat on his chest, and stopped his voice; but soon, obeying the order of another exorcist, he returned to the nun, spoke through her mouth, and showed himself extremely hideous and horrible on her face; and the father, returning to the fight, continued his duties as if he had never been attacked. In one afternoon he was thus attacked and released seven or eight times; but these assaults were followed by others still more violent, so that in his exorcisms he seemed to be struck with violent interior blows, borne to earth, and violently shaken by his adversary. He remained in this state sometimes half an hour, sometimes an hour. The other exorcists applied the Holy Sacrament to the places where he felt the demons, sometimes to his chest, sometimes to his head. When the devil left him he reappeared on the face of the Mother Superior, where the monk, with holy vengeance, pursued him and constrained him to adore the Holy Sacrament. Once the devil threw him out of a window onto the rock where stands the convent of the Jesuits and broke one of his thighs. After having sustained these terrible trials for many years with perfect patience and resignation, he was freed from them and at length died in the odor of sanctity.

As to the Mother Superior, toward the end of the year 1635, something of a most extraordinary nature happened to her. Lord Montague came to Loudun, accompanied by two other English noblemen. He brought the exorcists a letter from the Archbishop of Tours, ordering them to edify his lordship as much as possible. The Mother Superior, in the midst of a convulsion, stretched out her left arm and the name JOSEPH appeared on it, written in capital letters. The report of this event was signed by the English noblemen. Lord Montague hastened to Rome, abjured his heresy, embraced the ecclesiastical career, and, under another name, settled in France, where he lived many years. He is mentioned in the memoirs of Mme. de Motteville.

At the beginning of 1636, on Twelfth Night, Father Surin resolved to compel the last demon that remained in the Mother Superior to adore Jesus Christ. He had the lady tied to a bench. The exorcisms drove the demon into a fury; and instead of obeying, he vomited a multitude of maledictions and blasphemies against the three Persons of the Holy Trinity, against Jesus Christ, and against his Holy Mother, so execrable that one would be horrified to read them. The father knew that he was about to come out and had the lady unbound. After tremblings, contortions, and horrible howlings, Father Surin pressed him more and more with the Holy Sacrament in his hand and ordered him in Latin to write the name of Mary on his lady's hand. Raising her left arm into the air, the fiend redoubled his cries and howls and in a last convulsion he issued from the lady, leaving on her hand the holy name MARIA in letters so perfectly formed that no human hand could imitate them. The lady felt herself free and full of joy, and a *Te Deum* was sung in honor of the event.

The Saint and the Devil

(England)

S aint Cuthman, when a lad, faithfully attended to his duties as a shepherd, and after the death of his father, worked hard for his mother's support in a place called Steyning, near Brighton, where he built a hut and a wooden oratory. His holy life and good works gained the love and reverence of the people about, who attributed to him many miracles. One afternoon he walked forth to visit a recluse named Sister Ursula, who dwelt in a solitary cell on the summit of a hill adjoining Poynings, and whom he had been told was sick and desirous of being shriven by him. Now Saint Cuthman, with his staff in hand, walked on until he reached the eminence for which he was bound. On the brow of this hill in former times the heathen invaders of the land had made a camp, vestiges of which may still be traced. But it was not with these memorials of a bygone and benighted age that the saint concerned himself, but he was filled with thanksgiving that it had given place to the pure light of the gospel.

From: James Charles Wall, *Devils* (London: Methuen & Co., 1904).

Thus communing with himself, Saint Cuthman reached the northern boundary of the rampart surrounding the old Roman camp and
cast his eyes over the vast Weald of Sussex. From his bird's-eye view
he was rejoiced to see the great number of churches that had been
built since his first recollections of the country, and in audible tones
gave praise for so great a change. While thus absorbed in contempla-
tion, he beheld a tall man of singularly swarthy complexion, haughty
mien, and eyes that seemed to burn like fire. This mysterious
personage was vested in a crimson dress of costly materials, yet
carried the implements of a common laborer, a pickax and shovel. At
the first glance Saint Cuthman knew that it was the Evil One. "Comest
thou to tempt me, accursed one?" he sternly demanded. "If so, learn
that I am proof against thy wiles. Depart from me, or I will summon
good spirits to cast thee hence."

"Thou canst not do so," laughed the stranger. "I am master here.
Altars have been reared to strange gods upon this hill and sacrifices
made to them—nay, I myself have been worshipped as Dis, and the
blood of black bulls has been poured out upon this ground in mine
honor. Therefore the hill is mine, and thou art an intruder upon it, and
deservest to be cast down headlong into the plain. Yet will I spare
thee———"

"Thou darest not so much as injure a hair of my head, Sathanas,"
interrupted the saint.

"I tell thee I have no design to harm thee," replied the fiend, "but
give heed to what I'm about to say. Vainly hast thou essayed to count
the churches in the Sussex Weald, and thou hast glorified heaven
because of the number of the worshippers gathered within those
fanes. Now, mark me, thou hast taken a farewell look of that plain, so
thickly studded with structures pleasing to thy sight but an abomination to me. Before tomorrow morn, that vast district, far as thine eye
can stretch, even to the foot of yon distant Surrey hills, the whole
Weald of Sussex, with its many churches, its churchmen, and its
congregations, shall be overwhelmed by the sea."

"Thou mockest me, but I know thee to be the Father of Lies," cried
the saint.

"Disbelieve me if I fail in my task—not till then," said the devil.
"With the implements which I hold in my hand I will cut such a dyke
through this hill, and through the hills lying between it and Hove, as

shall let in the waters of the deep, so that all dwelling within yonder plain shall be drowned by them."

The holy man was for a time troubled, but his confidence was presently restored. "Thou deceivest thyself," he said. "The task thou proposest to execute is beyond thy power."

"Beyond *my* power," cried the devil. "It is a trifle in comparison with what I can achieve. I have had a hand in many wonderful works, some of which are recognized as mine, though I have not received credit for a tithe of those I have performed. Devil's bridges are common enough, methinks; devil's towers are by no means rare; the very rampart upon which we stand was partly my work. The first Caesar has the credit of many of my works, and he is welcome to it. He is not the only one who has worn laurels belonging by right to others. Saint as thou art, you must give the devil his due. Do so, and thou must needs praise his industry."

"And thy present feat is to be performed before tomorrow, thou sayest?" asked Saint Cuthman.

"Between sunset and sunrise, most saintly sir."

"That is but a short time for so mighty a task; bethink thee a September night is not a long night."

"The shortest night is long enough for me," replied the fiend. "If the dawn comes and finds my work incomplete, thou shalt be at liberty to deride me."

"I shall never treat thee otherwise than with scorn; but thou hast said it, and I hold thee to thy word. Between sunset and sunrise thy task must be done. If thou failest—from whatever cause—thy evil scheme shall be forever abandoned."

"Be it so! I am content," said the devil. "But I shall *not* fail. Come hither at sunset, and thou wilt see me commence my work. Thou mayst tarry nigh me, if thou wilt, till it be done."

After this the devil suddenly disappeared, leaving the saint troubled in mind. But no time must be lost; that doomed district must be delivered from the power of the Evil One. Saint Cuthman quitted the Roman camp and hastened in the direction of the cell of Sister Ursula.

The recluse, one of the noble house of Braose, once celebrated for her beauty, was now through age and severe discipline more like a living skeleton, but the report of her sanctity had spread far and wide. Her health was fast failing, and as her emaciated form met the gaze of

Saint Cuthman, he clearly perceived her hours in this world to be but few.

The saint exhorted the anchorite to fast and watch throughout that night. When the sun had gone down she was to turn the hourglass and let the sand run out six times; that would bring it to the first hour after midnight. Next, she was to light a taper and set it between the bars of the window of her cell, which looked toward the east, until it burned out. All this Sister Ursula promised to perform, and Saint Cuthman departed as the sun was sinking into the sea.

As he took his way toward the northeastern boundary of the ancient encampment, a noise as of thunder reached his ear, and the ground shook so violently beneath his feet that he could scarcely stand. Nevertheless, on he went until he reached the eminence overlooking Poynings.

Here, as he expected, he beheld the archfiend at work. He had already made a great breach into the down, and enormous fragments of chalk and flintstones rolled down with a terrific crash. Every stroke of his pickax shook the hill to its center.

Saint Cuthman firmly planted his staff in the ground and looked on, the only spectator of the astounding scene. The devil's proportions became colossal; he looked like one of that giant race whom poets of heathendom tell us warred against Jove. His garb was suited to his task and resembled that of a miner. His sinewy arms were bared to the shoulders, and the two curled horns were visible on his uncovered head. His implements had become enormous as himself. Each stroke plunged fathom deep into the ground and tore up huge boulderlike masses of chalk, the smallest of which might have loaded a wain. The fiend worked away with might and main, and the concussion produced by his tremendous strokes was incessant and terrible, echoing far over the weald like the rattling of a dreadful thunderstorm.

But the sand ran out, and Sister Ursula turned her glass for the first time.

Suddenly the fiend stopped and clapped his hand to his side as though in pain. "A sharp stitch," quoth he. "My side tingles as if pricked by a thousand pins. The sensation is by no means pleasant, but 'twill soon pass." Then, perceiving the saint watching him, he called out derisively, "Aha! art thou there, thou saintly man? What thinkest thou now of the chance of escape for thy friends in the weald?

Thou art a judge of such matters, I doubt not. Is my dyke broad enough, think you, or shall I widen it and deepen it yet more?" And the chasm resounded with his mocking laughter.

"Thou art but a slovenly workman, after all," remarked Saint Cuthman. "The sides of thy dyke are rough and uneven; they want leveling. A mortal laborer would be shrewdly reprimanded if he left them in such an untidy condition."

"No mortal laborer could make such a trench," he cried. "However, it shall never be said that I am a slovenly workman."

Whereupon he seized his spade and proceeded to level the banks of the dyke, carefully removing all roughness and irregularity.

"Will that satisfy thy precise notions?" he at last called out.

"I cannot deny that it looks better," replied the holy man, glad to think that another hour had passed—for a soft touch upon his brow made him aware that at this moment Sister Ursula had turned the hourglass for the second time.

A sharp sudden pain smote the devil and made him roar out lustily, "Another stitch, and worse than the first! But it shall not hinder my task."

Again he fell to work. Again the hill was shaken to its base. Again mighty masses of chalk were hurled into the valley, crushing everything upon which they descended.

It was now dark. But the fiery breath of the demon sufficed to light him in his task. He toiled away with right goodwill but suddenly suspended his labor. The hourglass had been turned for the third time.

"What is the matter with thee?" demanded the saint.

"I know not," replied the writhing fiend. "A sudden attack of cramp in the arms and legs, I fancy. I must have caught cold on these windy downs. I will do a little lighter work till the fit passes off." Upon this he took up the shovel to trim the rough sides.

While thus engaged, the further end of the chasm closed up, so that when he resumed the pick once more, he had all his work to do over again. This made him snort and roar like a mad bull, and so much flame and smoke issued from his mouth and nostrils that the bottom of the dyke resembled the crater of a volcano.

Sister Ursula then turned the glass for the fourth time. Hereupon an enormous mass of breccia, or goldstone, rolled down upon the devil's hoof. This so enraged him that he sent the fragment whizzing over the hills to Hove. What with rubbing his bruised hoof and roaring, some time elapsed before he resumed his work.

The fifth turning of the glass gave him such pains in the back that for some minutes he was completely disabled.

"An attack of lumbago," he cried. "I seem liable to all mortal ailments tonight."

Once more he began to ply his pickax with greater energy than ever, toiling on without intermission, filling the chasm with flame from his nostrils, and producing the effect of a continuous thunderstorm over the weald.

At the end of another hour the sister turned the glass for the last time.

The devil was again checked in his work. This time he had struck his pickax so deep into the chalk that he couldn't move it. In his attempts to do so the helve, which was thick as the mainmast of a ship, broke in his grasp. In the midst of his rage he heard Saint Cuthman calling to him to come forth.

"Wherefore should I come forth? Thou thinkest I am baffled, but art mistaken. I will dig out my ax head presently, and my shovel will furnish me with a new handle."

"Cease, if thou canst, to breathe forth flame and smoke for a short time and look toward the east," shouted the saint.

"There is a glimmer of light in the sky over there, but dawn cannot be come already," said the devil.

"The streak of light grows rapidly wider and brighter," said Saint Cuthman. "The shades of night are fleeing fast away. The larks are beginning to rise and carol forth their matin hymns on the downs. The rooks are cawing amid the trees of the park beneath us. The cattle are lowing in the meads—and hark! dost thou not hear the cocks crowing in the village of Poynings?"

"Cocks crowing at Poynings!" yelled the devil. "It must be the dawn. But the sun shall not behold my discomfiture."

"Hide thy head in darkness, accursed being! Hence with thee! and return not to this hill. The dwellers of the weald are saved from thy malice and may henceforth worship without fear. Get thee hence! Go! Make tracks!" cried Saint Cuthman.

Abashed by the awful looks of the saint, the devil fled. Howling with rage, he tore to the northern boundary of the encampment, where the marks of his hoofs may still be seen indelibly impressed on the sod. Then springing off and spreading his sable wings, he disappeared.

As he took flight, Sister Ursula's taper went out. Instant darkness fell over the hill, and Night resumed her former sway. The cocks ceased to crow, the larks returned to the ground, the rooks returned to their nests, and the cattle ceased their lowing.

As the taper went out, Sister Ursula expired. Her last hours had been given for the benefit of the reposing inhabitants of the weald. Thus was the devil frustrated, leaving unfinished the "Devil's Dyke."

The Blacksmith and Beelzebub's Imps

(Alsace)

Once upon a time there lived in a certain town in Alsace a blacksmith who had sold himself to the devil. This devil gave him the power to hold the person who picked nails out of his shoeing box, sat in a certain chair in his house, or ascended a high pear tree in his garden. Wishing to obtain some more money, the blacksmith again sold himself, but this time to Beelzebub, the Prince of Devils, who was supposed to be fabulously rich. The blacksmith was to get several thousands of dollars, Beelzebub having the right to claim him, body and soul, at the end of twenty years.

When this time had expired, Beelzebub sent one of his imps to claim the blacksmith. The latter asked the imp if he would help him, for he was very busy. The imp was willing, so the blacksmith told him to pick the bent horse nails out of his shoeing box, but as soon as he put his hand into the box, he became powerless and could not move. Then the blacksmith, in great glee, heated a pair of tongs and began to pinch

From: W. J. Wintemberg, "German Folk-Tales Collected in Canada," *Journal of American Folk-Lore* 19 (1906): 241–44.

the imp. After torturing him to his heart's content, he released him from the spell, and the imp returned to Beelzebub.

Beelzebub then sent another imp, and the other one having related his experience, this one was a little more cautious. When the imp arrived, the blacksmith was just going into the house to eat his dinner, so he invited him to come in also and told him to sit down while he washed and got ready for dinner. The unsuspecting imp, seeing no other chair in the room, sat down in the magic chair, and thereupon came under the influence of the blacksmith's spell. The blacksmith returned to his shop and heated some irons, with which he tormented the unlucky imp more than he did the other; then releasing him from the spell, he sat down and ate his food, confident that Beelzebub would now be willing to let him live in peace.

But the fiend, undaunted, sent another imp. The blacksmith had still another method of escape—the high pear tree. At this particular time the topmost branches bore some large juicy pears. When the imp appeared, the blacksmith told him about his pear tree and the pears that were ripe and which, owing to the fact that he and his apprentice were busy, and also because his wife and daughter were unable to climb to such a height, would spoil if they were not soon picked off the tree. So he asked the imp if he would kindly undertake to pick them for him. The imp, eager to claim this troublesome soul for his master, climbed the tree, but as soon as he was up amidst the branches, he became powerless. The blacksmith then called his apprentice, and they heated some long iron rods with which they tormented him until they thought he had enough.

Beelzebub could not get another imp to go for the blacksmith, and so he was left in peace.

The Devil's Bridge

(Alsace)

There is a curious legend connected with a bridge that spans some tributary of the Rhine forming the boundary between Alsace and Switzerland. When this bridge was being built, an almost insurmountable difficulty arose. Beelzebub, always willing to win a human soul, offered to aid the builders on condition that the first living being that crossed the bridge should be his, and he sent one of his imps to help. The bridge builder, being aware of the extreme gullibility of the fiend, consented, but outwitted him, for as soon as the bridge was completed, he brought a black goat, and placing it before him, pushed it across the bridge. Beelzebub's imp, in his rage at being outwitted, grasped the goat by the horns, and hurled it through the floor of the bridge. Every old Alsatian who comes from this part of Alsace will solemnly aver that the hole is still there, because all efforts at repairing the breach are frustrated by Beelzebub's imps.

From: W. J. Wintemberg, "German Folk-Tales Collected in Canada," *Journal of American Folk-Lore* 19 (1906): 241–44.

The Precolitsch

(Transylvania)

Down in the wild southeastern corner of Europe, where Serb, Bulgar, Walach, and Turk have so long been striving for the mastery—a contest that now at last seems to be in a fair way of settlement—many curious superstitions flourish that are little known outside the boundaries of those war-wasted lands.

From: Philip MacLeod, "The Precolitsch," *Occult Review* 29 (1919): 156–59.

One of the strangest, and at the same time most terrible, of these superstitions is the belief in what is called the Precolitsch (or *Prikulics*). This name is given, in the Walachian Mountains, to a being somewhat resembling the Bunyip of Australia, though the stories related of him are of a more terrifying character. The Precolitsch is described as a species of wandering terror, gifted, as the Bunyip apparently is, with the power of assuming various forms and possessing unheard-of strength.

One story concerning this mysterious being has been placed upon record as matter of fact. It has been well said that it is characterized by a "horrible sort of originality." The authority for this strange narrative is an officer in the Austro-Hungarian army, whom I will call Captain Mueller, that not being his real name. He was, as will be seen, closely concerned in the incident related. At the period in question, he was a *Faehnrich*, or ensign. I keep, as closely as possible, to the terms of his narration.

Captain, or rather Ensign, Mueller was at one time stationed at the Pass of Temesn in Transylvania, with about forty men under his command. The pass consists of a long, narrow ravine, walled in on each side by rocky precipices, inaccessible to human foot. It is about fifty yards wide. A wall with a strong gate has been built across it. Inside the wall are, or were, the buildings occupied by the officer in command of the guard, his men, and the officials of the *Contumaz*, or quarantine. It was usual to post two sentries outside the wall, one close to the gate and the other a short distance farther out.

Christmastime had come, welcomed no doubt by such festivities as could be made in such a place. The weather was cold, and the pass, with the mountains around it, was covered with snow.

One morning a soldier of the guard, a Hungarian Gypsy, came before his officer and begged leave to make a request. It seems that, in the ordinary routine of duty, it would be his turn to mount guard that night, from ten o'clock till twelve at the outer of the two posts above mentioned, beyond the gateway; and he begged most earnestly to be allowed to exchange turns with some other soldier so as not to be on guard there at that time. He would willingly take two other turns if he might be allowed to avoid that one; and he entreated that, for the love of God, his officer would grant his request.

Ensign Mueller was very much surprised at all this and asked the man what reason he had for making a petition so unusual in the service. The soldier replied that he had been born on what he called "New Sunday" and therefore possessed a power of knowing things hidden from ordinary people—a kind of second-sight. He had thus, he said, become aware that, if he mounted guard at that particular time, a great misfortune would inevitably befall him. After midnight, however, he would have nothing more to fear, and he renewed his request with the most earnest manner of supplication.

Ensign Mueller afterward confessed that he at first felt a great impression from the evident sincerity and conviction with which the private spoke, all the more so as the man was in other respects quite faultless as a soldier. But (as he afterward had great reason to regret) common sense soon resumed its sway and removed the strong impression produced by the Gypsy's manner. Besides, to grant a request so unusual would have led to all sorts of irregularities and would have been subversive of the interests of the service. So instead of acceding to the man's petition, Ensign Mueller, with excellent intentions, gave him a good lecture upon the silliness of superstition and told him that he would have to keep his number and mount the outer guard from ten till midnight.

The Gypsy seems accordingly to have made up his mind to do battle with his terrors and fulfill his duty, "since no better it mote be." He was moreover encouraged by being reminded that his comrade at the inner post would have him constantly in his sight and would instantly come to his assistance if he required it, while the whole guard would be prepared to turn out at a moment's notice if anything suspicious should take place.

That evening, Ensign Mueller went over to the quarantine superintendent's quarters to play chess with him, and they were soon engaged in their game. It was about half past nine o'clock. Suddenly, they both saw a man's face, strange and wild, outside the window, close to the glass—the room was situated on the ground floor—and staring in upon them with, as it seemed, an expression of mockery or derision. They could see the body, which appeared to be wrapped in a white cloak such as is worn by the peasantry in those parts. Next moment, the figure turned from the window and slowly went away.

At so lonely a post as the Pass of Temesn, the sight of a strange face is quite an event, especially at such an unusual hour. Ensign Mueller ran out, accompanied by his friend. It was a clear moonlit night (a full moon shone until after midnight); the snow was lying deep upon the ground. They saw the figure pass along the wall as far as a small niche or recess, into which it turned; they followed and found the niche empty! There was apparently no possible way out except by passing through the solid wall. Ensign Mueller and his friend could make nothing of it. They shook their heads, looked at each other, and returned to their game.

Ten o'clock passed over; the Gypsy must have begun his watch. The game of chess went on, till suddenly it was interrupted by the sound of a shot from without, closely followed by another, then by a confused noise and shouting. The guard turned out, Ensign Mueller rushing up to join them, and went out through the gateway at the double.

The inner sentry was standing in the snow, convulsively grasping his smoking gun and staring toward the place where the other sentinel should have been but was not—the Gypsy had disappeared.

Ensign Mueller rushed on to the spot where the man had been standing. Not a sign of him was to be seen, but his gun was lying in the snow, *with the barrel bent into a semicircle,* like a sickle blade. (The musket had not burst; the barrel was a strong one, with neither crack nor flaw in it.) In the snow were the tracks of the soldier's shoes; there were other footmarks there too, shapeless ones.

Further search was made, and the soldier was found lying some thirty paces away, below the crest of a slope. He was unconscious and moaning piteously. They carried him into the hospital. It was found that his whole body was as it were burned, especially the face and breast, which were quite blackened. He never recovered consciousness for even a moment but lay crying and moaning terribly all night and the next day till the afternoon, when he died.

The other sentry reported that, being aware of his comrade's fears, he had never once taken his eyes off him from the moment of going on guard. It was, as before observed, a bright moonlit night, and he could see every motion of the Gypsy, as he paced quietly up and down. Suddenly (continued the inner sentry), a black shape was standing on the snow at a short distance beyond the other man; how it had come there, all at once as it were, he could not tell. It was an ugly black shape and seemed to him rather animal than human. It was not very big. The moment he saw it, it began to approach the outer sentry, who challenged it, but it continued to come on. The Gypsy then fired at it, and the Black One made a huge spring toward him.

The inner sentry fired in his turn, whether with or without effect he could not tell; but he saw the thing seize the Gypsy by the breast. Next instant, they were both gone from his sight, he knew not how.

This is all that is ever likely to be known of the matter. The unfortunate soldier died, as above related, without word or sign; and "where or in what realm of creatures the Other is to be sought for is a matter best left to each man's unprejudiced judgment." It is possible that the bent musket may still be preserved in some arsenal in Transylvania.

A learned Romanian gentleman of Budapest informs me that a swineherd on his estate once ascribed an unusual mortality among the pigs to the malignant operations of the *Prikulics*. He (the swineherd) performed some secret magical rites as a precaution. "Ha!" said he defiantly, snapping his fingers, "the Prikulics won't be able to hurt our pigs anymore!"

Hungarian authorities (I am writing in Budapest) seem to identify the Precolitsch with the Hungarian *Farkaskoldus,* or wolf-beggar (cf. the Old English *bull-beggar*). The Farkaskoldus is a kind of vampire. It is said that shepherds, especially when they have been unjustly treated during life, are apt to become Farkaskolduses after death and ravage the flocks of those who have injured them; they also kill human beings. When their revenge is accomplished, they return to the grave.

The Vampire
Honoria Westcar

(England)

When I first saw Honoria Westcar, I thought she was the prettiest woman I had ever met. Her eyes and hair were dark and her color a rich carmine, while the rest of her complexion was of a creamy tint. She had winning ways, and I was altogether charmed with her.

Her visit was professional. She told me she would be much pleased to come and see me again on her return from an operatic tour, which was to extend for some months; she had a fine voice and was singing in a grand opera.

I neither heard from her nor saw her for over a year. I often remarked to my companion with whom I live, "I wonder what has become of the pretty Miss Westcar?"

One day a visitor was ushered into my consulting room. I could not recognize her in the least. She said, "Don't you know me? I am Miss Westcar."

I started. Changed isn't the word; she was simply a wreck.

Her lovely color had gone, the creamy tint of her complexion had become a dirty drab, quantities of deep furrows and wrinkles marred the former smoothness of her skin, her beautiful dark eyes were dull and sunken with deep circles beneath them. Instead of a girl of twenty-six to twenty-seven which I knew her to be, she looked like a haggard old woman of seventy. I could only gaze at her in amazement.

"Have you been ill?" I asked at length.

"Oh no," she replied, "I have gone in for spiritualism and have had some very strange happenings."

"Indeed," I said, vaguely uncomfortable.

From: Zuresta, "A Weird Experience," *Occult Review* 8 (July–December 1908): 103–5.

She told me thirteen was her lucky number. She always did everything in thirteens. She had repeatedly found mysterious presents put in her workbasket when no one had been near the room, and once a golden horseshoe was dropped in front of her on the table without visible hands. I let her ramble on, for I could hardly credit these, to me, foolish stories.

Meanwhile she had edged quite close to me and took my hand in both hers. "You comfort me so," she remarked, as she held it tightly clasped and every now and then rubbed her fingers up and down my arm.

For a while I took no heed, and then a most peculiar sensation came over me and I felt myself getting pale and faint. I noticed her color was gradually returning, and I grew every moment fainter and fainter. My friend at this moment came into the room and, seeing how tired I was, insisted on my having some lunch and going to lie down. In fact, she had almost to turn Miss Westcar out of the room, so reluctant was she to go. As she said good-bye she remarked, "I shall be with you in spirit."

(I may mention I have a very bright color which hardly ever fades, even in illness.)

I went to lie down, being thoroughly exhausted. I had hardly lain ten minutes when a most excruciating pain shot through me, as though body and soul were being violently wrenched asunder, and I lay still and rigid on the bed.

When I opened my eyes I found, to my surprise, I was not in my own room at all. It was quite unfamiliar to me and was furnished with six chairs and a sofa all covered in dingy green rep; faded rep curtains hung before the windows, which, though it was summertime, were closed and the curtains drawn across.

I was seated in a high-backed oak chair, one of the only things of value in the room.

A fair man, thin and with a deathly white complexion, stood on one side. His eyes were close set and of a hard cold steel blue; his face was adorned with a blond mustache and beard, but the little I could see of the mouth was cruel. Miss Westcar stood on the opposite side to him.

"Have you locked the door?" she asked anxiously; "it would be awkward if we are disturbed."

"No one will come, we are alone in the house; I have seen to that. Yes, this is just the subject we need. We both want a fresh supply of ozone, shall I call it? I am glad you secured her"; and he laughed cynically.

"I hardly thought I should, but she is evidently sympathetic."

"All the better for us. Let us waste no more time."

I could not move hand or foot, and yet with the horror of the whole thing, I tried to scream for help, but I was voiceless. Miss Westcar approached me and opened my dress at the neck.

"Yes," he said gloatingly, "she has a fine throat and neck. Will you begin?"

"Very well." She took one of the instruments and punctured my neck. She then started to suck where she had made the incision. In a very short time her face became a glow of color; a glass was opposite me and I saw myself become whiter than I ever remember.

"That's enough," he said; "it's my turn now."

He started to do the same in two or three places, lower down in my neck, and, oh! the sickening sense of repulsion I felt when his lips touched my bare skin.

"Oh," he remarked with a ghoulish smile, "this is something like; it gives one new life. You must visit her again in a day or two." He made another puncture and again applied his lips, and I could neither speak nor move. When I looked at him, he had a fine, fresh color and appeared ten years younger.

"I think that's enough for today. Release her or she won't be any use for some days, and she is too good a subject to lose." Then they went through some incantations with the chafing dish and burnt some powders which gave out a greenish-blue flame, and I knew no more till I found myself undergoing the same horrible pain as before.

I had no idea how long I had been abstracted, but my friend told me I had been in a deathlike trance for two hours, and nothing could rouse me.

She now brought me a cup of strong tea, and though I was very white and shaken, that revived me somewhat.

I should have thought the whole was a ghastly dream had I not, when undressing that night, noticed five or six punctures on my neck and throat like the prick of a needle or pin; then I knew it had really happened.

Two days after, she called and was admitted without my knowledge, and before I could prevent her, she had seized my hand and begun fondling it as before. I snatched it away, but not before the mischief was done, for that day again I had the same attack, though not quite so long nor so violent.

Both again punctured me and pressed their lips to my neck and throat, but whether they were disturbed in their unholy work or had had enough, I cannot say. I was released under the hour.

The next time she came, a few days later—hoping, I suppose, to renew supplies—she was told I was not at home, nor would anything induce me to see her again. Though she called frequently, she was never admitted, and I never saw her again.

But the extraordinary part of this horrible, and I venture to say unique, experience happened quite four or five years later. A lady who is a very good medium herself came to spend an evening, and I related these facts to her.

"Oh yes," she exclaimed, "I know that room quite well and Honoria Westcar. The man you describe is, or was, her fiancé; they both went in strongly for black magic. The last time I saw them they were absolute wrecks."

Elga

(Austria)

Two years ago I was living at Hermannstadt, and being engaged in engineering a road through the hills I often came within the vicinity of the old castle, where I made the acquaintance of the old castellan, or caretaker, and his wife, who occupied a part of the wing of the house, almost separate from the main body of the building. They were a quiet old couple and rather reticent in giving information or expressing an opinion in regard to the strange noises that were often heard at night in the deserted halls, or of the apparitions that the Walachian peasants claimed to have seen when they loitered in the surroundings after dark. All I could gather was

From: Franz Hartmann, M.D., "An Authenticated Vampire Story," *Occult Review* 10 (July–December 1909): 144–49.

that the old count was a widower and had a beautiful daughter, who was one day killed by a fall from her horse, and that soon after the old man died in some mysterious manner, and the bodies were buried in a solitary graveyard belonging to a neighboring village. Not long after their death, an unusual mortality was noticed among the inhabitants of the village: several children and even some grown people died without any apparent illness; they merely wasted away. And thus a rumor was started that the old count had become a vampire after his death. There is no doubt that he was not a saint, as he was addicted to drinking, and some shocking tales were in circulation about his conduct and that of his daughter; but whether or not there was any truth in them, I am not in a position to say.

Afterward the property came into possession of ———, a distant relative of the family, who is a young man and officer in a cavalry regiment in Vienna. It appears that the heir enjoyed his life at the capital and did not trouble himself much about the old castle in the wilderness; he did not even come to look at it but gave his directions by letter to the old janitor, telling him merely to keep things in order and to attend to repairs, if any were necessary. Thus the castellan was actually master of the house and offered its hospitality to me and my friends.

One evening myself and my two assistants, Dr. E———, a young lawyer, and Mr. W———, a literary man, went to inspect the premises. First we went to the stables. There were no horses, as they had been sold; but what attracted our special attention was an old queer-fashioned coach with gilded ornaments and bearing the emblems of the family. We then inspected the rooms, passing through some halls and gloomy corridors such as may be found in any old castle. There was nothing remarkable about the furniture, but in one of the halls there hung in a frame an oil painting, a portrait representing a lady with a large hat and wearing a fur coat. We all were involuntarily startled on beholding this picture, not so much on account of the beauty of the lady but on account of the uncanny expression of her eyes, and Dr. E———, after looking at the picture for a short time, suddenly exclaimed, "How strange! The picture closes its eyes and opens them again, and now it begins to smile!"

Now Dr. E——— is a very sensitive person and has more than once had some experience in spiritism, and we made up our minds to form a circle for the purpose of investigating this phenomenon. Accordingly, on the same evening we sat around a table in an adjoining room, forming a magnetic chain with our hands. Soon the table began to move and the name ELGA was spelled. We asked who this Elga was, and the answer was rapped out: "The lady, whose picture you have seen."

"Is the lady living?" asked Mr. W———. This question was not answered, but instead it was rapped out: "If W——— desires it, I will appear to him bodily tonight at two o'clock." W——— consented, and now the table seemed to be endowed with life and manifested a great affection for W———; it rose on two legs and pressed against his breast, as if it intended to embrace him.

We inquired of the castellan whom the picture represented; but to our surprise he did not know. He said that it was the copy of a picture painted by the celebrated painter Hans Markart of Vienna and had been bought by the old count because its demoniacal look pleased him so much.

We left the castle, and W——— retired to his room at an inn, a half hour's journey distant from that place. He was of a somewhat skeptical turn of mind, being neither a firm believer in ghosts and apparitions nor ready to deny their possibility. He was not afraid, but anxious to see what would come out of his agreement, and for the purpose of keeping himself awake he sat down and began to write an article for a journal.

Toward two o'clock he heard steps on the stairs, and the door of the hall opened. There was a rustling of a silk dress and the sound of the feet of a lady walking to and fro in the corridor.

It may be imagined that he was somewhat startled, but taking courage, he said to himself, "If this is Elga, let her come in." Then the door of his room opened and Elga entered. She was most elegantly dressed and appeared still more youthful and seductive than the picture. There was a lounge on the other side of the table where W——— was writing, and there she silently posted herself. She did not speak, but her looks and gestures left no doubt in regard to her desires and intentions.

Mr. W——— resisted the temptation and remained firm. It is not known whether he did so out of principle or timidity or fear. Be this as it may, he kept on writing, looking from time to time at his visitor and silently wishing that she would leave. At last, after half an hour, which seemed to him much longer, the lady departed in the same manner in which she came.

This adventure left W——— no peace, and we consequently arranged several sittings at the old castle, where a variety of uncanny phenomena took place. Thus, for instance, once the servant-girl was about to light a fire in the stove, when the door of the apartment opened and Elga stood there. The girl, frightened out of her wits, rushed out of the room, tumbling down the stairs in terror with the petroleum lamp in her hand, which broke and came very near to setting her clothes on fire. Lighted lamps and candles went out when brought near the picture, and many other "manifestations" took place, which it would be tedious to describe; but the following incident ought not to be omitted.

Mr. W——— was at that time desirous of obtaining the position as co-editor of a certain journal, and a few days after the above-narrated adventure he received a letter in which a noble lady of high position offered him her patronage for that purpose. The writer requested him to come to a certain place the same evening, where he would meet a gentleman who would give him further particulars. He went and was met by an unknown stranger, who told him that he was requested by the Countess Elga to invite Mr. W——— to a carriage drive and that she would await him at midnight at a certain crossing of two roads, not far from the village. The stranger then suddenly disappeared.

Now it seems that Mr. W——— had some misgivings about the meeting and drive, and he hired a policeman as detective to go at midnight to the appointed place, to see what would happen. The policeman went and reported next morning that he had seen nothing but the well-known, old-fashioned carriage from the castle with two black horses attached to it standing there as if waiting for somebody, and that he had no occasion to interfere and merely waited until the carriage moved on. When the castellan of the castle was asked, he swore that the carriage had not been out that night, and in fact it could not have been out, as there were no horses to draw it.

But this is not all, for on the following day I met a friend who is a great skeptic and disbeliever in ghosts and always used to laugh at such things. Now however, he seemed to be very serious and said, "Last night something very strange happened to me. At about one o'clock this morning I returned from a late visit, and as I happened to pass the graveyard of the village, I saw a carriage with gilded ornaments standing at the entrance. I wondered about this taking place at such an unusual hour and, being curious to see what would happen, I waited. Two elegantly dressed ladies issued from the carriage. One of these was young and pretty, but threw at me a devilish and scornful look as they both passed by and entered the cemetery. There they were met by a well-dressed man, who saluted the ladies and spoke to the younger one, saying: 'Why, Miss Elga! Are you returned so soon?' Such a queer feeling came over me that I abruptly left and hurried home."

This matter has not been explained, but certain experiments which we subsequently made with the picture of Elga brought out some curious facts.

To look at the picture for a certain time caused me to feel a very disagreeable sensation in the region of the solar plexus. I began to dislike the portrait and proposed to destroy it. We held a sitting in the adjoining room; the table manifested a great aversion against my presence. It was rapped out that I should leave the circle and that the picture must not be destroyed. I ordered a Bible to be brought in and read the beginning of the first chapter of St. John, whereupon the above-mentioned Dr. E—— (the medium) and another man present claimed that they saw the picture distorting its face. I turned the frame and pricked the back of the picture with my penknife in different places, and Dr. E——, as well as the other man, felt all the pricks, although they had retired to the corridor.

I made the sign of the pentagram over the picture, and again the two gentlemen claimed that the picture was horribly distorting its face.

Soon afterward we were called away and left that country. Of Elga I heard nothing more.

A Vampire in Crete

(Greece)

Once upon a time the village of Kalikrati was haunted by a vampire, which destroyed both children and many full-grown men and desolated both that village and many others. They had buried him in the Church of St. George at Kalikrati, and as in those times he was a man of note, they had built an arch over his grave.

Now a certain shepherd, his mutual *syntaknos*, was tending his sheep and oats near the church, and on being caught in a shower, he went to the sepulchre for shelter. Afterward he determined to pass the night there, and after taking off his arms, he placed them crosswise by the stone which served him for a pillow, and because of the sacred symbol they formed, the vampire was unable to leave his tomb.

During the night, as the vampire wished to go out again that he might destroy men, he said to the shepherd, "Gossip, get up hence, for I have some business to attend to."

The shepherd answered him not, either the first or the second or the third time, for he concluded that the man had become a vampire and that it was he who had done all these evil deeds. But when he spoke for a fourth time, the shepherd replied, "I shall not get up hence, gossip, for I fear you are no better than you should be and may do me a mischief. But swear to me by your winding sheet that you will not hurt me, and then I will get up."

The vampire did not, however, pronounce that oath but said other things. But finally, when the shepherd did not suffer him to get up, the vampire swore to him as he wished. On this the shepherd rose, and on taking up his arms, the vampire came forth, and after greeting the shepherd, said to him, "Gossip, you must not go away, but sit down here, for I have some business which I must go after. But I shall return within the hour, for I have something to say to you." So the shepherd waited for him.

From: Lucy Mary Jane Garnett, *The Women of Turkey and Their Folk-Lore. Part 1: The Greek Women* (London: David Nutt, 1890).

And the vampire went a distance of about ten miles, where there was a couple recently married, and he destroyed them. On his return the shepherd saw that he was carrying some liver, his hands being wet with blood, and as he carried it he blew into it, just as the butcher does, to increase the size of the liver. And he showed his gossip that it was cooked, as if it had been done on the fire. "Let us sit down, gossip, and eat," said he. And the shepherd pretended to eat it, but only swallowed dry bread and kept dropping the liver into his bosom. Therefore, when the hour of separation arrived, the vampire said to the shepherd, "Gossip, this which you have seen you must not mention, for if you do, my twenty nails will be fixed in your children and yourself."

Yet the shepherd lost no time but gave information to the priests and others, who went to the tomb and found the vampire just as he had been buried, and all were satisfied that it was he who had done all the evil deeds. So they collected a great deal of wood, and they cast him on it and burnt him. When the body was half consumed, the gossip too came forward in order that he might enjoy the ceremony. And the vampire cast, as it were, a single spot of blood, which fell on his foot; and the foot wasted away as if it had been burned with fire. On this account they sifted even the ashes, and they found the little fingernail of the vampire and burnt that too.

The Vampires of Kisilova

(Eastern Europe)

I n 1718, after parts of Serbia and Walachia had fallen to Austria, the Austrian government received several reports from the commanders of the troops cantoned in those countries. They stated that it was a general belief among the people that dead persons, but still living in the grave, came out under certain conditions to suck the blood of the living and thus sustain underground a remnant of health and strength. As early as 1720, one report announced that at Kisilova, a village situated in Lower Hungary, a certain Pierre Plogogowitz, about ten weeks after his sepulture, had appeared by night to several residents and so squeezed their necks that they had died within twenty-four hours, so that in the course of a week nine persons, some young, some aged, had died in this manner. His widow herself had been annoyed by him and had left the village on this account. The inhabitants demanded permission of the commandant to exhume and burn the body. The commandant having refused it, they declared that they would all leave the village unless their request was complied with. The commanding officer thereupon came to the village in the company of the cure of Gradisca. He caused the coffin of Pierre to be opened, and they found his body intact, except the end of his nose, which was a little shriveled. The body exhaled no bad odor but seemed rather the body of a man asleep than of the dead. His hair and beard had grown, and fresh nails had replaced the old ones, which had fallen off. Under the external skin, which appeared pale and dead, had formed a new living skin; the hands and feet resembled those of a man in perfect health. As they found in his mouth fresh blood, the people believed it must have been he who had sucked the blood of those who had quite recently died, and nothing could prevent their

From: Adolphe d'Assier,. *Posthumous Humanity: A Study of Phantoms* (with an appendix of beliefs current in India) (London: George Redway, 1887).

plunging into the breast of the corpse a sharpened stake. There then gushed a quantity of fresh and pure blood from the mouth and nose. The peasants threw the body on the pyre and burned it.

Also in the last century there died at the village of Kisilova an old man of about sixty-two years of age. Three days after his interment, he appeared at night to his son and asked for something to eat. The latter having served him, he ate and disappeared. The next day, the son related to his neighbors what had occurred, but the specter did not show himself on that day; but the third night he again appeared and asked for food. It is not known whether the son gave it or not, but they found him in the morning dead in his bed. The same day five or six persons fell suddenly ill in the village and died, one after the other, a few days after. The bailiff of the place, being informed of what had happened, sent an account to the court of Belgrade, which ordered two of its officers to go to the village, in company of the executioner, to inquire into the affair. The imperial officer, from whom the present narrative emanates, himself went there from Gradisca to personally verify a story of which so much had been heard. They had the tombs of all who had died within the previous six weeks opened. When they came to that of the old man, they found him with his eyes open, his complexion rosy, breathing naturally, although motionless and dead, whence they concluded that he must be an unmistakable vampire. They erected a pyre and reduced the corpse to ashes. No sign of vampirism was found in either the body of the son or in that of any of the others.

Two Cases of Vampirism

(Hungary)

D r. Ennemoser gives two authenticated accounts of vampirism in Hungary. In the first, the report is made by the bailiff of Kisilova, to the tribunal of Belgrade, which dispatched to the village two officers and the executioner to examine into the affair. An imperial officer also went, expressly to be witness of the circumstance. A number of graves of those who had been dead six weeks were opened, and one corpse, that of an old man of sixty-two years of age, was found "with the eyes open, having a fine colour, with natural respiration, nevertheless motionless as the dead. The executioner drove a stake into his heart; they then raised a pile and reduced the corpse to ashes." The deceased had appeared in the night to his son three days after his funeral, had demanded food, eaten it, and then disappeared; the second night after he had again appeared, the son was found dead in his bed. On the same day five or six other persons had fallen suddenly ill in the village and died one after the other in a few days.

Dr. Ennemoser's other narrative relates to a bad case of vampirism in another Hungarian canton. A dead man named Arnald Paul, who formerly had been tormented by a Turkish vampire, turned vampire himself. On the thirtieth day after his death, he vampirized and killed four persons, and on the fortieth day his body was exhumed.

His body was red, his hair, nails and beard had all grown again, and his veins were replete with fluid blood, which flowed [oozed?] from all parts of his body upon the winding-sheet which encompassed him. The Hadnagi, or baillie of the village, in whose presence the exhumation took place and who was skilled in vampirism, had, according to custom, a very

From: Anon., "The Vampire," reprinted from *The Theosophist* 12 (1891).

sharp stake driven into the heart of the defunct Arnald Paul, and which pierced his body through and through, and made him, as they say, utter a frightful shriek, as if he had been alive (which, of course, he was): that done, they cut off his head and burnt the whole body.

They also cremated four bodies of other persons who had died of the vampire.

These precautions availed not, however, for three years later within the space of three months, seventeen persons of the same village, of both sexes and all ages, fell victims to vampirism. A close inquiry into this unprecedented survival of the scourge after resort to cremation, made by the doctors and surgeons, elicited the significant fact that the vampire Arnald Paul had sucked to death not only human beings but also "several oxen, which the new vampires had eaten." So it seems that the vampiric mania, like rabies, may be communicated through bacilli nourished in the bodies of animals, to other persons not touched by the first vampire, when they partake of the flesh of a vampirized beast. Recent experiments in the Paris hospitals in curing paralysis by transmission in a modified form through the body of a third person appear to throw some light upon the psychical part of this subject.

The Vampire State

(Czechoslovakia)

In the spring of 1727 Arnod Paole returned from the Levant to his native village near Belgrade, a prosperous, honest, and clean-living man. But there was a shadow brooding on him. He confided to one or two a strange tale of how in the East he had been bitten by a phantom, and it seemed to have affected his mind. One day he fell off his haycart and was picked up insensible. He never regained

From: Reginald Hodder, "Vampires," Occult Review 19 (1914): 223–26.

consciousness but died, or seemed to die, some few hours afterward. He was buried. Three or four weeks later several people in the neighborhood made complaints to the authorities that they had been haunted by Arnod, and very soon four of them died. Then, says the official report, the body of Arnod Paole was disinterred *forty days after his burial,* and it was discovered that the body was in a perfectly fresh state, with no sign of decomposition. The eyes were wide open and the shroud was stained with fresh blood. His nails had come off, and new nails, talon-shaped, were growing. The wisest men of the place pronounced him to be "in the vampyr state"; accordingly a stake was driven through his heart, "whereupon he gave an audible groan and a quantity of blood flowed from him." The four who had died and were supposed to have been infected by Arnod were treated in the same way, lest they in turn should infect others.

It was not until five years later that the neighborhood again began to show signs of the evil. Gruesome tales of mysterious midnight visitants began to get about, and people began to sicken quickly and die. Again the churchyard was resorted to, and this time a great number of graves were opened. The medical report on the subject, signed by three regimental surgeons and countersigned by the lieutenant-colonel and a sublieutenant, gives a full account of the disinterment of thirteen people, after periods of from eighteen days to ninety days in the grave, most of them being in the "vampyr condition." This document seems to establish the fact that *human bodies have been buried in a state of deathlike trance and so remained for months.* It also proves that, if these entranced subjects were not vampires, then the medical men who drove stakes into their hearts were butchers and murderers.

The Werewolf Trials

(France)

n Poitou the peasants have a curious expression, *"courir la galipote,"* which means to turn into a werewolf or other human-animal by night and chase prey through the woods. The *galipote* is the familiar or imp which the sorcerer has the power to send forth.

In the Dark Ages sorcerers capable of this accomplishment were dealt with according to the law, and hundreds were sent to trial for practicing black arts, being condemned, in most instances, to be burnt alive or broken on the wheel. One of the most notorious historical cases was that of Pierre Bourgot, who served the devil for two years and was tried by the Inquisitor-General Boin.

Johannus Wierius gives in full the confession of Bourgot, otherwise called Great Peter, and of Michael Verding. The prisoners, who were accused of wicked practices in December 1521, believed they had been transformed into wolves.

About nineteen years before Pierre's arrest at Pouligay, a dreadful storm occurred which scattered the flock of sheep of which he was shepherd, and while he went far afield to search for them he met three black horsemen, one of whom said to him, "Where are you going, my friend? You appear to be in trouble."

Pierre told him that he was seeking his sheep, and the horseman bade him take courage, saying that if he would only have faith, his master would protect the straying sheep and see that no harm came to them.

Pierre thanked him and promised to meet him again in the same place a few days later. Soon afterward he found the stray sheep.

The black horseman, at their second meeting, told Pierre that he served the devil, and Pierre agreed to do likewise if he promised him protection for his flock. Then the devil's servant made him renounce God, the Virgin Mary, and all the saints of paradise, his baptism, and the tenets of Christianity. Pierre swore that he would do so, and kissed

From: Frank Hamel, *Human Animals* (New York: Frederick A. Stokes Co., 1916).

the horseman's left hand, which was as black as ink and felt stone cold. Then he knelt down and took an oath of allegiance to the devil, and the horseman forbade him thenceforth to repeat the Apostles' Creed.

For two years Pierre remained in the service of the Evil One, and during that time he never entered a church until mass was over, or at least until after the holy water had been sprinkled.

Meanwhile his flock was kept in perfect safety, and this sense of security made him so indifferent about the devil that he began to go to church again and to say the creed. This went on for eight or nine years, when he was told by one Michael Verding that he must once more render obedience to the Evil One, his master. In return for his homage Pierre was told that he would receive a sum of money.

Michael led him one evening to a clearing in the woods at Chastel Charlon, where many strangers were dancing. Each performer held in his hand a green torch which emitted a blue flame. Michael told Pierre to bestir himself and that then he would receive payment, so Pierre threw off his clothes and Michael smeared his body with an ointment which he carried. Pierre believed that he had been transformed into a wolf and was horrified to find that he had four paws and a thick pelt. He found himself able to run with the speed of the wind. Michael had also made use of the salve and had become equally agile. After an hour or two they resumed human shape, their respective masters giving them another salve for this purpose. After this experience Pierre complained that he felt utterly weary, and his master told him that was of no consequence and that he would be speedily restored to his usual state of health.

Pierre was often transformed into a werewolf after this first attempt, and on one occasion he fell upon a boy of seven with the intention of killing and eating him, but the child screamed so loudly that he beat a hasty retreat to the spot where his clothes lay in a heap, rubbed himself hurriedly with the ointment, and resumed human form to escape capture. Another time Michael and he killed an old woman who was gathering peas, and one day while in the shape of wolves they devoured the whole of a little girl except for one arm, and Michael said her flesh tasted excellent, although it apparently gave Pierre indigestion. They confessed also to strangling a young woman, whose blood they drank.

Among other disgusting crimes, Pierre murdered a girl of eight in a garden by cracking her neck between his jaws, and he killed a goat near the farm of one Master Pierre Lerugen, first by setting on it with his teeth and then by gashing its throat with a knife. The latter operation leads to the belief that he had resumed his original shape at the time.

A peculiar point worth noticing about the case of Michael and Pierre was that the former was able to transform himself at any moment with his clothes on, while the latter had to strip and rub in ointment to achieve the same result. At the time of his confession Pierre declared that he could not recollect where the wolf's fur went when he became human again.

He also deposed that an ash-colored powder was given to him, which he rubbed upon his arms and left hand and thus caused the death of every animal he touched. Here there would seem to be some discrepancy, for he declared that in many instances he strangled, bit, or wounded his victims!

Garinet gives a good account of the important trial in 1573 of Gilles Garnier, who was arrested for having devoured several children while in the form of a werewolf.

The prisoner was accused of seizing a young girl aged ten or twelve in a vineyard near Dôle, of killing her and dragging her into a wood, and of tearing the flesh from her bones with his teeth and claws. He found this food so palatable that he carried some of it away with him and offered to share it with his wife. A week after the feast of All Saints, he captured another young girl near the village of La Pouppé and was about to slay and devour her when someone hastened to her rescue and he took flight.

A week later, being still in the form of a wolf, he had killed and eaten a boy at a spot between Gredisans and Menoté, about a league from Dôle. He was accused also of being in the shape of a man when he caught another boy of twelve or thirteen years of age and carried him into the wood to strangle him, and, "in spite of the fact that it was Friday," he would have devoured his flesh had he not been interrupted by the approach of some strangers, who were too late, however, to save the boy's life. Garnier, having admitted all the charges against him, the judge pronounced the following sentence: "The condemned man is to be dragged to the place of execution and there burnt alive and his body reduced to ashes."

The account of the trial, which took place on the 18th day of January,

1573, was accompanied by a letter from Daniel d'Ange to the Dean of the Church of Sens which contained the following passage:

> Gilles Garnier, lycophile, as I may call him, lived the life of a hermit, but has since taken a wife, and having no means of support for his family fell into the way, as is natural to defiant and desperate people of rude habits, of wandering into the woods and wild places. In this state he was met by a phantom in the shape of a man, who told him that he could perform miracles, among other things declaring that he would teach him how to change at will into a wolf, lion, or leopard, and because the wolf is more familiar in this country than the other kinds of wild beasts, he chose to disguise himself in that shape, which he did, using a salve with which he rubbed himself for this purpose, as he has since confessed before dying, after recognizing the evil of his ways.

The affair made such a stir in the neighborhood, and the dread of werewolves had risen to such a pitch, that it was found necessary to ask the help of the populace in suppressing the nuisance. A legal decree was issued which empowered the people at Dôle to "assemble with javelins, pikes, arquebuses, and clubs to hunt and pursue the werewolf, and to take, bind, and kill it without incurring the usual fine or penalty for indulging in the chase without permission."

Boguet is the authority who cites the following cases of lycanthropy:

A boy called Benedict, aged about fifteen, one day climbed a tree to gather some fruit, when he saw a wolf attacking his little sister, who was playing at the foot of the tree.

The boy climbed down quickly, and the animal, which was tailless, let go of the little girl and turned upon her brother, who defended himself with a knife. According to the boy's account, the wolf tore the knife out of his hand and struck at his throat. A neighbor ran to the rescue and carried the boy home, where he died a few days after from the wound. While he lay dying he declared that the wolf that had injured him had forepaws shaped like human hands, but that its hind feet were covered with fur.

After inquiry it was proved that a young and demented girl called Perrenette Gandillon believed herself to be a wolf and had done this horrible deed. She was caught by the populace and torn limb from limb. This case occurred in the Jura Mountains in 1598.

Soon afterward Perrenette's brother Pierre was accused of being a werewolf, and confessed that he had been to the witches' Sabbath in this form. His son George had also been anointed with salve and had killed goats while he was in animal shape. Antoinette, his sister, was accused of sorcery and of intercourse with the devil, who appeared to her in the form of a black goat. Several members of the Gandillon family were arrested, and in prison Pierre and George conducted themselves as though they were possessed, walking on all fours and howling like wild beasts.

Not long after the Gandillon family had been disposed of, one Jeanne Perrin gave evidence that she was walking near a wood with her friend Clauda Gaillard, who disappeared suddenly behind a bush, and that the next moment there came forth a tailless wolf which frightened her so much that she made the sign of the cross and ran away. She was sure that the hind legs of the wolf were like human limbs. When Clauda saw her again she assured Jeanne that the wolf had not meant to do her harm, and from this it was thought that Clauda had taken the shape of the wolf.

One of the best known of the werewolf trials concerns Jacques Rollet, the man-wolf of Caude, who was accused of having devoured a little boy.

He was tried and condemned in Angers in 1598. Rollet came from the parish of Maumusson, near Nantes, and he carried on his practices in a desolate spot near Caude, where some villagers one day found the corpse of a boy of about fifteen, mangled and blood-bespattered. As they approached the body three wolves bounded into the forest and were lost to sight, but the men gave chase, and following in the animals' tracks, came suddenly upon a half-naked human being, with long hair and beard, his hands covered with blood and his teeth chattering with fear. On his clawlike nails they found shreds of human flesh.

This miserable specimen of man-animal was hauled up before the judge, and under examination he inquired of one of the witnesses whether he remembered shooting at three wolves. The witness said he remembered the incident perfectly. Rollet confessed that he was one of the wolves and that he was able to transform himself by means of a salve. The other wolves were his companions, Jean and Julian, who knew the same means of acquiring animal shape. All the particulars he gave as to the murder were accurate, and he confessed to having killed and eaten women, lawyers, attorneys, and bailiffs, though the last-named he found tough and tasteless. In other respects his evidence was confused, and he was judged to be of weak intellect, and though condemned to death was sent finally to a madhouse, where he was sentenced to two years' detention.

There was an epidemic of lycanthropy throughout this year, and on the 4th of December a tailor of Châlons was burnt in Paris for having decoyed children into his shop, a cask full of human bones being discovered in the cellar. For the space of a few years no notorious werewolf trials appear to have taken place, but the year 1603 was almost as prolific in this respect as 1598.

Information came before the criminal court at Roche Chalais that a wild beast was ravaging the district, that it appeared to be a wolf, and that it had attacked a young girl called Margaret Peiret in full daylight.

A youth of thirteen or fourteen in the service of Peter Combaut deposed to the fact that he had thrown himself upon the said Margaret, while transformed into a wolf, and that he would have devoured her had she not defended herself stoutly with a stick. He also confessed to having eaten two or three little girls.

Evidence was given on May 19, 1603, by three witnesses, one of whom was Margaret herself. She said she had been accustomed to mind cattle in the company of the boy, Jean Grenier, and that he had often frightened her by telling her horrible tales about being able to change into a wolf whenever he wished, and that he had killed many dogs and sucked their blood, but that he preferred to devour young children. He said he had recently killed a child, and after eating part of her flesh had thrown the rest to a companion wolf.

Margaret described the beast which had attacked her as stouter and shorter than a real wolf, with a smaller head, a short tail, and reddish hide. After she struck at it, the animal drew back and sat down on its haunches like a dog, at a distance of about twelve paces. Its look was so ferocious that she ran away at once.

The third witness was Jeanne Gaboriaut, who was eighteen years old. She gave evidence that one day, when she was tending cattle in company with other girls, Jean Grenier came up and asked which was the most beautiful shepherdess among them. Jeanne asked him why he wanted to know. He said because he wished to marry the prettiest, and if it was Jeanne he would choose her.

Jeanne said, "Who is your father?" and he told her that he was the son of a priest.

Then she replied that he was too dark in appearance for her taste, and when he answered he had been like that for a long time, she asked him whether he had turned black from cold or whether he had been burnt black.

He said the cause was a wolfskin he was wearing, which had been given to him by one Pierre Labourant, and when he wore it he could turn into a wolf at will or any other animal he preferred, and he went on with details similar to those he had disclosed to Margaret Poiret.

It was proved, however, that Grenier was not the son of a priest, but of a laborer, Pierre Grenier, and that he lived in the parish of St. Antoine de Pizan.

When questioned as to his crimes, he confessed to the assault upon Margaret Poiret as described by her, and also that he had entered a house in the guise of a wolf, and finding no one there but a babe in its cradle he seized it by the throat and carried it behind a hedge in the garden, where he ate as much of the body as he could and threw the remainder to another wolf.

At St. Antoine de Pizan he attacked a girl in a black dress who was tending sheep, and he killed and devoured her, a strange point being that her dress was not torn, as happens in the case when real wolves make the assault.

When questioned as to how he managed to turn into a wolf, he said that a neighbor, called Pierre la Tilhaire, had introduced him in the forest to the lord thereof, who had given wolfskins to both, as well as a salve for anointing themselves. When asked where he kept the skins and the pot of ointment, he replied that they were in the hands of the Lord of the Forest, from whom he could obtain them whenever he wished.

He declared that he had changed into a wolf and gone coursing four times with his companion Pierre la Tilhaire, but they had killed no one. The best time for the hunt was an hour or two a day when the moon was on the wane, but he also went out at night on some occasions.

When asked whether his father knew of these proceedings, he replied in the affirmative and declared that his father had rubbed him three times with the ointment and helped him into the wolfskin.

The inquiry into Jean Grenier's case was a very lengthy one and was adjourned several times, but eventually he was sentenced to imprisonment for life at Bordeaux on September 6, 1603, his youth and want of mental development being pleaded in extenuation of the crimes of infanticide he had undoubtedly committed. The president of the court declared that lycanthropy was a form of hallucination and was not in itself a punishable crime. Jean's father was acquitted of complicity and allowed to leave the court without a stain on his character, and Jean was sent to a monastery.

In 1610, after Jean had been at the Monastery of the Cordeliers in Bordeaux for seven years, de Lancre, who relates his story, went to see him. He was then about twenty years of age and of diminutive stature. His black eyes were haggard and deep-set, and he refused to look anyone straight in the face. His teeth were long, sharp, and protruding; his nails were also long and black and his mind was a mere blank.

He told de Lancre, not without pride, that he had been a werewolf but that he had given up the practice. When he first arrived at the monastery he had preferred to go on all fours, eating such food as he found on the ground. He confessed that he still craved raw human flesh, especially the flesh of little girls, and he hoped it would not be long before he had another opportunity of tasting it. He had been visited twice during his confinement by the Lord of the Forest, as he called the mysterious person who had given him the wolfskin, but that both times he had made the sign of the cross and his visitor had departed in haste.

In other respects his tale was identical with the experiences he had related before the court.

De Lancre thought that the name Grenier or Garnier was a fatal name in connection with werewolves.

Evidence was given as to the times, places, and number of murders, and many of the facts were proved incontestably.

Jean's evidence as to the part his father had played in his misdeeds was hazy. He said that on one occasion his father had accompanied him, also wearing a wolfskin, and that together they had killed a young girl dressed in white, and that they had devoured her flesh, the month being May of 1601.

He also added curious details regarding the Lord of the Forest, who had forbidden him to bite the thumbnail of his left hand, which was thicker and longer than the others, and that if he lost sight of it while in the form of a wolf he would quickly recover his human shape.

When confronted with his father Jean altered some of the details of his story, and it was agreed that long imprisonment and extended cross-examination had worn out his already feeble intellect.

The Phantom of the Pharmacy

(Eastern Europe)

In 1659 there died at Crossen, in Silesia, an apothecary's apprentice named Christopher Monig. Some days after, they perceived a phantom in the pharmacy. Everyone recognized Christopher Monig. This phantom seated itself, rose, went to the shelves, seized pots, flasks, etc., and changed their places. It examined and tasted drugs, weighed them in the scales, pounded the drugs with a noise, served the persons who presented prescriptions, received the money, and placed it in the drawer. No one, however, dared to speak to it. Having doubtless some grudge against the master, then very seriously ill, it busied itself with giving him all sorts of annoyances. One day it took a cloak which was in the pharmacy, opened the door, and went out. It walked through the streets without looking at anyone, entered the houses of several of his acquaintances, gazed at them a moment without speaking a word, and withdrew. Meeting a servant-girl in the cemetery, it said to her, "Go to your master's house and dig in the lower room; you will find there an inestimable treasure."

The poor girl, overcome with terror, fell senseless on the ground. It stooped down and lifted her but left a mark that was long visible. Returning home, and although suffering from great terror, she related what happened to her. They dug at the spot indicated and found, in

From: Adolphe d'Assier, *Posthumous Humanity: A Study of Phantoms* (with an appendix of beliefs current in India) (London: George Redway, 1887).

an old pot, a pretty [bloodstone?]. It is well known that alchemists attributed occult properties to this stone. The rumor of these prodigies having reached the ears of Princess Elizabeth Charlotte, she ordered that the body of Monig should be exhumed. It was thought that this was a case of vampirism; but nothing was found except a corpse in rather an advanced state of putrefaction. The apothecary was then advised to get rid of all the things that had belonged to Monig. The specter reappeared no more from that time.

The Haunted Villa

(France)

D r. Durnford three years ago lay basking on the verandah of one of the prettiest villas on the outskirts of the town of M——— in the south of France. The villa had been rented by his sister, a Mrs. Norris, a charming widow who, with her two children and English servants, had taken up her residence at M———.

Her favorite brother (Dr. Durnford) had been very ill, and a couple of months' complete rest were ordered him by his medical colleagues. "Get away from England and forget you ever had an overworked heart, and rest, rest, rest," were the words of parting advice. So it came to pass that Dr. Durnford found himself comfortably settled in his favorite sister's villa at M———. That evening after a cozy dinner and a long and intimate chat with Mrs. Norris, he went to his room. A wood fire crackled cheerfully in a wide fireplace. A quaint round mirror hung over the mantelpiece, and the rest of the room was furnished scantily but with refined taste. The floor was inlaid, brightly polished, and an electric switch was conveniently placed beside him, with a reading lamp. He went off to sleep directly, and was awakened by the feeling that someone was gazing intently at him. To his horror

From: C. Milligan Fox, "The Haunted Villa: A True Story," *Occult Review* 11 (1910): 158–60.

the doctor saw an evil face belonging to a man of huge bulk, and he felt powerless to withdraw his eyes from this sinister-looking being. Hours seemed to pass in that long and compelling gaze. At last the figure raised itself and the doctor noticed again the enormous height of this unwelcome visitor. The figure then moved toward the fire, and stood with its back against it. Then Dr. Durnford noticed that his visitor's head reached the top of the *mirror*, which hung over the mantelpiece. "Now!" thought the doctor, "is my time"; and he threw out one hand and seized hold of the electric switch, but before he could say or do anything, the figure dissolved into air, just as if it had been made of vapor. No more sleep came to soothe his excited nerves, and in turning over the matter in his mind, he decided to say nothing to his sister, who was a high-strung nervous woman, and keep the unpleasant visitation to himself.

That morning his sister told him he did not look very well, but he put her off by saying that he never slept extra well for the first time in a strange house. The day passed quickly, and a long spin with friends in a delightful motorcar made the doctor completely forget his strange nocturnal experience.

That evening after dinner his little niece Muriel came bounding into the room, and going up to her mother, whispered something. "What!" said Mrs. Norris, "Gerald refuses to go to bed? What has he been reading?"

"No, no, indeed, mother, he has not been reading anything, but he keeps on saying, 'I saw your burglar, and he was such a big giant.'" Turning to Dr. Durnford, his little niece continued, "You see, uncle, the burglar came one night and stole all my nice pretty things, and he was so very very *big*."

"There, there," said the doctor's sister, "don't think of that wicked burglar; I'll go and quiet Gerald."

On Mrs. Norris's return she looked quite distressed and said Gerald seemed terrified to be left alone, and that she had arranged for one of the maids to sleep in the room with him. "The poor child insists on the burglar being alive, when we all know he killed himself a year ago."

"Tell me the whole story," said the doctor, now thoroughly roused, and remembering his own strange experience, he felt sorry for his little nephew and for the fright he must have had.

"We certainly had an ugly experience," said the doctor's sister. "One night Muriel was awakened by seeing a giant bending over her. She then saw him crawl on the floor toward my room, which opened into Muriel's. Muriel said she simply screamed, and held her finger on the electric bell till the servants came running; and the burglar, she said, crawled into the balcony and disappeared, taking with him all Muriel's little silver ornaments, but she certainly saved me, and my jewelry, and was a good plucky child," said Mrs. Norris proudly.

"What happened to the burglar?" Dr. Durnford asked.

"A few months later he was arrested from Muriel's description in the town of M———, and being of great strength he was able to overpower the gendarme. Drawing out a revolver, he fired on him, and then turned and shot himself through the head. He was a notorious criminal, and I shudder to think of what might have been."

"Let us go up and see Gerald," said the doctor thoughtfully.

On going into the room, they saw the little boy was wide awake and talking to the maid. "Yes! I saw him go right up the chimney like a puff of smoke."

"Why, to be sure," said the doctor, "no doubt you did, for it must have been dear old Father Christmas, who came to pay you a visit in France and wanted you to tell him what nice present you would like for next Christmas."

"But I thought he always had a long white beard, and this man was not dressed up like Father Christmas and was just an ugly big giant like Muriel's burglar."

"Ah!" said Dr. Durnford, "he had to disguise himself, no doubt, and besides, what would have brought him to see you? Perhaps Father Christmas may have left something for you. Just look! What is this?" picking up something from the floor. "A gold coin. Ah! well, little boy," said the doctor, "when he comes again you won't be afraid of him, will you?"

"No!" said Gerald decidedly. But he never came again, and the villa was left in peace.

The Restless Ghost

(England)

The person that is the original author of this account (from whose own mouth the same is taken) is an honest, substantial man named William Clark, by profession a maulster but living at present in a farmhouse at a town called Hennington, within four miles of Northampton. The house is usually called Old Pells house, persons of that name having for several generations lived in it; nor was it within the memory of man any way haunted or disturbed, till within this twelve-month last past or thereabouts. Since which time this Goodman Clark and his family have been often alarmed and affrighted, sometimes the doors in the night all unlocked, unbolted, and flung off the hinges; at other times the windows broken so lamentably as if the devil had been got into one of the frolics of our London hectors to make work for the glaziers in his nocturnal rambles. Oftentimes the Goodman would get up in his shirt to see what was the matter or occasion of so much confusion, but still nothing appeared till about three weeks since. He being walking a little way off from his house, the spirit on a sudden became visible to him, at first in a very horrid, but immediately after in a more familiar and humane shape. Yet was the man much frighted at it for the present, till recollecting his scattered spirits, he took the courage (in the name of almighty God, blessed forever) to demand *what it was*, and *what it would have*. To which the apparition, with a pleasant friendly countenance and distinct voice, answered in these words (as near as he can remember them) or at least to this effect: "I am the disturbed spirit of a person long since dead. I was murdered near this place two hundred sixty and seven years, nine weeks, and two days ago, to this very time. And come along with me and I will show you where it was done."

This being said, it conducted him into the next close to the side of a hedge and then said, "Here was I killed, my head being separated

From: John Millet, *The Rest-less Ghost; or, Wonderful News from Northamptonshire and Southwark* (Northampton: Taylor & Son, 1878, reprint).

from my body." Goodman Clark asked him how he came to be killed. He answered, "For lucre and covetousness of my estate." The man demanded whether he dwelt thereabouts in his lifetime; he replied no, he inhabited at London in Southwark, where he had some money and writings that had ever since lain buried in the earth, and that till the same was taken up and disposed of according to his mind, he should never be at rest. The man further inquired why he had not discovered the same sooner, rather than now after so very long a space of time. He answered that he did for several years after his murder haunt and disturb that place, but was at last laid and bound down by the magical art of a certain friar (whose name he mentioned but the man has forgot it) for two hundred and fifty years, during which time he was confined from appearing on earth, but now the same being expired he was come and resolved this man should do what he desired or else should never have any peace. The man inquired what was his request. The phantasm or ghost said that he should go to London the very next day and that it would meet him there and show him the place where the things were hid. The man replied he could not without great prejudice go so soon, but within a fortnight he would be there. At last they concluded he should come within that time and that the ghost would meet him upon London Bridge or going into Southwark, and so for that time it disappeared.

Clark, strangely surprised with this accident, coming home acquaints his neighbors, but more especially the minister of the parish he dwelt in and several other learned and godly men, with the story and all the strange circumstances, who unanimously advised him to keep his word and not fail to meet it, but not to eat or drink in any place whether it should lead him, etc.

Several times in this fortnight it appeared to him, but in a very gentle manner, putting him in mind of his promise, which Clark gave it fresh assurances he would make good and, being now familiarized, talked as freely to it as to any of his companions. One time it told him it left a wife and two children behind at its death and that its estate had now run through four several families. At another time he demanded whether it had been all this while in joy or torment, and whether when he had done and performed its will, it would go into a state of eternal happiness. But to neither of these questions would it answer one word, but when it was minded to be gone would still bid him go on before and not look back, and so left him.

The carrier from that town told all this of the story at the Castle Inn without Smithfield Bars near three weeks ago, and that Clark was to come up about it, and accordingly on Saturday the ninth of January, 1675, made a journey purposely and solely to London, on that occasion and on Sunday in the afternoon (being somewhat impatient to know the upshot of the matter) would needs walk over the bridge into Southwark. But no sooner was he going off from the footbridge into the burrough but the spirit appeared in the common habit of a man, standing right before him, and with an inviting smile turned about and led him on to a place in Southwark (which I am forced to omit naming, particularly for fear of adding to the people's trouble by sending more inquirers, of whom thousands have already been there so that 'tis sufficiently known to most on that side of the water). Being come there, he would not for some time appear to go in, because as he alleged there were some strangers present that were nothing concerned, but as soon as they were gone he went invisible both to Clark and two women and others that were in the house, where it very mildly told them the whole story aforesaid and that they were some of his posterity, and then shewed them a place, bidding them dig there next day and then he would be with them again. Next day Clark going over early, they dug accordingly in that place and, about eight feet deep, found a pot and in it a considerable quantity of gold, and at the bottom of that some writings, some of paper which did molder away and crumble to dust if they touched them, but others of parchment were whole, by whose dates it appeared they had lain there as long as he had said before it was since he was murdered. Clark was the man took up the pot, the spirit visibly standing by in human shape in the presence of several persons, and then it gave him particular orders how he should dispose of what he found, which he distributed accordingly, and then the spirit appeared to him again in a very joyful contented manner, saying, "Thou hast done well, and henceforth I shall be at rest, so as never more to trouble thee."

The Phantom Coach

(Ireland)

O f legends that appeal to the imagination, few compare in effect with that of the Phantom Coach. In my childhood I have often lain awake and trembled while I fancied that I heard the sound of its ghostly wheels. It was said to start at midnight from an old churchyard where many generations of the dead lay sleeping and, after calling at a ruined castle, to visit every burying place in the neighborhood. I have been told that many belated wanderers have been met by the spectacle of a mourning coach with headless horses, while others have seen nothing but been alarmed by the sound of wheels and hoofs. In Italy and Spain there is a belief in just such a ghostly hearse; and to the same class belong the headless steed of the Alhambra and horsemen who gallop about, as well in Andalusia as in Dunkerron, carrying their heads in their hands or destitute of them. There is in Cumberland a family that for centuries has lived in the old seat. Whenever any of the race is about to die, a hearse with four horses is heard to drive before the house. It may not be audible to a member of the family, but someone, guest or servant, is sure to hear it.

From: Maurice McCarthy O'Leary, "Notes and Queries: Certain Irish Superstitions," *Journal of American Folk-Lore* 10–11 (1897–98): 234–37.

The White Lady of the Hohenzollerns

(Germany)

A great deal has been written and said concerning the various appearances of the famous White Lady of the Hohenzollerns. As long ago as the fifteenth century she was seen, for the first time, in the old Castle of Neuhaus in Bohemia, looking out at noonday from an upper window of an uninhabited turret of the castle. And numerous indeed are the stories of her appearances to various persons connected with the Royal House of Prussia, from that first one in the turret window down to the time of the death of the late Empress Augusta, which was, of course, of comparatively recent date. For some time after that event, she seems to have taken a rest; and now, if rumor is to be credited, the apparition that displayed in the past so deep an interest in the fortunes—or perhaps one would be more correct in saying misfortunes—of the Hohenzollern family has been manifesting herself again!

The remarkable occurrences of which I am about to write were related by certain French persons of sound sense and unimpeachable veracity, who happened to be in Berlin a few weeks before the outbreak of the European War. The Kaiser, the most superstitious monarch who ever sat upon the Prussian throne, sternly forbade the circulation of the report of these happenings in his own country, but our gallant Allies across the Channel are fortunately not obliged to obey the despotic commands of Wilhelm II, and these persons, therefore, upon their return to France, related to those interested in such matters the following story of the great war lord's three visitations from the dreaded ghost of the Hohenzollerns.

Early in the summer of 1914 it was rumored in Berlin that the White Lady had made her reappearance. The tale, whispered first of all at

From: Katharine Cox, "Wilhelm II and the White Lady of the Hohenzollerns," *Occult Review* 25 (1917): 17–22.

court, spread gradually among the townspeople. The court, alarmed, tried to suppress it, but it refused to be suppressed, and eventually there was scarcely a man, woman, or child in the neighborhood who did not say—irrespective of whether they believed it or not—that the White Lady, the shadowy specter whose appearance always foreboded disaster to the imperial house, had been recently seen, not once but three times, and by no less a person than Kaiser Wilhelm himself!

The first of these appearances, so rumor stated, took place one night at the end of June. The hour was late. The court, which was then in residence at the palace of Potsdam, was wrapped in slumber. All was quiet; there was an almost deathlike silence in the palace. In one wing were the apartments of the empress, where she lay sleeping; in the opposite wing slept one of her sons; the other princes were in Berlin. In an entirely different part of the royal residence, guarded by three sentinels in a spacious antechamber, sat the emperor in his private study. He had been, lately, greatly engrossed in weighty matters of state, and for some time past it had been his habit to work thus, far into the night. That same evening the Chancellor, von Bethman-Hollweg, had had a private audience of His Majesty and had left the royal presence precisely at 11:30, carrying an enormous dossier under his arm. The emperor had accompanied him as far as the door, shaken hands with him, then returned to his work at his writing desk.

Midnight struck, and still the emperor, without making the slightest sound, sat on within the room. The guards without began to grow slightly uneasy, for at midnight punctually—not a minute before, not a minute after—it was the emperor's unfailing custom, when he was working late at night, to ring and order a light repast to be brought to him. Sometimes it used to be a cup of thick chocolate with hot cakes; sometimes a few sandwiches of smoked ham with a glass of Munich or Pilsen beer—but as this particular midnight hour struck, the guards awaited the royal commands in vain. The emperor had apparently forgotten to order his midnight meal!

One o'clock in the morning came, and still the emperor's bell had not sounded. Within the study silence continued to reign—silence as profound indeed as that of the grave. The uneasiness of the three guards without increased; they glanced at each other with anxious faces. Was their royal master taken ill? All during the day he had seemed to be laboring under the influence of some strange, suppressed excitement, and as he had bidden good-bye to the chancellor, they had noticed that the expression of excitement on his face had increased. That something of grave import was in the air they, and indeed everyone surrounding the emperor, had long been aware; it was just possible that the strain of state affairs was becoming too much for him, and that he had been smitten with sudden indisposition. And yet, after all, he had probably only fallen asleep! Whichever it was, however, they were uncertain how to act. If they thrust ceremony aside and entered the study, they knew that very likely they would only expose themselves to the royal anger. The order was strict, "When the emperor works in his study, no one may enter it without being bidden." Should they inform the lord chamberlain of the palace? But if there was no sufficiently serious reason for such a step, they would incur *his* anger, almost as terrible to face as that of their royal master.

A little more time dragged by, and at last, deciding to risk the consequences, the guards approached the study. One of them, the most courageous of the three, lifted a heavy curtain and slowly and cautiously opened the door. He gave one rapid glance into the room beyond, then, returning to his companions, said in a low voice and with a terrified gesture toward the interior of the study, "Look!"

The two guards obeyed him, and an alarming spectacle met their eyes. In the middle of the room, beside a big table littered with papers and military documents, lay the emperor, stretched full length upon the thick velvet pile carpet, one hand, as if to hide something dreadful from view, across his face. He was quite unconscious, and while two of the guards endeavored to revive him, the other ran for the doctor. Upon the doctor's arrival, they carried him to his sleeping apartments, and after some time succeeded in reviving him. The emperor then, in trembling accents, told his astounded listeners what had occurred.

Exactly at midnight, according to his custom, he had rung the bell which was the signal that he was ready for his repast. Curiously enough, neither of the guards, although they had been listening for it, had heard that bell.

He had rung quite mechanically, and also mechanically had turned again to his writing desk directly he had done so. A few minutes later he had heard the door open and footsteps approach him across the soft carpet. Without raising his head from his work he had commenced to say, "Bring me————"

Then he had raised his head, expecting to see the butler awaiting his orders. Instead his eyes fell upon a shadowy female figure dressed in white, with a long flowing black veil trailing behind her on the ground. He rose from his chair, terrified, and cried, "Who are you, and what do you want?"

At the same moment, instinctively, he placed his hand upon a service revolver which lay upon the desk. The white figure, however, did not move, and he advanced toward her. She gazed at him, retreating slowly backward toward the end of the room and finally disappeared through the door which gave access to the antechamber without. The door, however, had not opened, and the three guards stationed in the antechamber, as has been already stated, had neither seen nor heard anything of the apparition. At the moment of her disappearance, the emperor fell into a swoon, remaining in that condition until the guards and the doctor revived him.

Such was the story, gaining ground every day in Berlin, of the first of the three appearances of the White Lady of the Hohenzollerns to the Kaiser. The story of her second appearance to him, which occurred some two or three weeks later, is equally remarkable.

On this occasion she did not visit him at Potsdam but at Berlin, and instead of the witching hour of midnight, she chose the broad, clear light of day. Indeed, during the whole of her career, the White Lady does not seem to have kept to the time-honored traditions of most ghosts, and appeared to startled humanity chiefly at nighttime or in dim uncertain lights. She has never been afraid to face the honest daylight, and that, in my opinion, has always been a great factor in establishing her claim to genuineness. A ghost who is seen by sane people, in full daylight, cannot surely be a mere legendary myth!

It was an afternoon of bright summer—that fateful summer whose blue skies were so soon to be darkened by the sinister clouds of war! The royal standard, intimating to the worthy citizens of Berlin the presence of their emperor, floated gaily over the imperial residence in the gentle breeze. The emperor, wrapped in heavy thought—there was much for the mighty war lord to think about during those last pregnant days before plunging Europe into an agony of tears and blood!—was pacing, alone, up and down a long gallery within the palace.

His walk was agitated; there was a troubled frown upon his austere countenance. Every now and then he paused in his walk and withdrew from his pocket a piece of paper, which he carefully read and reread, and as he did so, angry muttered words broke from him and his hand flew instinctively to his sword hilt. Occasionally he raised his eyes to the walls on either side of him, upon which hung numerous portraits of his distinguished ancestors. He studied them gravely, from Frederick I, Burgrave of Nuremberg, to that other Frederick, his own father, and husband of the fair English princess against whose country he was so shortly going to wage the most horrible warfare that has ever been waged in the whole history of the world!

Suddenly, from the other end of the long portrait gallery he perceived coming toward him a shadowy female figure, dressed entirely in white and carrying a large bunch of keys in her hand. She was not this time wearing the long flowing black veil in which she had appeared to him a few weeks previously, but the emperor instantly recognized her, and the blood froze in his veins. He stood rooted to the ground, unable to advance or to retreat, paralyzed with horror, the hair rising on his head, beads of perspiration standing on his brow.

The figure continued to advance in his direction, slowly, noiselessly, appearing rather to glide than to walk over the floor. There was an expression of the deepest sadness upon her countenance, and as she drew near to the stricken man watching her, she held out her arms toward him, as if to enfold him. The emperor, his horror increasing, made a violent effort to move, but in vain. He seemed indeed paralyzed; his limbs, his muscles, refused to obey him.

Then suddenly, just as the apparition came close up to him and he felt, as on the former occasion when he had been visited by her, that he was going to faint, she turned abruptly and moved away in the direction of a small side door. This she opened with her uncanny bunch of keys and, without turning her head, disappeared.

At the exact moment of her disappearance, the emperor recovered his faculties. He was able to move, he was able to speak; his arms, legs, tongue obeyed his autocratic will once more. He uttered a loud terrified cry, which resounded throughout the palace. Officers, chamberlains, guards, servants came running to the gallery, white-faced, to see what had happened. They found their royal master in a state bordering on collapse. Yet, to the anxious questions which they put to him, he only replied incoherently and evasively; it was as if he knew something terrible, something dreadful, but did not wish to speak of it. Eventually he retired to his own apartments, but it was not until several hours had passed that he returned to his normal condition of mind.

The same doctor who had been summoned on the occasion of Wilhelm's former encounter with the White Lady was in attendance on him, and he looked extremely grave when informed that the emperor had again experienced a mysterious shock. He shut himself up alone with his royal patient, forbidding anyone else access to the private apartments. However, in spite of all precautions, the story of what had really occurred in the picture gallery eventually leaked out—it is said through a maid of honor, who heard it from the empress.

The third appearance of the White Lady of the Hohenzollerns to the Kaiser did not take place at either of the palaces but, strangely enough, in a forest, though exactly where situated has not been satisfactorily verified.

In the middle of the month of July 1914, while the war clouds were darkening every hour, the emperor's movements were very unsettled. He was constantly traveling from place to place, and one day—so it was afterward said in Berlin—while on a hunting expedition, he suddenly encountered a phantom female figure dressed in white who, springing apparently from nowhere, stopped in front of his horse and blew a shadowy horn, frightening the animal so much that its rider was nearly thrown to the ground. The phantom figure then disappeared as mysteriously as it had come—but that it was the White Lady of the Hohenzollerns, come perchance to warn Wilhelm of some terrible future fate, there was little doubt in the minds of those who afterward heard of the occurrence.

According to one version of the story of this third appearance, the phantom was also seen by two officers who were riding by the emperor's side, but the general belief is that she manifested herself, as on the two former occasions, to Wilhelm alone.

There are many who will not believe in the story, no doubt, and there are also many who will. For my own part, I am inclined to think that, if the ghost of the Hohenzollerns was able to manifest herself so often on the eve of any tragedy befalling them in the past, it would be strange indeed if she had not manifested herself on the eve of this greatest tragedy of all—the War!

The Hunting Lodge of Griesheim

(Germany)

When the Landgrave of Hesse-Darmstadt had the Hunting Lodge at Griesheim pulled down, his action caused some surprise, as the house was only some fifty years old, had cost much to build, and was still in excellent condition. But those who knew the reasons for the Landgrave's action greatly approved of it. True, it would not have commended itself to the Society for Psychical Research, but then all this happened long before that excellent body was founded.

The circumstances leading to the demolition of the Lodge are of a somewhat singular nature. They were recorded shortly afterward from the evidence of eyewitnesses and persons immediately concerned in them, so "the thing is, in a manner, history." So far as the present writer is aware, the story has never before been told in English. He has kept as closely as possible to the particulars of the original record.

By all accounts, the adventures to be met with in Griesheim Wood were not, during a certain period at least, to everybody's taste. The period referred to was that which followed Freiherr von Mingerod's death, which took place in 1750.

Freiherr von Mingerod was the then Landgrave's Master of the Hounds, which explains his connection with the Hunting Lodge. He seems to have been a mighty hunter and a keen sportsman, and was certainly a faithful servant to his master, who wrote a quaintly touching little elegy on his death—verses that have the queer pathos of an old-fashioned tune, tinkled faintly and slowly by some old clock or *tabatiére* come down from the days of sword and *perruque*. One likes to think of the old prince, sitting in his Hunting Lodge with powdered

From: Philip MacLeod, "Why the Hunting-Lodge at Griesheim Was Pulled Down: A True Story," *Occult Review* 18 (1913): 86–90.

hair and red coat and great boots, looking dreamily out through the open window while he shapes his verses, with the drowsy murmur of the summer wood coming in to him.

Why Freiherr von Mingerod should have haunted the wood after his death is not clear. Perhaps, as in the case of poor Goldsmith, his mind was not at ease when he died. His memory is charged with no crime, nor even with suspicion, and yet it seems that he could not rest in the grave. Certain it is that after his death the wood of Griesheim began to have a most uncanny reputation.

People said that unaccountable winds arose in the forest at night, winds that grew more violent as they approached the Lodge, and kept on blowing till long after midnight, ceasing as suddenly and mysteriously as they had begun. And, though it was known that the Lodge was well secured and that not a soul was in it, yet every window would at such times be seen brilliantly lighted up. Many persons declared that they had met a hunter in the twilight, a hunter that rode noiselessly by, without sound of hoof. An old forester deposed one day that the evening before he had seen in a woodpath a dog of a breed that had long died out. Quite astonished, he had approached it, while his own dog, an animal both courageous and vicious, slunk close at heel; but the nearer he approached the creature, the huger and vaguer it grew till, as he was close upon it, there was nothing but a mist that he found all about him. Full of fear, he hastened home and next day made the official report that has come down among the records of the case.

Herr E——, who had the care of the Lodge, once sent his two young sons there with an elderly servant to make some preparations for an approaching visit from the Landgrave. Night came on before all things were ready, but at last lights were put out, window shutters and doors carefully secured, and the little party set out for home. They had hardly gone a hundred and fifty paces from the house when one of the brothers, chancing to look back, saw every window brilliantly lighted! What hand could in those few seconds have lighted all the candles and opened the well-bolted shutters? The terrified spectators did not stay to inquire, but made off as quickly as they could.

There was a certain Fuchs, a captain in the White Dragoon Regiment, which at that time furnished part of the guard for Kranichstein, the Landgrave's palace. Fuchs had formerly been in the Prussian Army, served in one of Frederick II's campaigns, and obtained an order. He was a man of great determination and presence of mind, and he often said that if the Landgrave would only grant him permission and the necessary means, he would soon put an end to the hauntings at Griesheim. This came to the Landgrave's ears, and he one day asked Fuchs what means he considered necessary to banish the ghost. Fuchs replied that if twenty dragoons, picked by himself, were placed under his orders, together with a supply of food and drink adequate to sustain them during the watch, he would undertake the task of exorcism.

The Landgrave readily acceded to the captain's request, directing only that every possible precaution should be taken; and about noon on a fine autumn day not long afterward, Rittmeister Fuchs and his merry men were assembled in the haunted Lodge. Needless to say, the captain had chosen fellows of courage and without the smallest trace of superstition. He had issued stringent orders: "No man is to leave his post before he is relieved, let him see or hear what he pleases. If any one approaches and does not immediately answer when challenged, fire upon him with the carbine. Any man guilty of the slightest insubordination will at once be shot down by me."

The Rittmeister quartered his men on the ground floor of the house, while he himself examined every room above, every fireplace, every corner, and even the chimneys; he locked every door behind him and took the keys. The back door was locked and bolted; the cellars were searched; the wood was thoroughly beaten. Nothing suspicious; Fuchs was already groaning at the prospect of having to begin his next morning's report at Kranichstein with "All's well, Herr Landgraf."

The day wore on; the shadows of the firs grew longer and longer till they vanished as evening came. There was no moon that night. But even before sunset, eight dragoons with carbines and sidearms had been posted all round the house in a sort of ring. The sentries were relieved every half hour.

All the rooms on the ground floor were brightly lighted with candles, which were carefully renewed whenever necessary. The Rittmeister sat for the most part in the drawing room, but every now and then he walked among the other chambers or about the house outside.

So things went on till near midnight. The sentries reported nothing suspicious, though they had been exceptionally vigilant and "had tried different ruses" to entrap all possible tricksters. Nobody guessed how near the catastrophe was!

The sentries on the southwest suddenly noticed a dull rustling at some distance, which came nearer and nearer. All at once it became a violent gale that bent the young trees like whips, tore the tops off the old ones, and hurled them roaring by. To make matters worse, bands of fire came darting through the wood, flashing and vanishing, and often passing close to the dazzled eyes of the sentries.

It was too much for those honest fellows, and they retired to the house on the double, where they received anything but a warm welcome from their commander. He himself, of course, had observed the storm and felt the house rock to its foundations before it; but the unexampled insubordination of his men greatly incensed him, and he chased them back to their posts with what are described as "all the oaths of an old soldier."

The gale continued to roar, and bluish flames flickered through the dark over and about the house. After midnight, however, the wind dropped, the "ghostly messengers" flashed no more, and the wood became as dark, to use the dragoons' expression, as the inside of a cartridge pouch. Rittmeister Fuchs began to believe that he had nothing but the elements to deal with. The sentries found it exceedingly dull; everything was quiet.

Hark! A shot! Several other shots! The Rittmeister, followed by his men, rushed out of the house. Nothing further to be heard, nothing to be seen but the dark masses of the trees. The party returned, resolving to await the time of relief. One Z———, a private, reported that the nearest sentry had quit his post. The Rittmeister was just about to sally forth again, when something happened.

The house suddenly rocked as if it had been struck by a thunderbolt; a hurricane was roaring about it all at once; the well-secured casements flew wide, and the gale, rushing in, tore all the doors on the ground floor open and extinguished every light. Then the wind sunk as suddenly as it had risen.

Fuchs ordered the candles to be lighted, and it was then found that every door and window was as well secured as ever! This baffled the party; they cudgeled their brains to no purpose, till Fuchs suddenly noticed that it was twelve minutes past the time of relief and that six of his men were missing. He sent his sergeant to look for them, and then went out himself with four men, but there was no trace either of the six men or of the sentries. The captain resolved to keep his remaining half dozen troopers in the house.

The night wore on, and the hands of the clock were pointing to three when, first outside and then inside the house, there arose a hissing, and a whistling, and a howling and roaring through which there sounded peals of loud and seemingly scornful laughter. The captain rushed out into the hall, with his men behind him, and shouted as he stood in the doorway, "And if the devil and all the hosts of hell are coming to quarter here, *still* I will not move from the place!"

That moment a raging blast, arising in the house itself, seized upon the commander and his men, drove them forward, and was within an ace of throwing them down the steps. Every light went out, and they stood in Egyptian darkness. Next moment there was not a breath of wind about the house.

The captain ordered the candles to be lighted. Not a trace of damage was to be found, but two more dragoons had disappeared! In the circumstances, the Rittmeister thought it useless to stay there any longer. The doors and the shutters were all secured, the lights put out, and the retreat begun. But hardly had the party got twenty paces from the house than they saw every window brightly lighted, so that the curtains could be seen, and the bolted shutters had all been drawn back. In spite, however, of this tempting opportunity for investigation, the party continued its homeward march.

But what had happened to the fourteen missing troopers? Had they fallen victims to the infernal powers?

Not at all. They all reached their respective squadrons that night in fairly good condition. The eight sentries had some additional particulars to relate.

It seems that, some time after taking up their stations, a noise had been heard, as if something were breaking through the bushes toward them. (This noise seems to have drawn them all together.) As the noise approached, they began to hear a hollow groaning, and as a flame flashed through the wood about them, they had distinctly seen a large formless mass, covered with hair, rolling its way toward them and groaning as it came. Without pausing to reason about the matter, they had fired upon the object at some twenty-five paces; all became dark again and, conscious of having done their duty, the gallant fellows now thought it well to retreat—not, however, toward the house and their fiery commander (who would, very probably, have shot them) but as fast as possible in an opposite direction. The other eight men had silently stolen away under the compulsion of similar feelings.

No record remains to show whether the sixteen deserters were punished or pardoned. Neither is anything known of the results of Rittmeister Fuchs's report to his gracious Landgrave in the morning, or of the subsequent history of that commander. But certain it is that not long after these events, the Lodge at Griesheim was pulled down.

The Ghost and the Phantom Cat

(England)

T he lady was living with her father about 1840 in an ancient country house which he had rented from an elderly heiress. The inmates soon discovered that the house was haunted. Strange noises were heard from time to time in the dining room at night. A mysterious black cat used to appear in the entrance hall in the evening and scamper straight up the main staircase—not ascending it in the manner of mortal cats but by winding itself in and out of the balustrade in a decidedly uncanny and preternatural way. And worst of all, an old gentleman in a black skullcap, yellow dressing gown, and red slippers would come at midnight out of a certain door, cross the hall, go upstairs (in a dignified manner and not as the cat did), and vanish into an empty bedroom on the first floor. All the members of the household used to hear the noises and see the old gentleman whenever they were awake and downstairs at midnight. As to the "tortuous cat," it was vouched for by the servants and duly recorded by the lady who told the story. At length the inmates, finding the situation unpleasant, courageously determined to beard the ghost and give the old gentleman a practical and straightforward remon-

From: Frank Hamel, *Human Animals* (New York: Frederick A. Stokes Co., 1916).

strance about his conduct. On a certain night four menservants were accordingly posted on the staircase at the head of the first flight of stairs, it having been arranged that they should stop the intruder if they could, while their master, with a loaded pistol, should follow him and cut off his retreat.

At midnight the venerable gentleman emerged from his accustomed door. "Here he is!" cried the master of the house, and the servants on the staircase held their ground while the old gentleman approached silently, apparently unconscious of their presence. He came close up to the dauntless four, and then, to their amazement, he passed straight through them and reappeared on the other side. Turning around, they saw him calmly gliding up the second flight of stairs, above that on which they were posted. The master of the house, calling on them to follow, gave chase and fired his revolver. The old gentleman took no notice of the shot and entered the empty bedroom as usual, through its closed door. His pursuers opened the door only to find the room empty. A thorough search was made, the wainscoting sounded, the chimney explored, the cupboards turned out, and so forth, but nothing was found but a box containing deeds and some money in a forgotten closet.

The next morning the occupier wrote to the owner of the house to tell her of the discovery of the deed box, and at the end of his letter, he inquired casually whether any of her relatives had been noted for a peculiarity of dress.

She replied that her grandfather always used to wear, when he was at home and in his study, *a black skullcap, a yellow dressing gown, and red slippers.*

After the finding of the deed box, the ghost failed to reappear and the companion cat no longer did gymnastic exercises on the balustrade.

The Ghost-Bull

(England)

The Roaring Bull of Bagbury is a famous Shropshire ghost. Miss Georgina Jackson recites the story as it was told by an old farmer called Hayward.

A very bad man lived at Bagbury Farm, and when he died it was said of him that he had only done two good deeds in his life, one being to give a waistcoat to a poor old man and the other a piece of bread and cheese to a poor village lad. After he was dead, his ghost refused to rest and haunted the farm buildings in the shape of a bull, roaring till the boards, the shutters, and the tiles seemed to fly off the outhouses. It was quite impossible for anyone to live within range of this roaring, which usually began about nine or ten o'clock at night, sometimes even earlier, and at last became so troublesome that the people at the farmhouse sent for twelve parsons to lay the ghost.

When the parsons came, "they got him under" but could not lay him, and at last they drove him, still in the shape of a bull, into Hessington Church. All the parsons carried candles, and one of them, who was blind, knowing that there was danger from a stampede, placed his lighted candle in his top boot. It was a good thing that he did so, for presently the animal made a great rush, and out went every candle except that belonging to the blind parson who said, as though prepared for the event, "You light your candles by mine." But before he was laid, the bull made such a "burst" that he cracked the wall of the church from top to bottom, as hundreds of witnesses have asserted from that day to this.

At last they secured the ghost "down into a snuffbox," as the custom is, and he begged that he might be laid under Bagbury Bridge, declaring that every mare that passed over the bridge should lose her foal and every woman her child. This threat made them refuse his request, and they laid him in the Red Sea, where he has to remain for a thousand years. The knowledge that he was so far away did not prevent the villagers being very chary of crossing Bagbury Bridge at nighttime.

From: Frank Hamel, *Human Animals* (New York: Frederick A. Stokes Co., 1916).

Phantom Funerals and Corpse Candles

(Wales)

When Saint David of blessed memory lay dying, his soul was greatly troubled by the thought of his people, who would soon be bereft of his pious care and exhortations. He remembered the Celtic character, apt to be lifted to heights of enthusiastic piety by any passing influence of oratory or a strong personality such as his own and, alas! prone to sink to depths of indifference, or even skepticism, when that influence was removed. So the saint prayed very earnestly for his flock that some special sign of divine assistance might be granted them. Tradition says that his prayer was heard and a promise given that henceforth no one in the good Archbishop's diocese should die without receiving previous intimation of his end, and so might be prepared. The warning was to be a light proceeding from the person's dwelling to the place where he should be buried, following exactly the road which the funeral would afterward take. This light, visible a few days before death, is the *canwyll corph* (corpse candle).

All authorities agree that the most characteristic feature of the corpse candle's appearance is that it invariably follows the exact line that will be taken by the funeral procession. This is well illustrated by an instance that occurred some years ago at a house in Cardiganshire. Instead of going straight along the drive, the light was seen to flicker down some steps and around the garden pond. And when the death occurred, the drive was partly broken up under repair and the coffin had to be taken the way indicated by the corpse candle. Another story from Carmarthenshire relates how shortly before a death in the family owning a certain house, the woman living at the lodge saw a pale light come down the drive one evening. It pursued its way as far as the

From: M. L. Lewes, "Corpse-Candles and the *Teulu*," *Occult Review* 8 (July–December 1908): 75–78.

lodge, where it hovered a few moments, then through the gates and out on the road, where it stopped again for several minutes under some trees. On the day of the funeral the hearse, for an unexpected reason, was pulled up for some time at the exact spot under the trees where the *canwyll* had halted.

Not long ago the writer was talking about the *canwyll corph* and kindred subjects with the postmistress of a Cardiganshire village, who remarked that she had only known one person who had ever seen a "corpse light." This was a woman—now dead—called (for this occasion) Mary Jones and, to use the words of the postmistress, "a very religious and respectable person." At one time in her life she lived in a village called Pennant (a place well known to the writer), where the church is rather a landmark, being set on the top of a hill. Mary Jones invariably and solemnly declared that whenever a death occurred amongst her neighbors, she would always previously see a corpse candle wend its way up the hill from the village into the churchyard. And at the same place she once saw the *Teulu* (a phantom funeral). This last experience was in broad daylight and was shared with several other people, who were haymaking at the time and who all clearly saw the spectral procession appear along a road and mysteriously vanish when it reached a certain point. Belief in the *Teulu* used to be very widespread in Cardiganshire, especially, it is said, in the northern part of the county. Meyrick writes, "The *Teulu* . . . a phantasmagoric representation of a funeral, and the peasants affirm that when they meet with this, unless they move out of the road, they must inevitably be knocked down by the pressure of the crowd. They add that they know the persons whose spirits they behold, and hear them distinctly singing hymns."

But the *Teulu* was not always visible; sometimes the presence of the ghostly cortege would be known merely by the sudden *feeling* of encountering a crowd of people and hearing a dim wailing like the sound of a distant funeral dirge.

The writer has heard of two cases of people being involved in these invisible funeral processions, which must truly be a most disagreeable experience. One story relates to a Mrs. D———, who lived in the parish of Llandewi Brefi in Cardiganshire. Her husband was ill, and one day as she was going upstairs to his room, she had a feeling as of being in a vision, though she could *see* nothing. But the staircase seemed suddenly crowded with people, and by their shuffling, irregular footsteps, low exclamations, and heavy breathings, she knew they were carrying a heavy burden downstairs. So realistic was the impression that when she had struggled to the top of the stairs she felt actually weak and faint from the pressure of the crowd. A few days later her husband died, and on the day of the funeral, when the house was full of people and the coffin carried with difficulty down the narrow stairs, she realized that her curious experience had been a warning of sorrow to come.

The other instance was told by the Rev. G. Eyre Evans, of Aberystwith, a minister, and writer on archaeological subjects of considerable local fame. In his own words, "As to the *Teulu*, well, if ever a man met one and got mixed in it, I certainly did when crossing Trychrug [a high hill in Cardiganshire] one night. I seemed to feel the brush of people, to buffet against them, and to be in the way. Perhaps the feeling lasted a couple of minutes. It was an eerie, weird feeling, quite inexplicable to me, but there was the experience, say what you will." Mr. Eyre Evans also relates two experiences regarding the *canwyll corph*, but the writer will not repeat them here, as, though interesting, neither story has any specially significant feature to distinguish it greatly from other instances of a similar type.

Another belief relating to the *canwyll* was that it not only boded future trouble, but that it was positively dangerous for anybody who saw one to get in its way. The writer had never heard of this disagreeable attribute of the corpse light until she talked with the postmistress already quoted. This woman said that long ago she and other children were always frightened from straying far from home by tales of "Jacky Lantern," a mysterious light which, encountered on the road, would infallibly burn one up. Perhaps this idea is peculiar to Cardiganshire, as Borrow (*Wild Wales*, chap. 88) mentions meeting with the same belief when talking to a shepherd who acted as his guide from the Devil's Bridge over Plinlimmon. Borrow said: "They [corpse candles] foreshadow deaths, don't they?" "They do, sir; but that's not all the harm they do. They are very dangerous for anybody to meet with. If they come bump up against you when you are walking carelessly, it's generally all over with you in this world." Then followed the story of how a man, well known to the shepherd, had actually met his death in that weird manner.

This idea certainly adds to the fear inspired by the sight of the *canwyll,* but the more general belief seems to have been that the lights were quite harmless in themselves and, when seen, were regarded with awe only as sure harbingers of future woe.

Of the Banshee

(Ireland)

As a rule, the weird warning of the Banshee takes place a day or two before the death of which it is the knell. But cases are cited in which it has been heard when some action is being taken that is to end in disaster. A story is told of Kerry, where the low, sad notes were heard at the moment of the betrothal of a beautiful young girl to her lover. Cruelly jilted, the poor girl died of a broken heart, and the night before her death the dirge of the Banshee was heard once again, loud and clear, outside the window of her mother's cottage.

As a rule, the spirit comes alone, but instances are given in which a number of voices are heard singing in chorus. It is said that some years ago a much-loved lady of the O'Flaherty family was taken ill at the family mansion near Galway, but as her ailment seemed nothing more serious than a slight cold, no uneasiness was felt on her account. Some friends who had called to see her were merrily chatting with their sick friend, when suddenly weird, wild music was heard. All turned pale and trembled as they recognized the fateful singing of a chorus of Banshees. In the course of a few hours the lady's ailment developed into pleurisy and terminated fatally. As the sufferer lay dying, the unearthly chorus burst forth again in a sweet, plaintive requiem.

From: A. W. Jarvis, "The Weird-Wailing Banshee," *English Illustrated Magazine* 35 (1906): 97–102.

The Banshees of Doom

(Ireland)

Never, it is to be hoped, has the Banshee appeared in a more revoltingly horrible shape than that seen by Brian Roe on the fatal August morning, in 1317, as he marched on Corcomroe to give battle to the forces of Dermot O'Brien. When they reached the shore of Lough Rask, and while all were looking at the shining mere, "they saw," says Magrath, "the monstrous and distorted form of a lone, ancient, hideous hag, that stopped over the bright lough's shore. The loathly creature's semblance was this: she was thatched with elf locks, foxy gray and rough as heather, long as sea wrack, inextricably tangled; that had a bossy, wrinkled, foul ulcerated forehead, every hair of her eyebrows was like a strong fishhook, and from under them, blearing, dripping eyes peered with malignant fire between the lids all rawly crimson-edged. . . . The crone had a cairn of heads, a pile of arms and legs, a load of spoil, all of which she rinsed and diligently washed, so that by her labor the water of the lake was covered with hair and gory brains.

The army, hushed, intently and long gazed at her, but the chief spoke to the beldam: "What is thy name, what people are thine, of whom are kin, these the so maltreated dead on this moist shore?"

"The Dismal of Burren I am named always," came the reply. " 'Tis of the *Tuathe De Danann* I declare myself, and, royal chief, this pile stands for your heads, in their midst thine own head, which now thou carriest it yet no longer is thine. Proudly as thou goest to battle, the time is not far from you when all to a very few ye must be slain."

Terror-stricken and maddened by the hag's blood-chilling prophecy, the soldiers were about to throw their javelins at her when, on a rushing wind, she rose above them screeching forth their doom.

"Never heed ye the daft thing's rambling prophecy," cried the ill-fated prince, as he marched on Corcomroe—and his fate. Ere the dawn of another day he lay beneath the abbey pavement.

From: A. W. Jarvis, "The Weird-Wailing Banshee," *English Illustrated Magazine* 35 (1906): 97–102.

The following year de Clare set out to make his last and ill-fated effort to overthrow the Celtic chiefs of Clare. As he passed over the Fergus, a strange female is said to have confronted him. Magrath states that she spoke Gaelic, and so de Clare asked his Irish followers to tell him who she was and what she meant by washing a quantity of blood-stained robes in the river. The Banshee replied that she was "Bronach, and abode in the fairy hills of the land, but that her permanent residence was among the dwellers of hell, from which place she had come to invite De Clare to follow her." Scoffing at the creature, the knight passed on to attack the stronghold of the O'Deas; but before many hours had passed, his army was routed and he and his gallant son, together with many of his bravest followers, lay cold and stark on the battlefield.

The Fiery Man

(Germany)

In some parts of Germany, notably in Franconia, the peasantry believe, or used to believe, in a supernatural phenomenon called the *Puhu,* or Fiery Man. The nature of this phenomenon may be gathered from the narratives given below. It is stated that the Fiery Men are the souls of persons who in life removed their neighbor's landmark. Why these persons should be punished in this particular manner does not appear; we are not justified in assuming that the spiritual world uses our weights and measures, or takes our ideas to guide its operations. "We do not," says Charles Lamb, "know the laws of that country"—and perhaps we are hardly qualified to lay them down, even when we have passed the very highest examinations.

There is a curious legend of a girl who was induced to call from a window, "Come and kiss me, Fiery Man!" Presently the terrified company heard a swift foot upon the stair and a panting breath at the door, which they dared not open. Suddenly two hands were struck on

From: Philip MacLeod, "The Fiery Man," *Occult Review* 21 (1915): 286–88.

the wood, and the steps retreated again, but on the door there remained the deep charred marks of two fiery hands.

This, however, is merely a legend, which may or may not be true. Not so the following strange experiences of good Pastor H——, communicated by that excellent Evangelical clergyman to the *Homiletisch-Liturgische Correspondenzblatts* in the year 1834, as an example of a discussion on a certain point of theology. Here we have, as above observed, firsthand experience.

The pastor tells us that he made a little walking tour, in the course of which he stopped at a house in a small town near Neustadt a.d. Linde. Having made a call at a village some distance off, he was returning late at night and had come to within two miles of his temporary abode, when he noticed a will-o'-the-wisp flying from a village on a steep hill beyond the river, over to the road, and back again. Apparently, he then lost sight of it for a moment or two. But his experiences are best given in his own words, which the present writer translates, as literally as possible, from the original:

> Then I noticed in the window of the castle there [on the hill] a light that I had not observed before. But I never thought that this light could be the same as the will-o'-the-wisp I had seen, till it suddenly drove out from the window, sank to the ground, sprang up and down once or twice, rolled, looking like a great fire, down the steep hill, took the river in a curving leap, and flew, having become small again, over the meadows and the plowed land, up the slope straight toward me.
>
> It took eight or ten seconds to come all this way—a good quarter of an hour's walk. It stopped for a moment in the plowed land, some twenty or twenty-five paces from me, and then set off moving, exactly like a man carrying a lantern; and I quite clearly saw the hand that held the light, and it swaying to the pace, and the movement of the legs was visible to me behind the light, which kept up with me step for step. . . .
>
> Now I got into such a fright that I began to pray for courage and heart, in case this uncanny thing should approach me. But after it had gone with me some hundred paces, it turned and flew, in the same manner that it had come, and just as quickly, back to its home, where in a few seconds it vanished.
>
> And now I began to blame myself for my foolish fears and to wish that I could see this curious thing again. My wish was

soon granted; in seven or eight minutes, the light appeared again in the castle, flew over the valley, just as before, tore up the slope at the same wild speed, straight toward me, and again began to keep step with me in the plow, at a distance of twenty paces. But if I had trembled before, now I shook indeed, and began to pray to my Savior, that He would grant me such heart and courage that I should fear no creature, but only Him, my just Judge. I pronounced the last words aloud, and the ghost fled away as before. And now I thought of what I had written in the *Correspondenzblatt:* How ill it beseemed a Christian to be affrighted by such apparitions; so I resolved never more to make light of such fears.

Next evening the pastor consulted Herr S———l, a Town Council- lor of Neustadt a.d. Linde. This man, as we learn from another source, had been from his twentieth year, and without any preceding illness, gifted with the power of seeing apparitions. Curiously enough, this power in him seems to have been accompanied by extraordinary bodily health and vigor and an unusual capacity for normal affairs. He took the pastor's revelation as something of everyday occurrence and said that he had often met that spirit; if he walked that way at night, it would accompany him for a quarter of an hour along the road. Herr S———l had never spoken to him. He described the spirit as of a shining sulfur yellow and quite transparent.

Our next evidence upon this subject comes from Pastor Schneider of Feldberg, a Lutheran clergyman. His relation was published in 1850.

Pastor Schneider tells us that he once had the cure of Lutheran souls at O.E. Having had occasion one November to visit the town of Freiburg, he left that place for home at eleven o'clock in the evening by mail coach. The coach brought him to a point about two hours' walk from O.E., and there he got down, intending to finish his journey on foot.

It was a fine night; there was a moon, but it was not very bright, being in its last quarter. Herr Schneider met nobody on the way. About four in the morning he came into the outskirts of the village where his parsonage was situated. His experience may be given in his own words:

Suddenly I saw a bright fire, in the middle of the village street, about twenty or thirty paces from me. It was as round as a round basket, burning briskly, with many flames, pale, something like the flames of spirits of wine. I took a rest and propped myself on my stick, looking quietly at the fire. I thought some boys must have lighted it. Thus several minutes passed, while I continued to look at the fire.

At length I began to walk quietly on toward the fire, which was still burning in the same way, neither increasing nor diminishing; when suddenly, just as I was close to it, it rose up to about twenty feet above the earth, hung still for a moment, and then swiftly sped through the air toward the churchyard. I could see it distinctly, and watched it suddenly sink down into the churchyard and disappear. The moonlight was strong enough to enable me to see that there was not a trace of wood, coal, or ash on the spot where the fire had been, and in all the houses about all was sleep; not a sound of life or of light. . . .

Last year [1849?] I saw a *puhu* again. It was in the autumn; I was returning with my children from a walk to M———. As we came into our little vale, a puhu was hurrying to and fro on the top of the hill between this place [Felding?] and O.E. We followed the burning apparition with our eyes for a long time. When we got home, I took the telescope and very attentively observed the apparition with that instrument. It was just like the other appearance described above: round, and blazing with many pale flames, and of the size of a basket [v.n. sup.]. For a long time it ran to and fro upon the hill opposite the parsonage, till at length it went down into the valley and disappeared among the houses.

For the rest, I testify, with my signature, to the plain truth of the incidents here related.

J. J. SCHNEIDER, *Pastor.*

It is remarkable that the belief in the puhu seems to have prevailed in the neighborhood of the Feldberg before Schneider's time. A German poet alludes to this belief, very contemptuously, as a sort of old wives' tale. In the face of the pastor's quite unexceptionable evidence, it would seem that the story of the puhu is something more than that.

A Fairy-Wife

(Alsace)

The gable ends of the Alastian peasant's log house were covered with boards, and between these were cracks which were sometimes not closed even in the depth of winter, although this part of the hut often was the sleeping apartment of some member of the peasant's family.

It was in a room of this sort that a young Alsatian slept. He was visited every night by a beautiful woman—a sort of fairy—who always entered and disappeared through one of the crevices between the boards.

As is usual in such cases, the young man fell in love with the beautiful visitant and resolved to secure her for his wife, so he told his father of his determination. His father advised him to have all the cracks between the boards, excepting one, closed, and when the maiden was in the room, he was to take a knife and insert it in the aperture through which she entered. This was done, and one morning the young man was overjoyed to find his beautiful visitor still in his room.

They were married and lived together nearly eleven years, and had five children. The man felt confident that his wife would now stay with him, and one day while making some improvements in the house, he removed the knife, and at the same moment his wife vanished and never returned.

From: W. J. Wintemberg, "German Folk-Tales Collected in Canada," *Journal of American Folk-Lore* 19 (1906): 241–44.

Fairy Gold

(Ireland)

It is still common to meet with persons who get what they call a "warning" in a dream. They are advised to dig by night in some old "fort" or *rath* for the fairy gold which is always hidden in such places. It is a dangerous task, which the natural covetousness of the poor induces them to undertake.

A year ago, the sister of a poor laborer returned from the United States. Before leaving America, she had twice dreamt of finding gold in a fort near her brother's cottage, and on the very night of her arrival the two repaired thither. They were unsuccessful, and the brother refused to make any further attempt. The woman persuaded her cousin, an elderly, industrious, and most sensible man, to aid her, and the pair pursued their quest day and night, until they had completely undermined the rampart of the fort. In spite of ill success, they continued their labors, which ended only by the sudden death of the cousin. The doctor gave heart disease as the cause; but according to the unanimous verdict of the neighbors, death resulted from the anger of the fairies, which had been aroused by their temerity in interfering with their possessions.

From: Maurice McCarthy O'Leary, "Notes and Queries: Certain Irish Superstitions," *Journal of American Folk-Lore* 10–11 (1897–98): 234–37.

The Hobyahs

(Scotland)

Once there was an old man and woman and a little girl, and they all lived in a house made of hemp stalks. Now the old man had a little dog named Turpie; and one night the Hobyahs came and said, "Hobyah! Hobyah! Hobyah! Tear down the hemp stalks, eat up the old man and woman, and carry off the little girl!" But little dog Turpie barked so that the Hobyahs ran off, and the old man said, "Little dog Turpie barks so that I cannot sleep nor slumber, and if I live till morning I will cut off his tail." So in the morning the old man cut off little dog Turpie's tail.

The next night the Hobyahs came again and said, "Hobyah! Hobyah! Hobyah! Tear down the hemp stalks, eat up the old man and woman, and carry off the little girl!" But little dog Turpie barked so that the Hobyahs ran off, and the old man said, "Little dog Turpie barks so that I cannot sleep nor slumber, and if I live till morning I will cut off one of his legs." So in the morning the old man cut off one of little dog Turpie's legs.

The next night the Hobyahs came again and said, "Hobyah! Hobyah! Hobyah! Tear down the hemp stalks, eat up the old man and woman, and carry off the little girl!" But little dog Turpie barked so that the Hobyahs ran off, and the old man said, "Little dog Turpie barks so that I cannot sleep nor slumber, and if I live till morning I will cut off another of his legs." So in the morning the old man cut off another of little dog Turpie's legs.

The next night the Hobyahs came again and said, "Hobyah! Hobyah! Hobyah! Tear down the hemp stalks, eat up the old man and woman, and carry off the little girl." But little dog Turpie barked so that the Hobyahs ran off, and the old man said, "Little dog Turpie barks so that I cannot sleep nor slumber, and if I live till morning I will cut off another of his legs." So in the morning the old man cut off another of little dog Turpie's legs.

From: S. V. Proudfit, "Notes and Queries: The Hobyahs—A Scotch Nursery Tale," *Journal of American Folk-Lore* 4 (1891): 173–74.

The next night the Hobyahs came again and said, "Hobyah! Hobyah! Hobyah! Tear down the hemp stalks, eat up the old man and woman, and carry off the little girl!" But little dog Turpie barked so that the Hobyahs ran off, and the old man said, "Little dog Turpie barks so that I cannot sleep nor slumber, and if I live till morning I will cut off another of his legs." So. in the morning the old man cut off another of little dog Turpie's legs.

The next night the Hobyahs came again and said, "Hobyah! Hobyah! Hobyah! Tear down the hemp stalks, eat up the old man and woman, and carry off the little girl!" But little dog Turpie barked so that the Hobyahs ran off; and the old man said, "Little dog Turpie barks so that I cannot sleep nor slumber, and if I live till morning I will cut off little dog Turpie's head." So in the morning the old man cut off little dog Turpie's head.

The next night the Hobyahs came and said, "Hobyah! Hobyah! Hobyah! Tear down the hemp stalks, eat up the old man and woman, and carry off the little girl!" And when the Hobyahs found that little dog Turpie's head was off, they tore down the hemp stalks, ate up the old man and woman, and carried the little girl off in a bag.

And when the Hobyahs came to their home, they hung up the bag with the little girl in it, and every Hobyah knocked on top of the bag and said, "Look me! look me!" and then they went to sleep until the next night, for the Hobyahs slept in the daytime.

The little girl cried a great deal, and a man with a big dog came that way and heard her crying. When he asked her how she came there and she had told him, he put the dog in the bag and took the little girl to his home.

The next night the Hobyahs took down the bag and knocked on the top of it and said, "Look me! look me!" and when they opened the bag the big dog jumped out and ate them all up; so there are no Hobyahs now.

Monsters of the Lake

(Ireland)

I n the mountainous region that extends from the western limits of the County Cork throughout the most picturesque portions of Kerry, there are many deep and gloomy lakes, nestling under rugged cliffs and removed from the noise of human activity. Such are the loughs along the Caha ranges, and the well-known Devil's Punch Bowl upon Mangerton. Many of these lakes are regarded with superstitious veneration, for in their depths is supposed to dwell a monster, shaped like a foal or calf, of great size. This creature is never visible in the daytime, but by night it sallies forth to feed upon the pasture by the shore. As a rule the herbage is stunted and of little value, but it sometimes happens that a meadow coaxed into being with infinite pains will be found to have suffered from nocturnal trespass.

On one occasion, when this had been the case, a poor farmer and his two sons determined at whatever risk to intercept the marauder. For this purpose they provided themselves with sticks and concealed themselves beside the low stone wall that girt the little field. It was moonlit, and every object was distinctly visible. The lake was as clear as by day, and every ripple could be heard. The watchers had remained upon their post for some time and were already growing drowsy. The party was about to depart, when their attention was attracted by a violent disturbance in the waters. They saw something rise to the surface and swiftly swim ashore. As it landed they could make out a curious four-footed animal, rather taller than a horse, which leaped over the low wall and entered the meadow. After watching for some time, their fears gave way to indignation. They held a whispered consultation, and then crept cautiously around in such way as to cut off its retreat toward the lake. When the creature had satisfied its hunger, it turned toward the water and was confronted by the men. They advanced boldly, seeking to intimidate it

From: Maurice McCarthy O'Leary, "Notes and Queries: Certain Irish Superstitions," *Journal of American Folk-Lore* 10–11 (1897–98): 234–37.

with shouts and flourishing their sticks. Presently, however, they shrank before the threatening aspect of the beast, which advanced on them in apparent fury, while sparks seemed to fly from its mane and tail. They instantly took flight and never again ventured to interfere with the depredator.

Black Dog Stories

(England)

A young lady of a well-known family was sitting at work, well and cheerful, when she saw to her great surprise a large black dog close to her. As both door and window were closed, she could not understand how he had got in, but when she started up to put him out she could no longer see him. Quite puzzled and thinking it must be some strange illusion, she sat down again and went on with her work, when presently he was there again. Much alarmed, she now ran out and told her mother, who said she must have fancied it or else that she must be ill. She said that she was quite well and that she was sure she had seen the animal. Then her mother promised to wait outside the door, and if the dog appeared again her daughter said she would call her. Presently the daughter saw the dog again, but he disappeared when she called her mother. Soon afterward the mother was taken ill and died. Before her death she said to her daughter, "Remember the black dog."

Another family in the east of England has a tradition that the appearance of a black dog portends the death of one of its members. It was not said that no death took place without such warning, but only that when the apparition occurred, its meaning was certain. The eldest son of this family married. He knew not whether to believe or disbelieve the legend. On one hand he thought it superstitious to receive it, and on the other he could not altogether reject it in the face of much testimony. In this state of doubt—the thing itself being

From: Frank Hamel, *Human Animals* (New York: Frederick A. Stokes Co., 1916).

unpleasant—he resolved to say nothing on the subject to his young wife. It could only, he thought, worry and harass her and could not by any possibility do any good, and he kept this resolution. In due course of time he had a family, but of the apparition he saw nothing. At length, one of his children was taken ill with smallpox, but the attack was slight and not the least danger was apprehended. He was sitting down to dinner with his wife, when she said, "I will just step upstairs and see how baby is going on, and I will be back again in a moment." She went and, returning rather hastily said, "Baby is asleep, but pray go upstairs, for there is a large black dog lying on his bed. Go up and drive it out of the house." The father had no doubt of the result. He went upstairs. There was no black dog to be seen; but the child was dead.

The Highlanders have also a legend of an ownerless black dog, which caused all kinds of misadventure in the vicinity where he prowled. A hunter shot at the dog with a silver bit, and the aim was so successful that nothing more was seen of the animal. Suddenly a small boy ran up to the hunter with a terrible story of his grandfather who had died within sight of his home as though stricken by a gunshot wound, and on examination it was found indeed that the silver piece was embedded in his flesh. There was no further misfortune in the village after this double event, but the tale has more of witchcraft about it than ghostliness.

The Black Dog of Hergest was famous all over the countryside, and no one ventured to enter the room he was said to haunt. At night he clanked a chain, but at other times he was seen wandering about without one, often near a pond on the high road to Kingston.

Another phantom dog story comes from the parish of Dean Prior, a narrow woodland valley watered by a stream. Below a beautiful cascade is a deep hollow called the Hound's Pool. At one time there lived near this spot a skillful weaver. After his death he was seen by his family working as diligently as ever at his loom, and this being regarded as uncanny, application was made to the vicar of the parish as to what steps were to be taken to remove the apparition. The parson called at the cottage where the weaver had lived and, hearing the noise of the shuttle in the upstairs room, called to the ghost of the weaver to descend.

"I will," replied the weaver's voice, "as soon as I have worked out my shuttle."

"No," replied the vicar, "you have worked long enough. Come down at once."

So the phantom appeared, and the vicar, taking a handful of earth from the churchyard, threw it in his face. In a moment the apparition turned into a black hound. "Follow me," said the vicar, and the dog followed to the gate of the wood, where a mighty wind was blowing. The vicar picked up a nutshell with a hole in it and, leading the hound to the pool below the cascade, said, "Take this, and dip out the pool with it. When it is empty thou shalt rest."

The hound still haunts the spot, and to those who can see is ever at work on the waters of the pool.

Supernatural Hounds as Death Omens

(Ireland)

Dogs are still believed in Ireland to be affected by the approach of death, and this belief is not confined to the uneducated. Packs of supernatural hounds are heard to mourn the death of some staunch old sportsman, and I remember an account of such a case. A man had been spending the day at Newmarket, a little village in the County Cork. He had accomplished about half his journey and was traveling at an easy pace, when his attention was roused by the cry of a pack of foxhounds. Fancying that he was mistaken, he paused to listen and could plainly hear the sound as if from among the graves. His horse pricked up his ears but manifested no further uneasiness beyond the natural inclination of an old hunter to take part in the chase. As he resumed his course, he could at intervals hear the cry, which lasted

From: Maurice McCarthy O'Leary, "Notes and Queries: Certain Irish Superstitions," *Journal of American Folk-Lore* 10–11 (1897–98): 234–37.

until the pack apparently killed in the little wood of Lisdargan. On reaching home, he learned of the death of his uncle, which had taken place about a quarter of an hour before, and who had died quite unexpectedly, after raising himself in bed in the act of cheering on a pack of hounds.

A few years ago, toward the end of August, after a day spent in shooting on the hills, I sat down to rest on the mountainside in company with an old keeper who was a firm believer in ghosts and fairies, whom, in common with his neighbors, he preferred to mention as "the good people." After entertaining me with several marvelous anecdotes of the experiences of his friends, favored ghost-seers, I asked him if he himself had ever seen anything supernatural. I give his story as nearly as possible in his own words:

"'Twas of an evening, for all the world like this, that I went up the Sligo to drive hither a share of goats that I had, that were facing west into the Cummeens. I found the goats, and as well became me, I turned them in toward the cliff when, the Lord save us! I heard a noise like the cry of hounds. What must this be? says I to myself; sure there isn't a hound in the barony, good or bad, these times, and who'd be hunting in summer? Well, with that I hear the noise again; and I heard it first back west at Ballydaly, it was now seemingly coming down the hollow betwixt Shanacknock and Ounaglure. The sun was fast setting, and I put my two hands to my eyes to shelter them from the blaze that was blinding me entirely. I waited so for a piece, and not one happort did I see, only the noise ever and always coming nearer and nearer.

"Of a sudden I thought there was something moving down on the inch at the bottom of Conny the law's land, and my dear, what was it but a man in a red coat, and he riding a big black horse in a full gallop! The man was waving his hand as he faced in for the big ditch bounding Jerry Looney's. He took it in one fly, and then he turned his horse and leaped the *bareen*, as your honor'd leap the *kippen* I'm holding in my hand. As he came along, I could hear the cry of the hounds plainer and plainer from all around him, but not a sketch of a dog could I see if you were to give me Ireland that minute. Well, to make a long story short, I was that frightened that I was, saving your presence, pouring out with the perspiration. But anyway, I couldn't take my eyes off the man, and I watched him going like mad through the cornfield on the widow's farm. 'Whoever you are, you're done now, my man,' says I, 'for that horse of yours'll never carry you safe over the wet montanes beside the river.' But man alive, he made nothing of them same! He went over them as if they were the driest field in the old master's place; and what's more, though your honor minds well what Colley's vein was like before 'twas drained, I'm blessed this minute if he didn't ride it down where you'd hardly say there was footing for a snipe, let alone for a man on horseback! When he got well in toward the old bog road, what does he do, only wheel around as if he had a mind to cross the coast road and come up upon the mountain. 'It's me he's after, sure enough,' thinks I, and I tried to get up, and let a screech out of me, but if you'll believe me, I could only set where I was, so wake as the child in the mother's arms. 'If he crosses the road, I'm a dead man,' says I, and I really believe if he had, the life would have left me that very minute.

"Glory be to God, 'twas a terrible time, and you may say I was thankful when he changed once more and, driving over by the Dawheen's, went straight for Duhallow. Right opposite him now was the holy well of Tubberit. As he came nearer and nearer to the blessed place, I seen a wonderful change come over him. So far that horse of his was racing like the wind, with the head on him stretched out, pulling and dragging as if he'd make garters of the reins. The man, too, was sitting up straight, and 'twas an admiration the way them dogs, for all I couldn't see one bit of them, was giving tongue all through. But now, why, I couldn't rightly hear the hounds at all, and the horse seemed all as one dead beat. As to the man—well, I never seen its equal in all my born days; you'd say 'twas the way he was drunk, or sick, or someways queer in himself, if 'twas only the way he'd roll about and nearly tumble to the ground. They were just about three spades off the well, when the horse stopped dead up as if he was shot. What does my man do then, only seemingly try and coax him in every whole way he could. It wasn't the least good on earth. At last he up with his whip, and he hits him one clout. Man dear! it sounded for all the world like the blast out of a quarry; and that the two hands may stick to me if the sparks didn't fly out of his ribs like chaff out of a machine. 'Twas then, you may say, he threw a leap into the air and, as he rug up upon his hind legs, I thought every whole minute he'd be back upon his rider.

"When he had gone on that way for a good piece, without setting one foot nearer to the well, I heard quite plain the most elegant music in the whole wide world. It seemed louder than the strongest pipes, and all through there was a soft crawnawning, mostly like a fiddler but a deal sweeter. And whereon before I was that dead out from the fright, I grew now bolder and bolder, till faith I didn't care so much as one happorth for ever a thing living or dead. Howsomever, I watched the man all through, and I won't belie him to your honor; whatever he was, he began to fade away, just as you'd see—the Lord between us and harm!—the fog melting away at sunrise from the mountain. Every whole minute I had harder work to see him, till when at last the music gave one long loud report, and he was gone! And if I put my two eyes on sticks, I couldn't see or hear him, or his horse, or the music, forever again."

Animals that Omen Death

(England)

Certain animals are associated with certain families, and in many such instances the animal makes its appearance as a death warning. Sometimes the animal in question, which is in the nature of a totem of the clan, is the family crest and has an occult connection with its traditions and history.

The Ferrers, whose countryseat is at Chartley Park, near Litchfield, have a peculiar breed of cattle on their estates. The color of the cattle is white with black muzzles. The whole of the inside of the ear, and one-third of the outside from the tip downward is red, and the horns are white with black tips, very fine and bent upward.

In the year in which the Battle of Burton Bridge was fought and lost, a black calf was born into this stock, and the downfall of the Ferrers family occurred about this time, giving rise to a tradition which has

From: Frank Hamel, *Human Animals* (New York: Frederick A. Stokes Co., 1916).

never been falsified, that the birth of a dark or particolored calf from the Chartley Park breed is an omen of death within the year to a member of the Ferrers family.

The *Staffordshire Chronicle* of July 1835 says:

> It is a noticeable coincidence that a calf of this description was born whenever a death happened in the family. The decease of the seventh Earl Ferrers and of his countess, and of his son, Viscount Tamworth, and of his daughter, Mrs. William Jolliffe, as well as the deaths of the son and heir of the eighth earl and of his daughter, Lady Francis Shirley, were each preceded by the ominous birth of the fatal-hued calf. In the spring of 1835 a black calf appeared at Chartley, and before long the beautiful countess, second wife of the eighth earl, lay on her deathbed.

Birds of various kinds frequently make their appearance in families as harbingers of death. When the Oxenhams of Devonshire were visited by the apparition of a white bird, they knew that one of the family was doomed. The well-known story is told by James Oxenham in a tract titled "A True relation of an Apparition in the likenesse of a Bird with a white breast that appeared hovering over the deathbeds of some of the children of Mr. James Oxenham, of Sale Monachorum, Devon, Gent."

One of the first members of the family to see the apparition was the famous John Oxenham, a young man of twenty-two, who was taken ill in the vigor of his youth, a great strapping fellow six feet and a half in height, well built, of comely countenance, and of great intellectual gifts. He died on the fifth day of September 1635, and two days before his death the bird with the white breast hovered over his bed. Charles Kingsley made use of this incident in *Westward Ho!* John Oxenham, in the midst of drinking a toast, suddenly drops his glass on the table and, staring in terror at some object which he seems to see fluttering round the room, he cries out, "There! Do you see it? The bird! The bird with the white breast!"

No sooner was John Oxenham in his grave than the apparition showed itself to Thomasine, wife of James Oxenham, who died on the 7th of September, 1635. She was quite a young woman and, according to the witnesses, Elizabeth Frost and Joan Tooker, the strange phantom was seen clearly fluttering above her sickbed. The next member of the Oxenhams to whom the warning appeared was Thomasine's little sister, Rebecca, a child of eight, who breathed her last on September the 9th following. And no sooner had the little girl been laid in her grave than Thomasine, infant of the above-mentioned Thomasine and James Oxenham, was taken sick and died on the 15th of September, 1635, the bird appearing also in this case.

It is impossible not to wonder what disease it was that carried off so many members of the Oxenham family within a few days of one another, and whether the bird was fluttering through the rooms the whole of the time or disappeared between the various deaths. Certain it is that it was not seen hovering over the sickbeds of other members of the family who recovered health. An earlier visitation had occurred in 1618, when the grandmother of the said John, a certain Grace Oxenham, had yielded up her soul into the hands of her Maker. Many later appearances of the famous bird are on record. A Mr. Oxenham who lived in Sidmouth for many years and who died between 1810 and 1821, was attended by an old gardener and his wife, who gave evidence that they had seen a white bird fly in at the door, dart across the bed in which their master lay dying, and *disappear in one of the drawers of the bureau,* but when they opened all the drawers to find the apparition, they could discover no signs of it.

In 1873 the Rev. Henry Oxenham gave the following version of the family story, which may be found in Frederick George Lee's *Glimpses of the Supernatural:*

> Shortly before the death of my late uncle, G. N. Oxenham, Esq., of 17 Earl's Terrace, Kensington, who was then head of the family, this occurred: His only surviving daughter, now Mrs. Thomas Peter, but then unmarried and living at home, and a friend of my aunt's, Miss Roberts, who happened to be staying in the house but was no relation and had never heard of the family tradition, were sitting in the dining room immediately beneath his bedroom about a week before his death, which took place on December 15, 1873, when their attention was aroused by a shouting outside the window.
>
> On looking out they observed a white bird—which might have been a pigeon, but if so was an unusually large one—perched on the thorn tree outside the windows and it remained there for several minutes, in spite of some workmen on the opposite side of the road throwing their hats at it in the vain effort to drive it away.

Miss Roberts mentioned this to my aunt at the time, though not, of course, attaching any special significance to it, and my aunt (since deceased) repeated it to me soon after my uncle's death. Neither did my cousin, though aware of the family tradition, think of it at the time. My cousin also mentioned another circumstance, which either I did not hear of or had forgotten, *viz.* that my late aunt spoke at the time of frequently hearing a sound like the fluttering of a bird's wings in my uncle's bedroom, and said that the nurse testified to hearing it also.

A more tragic incident connected with the same legend was that when Lady Margaret Oxenham was about to be married, a white bird appeared and fluttered about her head, and that she was stabbed at the altar by a rejected lover.

Familiars

(France)

The basic belief that it is possible to send forth a familiar to wreak harm on others is found fully developed in black magic, and to such occult powers no doubt many strange phenomena may be attributed.

A peculiarly uncanny story about a witch and her familiar comes from Poitou. A young man who lived near Champdenois went to spend the evening with some friends. He was jumping over a stone fence which separated the neighboring estates, when a familiar settled on his back. The young man caught hold of the demon with all his strength and strangled him, flinging him on the ground, where he lay apparently lifeless. Curiosity induced the young man to lift the inert body on to his shoulders, as he wished to look at it by candlelight and show it to his friends.

From: Frank Hamel, *Human Animals* (New York: Frederick A. Stokes Co., 1916).

When he arrived at his friends' house, the inmates were sitting in a circle about the hearth and the mistress of the house was spinning, surrounded by her maids. They all looked wonderingly at the demon, but the mistress appeared to be strangely ill at ease.

"I believe," said the young fellow, "it's a sorcerer. There's only one way of finding out. We'll put it in the fire, then we shall know what sort of being it is."

When she heard this cruel suggestion, the mistress gripped the arms of her chair in obvious anxiety and let her spindle drop to the ground, saying she was feeling very ill. When the demon was put on to the glowing cinders, she shrieked out and was forced to confess, in a shamefaced manner, that she had been wandering in the woods that evening in the shape of an animal, and that the young man had captured her double. Whether this witch intended to work harm is not divulged.

Two Tales of Familiars

(Italy)

A certain man lived at Trapani in Sicily in the year 1585, whose house was greatly disturbed by a spirit typical of this species. It threw huge stones about and juggled with crockery and kitchenware in the manner peculiar to these tricksy sprites. If one played the lute, the spirit accompanied the music with songs of the most questionable description, and even accompanied the master of the house when he traveled abroad on business. The unfortunate recipient of these attentions resolved, at all costs, to rid himself of such an incubus, and this he succeeded in doing by the aid of priestly exorcism.

In a town near Venice a certain magician possessed a ring inhabited by a familiar which he had bound to his service, and repenting of his

From: Lewis Spence, "The Familiar: Its Nature and Origin," *Occult Review* 30 (1919): 130–37.

sorceries, betook himself to a priest for advice. The holy man advised him to have the trinket destroyed, "at which word the familiars were heard (as it were) to mourn and lament in the ring, and to desire that no such violence might be offered unto them, but rather than so, that it would please him to accept the ring and keep it, promising to do him all service and vassalage." But the churchman was sufficiently strong-minded to reject the offer and, being zealously enraged, seized a great hammer and broke the ring almost to dust.

Two Familiars of the Angel-Demon Type

(Spain)

Perhaps the best-known instance of a familiar of the angel-demon type was that which attached itself to Dr. Torralva, a Spanish physician of the sixteenth century, who came safely through the fearsome ordeal of the Inquisition of his day. This being is described as "an angel of the order of good spirits," who was so gifted in his knowledge of the future and of hidden things that he was without peer in the spiritual world, and of such a peculiar temperament that he disdained to make any bargain with those he served. He is described as having the appearance of a fair young man with light hair, and dressed in a flesh-colored habit and black surtout. He was called Zequiel, and his services were put at the disposal of Torralva by a Dominican monk, who seems to have had no further occasion for them. He visited the doctor at every change of the moon, or as often as the physician required his advice, accompanying him on his travels, which were usually accelerated by some magical device suggested by the obliging Zequiel. He even accompanied Torralva to

From: Lewis Spence, "The Familiar: Its Nature and Origin," *Occult Review* 30 (1919): 130–37.

church, said nothing contrary to Christianity, and never counseled his patron to evil. When the doctor exacted exorbitant fees from his patients, Zequiel rebuked him, telling him that since he had received his knowledge for nothing he ought to impart it gratuitously, and whenever Torralva was in want of money he found a supply in his chamber which he knew had been furnished by this beneficent spirit. Through acting on the counsel of Zequiel, the physician achieved considerable fame and fortune, but as he made no secret of his intercourse with his supernatural assistant, he shortly incurred the attentions of the Inquisition, which, however, set him at liberty upon receiving his assurance that he repented of his suspicious conduct and renounced all magical practices.

Another instance is that of the Lord of Corasse, a castle situated about twenty miles from Orthes, who having about 1365 unjustly deprived a clerk of Catalonia of certain tithes, was subjected by his victim to the usual poltergeist annoyances. Arriving one night at the castle, says Froissart, this spirit began to hurl and fling about all the movables capable of being treated in such a manner. When the invisible mischief maker was challenged by the Lord of Corasse as to his identity, he replied that his name was Orton and that he had been dispatched by the said clerk to torment the tyrannous lord who had kept him from the enjoyment of his revenues. The Seigneur scoffed at the idea that a spirit of such powers should attach himself to a mere clerk, and suggested that Orton should enter his service. Orton accepted the position and became inseparable from the Lord of Corasse, much to the annoyance of his wife, who was terrified at the spirit's manifestations. He would wake his master in the watches of the night to acquaint him with notable happenings in England, Germany, or Hungary, giving him good advice as regards his private affairs until shortly before his death.

Wizard-Cats

(England)

An inhabitant of Toulon told Berenger-Feraud in 1875 that one of his friends had a wizard-cat. Every evening the cat used to listen to their conversation, and if the subject interested him, he expressed his own opinion, usually saying the last word on the topic. If his mistress had any plans on hand, she consulted the cat, giving her reasons for taking one course or another. After having weighed the pros and cons carefully, the cat used to advise her by saying yes or no as to whether her plans could be carried out or not.

The cat used to speak whenever he wanted food, asking either for fish or meat to be purchased, and he talked very indignantly if the required dainty was not forthcoming.

From time to time this uncanny animal disappeared for many days at a stretch, and the members of the household were convinced that he had taken human form in his absence. He always used to speak before leaving and after returning.

When he lay on the point of death, he prayed that his body might be decently buried, and his mistress gave him a solemn promise to this effect and laid the corpse in a box which she interred behind the cemetery wall. She dare not bury it in the grave prepared for human beings, but the coffin was laid alongside a Christian tomb, and at the funeral the cat's soul was recommended to the care of his Creator.

Wizard-cats have been known to do serious harm to those against whom they have a grudge, and it is well to be sure, if you value your life, whether you are dealing with a real animal or a "familiar" when you feel angry.

A young man in Radnorshire had the reputation of being very cruel to cats. On the day he was to be married he saw a cat cross his path, and he threw a stone at it. From that moment he weakened in health and had to go away frequently to recuperate. The neighbors said that during these absences he was changed into a cat and ran wild in the

From: Frank Hamel, *Human Animals* (New York: Frederick A. Stokes Co., 1916).

woods and, after his death, tradition declared that he wandered through the district at night in the shape of a cat and struck terror in the hearts of naughty children.

Cat- and Dog-Witches

(Scotland)

One of the most celebrated Scottish witch-cat trials took place at Caithness when Margaret Nin-Gilbert was interrogated on February 8, 1719, by William Innes, minister of Thurso, and confessed that she was traveling one evening when she was met by the devil in the likeness of a man who "engaged her to take on with him," which she agreed to do. From that time she became familiar with him, and sometimes he appeared to her in the likeness of a huge black horse, sometimes riding a horse, sometimes like a black cloud, and again in the shape of a black hen. She apparently obtained the powers of a witch with the help of this apparition, and the use she made of them appears in the following story told by one William Montgomery, a mason, whose house was invaded by cats in such numbers that his wife and maidservant could not endure to remain in the place.

One night on Montgomery's return he found five cats by the fireside, and the servant told him they were "speaking among themselves."

The cat-witch on the preceding November 28 had climbed in at a hole in a chest, and Montgomery watched his opportunity, intending to cut off her head when she should put it out of the hole. "Having fastened my sword on her neck," he continues, "which cut her, nor could I hold her; having [at length] opened the chest, my servant, William Geddes, having fixed my durk in her hinder quarters by which stroke she was fastened to the chest; yet after all she escaped out of the chest with the durk in her hinder quarter, which continued

From: Frank Hamel, *Human Animals* (New York: Frederick A. Stokes Co., 1916).

there till I thought, by many strokes, I had killed her with my sword; and having cast her out dead, she could not be found next morning." Four or five nights after, the servant cried out that the cats had come again, and Montgomery "wrapped his plaid about the cat and thrust the durk through her body, and having fixed the durk in the ground, I drove at her head with the back of an ax until she was dead, and being cast out could not be found next morning."

He further declared that no drop of blood came from the cats, also that they did not belong to anyone in the neighborhood, although one night he saw eight of them and took this to be witchcraft for certain.

On February 12, Margaret Nin-Gilbert, who lived about half a mile from Montgomery's house, was seen by some of her neighbors to drop one of her legs at her own door, and she being suspected of witchcraft, the leg, black and putrefied, was taken before the deputy sheriff, who immediately had the maimed woman arrested and imprisoned. By her own confession she admitted that she was bodily present at Montgomery's house "in the likeness of a fettered cat" and that Montgomery had broken her leg either with his durk or ax, which leg since had fallen off from the other part of her body. Also that one Margaret Olsone was also there in the likeness of a cat, and several other women, and that they were invisible because "the devil did hide and conceal them by raising a dark mist or fog to screen them from being seen."

Sometimes the apparition of a witch as a cat foretells death.

In 1607 a witch of the name of Isobel Grierson was burnt after being accused and convicted of entering the house of Adam Clark, in Prestonpans, in the likeness of his own cat and in the company of a mighty rabble of other cats, which by their noise frightened Adam, his wife, and their maid, the last-named being dragged up and down the stairs by the hair of her head, presumably by the devil in the shape of a black man. Isobel also visited the house of a certain Mr. Brown in the shape of a cat, but once being called upon by name she vanished, but Brown himself died of a disease she had laid upon him.

In 1629 another Isobel, wife of George Smith, was indicted as follows:

> *Item* she resett Cristian Grinton, a witch in her house, whom the pannel's husband saw one night to come out at one hole in the roof, in the likeness of a cat, and thereafter transform herself

in her own likeness, whereupon the pannel told her husband that it should not fare well with him, which fell out accordingly, for next day he fell down dead at the plough.

The witches of Vernon frequented an old castle in the shape of cats. Three or four brave men determined to pass the night in the stronghold, where they were assailed by the cats and one of them was killed, several of the others being hurt, and many of the cats received wounds. Afterward the women were found to have returned to human shape and suffered from corresponding gashes.

The witches of Vernon had their imitators in three witches of Strasbourg who, in the disguise of huge cats, fell upon a workman. He defended himself courageously and chased away the cats, wounding them. They were found instantaneously transformed into women, badly hurt and in their beds.

Another story describes how several cat-witches tormented a poor laborer who, wearying of their persistence, drew his broadsword and sent the animals flying. One less nimble than the rest received a cut from the sword which severed one of its hind legs, when, to the laborer's amazement, he discovered on picking up the limb that it was human in shape, and next morning one of the old hags was discovered to have only one leg left.

M. Henri Gelin tells a good story of a witch who transformed herself into a dog.

One winter evening dogs were barking all around a lonely house in Niort far more loudly than usual. The farmer rose from his bed and carefully opened the shutters. In the middle of the yard he saw a black and white greyhound, which apparently was enjoying itself molesting the other dogs, knocking them over with its paws without the least difficulty, and then picking them up in its jaws and throwing them to some distance as soon as they ventured within reach. The farmer drew on his trousers, into the seat of which his wife had sown a horse chestnut as a talisman against witchcraft, loaded his gun, and fired on the animal which fell dead. The next day he rose at an early hour to go and examine the corpse of his prey and was greatly astonished to see the body of a beautiful woman dressed in gorgeous clothes lying in the very spot on which the dog was shot. Around her neck there hung a rich chain made of five strings of jewels bearing enameled medallions beautifully chased, and on her fingers were a profusion of precious gems. In order to cover all traces of his involuntary murder, he quickly dug a hole in a corner of the yard and made a pile of faggots above the newly replaced earth. He had only just finished his task when a gentleman came into the yard and asked whether he had seen a lady pass that way. From the particulars given, the farmer soon felt certain that the woman in question was the witch he had killed. Tremblingly he replied that he had not seen the lady. But a little dog that followed the gentleman ran to the heap of faggots and began turning them over, howling piteously. "You have killed my poor wife," cried the gentleman. "I am certain she came here." But he did not insist on looking into the pile and presently withdrew, followed by the still whimpering dog.

The Bird-Witches

(France)

A beautiful girl of about twenty years of age lived in a Provençal village. Her figure was good, she had an engaging carriage, fine hair, lovely eyes and teeth, and, in short, she was very attractive, but none of the young men of the village ever attempted to make love to her, and she had never had an offer of marriage. Whenever she met a young man who was new to the neighborhood, he said, "Oh, what a pretty girl!" But his friends whispered in his ear, "Yes, she's lovely, but she's a witch," and the mere suspicion of such a thing was so unpleasant that the young man knew it was quite impossible to give the lady a second sympathetic thought.

A few courageous young men, it is true, were anxious to hear further details about her sad story, and their friends gave them the following account as soon as they were out of earshot of any curious listener.

The young girl's mother, it appeared, had become a witch in her

From: Frank Hamel, *Human Animals* (New York: Frederick A. Stokes Co., 1916).

early youth, because, finding herself at the bedside of an old neighbor who lay at death's door and who was a notorious witch, she had been imprudent enough to take hold of her hand. Her indiscretion had not at the time become public property, and she had no difficulty in getting a husband, but a very short time after the marriage had taken place, the man had fallen ill, and died soon afterward in a mysterious decline.

Under these circumstances there could be no doubt that the daughter was a witch as well as the mother and it was equally certain that any bold gentleman who might venture to marry her would be condemned to an early death.

Whether the young lady in question was pleased at the prospect of being laid on the shelf is very doubtful. Most girls of twenty have not an idea in the world beyond getting married, and she did not seem to be an exception to the rule.

One day a nice-looking young man who had recently come to the district to take up a position of some importance was much struck by the young lady's good looks. When a friend told him she was undoubtedly a witch, he shrugged his shoulders in contemptuous incredulity and continued to glance at her with interest and even tenderness in his gaze.

He was specially favored by the girl, who received his attentions with pleasure and returned his glances. They soon made one another's acquaintance and, before long, an engagement was arranged between them.

The young man's family looked upon the forthcoming marriage with anything but goodwill. But the young lover was obstinate, and as the girl and her mother did their best to keep him to his intentions, the arrangements were settled and the wedding day fixed.

The fiancé was allowed to pay court to his ladylove every evening, and he made good use of this privilege. Autumn was approaching and the evenings were drawing in, and as the wedding was to be in November, there were many things to arrange and discuss every day, which made long visits a matter of course.

Time and time again one of the young man's friends pointed out the danger into which he was running by marrying a witch, but all advice was useless. It had an effect in one way, however, as it made the young man anxious to know whether the accusation could possibly be true. After a long time, in which his friend's suggestions had slowly made an impression, the young man decided to take steps to make sure what sort of a woman he was about to marry.

It is a well-known fact that the witches' Sabbath begins exactly at midnight, and once or twice when it grew very late while he was visiting his fiancée, her mother had suggested it was time he took his leave as it was close on midnight. This occurrence had made him slightly suspicious, and he decided to resort to a ruse.

One evening, having arrived at the usual hour, he complained of fatigue and pretended to fall asleep. Being Friday, the meeting of the witches was a specially solemn one, and not a single witch could afford to be absent. As time wore on, mother and daughter tried to wake the young man, but this was impossible, as he was sleeping too heavily, even snoring in a marked fashion, although all the time he was prepared to glance out of one eye if anything extraordinary went on in the room.

Presently, finding all their efforts in vain, the two women began talking in whispers and were seemingly in great trouble. Then, as time pressed on, they took a mighty resolution. They put out the light so that the room was in utter darkness save for the glowing embers on the hearth, then they took from a hidden press a jar of ointment which they placed on the table. They quickly divested themselves of their clothes and, dipping their fingers into the jar, rubbed themselves all over very carefully with the ointment. Every time they rubbed a limb, they cried out, "*Supra fueillo*—above the foliage!"

As soon as they had finished this ritual, they suddenly became owls, flew up the chimney, uttering the lugubrious hoot of the night bird and leaving behind them no signs of their presence except their discarded clothes on a chair in the room which had been the stage of this strange transformation.

As soon as he was left alone, the young man opened his eyes in a state of indescribable stupefaction. He rose, lit the lamp, looked carefully all round the room, touching many of the things to make sure that he was really awake and that he had not been the subject of a hallucination. When he came to the clothes, which still felt warm from their owners' bodies, and saw on the table the jar of black ointment which smelt as though it had been made of burnt animal fat, he knew he was not dreaming.

Just then a clock close by struck the hour of twelve, and the young man, shaking and quaking with the strangeness of what had taken place, looked around in fear lest some awful apparition should greet his eyes. But nothing happened, for all the witches were at the Sabbath by that time.

Then a mad idea entered his head! Why should not he, too, transform himself into an owl and go to join his future wife and her mother, who had effected the transformation without apparently the slightest difficulty. The idea had no sooner struck him than he prepared to carry it out. In the twinkling of an eye he slipped off his clothes, dipped his fingers into the magic jar, and rubbed himself exactly as the women had done. Unfortunately, however, he could not remember the exact phrase they had used, and instead of crying, "*Supra fueillo,*" he said, "*Souto fueillo*—under the foliage," with every rub.

Scarcely had he completed his exercises and said, "*Souto fueillo,*" for the last time than he was immediately changed into an owl and flew toward the chimney.

Scarcely had he reached the grate, however, when he knocked against the smoldering green fagots and burnt himself.

He attributed this misadventure to his want of address, not being accustomed to the shape and movements of a bird, and he assured himself that as soon as he was free of the house he would manage better. But when he reached the open country, he began to suffer tortures. Where the fields were bare he found himself easily able to fly, just like any ordinary owl, but as soon as he came to the smallest hedge or thicket, he was obliged to pass through it instead of clearing it from above, and every branch, twig, or thorn hit and stung him like a whip.

He wished to stop flying, for every moment his suffering grew more unendurable, but it was impossible to stop, for he was induced by some superior power to go straight ahead, and however much he tried, he could not avoid the shrubs and trees which lay in his path. The words "*souto fueillo*—under the foliage" which he had used were literally true, in the most cruel sense. He was bruised and torn all over, and felt as though he were at the point of death and that his last moment had come, when suddenly he heard a cock crow and the first ray of light appeared in the sky, heralding the dawn. The witches' Sabbath had ended, he fell heavily to earth, finding himself lying naked on the wet soil. Bruised and bleeding, and smarting from a hundred scratches, his condition was pitiable, but he took heart when he realized that his experiment, so foolishly attempted, had not turned out even worse. He stood up and, limping and sore, hastened to his own house, slinking into bed, where he developed a serious fever which kept him there for many weeks. No one ever guessed the real cause of his illness, but as soon as he had recovered his ordinary state of health he went to live in another town and never even called on his ex-fiancée and her mother to ask them for the clothes which he had left on a chair in their sitting room.

The Horse-Witch

(Denmark)

In the neighborhood of Ostrel in Denmark, a man served on a farm, the mistress of which, unknown to him, was a witch. Although she gave him good and wholesome food, he never thrived but became thinner every day. At this, being much troubled, he went to a wise man, to whom he communicated his case. From this man he learnt that his mistress was a witch and that at night, while he slept, she transformed him into a horse and rode upon him to Troms Church in Norway, so that it was not to be wondered at that his strength decreased. The wise man at the same time gave him an ointment with which to rub his head at night, and said when he fell asleep he would have a violent itching on his head, and then he would wake up and see that he was standing outside Troms Church.

The man did as he had been told, and on waking up the following night, he found that he was standing by the church, holding in his hand a bridle which he had torn off whilst scratching his head. Behind him he saw many horses bound together by each other's tails. Presently his mistress came out and cast a friendly look at him, but he nodded for her to come nearer, and when she stood by, he cast the bridle over her head and she became a handsome mare on the spot. He mounted and rode her home. On the way he called at a farrier's

From: Frank Hamel, *Human Animals* (New York: Frederick A. Stokes Co., 1916).

and made him shoe the mare. When he reached home he told his master that he had been out to buy a fine mare, which would go handsomely in harness with one already in the stables. The master paid him a good round sum for the animal, but when he took off its bridle, there stood his wife with horseshoes on her hands and feet. He turned her straight out of doors, but she never managed to get rid of the horseshoes.

Bewitching Cattle

(Germany)

C oncerning the bewitching of cattle and horses, the possibility of it is believed in, or (to express it more correctly) known to almost every peasant in Bavaria and Austria, especially in the mountainous districts, where the farmers will often refuse to permit a stranger to enter their stable unless he pronounces a blessing. If a cow is "bewitched," the milk soon after the milking turns dark blue and emits a putrid odor, rendering it unfit for use. Such a case happened at the dairy of my sister at her residence at S———, near Munich.

At a farmhouse in the vicinity of the castle of S———, where my sister lives, the milk one day became "blue." After having been deposited in the usual place, it began to darken, became light blue, and that color after a while deepened into an almost inky black, while the layer of cream on the top exhibited zigzag lines. Soon the whole mass began to putrify and to emit a horrible odor. This occurred again and again every day, and the farmer was in despair. Everything was tried to find out the cause of the trouble: the stable was thoroughly cleaned and disinfected, the place where the milk was kept was changed, new pails were bought, a different kind of food given to the cows, samples of the milk were sent to the university professors to be

From: Franz Hartman, "Witchcraft in Germany," *Occult Review* 3 (January–June 1906): 237–39.

examined by chemists, veterinary surgeons were called in, and everything possible was done without any effect.

At last my sister, hearing of these things and being incredulous, went to the farm for the purpose of investigating the matter. She took with her a clean, new bottle and filled it with the milk directly from the cow. This she took home with her and deposited it in her pantry. On the following day her cows became bewitched and their milk became blue, while the trouble in the house of the neighbor ceased.

Now again everything possible was tried to find out the cause, but without any success. University professors and veterinary surgeons came and examined and went away as wise as before, and the trouble continued for about three months. Finally, my brother-in-law was advised to apply to an old woman reputed to be able to cure such things. She lived at K———, about three hundred miles distant. The count went to see her and told her about this affair, whereupon she wrote certain signs upon slips of paper and gave them to him, asking him to put one of these slips over each opening in the stable and told him that soon after that, something curious would happen.

My brother-in-law followed her advice, and a couple of days afterward, as the milkmaid went to the dairy in the morning before sunrise, carrying a lantern, when she opened the stable door something like a black animal of the size of a big dog rushed out, knocking the milkpail and lantern out of her hands and disappearing. After this event, all was right again.

Another similar case happened about two years ago at Berehtesgaden (Bavaria). In this case the owner of the cattle accused one of his neighbors of having bewitched his cows, but as he could not prove it he had to pay a fine for defamation of character. Those who do not believe in magic and obsession may consider these stories incredible, but for my part, I am satisfied that the said troubles had occult causes, and I know that there are still forces existing in nature whose qualities and activity are not yet recognized by the world in general.

Matthew Hopkins and the Witches of Chelmsford

(England)

Matthew Hopkins of Manningtree, Essex, a witch-finder of ill fame, was the cause of bringing thousands of supposed witches to judgment and so to the stake. He was paid twenty shillings, in each town he visited and managed to rid it of its suspicious characters, and he appeared to have found his profession extraordinarily lucrative. In 1644 he was commissioned by Parliament to make a circuit through several counties with a view to discovering witches. He traveled in the company of several boon companions for three years and was instrumental in having sixteen persons hanged at Yarmouth, forty at Bury, and at least sixty in other parts of Suffolk, Norfolk, and Huntingdonshire.

During a notorious trial of a number of witches at Chelmsford, Essex, on July 29, 1645, Hopkins made a deposition about an alleged witch, Elizabeth Clarke, who confessed that she had known the devil intimately for more than six years and that he visited her between three and fives times a week. She invited Hopkins and his companions, one of whom was a man called Sterne, to stay at her house for a time until she could call up one of her white imps for them to see. Presently there appeared on the scene an imp like a dog, white and with sandy spots, which seemed to be very fat and plump, with short legs. The animal forthwith vanished away. The said Elizabeth gave the name of this imp as Jarmara. And immediately afterward there appeared another imp, which she called Vinegar Tom, in the shape of a greyhound with long legs. The said Elizabeth then remarked that the next imp should be black in color and that it should come for Master

From: Frank Hamel, *Human Animals* (New York: Frederick A. Stokes Co., 1916).

Sterne (the other witness already mentioned), and it appeared as she promised but presently vanished without leaving a sign. The last imp of all to come before the spectators was a creature in the shape of a polecat, but the head somewhat bigger. The said Elizabeth then disclosed to the informant that she had five imps of her own. And two other imps with which she had dealings belonged to a certain Beldam Anne West.

The said Matthew Hopkins, when going from the house of a Mr. Edwards of Manningtree to his own house one night between nine and ten o'clock, accompanied by his favorite greyhound, noticed the dog give a sudden leap and run off as though in full course after a hare. Hastening to see what the greyhound pursued so eagerly, he espied a white thing about the size of a kitten, and the panting dog was standing aloof from the creature. By and by the imp or kitten began to dance about and around the said greyhound and, viciously approaching him, bit or tore a piece of flesh off the dog's shoulder.

Coming later into his own yard, the informant saw a black thing proportioned like a cat, only that it was thrice as big, sitting on a strawberry bed and fixing its luminous eyes on him. But when he went toward it, it leaped suddenly over the palings and ran toward the informant as he thought, but instead it fled through the yard with his greyhound in hot pursuit after it to a great gate which was "underset with a pair of tumbrel strings," and it did throw the said gate wide open and then vanished. And the said greyhound returned again to the informant, shaking and trembling exceedingly.

Sterne gave evidence on the same day and much to the same effect, but said that the white imp was like a cat but not so big, and when he asked Elizabeth whether she was not afraid of her imps she answered, "What! do you think I am afraid of my children?" and she called the imp Jarmara as having red spots, and spoke of two more called Sack and Sugar. Four other witnesses confirmed the story practically in its entirety.

Elizabeth Clarke herself gave evidence then, and said Anne West had sent her a "thing like a little kitlyn," which would obtain food for her. Two or three nights after this promise, a white thing came to her in the night, and the night after a gray one spoke to her and said it would do her no hurt and would help her to get a husband. After various charges against the said Elizabeth Clarke and her accomplice, Elizabeth Gooding, Anne Leech, a third woman accused of witchcraft, deposed on April 14 that she and the other two accused sent their respective gray, black, and white imps to kill cattle belonging to various neighbors, and that later they had sent them to kill neighbors' children, and she added that her imps spoke to her in a hollow voice which she plainly understood, and that these accused witches had met together at the house of the said Elizabeth Clarke, when a book was read "wherein she thinks there was no goodness."

Another woman suspected of witchcraft was Helen Clark, who confessed on April 11 that the devil had appeared to her in the likeness of a white dog, and that she called her familiar Elimanzer and that she fed him with milk potage and that he spoke to her audibly and bade her deny Christ.

With the witch Anne West was implicated her daughter Rebecca West, who, however, was acquitted, and the notorious Matthew Hopkins deposed that she had told him of visiting the house of Clarke with her mother, and that they had found Leech, Gooding, and Helen Clark, and that the devil had appeared in the shape of a dog, afterward in the shape of two kittens, then in the shape of two dogs, and that the said familiars did homage in the first place to the said Elizabeth Clarke and slipped up into her lap and kissed her, and then went and kissed all that were in the room except the said Rebecca, who was then made to swear on a book that she would not reveal what she saw or heard—on pain of the torments of hell—and that afterward the devil came and kissed her and promised to marry her, and she sent him to kill a neighbor's child, of the name of Hart, who died within a fortnight.

Susan Sparrow, who gave her evidence on the 25th of April, said that the house in which she lived with one Mary Greenleif was haunted by a leveret which usually came and sat before the door, which, when coursed by a dog, never stirred, "and just when the dog came at it, he skipped over it and turned about and stood still, and looked on it, and shortly after that the dog languished and died."

Another of the witches, called Margaret Moone, had a familiar "in the likeness of a rat for bigness and shape, but of a grayer color." She confessed to two of the witnesses that she had twelve imps and called these by such names as Jesus, Jockey, Monsieur Sandy, Mrs. Elizabeth, and Collyn, etc. Moone was a "woman of very bad fame," who confessed to many crimes, especially of causing the death of animals and children.

Rose Hallybread, who died in gaol before execution, was accused of being implicated with Joyce Boanes in sending four familiars to the house of a carpenter, Robert Turner, whose servant was then taken sick and "crowed perfectly like a cock, sometimes barked like a dog," sang tunes, groaned, and struggled with such strength that five strong men were needed to hold him. Boanes confessed that her imp made the victim bark like a dog, Hallybread's imp caused him "to sing sundry tunes in great extremity of pains," and Susan Cork compelled him to crow. The torture was inflicted because Turner's servant had refused to give Susan Cork a sackful of chips.

Anne Cate, another of the witches who was executed at Chelmsford, said she had three familiars like mice and a fourth like a sparrow. They were called James, Prickeare, Robyn, and Sparrow, and she sent them to kill both cattle and human beings.

It was thought impossible to kill these familiars, and one Goff, a glover and very honest man of Manningtree, confessed to passing Anne West's house about four o'clock on a moonlit morning and seeing her door was open, he looked into the house. "Presently there came three or four little things in the shape of black rabbits leaping and skipping about him, who, having a good stick in his hand, struck at them thinking to kill them, but could not, but at last caught one of them in his hand, and holding it by the body, he beat the head of it against his stick, intending to beat the brains out of it. But when he could not kill it that way, he took the body in one hand and the head in another and endeavored to wring off the head, and as he wrung and stretched the neck of it, it came out between his hands like a lock of wool." Then he tried to drown it in a spring but kept falling down. At last he crept to the water on hands and knees, holding the familiar under the water for a good space. But as soon as he let go, it sprang out of the water up into the air and so vanished.

He went and asked Anne West why she had set her imps on him to molest and trouble him, but she said "they were sent out as scouts upon another design."

Joan Cariden, widow, examined September 25, 1645, said that about three quarters of a year ago, as she was in bed about twelve or one of the clock in the night, there lay a rugged soft thing on her bosom which was very soft, and she thrust it off with her hand; and she said that when she had thrust it away she thought God forsook her, for she could never pray so well as she could before, and further she said that she verily thought it was alive. Examined further, she said the devil came to her in the shape of a black rugged dog in the nighttime and crept into bed with her and spoke to her in mumbling language. The next night he came again and required her to deny God and lean on him.

Jane Hott, widow and associate of the above, also examined on September 25, 1645, confessed that a thing like a hedgehog had usually visited her, and when it lay on her breast she struck it off with her hand, and that it was as soft as a cat.

An Alsatian Witch Story

(Alsace)

In Alsace the chimneys of houses are very wide, and it was through these the witches left the house without being seen. At a certain farmhouse there were two women—mother and daughter—who were witches. With them lived an inquisitive young farmhand. He had noticed that something unusual was taking place in the house every month, so one night he hid in the kitchen and watched. About midnight the women came and stood naked before the fireplace, beneath the chimney, and after anointing themselves with an oil which the Germans call *Hexenfett* (i.e., witch's fat), uttered some magic words, and up they went through the chimney.

The young man then emerged from his hiding place, and seeing the vessel containing the oil, he anointed himself to see what effect it would have on him. He had scarcely pronounced the mystic words when he went up the chimney with a suddenness that was surprising, and when he reached the ground he found himself astride a large black sow which carried him with great speed across the country. They soon arrived at a broad and swift-flowing river, but this did not hinder the onward advance of the sow, for it cleared the broad expanse of water at a single bound.

From: W. J. Wintemberg, "German Folk-Tales Collected in Canada," *Journal of American Folk-Lore* 19 (1906): 241–44.

The young man looked back, and admiring its leaping powers, he said to the sow, "That was a long leap you made," but as he spoke the spell was broken, the sow disappeared, and he found himself in a strange country many miles from home.

The Witch Ann Forster

(England)

Notwithstanding that many have taken very great pains to confute, by reason of the opinion so long held in the world, that there have been and are witches, arguing against the express text of Scripture, "Thou shalt not suffer a witch to live," and falsely finding out sophisms to make the Witch of Endor I know not what kind of cunning woman, taught only to play tricks by the idolatrous priests; for why should a law be made so severely against witches if there had been none, or why should the Scripture record so peculiar a story of the Witch of Endor, if she had known no more than some few tricks of legerdemain and had not had a particular converse with infernal spirits?

I say, notwithstanding all the clutter these men have made to introduce this unbelief of witches into the world, by alleging first that there is no such thing as a witch in Scripture. And secondly, that the opinion of witchcraft first took birth from heathen fables, and was afterward improved by popish impostures, and laughing at all the strange and wonderful stories related by so many credible witnesses in confirmation of it. Yet certain there are such lewd and wicked people who give themselves over to the dominion of the Prince of the Power of the Air to have his aid and assistance in executing their malice and revenge. Of what follows will be a very pregnant testimony, which being no less true than it is sad and wonderful.

There lived and still lives in the town of Eastcoat near Fosters Booth

From: D. M., *A Full and True Relation of the Tryal, Condemnation and Execution of Ann Forster* (Northampton: Taylor & Sons, 1878, reprint).

in Northamptonshire a rich and substantial grazier, who happening about April last (when mutton was very dear and scarce) to have killed a sheep for the use of his own family, there came into his house an old woman who long had been observed to be muttering to herself, came into his house and would needs have some of his mutton, but he neither willing to spare it nor she to give the price it was then worth, he utterly refused to let her have any. Whereupon she went away murmuring and grumbling, and told him he had as good have done what she desired and took her money. He took so little notice of what she said that some few days after, he did not at all remember it when it happened that, going into his pasture, he found thirty of his sheep in a condition dead and in a strange and miserable manner, their legs broken in pieces and their bones all shattered in their skins. Whereupon amazed at the strangeness of the spectacle, he sent for several of his neighbors to view them, who no less wondering at it than he, entered into a suspicion that they must needs be bewitched and advised him to take one of them and burn it, for they said that they had heard it confidently affirmed by men of reputed knowledge that upon doing so the witch would appear. Whereupon the honest grazier, overpersuaded by his neighbors, took one of the sheep and threw it into the fire; but though they could by no means burn it, yet immediately came the same old woman running in a great hurry who would some days before have bought some of this mutton, and in a mighty chase asked him what he meant to offer to burn his sheep, which fully increasing his suspicion, having a knife in hand, and led perhaps by that general opinion that fetching blood of the witch takes away her power of doing any harm, he gave her a little cut over the hand and fetched blood of her. She little regarding and neglecting to apply any remedy to it, it rankled and swelled extremely, whereupon she came again and threatened that she would arrest and trouble him for it. And he, to avoid anything of trouble, being a quiet man, was content to give her twenty shillings toward her cure, which she had no sooner received of him but she returned these or the like words, that that was the devil's money and that now she had power enough to punish him. Nor did she delay to execute her malice, but soon after, being assisted by Satan, her colleague, about the 22nd of May last set his house and barns on fire, and notwithstanding all the help of his neighbors to quench it, they could nothing prevail, but that one of his barns was quite burned to the ground. And sometimes the fire would be in his wheat, and sometimes in his chambers, so that they knew not which way to turn themselves to extinguish it. At length with much pain and labor and the good spirit prevailing over the bad, they made a shift to put it out, without any considerable damage to his household goods, save only that the barn before-mentioned was quite consumed. Among the rest of the neighbors that came to assist at this fire came likewise this old woman, who was observed to tell several of the others that all they did was but in vain, and that do what they could, they should never be able to quench the fire. Whereupon they were more and more confirmed in the former strong presumptions they had, that all this mischief was done by her devilish art, and thereupon laying hands on this suspected witch, carried her before the next justice of the peace, where being charged for having by devilish practices and combination with the Prince of Darkness, first caused this poor man's sheep to die in that strange and miserable manner and afterward to have kindled the fire in his barns and houses, she freely confessed all, and boasted that she would make many more die as well as herself. Upon which confession of hers, she was by mittimus from the justice of peace committed to Northampton Gaol, there to remain till the next assizes.

No sooner was she brought in but the keepers of the gaol caused her to be chained close to a post that was in the gaol; but she had not been long so tied before she began to swell in all parts of her body, that her skin was ready to burst, which caused her to cry out in a most lamentable manner, insomuch that they were forced to unchain her again and to give her more liberty that the devil might come to have intercourse with her, the which he usually did, coming constantly about the dead time of the night in the likeness of a rat, which at his coming made a most lamentable and hideous noise which affrighted the people that did belong to the gaol, which caused many to come and see her during her abode there, and several hath been with her when the devil hath been coming to her, but could see nothing but things like rats and heard a most terrible noise. Not long after, the assizes being come, this witch that went by the name of Ann Forster was called to the bar, and being asked whether she were guilty of those crimes that were there alleged against her, she at first pleaded not guilty, but it being so evidently proved that she was the person that had committed all those things before-mentioned, she then confessed and said that the devil did provoke her to do all those mischiefs. And seeing that a sentence of death was passed upon her, she prayed to God to forgive her and desired the man (on whom she had so much spent her malice, which was to the ruin of him) to forgive her likewise, for she could no way make him amends but only by satisfying the law, according to the sentence which was pronounced against her. She said that she could bring out many more that were as bad as herself. After the sentence of death was passed upon her, she mightily desired to be burned; but the court would give no ear to that, but that she should be hanged at the common place of execution, which accordingly was performed on Saturday last, being the 22nd of this instant August.

The Witches and the Boat

(Italy)

There were two witches, mother and daughter, who lived by the seaside, and the younger was a beautiful girl who had a lover, and they were soon to be married. But it began to be reported that the women were given to sorcery and had wild ways, and someone told the young man of it, and that he should not take such a wife. So he resolved to see for himself by going to their house, but intending to remain till midnight, when he knew if they were witches they could not remain longer at home. And he went and made love, and sat till it was after eleven, and when they bade him go home he replied, "Let me sit a little longer," and so again, till they were out of patience.

Then seeing that he would not go, they cast him by their witchcraft into a deep sleep, and with a small tube sucked all his blood from his

From: Charles Godfrey Leland, *Etruscan Roman Remains in Popular Tradition* (New York: Charles Scribner's Sons, 1892).

veins and made it into a blood pudding or sausage *(migliaccino),* which they carried with them. And this gave them the power to be invisible till they should return.

But there was another man on the lookout for them that night, and that was the brother of the youth whom they had put to sleep, for he had long suspected them, and it was he who had warned his brother. Now he had a boat, and as he observed for some time every morning that it had been untied and used by someone in the night, he concluded it was done by these witches. So he hid himself on board carefully and waited and watched well.

At midnight the two witches came. They wished to go to Jerusalem to get *garofani* (clove gilly flowers, or the clove plant, much used in magic). And when they got into the boat the mother said:

"Boat, boat, go for two!"

But the boat did not move. Then the mother said to the daughter, "Perhaps you are with child—that would make three." But the daughter denied it. Then the mother cried again:

"Boat, boat, go for two!"

Still it did not move, so the mother cried again:

*"Vai per due, vai per tre,
Per quattro, per cuanto tu vuoi!"*

("Go for two or three or still
For four, as many as you will!")

Then the boat shot away like an arrow, like lightning, like thought, and they soon came to Jerusalem, where they gathered their flowers and reentering the boat, returned. Then the boatman was well satisfied that the women were witches and went home to tell his brother, whom he found nearly dead and almost out of his mind. So he went to the witches and threatened them, till they gave the youth the *migliaccino.* And when he had eaten it, all his blood and life returned, and he was well as before. But the witches flew away as he arose, over the housetops and over the hill, and unless they stopped they are flying still.

The Mother-in-law Witch

(France)

A woman whose children were always ailing lived in the village of Ceyreste near to Ciotat. As soon as one child recovered another fell ill, and their mother was in despair, because she could not account for their ailments.

One day, one of her neighbors said, "Do you know, I feel sure your mother-in-law is injuring the health of your little ones. She may be a witch."

The woman spoke to her husband about the matter, and they decided to watch over their children carefully to see whether their illness was due to evil influence.

One night they were watching without appearing to do so, when suddenly a black cat approached the cradle of one of the children, moving with stealth and quite silently. The husband raised a stick he had picked up for the purpose and struck the animal violently, intending to kill it. But the blow was not carefully aimed and he only succeeded in crushing one of the evil animal's paws. With a bound it escaped him.

For a day or two afterward nothing was seen of the children's grandmother, who usually came on a visit every day to inquire after the health of her grandchildren.

Then the neighbor said, "She is hiding something from you. Go and see why she does not come."

The husband followed her advice and went to see his mother, whom he found with her hand bound up and in an extremely bad temper. He pretended not to see that she had been hurt, and he asked her in the most natural tone he could summon why she had not been to visit them as usual.

"Whatever should I come to your house for?" she asked angrily.

From: Frank Hamel, *Human Animals* (New York: Frederick A. Stokes Co., 1916).

"Look at the state of my fingers. If I had been struck by a hatchet instead of a stick, my fingers would have been cut off and I should have nothing left but a stump."

The Vengeance of Pippo

(Italy)

There was a man named Pippo, and he had not been long married to a young and beautiful wife when he was obliged to go on a long journey. And it so chanced that this journey was by accident prolonged, nor did his letters reach home, so that his wife, who was young and very simple, believing all the gossip and mischievous hints of everybody, soon thought that her husband had run away. Now there was a priest in the village who was *bastanza furbo*—not a little of a knave—and to him she bitterly complained that her husband had abandoned her, leavening her *incinta*, or with child.

At this the priest looked very grave and said that it was very wicked of her husband to act as he had done; yes, that it was a mortal sin for which both she and Pippo would be damned, even to the lowest depth of hell, because she would give birth to a child that had only been begun and not finished, for that it would probably be born without a head or limbs, and she would be very lucky if only a hand and foot or the eyes were wanting. And that all women who bear such monsters would be certainly condemned to the worst.

Now the wife, being only a simple *contadina*, was very devout and went frequently to confession, and believing every word which the priest said, was terribly frightened and asked him what could be done in this case. Then he replied that there was a way to remedy it, which he should most unwillingly employ, yet still to save her soul, and for the child's sake, he would try it. And this was that she should pass the

From: Charles Godfrey Leland, *Etruscan Roman Remains in Popular Tradition* (New York: Charles Scribner's Sons, 1892).

night with him, when by his miraculous power as a priest, and by his prayers, he would so effect it that the infant would be perfected—and she could be freed from sin. But he made her swear an oath not to tell a word of all this to any human being, and especially not to Pippo, else all would fail. So she assented, and the priest had his will.

Now no one knew it, but Pippo was a *streghone*, or wizard, and casting his mind forth to know how all was going on at home, learned all this fine affair which had passed. Then returning, instead of going to his house, he put on the form of a beautiful nun and went to the priest's. The priest had two young sisters, famous for their extraordinary beauty, and Pippo was very kindly received by them as well as by the brother. And when he begged for a night's lodging, the two young girls bade him sleep with them, which he did, of course seducing them thoroughly.

The next morning, being alone with the priest, he first ogled him, and as the other caught eagerly at the chance of sinning with a nun, he plainly asked him if they should not go into the cellar, *per fare l'amore.* At which the priest was enraptured; but when they were alone together Pippo assumed his natural form, which was a terrible one, and said, "I am Pippo, whose wife thou didst wrong with thy lies. Evil hast thou done to me, but I have done worse to thy sisters, and worst of all to thee, for now thou art accursed before God, thou false priest!" And the *prete* could do nothing and say nothing. And there came before him all the time many spirits who mocked him, and he had to leave holy orders. And this was the revenge of Pippo.

Gerald the Warlock

(Ireland)

The fourth Earl of Desmond, Gerald, was commonly known as the "Great Earl." He was betrayed and killed in 1583 and passed from the region of history to that of mythology, as he is credited with being the husband (or son) of a goddess. Not many miles from the city of Limerick is a lonely, picturesque lake, Lough Gur, which was included in his extensive possessions, and at the bottom of which he is supposed to lie enchanted.

According to the legend, he was a very potent magician and usually resided in a castle which was built on a small island in that lake. To this he brought his bride, a young and beautiful girl whom he loved with a too fond love, for she succeeded in prevailing upon him to gratify her selfish desires, with fatal results. One day she presented herself in the chamber in which her husband exercised his forbidden art and begged him to show her the wonders of his evil science. With the greatest reluctance he consented, but warned her that she must prepare herself to witness a series of most frightful phenomena, which, once commenced, could neither be abridged nor mitigated, while if she spoke a single word during the proceedings the castle and all it contained would sink to the bottom of the lake. Urged on by curiosity, she gave the required promise, and he commenced. Muttering a spell as he stood before her, feathers sprouted thickly over him, his face became contracted and hooked, a corpselike smell filled the air, and winnowing the air with beats of its heavy wings a gigantic vulture rose in his stead and swept around and around the room as if on the point of pouncing upon her. The lady controlled herself through this trial, and another began.

The bird alighted near the door, and in less than a minute changed, she saw not how, into a horribly deformed and dwarfish hag who, with yellow skin hanging about her face, and cavernous eyes, swung herself on crutches toward the lady, her mouth foaming with fury and

From: St. John D. Seymour, *Irish Witchcraft and Demonology* (Dublin: Hodges, Figgis & Co., Ltd., 1913).

her grimaces and contortions becoming more and more hideous every moment, till she rolled with a fearful yell on the floor in a horrible convulsion at the lady's feet, and then changed into a huge serpent, which came sweeping and arching toward her with erect crest and quivering tongue. Suddenly, as it seemed on the point of darting at her, she saw her husband in its stead, standing pale before her, and with his finger on his lips enforcing the continued necessity of silence. He then placed himself at full length on the floor and began to stretch himself out, longer and longer, until his head nearly reached to one end of the vast room and his feet to the other. This utterly unnerved her. She gave a wild scream of horror, whereupon the castle and all in it sank to the bottom of the lake.

Once in seven years the great earl rises, and rides by night on his white horse around Lough Gur. The steed is shod with silver shoes, and when these are worn out the spell that holds the earl will be broken, and he will regain possession of his vast estates and semiregal power. In the opening years of the nineteenth century there was living a man named Teigue O'Neill, who claimed to have seen him on the occasion of one of his septennial appearances under the following curious conditions. O'Neill was a blacksmith, and his forge stood on the brow of a hill overlooking the lake, on a lonely part of the road to Cahirconlish. One night, when there was a bright moon, he was working very late and quite alone. In one of the pauses of his work he heard the ring of many hoofs ascending the steep road that passed his forge, and standing in his doorway he saw a gentleman on a white horse, who was dressed in a fashion the like of which he had never seen before. This man was accompanied by a mounted retinue in similar dress. They seemed to be riding up the hill at a gallop, but the pace slackened as they drew near, and the rider of the white horse, who seemed from his haughty air to be a man of rank, drew bridle and came to a halt before the smith's door. He did not speak, and all his train were silent, but he beckoned to the smith and pointed down at one of the horse's hoofs.

Teigue stooped and raised it, and held it just long enough to see that it was shod with a silver shoe, which in one place was worn as thin as a shilling. Instantly his situation was made apparent to him by this sign, and he recoiled with a terrified prayer. The lordly rider, with a look of pain and fury, struck at him suddenly with something that whistled in the air like a whip. An icy streak seemed to traverse his body, and at the same time he saw the whole cavalcade break into a gallop and disappear down the hill. It is generally supposed that for the purpose of putting an end to his period of enchantment the earl endeavors to lead someone on to first break the silence and speak to him, but what, in the event of his succeeding, would be the result or would befall the person thus ensnared, no one knows.

In a letter written in the year 1640, the earl assumes a different appearance. We learn from it that as a countryman was on his way to the ancient and celebrated fair of Knockaney, situated a few miles from Lough Gur, he met "a gentleman standing in the way, demanding if he would sell his horse. He answered yea, for £5. The gentleman would give him but £4 10s., saying he would not get so much at the fair. The fellow went to the fair, could not get so much money, and found the gentleman on his return in the same place, who proffered the same money. The fellow accepting of it, the other bid him come in and receive his money. He carried him into a fine spacious castle, paid him his money every penny, and showed him the fairest black horse that ever was seen, and told him that that horse was the Earl of Desmond, and that he had three shoes already. When he hath the fourth shoe, which should be very shortly, then should the earl be as he was before, thus guarded with many armed men conveying him out of the gates. The fellow came home, but never was any castle in that place either before or since." The local variant of the legend states that the seller of the horse was a Clare man, and that he went home after having been paid in gold the full amount of a satisfactory bargain, but on the following morning found to his great mortification that instead of the gold coins he had only a pocketful of ivy leaves. Readers of Victor Hugo's *Notre Dame* will recall the incident of the *écu* that (apparently) was transformed by magic into a withered leaf. Similar tales of horse dealing with mysterious strangers are told in Scotland in connection with the celebrated Thomas the Rhymer, of Erceldoune.

Witches' Unguents

(Various)

We have all heard of the strange visions and exalted state of mind brought about by such drugs as opium, morphine, and the like, and it is highly probable that witches' ointments produced the same results. The latter were composed of the most powerful narcotics made into an ointment by the addition of certain fatty substances.

The body of the witch was anointed from head to foot with this, and she then either went to bed or lay down and relapsed into a heavy sleep, producing all manner of weird dreams.

There is an old tale of a witch who promised of her own accord to perform an errand in a far country without even going out of her house. She insisted upon her audience leaving the room. They did so, but looking through a chink in the door saw her undress and cover herself with ointments, after which she fell down in a heavy sleep. They thereupon broke open the door which she had carefully bolted, and as the quaint old chronicles have it, "beat her exceedingly," but she had no more sense of feeling than we find in patients under the influence of magnetic somnambulism, and they finally went away.

When the potency of her strange powers was exhausted, she awoke of her own accord. She swore quite calmly that she had passed over seas and mountains and had done what she set out to perform. Now this was only a poor ignorant woman in no way clever enough to invent these visions, so that the only feasible solution seems to be that the narcotic in her unguents caused the hallucinations.

It appears that practically all the witches who attended the Sabbath used these unguents. If you read the accounts of witch trials in any of the old histories or chronicles of those times, you will be struck by the remarkable concurrence of their testimonies as to the scenes they declared they had witnessed.

Although, of course, a good deal of this may be accounted for by the

From: Arthur Gay, "Witches' Unguents," *Occult Review* 15 (1912): 207–9.

power of "suggestion" and mental infection, as well as by the leading questions of the inquisitors, it is still more than probable that similar anointments and preparations produced almost similar dreams.

Students of magnetism, mesmerism, and hypnotism have often proved that somnambulism is much heightened by certain chemical aids; moreover, they have found that there are drugs that produce a strange sympathetic effect upon the imagination of patients possessing highly excitable nervous temperaments. Many an ignorant, foolish old woman during the witch epidemic, to her own undoing, laid claim to powers of sorcery only because she knew how to mix a potion or an unguent that produced certain visions.

Paolo Minnucci tells us that a witch, being brought before a magistrate at Florence upon the usual accusation of sorcery, not only confessed that she was guilty but swore that if she were only permitted to return home and anoint her body, she would that very night attend the Sabbath. Wishing to test her vaunted powers, the magistrate permitted her to do this, whereupon she went home, used her unguent, and immediately fell into a profound sleep.

They then, in the brutal manner peculiar to those times, tied her to the bed and tested the reality of her unconsciousness by burns, blows, and pricking her with sharp instruments. It was, however, all in vain. The woman still remained sound asleep, nor did she awake till the next day, when she declared she had been to the Sabbath.

A Gypsy Cure for Warts

(Germany)

This narrative will contain only a plain and ungarnished, yet truthful, account of the incidents that I have to relate and will be given without bias or prejudice. When I was a boy I suffered very much from unsightly corneous excrescences—commonly called warts—which so disfigured my hands that my companions

From: David Gordon Morrison, "How Warts Were Mysteriously Removed from the Hands," *Occult Review* 15 (1915): 31–34.

called me "Warty." They no doubt thought that this nickname was fairly descriptive of my condition. My mother had tried all the remedies known to the pharmacopoeia to remove those hardened protuberances, but without success. When I had reached that age at which I had to begin to earn a little to help the family exchequer, my initial efforts in this direction were in the humble capacity of message boy to a shoemaker. A few weeks after I had started in this way, I was sent to a Gypsy encampment with a pair of shoes which had been ordered by the "Queen" of this contingent of Romanies who periodically visited Brechin, where our family then resided.

"When you enter the camp be sure that you ask for the Queen." Such were my instructions, not because my employer did not know the family name of this lady but because this was the recognized etiquette of a Gypsy encampment. I looked forward with much interest to this visit, as I fancied it would bring me no inconsiderable distinction among my companions, we as boys having from a respectful distance often viewed with inquisitive eyes this particular encampment of peculiar people.

With the parcel tucked under my arm and feeling big with importance, I wended my way toward the Gypsy camp. Before entering within its precincts, however, I was accosted by a big burly chap, who demanded of me if I knew where I was going. To his inquiry, I told him that I had a message for the Queen. "Oh! indeed," said he, "then follow me." He guided me to a tent, at the entrance to which he stopped and whispered something to someone within in a language that I did not understand. A voice from the tent politely requested me to enter. I did so with some hesitancy, and at the same moment— clumsily, no doubt—handed to the lady the parcel which I had been commissioned to convey to her. The Queen desired me to sit down on a skin mat spread on the floor of the tent and to open the parcel immediately. While I was struggling to undo the string which bound it, in my nervousness one of the loops kinked on my warty hands, causing them to bleed. Noticing the state of my hands, the Queen carefully examined them. While she was thus engaged, I shyly looked at her through my half-closed eyes. Her quiet manner impressed me with feelings of awe unmingled with fear. When she spoke, her voice sounded sweet and mellow, like the cooing of doves.

"Your hands," she remarked, "are in a very bad state and must cause you much pain and trouble."

"Yes, mem," I replied.

"Would you like these unsightly things removed?" asked the Gypsy.

"Yes, mem," I again replied.

She, suspending her examination of my hands for a moment, eyed me keenly and seemed satisfied with this close inspection of my face and general makeup.

"How old are you?" she then asked.

"I am twelve years of age," I replied.

"You are very small for your age," she observed, as if whispering to herself.

Then she inquired if my mother had tried anything to remove the warts from my hands.

"Ay! but she cannot cure them," I said.

"Just what I expected you would tell me. I can, however, do something," said the Gypsy.

This for me, as a boy, was a somewhat prolonged conversation. It was getting on my nerves, and I was beginning to feel the wet hand of fear closing around my heart. Observing that my eyes were moist with rising tears, the Queen, to reassure me, gently stroked my head and gave me bread and honey to eat. I nevertheless became restless and fidgety—it may have been from ungrounded apprehensions of danger arising from the unusual position in which I found myself. The bread and honey did not taste as pleasant to me then as it would have done on a special occasion at home. She, however, succeeded in diverting my attention from the subject of my warty hands by showing me several very curious things, by means of which, together with her kind and gentle ways, she soon gained my confidence and restored me to a state of composure.

"You are yourself now, are you not? so listen to what I have to say," said the lady, in a somewhat imperative manner. "I will tell you what you must do in order to remove those warts forever from your hands. You must, however, promise me this much, that you will never divulge to anyone—not even to your mother—what I am about to tell you," said the Gypsy.

I felt for a moment that, in giving such a promise, I should be placed under the necessity of concealing something from my mother, and this to me did not seem the correct thing to do. Reluctantly, however, I gave the Gypsy the desired promise. As this adventure with the Gypsy occurred more than fifty years ago, and as its results relieved me from continuous pain, I can now, without fear of consequences, not only divulge the nature of the "spell" that ended, as it did, in the removal of the warts from my hands, but also discharge an obligation to those who may suffer from similar afflictions and who may be inclined to try the effects of this charm.

"You must," continued the Gypsy, "steal from some woman's knitting basket—but not from that of your mother—a length of gray woolen thread. On this thread you must tie a knot for every wart now on your hands. Moreover you must hide this knotted thread under a stone. When you have done this, you must endeavor to forget about me and also this hidden charm."

This finished my interview with the Gypsy Queen; then she unceremoniously bundled me out of the tent. As I trudged homeward, my mind began to fill with conflicting thoughts regarding this Gypsy and the "spell" that was to work such wonders. I seemed urged to think that she was serious in her desire for my good. I felt some compunction in regard to stealing the indispensable piece of woolen thread, as I was afraid of the punishment that would inevitably follow should this nefarious act of mine be discovered by my mother. Spartanlike, however, I risked the danger of being caught in the act and so purloined the necessary piece of thread. In order to avoid discovery while preparing this "mystic spell," I secluded myself in a neighbor's garden toolshed, where I proceeded to tie knots corresponding in number to the warts on both hands—there being eight on my left and nine on my right hand. Then I hid this knotted woolen thread—this so-called mysterious charm—under a stone. The next thing was to take heed to the Gypsy's injunction, and that was to forget all about the "charm" and even the Gypsy. A very few days sufficed for this purpose, for very soon all remembrance of the Gypsy, the spell, and even of my warts slowly faded from my active brain into my subconscious being without any mental effort on my part. I have often since that period of my boyhood regretted that I did not take particular note of the number of days which intervened between the cause and the effect. My recollection, however, is that the "spell" accomplished its desired results within the limit of a few weeks. My mother incidentally remarked that I had ceased to complain of my warty hands, and asked to see them. She was surprised and pleased to discover that all the warts which had formerly disfigured my hands had entirely disappeared, and that not even a trace of them was left to indicate their previous existence. I had been quite successful in excluding from my mind any thought concerning them, and was surprised that the Gypsy's "spell" had been the means employed in securing to me such wonderful benefit. Since that time, now over half a century, no warts, big or little, have grown on my hands or on any other part of my body.

Nostradamus

(Various)

Nostradamus very early gave evidence of his remarkable genius. When little more than a child, he was sent by his father to study at Avignon, and it is said of him that he assimilated the teachings of his professors with such facility that these marveled. Possessed of a wonderful memory, he added to this precious faculty a sound judgment, penetration, tact, vivacity, gaiety, and finesse in conversation. While yet young, he instructed his fellow students and frequently explained to them numerous terrestrial and celestial phenomena, exhibiting thus early a profound interest in the science of astronomy.

At this period astronomy formed part of the science of philosophy, and Nostradamus proved better qualified to instruct his schoolfellows upon the movements of the planets and the annual revolution of the earth around the sun than were the learned professors of the college of Avignon, and his own tutor frequently charged him to teach in his stead. His father, however, unwilling that his son should devote himself to astronomy, desired him to undertake the study of medicine and, accordingly for this purpose, sent him to Montpellier, where his prodigious faculty for assimilating knowledge rapidly brought him to the front.

Let us glance at the outer man. Nostradamus was well made, but of no more than medium height. His face was oval, his forehead high,

From: Sax Rohmer, *The Romance of Sorcery* (New York: Dutton, 1914).

broad, and bulging, and his eyes were gray and brilliant; his nose was aquiline, his cheeks were fresh and rosy, and his hair was of a deep chestnut hue. He wore his beard long and was noticeable for his expression of abstraction.

I do not propose to dwell upon the career of Nostradamus as a student but to deal with his life as physician, philosopher, and prophet, and I come to the first great event in his history when, at the age of twenty-two years, even before he had had conferred upon him the degree of doctor, he gained for himself a reputation that surpassed that of the most learned physicians of his time.

In 1525 a pestilence broke out and ravaged Montpellier and the surrounding country, and Nostradamus, aware that certain districts were without doctors, quit Montpellier and set out upon a tour of the villages attacked by the contagion. Departing from the methods employed by the faculty of Montpellier, he made up new remedies, and while those of his colleagues proved of no avail against the dread disease and frequently hastened death, his own effected marvelous cures. His devotion to the stricken people was equaled only by the wonderful skill that he displayed in dealing with the cases to which he attended, and although many refrained from entrusting themselves to the care of so young a physician, the excellence of his remedy soon became known, even as far as Toulouse and Bordeaux, and he had ultimately many more patients than he found it possible to cope with.

Astonished at his phenomenal success, the other doctors invited him to name the composition of the drug with which he had succeeded in arresting the progress of the pestilence. But he merely replied that he held a certain powder, the recipe for which was in the possession only of his own family. That this was nothing less than the great Elixir, more than one student of alchemy has believed.

The old and learned professors of the faculty of Montpellier, having heard of the successes attained by their young pupil during his journey, recalled him after the pestilence had been stayed, to confer upon him the degree of doctor. In 1529, after having effected a great number of marvelous cures and having established a reputation, he returned to Montpellier, loaded with honors, but, for all that, poor.

Nostradamus, having as we have seen employed remedies that were unauthorized by the faculty, was interrogated with defiance, but it is said that he was received as doctor amid the applause and admiration of the learned assembly. History has preserved to us the name of the person who most frequently interrogated Nostradamus. This was the celebrated Antoine Romier, one of the most noted physicians of the sixteenth century.

Before the French Revolution there was still to be seen, on the registers of the faculty of Montpellier the signature of Nostradamus, and beneath the following date, written in his hand: XXIII OCTOBRE MDXXIX.

Some time later, his name had become so popular that the students actually demanded that he should be appointed as their professor. Their wishes were acceded to, and, if we are to believe Astruc, and Bouche's *Histoire de Provence*, the young doctor Nostradamus was named professor to the faculty of Montpellier.

Ere long, however, Nostradamus, who loved travel, tired of Montpellier. He left this city, his chair, his pupils, his friends, and revisited the country of Provence, the scene of his former successes. Everywhere he was received with acclamation and affection; every town was *en fête* to welcome him.

At the gates gathered those whom he had restored to health, and before their preserver marched young boys and girls who strewed his path with flowers.

The notable people of the district extended to him invitations to visit them and to remain for several months in their families. In fact, according to the chronicles of the time, never had king, prince, or mighty noble a more genuinely affectionate welcome from the Midi than that accorded the young professor of the faculty of Montpellier.

One of the greatest savants of the century, Jules César Scaliger, having heard—as all France had heard—of the immense reputation of Nostradamus, communicated with him in order that he might judge for himself if the commotion had any real foundation.

Although it has been said that Scaliger was the son of an obscure sign painter, he was in reality a descendant of the famous Della Scala family of Verona, one member of which had been the patron of Dante. A physician of no small repute, he was also one of the most renowned classical scholars that Europe has produced.

The young professor, then, immediately availed himself of the invitation extended and proceeded to the town of Agen. During his sojourn there, Scaliger frequently plied his colleague with questions concerning the manner in which the latter had practiced his profession during the recent plague, and the replies he received, says a contemporary chronicler, were of so learned a nature that the classic was constrained to confess that this was no ordinary man. A friendship sprang up between these two—a bond so strong that Nostradamus was persuaded to set himself up in Agen.

This town, honored in the presence among its citizens of two such remarkable intellects, offered them considerable presents to induce them to remain permanently within its walls. These they declined, however, saying that they could not belong solely to the town of Agen, since they did not belong even to themselves, and that if the authorities had presents to give, they should, rather than occupy themselves with them, think of the unfortunate, of the infirm, of the sick, and of the aged. This response appealed to the people so keenly that on the morrow they went to meet Scaliger and Nostradamus, who were out walking, and carried them in triumph through the town.

A man of the age of Nostradamus, handsome and enjoying so great a reputation, naturally excited the attentions of family men who possessed marriageable daughters, and several people of considerable standing presented themselves with a view to arranging an alliance. They were, however, refused by the young savant, and many of the disappointed had convinced themselves that he would never marry, when at last he espoused a young girl of high station, "very beautiful and of an amiable disposition," by whom, says his great friend Chavigny, he had two children—boy and girl. But his wife and children died young, and Nostradamus, stricken with grief, resolved upon leaving Agen, where he had lived for four years, in order to travel far from the scene of his triple bereavement and to make new acquaintances.

He now journeyed in turn through La Guienne, Languedoc, Italy, and France.

One of the earliest signs of his ability in divination was demonstrated while he was traveling through Lorraine. In this country he made the acquaintance of the Seigneur de Florinville, who requested Nostradamus to visit his château to treat his wife, who was stricken by some infirmity.

While walking one day with his host in the courtyard, the two fell to discussing omens. During their conversation two suckling pigs— one white, the other black—strayed into the yard and approached them. The seigneur took this opportunity to ask of Nostradamus what would be the destiny of these two pigs.

"You," replied Nostradamus, "will eat the black one, but the other will be devoured by a wolf."

The answer was in accordance with the wishes of de Florinville, for although in public he treated his guest as an intimate friend, he seems secretly to have regarded him as an impostor. Certain that it was now in his power to expose Nostradamus, he gave instructions to his chef to kill the white pig and to serve it for supper.

In obedience to his master's command, the cook killed the white pig, dressed it, and placed it upon the spit ready for roasting at the proper time. Shortly afterward, however, he was called away from the kitchen upon some errand, and during his absence a tame wolf cub, the property of the seigneur, entered and, discovering the carcass of the white pig, immediately set to eating it. The animal had eaten about half of his delicacy when the chef returned and surprised the wolf at his meal.

Fearing that he would be reprimanded for his carelessness, the cook immediately seized the black pig, killed it, and prepared it for supper in place of the white one.

Supper was served, and all the guests took their places at the board. The Seigneur de Florinville, who of course knew nothing of what had taken place in the kitchen, felt assured that he would now achieve his ill-mannered triumph over Nostradamus, and addressing the latter with a confident air, he remarked that they were about to eat the white pig, inasmuch as the wolf had not done so.

Nostradamus replied that he was in error and expressed his conviction that the meat now placed before them was the flesh of the black pig. Thereupon de Florinville sent for the chef and asked him before all whether that which was upon the table was the white pig or the black.

The poor servant cowered with confusion—he had known nothing of his master's evil scheme—and stammered out that he had cooked the black pig, as the white one had been devoured by the wolf cub during his absence from the kitchen.

De Florinville's state of mind may be better imagined than de-scribed, and certainly his discomfiture was well merited. Reports of this absurd incident were very soon noised abroad and, as such things are usually made much of, were considerably exaggerated. But the episode served, nevertheless to show the ability of Nostradamus as a diviner.

Count Cagliostro

(Various)

W ho has not heard of Cagliostro? And yet who but a few students have any real knowledge of that mysterious character, of whom it may be said, as it was of Melchizedek, that he had "neither beginning of life nor end of days." Both at least, like the king of Salem's, are wrapped in uncertainty, and though popular tradition, repeated again and again by the uncritical historian, has identified Cagliostro's early life with that of the Italian scoundrel Joseph Balsamo, the evidence is as near conclusive as presumptive evidence can well be that the two had no connection whatever with one another, beyond having married Italian wives with the same surname—and that by no means an uncommon one—and the fact that Balsamo is said to have had an uncle of the name of Cagliostro. From what we know of Balsamo it may fairly be said that two people more opposite in character than himself and Count Cagliostro would be difficult to discover, and the identification of the two would seem to involve the assumption that Cagliostro had discarded his first wife and taken a second, a supposition which would render worthless the argument based on the identity of their surnames.

Cagliostro's whole career, as far as we know it, shows a character in which generosity is perpetually being carried to the verge of folly. His credulity was constantly making him the dupe of designing knaves, in whose honesty he placed a pathetic faith, and had he ever had the misfortune to encounter his alter ego, a common rogue of the most

From: Ralph Shirley, "Count Cagliostro," *Occultists & Mysteries of All Ages* (London: William Rider & Son, Ltd., 1920), 120–44.

ordinary type, it is safe to predict that he would not have escaped from his clutches till he had been fleeced of the bulk of his possessions. As late as the date of his trial in the affair of the Diamond Necklace, no suggestion of the identity of the two characters was even mooted. The story owes its origin to the fertile brain of one of the greatest scoundrels of whom European history holds record, the notorious blackmailer Thèveneau de Morande.

Who, then, was Cagliostro? The answer to this question must ever remain among the unsolved problems of history. There is, however, no reason to dismiss as incredible—even if there is reason to doubt—the account which he gave of himself on the occasion of the Diamond Necklace trial. From what we know of Cagliostro we may, I think, say that his character was far too ingenuous for him to have been likely to invent so remarkable a tale. Everything, however, in his history points to the fact that he was just the person to take a record of the kind and color it with the hues of his own fertile imagination. In any case, the impartial historian, while dismissing as preposterous the Balsamo fiction, is bound to give some weight—however slight—to the only evidence on the subject we possess which is not manifestly untrue. Cagliostro himself, however, did not pretend to have knowledge of his parentage. "I cannot," he states, "speak positively as to the place of my nativity nor as to the parents who gave me birth. All my inquiries have ended only in giving me some great notions, it is true, but altogether vague and uncertain, concerning my family." The gist, however, of his story was that he spent his childhood in Arabia, where he was brought up under the name of Acherat. He had then, he states, four persons attached to his service—the chief of whom was a certain Althotas, a man between fifty-five and sixty years of age. This man (whom it has been attempted to identify with a certain Kölmer, a Jutland merchant who had traveled extensively and had the reputation of being a master magician) informed Cagliostro that he had been left an orphan when three months old and that his parents were Christian and nobly born. All his attempts, however, to discover the secret of his birth were doomed to disappointment. The matter was one that was treated as taboo. In his twelfth year (to follow his own story) he left Medina for Mecca, where he remained three years until, wearying of the monotonous round of the sharif's court, he obtained leave to travel.

> One day [he narrates], when I was alone, the prince entered
> my apartment; he strained me to his bosom with more than
> usual tenderness, bid me never cease to adore the Almighty,
> and added, bedewing my cheeks with his tears: "Nature's
> unfortunate child, adieu!"

From this date commenced, according to his own account, Cagliostro's travels, first in company with Althotas, for whom he ever
expressed the warmest affection, afterward with the wife whom he
chose for himself in Italy. For upward of three years he claims to have
traveled through Egypt, Africa, and Asia, finally reaching the island of
Rhodes in the year 1766 and thence embarking on a French ship
bound for Malta. Here he and his guardian were received with all
honor, Pinto, the Grand Master of the Knights of Malta, giving them
apartments in his palace.

> It was here [he notes] that I first assumed European dress and
> with it the name of Count Cagliostro; nor was it a small matter
> of surprise to me to see Althotas appear in a clerical dress with
> the insignia of the Order of Malta.

The Grand Master Pinto was apparently acquainted with Cagliostro's history. He often spoke to him, he says, of the sharif but always
refused to be "drawn" on the subject of his real origin and birth. He
treated him, however, with every consideration and endeavored to
induce him to "take the cross," promising him a great career and rapid
preferment if he would consent to do so. Cagliostro's love of traveling
and of the study of medicine drew him in another direction, and on
the death of his guardian Althotas, which occurred shortly after, he
left Malta forever. After visiting Sicily and the Greek Archipelago
in company with the Chevalier d'Aquino he proceeded thence to
Naples, where he took leave of his companion. Provided with a letter
of credit on the banking house of Signor Bellone, he left Naples for
Rome, where his destiny awaited him in the shape of Seraphina
Feliciani, who shortly after became his wife and to whom he showed
throughout his married life a most unfailing devotion. Cagliostro
states that he was then (*anno* 1770) in his twenty-second year, and he
appears to have continued to pursue that nomadic life which was so
dear to him, traveling from town to town on the Continent of Europe
till he at length emerged into the light of day in the city of London, in

the month of July 1776, in furnished apartments in Whitcombe Street, Leicester Fields.

London seems always to have been an unfortunate place for Cagliostro, and here he was destined, on the first of many occasions, to become the victim of his own too trustful and generous disposition and to be fleeced of the greater part of his possessions by a nest of rogues, who took advantage of a foreigner entirely ignorant of London. Eventually he was rescued from this gang of knaves by a good Samaritian in the shape of a certain O'Reilly. Now O'Reilly was a prominent member of the Esperance Lodge of Freemasons, and here we first find Cagliostro brought into contact with that celebrated secret society, his connection with which was destined to play so all-important a part in the subsequent years of his life. O'Reilly, it appears, was the proprietor of the King's Head in Gerard Street, where the Esperance Lodge assembled, and it was only natural that one so fascinated with the occult as Cagliostro should be readily persuaded by his benefactor and rescuer to become initiated into the order of Freemasons. It is not necessary here to follow in detail the sordid intrigues of which, during his sojourn in England, he was made the victim. He was, however, glad eventually to escape from the country, with "no more than £50 and some jewels" in his possession, having lost in all, through fraud and consequent legal proceedings, some three thousand guineas during his sojourn. Cagliostro's star, however, had not yet set, and his all too brief spell of fame and triumph was still in front of him. Providence, in the shape probably of the emissaries of Freemasonry, was waiting at Brussels to replenish his purse, and the same Providence, probably in the same guise, replenished it many times afterward with no niggardly hand.

From Brussels to The Hague, from The Hague to Nuremberg, from Nuremberg to Berlin, from Berlin to Leipzig, we trace the count's peregrinations, gathering fame and founding Egyptian Mason Lodges as he went. It is true he met with setbacks and reverses, and the capital of Frederick the Great would have none of him, but it is clear that, in spite of these, his credit and reputation as a healer and clairvoyant grew steadily in volume. It was, in fact, on these two gifts that his fame rested. Though he claimed to have been taught the secrets of occultism by Althotas, or to have learned them from the Egyptian priests, there is no evidence throughout the records of his career of his possessing anything but a smattering of such abstruse knowledge, and on several occasions, notably at St. Petersburg, there is something more than a suspicion that his attempt to make good his claim to the name of occultist involved him in serious humiliation and rebuffs. The tales, however, of his predictions and their fulfillments were handed on from mouth to mouth, doubtless losing nothing on the way, while his reputation as a healer and the stories of the cures that he effected assured a perfect furor of enthusiasm in every fresh town to which he paid a visit. He took advantage of this enthusiasm to found fresh Masonic Lodges in all directions, and while he consistently refused to receive payment of any kind for his cures, the shekels of an endless file of initiate converts poured into the coffers at the headquarters of Egyptian Masonry. Never was man at once more lavish with money and more indifferent to the comforts that money brings. "He slept in an armchair," said Mme. d'Oberkirch contemptuously, "and lived on cheese." Whatever he spent, however, he appeared to draw from an inexhaustible widow's cruise. As in spite of his refusal to accept fees, he paid his own bills with the greatest promptitude, the problem whence this continuous stream of gold flowed excited unbounded curiosity, and many were the fantastic stories invented to account for it.

Meanwhile, after visiting Mittau, where he was enthusiastically taken up by Marshal von Medem, the head of the Masonic Lodge at that place, he passed on to Petersburg, Warsaw, and thence to Strasbourg. Here he was destined to enjoy a great triumph and to win a powerful friend, who was eventually, through a pure accident, to prove the cause of his undoing. This was none other than the notorious Cardinal de Rohan. It is hardly necessary to state that the ecclesiastical dignitary of the eighteenth century in France was not selected for his high office by reason of his exemplary life or his Christian virtues. To neither of these did Cardinal de Rohan make any claim. Yet honors had fallen thick and fast upon him. He was Bishop of Strasbourg, Grand Almoner of France, Cardinal, Prince of the Empire, Landgrave of Alsace in addition to being Abbot of the richest abbey in France, the Abbey of St. Waast Handsune. Of fascinating manner, an aristocrat of the aristocrats, there was no position in the kingdom to which he did not feel justified in aspiring. The fact that he enjoyed a reputation for dissipation and extravagance did not appear calculated to tell against him in such an age.

Surprising as it may seem, the cardinal combined with a pleasure-loving disposition a passion for alchemy and the pursuit of the occult sciences, and the arrival of Cagliostro at Strasbourg naturally enough excited his interest to no small degree. The cardinal determined to lose no time in making the acquaintance of the man about whom and whose marvelous cures the whole town was already talking almost before he set foot in its streets. But Cagliostro was inclined to ride the high horse. "If the cardinal is ill," he replied to the great man's messenger, "let him come to me and I will cure him. If not, he has no need of me nor I of him." In spite of the count's standoffishness, the cardinal was not to be denied, and the acquaintance once made soon ripened into the closest intimacy. Cagliostro was told to consider the palace his own, and he and his wife resided there on the footing of the most honored guests.

Marvelous tales are told of the results of his experiments in the cardinal's laboratory, how he manufactured gold and jewels and finally showed de Rohan in the crystal the form of the woman whom he had loved. It is on these stories alone that the reputation of Cagliostro as an alchemist really rests, and in the absence of further confirmatory evidence one is inclined to take them with a grain of salt. However this may be, it is certain that the cardinal was completely won over, and Cagliostro took care not to lose caste by assuming airs of humility or deference. Never, certainly, was there less of a snob than this marvelous adventurer. "Cagliostro," says Mme. d'Oberkirch, "treated him and his other distinguished admirers as if they were under the deepest obligation to him, but he under none whatever to them." As usual, our hero was besieged at Strasbourg by those who would profit by his medical knowledge and skill as a healer, for he really appears to have possessed both, and as usual by obliging his clients, he incurred the inveterate hostility of the medical profession.

In all ages of the world's history the natural healer has had the doctor as his enemy, and the prophet, the priest. Orthodoxy has ever closed its ranks against those who poach on its preserves. Doubtless it is the natural instinct of self-defense. For Cagliostro, however, it was extremely inconvenient. The people would throng his doorsteps to be cured and make him heal them willy-nilly, and the medical profession were equally determined to make each place in which he practiced his medical skill too hot for him. Others might have been willing to let the dogs bark, but a fatal sensitiveness to criticism made the count an all too easy target for their venom. They drove him from Strasbourg as they had driven him from other places, in spite of the entreaties of de Rohan, who pressed him to stay and disregard their clamor.

We need not follow Cagliostro from Strasbourg to Bordeaux and from Brodeaux to Lyons, where he added further laurels to his reputation and founded further Lodges of Egyptian Masonry. He might have remained indefinitely to all appearance at the latter place if it had not been for the solicitations of Cardinal de Rohan, who urged him to respond to the appeals of Parisian society and visit the gay capital, where he guaranteed him an enthusiastic reception. He even sent a special messenger to back his request, and perhaps Cagliostro himself had heard the capital of cultured Europe calling. Anyhow he came, his evil fate—if not Paris—summoning him. Cagliostro declared that he took the greatest precaution on arriving there to avoid causing ill will. However this may be, he immediately became "the rage" in fashionable circles. People flocked to him by hundreds to be cured, and the stories of the miracles that he was supposed to have effected were the talk of every dinner party in the capital. Mesmer had already left Paris with a fortune of 340,000 livres, made by his lucrative practice, in his pocket. Paris, craving for a new excitement, was ready to receive with open arms the wonder-worker of whom it was said that no one of all his patients ever succeeded in making him accept the least mark of gratitude.

Cagliostro was here surfeited with flattery. Houdin executed his bust. His statuettes were in every shop window; his portrait was in every house. Those who claimed to have been cured by him were met with on all sides. Angels, it is said, and heroes of biblical story appeared at his séances. No story was too absurd for Paris to believe about him.

But a train of events in which he had no hand, and a catastrophe for which he had no responsibility, were destined, while wrecking other reputations and undermining the throne itself, to bring his career of triumph to a sudden and tragic close and eventually to drive him, a forsaken and persecuted outcast, to his final doom. Cagliostro, as already stated, had nothing whatever to do with the affair of the Diamond Necklace. But for all that, he was caught in the web of deceit that an unscrupulous woman had woven to suit her own purposes.

The Countess de Lamotte-Valois, a descendant of a natural son of Henri II and an adventuress of the most reckless type, had found a protector in the person of the susceptible Cardinal de Rohan. Now the cardinal was by no means persona grata at the court of Versailles. As a matter of fact, he was never seen there except at the Feast of the Assumption, when it was his duty as Grand Almoner to celebrate mass in the royal chapel. The cause of this was the enmity of Queen Marie Antoinette. The cardinal had been recalled from the embassy at Vienna at the instance of her mother, Maria Theresa, and doubtless the mother had communicated to the daughter a distrust for the brilliant but pleasure-loving cardinal. This was a fatal obstacle to de Rohan, whose ambition it was to become First Minister to the king. The countess de Lamotte saw her chance in the thwarted ambitions of her protector and took care to pose as an intimate friend of the queen, a story to which her frequent visits to Versailles in connection with a petition for the recovery of some family property which had passed into the possession of the state lent a certain appearance of truth. She represented to the cardinal the interest the queen took in him but which matters of policy compelled her to dissemble.

In the sequel, a series of letters—of course forged—passed between de Rohan and the supposed queen. The queen, through the intermediary of the countess, borrowed large sums of money of the cardinal, which the cardinal, on his part being head over ears in debt in spite of his enormous income, was compelled to borrow of the Jews. Then, when the cardinal was becoming suspicious, the countess arranged a bogus interview, at which another lady—admittedly remarkably like her—posed as the queen and permitted de Rohan to kiss her hand. Finally, Mme. de Lamotte got in touch with Böhmer, the owner of the famous necklace. This she represented to the cardinal that the queen had set her heart on obtaining, but could not at a moment's notice find the ready cash. Would he become security?

Needless to say, de Rohan fell into the trap. The first installment of the bill fell due, and the cardinal, who had not expected to be called on to pay, was unable offhand to find the money. At this point Böhmer, feeling nervous, consulted one of the queen's ladies-in-waiting, who informed him that the story of the queen's having bought the necklace was all moonshine. He then went to the countess de Lamotte, who had the effrontery to say she believed he was being victimized and advised him to go to the cardinal, thinking doubtless that de Rohan would take the entire responsibility when the alternative was his ruin. The jeweler, however, instead of taking her advice, went straight to the king. The king immediately communicated with the queen, who was furious and insisted on having the cardinal arrested forthwith. The fat was now in the fire with a vengeance. The arrest of the cardinal was followed by that of the countess de Lamotte, of Cagliostro and his wife (whom the countess in utter recklessness accused of the theft of the necklace), of the Baroness d'Oliva, who had "played" the queen, of de Vilette, the forger of the letters, and various minor actors in this astounding drama.

In the celebrated trial that followed, Cagliostro was acquitted, but not until he had spent nine months in the Bastille. There was, in fact, not a shadow of evidence against him. His wife was released before the trial took place. Cagliostro received an ovation from the people of Paris on the occasion of his release, as well as de Rohan, who was also acquitted, the popularity of the verdict being due to the hatred with which the royal family were now everywhere regarded. But on the day after, by a royal edict, de Rohan was stripped of all his dignities and exiled to Auvergne, while Cagliostro was ordered to leave France within three weeks. The count retired to England, fearful lest worse might befall him, but even here the relentless malignity of the discredited queen, who regarded his acquittal as equivalent to her own condemnation, followed his footsteps. The unscrupulous de Morande was paid by the court to ruin his reputation and to identify him with the thief and gaolbird Joseph Balsamo. London was soon made so hot for him that he returned once more to the Continent and made his home for a short time in Switzerland. Later on he went to Trent, where the prince-bishop, who had a passion for alchemy, made him a welcome guest. But the count's day was over, and misfortune continued to dog his footsteps. The Emperor Joseph II would not permit his vassal to harbor the man who had been mixed up in the Diamond Necklace affair, and the bishop was reluctantly obliged to bid him begone.

Cagliostro now found himself driven from pillar to post, his resources were at an end, and his friends were dead or had deserted him. He turned his steps toward Italy, and eventually arrived at Rome. Here his presence becoming known to the papal authorities, he and his wife were arrested as members of the Masonic Fraternity. In those days within the papal states, Freemasonry was a crime punishable by death. After a mock trial the death sentence was commuted to imprisonment for life, while his wife was confined in a penitentiary.

Rumor, which wove a web of romance around all his doings, did not leave him even here, and stories were circulated that he had escaped from his dungeon and was living in Russia. There appears, however, to be no doubt that neither count nor countess long survived their incarceration, and when the French soldiers invaded the papal states in 1797 and the Polish Legion under General Daubrowski captured the fortress of San Leo, in which the count had been confined, the officers who inquired after the once famous magician, hoping to set him free, were informed that it was too late and that he was already dead. The queen, whose vindictive spite had ruined these two lives, went to her doom first; but her instrument, the blackmailer Morande retired to a quiet corner of France on his ill-gotten fortune, escaped the furies of the French Revolution and ended his life surrounded by an atmosphere of the most unquestioned respectability.

And what of the man with whom not only his own fate but the misrepresentations of history have dealt so hardly? What manner of man was he for whom even those who denounce him as mountebank might not unreasonably, one would think, feel a passing sympathy? On two points we have ample testimony. All those who knew him bore witness to the marvelous magnetism of his personality and to the fascination and beauty of his extraordinary eyes. "No two eyes like his were ever seen," says the Marquise de Crégny, "and his teeth were superb." "He was not, strictly speaking, handsome," says Mme. d'Oberkirch, "but I have never seen a more remarkable face. His glance was so penetrating that one might almost be tempted to call it supernatural. I could not describe the expression of his eyes; it was, so to speak, a mixture of flame and ice. It attracted and repelled at the same time, and, whilst it inspired terror, it aroused along with it an irresistible curiosity. I cannot deny," she adds, "that Cagliostro possessed an almost demoniacal power." Not less noteworthy is the opinion of so hostile a witness as Beugnot, who confesses, while ridiculing him, that his face, his attire, the whole man in fact, impressed him in spite of himself. "If gibberish can be sublime," he continues, "Cagliostro was sublime. When he began speaking on a subject, he seemed carried away with it and spoke impressively in a ringing, sonorous voice."

This was the man whose appearance Carlyle caricatured in the following elegant phraseology:

A most portentous face of scoundrelism; a fat snub abominable face; dew-lapped, flat-nosed, greasy, full of greediness,

sensuality, ox-like obstinacy; the most perfect quack face produced by the eighteenth century.

Carlyle, however, who would say anything or write anything in his
moods of irritability, also alluded to the late Cardinal Newman as "not
possessing the intellect of a moderate-sized rabbit"; and the two
statements may fairly be juxtaposed.

Mr. W. R. H. Trowbridge, to whose recent book I am greatly
indebted for material for this brief sketch of Cagliostro's life, well
observes that "there is perhaps no other equally celebrated personality in modern history whose character is so baffling to the biographer." History has condemned him purely on the evidence of his most
unscrupulous enemies. But while dismissing such one-sided portraits,
it is no easy matter to arrive at an unprejudiced valuation of the real
man. Of his latest biographer's impartiality and candor, as well as his
careful research of authorities, it is impossible to speak too highly. His
conclusions will be all the more widely accepted in view of the fact
that he is himself in no sense an occultist. In spite of a rather long
chapter dealing with "Eighteenth-Century Occultism," we feel instinctively and at every turn that the subject is one in which he is
obviously out of his depth. Indeed, only on the second page of his
biography we come across the following surprising statement. Speaking of "theosophists, spiritualists, occultists," all of whom are unceremoniously lumped together, he observes:

> By these amiable visionaries Cagliostro is regarded as one of
> the princes of occultism whose mystical touch has revealed the
> arcana of the spiritual world to the initiated, and illumined the
> path along which the speculative scientist proceeds on entering
> the labyrinth of the supernatural.

Every occultist knows this to be sheer rubbish. Cagliostro has never
been regarded as an authority in any school of occultism. Many, if not
most occultists, have been inclined to believe that he was more than
half a quack. Mr. Trowbridge—it is to be said to his credit—has
judged him in the light of the evidence more fairly than they. The truth
is that Cagliostro, with all his good qualities, with all his generosity of
heart, his human sympathy, his nobility—yes, it really was nobility—of character, was beyond and above all things a poser and a
mysterymonger. He had a magnetic personality, a mediumistic tem-

perament, and almost certainly some clairvoyant power, though it is noticeable that he invariably employed a little boy or girl whose assistance was essential to his predictions. Beyond this and, I think we must say, more important than all this, he had an incontestable natural healing gift, which he aided by no small knowledge of practical medicine. In these qualifications we have the secret of his success and also the clue to his failure. He was excessively vain and loved to impress the multitude. He loved moreover to impress them by surrounding himself with an atmosphere of mystery and posing as an occultist, which (probably) he never was. He has left no body of teaching behind him. He has left no followers, no disciples. He was merely the comet of a season, though an exceptionally brilliant one. It would be absurd to class him in the same category as such master occultists as Cornelius Agrippa and Paracelsus, or indeed even as Eliphas Levi. He was not cast in the same mold. He belonged to another and a lower type. But his was withal a striking as well as a sympathetic personality, a personality that makes appeal, by a certain glamor heightened by the tragedy of his inglorious end, to all that is warm, and chivalrous, and romantic in the human heart.

Cagliostro and the Suspicious Husband

(France)

A daring cat story is of French origin and bears distinctive national characteristics on the face of it. On the 26th of March, 1782, a gentleman of wealth who was jealous of his wife's honor, decided he would consult Count Cagliostro in order to find out whether his wife, who was young and beautiful, had always been faithful to him. He told the count the reason of his visit and

From: Frank Hamel, *Human Animals* (New York: Frederick A. Stokes Co., 1916).

begged him to assist him in discovering the truth. Cagliostro said that this was quite an easy matter and that he would give him a small vial containing a certain liquid which he was to drink when he reached home and just before he went to bed. "If your wife has been unfaithful to you," said Cagliostro, "you will be transformed into a cat."

The husband went home and told his wife how clever the count was. She asked him the reason of his journey. At first he refused to tell her, but when she insisted he told her the exact means by which he was going to test her fidelity. She laughed at his credulity, but he swallowed the draft and they went to bed. The wife rose early to attend to her household duties, leaving her husband asleep. At ten o'clock, as he did not appear, she went up to wake him, and to her intense astonishment, she found a huge black cat in the bed in place of her husband. She screamed, called her dear husband's name, and bent over the cat to kiss it, but without avail. *Her husband had vanished!* Then, in her despair, she knelt beside the bed and prayed for pardon, saying that she had committed a sin and that a handsome young soldier had cajoled her, by means of vows, of tears, and stories of heroic battles, to forget her marriage vows.

The Comte de St. Germain

(France)

How do we distinguish the false from the real? How do we separate the mass of facts from the mass of fiction? How do we disentangle from the mazes of mystery and magic the bewildering personality of the Comte de St. Germain—is a task well-nigh possible of accomplishment. For we have not only the

From: Virginia Milward, "The Comte de St. Germain," *Occult Review* 15 (1912): 284–88.

difficulty of obtaining any authentic information concerning him, but we have to contend with the eternal prejudice against anyone or anything occult, the baffling secrets of state in the past, the apparent conspiracy of kings and governments to reveal nothing definite about the count, and also the mystery with which he chose to surround himself—a powerful combination of circumstances which makes it difficult to judge or even to understand the man.

Who was he? What were his aims in life? What were his powers and privileges? These are only a few of the questions that occur to us, as we read the little that is known of his varied life.

His birth and parentage seem to be shrouded in the same uncertainty and mystery that surround every action in his curious career. It is known that he did not belong to the French family of St. Germain, as was popularly supposed. He was not the son of a Portuguese Jew, or an Alsatian Jew, or a tax gatherer in Rotondo; neither was he the illegitimate offspring of the King of Portugal nor of the widow of Charles II (King of Spain). But we have every reason to believe that he was the son of Franz Leopold, Prince Ragoczy of Transylvania, and was during his entire childhood under the protection of the powerful Duc de Medici.

Each succeeding Ragoczy endeavored, more or less unsuccessfully, to maintain the freedom of their beloved principality intact from the ambitious designs of the Austrian Empire, and all the early years of the mystic count were clouded and obscured by bitter political intrigue.

According to the terms of the will of Prince Franz Leopold Ragoczy, his three sons, including our Comte de St. Germain, were left amply provided for, thus establishing the important fact that he was in no way the penniless adventurer he has been labeled, making vast sums of money by unlawful means.

"A hero of romance," "the wonder man," "a charlatan," "a mystic," "a swindler," are only some of the many names by which this man was called, and he answered to some of them, perhaps, but not to all.

That he was a man of family, and that he was a man of means, have been proved beyond dispute, but his age, his aim and purpose in life, and his abnormal powers seem shrouded in a mystery it is impossible to penetrate.

He assumed for purposes of traveling, and especially when on those diplomatic journeys which occupied a considerable portion of his

time, quite an amazing and bewildering number of different pseud-
onyms, and we hear of him as the Marquis de Montferrat, Comte
Bellamare, Chevalier Schoening, Chevalier Weldon, Comte Soltikoff,
Graf Tzarogy, Prinz Ragoczy, in turn, at the different cities where he
stayed—a very common custom, however, among the nobility on
their travels.

The Baron de Cleichen states on the authority of Rameau, who knew
the count in 1710, that at that date he had the appearance of a man of
some fifty years of age. He possessed regular features, black hair,
brown complexion, was neither stout nor thin, dressed always very
simply, but wore magnificent diamonds in his shoe buckles and on
every finger. He was of medium height, very intellectual looking, and
combined excessive courtliness with great charm of manner.

He spoke French, English, German, Spanish, Italian, and Portuguese
fluently and was perfectly at home in Chinese, Arabic, Sanskrit, and
the language of Homer and Virgil.

He was a good musician, and his improvising earned the admiration of the master Rameau. He also painted in oils and with such
success, giving so peculiar a brilliancy to his colors, the result of a
secret known only to himself, that Vanloo, who admired his produc-
tions, implored him to divulge his secret.

He was an expert chemist, had a profound knowledge of alchemy,
and in the Château de Chambord there existed a laboratory fitted up
for all kinds of experiments.

He could also write easily, legibly, and well with both hands at the
same time—a really remarkable feat. But undoubtedly the most
striking and extraordinary of his gifts was his capacity for being able
to "improve" precious stones and considerably add to their value.
Possibly in his extensive travels in Africa, India, and China he learned
some of these arts and sciences, which no doubt caused him to be
considered a magician of no mean merit in the eyes of eighteenth-
century France.

He is stated to have said that he knew the secret of prolonging life
and successfully concealing the ravages of time and to have promised
the Comtesse de Genlis, when but a child of ten years, that if she
desired it he could and would bestow upon her the gift of eternal
youth. To discover the elixir of life or the philosopher's stone was the
ambition and aim of every alchemist of that date.

A curious story is told of the count, illustrating his magical powers or what we might now be disposed to call his conjuring tricks. One day he asked Mme. de Pompadour to place near the fire the beautiful little bonbonnière in black enamel which he had previously given her. The marquise did so, and a few minutes afterward, when she went to pick it up, she discovered to her astonishment that the magnificent agate in the lid had disappeared, and in its place was a shepherdess with her flock. The count entreated her to again place it by the fire, when in course of time the agate reappeared and the shepherdess vanished.

If this incident really took place, and we have every reason for believing it did, what are we to conclude? That assuredly the count had very abnormal gifts, and such occurrences might easily give rise to the legend, if it was a legend, that he could also appear and disappear at will.

That this man was not a charlatan we may feel confident, for the reason that he enjoyed the friendship and confidence of kings and councillors, and spent many long evenings at Versailles in the company of Louis XV, who gave him the Château de Chambord as a token of his esteem and favor.

But like other great men of those times he probably loved to surround himself with an atmosphere of mystery, which considerably enhanced the awe and veneration in which he was held, and any gifts outside the commonplace, however simple in themselves, were no doubt grossly exaggerated and attributed to magic.

The count was most frugal in his habits, ate no meat and drank no wine, and never took his repast in public. He claimed that he could tame bees and make snakes listen to music; the latter accomplishment he doubtless learned in the East.

He would sometimes fall into a trance and, when he recovered consciousness again, declare he had been in another world, communing with the spirits.

From 1737 to 1742 he lived in Persia at the shah's court. In 1745 we hear of him in England, arrested as a Jacobite spy, a letter from the Young Pretender being found in his pocket, placed there by an enemy—but he was honorably acquitted.

However, apart from his magic gifts and extraordinary personality, we think his great claim to interest lies in the fact that he was undoubtedly the secret agent of Louis XV, who used him on many a diplomatic and dangerous errand, notably to England, when he was desirous of securing the peace his ministers for purely personal reasons did not desire. The Comte de St. Germain incurred the bitter hatred of the Duc de Choiseul in consequence, who had his own "fish to fry," wished the war to continue, and would gladly have consigned the king's private peacemaker to the oblivion of the Bastille.

Both the king and Mme. de Pompadour had the greatest faith and trust in the count, but his position as a secret agent was not an enviable one. Whatever transpired, he had to bear the blame, and when the negotiations with England, which he had been authorized to try and arrange, broke down, it was the count who fell into disgrace. Such was ever the fate of the secret agent!

Voltaire evidently knew of his missions to foreign countries, for he spoke of him as "a man who never dies, and who knows everything."

The count was a Freemason and was associated with Mesmer in his mystical work; he had also much in common with Cagliostro, with this difference, that that strange being died disgraced in the prisons of the Inquisition, while the count was all his life reputed to be a man of honor.

The mystery and magic that surrounded him is largely due, we think, to the crass credulity of the people of the times in which he lived, which credulity doubtless he helped to foster.

The Comte de St. Germain's political work did not end entirely with Louis XV's reign, for though no longer employed as a secret agent, he would have rendered a great service to Louis XVI had that monarch chosen to listen to him and heed his warning. For the count foretold the Revolution of 1789, the downfall of the monarchy, the death of the queen, the disaster to the government, the anarchy and bloodshed to follow, and Lafayette's conceited incompetence. Moreover, he prophesied the complete ruin of the house of Bourbon, adding that they would become in course of time merely a private family. These were naturally unpleasant tidings to the king and queen and as such seemed scarcely credible in their then position of false security.

By means of the Comtesse d'Adhémar, the count obtained an audience with Marie Antoinette, who communicated his gloomy and terrible prognostications to the king, who in turn immediately summoned Maurepas, the minister the count had so sternly denounced for his obstinacy and incapacity. Maurepas advised the arrest of the prophet at once and his confinement in the Bastille till he should divulge where he had obtained all his information, but the farseeing count had foreseen this move on the part of his enemy and disappeared, and the police searched for him in vain. Each self-seeking minister in turn disliked the count, the famous freelance, and abhorred his views.

The predictions came true, and the monarchy fell and France came upon evil days, but from time to time and even up to the days of her imprisonment and death, Marie Antoinette received strange warning messages from the mysterious count she had seen but once, which messages, alas! were powerless to avert her fate.

The date of the count's death is not known, nor where he died. Mme. d'Adhémar says he was believed "to have deceased in 1784 at Schleswig," but she goes on to relate that the Comte de Châlons, returning from Venice in 1788, declared he had seen and spoken to St. Germain in the Place St. Marc the day before he left—so there is no direct evidence of the date of his death or of his place of burial.

What his aims were exactly, or if he had any at all, does not appear very clear. He was patriotic, undoubtedly, in the best sense of that much abused word, but beyond many acts of personal kindness to individuals and the secret services he rendered to Louis the Well-Beloved, it is difficult to determine in what precisely lay his "great work."

As a "messenger" or prophet he appears to have failed, as political agent he was disgraced, but as a close friend and councillor of kings he shows in a more favorable light, and as a nobleman of untarnished honor, blameless life, and great attainments we may regard him with admiration and respect.

His was one of those little-known characters whose meteoric appearance dazzles and puzzles the world—a man charged with a mission (self-imposed, perhaps) he never fully accomplished, with aims in life revealed only to the few—who lived and died a lonely figure, surrounded by mystery to the end.

The Story of Urbain Grandier

(France)

A
t the beginning of the seventeenth century, the curate of
Loudun was Urbain Grandier. To those talents which lead to
success in this world, this man united a corruption of morals
which dishonored his character. His conduct had made him
many enemies. There were not merely rivals but husbands and
fathers, some of high position who were outraged at the dishonor he
brought on their family. He was nevertheless a wonderfully proud
man, and the bitterness of his tongue and the harshness with which he
pursued his advantages only excited them the more. And these
advantages were numerous, for he had a marvelous faculty for
pettifogging. His iniquities had rendered him the scourge of the town,
whose principal curate and greatest scandal he was at one and the
same moment. This is proved by the dispensation obtained by many
fathers of families to assist at the divine service in some other parish
and by the permissions granted them to receive the sacrament from
some other hand.

Six years previously, a convent of nuns of the order of Saint Ursula
had established itself at Loudun. This community, like every new
institution, was in somewhat straitened circumstances, though the
social position of its members was good. Most of them were daughters
of the nobility, while the remainder belonged to the best Bourgeoisie
of the country. The good reputation of the new order (it was not quite
fifty years old), and the high character it bore in Loudun, had also
attracted to it a great number of pupils. The nuns were therefore
enabled, with economy, to make ends meet and could look forward to
the future with confidence.

From: Anon. [des Niau], *Collectanea Adamantaea.—xxi., The History of the Devils of
Loudun, the Alleged Possession of the Ursuline Nuns, and Trials and Execution of Urbain
Grandier, Told by an Eye-Witness* (trans. and ed. Edmund Goldsmith), 3 vols.
(Edinburgh: privately printed, 1887).

The Mother Superior, Mme. de Belfiel, daughter of the Marquis de Cose, was related to M. de Laubardemont, Councillor of State and afterward Intendent of the Provinces of Touraine, Anjou, and Maine. Mme. de Sazilli was a connection of the Cardinal de Richelieu. The two ladies de Barbesiers, sisters, belonged to the house of Nogeret. Mme. de le Mothé was daughter of the Marquis de la Motte Barace in Anjou. There was also a Mme. d'Escoubleau, of the same name and family as the Archbishop of Bordeaux. Thus they could flatter themselves with dreams of future successes, when they happened to lose their Prior Moussaut, who had charge of their spiritual welfare.

A successor had now to be sought. Grandier, who had never had any connection with the convent, offered himself nevertheless as a candidate. The proposal was scornfully rejected; and the Mother Superior, Mme. de Belfiel, had a great quarrel with one of her friends, who urged her to appoint this priest. The choice of the convent fell on Canon Mignon, a man of considerable merit and in whom spiritual gifts were only equaled by intellectual ones. Grandier, already irritated at his own want of success, was still more annoyed at Mignon's appointment. He consequently determined to give plenty of work to the confessors and to his penitents.

However this may be, extraordinary symptoms began to declare themselves within the convent, but they were hushed up as far as possible and not allowed to be known outside the walls. To do otherwise would have been to give the new institution a severe blow and to risk ruining it at its birth. This the nuns and their confessor understood. It was therefore decided to work in the greatest secrecy to cure, or at least mitigate, the evil.

As usually happens, the extraordinary phenomena displayed in the persons of the nuns were taken for the effects of sexual disease. But soon suspicions arose that they proceeded from supernatural causes and that they perceived what God intended everyone to see.

Thus the nuns, after having employed the physicians of the body, apothecaries, and medical men, were obliged to have recourse to physicians of the soul and to call in both lay and clerical doctors, their confessor no longer being equal to the immensity of the labor. For they were seventeen in number; and everyone was found to be either fully possessed or partially under the influence of the Evil One.

All this could not take place without some rumors spreading abroad. Vague suspicions floated through the city. Had the secret even been kept by the nuns, their small means would soon have been exhausted by the extraordinary expenses they were put to in trying to hide their affliction, and this, together with the number of people employed in relieving them, must have made the matter more or less public. But their trials were soon increased when the public was at last made acquainted with their state. The fact that they were possessed of devils drove everyone from their convent as from a diabolical residence or as if their misfortune involved their abandonment by God and man. Even those who acted thus were their best friends. Others looked upon these women as mad and upon those who tended them as visionaries. For in the beginning, people, being still calm, had not come to accuse them of being impostors.

It became necessary to have recourse to exorcisms. This word alone is for some people a subject of ridicule, as if it had been clearly proved that religion is mere folly and the faith of the church a fable. True Christians must despise these grinning impostors. Exorcisms, then, were employed. The demon, forced to manifest himself, yielded his name. He began by giving these girls the most horrible convulsions; he went so far as to raise from the earth the body of the Mother Superior who was being exorcised and to reply to secret thoughts, which were manifested neither in words nor by any exterior signs. Questioned according to the form prescribed by the ritual as to why he had entered the body of the nun, he replied it was from hatred. But when being questioned as to the name of the magician he answered it was Urbain Grandier, profound astonishment seized Canon Mignon and his assistants. They had indeed looked upon Grandier as a scandalous priest, but never had they imagined that he was guilty of magic. They were therefore not satisfied with one single questioning; they repeated the interrogation and always received the same reply.

The declaration of the Evil Spirit could not fail to make a great commotion and to have results that required precautions to be taken at once. The canon, like a wise man, put himself in communication with justice and informed the magistrates of what was passing at the convent, on October 11, 1632. Grandier, prepared for all contingencies, had already taken his measures. Many of the magistrates belonged to the new religion and were favorable to him, looking upon him as a secret adherent; they served him as he expected. At the same time, he made all possible use of his extraordinary talents for pettifogging, presented petition on petition, questioned every statement of the exorcists and of the nuns, threatened their confessor Mignon, complained that his reputation was attacked and that the means were thus taken from him of doing the good his position required, and demanded that the nuns should be locked up and exorcists put an end to. He knew well enough that his demands were out of the question and that civil justice has nothing to do with the exercise of religious functions. But he wished, if possible, to embarrass the exorcists and commit the judges with the bishops or, at any rate, throw discord among them and give his Calvinists an opportunity of crying out. He succeeded.

The magistrates separated. Only those who were favorable to him remained; the rest ceased to appear at the exorcisms, and Mignon soon withdrew from the convent. Excitement rose in the public mind, a thousand arguments on this or that side permeated the town, and a thousand quarrels took place on all sides.

The excitement, however, and these disputes settled nothing, and the exorcisms, which continued, had no better result. Grandier triumphed, and his friends admired his wit, his skill, and proclaimed aloud that he could not be convicted of anything, not even as regards women, although they knew well how far he had gone in this matter. Until now, the court had taken no notice of the affair; but the noise it had made in the world since the first days of October 1632 had reached the queen's ears. She requested information, and the Abbé Marescot, one of her chaplains, was sent to examine into the matter and report to her. He arrived at Loudun on November 28 and witnessed what was going on. No immediate consequences followed, but an incident soon occurred which caused a sudden change in the position of the affairs.

The king had resolved to raze the castles and fortresses existing in the heart of the kingdom and commissioned M. de Laubardemont to see to the demolition of that of Loudun. He arrived, and saw what a ferment the town was in, the animosity that reigned there, and the kind of man who caused the commotion. The complaints of those who were victims of the debaucheries, of the pride, or of the vengeance of the curate touched him, and it seemed to him important to put an end to the scandal. On his return he informed the king and the cardinal-minister of the facts. Louis XIII, naturally pious and just, perceived the realness of the evil, and deemed it his duty to put a stop to it. He appointed M. de Laubardemont to investigate the matter without appeal and ordered him to choose in the neighboring jurisdictions the most straightforward and learned judges. The commission is dated November 30, 1633.

Nothing less was needed to bring to justice a man upheld by a seditious and enterprising party, and so well versed in the details of *chicanerie,* an art always shameful in any man, but especially to an ecclesiastic. The king issued at the same time two decrees to arrest and imprison Grandier and his accomplices. Armed with such powers, the commissioner did not fear to attack a man who had often succeeded in gaining either a nonsuit on some question of form, or in turning accusations to his own advantage or else dragging out proceedings to such a length as to weary his adversaries and his judges.

The Calvinists, already irritated at the razing of the castle which served them as a rallying place in times of rebellion, cried out against this new tribunal, because they saw it was the sole means of rendering useless the knaveries of their friend. But they cried out much louder when the commissioner arrested the accused, without waiting for information, and seized all his papers. As if it were not well known that in criminal matters this mode of proceeding is usual, in this case it was absolutely necessary. For without this precaution, Grandier might have fled and defended himself from afar, engaging the attention of the judges, who had plenty of work elsewhere. He might even have raised tumults in the city, which might have necessitated violent remedies.

These precautions being taken, the commissioner commenced his investigation and proceeded to hear witnesses on December 17, 1633.

The commissioner now learned of what Grandier and his party were capable. The witnesses were so intimidated that none would speak, and it required all the Royal Authority to reassure them. He therefore issued a proclamation forbidding the intimidation of witnesses, under penalty of prosecution; and the Bishop of Poitiers, having supported the king's decision, and the two priests Gervais Mechin and Martin Boulieau, having been forced to retract their evidence in the former trial, presented a petition in which they declared that they had been seduced and constrained by several persons in authority in order to recall evidence, and they now affirmed their first evidence to be true. The evidence of the nuns was also heard and that of laypersons of both sexes, as well as that of two women, the one of whom confessed that she had had criminal relations with Grandier and that he had offered to make her Princess of the Magicians, while the other confirmed the evidence of the first.

As regards the nuns, they deposed that Grandier had introduced himself into the convent by day and night for months, without anyone knowing how he got in; that he represented himself to them while standing at divine service and tempted them to indecent actions both by word and deed; that they were often struck by invisible persons and that the marks of the blows were so visible that the doctors and surgeons had easily found them; and that the beginning of all these troubles was signaled by the apparition of Prior Moussaut, their first confessor. The Mother Superior and seven or eight other nuns, when confronted with Grandier, identified him, although it was ascertained that they had never seen him save by magic and that he had never had anything to do with their affairs. The two women and the two priests formerly mentioned maintained the truth of their evidence. Besides the nuns and six laywomen, there were "sixty witnesses deposed to adulteries, incests, sacrileges, and other crimes committed by the accused, even in the most secret places of his church, as in the vestry where the Holy Host was kept, on all days and at all hours."

The king and his council thought it right to furnish him with means to overcome all obstacles to a speedy decision. This precaution was necessary, for letters from the bailly of Loudun, Grandier's chief supporter, to the procurator-general of the Parliament, were intercepted, in which it was asserted that the "possession" was an imposture. The latter's reply was also seized. M. de Laubardemont returned therefore to Loudun with a Decree of the Council, dated May 31, 1634, confirming all his powers and prohibiting Parliament and all other judges from interfering in this business, and forbidding all parties concerned from appealing, under penalty of a fine of five hundred francs. He caused Grandier to be transferred from the prison of Augers to that of Loudun, so as to have him at hand to confront the witnesses, if need be. But first of all, he considered it necessary to examine the nuns carefully. For this purpose, with the consent of the bishop, he sequestered them in different convents and interrogated them so severely that one might have thought they themselves were the magicians. "He saw them all, the one after the other, for several days and listened to their conversations, to observe their mode of thought. He enquired minutely into their lives, their morals, their behavior, not only secular but religious. His depositions, or notes, which represented the evidence of the twenty girls, including not a few nuns, filled fifty rolls of official paper, and were the admiration of all judges, so great was the prudence and care they demonstrated."

On the other hand, the Bishop of Poitiers, after having sent several doctors of theology to examine the victims, came to Loudun in person and exorcised them himself or had them exorcised by others in his presence for two and a half months. Never was work done with such care and attention.

All precognitions over, the commissioner began to confront the accused with the witnesses, and the latter maintained, face to face with Grandier, the evidence they had given against him.

As regards the nuns, it was observed that they never contradicted themselves, whether questioned together or separately, though they were examined often, by different persons and as skillfully as possible. Now, criminals do not manage this, for the cleverest have the greatest difficulty in avoiding contradictory statements. Those writers who have supported Grandier have never discovered the least discrepancy in the evidence of the nuns. Nor did Grandier ever plead malice on their part as a defense, for they had never seen him nor had he anything to do with their affairs, as we have said.

Thus, as it was a matter rather of religion than of jurisprudence, they resolved to begin by prayer to God, Who is the Father of all Light, rightly considering that all France was watching the trial with eager eyes, that the trial was shrouded in a thick veil of obscurity, and that their verdict would entail important consequences. They therefore prepared to receive divine assistance and grace by frequent confessions and by often receiving the Holy Sacrament. They then decreed a general procession to implore celestial aid in so difficult a matter. To excite the devotion of the masses by their example, they went in a body during the whole of the trial to visit the churches of the city, set aside by the bishop for forty hour services, and reached each in time for the elevation of the Host. Thence the exorcists went to the church fixed upon for exorcisms, and the judges proceeded to the tribunal to continue the case. In the evening all returned to church for evensong.

The examination lasted forty days, during which demons gave them the clearest proofs of their presence in the bodies of the persons exorcised. Every day new evidence was added against Grandier, and yet nothing was ever said against him that did not turn out strictly true. These assertions merit distinct proof, which will be found interesting.

On Friday, June 23, 1634, about three o'clock in the afternoon, the Bishop of Poitiers and M. de Laubardemont being present, Grandier was brought from his prison to the Church of Ste. Croix in his parish to be present at the exorcisms. All the possessed were there likewise. And as the accused and his partisans declared that the possessions were mere impostures, he was ordered to be himself the exorcist, and the stole was presented to him. He could not refuse; therefore, taking the stole and the ritual, he received the pastoral benediction, and after the *Veni Creator* had been sung, he commenced the exorcism in the usual form. But where he should haughtily have given commands to the demon, instead of saying *"Impero"* (I command), he said, *"Cogor vos"* (I am constrained by you). The bishop sharply reprimanded him, and as he had said that some of the possessed understood Latin, he was allowed to interrogate in Greek. At the same time, the demon cried out by the mouth of Sister Clara, "Eh! speak Greek, or any language you like; I will answer." At these words, he became confused and could not say anything more.

To behave thus or to acknowledge the truth of the accusation is one and the same thing, but other circumstances strengthened this certainty.

Any man whose own writing testifies against him is lost. Now this is what Grandier experienced. The devils, in several instances, confessed four pacts he had entered into.

This word *pact* is somewhat equivocal. It may mean either the document by which a man gives himself to the devil or the physical symbols whose appreciation will produce some particular effects in consequence with the pact. Here is an example of each case. Grandier's pact, or magical characters, whereby he gave himself to Beelzebub was as follows: "My Lord and Master, Lucifer, I recognize you as my God, and promise to serve you all my life. I renounce every other God, Jesus Christ, and all other saints; the Catholic, Apostolic, and Roman Church, its sacraments, with all prayers that may be said for me; and I promise to do all the evil I can. I renounce the holy oil and the water of baptism, together with all the merits of Jesus Christ and his saints; and should I fail to serve and adore you, and do homage to you thrice daily, I abandon to you my life as your due." These characters were recognized as being in Grandier's own hand.

Now there is a specimen of the other kind of pact, or magical charm. It was composed of the flesh of a child's heart extracted in an assembly of magicians held at Orleans in 1631, of the ashes of a holy wafer that had been burnt, and of something else which the least straitlaced decency forbids me to name.

A most convincing proof of Grandier's guilt is that one of the devils declared he had marked him in two parts of his body. His eyes were bandaged and he was examined by eight doctors, who reported they had found two marks in each place, that they had inserted a needle to the depth of an inch without the criminal having felt it, and that no blood had been drawn. Now this was a most decisive test, for however deeply a needle be buried in such marks, no pain is caused and no blood can be extracted if they are magical signs.

But if the devils, overcome by the exorcisms, at times gave evidence against the criminal, at others they seemed to conspire to blacken him still more under the semblance of an apparent justification. Thus several of the possessed spoke in his favor, and some even went so far as to confess that they had calumniated him. Indeed, the Mother Superior herself, one day when M. de Laubardemont was in the convent, stripped herself to her shift and, with a rope around her neck and a candle in her hand, stood for two hours in the middle of the yard, although it was raining heavily; then entering the room in which M. de Laubardemont was seated, she threw herself on her knees before him, declaring she repented of the crime she had committed in accusing Grandier, who was innocent. She then withdrew and fastened the rope to a tree in the garden, attempting to hang herself, but was prevented by the other nuns.

When the devil played these kinds of tricks, they forced him to retract by calling on him to take Jesus Christ present in the Eucharist as witness of the truth of his statement, which he never dared to do.

What criminals could ever be condemned if such proofs were not deemed sufficient? The certainty of the possessions; the depositions of two priests who accused him of sacrilege; those of the nuns declaring that they saw him day and night for four months though the gates of the convent were kept locked; those of the two women who bore witness that he offered to make one of them Princess of the Magicians; the evidence of sixty other witnesses; his own embarrassment and confusion on so many occasions; the disappearance of his three brothers who had fled and were never seen again; his pact and the magic characters that were afterward burnt with him—all these placed his guilt beyond doubt.

The trial being completed and the magician duly convicted, there only remained to sentence the evildoer. The commissioners assembled at the Carmelite convent, and it was noticed that there was not the slightest difference of opinion among all the fourteen judges, though they had never seen or known one another. They were all agreed as to the daily penalty to be inflicted, and having pronounced their sentence, they were filled with joy and their conscience was perfectly at rest. It was as if God, Whose honor was so invested in this affair, had intended to give them this consolation.

No one among the Catholics, or indeed among all honest men, failed to applaud the sentence on Grandier. It was as follows:

> We have declared, and declare, the said Urbain Grandier attainted and convicted of the crimes of magic, maleficence, and possession occurring through his act, in the persons of certain Ursuline Nuns of this Town of Loudun and other women; together with other crimes resulting therefrom. For reparation whereof we have condemned, and do condemn, the said Grandier to make *amende honorable* bareheaded, a rope round his neck, holding in his hand a burning torch of the weight of two pounds, before the principal gate of Saint Pierre du Marche, and before that of Saint Ursula of the said town; and there, on his knees, to ask pardon of God, the King, and Justice, and that done, to be led to the public square of Sainte Croix, to be there tied to a stake, which for that purpose shall be erected in the said square, and his body to be there burnt with the pacts and magical inscriptions now in custody of the Court, together with the manuscript book written by him against the celibacy of priests, and his ashes to be scattered to the wind. We have declared all his property forfeited and confiscated to the Crown, less a sum of 150 livres, which shall be expended in the purchase of a copper plate, on which shall be engraved the present sentence, and the same shall be placed in a prominent position in the said church of Saint Ursula, there to be preserved forever. And before this present sentence shall be carried out, we order that the said Grandier shall be put to the question ordinary and extraordinary, to discover his accomplices.—

Pronounced at Loudun on the said Grandier, and executed the 18th of August, 1634.

In execution of this sentence, he was taken to the Court of Justice of Loudun. His sentence having been read to him, he earnestly begged M. de Laubardemont and the other commissioners to mitigate the rigor of their sentence. M. de Laubardemont replied that the only means of inducing the judges to moderate the penalties was to declare at once his accomplices and by some act of repentance for his past crimes to implore divine mercy. The only answer he gave was that he had no accomplices, which was false, for there is no magician but must be accompanied by others.

For the last forty days the commissioner had placed at his side two monks to convert him. But all was in vain; nothing could touch this hardened sinner. It is true, however, that the conversion of a magician is so rare an occurrence that it must be placed in the rank of miracles. "I am not astonished," says one who was present, "at his impenitence, nor at his refusing to acknowledge himself guilty of magic, both under torture and at his execution, for it is known that magicians promise the devil never to confess this crime, and he in return hardens their heart, so that they go to their death stupid and altogether insensible to their misfortunes." Before being put to the torture, the prisoner was addressed by Father Lactance, a man of great faith chosen by the Bishop of Poitiers to exorcise the instruments of torture, as is always done in the case of magicians, in order to induce them to repent. Everyone shed tears except the prisoner. M. de Laubardemont also spoke to him, together with the Lieutenant-Criminel of Orleans, but notwithstanding their efforts, they made no impression. This determined M. de Laubardemont to try the effects of torture. The boots were applied, and the judge repeated his questions as to his accomplices. He always replied that he was no magician, though he had committed greater crimes than that. Questioned as to what crime, he replied, "Crimes of human frailty," and he added that were he guilty of magic he would be less ashamed of that than of his other crimes. This speech was ridiculous, especially in the mouth of a priest, who must know better than a layperson that of crimes the greatest is that of sorcery.

Torture drew from him nothing but cries, or rather sighs from the depth of his bosom, unaccompanied by tears though the exorcist had abjured him, according to the ritual, to weep if he were innocent but if guilty to remain tearless. Though he was very thirsty, he several times refused to drink holy water when it was presented to him. At length, pressed to drink, he took a few drops, with glaring eyes and a horrible look on his face. Never in the greatest agony of torture did he mention the name of Jesus Christ or of the Holy Virgin, save when repeating words he was ordered to speak, and then only in so cold a manner and with such constraint that he horrified the assistants. He never cast his eyes on the image of Christ nor on that of the Virgin, which were opposite to him, and they were offered to him in vain; whereupon the judges remonstrated with him. They were still more scandalized when they tried to make him say the prayer that every good Christian addresses to his guardian angel, especially in great extremities, and he said he did not know it. Such was his conduct under torture; in such a crisis every feeling of religion would be awakened in an ordinary man.

His legs were then washed and placed near the fire to restore circulation; he then began to talk to the guards, joking and laughing, and would have gone on had they allowed him. He spoke neither of receiving the sacrament of penitence nor of imploring God's pardon. They had given him for a confessor the Father Archangel, who asked him if he did not wish to confess. He replied that he had done so the previous Tuesday, after which he sat down and dined with the same appetite as usual, drank three or four glasses of wine, and spoke of all kinds of things except God. Instead of listening to what was said to him for the good of his soul, he made speeches he had prepared beforehand as if he were preaching. They consisted of complaints as to the pain in his legs and a feeling of chilliness about his head, in asking for something to drink or to eat, and in begging that he might not be burnt alive.

When he was carried to the courthouse, where the Holy Fathers began to prepare him for death, he pushed back with his hand a crucifix which was presented to him and muttered between his teeth some words which were not heard. His guards, witnessing this action, were scandalized and told the monk not to offer him the crucifix again since he rejected it. He recommended himself to no one's prayers, neither before nor during execution of the sentence—only, as he passed through the streets, turning his head to one side and the other to see the people, it was noticed that he said twice, with an appearance of vanity, "Pray God for me," and that those to whom he spoke were Huguenots, among whom was an apostate. The monk who was with him exhorted him to say, *"Cor mundum crea in me, Deus."* Grandier turned his back on him and said with contempt, *"Cor mundum crea in me, Deus."*

Having reached the place of execution, the fathers redoubled their charitable solicitude and pressed him most earnestly to be converted to God at that moment, offered to him the crucifix, and placed it over his mouth and on his chest. He never deigned to look at it, and once or twice even turned away; he shook his head when holy water was offered to him. He seemed eager to end his days and in haste to have the fire lighted, either because he expected not to feel it or because he feared he might be weak enough to name his accomplices, or perhaps, as is believed, in fear lest pain should extract from him a renunciation of his master Lucifer. For the devil, to whom magicians give themselves body and soul, so thoroughly masters their mind that they fear him only and expect and hope for nothing save from him. Therefore did Grandier protest, placing his hand on his heart that he would say no more than he had already said. At last, seeing them set fire to the fagots, he feared they did not intend to keep their promise to him but wished to burn him alive, and he uttered loud complaints. The executioner then advanced, as is always done, to strangle him; but the flames suddenly sprang up with such violence that the rope caught fire, and he fell alive among the burning fagots. Just before this, a strange event happened. In the midst of this mass of people, notwithstanding the noise of so many voices and the efforts of the archers who shook their halberts in the air to frighten them, a flight of pigeons flew around and around the stake. Grandier's partisans, impudent to the end, said that these innocent birds came in default of men as witnesses of his innocence; others thought very differently and said that it was a troop of demons who had come, as sometimes happens on the death of great magicians, to assist at that of Grandier, whose scandalous impenitence certainly deserved to be honored in this manner. His friends, however, called this hardness of heart constancy and had his ashes collected as if they were relics, they who did not believe in such things, for the Huguenots looked upon him as one of themselves, especially when they noticed that he never called on the Virgin nor looked upon the crucifix.

Thus did he close his criminal career by a death that horrified not only Catholics but even the most honorable of the Calvinist party. But the end of the magician was not the end of the effects of his sorcery; and the possessions, far from ceasing, as had been hoped, continued for a time. God permitted that a great number of those who had been connected with the affair should be more or less vexed by demons. The Civil Lieutenant, Louis Chauvet, was seized with such fear that his mind gave way, and he never recovered. M. Mannouri, the surgeon who had sounded the marks which the devil had impressed on the magician priest, suffered from extraordinary troubles and was of course said by the friends of Grandier to have been the victim of remorse. Here are particulars of the death of this surgeon:

One night at about ten o'clock as he was returning from visiting a sick man, walking with a friend and accompanied by a man carrying a lantern, he cried all of a sudden like a man awakening from a dream, "Ah! There is Grandier! What do you want?" At the same time he was seized with trembling. The two men took him back to his home, while he continued to talk to Grandier whom he thought he had before his eyes. He was put to bed filled with the same illusion and shaking in every limb. He only lived a few days, during which his state never changed. He died believing the magician was still before him and making efforts to keep him at arm's length.

Part II

Tales from Africa & the Near East

The Devil Bush

(Liberia)

What is the Devil Bush? you are ready to ask and so were we, but the question, though asked a thousand times over, remained unanswered. At its sound every native would close his lips and veil even his eyes with an impenetrable expression. We would be walking along a path, when suddenly the guide would stop, point to a small handful of grass taken on each side of the path, bent over and tied across it. That just meant you had to turn back, for a little farther on was the Devil Bush, and to intrude into those sacred precincts meant—ah, well, he never told you what, but from his manner something as terrible as death. Men would bring their children into school, and the more honest and open of them would say, "Daddy, I leave my gal in your hand until time for her to go in Devil Bush." Others would give you no such warning, but about the time the girl reached her eleventh year, or a little later, she would receive word by a hurried messenger to come at once; her mother or father or grandmother was ready to die, or as they expressed it, "live die." They of course left hurriedly, never to return to the mission again, save as somebody's wife, after two or three years' absence. Upon asking them why they did not return sooner, as they invariably promised to do, the one answer came: "I have been in Devil Bush." Nor was the success with the boys much greater. The nearer a boy was united to a noble family, the more certain he was to be torn from the mission on one pretext or another, whether he were willing or not, and

From: "Folk-Lore Scrap-Book: The Devil Bush of West Africa," *Journal of American Folk-Lore* 9 (1896): 220–22.

once in the confines of that unknowable thing, the Devil Bush, you would see him no more for months, and sometimes for years.

A missionary had drawn into his school the son of the Queen of the Woman's Devil Bush, and after this youth had returned to his home in order to receive initiation, the missionary was invited to visit the town of the queen. Refused admission to the precincts of the Devil Bush, he nevertheless bought entrance by a bribe but was allowed to behold only meaningless performances. On the same day, however, a native from a distance entered the town intoxicated and began to make an uproar; he was remonstrated with and informed that this was the town of the Queen of the Devil Bush, to which he replied that he did not care for the Devil Bush or its queen. He was left undisturbed on the same night, but on the morrow taken before the queen, to whom it is said that he repeated the blasphemy, as it was considered, although warned that he would be excused on an apology. He was immediately seized, hurried to an open space in the center of the town, stripped, tied, and so fixed that he could not move. Then many bunches of small rattan splints were brought, and skillful fingers began to wrap his fingers and toes, drawing the splints with all their might. After five hours of suffering he was ransomed by a friend, but died as a consequence of his treatment. This the missionary witnessed.

It is said that if a man is unusually cruel to one of his wives (for he may have as many as he is able to buy) the matter is brought before the Woman's Devil Bush. The case is tried, and if it is a true one, the man is condemned to die. A person is appointed, skilled in the art, to poison him, and in due course of time he dies. The death is made a long and painful or a quick one, according as they wish to inflict greater or less punishment. Again, if the tribe decides to go to war, that declaration of war is not complete until it has been referred to the women and they pass upon and approve it. In addition to these powers that we see cropping out, it is certain that the women are instructed in all the arts that are considered necessary to a good wife and mother, ere she is permitted to leave the Devil Bush and be taken by her betrothed husband.

When I sought information as to the Man's Devil Bush, I found myself at first completely foiled. It was not until many of the boys grew up and learned to trust me that, little by little, I gathered the links which, when woven together, gave me some idea of its mysteries. It is an institution for instructing every man in the tribe as to his duty to the commonwealth. It seems that no one can hold office until he has gone through the Devil Bush. The diploma is not given on sheepskin but on that of the graduate by a number of deep scratches from the back of the neck a short distance down the backbone. When these heal, they leave rectangular scars, raised so as to be distinctly seen and known. When a boy enters the Devil Bush, he is stripped and a most careful examination made of all his scars, and these are noted in the records.

It is said that the devil never lets one in his bush get hurt or scarred save with the diploma mark. This is a most unfortunate assertion and has cost many a life. Should a boy get hurt in any way, it matters not how, he is carefully watched and every effort made to heal him without a scar; but should these efforts fail and scars be left, those scars seal his doom. He is killed, and his family is notified in the following way: Whenever the inmates of the Devil Bush wish to obtain food, they disguise themselves so as not to be recognized by anyone; they then make a raid on the nearest town, blowing a peculiar note on a trumpet made of an elephant's tusk, with a lizard's skin so stretched over it as to produce weird vibrations. At this sound the inhabitants of the town hurriedly place food out in the streets and, entering their houses, close their doors so as not to see the devil. The whole raiding party then pass through the town, taking charge of all the food they find and leaving a broken earthen pot at the door of the mother of the boy who has been killed. That broken pot says, "Your part is spoiled and broken," or in other words, "Your boy is dead." This is all she ever learns of the fate of her boy—just the story the jagged lips of a broken earthen pot tell. Henceforth she mourns with a great void of heart, facing the deep mysteries of the terrible Devil Bush.

It is certain death for one of the boys to see or speak to a woman or girl while in the Devil Bush unless he has been released on furlough. An eyewitness describes the manner in which an inconsiderate offense of this sort was punished by death, the boy being bound to a long pole, which was then raised and allowed to fall with the culprit. The instruction is said to include, as a sort of advanced course, the use of magic arts.

Spirit Beliefs

(Nigeria)

Reducing these principles into plain facts, and having established this fact of God supremacy beyond all question, it is
next of all evident that there are between the Supreme God
and humanity a certain more or less definite number of
spiritual beings—local or communal deities—who live in trees,
stones, rivers, mountains, and other natural phenomena, as well as in
artificial objects of various kinds—in a few words, whose emblems
are natural or artificial deities who, although created and deputed by
the Supreme Being, occupy an independent position with regard to
the management and administration of human affairs, and indeed so
far as these—inseparable as they are from the spiritual—are concerned, of the spiritual: every human community having its own
community in spirit land, which although shorn of all materialism, as
the vitalizing shadow of the substance is identical.

These deities, made as they are in man's own image, are as a matter
of course anthropomorphic in form, consequently human or natural in
their character, which means in plain English that they are capable
both of good and evil; and having their own specific attributes and
functions, they immediately and specifically represent the varying
interests of the various social elements. Known among the Efik and
Ibo as Idems, they have priests, and in some instances priestesses, the
latter of whom are consecrated from birth and always remain celibate,
to make sacrifice and prayer to those particular gods to whom they
have been dedicated. In spite of the fact that the Creator is seldom
approached or referred to except in crises or under very exceptional
emergencies, these departmental divinities are in popular estimation
regarded as distinctly inferior to him in power and magnitude. Yet
placing a purely human construction on the matter as the people do,
and looking at it from the standpoint of a mentality that is eminently
human and in no sense either influenced or inspired by any outside or

From: Arthur Glyn Leonard, "Southern Nigeria: Religion and Witchcraft," *Imperial and Asiatic Quarterly Review* (3rd series) 23 (1907): 279–311.

higher element, it is not in the least surprising that in some respects these inferior deities are deemed to occupy a position not only of considerably greater congeniality but also of more immediate consequence, merely because of the fact of their association with the earth and of their connection with humanity, which brings them into touch with the more substantial, therefore more enjoyable, pleasures of human existence.

If, then, we compare their thoughts with their actions, and in this practical way learn to comprehend their beliefs through a thorough and systematic knowledge of their practices, it is in no sense difficult to condense the principles contained therein into an exceedingly limited and compact compass. On these sensible lines, by consolidating the information and knowledge that have been placed at my disposal with regard to their sociology, but more especially in connection with the two main elements—the spiritualism and emblemism of their belief—certain facts at once become prominent. Thus, for example, that life or existence is a dual element or combination of the material and the spiritual; in other words, that the world as it appears to them is divided into these two main or principal phases, which in their turn are subdivided into the following units: (1) human beings; (2) animal beings; (3) vegetal beings; (4) material beings—the three latter of various kinds and descriptions, the entire vitality of the material phase being due to the animation or inspiration of the spiritual or life-giving principle. It is also evident that, while for the most part the countless host of spiritual beings who divide their existence between this world and spirit land are for the most part anthropomorphic, there is also in evidence a specific form of spirit of like kin, but varying in degree, which is confined to the animal, vegetal, and material elements. But while the spirit essence of vegetal and material—also of the animal, except in specific cases and under certain conditions—is confined exclusively to its own species, the anthropomorphic spirit essence is not only interchangeable with the zoomorphic but possesses the ability to enter into matter of every sort, a characteristic that with regard to the latter is limited to human bodies only.

From this extremely fundamental standpoint, beyond certain superficial differences which I will point out, there is no further classification of the spirit element that I am aware of; nor in fact within such limitations as have been defined could this be either possible or probable. Spirits, then, are accordingly divided, first of all into two main classes: (1) the embodied; (2) the disembodied, or regarded from another standpoint, the ancestral and the nonancestral; while these again may be subdivided into (1) the ancestral embodied; (2) the nonancestral embodied; (3) the ancestral disembodied; and (4) the nonancestral disembodied. In plain English, then, this means that those who are ancestral are capable of good and evil, while those who are not ancestral are at all times inimical; all outcasts and disembodied spirits being also, as a matter of course, malignant and vicious. For embodiment of the material is the distinguishing characteristic which divides the natural world of the Supreme God or Creative Power from the unnatural domain of the evil or destroying power, because this latter element, under an omnipotent cloak of disembodiment, is neither confined by limits nor regulated by balance of any kind.

It is quite obvious, then, that apart from all polemic or prejudice, these natives have a clear and distinct concept of God, whom they look upon as the Creator, by whose action the conception of all things human, animal, and vegetal takes place—the male and female energies of the various elements being nothing but mere agents or instruments in His hands. So in continuation of this idea, it is also evident that the sun, moon, stars, rain, dew, lightning, thunder, and other natural phenomena are likewise instruments created by Him, into which He has infused His own animating spirit, in the same mysterious way that He has given to humanity that personal gift of reason which enables it to appreciate and express its appreciation of the various spiritual influences which surround it as well as to discriminate between the positive and the negative, or what appeals to it as good and evil.

So, too, the spirits of disease, which are for the most part, if not entirely, evil, are not adored as gods, nor are sacrifices made to them in a divine sense but only in that of propitiation—a most tremendously significant feature, demonstrating plainly and vigorously as it does that, brutal and ignorant as the people are from a civilized standpoint, the worship of their ancestors, which as an evolution from Nature herself is their natural religion, is an element outside and apart from demonology. For demonology, as they believe in and practice it, is altogether an outcome of that branch of human thought and desire which has been mentally, and so to speak deliberately, concentrated on the wrong side of the social balance and put into practice with the object of consummating the destruction of all that is evil or good on the right side of the balance—in a word, the unnatural or all-destroying factor in humanity as opposed to the natural or dual element which, although dual, is more on the side of construction; a concept which in principle is very similar, if not identical, to that which they believe to be the motive principle of suicide which, although a seemingly deliberate act of the person, is regarded as due to obsession on the part of a unit of that detached power of evil which they can only express by the one and single term of witchcraft.

This very essential principle of embodiment is to them the actual line of demarcation between the normal human spirit and the abnormal human demon—in other words, between the divided energies of Good and Evil and the indivisible unit of Evil, pure and unadulterated, only.

Spiritual Beliefs of the Hottentots

(South Africa)

The Hottentots were a superstitious people who place great faith in the efficacy of charms to ward off evil. They even besought favors from certain pieces of root so used, and if their wishes were successful, they praised and thanked the charms. This superstition might in time have developed into idolatry, but it was arrested before it reached that stage. They believed that certain occurrences foreboded good or ill luck, and were always on the watch for omens. Their veneration of the mantis, an insect that bears so close a resemblance either to a withered leaf or to a dry stalk of grass that its presence cannot be detected except when it is in motion, has been

From: George McCall Theal, *The Yellow and Dark-Skinned People of Africa South of the Zambesi* (London: Swan Sonnenschein and Co., Ltd., 1910).

asserted by many writers, some of whom have even termed it the Hottentot god, but it has been called in question by others. The reason of this contradiction is that their notions regarding the insect were acquired from their Bushman female captives, who had been taught by their parents that it was endowed with the power of exchanging its form for that of any other animal, and that it could confer good or bad fortune upon human beings. Clans in which Bushman blood was strong would therefore venerate the mantis, and others would pay little or no regard to it.

They lived in dread of ghosts and evil spirits, but with no more conception of the nature of such shadowy beings, or of the mode of receiving harm, than little children have. They invoked blessings from the moon, the harbinger of their festivities, to whose praise they sang and danced when it appears as new. In later times those who had come in contact with Bantu prayed for blessings from dead ancestors, to whose shades sacrifices were offered by priests on important occasions, but this was evidently a custom of foreign origin. Generally they implored protection and favor from a mythical hero named Tsui‖goab or Heitsi-eibib, who was believed by them to have lived on the earth and to have died and risen again many times, and whose worship consisted in throwing a branch of a tree, a bit of wood, or an additional stone upon a cairn at a place where he was supposed to have been once buried. Tales of the wonderful deeds of this Heitsi-eibib were commonly narrated by old men and were implicitly believed by everyone who heard them. All the actions ascribed to him were those of a man, but of one endowed with supernatural power.

Thus he was said on one occasion to have been pursued by an enemy, and with his family and his followers to have come to a large river. He said, "My grandfather's father, separate thyself that we may pass through, and close thyself afterward." The river did so. Heitsi-eibib and his people passed through in safety, and when the enemy followed them, the river closed again and they were all drowned. This tale may seem to have had its origin in the teaching of missionaries, but it has been obtained from so many sources, some of which were never directly or indirectly under missionary influence, that it is beyond doubt original.

Another of the tales related of Heitsi-eibib is as follows: ‡Gā‡gorib sat by a large hole in the ground, and when people passed by he told them to throw a stone at his forehead. When they did this, the stone rebounded and stunned them, and they fell into the hole and died. Heitsi-eibib heard of this, so he went to the place, and ‡Gā‡gorib challenged him to throw a stone. He declined to do so, and they then began to chase each other round the hole, saying "Push Heitsi-eibib down! Push ‡Gā‡gorib down! Push Heitsi-eibib down! Push ‡Gā‡gorib down!"

At last Heitsi-eibib was pushed down, but he said, "My grandfather's father, raise up thy bottom and let me out." The hole did so, and he came out.

They began to chase each other around it again, saying "Push Heitsi-eibib down! Push ‡Gā‡gorib down! Push Heitsi-eibib down! Push ‡Gā‡gorib down!" and Heitsi-eibib was thrown in the second time.

He said, "My grandfather's father, raise up thy bottom and let me out." The hole did so. This happened many times, but at last when ‡Gā‡gorib was looking on one side, Heitsi-eibib struck him behind the ear and stunned him, so that he fell into the hole and could not get out again. From that time onward the people had rest, because ‡Gā‡gorib was conquered.

Still another of these tales is given, as it records one of the deaths of Heitsi-eibib and of his coming to life again. It is in the words of the Reverend G. Krönlein, as translated by him from the Nama original.

When Heitsi-eibib was traveling about with his family, they came to a valley in which the raisin tree was ripe, and he was there attacked by a severe illness. Then his young (second) wife said, "This brave one is taken ill on account of these raisins. Death is here at the place."

The old man (Heitsi-eibib), however, told his son !Urisib (the whitish one), "I shall not live, I feel it; thou must, therefore, cover me when I am dead with soft stones." And he spoke further, "This is the thing which I order you to do: of the raisin trees of this valley you shall not eat, for if you eat of them I shall infect you, and you will surely die in a similar way."

His young wife said, "He is taken ill on account of the raisins of this valley. Let us bury him quickly, and let us go."

So he died there and was covered flatly with soft stones according as he had commanded. Then they went away from him.

When they had moved to another place and were unpacking there, they heard always from the side whence they came a noise as of the people eating raisins and singing. In this manner the eating and singing ran:

> I, father of !Urisib,
> Father of this unclean one,
> I, who had to eat the raisins, and died,
> And dying live.

The young wife perceived that the noise came from the side where the old man's grave was, and said "!Urisib, go and look." Then the son went to the old man's grave, where he saw traces which he recognized to be his father's footmarks, and returned home. Then the young wife said, "It is he alone; therefore act thus":

> Do so to the man who ate raisins on the windward side,
> Take care of the wind that thou creepest upon him
>   from the leeward;
> Then intercept him on his way to the grave,
> And when thou hast caught him, do not let him go.

He did accordingly, and they came between the grave and Heitsi-eibib, who, when he saw this, jumped down from the raisin tree and ran quickly, but was caught at the grave. Then he said, "Let me go, for I am a man who has been dead, that I may not infect you."

But the young wife said, "Keep hold of the rogue."

So they brought him home, and from that day he was fresh and hale.

Dr. Theophilus Hahn, the son of a missionary, who spent his youth among the Namaqua and learned to speak their language as soon as he did that of his parents, in his *Tsuni‖Goam, the Supreme Being of the Khoikhoi*, published in London in 1881, states that the Namaqua believe Tsui‖goab, or Heitsi-eibib as otherwise called, to be a powerful and beneficent being who lives in the red sky. There is also a powerful evil being, named ‖Gaunab, who lives in the black sky and does harm to men who on that account fear and worship him. In a series of combats with ‖Gaunab, Tsui‖goab was repeatedly overcome, but after every struggle grew stronger, till at last he killed ‖Gaunab by a blow behind the ear. He was, however, wounded in the knee and has been lame ever since, whence his name, the wounded knee. At early dawn the Namaqua look towards the east and implore blessings from him.

Saint Worship

(Turkey)

The tomb of a reputed saint is often set off by a rough enclosing wall, and is sometimes covered by a building. The occupant is termed an Evliya (plural of the Arabic *vely* or *wely*). The site is frequently "on a high hill" and "under a green tree," just as was so often the case in the Old Testament times and countries. Many are in secluded spots, but every worshipper is welcomed. In and near a city, Evliyas are abundant. One saint has the reputation of curing headache, another stomachache, and another toothache. Some are good for weak eyes. At one such spot it is the prescribed custom to burn pine fagots and rub the eyes with the soot, while at another one must wash his eyes in the water of a fountain close at hand. One is visited by persons hard of hearing, another by anyone whose mouth is awry. In the latter trying condition, the suppliant pays a small fee and is slapped on the mouth by the attendant with the slipper of the deceased saint. Certain graves are much resorted to by barren women who desire children, as Hannah visited Shiloh (I SAM. 1:9–11); to others children are taken who cannot properly walk or talk, or who seem deficient or belated in the use of some ordinary faculty.

The ceremonies at such shrines are simple and vary with local customs and with the worshipper's sense of the fitness of things and of the urgency of his case. There is of course a prayer, "uttered or unexpressed," understood to be offered to the Almighty through the medium of the saint. Sacrifice is common. Earth taken from beside a sacred tomb is called "precious" and is supposed to possess great efficacy. This seems to be on the principle of sympathetic magic. The dust, having been in contact with or close proximity to the holy man, has partaken of his virtues and retains his power. A little of such earth is mixed with water and smeared upon the person of a child ailing or in any way deficient, or the child is made to drink the muddy water. One general panacea for the sick is to bring earth from a sacred grave,

From: George E. White, "Saint Worship in Turkey," *Moslem World* 9 (1919): 8–18.

dissolve it in water, and give it to the patient to drink. It is more in keeping, however, for the patient, if possible, to walk, ride, or be carried to the sacred spot, to offer his petition there in person, and to smear the precious earth on his body, or to swallow it moistened with water. To fertilize a field or rid it of pests like mice, handfuls of earth are taken from beside the tomb of the saint, whose living representatives collect the farmer's religious dues, and the precious earth is sprinkled over the soil. Another way of approaching the being once human, but now having access to the superhuman realm, is especially employed by those who are afflicted with malaria or with some of the other sorts of fever prevalent in a country where sanitary science is yet almost absent. This consists in tying a rag or a bit of rope or hair taken from the person to the fence or wall about the grave or to a tree standing near. Horseshoes and nails are also driven into the trees, constituting a visible, tangible, permanent bond between the suppliant and the saint.

Men fear to steal or commit other depredation within or near such sacred precincts. I once climbed over the log enclosure around a grave to pick some alpine violets, those early harbingers of spring. A friendly passerby advised me to get out, lest the offended "lier" there should kick me out. Trees are not cut from a grove made sacred by the presence of an Evliya, lest the wood fly back to its place in the night or lest the woodcutter's house burn before morning. Even sticks brought home by children are sometimes carried back by an old granny before night, lest some "stroke" overtake the dwelling or its inmates. This fear, however, has been very useful in retaining some trees on the mountains, which are fast being deforested to the serious damage of the plains and valleys below. In the event of death, however, wood may be cut from even the most sacred grove for the purpose of making a coffin.

To their own people and to reverent worshippers, these "lords many and gods many" are held to be indispensable protectors and kind benefactors. Immigrants from the province of Shirwan in Russia are unwilling to settle more than six hours distant from the grave of Hadji Hamza in Amasia, because their great Hoja promised his intercession for all his people living within six hours of his burial place when they come before the Judge of all the earth. Strange whims are attributed to these characters. For instance, a woman once related to us how Hadji Veli, their village patron, could not endure the color red nor the sound of a drum. As a consequence the village women forgo the beauty of red dresses, the color they love best, and they never beat a drum there, even at a wedding.

One summer day, beside a clear, cold mountain spring, I fell in with a man who talked familiarly, almost lovingly, of the *dedes,* the venerable religious characters entombed here and there upon the sunny mountain slopes about. The enclosure of one grave, he told me, was built by deer, who brought the material on their backs for the purpose. At another of the graves, miles away across the valley, a camel was formerly sacrificed every year. Then, becoming interested as I listened, he related how the dedes occasionally fire a cannon and how he had once plainly heard them on the very spot where we then were sitting, the echo of the great guns booming from peak to peak around. On going to the city, he found at least ten men who had heard the same cannonading, and all were sure that something portentous was at hand. My informant was then a soldier under arms, and in just a week came news of the Greek war of 1896, with orders for the troops to leave for the front. And the men went with light hearts, for they felt that God and the saints were stirring in their behalf.

On another day a party of us visited the grove and tomb of Chal Dede, Saint Chal—a spot to kindle the imagination of the most prosaic. Picture to your mind's eye a mountain peak fifteen hundred feet above the fertile plain unrolled like a map below; lower peaks separated by winding valleys roundabout; over yonder Bulak Mountain, crowned with the ruins of an ancient castle; the missionary compound in sight in the city a dozen miles away, where five hundred young people gather to attend the schools of the historic Halys River over there to the west; a pine grove below our feet, with the cool breeze soughing up through the trees; the flattened top of the grassy hill offering accommodation for a concourse of hundreds or even thousands of people; and in the center of the greensward the tomb of the saint, Chal Dede.

A substantial stone wall about forty feet square enclosed the little low building within which was the tomb. This last was perhaps three feet high by six feet long, and was a whitened sepulchre plastered outside. The outline of a neck and head of plaster at the west indicated the head of the saint, and a string of ninety-nine beads was hanging around this neck to be run through the fingers of a worshipper while repeating the "beautiful names" of God. A cloth of green was thrown over the tomb, and a turban of the same sacred color was wrapped about the headpiece. The walls were stained with the smoke of many candles burned in reverence.

Our guide, a Sunni Turk, at once began to pray, prostrating himself toward the south, the direction of Mecca, and intoning over such standard phrases as "God is great," "There is no good but Allah," and the like. He wiped his eyes with the green cloth from upon the tomb, remarking that they were diseased, and he hoped the saint would help them. He tore a rag from his ragged clothes and added another to the many rags tied to nails in the wall. He took dust from the graveside and rubbed it on his forehead. Then, as the rain clouds discharged their contents, our Turk explained that Chal Dede is one of the beloved of God and is of great mercy toward men. The region belongs to him. No man can cut a tree from the grove or carry away stones or earth without the risk of incurring his displeasure and some consequent penalty. The trespasser may die, or fall sick or paralytic, or his cattle be stricken with disease, or his crops fail. Chal Dede roams about at will, especially by night, visiting other dedes, his friends, and inspecting things generally. He sews—and the speaker directed our attention to a needle and thread always kept hanging on the wall—and makes presents of garments where they are least expected, or he repairs rents in the cloth thrown over his grave.

"So," continued the Turk simply, "my dead father and mother revisit my house every Friday night. I cannot see them, but they are there and inspect my dwelling to see whether there is sin there or right conduct, whether we quarrel or are at peace. Just so every man has a recording angel looking over his shoulder, who puts down all his acts and utterances, whether good or bad, and at the end the account is struck, and according to the balance, one goes to heaven or hell."

The Spirits of Dead Ovaherero

(South Africa)

The funeral customs of the Ovaherero were somewhat different from those of the other tribes. The backbone of a dead man was broken, to prevent his spirit from practicing mischief, and the body was then doubled up and buried in a deep grave with the face toward the north, the home of his ancestors. These people believed that the eyes of the spirit of a dead man were in the back of the head. They slaughtered a favorite oxen of the deceased, in order that the shades of these might accompany him to the spirit world, but they did not eat the flesh of the dead animals, as was the practice with other Bantu. In such cases the Ovaherero killed the oxen by shedding their blood, whereas cattle killed by them on all other occasions were bound fast and suffocated, with their faces turned toward the north.

From: George McCall Theal, *The Yellow and Dark-Skinned People of Africa South of the Zambesi* (London: Swann Sonnenschein and Co., Ltd., 1910).

Spirit Customs of the Bantu

(South Africa)

The Bantu believed that the spirits of the dead visited their friends and descendants in the form of animals. Each tribe regarded some particular animal as the one selected by the ghosts of its kindred and therefore looked upon it as sacred. The lion was thus held in veneration by one tribe, the crocodile by another, the python by a third, the blue buck by a fourth, and so on. When a division of a tribe took place, each section retained the same ancestral animal, and thus a simple method is afforded of ascertaining the wide dispersion of various communities of former times. For instance, at the present day a species of snake is held by people as far south as the mouth of the Fish River and by others near the Zambezi to be the form in which their dead appear.

This belief caused even such destructive animals as the lion and the crocodile to be protected from harm in certain parts of the country. It was not indeed believed that every lion or every crocodile was a disguised spirit, but that anyone might be, and so none were molested unless under peculiar circumstances, when it was clearly apparent that the animal was an aggressor and therefore not related to the tribe. Even then, if it could be driven away it was not killed. A Xhosa of the present time will leave his hut if an ancestral snake enters it, permitting the reptile to keep possession, and will shudder at the thought of anyone hurting it. The animal thus respected by one tribe was, however, disregarded and killed without scruple by all others.

The great majority of the people of the interior have now lost the ancient belief, but they still hold in veneration the animal that their ancestors regarded as a possible embodied spirit. Most of them take their tribal titles from it, thus the Bakwena are the crocodiles, the

From: George McCall Theal, *The Yellow and Dark-Skinned People of Africa South of the Zambesi* (London: Swan Sonnenschein and Co., Ltd., 1910).

Bataung the lions, the Baputi the little blue antelopes. Each terms the animal whose name it bears its *siboko,* and not only will not kill it or eat its flesh but will not touch its skin or come in contact with it in any way if that can be avoided. When one stranger meets another and desires to know something about him, he asks, "To what do you dance?" and the name of the animal is given in reply. Dos Santos, a Portuguese writer who had excellent opportunities of observation, states that on certain occasions, which must have been frequent, men imitated the actions of their siboko; but that custom has now almost died out, at least among the southern tribes.

Nearer than the spirits of deceased chiefs or of their own ancestors was a whole host of hobgoblins, water spirits, and malevolent demons, who met the Bantu turn which way they would. There was no beautiful fairyland for them, for all the beings who haunted the mountains, the plains, and the rivers were ministers of evil. The most feared of these was a large bird that made love to women and incited those who returned its affection to cause the death of those who did not, and a little mischievous imp who was also amorously inclined. Many instances could be gathered from the records of magistrates' courts in recent years of demented women having admitted their acquaintance with these fabulous creatures, as well as of whole communities living in terror of them.

The water spirits were believed to be addicted to claiming human victims, though they were sometimes willing to accept an ox as a ransom. How this belief works practically may be illustrated by facts which have come under the writer's cognizance.

In the summer of 1875 a party of girls went to bathe in a tributary of the Keiskama River. There was a deep hole in the stream, into which one of them got, and she was drowned. The others ran home as fast as they could, and there related that their companion had been lured from their side by a spirit calling her. She was with them, they said, in a shallow part, when suddenly she stood upright and exclaimed, "It is calling." She then walked straight into the deep place, and would not allow any of them to touch her. One of them heard her saying, "Go and tell my father and my mother that it took me." Upon this, the father collected his cattle as quickly as possible and went to the stream. The animals were driven into the water, and the man stood on the bank imploring the spirit to take the choicest of them and restore his daughter.

On another occasion a man was trying to cross one of the fords of a river when it was in flood. He was carried away by the current, but succeeded in getting safely to land some three or four hundred meters farther down. Eight or ten stout fellows saw him carried off his feet, but not one made the slightest effort to help him. On the contrary, they all rushed away frantically shouting to the herd boys on the hillsides to drive down the cattle. The escape of the man from the power of the spirit was afterward attributed to his being in possession of a powerful charm.

Besides these spirits, according to the belief of the Bantu, there are people living under the water, pretty much as those do who are in the upper air. They have houses and furniture, and even cattle, all of their domestic animals being, however, of a dark color. They are wiser than other people, and from them the witch finders are supposed to obtain the knowledge of their art. This is not a fancy of children but the implicit belief of grown-up men and women at the present day. As an instance, in July 1881 a woman came to the author of this volume, who was then acting as magistrate of a district in the Cape Colony inhabited by Bantu, and asked for assistance. A child had died in her kraal, and the witch finder had pointed her out as the person who had caused its death. Her husband was absent, and the result of her being "smelt out" was that no one would enter her hut or so much as speak to her. If she was in a path, everyone fled out of her way, and even her own children avoided her. Being under British jurisdiction, she could not be otherwise punished, but such treatment as this would of itself, in course of time, have made her insane. She denied most emphatically having been concerned in the death of the child, though she did not doubt that someone had caused it by witchcraft. The witch finder was sent for, and as the matter was considered an important one, a larger number of people than usual appeared at the investigation. On putting the ordinary tests to the witch finder, he failed to meet them, and when he was compelled, reluctantly, to admit that he had never held converse with the people under the water, it was easy to convince the bystanders that he was only an imposter.

The Demon Dance

(North Africa)

We must attribute the origin of the demon dance to a desire to get something from the spirit, I think, the latter being forced to come and listen to his worshippers when his proper movements were performed. Whereas the rite is now comparable to inoculation against disease, that idea was probably not the moving principle of the original cult, for although disease demons were exorcised then as now, it is probable that the nature gods were summoned so that prayers might be made to them—such a practice still surviving in the case of Doguwa and a few others. With the advent of Islam, however, these spirits would lose some of their importance and would have to fall into line with the others, for Muhammad recognizes the jinns though not the nature gods, and so at the present day all are summoned so that they may torment those people who are prepared for them and thus be more likely to leave the rest of the community in peace.

The power of summoning the Bori by means of the proper words and names so that they should be influenced by actions is not surprising. During a game of bowls, one will often see the man who has just sent down his ball still kneeling, with his hand stretched out, and at last turning it stiffly over in the direction of the bias, trying, as it were, to aid the bowl, even to force it in the required direction. While amusing to a European onlooker, such an act would be absolutely unintelligible to a Hausa—and to our remote forefathers. As the Bori cult progressed, there would be a separate dancer for each spirit honored (as is now almost always the case), and it is only natural to suppose that each Mai-Bori would try to introduce something from outside, both so as to outvie the others and also in order that he or she might have a monopoly of that particular rite. But there would be a real wish to honor the spirit too, and as soon as set steps had become recognized, the subsequent dancers would have to learn them and would not be allowed to make any alteration.

From: A. J. N. Tremearne, *The Ban of the Bori: Demons and Demon-Dancing in West and North Africa* (London: Heath, Cranton & Ousely, Ltd., 1914).

I am inclined to think that the present dances are mere survivals of much more complicated magical performances, for as other cults were being grafted on to the old one, an average would gradually establish itself. As they are religious ceremonies, they have persisted, for religion is always conservative, and no doubt they will continue for many years more, if allowed, on account of the profits earned by the professors. The dances are exciting and interesting, even in their present form, and probably no similar performance in the whole world can boast such a lengthy cast of characters, but what must they have been in the olden days in unknown savage Africa?

The Nature of the Soul

(Nigeria)

I t is hard, very hard," Bosa confessed, "in these busy days to say what we Onitshas really believe, because the Fathers have spoiled all our young people's minds with religions of different sorts. We have not properly understood. We are only half Christians. Yet we are no longer proper pagans. However, we still believe that there is, in the head and heart of every person, the Nkpulobe, which is the soul. Without that soul a man would not be a living being—he would simply be a body!"

"A dead body?" I asked.

"Sometimes a live body—when a person has lost his sense. A crazed man has lost his Nkpulobe."

"Can you describe it for me?"

"It is exactly the same as the body, for it is the man's own 'specially' self. Other people cannot touch it or feel it—but they can feel it at work near them, when a person whom they hate or love is beside them."

I take it that Bosa meant to imply the magnetic influence of one

From: John M. Stuart-Young, "Nigerian Supernaturalism: Part 2," *Occult Review* 31 (1920): 197–203.

nature over another—that hypnotic charm which some men seem to exert over their less fortunate and more impressionable fellows.

"There is only one soul in each person?" I catechized.

"Of course! Yet it is not possible to kill the Nkpulobe at all! If a man is slain by a leopard while out hunting, or if he is destroyed by an alligator while bathing; or if he be engineer and he is killed by an explosion on his boat; or if he be murdered; or if some person gives him poison, so that he dies in great pain; or if he kills himself in any way whatever, instead of waiting for God to call him; or if he suffers from some very bad skin disease that changes his body—*then* the soul is . . . mutilated. The Nkpulobe is maimed. The horrible kind of death he has died makes him an evil influence. That is why, if he is buried in the house of his family or in the usual graveyard, he may want others to die the same kind of bad death. So it is that we refuse, many times, power to his relatives to bury him in their compounds. In older times the body was thrown into the river. Many, many winches [witches] have a spirit of this sort for their big friend. They use the wicked Nkpulobe to damage all sorts of men and women and young children."

"What is the first act of the soul or spirit at death?" I asked.

"It reports itself to God."

"And does God give it work to do?"

There was a measure of hesitancy and a wrinkling of the brows.

"The Fathers have confused us," he exclaimed irritably. "We believe that the soul, if it has worked well, has finished with the world—at least insofar as that special body is concerned. God may do what He likes, you know. He may tell the Nkpulobe to be born again. He may take it back into Himself."

"What!" I cried. "You believe in the reincarnation of the soul and in the ultimate absorption of everything into God?"

"I don't understand those words. Let me show you. It is like this. The soul goes to God. God thinks. He does with each of His spirits what He deems best. He knows. The soul may be born again into the same family. Yes, we do believe that. But if it has been very evil, it may be condemned, as a *loose* spirit, to wander all around, looking for its own new home. It may become an animal. It often becomes a tree!"

"You amaze me, Bosa! This is karma!"

Bosa frowned his lack of understanding.

"*That?*" he asked apologetically. "I don't understand the word. But it is all very simple. We believe that a change of bodies is the only possible way to explain how soul and spirit are not the same. When a person is alive, he is both Nkpulobe and Moa Moa. He is a spirit, and he is also a soul. During the time that he is loose, after death, he has lost his Nkpulobe until God decides what work he shall do for the future. Therefore, for a short time, he is simply a wandering spirit."

"Tell me more of this rite of second burial," I said. "I begin to see now what it means. The soul has to be facilitated in its effort to sever all earthly bonds, so that God may have the greater freedom to deal with its future?"

"So!" Bosa nodded approvingly. "Immediately after death, there is a place where all the souls meet together. During the time that they are waiting for the second burial, they exist on a kind of leaf which we call Okazi. Until the priests have given them final release they are not properly Nkpulobe—they are simply Moa Moa. We fire guns, shout, and make plenty of noisy play, so as to frighten away the evil spirits, who might otherwise molest the newly dead or entice it away from its honest mission."

"Logical enough, in all truth," I confessed. "Is it at the time of the *second* burial that the soul seeks its Maker for a final verdict regarding the future?" Bosa nodded. "The first burial, then, is a sort of passport into the Great Land of the Dead. The second burial is the passport into the presence of God Himself, Who is the Ruler of the Land of Spirit? . . . Is that correct?"

"Yes. It is at the moment of our rite of second burial that God decides what He will do. The soul must either remain in the World of Heaven [I think that Bosa meant 'in paradise' or 'with God'] until Cuku gives it another body to hold. Maybe, because of its evil life, it is condemned to wander all around, learning sense, and watching other souls pass to and fro."

"When such spirits are seen, Bosa, do they inevitably belong to the same locality?"

The youth looked at me attentively.

"Do you mean whether spirits travel to strange places?"

"Yes. Or is there something that attracts them to the scenes of their earth life?"

My suggestion was confirmed by a grave nod. "If a native of our country dies far away, even so far away as England, his soul must come back straight to Onitsha. The place where are all the relations and friends who have already died, we call Ama Nri. The Nri is the best and most kingly family of all this Ibo country."

I asked Bosa about dreams. "Tell me," I said. "I know that you Onitsha people attach great importance to your thoughts during sleep. But when dead persons come to you at night, do you look upon them as souls? Or are they merely the thinkings of your own mind, while the body is fast asleep?"

Bosa opened his eyes widely and his lips curled.

"But . . . ! Don't you *know* that every soul has the power to leave its body while the body sleeps? And if this be so, how should you doubt that the dead are our friends and visitors? Of *course* the people, dead or alive, who come to us in our dreams are the *real* people we know! All men are free to dream, and all men are free to do what they like with their souls while in the dream state. When a man is asleep, whether at night or in the day, he can send his soul into the Unknown. Sometimes the dead pay visits—sometimes the living!

"Make you remember. We had a watchman once. He used to put his soul into the body of a fox. It was after the other watchman had been murdered. He said he preferred to wander all about the compound during the night. While he was a fox, he left his own body fast asleep inside the shed. Don't you remember the night we fought?"

I *did* remember, and I chuckled aloud.

I had been sitting, during the whole of a chilly night in March 1911, over my manuscripts. It had been a lonely vigil, but I was happy and full of life. The clock pointed to half past two. Suddenly there was a gunshot. This was succeeded by a wild clamor and the noise of angry voices. My nerves were none too steady in those disturbed days. But I seized my revolver from the bed and ran, hotfoot, into the compound.

Arriving there, I found Bosa struggling fiercely with the watchman.

The man seemed well-nigh demented, and was growling and yelling like some wild beast. Bosa had him by the shoulders. The legs of each assailant were clutched tensely, and I could see that Bosa's big task was to keep the man from reaching his gun, which was leaning, barrel upward, against the wall. Bosa's gun lay on the ground under their struggling feet. Only a few yards away a fox was kicking convulsively in its death agonies, the blood oozing sluggishly from its neck.

Meanwhile, Bosa's voice seemed to be wildly urging the watchman to recall who, what, and where he was—for the man appeared to be stupefied, bemused, or utterly crazy. . . . It was a full five minutes before he recovered his senses. Then he sank down on the ground, in a listless way, and began to sob. He asked what was the matter, as though he had only just awakened. The fox had just given its last kick and rolled over, quite dead.

I had watched this scene wonderingly. What it all signified I did not trouble to ask. Nor did the somnolence of a watchman amaze me. I went back to my manuscripts, and thence, as Mr. Pepys has it, "very tired to bed."

The trend of Bosa's present hint was too occult for serious consideration—that the fox *was* the watchman, that Bosa had (unwittingly) shot the fox, that the watchman had only recovered his reason when the fox was dead, and that during the prolonged period of the animal's death throes, the man was insane!

The Devil Worshippers

(Various)

The religion of the Yezidis, or devil worshippers, resembles in many respects that of the Baal worshippers. In Mesopotamia, in the highland district of Amadiyah, is the valley of Skeikh Adi. It is a picturesque glen, the hillsides well wooded, with rivulets babbling and sparkling in the sunshine, shut in from the other world by mountains. But charming as the valley appears, it is shunned by Christian, Jew, and Muslim alike as accursed, for it contains the tomb of Sheikh Adi, the founder of the sect who worships Satan, to which the Yezidi pilgrims resort annually on the occasion of their festival.

In the middle of the glen is the tomb, a fair-size white edifice with a double spire and spacious outbuildings. A little higher up in the valley is a small building of plain construction, windowless, with a

From: A. M. Judd, "Curious Forms of Worship: Devil-Worshippers," *Occult Review* 11 (1910): 250–57.

single spire, and dazzlingly white. The front faces the rising sun, and the slender point rising from the roof catches the last lingering rays of the same when sinking. At the back of this edifice are sheltered pens, in which are stabled seven white cows. These animals are sacred, dedicated to Sheikh Shems, "the sun," and the building to which they are attached is the Sanctuary of the White Cow, the temple of the devil worshippers.

Here, annually, generally in August, a solemn initiation is celebrated, at which the Kak, or fakir-saint of the Devil's Order, is present. The ceremony takes place at night, and as the shadows lengthen, the devil worshippers gather by hundreds in front of the Sanctuary of the White Cow. The men dress in spotless white robes and wear white turbans, above which rise the tops of the black caps from which they derive their designation Kara-bash or blackheads. The priests wear yellow stoles, and the fakirs of the fraternity black. All wear vests of white cotton and the twisted black cord, the *mahak* or bridle, which goes around the neck and falls down in front and never leaves a Yezidi night or day during life and is buried with him when he dies. This cord is the mark of the true Yezidi, the born and bred Satan worshipper, as the *Kissil mahak*, or red bridle, is the distinctive token of the Kissil Bashi, the Baal worshippers of the Upper Tigris.

The Yezidis use no form of prayer and have no written liturgy, reading and writing being prohibited to all, whether layman or cleric, with the solitary exception of a single family, to which is entrusted, as a hereditary charge, the reading of the Yezidi Bible, the Jalaoo, which with the Mashafi Rash constitutes their Black Book.

When the sun begins to dip below the hilltops, the worshippers rise and hold out their hands so as to catch its last rays. They cover their faces with both hands and kiss them, then fall upon their knees, bend their heads, touch the earth with their fingertips, and gently tap their foreheads.

When the sun has sunk, a white-robed priest, who has charge of the sanctuary, emerges from the pen in the rear and fixes half a dozen small lighted lamps in niches in front of the building. Immediately lights flash from every corner of the valley in answer to the signal that the ceremony is about to begin. The sound of music is heard in the distance, and the lights of a procession are seen approaching from the tomb of Sheikh Adi. It is the procession of the Angel Peacock, the sacred symbol of the devil worshippers. The Yezidis part right and left as the bearers of the Holy Sanjak come near to allow them to pass on to the temple. In front march the servitors carrying torches; then come five musicians playing upon flutes and tambourines; following these is a priest in yellow robes, holding aloft the sacred emblem of Satan worship, closely covered, the rear being brought up by a dozen black-robed fakirs. The party go around to the back of the temple and pass in by a low door in the rear and descend to the underground vault which is the sanctuary of the Yezidis. Here are assembled priests, elders, and fakirs, and at the farther end of the temple are ranged the white-robed women of the Faik-raya, or convent attached to the tomb with the lady superior in front wearing a white tuft in her headdress.

In the center of the sanctuary is a square stone altar, and behind this stand, the spiritual head of the Yezidis on one side and the emir of the community on the other. Between these is the Kak, or chief of the fakir brotherhood, who takes precedence of everybody and whose person and clothing are esteemed so holy that no one dares touch them.

Above the altar hangs a single lamp; in front of it, upon the ground, lie two human figures. One is attired in spotless white cerements, the other in the full robes of a fakir. One is the corpse of a dead mendicant brother, the other is the body of a living novice who is to become his successor in the order. In the gloom it is hard to distinguish the living from the dead, for both faces are livid and drawn. It is scarcely to be wondered at in the case of the novice, for he has been in underground solitude for forty days, fasting each day from sunrise to nightfall.

When all have taken their places, the bearer of the sacred emblem marches into the center and, taking his stand beside the Kak, unveils the Sanjak. It is the bronze image of a peacock, perched on the central branch of a triple candelabrum.

The connection of the peacock with the worship of the devil is thus explained. When the Almighty created the hawk, which destroys, Satan created the peacock, which is both beautiful and harmless, in order to show that all his works were not necessarily evil. It is also said that it was in the form of a peacock that the devil tempted Eve in paradise, and it is through a peacock that Satan will eventually regain his place in the celestial hierarchy.

At the sight of the Angel Peacock unveiled, the worshippers raise their hands above their heads, exclaiming, *"Khoda! Khoda!"* dropping them mechanically after. The *kawals*, or musicians, start a plaintive melody in a minor key, in which the women and the Pirs join, though they do not understand the words of the hymn. When the singing ceases, the Kak begins the ceremony of initiation. At a sign from him, two black-robed fakirs raise the neophyte from the ground. He prostrates himself before the sacred peacock and proceeds to divest himself of the white garment in which he is attired, and kneeling, shrouds with it the corpse of the dead fakir beside which he has been lying. Then the Kak invests him with the robes of his order, consisting of a coarse black gown worn over the white cotton drawers and vest which are obligatory portions of a fakir's costume, a black cord about the waist and a black cap, which the neophyte must have made with his own hands. Finally, the Kak throws over him the mahak, which never leaves him again in life or death. The Pirs wear the twisted cord short, so that its ends are concealed beneath their flaming yellow robes, but the fakirs wear it outside their black garments, so that it is always seen.

The initiate now walks slowly around the temple, passing the fakirs, each of whom spits in his face as he passes. This is done to avert evil and misfortune from him.

The first duty of the new-made fakir is to attend to his brethren present. He procures from the *tshavish* a pot of oil and some wick, which he immerses in it, and lights from the sacred lamp. He then walks around, holding the light, in front of the priests and fakirs. Each bends over it, holding his hand out as though to feel its warmth, then strokes his beard or chin, afterward kissing his fingers and lightly tapping his forehead.

The peacock procession is then re-formed, with the Kak, the emir, and the sheikh at its head, and regains the open air by a different ascent, which brings the members out of the opposite side of the small building above, where the white cows are stabled. The procession passes through the ranks of white-clothed worshippers, men and women, outside. The sacred peacock is now borne uncovered, and when the Yezidis see it, they fall prostrate on the ground with cries of ecstasy and devotion. The procession winds slowly down the glen toward the tomb of the founder of the sect. In the rear a Tshavish leads one of the sacred white cows dedicated to the sun, her horns adorned with garlands of flowers. The women chant hymns, to the accompaniment of flutes and tambourines, and the rest of the worshippers follow. When the tomb is reached, a halt is made in the courtyard surrounding the main building, the white heifer is killed, and its heart is cast in front of the emblem of the Angel Peacock. The carcass is then cut up and distributed among the Yezidi worshippers.

The ceremony is over. One by one the lights are extinguished, the Yezidis return to their respective abodes, and the sanctuary of the devil worshippers is given over to darkness and silence.

It would seem as though this worship was originally sun worship. The Semites, when they gained predominance in Mesopotamia, were, to a large extent, sun worshippers.

Curiously enough, in Acadian times, the moon was represented as masculine and the sun god as his offspring. The moon god was named Sin (the bright). Tammuz was his son. Istar, the evening star, was the latter's wife. Later she developed into Ishtar, or Ashtoreth of Semitic worship. At Sepharvaim there was a temple believed to have already grown old and decayed in 3800 B.C., which was the center of a vigorous worship, with many priests, scribes, and schools. The fact that the temple of the devil worshippers faces the rising sun, that the slender spire from the roof catches the last lingering rays of the westering orb, that the worshippers stretch their hands to catch these last rays, and that the white cows are dedicated to the sun, would seem to point to the fact of some connection of the Satan cult with that of the sun.

A short time ago an interesting account appeared in a daily paper of the seizure of a young Yezidi by a Turkish recruiting party. By the laws of conscription, a Yezidi is forced to serve in the Ottoman army. When the party arrives to take the recruit, wails and yells of despair are raised by the relatives. Men, women, and children kiss his eyes, cheeks, mouth, and hands. Throwing themselves on the ground, they even embrace his legs and feet with every manifestation of extreme grief. The conscript appears quite dazed with sorrow. He caresses over and over again his weeping kindred, whom he will never see again. He kisses the walls and hearth of the cabin in which he was born and wets them with his tears, for he well knows he is about to quit them forever. When, accompanied by his Turkish captors, he leaves the village, the lamentations of the villagers cease, and as though nothing has happened, they resume their work. Never again is the conscript's name mentioned. On joining his regiment, the young Yezidi becomes a Muslim. His kindred affect to forget him. Were he to approach the village from which he has been forcibly dragged away, every Yezidi, even his nearest and dearest—father, mother, sister, brother, friend, and sweetheart—would drive him away with curses, pelting him with stones, for he is accursed.

The Yezidis make no proselytes; a Yezidi must be born such and must marry in the sect. A candidate for the priestly office must be the son of a priest. There are six priests of a superior grade who with the Kak form the Seven Holy Ones, or hierarchy of the devil worshippers, and there are twenty-four of a subordinate grade. All wear the black cord around the neck, with the exception of the Kak, who wears one of white more intricately knotted in front.

The Yezidis say that their Black Book was written by the angel Reziel for the advantage of humankind but was withheld from Adam by the Creator of light. Satan, the great angel whom the Yezidis revere, stretched himself from the seven spheres wherein he was supreme and, reaching heaven, took the volume from Reziel and offered it to Adam. Adam, misled, refused it, and to punish him the book was withheld from his posterity for forty generations. At the expiration of that time, it was revealed to Sheikh Adi, who founded the sect of the devil worshippers. The book is written in an unknown character and cannot be deciphered save by the person who holds the office of Kak.

The Black Book is in the charge of the Seven Sleepers and is only removed from their custody on the occasion of the annual sacrifice. It is kept in the mausoleum of Sheikh Adi, in a vault cut in the rocky hillside. In the center is a square stone block, above which a flaring oil lamp is suspended; against one side are ranged seven smaller blocks, on each of which a figure is seated, propped up against the wall, attired in the robes of a Kak, with the distinctive white bridle. Each of these is a skeleton, and on the block in the middle lies the sacred book they guard. There are never more nor less than seven. When a Kak dies, it is here, in the presence of the departed, that the new head of the Yezidis always assumes the white mahak, which is the badge of supremacy, and with his own hands removes the oldest of his sleeping predecessors in the office of Kak and makes up the tale of seven with the latest, whom he succeeds.

Yezidis are enjoined to wear white, never to have anything of metal in their attire, to abstain from using anything that is blue, and to lead quiet orderly lives. In fact, they are said to be a quiet and peaceable people, which is somewhat singular, considering the abhorrence in which they are held by the general mass of the population round-about, and the records of blood-curdling tales told about them by the orthodox. To the Christian, Muslim, and Jew alike, the Yezidi is an object of detestation, and the mere sight of the black head covering that proclaims the devil-worshipping sectary is enough to send men, women, and children scurrying out of his way. By these persons the Kak, who only goes abroad at night, is looked upon as something worse than the satanic master he professes to serve.

The Kaks are supposed to be incarnations of the angel Reziel. Sheikh Adi was the first in whom Reziel became incarnate.

The Yezidis believe that the dead of their sect gather in the valley to celebrate the festival, just as the living do. When the first anniversary of Sheikh Adi's death came around generations ago, the faithful Yezidis flocked from all parts to join in the solemn yearly sacrifice. It was found on the day of the ceremony, when the worshippers met in the valley, that they were so tightly packed that there was no room to move; they could scarcely breathe, and began to cry out. Amazed at the sound, the Kak of those days turned from the sacrifice and saw that the dead of ages past were crowding there among the living. "Let each living man," he called out in sonorous tones, "remove the cord that is around his waist, and tie it around his neck." Each did so, and immediately the dead began to fade away and disappear, so there was ample room for the living. Since that time every living Yezidi wears the mahak around his neck as long as he breathes; also since then, the dead no longer mingle with the living in the valley but come to the shrine of the Sheikh only when the living, with the mahak to distinguish them, have completed the annual sacrifice and its accompanying rites.

The Yezidis believe that when the creation of man was resolved upon, Satan opposed it. In the shape of the beautiful bird he had created, not in that of the serpent, he entered the garden of Eden and in this guise induced Eve to taste the fruit of the tree of knowledge. If Adam had been willing to worship him, he would have helped the man and woman to eat of the tree of life also, and they and their posterity would never have known death. It was because Satan created the peacock that the Yezidis take it as the symbol of their worship.

It is only after long waiting that a priest has a chance of becoming one of the Seven Holy Ones of the sect. The candidate spends three days and nights alone in the underground temple, in company with the deceased, whose body is placed on the altar. Only bread and water is allowed him during the vigil. On the third night, in the presence of the remaining priests, he sacrifices a black cock upon the altar and sprinkles himself and the deceased with the blood; he then exchanges garments with the dead, lastly taking the mahak to the Kak, who secures it around his neck, thus making him a full priest of the higher grade and one of the sacred Seven Holy Ones.

It may be remarked as rather a curious circumstance that while the peacock and its beautiful feathers are accounted unlucky because of its connection with the fallen angel, the number seven, likewise connected with the Satan cult (there being seven white cows, and Seven Holy Ones, Seven Sleepers neither more nor less) has never lost its reputation of being a lucky one.

Dr. A. Hume Griffith, who conducted a medical mission among the people of Mesopotamia, acquired a good deal of information regarding the Yezidis, who inhabit the mountains around Mosul. He spent a week with the sheikh at his mountain castle at Baadai. This tribe numbered about twenty thousand and lived among the mountain fastnesses. They are very hostile to the Turks, who are unable to subdue them, owing to the inaccessibility of their homes. They will not admit that they worship the devil, although there is ample evidence to that effect. Their priests are clad in white and carry with them a wand of office, surmounted by a brass peacock. These are most sacred, and it is the boast of the Yezidis that none have ever been lost. No Yezidi will even utter a word containing the letters *sh*. At the entrance to their chief temple is the figure of a serpent. This is looked upon with great veneration and is kept black by means of charcoal. Each worshipper kisses this serpent before entering the temple. Their religious rites, which include the use of hypnotism, are only practiced between sunset and sunrise. Some time ago the Turks captured their shrine but were unable to make any progress with Muslim teaching and lately handed it back to the Yezidis. The devil worshippers are afraid to venture into the towns, though some of them used to come down to the doctor for medical treatment.

Demonic Possession of a Young Man

(Angola)

The following information is obtained from the verbal communication of Mr. Heli Chatelain:

A black servant named Jeremiah, who accompanied me to America, belonged on his father's side to the Mbacca and on his mother's to the Mbamba. Before coming in contact with Europeans, he had been subject, at irregular intervals, to the possession of a certain spirit, the name and individuality of this particular demon being supposed to be discoverable by the kind of gestures and actions performed by the person under his influence. In this condition, Jeremiah would rush to the woods, climb trees, and howl, the spirit being apparently a dweller in the forests. After the arrival of the missionaries, this tendency entirely disappeared, to his great relief. Of the reality of the spiritual possession, however, he continued to be profoundly convinced, conceiving that it stood on the same foundation as any other fact of experience.

While the patient is in this state, he is addressed as if he were the spirit himself, and his utterances are conceived to be those of the demon. It might happen that a possessed person would feel called on to prophesy, that is, to speak in the name of the demon, and in such case he might express himself in a remarkable way, using words the sense of which is understood but which are not employed save in prophetic utterance. Great reverence is paid to persons in this state, as representing the spirits, and their advice and counsel may be followed.

It may be added that belief in the fact of such possession is not confined to Africans, many priests in Angola entertaining a firm assurance of the real existence of the demons. Padre Cavazzi, the

From: "Demoniacal Possession in Angola, Africa (attributed to Heli Chatelain)," *Journal of American Folk-Lore* 6 (1893): 258.

author of a valuable work relating to Angola, writing in the seventeenth century, relates his own encounter with a goat locally worshipped, in whose aspect he saw the expression and fury of the fiend himself. A fetish, so-called, is merely a means of coming in contact with these spirits and acquiring power over them, in the same manner as in sorcery a hair of a person or some other article belonging to him must be owned in order to acquire control over that individual.

Possessed by an Animal-Spirit

(Abyssinia)

The possession by an animal-spirit is not always connected with totemism. In Abyssinia a person may imagine himself to be possessed by a hyena-spirit and behave in every way as does that animal. One woman fancied she would like a little donkey-flesh, so to satisfy her strange taste she seized hold by her teeth to the hinder part of one which happened to be near. Off went the astonished beast at a pace that nothing in the form of persuasion will lead him to adopt for the gratification of man. Off too, clinging tight with her teeth to his haunches, went the frenzied girl.

The exorcist makes the patient smell a rag in which a bone of a hyena and other things are tied—just as the Hausa in Nigeria holds out a bone—and after this a sacrifice is made, some fragments from the feast being buried for the demon should it return. In the Straits Settlements, a money-spirit may take possession of a person, causing him or her to behave like the animal.

The ordinary spirit possession then is an everyday affair, coming on naturally or being brought on by movement, music, or a narcotic, but

From: A. J. N. Tremearne, *The Ban of the Bori: Demons and Demon-Dancing in West and North Africa* (London: Heath, Cranton & Ousely, Ltd., 1914).

I have not seen in any book an indication that a long cast of characters behaves in a special set manner for each different spirit, as is the case with the Masu-Bori. Perhaps there has never been much more than the mere excitement and oracular speech with most other peoples, and yet this seems unlikely—though but few of the writers whose works I have seen have recorded anything further—for it is only natural that, by and by, particular steps should be associated with individual spirits, especially where they have become great gods with distinct powers.

The Bori performance includes both the Arab *zikr* (in which the dancers stand in line and gradually work themselves into a frenzy by swaying their bodies about and by calling upon Allah) and the *zar* (possession by which a spirit makes the person comatose and refuses to leave until the victim has been given a present), yet it is much more, for there is no representation of any special actions in either of these. Magajiya and some others whirl like the dervishes, and Bori dancing generally resembles the rite of the Aisawias to a great extent, for they also represent the movements of several animals; and here too the performers torture themselves and seem to feel no pain. Still, there seems to be no great festival during which scores of spirits are represented, as is the case among the Hausas, and we must look for another cause than that of the people running amok.

Stories of Bouda Possession

(Ethiopia)

I n the neighborhood of Adoua there was a woman who was said to have died, and was buried with ceremony in the churchyard. The following day a man came to one of the priests and offered him a sum of money for the body, pledging himself to strict secrecy. The bargain was concluded, and the unscrupulous priest allowed the stranger, who was a blacksmith, to disinter and carry off the corpse. On the way to the market the blacksmith passed the house where the deceased lady's family lived, and he usually rode or drove a remarkably fine donkey which, strangely enough, on passing the house or any of the old woman's children, brayed loudly and endeavored to run toward them.

At first no notice was taken of this odd behavior on the part of an ass, but at last one of the sons grew suspicious and exclaimed, "I am sure that ass is my mother!"

Accordingly Bouda (possessing spirit), ass, and all were seized and brought to the hut, much to the apparent satisfaction of the animal, which rubbed its nose against the young man and was even said to shed tears of joy on the occasion.

On being charged with the offense of sorcery, the Bouda tried to make light of it and denied the accusation, but at last by dint of threats and promises he was induced to confess that he had turned the old woman into a donkey, she having been not really dead but in a trance, into which he had purposely thrown her. His power, he asserted, was sufficient to change the external appearance, but not to alter the mind of his victim. Hence it was that the old woman, or rather donkey, possessed human feelings, which she had displayed in her endeavors to enter her former habitation and in her recognition of her children. The Bouda, moreover, agreed to restore her human appearance, and

From: Frank Hamel, *Human Animals* (New York: Frederick A. Stokes Co., 1916).

began his exorcism. As he proceeded, she by degrees assumed her natural form, and the change was almost complete, when one of the sons, blinded by his rage, forgot the promises of pardon which the Bouda had exacted and drove his spear through his heart. The incantation not being entirely finished, one foot remained in the shape of the hoof of an ass and continued so until her death, which was not till many years afterward.

Still another story belonging to the same class concerns two brothers who lived in Gojam. One of them, having transformed himself into a horse, ass, or cow, was sold in the market and driven out of town by his purchaser. Directly night had closed the eyes of his new master in sleep, the Bouda took on human form again and walked quietly home. The brothers were known to sell cattle in the market so frequently that people became suspicious, because they did not know where their stock was kept and they often had no beasts in their yard even the very day before the sales. Besides, it soon leaked out that every animal sold made its escape the same night and was never heard of again. Then a purchaser who had been twice taken in by the brothers determined to discover how the fraud was carried out. One market day he bought a fine horse from one of the brothers and rode off upon it, but no sooner had he left the market town behind him than he dismounted and drove a knife through the animal's heart. Then he walked back to the marketplace and, meeting the vendor, told him that in a fit of passion he had killed the beautiful animal he had just bought. The Bouda gave a start but managed to conceal his grief till he entered his house, when he burst forth into lamentations and rubbed the skin off his forehead, as is the custom when a near relative dies. To his inquisitive neighbors he declared that his favorite brother had been robbed and murdered in the Galla country, whither he had traveled in order to purchase horses. It was said, however, that he afterward sent no more animals to the marketplace for sale.

The Makololo also believe that certain people can transform themselves into animals, and they call such persons Pondoro. Livingstone came across a Pondoro in the Kebrasa Hills and heard that this gentleman was in the habit of assuming the shape of a lion, which he retained for days and sometimes even for a month, during which time he wandered in the woods where his wife had built a den for him and took care that he was provided with food and drink. No one was allowed into the den except the Pondoro and his wife, and no strangers were permitted even to lay a gun against any of the trees in the neighborhood of the den or against any shanty owned by the Pondoro. The were-lion used his gift to go hunting in the village. After a few days had passed, his faithful spouse scented her returning husband and provided him with a certain kind of medicine or ointment by which it became possible for him to change into a man again. But she had to hurry over this duty, so that the lion might not catch sight of her and, falling upon her, devour even her.

After the Pondoro was once more human, he returned to the village and asked the inhabitants to help him carry home his prey. One of the odd things about this were-lion was that he always trembled if he smelled gunpowder, and he sometimes overacted his part. Livingstone asked the natives to make him show off while he was watching, offering a reward for the performance, but they refused, saying, "If we ask him to do so, he may change while we are asleep and kill us." It was owing to his distaste for the smell of gunpowder that it was made punishable to rest muskets against his den.

In the same district the belief is also current that the souls of departed chiefs enter into lions "and render them sacred." Thus when a hungry lion prowled around the camp where a freshly killed buffalo lay, a native servant harangued him loudly in between his roars, saying, "What sort of a chief do you call yourself, sneaking around here in the dark trying to steal our buffalo meat? You're a pretty chief, you are! You've no more courage than a scavenger beetle. Why don't you kill your own dinner?" The Pondoro took no notice except to roar the louder, so a second native took the matter up and expostulated in most dignified terms as to the impropriety of the conduct of "a great chief like him" prowling around in the dark, "trying like a hyena to steal the food of strangers."

A piece of meat dipped in strychnine brought the lion-chief to his senses, and he took his departure. It is not to be wondered at that such things occur in a country where the natives regard their chiefs as almighty and infallible. The extent of their faith in him appears from the story of one Chief Chibisa, who placed a powerful "medicine" in the river and told his people they might safely enter the water as it was a protection against the bite of crocodiles. Thereupon the people bathed there without fear of these dangerous reptiles.

Du Chaillu in *Ashango Land* tells the story of a young lad, Akosho, who declared that he had been turned into a leopard and, feeling a craving for blood, had gone forth into the forest, where he had killed two men. After each murder he said he had taken on human shape. His chief Akondogo could not believe the story, but Akosho led him to the scene where lay the mangled bodies of the victims. It appears that the boy suffered from lycanthropy, and he was burned to death in full view of the tribe.

There once was a similar case of possession in which the patient thought herself to be a hyena. One evening when he was in his house at Gaffat, a woman began to cry fearfully and ran up and down the road on her hands and feet like a wild beast, quite unconscious of what she was doing. The natives said to him, "This is the Bouda, and if it is not driven out of her she will die." A crowd gathered around and everything possible was done to relieve her condition but without avail. She howled and roared in an unnatural manner and most powerful voice. At last a blacksmith, who was said to have secret connection with the Evil One, was called in to see what he could do. The woman obeyed his orders at once. He took hold of her hand and dropped the juice of a white onion or garlic into her nostril, and then he questioned the evil spirit by whom she was supposed to be possessed, as follows:

"Why did you possess this poor woman?"

"I was allowed to do so," came the answer through her lips.

"What is your name?"

"Gebroo."

"And your country?"

"Gojam."

"How many people have you already taken possession of?"

"Forty people—men and women."

"You must now leave this woman's body."

"I will do so on one condition."

"What is it?"

"I want to eat the flesh of a donkey."

The long cross-examination being concluded, the evil spirit was granted his strange request. A donkey was brought, and the possessed woman ran hastily upon the animal and bit the flesh out of the creature's back, and though the donkey kicked and started off, she clung to it as though fastened by leather thongs.

After the performance had continued for some time, the man recalled the woman, and a jar of prepared liquid with which much filth had been mixed was set down in a hidden spot where she could not see it. When, however, the exorcist exclaimed, "Go and look for your drink," she started off on all fours to the place where the jar stood and drank the whole of its contents.

When she returned, the blacksmith said, "Take up this stone." Although the stone in question was too large for her to move under natural conditions, she placed it on her head with ease and began spinning around, until the stone flew off on one side and she fell on to the ground. Then the exorcist said to the people around, "Take her away to bed. The Bouda has left her."

In a similar case the woman's symptoms began in a sort of fainting fit. Her fingers were clenched in the palms of her hands, the eyes were glazed, she nostrils distended, and the whole body stiff and inflexible. Suddenly a hideous laugh, like that of a hyena, burst from her and she began running about on all fours. The cure was brought about in much the same way as in the preceding case.

Asiki, or the Little Beings

(West Africa)

People believe that Asiki (singular Isiki) were once human beings, but that wicked men, wizards and witches, or other persons who assert that they have *memba* (witchcraft powers) caught them when they were children and could not defend themselves, nor could their cries for help be heard when playing among the bushes on the edge of the forest. These wicked persons cut off the ends of the children's tongues, so that they can never again speak or inform on their captors. They carry them away, and hide

From: Robert Hamill Nassau, *Fetichism in West Africa* (New York: Charles Scribner's Sons, 1904).

them in a secret place where they cannot be found. There they are subjected to a variety of witchcraft treatment that alters their natures so that they are no longer mortal. This treatment checks their entire physical, mental, and moral growth. They cease to remember or care for their former homes or their human relatives, and they accept all the witchcraft of their captors. Even the hair of their head changes, growing in long, straight black tresses down their backs. They wear a curious comb-shaped ornament on the back of the head. It is not stiff or capable of being used as a comb, and is made of some twisted fiber resembling hair. The Asiki value it almost as a part of their life.

These Asiki will sometimes be seen walking in paths on dark nights, and people meet them coming toward them. It is believed that in their meeting, if a person is fearless by natural bravery, or by fetish power as a wizard or witch, and dares to seize the Isiki and snatch away the "comb," the possession of this ornament will bring him riches. But whoever succeeds in obtaining that comb will not be allowed to remain in peaceful possession of it. The poor Isiki will be seen at night wandering about the spot where its treasure was lost, trying to obtain it again.

It happened in the year 1901 that there was a report, even in civilized Gabon, about these Asiki—that two of them were seen near a certain place on the public road at that part of the town of Libreville known as the "Plateau," where live most of the French traders and government officers. A certain Frenchman, who is known as a Free-mason, in returning from his 8 P.M. dinner at his boardinghouse to his dwelling place, observed that a small figure was walking on one side of the road, keeping pace with him. He accosted it, "Who are you?" There was no answer; only the figure kept on walking, advancing and retreating before him.

Also, a few nights later, a Negro clerk of a white trader met this small being on that very road and near the spot where the Frenchman had met it, and it began to chase the Negro. He ran, and came frightened to his employer's office and told him what had happened. His employer did not believe him, laughed at his fears, and told him he was not telling the truth. The very next night the Frenchman, the trader, and other white men and Negro women were sitting in conversation. The trader told the story of his clerk, whereupon the Frenchman said, "Your clerk did not lie; he told the truth. I have myself met that small being two or three times, but I made no effort to catch it." The women told him of the comb-ornament which Asiki were believed to wear, and of the pride with which Asiki regarded it and the value it would be to anyone who could obtain it. Then the Frenchman replied, "As the little being is so small, the very next time I see it I will try to catch it and bring it here, so that you can see it and know that this story is actually true."

On a subsequent night they two—the Frenchman and the trader—went out to see whether they could meet the Isiki. They did not meet with it that night, but a few evenings later the Frenchman went alone and met the Isiki near the place where it had first been seen. The Frenchman ran toward it and tried to catch it, but it being very agile, it eluded his grasp. But though he failed to seize its body, he succeeded in catching hold of its comb, and snatched it away and ran rapidly with it toward his house. It did not consist of any hard material as a real comb but was made of strands resembling the Isiki's hair and braided into a comb-like shape. The little being was displeased and ran after him in order to recover the ornament. Having no tongue, it could not speak, but holding out one hand pleadingly and with the other motioning to the back of its head, it made pathetic sounds in its throat, thus inarticulately begging that its treasure should be given back to it. On nearing the light of the Frenchman's house, it retreated, and he showed the ornament to other white men and some native women. (So positive was my informant that the names of these men and women were mentioned to me.) He said to the trader, "You doubted your clerk's story. Have you ever seen anything like this in all your life?" They all said they had not. It was reported that many other persons hearing of it went there to see it.

From that night, the little being was often seen by other Negroes. It was always holding out its hand and seemingly pleading for the return of its comb. This made the Negroes afraid to pass on that road at night. The Frenchman also often met it. It did not chase him but followed slowly, pleading with its hands in dumb show and occasionally making a grunting sound in its throat. It did this so persistently and annoyingly that the Frenchman was wearied with its begging and determined that the next night he would yield up the comb. But he went prepared with scissors. He found the little being following him. He stopped, and it approached. He held out his hand with the ornament. As the Isiki jumped forward to snatch at it, the Frenchman tried to lay hold of its body, but it was so very agile that, though it had come so near as to be able to take the comb from the Frenchman's hand, it so quickly twisted itself aside as to elude his grasp. He however succeeded in getting his hands in its long hair and snipped off a lock with his scissors. The Isiki ran away with its recovered treasure and did not seem to resent the loss of a portion of its hair. This hair the Frenchman is said to have shown to his companions at their next evening conversation, and I was given to understand that he had sent it to France. It was straight, not woolly, and long.

These Asiki are supposed not to die, and it is also believed that they can propagate; but so complete has been the parent's change under witchcraft power that the Isiki babe will be only an Isiki and cannot grow up to be a human being.

It is asserted that Asiki are now made by a sort of creative power (just as leopards and bush cats are claimed to be made, and used invisibly) by witch doctors.

King Solomon and Ashmedai

(Turkey)

When King Solomon was about to build the Temple, he was in great perplexity, for according to the command of the Lord, no iron tool was to be used in rearing the sacred edifice. He called all the wise men of Israel together and asked them what he was to do under the circumstances.

An aged counselor said, "O King, there is a worm called Shameer, which, when placed upon stone or iron, cuts it in pieces in any shape desired. Moses used it when he made the breastplate for Aaron the high priest. But his Shameer is now in the hands of the demons, and they have hidden it, none knows where."

From: Lucy Mary Jane Garnett, *The Women of Turkey and Their Folk-Lore: The Jewish Women*, part 2 (London: David Nutt, 1891).

King Solomon dismissed the assembly, and as he had power over the evil spirits, he made two of them appear before him and asked them, "Which of you keeps the Shameer concealed?"

They replied, trembling, "O King and Master, Ashmedai our lord only knows where this precious worm is to be found."

"And where is Ashmedai?" asked the king.

They replied, "He is far away, on such and such a mountain. There he has his abode, and has digged a well, out of which he drinks, and when he has done so, he puts a large stone on the mouth of the well, seals it with his seal, and lies down to sleep."

"That is enough. You may go," said Solomon.

He then called Benajah, his chief captain, told him all about the Shameer and Ashmedai, and commanded him to go and find them, at the same time advising him what to do in order to get possession of Ashmedai. He also gave the chief captain a chain, upon which was engraved the Holy Name, and a ring bearing also the Name, and dismissed him.

Benajah provided himself with several barrels of wine and a good quantity of wool, took the chain and the ring, and went in search of the mountain, which he found, and also the well. He made a hole in the well and let all the water out; then he filled the hole with the wool and bored another hole close to it, into which he emptied the barrels of wine. Having thus filled the well with wine and closed the hole, he hid himself to watch for the arrival of Ashmedai, who soon afterward came up. He examined the stone and the seal on the mouth of the well, found all was right, removed it, and as he was very thirsty, took a large draught of the wine, another, and yet another, and becoming quite intoxicated, fell asleep.

Benajah now approached the King of Evil Spirits with the chain upon which the Sacred Name was impressed. When Ashmedai awoke, he found himself bound and endeavored to break his chain. But Benajah said to him, "It is vain to resist, for thou art bound with the chain on which is the Holy Name. Follow me to King Solomon." Seeing that resistance was useless, he submitted. When they came into his presence, the King of Israel demanded of him the Shameer. Ashmedai was unwilling to reveal the place of its concealment, but was finally compelled to divulge how the worm might be procured, which was again done by the brave Benajah, and the Temple of

Solomon was built in all its glory. The King of the Demons meanwhile languished in chains, while Solomon reveled in luxury.

Said Ashmedai one day to his captor, "Take this chain off from me, and give me thy ring only for a moment, and I will make thee the greatest monarch of the world."

Solomon commanded the chain to be taken off and gave the demon his ring. But no sooner was Ashmedai free than he seized the king and hurled him thousands of miles away, took his ring and threw it into the sea, transformed himself into the likeness of Solomon, and reigned in his stead.

While Ashmedai ruled in Jerusalem, Solomon wandered from place to place announcing that he was the King of the Jews, but people only laughed at him and took him for a madman. Finally he came to Jerusalem, telling the same story, but none would listen to or believe him. Afflicted and cast down, he left the Holy City again, and went toward the seacoast. Before losing sight, however, of its sacred walls, he prostrated himself in prayer before God, asking for pardon and for his restoration to the throne, and then continued his journey to the nearest seaport town. As he approached he met a fisherman, who offered a fish for sale. Solomon bought it and, when he opened the fish, found within it his sacred ring, which Ashmedai had thrown into the sea. The moment he put it on, he felt himself a changed man, that he was again Solomon the King. He returned to his capital, made himself known to the Sanhedrin, and related to them his adventures.

The Council sent for Benajah, who confirmed Solomon's story. They then summoned the women of the royal household and asked them, "Have ye ever seen the feet of him who calleth himself King Solomon?"

They replied, "Nay, for he covers his person with a large mantle so that we cannot see his feet."

This question was put to ascertain whether the supposed king was a demon, for the demons have not human feet but claws like a cock. The Sanhedrin were now persuaded that it was Ashmedai and advised Solomon to enter the royal palace and hold the sacred ring before the impostor. When Ashmedai saw the ring, he shrieked aloud and vanished, and Solomon reigned as before.

Nimm the Terrible

(West Africa)

Just as the Calabar River is looked upon as the home of were-elephants and crocodiles, so the Kwa is the special dwelling place of Nimm the Terrible, who at the call of her women worshippers, sends forth her servants—the beasts which flock down to drink of her waters—to destroy the farms of any who have offended. Sometimes she manifests herself as a huge snake, sometimes as a crocodile. Her priestesses have more power than those of any other cult, and the society which bears her name is strong enough to hold its own against the dreaded Egbo Club itself.

It is during the rainy season that Nimm is most to be dreaded. Once, at the height of the rains, one of my best paddlers was returning with a consignment of goods from Calabar. The party in the canoe was a very friendly one, and all were talking and laughing. Suddenly, as his hand neared the water at the downstroke, the head of a crocodile appeared above the surface. The cruel jaws closed on the man's wrist, and in a flash he was dragged under. "Nimm," whispered the terrified survivors, as they paddled on. "Who knows? Perhaps he had angered his wife, and she prayed to Nimm to avenge her."

From: P. Amaury Talbot, "Through the Land of Witchcraft: Part 1," *Wide World Magazine* 31 (1913): 428–37.

The Demon-Lover

(Turkey)

In the village of Khassekul there lived a poor Jewish girl, fourteen years of age, who supported herself by weaving and dyeing kerchiefs for headdresses. A year had elapsed since her betrothal, and she worked all the more diligently in order to have something to lay by for her trousseau.

One night when the moon was shining brightly, she awoke and, thinking it was dawn, arose and hastened to the shore of the Bosporus to wash the cloth which she had already woven so as to prepare it for dyeing.

While she was thus busily engaged, a beautiful youth, who had approached unperceived, stood before her and asked, in a soft, insinuating voice, "What art thou doing here at this hour?"

The girl now observed what had before escaped her: that it was not day and that she had been deceived by the light of the moon. Still continuing her labor, however, she replied, "I am a maker of kerchiefs, and I am now washing them to make them ready for dyeing."

The youth dropped two pieces of English gold at her feet and disappeared as suddenly as he had come.

The following night she was again deceived by the light of the moon and returned to the shore of the Bosporus. Arriving there, she suddenly remembered for the first time the incident of the previous night. The youth was now waiting for her, and as she drew near, he advanced to meet her, placed gold bracelets on her finely molded arms, and said, "Thou for me; I for thee!"

The girl was very much startled and was about to make some reply to the youth, when he again disappeared.

Several months passed, and the girl still continued to weave and dye her kerchiefs. One day, when she was sweeping the room in which she lived, she found a gold piece similar to those which the youth had given her in the fair moonlight and with which she had

From: Lucy Mary Jane Garnett, *The Women of Turkey and Their Folk-Lore: The Jewish Women*, part 2 (London: David Nutt, 1891).

gradually purchased the materials for her trousseau. But from this time the image of the youth was always present to her sight, and his strange words, "Thou for me; I for thee," were constantly ringing in her ears. Yet though she frequently went by night to their former meeting place, he did not appear again. One day, however, he suddenly entered her apartment and offered flour in a silver dish to bake sweet cakes for him.

"I will do whatever my lord commands his slave," she replied, and began to mix the flour with wine, eggs, and sugar. While doing so, she observed that the youth had disappeared; but when the cakes were baked and ready for eating, he stood before her again, as if he had never left her.

The day of the betrothed girl's marriage at length arrived, and as is usual on such occasions, before the wedding night her relatives carried the painted wooden box containing her trousseau to the house of the bridegroom. When the marriage feast was ended, she went to the trunk to change her clothes but found it quite empty. On this the relations made great lamentation, and the bridegroom wept. But the bride attempted to console them by saying, "He will give me more pieces of gold to enable me to buy more clothes."

All cried out in astonishment, "Who?"

"He," she quietly replied. And to all the matrons who, suspecting that something must be wrong, pressed her to say who he might be, she only answered, "Thou for me; I for thee."

The relatives now hurried to the *beshdin* and submitted this very curious case to the rabbis. These learned men perceived at once that a demon had chosen the girl for his wife, and ostracized the newly married girl without further delay.

The Care of the Dead

(West Africa)

In the minds of most West African peoples, no hard-and-fast line seems to exist between the living and the dead. Ghosts are thought to exercise great influence over those who still dwell on earth. At all ceremonies of importance the names of the principal ancestors are invoked, and at feasts part of the food is always laid aside for them, in some such words as the following:

"Listen, my family! Here is the offering [goat, sheep, or cow] which we have killed for him who has died. Here is your portion. It is time for us to eat."

A libation is also poured out in order that the dead may drink with the living.

By a beautiful fancy, any stranger who dies in a town is buried on the road by which he entered it, so that his spirit may easily find the way back to his home, or at least watch the road thither and listen for the coming of friends.

Among many tribes those objects most used by the dead man while in life are broken and laid around his grave, so that their spirit, set free by the breaking of their earthly forms, may be borne by their owner into the world of ghosts.

The clubs or "companies" to which the dead formerly belonged usually come to give "plays" during the celebration of the funeral rites. In the case of one of the chief women's clubs, called *Ekpa*, on the occasion of the death of a member, the survivors run maenadlike around the town in a nearly naked state. Many brandish guns and swords, and all look fierce and wild. The men keep carefully out of sight, though their presence is not absolutely forbidden in daylight, but after dark no man must show his face. The women dance stark naked the whole night through, and should any man attempt so much as a glance at these mysteries, it is believed that his strength will ebb away and all his vitality leave him.

From: P. Amaury Talbot, "Through the Land of Witchcraft: Part 4," *Wide World Magazine* 32 (1913): 134–38.

Should a dying man have offended some powerful juju, or fear to meet the spirits of those he had formerly wronged, elaborate precautions are taken to placate them or protect his spirit.

A rather touching means to this end came to my notice some time ago. Outside the dead chief's door lay a cow which had been sacrificed, while above the deserted dwelling waved the Union Jack, so that in death, as in life, he might be safe beneath its protection.

To me, at least, this act of superstition seemed to express the outward and visible sign of what the Union Jack means to a people who, before its arrival, were liable to slaughter or torture at the behest of juju man or chief.

The Proud Grandfather-Ghost

(North Africa)

Over twenty years ago, when drinking green tea with a hostess whose windows overlooked the Mediterranean lapping the North African shore, she chanced to tell me the following anecdote, perhaps because we had been speaking of her early married life.

Herself an Englishwoman, she had ventured on an unusual marriage with a Muhammadan of high rank, whose title of sharif betokened his descent from the Prophet. The extraordinary fact of his choosing a Christian wife, as he was a spiritual prince, doubtless caused a stir not only among his tribal adherents but also among all true believers in the country, especially as the wedding took place at the British Legation, being safeguarded by all legal and international care. Perhaps the progressivist experiment was regarded with some

From: A. Roamer (pseud.), "Spirit Lights and Spirit Voices," *Occult Review* 23 (1918): 136–46.

anxiety not only on earth but also in the next plane of life, where it can hardly be doubted that news of earth friends is conveyed. Being holy by right of birth, the sharif could hardly do wrong. Yet the departure from Muhammadan custom was daring. What effect might this union between two people of opposing creeds produce upon their descendants? For the bride retained her Christian religion.

One night, this lady told me, she was lying awake in a bedroom in her villa, with her newborn son in a crib next to her bed. It was her very own villa, away from the crowded town—the same villa by the shore in which we then sat. The sharif bought it for her as a wedding gift, and it was built and furnished in English fashion so that she should feel truly at home. Therefore in the bedroom there was a fireplace, though this was then empty because the nights were no longer chilly as in midwinter. Except for the baby, she was at the time alone.

Presently through her closed eyelids, the young mother fancied there was some light in the room. She opened her eyes. Yes, an undoubted glimmer. Raising herself to look around, she was aware of what seemed to be a star near the fireplace. It grew larger and spread till in the midst of it a form became visible, surrounded by white radiance. As the sharifa gazed with fixed eyes, the figure became clearly an old man in Eastern dress, who moved slowly forward, passing the bed but pausing over the cradle.

If any momentary fear gripped the mother's heart, she was quickly reassured. For the spirit visitor, as she knew this to be, was only bending over the infant, studying its features with an expression of benignity. She discerned now that he wore the green turban of a sharif, (i.e., a descendant of the Prophet); her mind unconsciously registered his *jelab*, or cloak of rich stuff, his dress and whole air of dignity. Slowly the old man appeared to bestow his blessing on the little sleeping descendant of Fatima, daughter of Muhammad; then straightening his bent person, he glided back, fading as he went, across the room. Finally the apparition resolved itself into its original star-shape and disappeared near the fireplace.

Eagerly the sharifa told her husband next morning of the strange event. To her surprise he showed no astonishment.

"It is well! You saw my father," he replied with tranquil gravity. "It is natural he should wish to see his grandson, so he came. You have described his appearance and dress correctly."

My hostess on another occasion went on to tell me that once more she saw her deceased father-in-law, but this time by daylight.

Her husband decided to take her inland, to see the town whence he derived his title, on one of his visits thither. In a country without roads except for accustomed tracks made by herds driven in certain directions, the journey was made on horseback, as she disdained a litter. On the afternoon when they neared the white walls, domes, minarets, and palm trees of the sharif's ancestral abode, it chanced that his young wife found herself momentarily alone. Her husband and his followers had galloped off in quest of sport. Either they were hawking or hunting gazelle; the details escape my memory. But being a good horsewoman and knowing they would soon rejoin her, she rode ahead quietly.

Presently she found herself in a narrow place between rising ground, where there was no choice but to take a path trodden by droves of cattle, camels, and sheep. Here her horse hesitated and wished to stop.

Surprised, she looked around. Here, as elsewhere in that land, there were thickets of white broom, dry cactus, and underfoot, spires of pale pink asphodel. But also—what was more unusual—she saw on the other side an elderly sheikh of undoubted rank, standing on foot beside the track. Her surprise changed to amazement when she recognized him as the aged dead sharif. Of the wayfarer's identity she felt no doubt, remembering her midnight vision and the apparition's distinctive turban and dress.

A few moments passed during which she felt that she was being earnestly scrutinized by the figure. The inspection was apparently satisfactory, for his face wore a benevolent look. Then stepping aside, he disappeared. Her horse moved on of its own accord.

Again the sharif interpreted this as a natural and even flattering occurrence. That his wife should thus be met and welcomed to the city of his ancestors by his father's spirit gave him unfeigned filial pleasure.

The Hotel Poltergeist

(Egypt)

I think an account of an experience my husband, myself and my little boy had in the autumn of 1909 in a hotel in Egypt may be of interest. For obvious reasons I shall not mention the name of the hotel. I shall merely say it is not the one from which I am writing. My husband's and my room opened into our little boy's room; this was the only exit we had. The door of our boy's room opened into a long passage; two of his windows and one of ours opened onto a flat roof. At night we securely fastened the outside shutters, so that they could only be opened with some difficulty from the inside; the passage door was locked, but the windows, and the door between the bedrooms, were always left wide open.

One morning, after we had been in the hotel about ten days, one of the pair of socks my husband had taken off the evening before and had placed on the back of a cushioned chair was missing. We all hunted all over the room, but the sock could not be found. The following morning, exactly the same thing occurred—one sock was missing from the same place. As this also could not be found by us, we had the room thoroughly swept and searched, but neither the Arab nor the German chambermaid could find either of the missing socks. The following morning, one sock of another pair, placed in the same position, was missing. After much hunting by ourselves and the chambermaid, the socks which had disappeared on the previous three nights were found. The one which had disappeared on the second night was found on the roof some distance away, and those which had disappeared on the first and third nights were found woven in and out of the webbing under the seat of the cushioned chair, on the back of which they had been placed.

The next night we *pinned* the socks on the back of the chair with steel pins about four inches in length, with large heads. We watched that night but, unfortunately, could see nothing, as the electric light was

From: Mrs. Frank Currer Jones, "Does Egyptian Magic Still Exist?" *Occult Review* 15 (1912): 270–76.

always turned off before midnight. However, about 3.30 A.M. my boy and I heard a slight rustling sound. We immediately jumped up and felt for the socks, which were both there. At dawn both had disappeared. One pin was lying on the floor by the chair, while the other pin was stuck upright in the top of the chair but bent in the middle, so that one half was at right angles to the other half. The ashes from my husband's pipe on the dressing table were upset; so also was a glass for eye lotion. Nothing could be found.

The next night flour was sprinkled outside on the flat roof, so that it would be marked by the footsteps of any animal that should pass; and the headwaiter also kept watch. The following morning no socks were taken, my husband having put them away. But the ashes from one of his pipes were scattered over the dressing table; another pipe and a silver pencil case, which also had been left on the dressing table, had disappeared, as also the silver top of one of my dressing-bag bottles. The curious part about this latter disappearance was that the top had been picked off without the bottle being moved. This could plainly be seen, because the pipe ashes were sprinkled all about; but on lifting the bottle, a completely clean round spot was disclosed. There were no footmarks on the flour, nor did the headwaiter see anything. After much hunting, the pencil case was found on the floor in our boy's room; my silver top was found under his dressing table; one of the missing socks of the day before was found on the top of his wardrobe, under a bolster which had been there for some days; and the other missing sock was found some distance away on the flat roof. But the curious part was that, in spite of the wrench which the sock must have had, which the sharp bend in the pin made clearly evident, there was no hole in either sock. The pipe was not found till the afternoon, when our little boy found it on the iron laths of his bedstead, under the spring mattress of the bed. It was most carefully placed, exactly balanced so that it should not fall—with the bowl where the laths crossed, and the stem of the pipe along one of the laths.

The following night we shut the door between the two rooms and also one of the three windows opening onto the roof. We left the pipe under the bed where it was found, in order to see what would happen. The next morning the pipe was found on the dressing table, with the bowl propped up between two brushes, and the stem standing up against the mirror. In all we had seven visitations. And then they stopped as suddenly and unaccountably as they had begun. I must not omit to mention that we had a rattrap set in our rooms every night after the first two; and every morning it was down, but empty, and the cheese was untouched. We none of us walk in our sleep; there were no rats about; and even if there had been, no animal could, we think, have passed through the closed and tightly fastened outside shutters, for the pieces of wood were so exceptionally close that a bee got stuck one day when it tried to pass through. No hole was found anywhere in the room, and we blocked up the crack under the door opening into the passage. Of course the Arabs declared the devil was about. No one to whom we have told the story, or who had anything to do with it, can offer any satisfactory explanation. We know positively that none of ourselves did it in sleep, but even this would not explain how the socks found their way to the roof without footprints on the flour outside.

We have had further experiences, which are so astounding that we feel we should like them to be known, especially as friends out here, witnesses to some of the curious things that have happened, have urged us to report them.

Exactly seven weeks and two days after Pixie, as we named our mysterious visitor, had apparently finished playing tricks with our things, at another hotel it began its tricks again by taking one of my husband's socks during the night. During the eight nights it visited us on this occasion, the pipe was taken two or three times, and was once found on the top of the mosquito netting in the next room and another time inside an umbrella which was standing in a corner. One night our boy's collar and handkerchief, my husband's pipe, and a pen wiper disappeared. We had put flour down in the room the evening before. In the morning, after much hunting, the handkerchief was found in the springs under an armchair, the collar on top of the mosquito netting of one of the beds, the pen wiper upon the laths under the spring mattress of a bed, and the pipe, as I have already mentioned, on the top of the mosquito netting in the next room.

As always, the shutters and doors were locked, except the door between our little boy's room and ours. Much flour was sprinkled on the floor between the two rooms, but in the morning there was no mark upon it except a trail, which on examination we found could only have been made by the dragging of the pipe across it from one room to the other. On each side of this trail, and at the end of it, there was a little wall of flour made by the pipe. The little wall at the end could, we think, have been caused only by the sudden lifting up of the pipe from the floor, for there was no smudge at the end of the flour. Curiously enough, there was no mark on the flour by the dressing table, as there would have been had the pipe fallen from it. It was on this occasion that the pipe was found on the top of the mosquito netting, in the room next to that in which it had been left the night before. Several visitors to the hotel, to whom we had told our experiences, saw the trail and felt as much puzzled as we did ourselves.

In order to prove that our little boy did not do these things in his sleep, the following night—after he was asleep, so that he should have no knowledge of what we were doing—we placed chairs around his bed in such a manner that he would not be able to get out of bed without our hearing him or without his disturbing the chairs. In the morning, the chairs were undisturbed, but my husband's pipe had again disappeared, as also one stocking belonging to our little boy. The following night my husband was locked into our little boy's room, and the key of the door between the rooms was taken, and we hid our stockings. Our little boy rolled his up together and put them in the pocket of his ulster in his own room. In the morning one of these stockings had come through the locked door and was on top of the wardrobe in the room in which my boy and I slept. We found that the stocking could be dragged under the door between the rooms, but the mystery is—what had dragged it through and put it, or thrown it, onto the wardrobe?

Another curious point is that the stockings were rolled up together, and yet only one was taken, and this without the other being pulled out of the ulster pocket. The following night two pocketbooks and a pen wiper, taken from the table, were hidden behind the mirror which was fastened to the wall. It was with great difficulty, and only with the help of a stick, that one pocketbook and the pen wiper were recovered. The Arab and the *femme de chambre* promised to unfasten the mirror during the day, as only in this way could the other book be reached. We were going to pack next day, so I was anxious to get it back at once. We had up to this time found all the things, except one stocking, that had been missing for six days, and the pocketbook. On going to bed, I was vexed to find that the servants had not troubled to get the pocketbook, as taking down the mirror was troublesome, but they had hunted well for the missing stocking—even searching up the chimney. The next morning when we awoke, the stocking was lying over the back of a chair and the missing pocketbook was on the table! Our doors and shutters had been locked all night, as usual. We were glad to leave the hotel and to move further into Egypt, thinking we should escape at last from Pixie.

We only stayed about ten days at the next hotel, and for a week had peace. Then one morning, when my husband woke, he exclaimed, "Why, there is that cardboard box, which you put to be thrown away, on top of my mosquito netting! Pixie must have been here again!" But I would not believe this, and said that the Arab must have carelessly thrown it there and that we had not noticed it the night before. However, the next night—I fancy because I was an unbeliever this time—for the first time two stockings of mine were taken, one from each of two pairs I had in different parts of the room. We eventually found them on top of the wardrobe.

At the next hotel, where we stayed ten days, farther up the Nile, we had only one visitation from Pixie, when the cork sole was taken out of one of my husband's boots; it was eventually found behind a cupboard. We then came to this hotel from which I am writing, when such extraordinary things happened that I think perhaps I had better mention them in detail. On the second morning after our arrival, we found Pixie had taken the cork sole from my husband's boot again (it was found behind the chest of drawers), and one of our boy's stockings, which was found tightly twisted around and around the piece of wood which supports, underneath, the top of the round table in his room. After lunch that day, my husband and boy went out, while I rested a little. About twenty minutes later, on going to join them, I passed through our boy's room and found his coat in a bunch on the floor by the window, his waistcoat on top of his mosquito netting, and his knickers hanging from a nail on the wall behind the head of his bed, with the legs stretched out over the rail. Two pairs of shoes, stockings, and a boot bag with boots in it were strewn about in various parts of the room. I was much annoyed at my boy's untidiness, as I thought it, and decided that he must tidy up when he came in. They returned, and were as flabbergasted at the condition of the room as I had been.

The following morning both stockings, which our boy had hidden in a drawer, had been taken out; one was found under the dressing table and had to be got out with a stick, and the other had been neatly folded and was hidden in the lining of my husband's white helmet. But strangest of all, on the table a piece of paper, which was clean the night before, had several lines of writing on it, which we cannot decipher. It may be merely scribble, or it may be in some Eastern language. One dragoman, to whom it was shown, said it was a quotation from the Book of the Dead, but we doubt if he could read it or knew anything about it. He said the lines were "Twelve hours of the day, and twelve hours of the night, is the passage of the soul to the other world." Even if it is only scribble, how did it get on the paper? There is a distinct small bird at the beginning, which is frequently seen on the tombs and temples out here.

The afternoon of that day brought Pixie again. Our boy's heavy dressing gown was thrown on top of his mosquito netting, and his best jacket and two pairs of shoes were strewn about the room. While we were dressing for dinner that night and were all at the dressing tables, suddenly our boy's knickers came of their own accord from the chair on which they had been placed, flew across the whole width of his room, and fell on the floor inside our room. Up to this time our little boy had been very brave, but he owned he was now "terrified." We went down and had a quiet talk with the manager and began by asking him if our rooms were "haunted." We then told him our story, at which he was amazed, as was natural. He was much interested and wanted us to let him know if anything further happened. That evening, when our little boy came to bed and his father was with him, his waistcoat flew from the same chair right to the middle of our room, just as his knickers had done before dinner.

The following morning we found that nothing had been hidden during the night, but our boy's coat had been thrown down by the window and his waistcoat by the door. Before dressing for dinner, while I was busily writing in our room, I began to feel so "uncanny" that I thought I would go downstairs for a few minutes. Before leaving the rooms, I saw that everything was in its right place. On our returning to dress for dinner a few minutes later, we found our boy's jacket thrown on top of his bed—on top of the mosquito netting—his coat was thrown in a bunch on the floor in one place and his waistcoat in another. In the other room, my husband's pajamas had been taken from under the two pillows on his bed, where they had been placed in the morning, and one part was thrown across the room onto a table by my bed, and the other part was lying on the floor by the writing table at which I had been sitting only a few minutes before. We told the manager, who came up and was as much at a loss to understand the matter as we had been.

My husband remarked, "What does it mean? All this can't be for nothing."

A thought then suddenly flashed through my mind, and I said, "Perhaps some poor wandering restless soul needs our prayers and has been trying to attract our attention in this way, as possibly it may have had no other means of doing so." From that moment there has been absolutely no disturbance of any sort, and the last time it visited us is now some weeks ago.

I have written this account, stating facts only, as we are most anxious to hear what others may have to say. We are not Spiritualists and have never had any such experiences in our lives before.

I may add that, when we were at a hotel in which we had the smallest visitation and trouble, one of us accidentally overheard one gentleman visitor say to another that he had had "another curious experience." He then said that in the morning after he had been called, the heavy armchair in his room had moved of its own accord two or three feet across his room. We left the hotel and had no opportunity of making this visitor's acquaintance. There have also been accounts of one or two curious things of a somewhat similar sort in one of the Egyptian papers lately.

A Bushman Speaks of Two Apparitions

(West Africa)

We buried my wife in the afternoon. When we had finished burying her, we returned to the home of my sister Whāī-ttŭ and the other people, whence they had come forth. They had come to bury my wife with me, and we went away, crossing over the salt pan.

And we perceived a thing which looked like a child sitting upon the salt pan, seeming to sit with its legs crossed over each other.

And my sister Whāī-ttŭ spoke; she questioned us, "Look ye! What thing sits yonder upon the salt pan? It is like a little child."

And !kwe'iten-tā-‖kēn, another sister, spoke; she asked us, "Look ye! Why is it that this thing is truly like a person? It seems as if it had on the cap which Ddíä!kwãin's wife used to wear."

And my sister Whāī-ttŭ spoke; she answered, "Yes, O my younger sister! The thing truly resembles that which Brother's wife was like."

It did thus as we went along; it seemed as if it sat looking toward the place from which we came out.

And ‖kū-ăń spoke; she said, "The old people used to tell me that the angry people were wont to act thus. At the time when they took a person away, they used to allow the person to be in front of us, so that we might see it. Ye know that she really had a very little child; therefore ye should allow us to look at the thing which sits upon this salt pan. It strongly resembles a person; its head is there like a person."

And I spoke; I said, "Wait! I will do thus. As I return to my home, I will see whether I shall again perceive it as it sits."

And we went to their home, and we talked there for a little while. And I spoke; I said to them that they appeared to think that I did not

From: W. H. I. Bleek and L. C. Lloyd, *Specimens of Bushmen Folklore* (London: George Allen and Co., Ltd., 1911).

wish to return home, for the sun was setting. And I returned on account of it. I thought that I would go in the same manner as we had come, that I might, going along, look whether I should again perceive it as it sat. Going along, I looked at the place where it had sat, because I thought that it might have been a bush. I saw that I did not perceive it at the place where it had sat. And I agreed that it must have been a different kind of thing.

For my mothers used to tell me that, when the sorcerers (those who take us away) at the time when they intend to take us quite away, that is the time when our friend is in front of us. He desires that we may perceive him, because he feels that he still thinks of us; therefore his outer skin still looks at us, because he feels that he does not want to go away and leave us. For he insists upon coming to us; therefore we still perceive him on account of it.

My sister's husband, Mǎńsse, told us about it, that it had happened to him when he was hunting about. As he was going along, he espied a little child peeping at him by the side of a bush. And he thought, *Can it be my child who seems to have run after me? It seems to have lost its way, while it seems to have followed me.* And Mǎńsse thought, *Allow me to walk nearer, that I may look at this child to see what child it be.*

And Mǎńsse saw that the child acted in this manner: when the child saw that he was going up to it that he might see what child it was, he saw that the child appeared as if it feared him. The child sat behind the bush; the child looked from side to side. It seemed as if it wanted to run away. And he walked, going near to it, and the child arose on account of it. It walked away, looking from side to side. It seemed as if it wanted to run away.

And Mǎńsse looked to see why it was that the child did not wish him to come to it and why the child seemed to be afraid of him. And he examined the child as the child stood looking at him. He saw that it was a little girl. He saw that the child was like a person; in other parts of it, it was not like a person. He thought that he would let the child alone. For a child who was afraid of him was here. And he walked on, while the child stood looking from side to side. And as the child saw that he went away from it, it came forward near the bush, and it sat down.

The Invisible Attacker

(South Africa)

I had left my station, a camp called Bizana in Eastern Pondoland, for the purpose of "riding express," that is, taking dispatches to the town of Kokstad, the capital of East Griqualand and the headquarters of my squadron. It was the first time I had taken the journey, and I made several mistakes as to the road; however, about sunset I crossed the borderline of Pondoland into East Griqualand and passed the abandoned camp of Fort Donald.

I must explain that after leaving Fort Donald the road curves around under a stony precipitous hill called the Spitzkop, or Foggy Hill. I had been riding for five or six hours, and to my tired eyes the road seemed to stretch away interminably. As I rode along I noticed on the right-hand side of the road a track leading across the bare veld and joining the main road farther on, forming as it were the arc of a circle. It struck me that this was a most desirable shortcut. The veld was level, I could see that the grass-grown track joined the main road farther on, cutting off almost two miles, and I decided to follow it. The time was about 6:00 P.M. on a South African winter evening, that is to say about sunset, and perfectly light. I turned my horse onto the track, and proceeded along it at a slow canter for about a mile and then slowed down to a walk. Then hanging the reins on my bridle arm, I took out and proceeded to fill a pipe. While I was engaged in doing so, I suddenly felt my left shoulder grasped by what seemed to be a hand of enormous strength, and I received a wrench which nearly jerked me out of the saddle.

The country, I must state, was in a serious state of unrest—almost of rebellion—at the time, and as soon as I recovered my balance, I jerked my revolver out of the holster and swung my horse around to face whatever danger there might be. To my utter astonishment there was nothing whatever to be seen! There was still a certain amount of sunlight, and look as I might in every direction, I could see no sign of

From: Vere D. Shortt, "Two Experiences," *Occult Review* 29 (1919): 214–17.

any other human being except myself. Then I noticed that my horse was very restless and kept backing away and was covered with sweat. I particularly noticed this, as the day, being winter, had not been very warm and I had not been riding hard. Also at the same time, it began to be borne in on me that there was something wrong with the whole atmosphere of the place I was in. I can only explain what I mean by saying that I was conscious, in a sort of subconscious way, that there was something near me which was not natural and which was violently hostile to me. I felt an overmastering desire to leave the place, and getting my horse around (almost on his hind legs), I sent the spurs home and rode at a gallop until I struck the main road. I had no further experiences.

That night I stayed at the hotel at Brooke's Nek, about nine miles from Kokstad, and met there a comrade of mine named E———, who was going home from Kokstad to one of the outlying Pondoland stations. As I was going to bed, he came into my room and sat on the bed, chatting as I undressed. As I took my shirt off, he looked at me and then said, "Good Lord, man! What on earth have you been doing to your shoulder? Just look at it!" I turned to the glass and looked at my left shoulder. On the front of the shoulder were four deep, discolored bruises and one behind, nearer the neck—it looked exactly as if someone with a very large and powerful left hand had grasped my shoulder from behind and absolutely dug their fingers into the flesh. I told E——— what had happened that evening, and he said, "Oh! that's the old wagon road, that they had to stop using because they couldn't get a native to go along it at any time of the day or night. About five years ago they found a Negro driver lying in the road with his head twisted nearly around. There's something wrong with the place, but no one knows exactly what."

I may state in conclusion that this was all I could ever find out—simply vague stories of "something wrong" and the road avoided like the pestilence by natives. Personally I have no explanation to give, but then many strange things without explanations happen in Africa.

The Son of a Man and the Son of a Ghost

(West Africa)

O nce upon a time the son of a man and the son of a ghost dug pitfalls in the forest. So the son of the ghost said to the son of the man, "You select now the share of the animals which you will always take."

Therefore the man said, "I will always take the male animals."

The ghost said to him, "Choose now a good thing, so that you will have it always."

Thereupon the man said to the ghost, "Choose now the portion which you will have to eat all the time."

So the ghost said, "I will eat the females of all the animals, all that we shall catch; but you, the son of a man, you will eat all of the male animals."

Then the man said to the ghost, "You can also eat of the males."

But the ghost said, "No, I will not eat them, because it is forbidden to us ghosts to eat of male animals."

When two nights had passed, they went out to visit the traps, and they found that ten animals had been killed in the pitfalls. So the ghost said to the man, "You take all of them!" So he took them all. Then they went home. On another day they went to visit the traps, and they found a buffalo and an elephant standing in the pits; and these also were males, both of them. And again the man took them all. The man said, however, to the ghost, "Come, you may take one of the tusks." But the ghost said, "No, for it is forbidden to us ghosts to take ivory of a male animal, lest we die."

So the man took the whole elephant and carried the meat to his town.

But the wife of the man had forgotten the broken cutlass at the place

From: Adolph N. Krug, "Bulu Tales from Kamerun, West Africa," *Journal of American Folk-Lore* 25 (1912): 106–24.

where they had cut up the elephant. When the ghost saw the woman coming, he threw the broken cutlass into the pit for her. So he said to the wife of the man, "Go down into the pit and get your cutlass."

So the woman descended into the pit, and she said to the ghost, "Help me up out of the pit!"

When the man saw that his wife did not speedily return, he followed after her and found the ghost standing beside the pit. Then he asked him, "Where is my wife?"

And the ghost replied, "She is down there in the pit."

The man in turn said, "Help her up out of the pit!"

But the ghost replied, "No, I will not help her up, because I said I would not eat any male animals killed in these pits, but the females. At the present time there is a female down in the pit; there is nothing else for me to do but to take her."

To this the man replied, "But she is my wife!"

But the ghost said, "It is forbidden that a female animal, once it is caught in a pit the ghosts have dug, be released again, but the ghosts themselves must take it."

Upon this the man became angry and broke off a club with which to strike the ghost, but the ghost suddenly went down into the pit and took the woman, and they disappeared down there in the pit. And he was never seen anywhere again but in the streets of his father's village.

Thus the man lost his wife.

Man and His "Animal" Soul

(West Africa)

S hould any reader grow weary of the monotony of life in this prosaic twentieth century and long for the glamor and mystery of earlier ages, he has but to purchase a ticket for an Elder Dempster Liner and arriving on the West Coast of Africa, make his way into some part of the "bush" hitherto unstudied and unsurveyed.

Within a few hours familiar sights and sounds are left behind, the green forest curtain falls imperceptibly between our hypothetical traveler and all he has hitherto known. He is no longer in the twentieth century, with its strenuous struggle for existence and its matter-of-fact explanations of natural phenomena, but has stepped backward through the ages, to the childhood of the world. Here, in the eternal twilight of the bush, time is of little account. Mystery and terror lurk in each quivering shadow or half-heard sound. Every other flower and leaf has magical properties, while rivers, rocks, and trees are peopled with evil spirits, as hideous in nature as in shape, ever hovering around, eager to drag the unwary down to a terrible doom. That part of the forest belt that extends almost from the Gulf of Guinea to the German Cameroons, and indeed over the border, is peopled also by the so-called Calabar Bush Souls—akin to the were-tigers of India and the werewolves of our own northern lands.

It is an article of belief among the people of this uncanny region that every man has two souls, one of which always animates his human body, while the other, by means of a magic draught the secret of which has been handed down for untold ages, can leave the form in which it usually dwells and float invisibly into the depths of the forest, where it takes on its were-shape. The Calabar River is supposed to be

From: P. Amaury Talbot, "Through the Land of Witchcraft: Part 1," *Wide World Magazine* 31 (1913): 428–37.

the home of many such elephant and crocodile souls—Efumi, as they are called.

Early in 1911 a deputation from one of the larger towns brought two prisoners, father and son, before the commissioner at Oban. They were accused of having, in crocodile form, killed two women while the latter were crossing the river. As they refused to swear their innocence on the dominant juju of the town, they were brought before the white man, who naturally decided that there was no case against them. The deputation, however, had not finished with the matter. On returning home another juju was invoked, with the result that the son confessed that both he and his father were guilty, and that they had killed and eaten seven other men and women.

Strangely enough, people accused of this uncanny power nearly always acknowledge their guilt, even when fully aware that such confession will probably cost them their lives. Awa Ita, an old woman of Oban, was suspected of being a snake-soul and of sending out her familiar every night to lick a wound on her husband's ankle while he slept, and so prevent it from healing. The chiefs of the Ibo Society summoned her before their dreaded tribunal, which under native law had the right to condemn to death. In her own words: "They asked me, 'You possess a snake?' I answered, 'Yes,' because I have it for true." On this she was sentenced to death; but fortunately news of the threatened execution reached me, and she is not only still alive but cleared of suspicion in the opinion of the townsfolk, since the wound healed after the application of clean water and a little ointment.

Soon after my arrival, news was brought that a certain chief was about to suffer death on suspicion of having, in the guise of a were-leopard, killed several cows and goats. Fortunately my appearance on the scene put a stop to the proceedings.

Chief Agbashan, a well-known elephant hunter, is thought to owe his success in the chase to the fact that he is an elephant Efumi and can therefore approach his quarry unsuspected.

Such beliefs are deep-rooted, and when one imagines that a little headway has been made against them, coincidences seem to spring up to attest their truth and impress them on the minds of the people more deeply than before.

About a year ago, for instance, one of the bravest natives I know was out after elephant. He shot a bull over eleven feet in height and, on running up to examine it discovered to his horror that instead of the great, curved tusks which he expected and imagined he had seen, it only possessed two flat, ribbed protuberances about a foot long, the depth of a finger, and one and a half inches in breadth.

The sight of these abnormalities reduced the man to a state of abject terror, for he considered them proof positive that his kill was no true beast but a were-elephant. On returning to the nearest town, he learned that at the very hour at which the fatal shot had been fired, the son of one of the chiefs, long suspected as an elephant Efumi, had fallen dead! The deformed tusks, perhaps the most curious of their kind in the world, are now in the Museum of the Royal College of Surgeons.

Another striking case occurred among the Ododop tribe, the head chief of which, Awa Anjanna, was confessedly a buffalo-soul. He was a friend of mine and a man of great intelligence, scarcely touched by white influence. On our return to his country, after a sojourn in England and a tour through Central Africa, we looked for him in vain. Inquiries only brought the answer, "He die long since." It was obvious that his people did not wish to give further information, but later we learned that the commissioner at Oban had one day shot a buffalo in the station garden, about four o'clock in the afternoon. At almost the same moment, Awa Anjanna, in his little settlement some dozen miles away, struck his hand on his body, exclaiming, "They kill me for [i.e., at] Oban." A little while after, about the estimated time at which the wounded buffalo died, he passed away, after sending a message to all the buffalo-souls in his chief town to avoid Oban, as it was too dangerous.

The Dread of Witchcraft

(Nigeria)

There is nothing a native of Nigeria dreads more than witchcraft. A second terrible aversion is that of the enforced disembodiment of the soul. The "wandering spirit," without definite goal or ambition, is not merely an outcast from the peace which his relations have vainly sought to bestow, but he is also lost to all sympathetic communion with higher spirits and with willingly impressionable mortals.

According to Bosa's instruction, disembodied spirits are not constantly appearing. That they exist is more a matter of psychic perception than actual physical observation. Asked if he could describe the appearance of the soul and the spirit, in normal combination, during the life of a human being, he pointed to a large reading lamp on my worktable. In the heavy night air, this was diffusing two distinct circles of light. He compared the diffused outer circle of yellow radiance to the Nkpulobe, or what we would probably call the subliminal self, while the inner circle of reddish gold he likened to the normal consciousness, or the Moa Moa. It is an ingenious illustration, certainly, and it appeals to me; but whether it is his own inspiration or based upon a native illustration, I am unable to say.

A violent death is apparently the surest avenue toward visitation of the living by the dead, for then the poor spirit has been deprived of its full burial rights. The rite of burial which takes place immediately after death is that of the body only, and a second burial has to take place some months later, which is of purely spiritual significance. This second burial marks the soul's passage into eternity. The survivors dare not offer the two complete burial ceremonies to a relation who has met a death that has caused any kind of physical mutilation.

Many people in Europe are familiar with the word *juju* without knowing how this slang description of superstition was evolved. The actual word is *egugu*. In Ibo it is a term used to describe an immense

From: John M. Stuart-Young, "Nigerian Supernaturalism: Part 1," *Occult Review* 31 (1920): 138–46.

idol which contains a powerful spirit. This spirit acts the part of avenger and makes his appearance forty days after the death of a chief or of any person holding royal rank.

The word *egugu*, however, is not pure Ibo. I was amazed to find that it is identical with the Yoruba (Lagos) word *egugu*. The meaning attached to this word by the Yorubas is convincing—that of the spirit of a dead man. When we recall the fact that Sierra Leone, the Gold Coast, the Ivory Coast, all bear witness to the wanderings of the Yorubas, after the emancipation of the American slaves and the abolition of West African slavery, the universality of the term *juju* becomes comprehensible. It is highly probable that the lisped word *ejuju* was introduced to English notice by the first few drafts of freed slaves, that it seized on the imaginations of the sailors, and that it was carried to Europe and America in this way.

Witchcraft in the Bush

(West Africa)

It is, above all, during long bush tours that one comes nearest to understanding the minds of primitive peoples such as the forest folk of these regions. In the whole land there are no open spaces, save those which have been cleared for villages or farms. The heavenly bodies play but little part in their lives, for as one of the men remarked, "We do not trouble ourselves about the stars, because the trees always hide them." Everywhere the foliage presses around one like a solid wall, while creepers with stems like giant cables, often two and a half feet in circumference, hang in festoons from tree to tree, so tangled together that hours may be spent in cutting a short way through. Such bush, with its soft green twilight, dark shadows, and quivering lights, is peopled by many terrors, but among these that of *ojie* (witchcraft) reigns supreme. Some people, indeed, believe that

From: P. Amaury Talbot, "Through the Land of Witchcraft: Part 2," *Wide World Magazine* 31 (1913): 507–15.

there are good jujus which are stronger, but most think that none but Obassi himself can give protection against this ever-present terror, which walks by day or night and may manifest itself in the least expected ways. Mother, sister, or sweetheart may be witches in disguise. The bird that flies in at your open door in the sunshine, the bat that circles around your house at twilight, the small bush beasts that cross your path while hunting—all may be familiars of witch or wizard, or even the latter themselves, disguised to do you hurt. In this world of magic shape-shifting is an everyday occurrence, and it seems scarce harder of belief that a man should be able to change into leopard or crocodile than that tiny flowers, no bigger than a pinhead, should become huge fruits, hanging from tree and liana, ready to fall and stun the hapless passerby. To those who know the depths of virgin forests, with their strange solitudes filled by the thousand unexplainable sounds which together make up one vast silence, such beliefs seem not only natural but inevitable.

Should witches wish to kill a man, the people believe, they gather together at nighttime in front of his town and dance, not upon the ground but a few feet above. While dancing, they often grow to giant size. No noise can be heard, and they are invisible to all who have not second sight. Perhaps the most terrible power possessed by witch or wizard is that of "sucking out the heart" of a man without his knowledge. They sit on the roof of the victim's house at night and draw out his heart while he sleeps; and without the aid of some strong juju, he will never know what is killing him. A man wasting away from consumption or beriberi is usually thought to have been bewitched in this way.

When a witch knows that her victim's last hour draws near, she sends the giant bat (*Hypsignathus monstrosus*) in the nighttime to the town of the dying man. Its dull, monotonous cry, "Pang-pang," sounding out of the darkness, is taken for the blows on the nails driven into the coffin which it has been ordered to prepare for the burial of some victim. When such a sound is heard during the night, it is a matter of faith that at dawn there will be one dweller less in the little town.

In the old days, if a man was thought to be a wizard, he used to be taken into the bush to be "examined." There he was bound and a hole cut in his body just above the liver. From this the officiating juju man usually succeeded in withdrawing the suspected familiar, generally in the form of a bird, toad, or other small creature, but sometimes in that of a tiny man. If nothing was found, the victim was cleared of all suspicion, but alas! death invariably resulted from the treatment.

Even now the bodies of those who have fallen under the suspicion of witchcraft are examined in this way after death. Should the ceremony be omitted, and the familiar remain unkilled, it is thought that it will sally forth from the grave at nighttime and bring disaster on the dead man's town. As a precaution, the corrosive juice of a species of cactus is dropped into the eyes of the corpse and the mouth is filled with the leaves of the *egakk* tree, so that the soul should be unable to sally forth through these apertures.

Not long ago a woman died in one of the principal towns of this region. She was buried with the usual rites, and some time after, people began to fall sick and die. This was put down to witchcraft, practiced by someone in the town, but as government does not allow suspected characters to be tested in the way already described, the inhabitants could only seek safety by going to outlying farms. Then the juju "image" declared that every night he saw the ghost of the dead woman rise from her grave and walk through the town, spreading pestilence among its people. Two native officials went down to the grave to investigate. There they found a small hole, like the entrance to a rat's run—which it probably was. They sprinkled pepper on a piece of paper and laid it inside. On the morrow this had disappeared, which proved conclusively, they decided, that the ghost had come out by that way. All the townspeople accordingly collected together and made a great bonfire. Then they dug up the body and burned it, and after this there was no more sickness.

Some time ago in one of the larger towns, the people were dying so fast that it was thought witches must be killing them. To stop this the chief proclaimed that the inhabitants must assemble together on a certain day. When all were present he ordered that the juju *njomm aiyung* (the blood juju) should be practiced. A cut was made in the body of each person and a few drops of blood allowed to flow into a calabash half full of dry corn, which had been brought for the purpose. None were exempt; even the babies born that day gave one drop of blood. When all had been bled, each man, woman, and child was made to partake of the corn. This was done so that witchcraft might no longer be practiced against any of the townsfolk; for after mingling blood and then partaking of it, should one of the parties attempt to harm another, the blood juju would catch them, and the evil they had tried to inflict would fall on themselves.

Sometimes the terror of witchcraft will scatter the population of a whole town. Such was the case with Oberekkai, which stands on a little tributary of the Kwa River. In the old slave-dealing days, this was a large and prosperous town, and its chief, Nataba, was the wealthiest man in the district. As more labor was needed to develop his great cocoa and other plantations, he sent to buy workpeople from the Cameroons. In course of time the emissaries returned with a band of some thirty captives, whose big limbs and robust appearance gave promise of excellent labor material.

The newcomers kept apart from the people of Oberekkai and refused to take any share in the social life of the town. When "plays" were given, they hung together at the edge of the crowd, looking somberly on, but more often gathered by stealth in the nighttime at a farm hut belonging to one of them.

After a while strange stories began to spread of midnight rites practiced before unknown jujus brought by the newcomers from their own land. Then the townsfolk sickened. One after another they died, and the survivors whispered that the captives were wizards from the Cameroons and were "eating out the hearts" of those who had enslaved them, so that soon neither man, woman, nor child would remain of the freeborn folk of Oberekkai. Terror took possession of the people. Many fled, and in a comparatively short time the inhabitants were reduced to a mere remnant. Nataba and those of his family who still survived determined on desperate measures. One after another the slaves disappeared. Their "magic" was powerless to protect them from the vengeance of the infuriated people of the town, and finally they were all wiped out. Oberekkai remains today, with its untended plantations upon which the all-invading bush is rapidly encroaching, a mere shadow of its former greatness.

Tales of Voodooism

(West Africa)

I t was my good fortune in 19— to meet a gentleman who had traveled over a great part of the globe and who had made occultism a special study. No one was better qualified than he to give me interesting narratives on voodoo magic. The result of our conversations is embodied almost literally in the following pages.

It is generally conceded that the whole of the West Coast of Africa is the white man's grave, and I do not think that anyone who has ever been there will question the truth of this statement, but in addition to the climate there is a class of men and women equally deadly. These people are known as voodoos, the wonder-workers, the black magic men, the necromancers, the devil's own, and such like titles. There can be no doubt that these magicians flourish right throughout the whole of Africa and that their disciples are covering the face of the earth at the present day.

The followers of this cult, or art, or devil's own work, on the West Coast are far more numerous than is generally supposed and are also to be found in London, Paris, Vienna, etc. In America they increase in numbers, and according to my friend's experience of them there, the number seems to keep pace with the financial gain.

"One day," said my informant, "while at a place called Axim, on the Gold Coast, Prince Karatsupo came to me and asked if I had ever seen the voodoos at work, to which I replied that I had not. 'Then,' said he, 'a marvellous opportunity presents itself for you to see them, and with my introduction I do not think there will be any difficulty in allowing you to witness their work. Mind you, a lot of their business is what you will call hellish, beastly, and repugnant, but that they accomplish results there is no doubt on this earth.'

"Accordingly that afternoon I was conducted to the hut of a woman (who might have seen forty-five summers) and what seemed to me two daughters, aged eighteen and twenty-three respectively. The

From: Irene E. Toye Warner, ed., "Voodooism on the West Coast of Africa: Narratives by an Eye-Witness," *Occult Review* 20 (1914): 143–50.

woman eyed me very suspiciously at first, put two or three questions to me, and then said, 'He'll do!' for evidently I was considered worthy to be allowed to observe their ceremonies intact. (But whether this was intended as a compliment or not I have never been able to satisfy myself.)

"Through the prince, they explained to me that they were being paid a large sum of money by a native exporter to remove a certain white man, who was fast supplanting him in the palm oil business on the Gold Coast. The scene was laid at a place called Tacquah, situated roughly between Axim and Cape Coast Castle. The business carried on there I believe to be solely the bartering of palm oils and ivory tusks, in exchange for Hollands gin, gaudy striped calicoes, and such like.

"Accordingly, at about three o'clock, the hellish work commenced. Herbs were burned by way of incense, and to anyone standing by, they would quickly have known that the devil had got his own, for the stench was unbearable. Then certain chants and incantations took place, and to look at the faces of those three women, the elder one especially, you could easily conceive that hell and hate were typified therein. A poor innocent cockerel was then seized. I think three feathers were pulled out over his heart and his neck wrung off in very quick time. What incantations took place I am unable to say, but I am sure they were diabolical.

Then the younger girl tore open the skin over the heart and plunged the feathers into the blood, soaking them thoroughly. After which she proceeded to the residence of the white man and, being in touch with his servant, a Kroo-boy, got into his hut and safely planted the feathers, with their cursed weight of villainy and murder, in a crevice near the bed.

"To all intents and purposes this man was well and healthy at the time to which we refer. This at least was the unanimous opinion of the public.

"In the middle of the night the doomed man was reported to have yelled with excruciating pain, which continued at intervals until the morning, when he seemed to have revived. During the day he had the pains at intervals and consulted a medical man who was located at Axim, on one of the Gold Company's concessions. This doctor, believing it to be malarial fever coupled with a bad state of the digestive tract, ordered immediate rest. He returned home and went to bed, but in vain did he seek for relief, for at the same hours the next day the pains were intensified and his yells were distressing to hear, and the natives declared that he had got in the grip of the voodoos, although it is but fair to say that they did not know how or in what measure this quiet-going Englishman could have aroused their wrath. On the third day at the same hour, the man died, and great indeed were the lamentations of the people, for they were nearly all engaged in that village on his work, and his loss therefore meant much to them.

"Some time after, the Kroo-boy to whom we have before referred told how the younger member of the voodoo party had visited the hut. The natives thereupon made it their business to search it thoroughly, but found nothing of an incriminating nature against the voodoos. The boy, who was alike afraid of the voodoos and in love with the voodoo girl, made and recanted statements two or three times, until it was found that his evidence was unreliable, and it was thought that the sudden death of his master had somewhat upset his mentality. But when, about ten days after his master's burial, he had the same pains and aches, the people concluded that assuredly he had been, and was at this present time, in the grip of the voodoos.

"I am not absolutely certain, but I believe the boy died a few days afterward. If this was not the case, he must have conceived some incurable disease in the stomach, with prevented him attending the court to give evidence on oath. The voodoo women were arrested solely on his assertion, but as he was unable to attend the court, the case was struck out of the list and the three woman discharged.

"Now we come to a very interesting development in this case. The native exporter was called on from time to time to fund hush money to a considerable amount for these women. He bore this blackmailing as long as he could, but there comes an end to all things. Unable longer, or it may be unwilling, to comply with their demands, he threatened to make a clean breast of the whole affair and to stand the consequences. What actually took place between them we do not know, nor shall we ever know, but certain it is that on the third day after he was seen coming away from their hut, he was found dead in his own.

"These and hundreds of similar stories are known on the coast, and it is no wonder that the natives look with utmost dread on anything directly or remotely connected with voodooism; and I, from my experience of these people, quite sympathize with them."

So concluded my friend's narrative.

On another occasion, when the conversation again drifted to West African topics, I had the following interesting account from my friend:

"Some time in 1884, probably about June, I was the guest of a Mr. Dawson, a native interpreter near Kumasi, on the West Coast of Africa. I found him to be far superior, intellectually at least, to the surrounding natives. There was nothing very remarkable about this man, except that he had assumed the manners and habits of the Europeans with whom he came in contact as far as he possibly could, and it was because of this assimilation of European ideas that I found myself under his roof, with his daughter, a very charming young native woman who struck me as altogether generally superior to any woman I had seen on the West Coast of Africa during my residence there. She was young, vivacious, and not at all of a forward disposition.

"One evening, while sitting out on the verandah with these two, the conversation chanced to turn to the dreaded voodoos. A woman was passing at that moment, and Mr. Dawson, seeing her, somewhat excitedly drew my attention to her as one belonging to the class to which we had just referred. I had not a good look at the woman, and consequently cannot describe her, but I learned that she was between forty and fifty years of age and thoroughly dreaded by the community.

"Report has it," so my informant notified me, "that one evening when dark, she was evidently going with evil in her heart and devilish intent to lay a curse on someone, when a poor child crossed her path and in the dark knocked against her. She pulled up and cursed him, telling him that he would be dead in five days, and that when he got home he would have the fever. All of which turned out as she vowed it would.

"It happened that about a month after this incident there was a death in the community, and report had it that the man—who was undoubtedly the subject of the voodoo's vengeance—was probably the one to whose hut she was wending her way when the child was cursed by her. On seeking to know the cause of the man's death, the following strange story was told to me.

"Some two years before, a native, whom we will name Smith, with several others was secured by one of the English traders in the country and was consequently often down at the coast, where he came very much into contact with European notions and ideas; but returning later to Kumasi, he fell in love with one of the native women. The course of true love in this case did not run smoothly, for another native was anxious to secure this charming damsel, and kept a very sharp lookout on Smith.

"There were some things that Smith did not altogether approve, doubtless owing to European influences and impressions made upon him at the coast. A sort of quiet resentment seemed to permeate both men, and it was at this time that his rival for the woman's hand and heart received a visit from the same voodoo woman to whom we have already referred. Whether he had sent for her or she had come of her own accord to see him, we know not.

"One day Smith was taken ill, and the native medicine man was sent for; he looked very grave and said that he was uncertain whether a spell was being worked upon him then or not, but thinking that it must be so (for they all loved Smith), he decided if possible to break the power, if any, of the voodoo. Late that night the medicine man returned to his patient, bringing with him a bundle of herbs, three feathers from a hen, a cockscomb, and one (or both) of its legs. He deposited all these things in the center of the hut and, having closed the door, examined his patient carefully. Presently he burst into a loud laugh and said that he had discovered that a curse had been placed upon the patient, whom he directed to arise from his mat at once.

"I was unable to find out what form the curse took. Outside was the voodoo keeping guard, and as the medicine man left, report has it that she cursed him for interfering with Smith and trying to upset her work. This, of course, if true, showed her complicity in the evil work that was then being practiced on this unfortunate man. The strange part in this affair, however, is that the medicine man was never again seen in those parts, although he was reported to have gone to Cape Coast and located there. Doubtless he feared the working of the curse of the voodoo woman had he remained in her vicinity; be that as it may, Smith got better and altogether refused to believe that anyone had placed a curse upon him.

"On the first night of the new moon, however, the voodoo was seen near Smith's location, and the next day Smith had the fever. The neighbors came and did their best for him, but in vain, for that night he was delirious, and the next day was worse, and thus for nine or ten days he was in a feverish condition, when he died.

"It was reported that two green marks were found on his body, and it was surmised that on the night of his death the voodoo woman had entered his hut and injected deadly poison into him where those spots appeared. Whether this was so or not there is no means of proving, but such was the common talk of the people.

"Three days after the death of Smith, the rival married the girl, and both left Kumasi right away."

A clergyman, whom I met recently, had also had some experience of West Coast sorcerers. He informed me that they undoubtedly possess the knowledge of certain deadly poisons quite unknown to Europeans, by which it is supposed they accomplish much of their deadly work. One of these drugs, probably obtained from a plant that only grows in tropical swamps, produces madness, followed by death in a long or short period, according to the strength of the dose administered. The victim has no chance of recovery or respite when once he has swallowed the fatal draught.

A Scotsman had a Kroo-boy for a servant; the latter was very much attached to his master and thoroughly trustworthy. Now it happened that the Scotsman had gained the enmity of some native traders, and it was considered to their interests to remove the Kroo-boy from his service, that they might be able later to damage his master. Accordingly a dose of deadly poison was administered, and the poor Kroo-boy, feeling that he was becoming insane, begged his master to bind him up lest he should do him any injury. In a few days the faithful servant died—raving mad.

One day an Englishman saw a native and his wife quarreling, the former brutally assaulting the latter and wounding her badly. He interfered and knocked the native down, and assisted the woman to dress her wounds. The husband got up, muttering imprecations and vowing vengeance. A few days after, the Englishman became ill and went to a doctor. There seemed to be nothing definite the matter, but from that time he got steadily worse, becoming thinner and weaker as the weeks grew into months, and finally dying of exhaustion.

On one occasion my friend saw a sorcerer and his two disciples parading around the village armed with a sword and a long scourge, which they used on any natives who came near—apparently to overawe them—for these men are held in great fear amongst the natives. His face could not be seen, for it was closely veiled by a thick netting through which, no doubt, the man could see well. The sorcerer generally lived apart in a hut surrounded by thick foliage and situated some little distance from the village. He was consulted on all important matters and knew all that happened for miles around. There seemed to be only one sorcerer for each tribe, and when he died another took his place. He had power even to dethrone kings, should they dare to offend him.

It is probable that these higher class sorcerers are members of a secret brotherhood who have the keeping of secrets, such as the use of various plants for healing or otherwise, which have been most jealously guarded and handed down orally from a remote antiquity by those who had been initiated. The ordinary voodoos of Africa and America seem to belong to a lower order of magicians than do the sorcerers proper, and their services are more easily bought than are those of the latter class.

The Witch Doctor

(Angola)

The Ovimbundu are a southern division of an extensive group of people known as the Bundas, who, in turn, belong to the group of Bantu populations. They occupy the territory of the Bailundu and Bihe plateaus, from Benguela to the Quanza River, a tableland four thousand to upward of six thousand feet high, and in south latitude about twelve degrees. The Ovimbundu are described by Mr. Woodside as a dark-skinned people, varying from coffee brown to quite black, with thick curly hair. They are entirely uncivilized, but are a peaceable, kindly people. Their food is chiefly vegetal,

From: George A. Dorsey, "The Ocimbanda, or Witch-Doctor of the Ovimbundu of Portuguese Southwest Africa," *Journal of American Folk-Lore* 12 (1899): 183–88.

although they possess cattle, sheep, goats, pigs, and chickens. They practice polygamy, and the women prepare the food and do nearly all the field work. The men are famous as traders and journey to the interior for rubber, wax, ivory, and slaves; the latter they secure by purchase from the country of the Lubas. The principal medium of exchange is a cheap cotton cloth which is obtained from white travelers.

Among the Ovimbundu, as in nearly all parts of Africa, the witch doctor is an important personage. He is feared by all classes and often has more influence and power than the chief himself. Whenever anything is lost or stolen, they apply to the witch doctor to find out where the object is or who is the thief. As no one is supposed to die a natural death, the doctor is called in to discover the witch who caused the death. To him they go for all kinds of charms to protect themselves against all evils or to cast a spell on someone whom they wish to injure; to him they also go for help in case of sickness. He is also a diviner, reading both the past and future. At all spirit feasts, at the installation of a new chief, in preparation for war, and on almost every occasion, the witch doctor plays a prominent part. He bears an influential position among his people, and his art is the source of a considerable income, for always before he begins operations the pay must be brought and laid down before him. Thus it is that he is loath to part with even a few of his charms, much less a full set.

The *ocimbanda* does not inherit his power but must serve a long apprenticeship to some old witch doctor, whom he pays liberally. He is then given a small basket with a few charms, to which he adds from time to time. His idols and charms are not made by him but are purchased one by one. All of these objects are considered powerful, *cikola* (sacred), and the common people are afraid to touch them; even the touch of a white man is sacrilegious. One of the distinguishing features of a witch doctor's costume is a headdress, *ekufue*, made of long porcupine quills fastened together at one end, sewn to a cloth disk about two inches in diameter. Many of the quills are over a foot in length. This headdress is only worn when divining. He also occasionally wears about the loins a girdle, *uya*, consisting of a strip of antelope skin sewn together along the two edges, thus forming a pouch which contains medicines. Attached to the girdle are war charms and medicines, of which he partakes from time to time. There are also several kinds of small skins in the collection, on which the doctor kneels when about to perform. Two pigments should also be noticed. The first is a white, clayey substance, *ocikela*, with which the ocimbanda paints himself and with which he also marks the person whom by his divining he has discovered to be innocent, the sign of acquittal being a mark across the forehead and down the arms. The other pigment is a red clay, *onongo*, with which he also marks his own body and which he employs as the sign of guilt.

Of the various objects of the ocimbanda's outfit proper, the most important is the basket, *uhamba*, in which the outfit is kept. When it is said that So-and-so has a uhamba, it means that he is a witch doctor. The basket is thirteen inches high by nineteen in length, and eight inches in thickness. The ends are rounded, thus giving the basket, as seen from above, an elliptical form. The cover, three inches in height, fits closely down over the basket, after the manner of our telescope bag. The bottom of the basket is made separate and is fastened by means of an interlacing of grass braid. The sides of the basket are simply one long strip of interlaced reed and bark fiber, the ends overlapping and being fastened together by the grass braid, which passes up continuously from the bottom to the top of the basket which it circles, thus giving a decorative effect as well as affording additional strength. The lid is built in a similar manner.

Only second in importance is a small basket-shaped gourd, *ongombo*, used in divination. The basket is ten inches in diameter and three inches deep. Around the rim are bound two bands of grass fiber, thus affording strength and, by means of the manner of binding these in place, a certain amount of decoration. The basket has evidently seen much use, for the bottom is cracked in several places and has been mended with cotton thread. On two sides near the rim are two cowrie shells. The contents of this basket are extremely varied, all the objects being in the nature of charms. Among them may be enumerated several small images made of different kinds of wood, horn of a goat, ox hoof, piece of pig's foot, lion's tooth; skin from the nose of a hyena, to smell out crime; bone of a person, a supposed witch; chicken bones and a chicken head with open mouth, which is supposed to represent a gossip; and dozens of other trinkets, each having its own significance in the eyes of the witch doctor.

During the process of divination, two images, *ovitekas*, representing male and female, are set up before the ocimbanda, that he may cause them to be inhabited by spirits. These are not worshipped as idols yet are venerated in a sense by the common people, especially by women and children. The images are carved out of hardwood and stand a little over a foot in height. Each one is partially clothed in a cotton wrapper and bears about the neck several strands of native beads. They possess unusual interest, as on the back of the head of each the manner of wearing the hair of each sex is carefully portrayed. Attached to the male by a string around the neck is a rosette of dull red and yellow feathers, one of which has been artificially notched. To enable the ocimbanda to call the spirits into these images, he uses a whistle, *ombinga,* consisting of the horn of a small antelope inserted into an oxtail wrapped with beads arranged into broad bands of white, black, and red. Furthermore, when about to divine, the doctor eats a number of ants. He also has some medicines known collectively as *ovihemba,* which are kept in a skin, from which he takes and eats before and during divining. Of rattles, *ocisikilo,* shaken by the ocimbanda during the practice of his art, there are two, both bottle-shaped gourds containing canna lily seeds.

When the ocimbanda goes to divine, he first carefully spreads his skins one upon the other, and upon these he places his basket of charms. He puts white and red clay on his eyebrows, cheekbones, shoulders, and elbows; also stripes his body with these clays, and puts on his necklace and headdress, which gives him a strange, wild appearance. Taking one of the gourd rattles and giving the others to the parties interested, setting up the images, he is ready for operations. He begins by shaking the gourds and blowing the horn whistle, at the same time chanting in a minor strain, all the rest responding in chorus. In this way he works himself up into a sort of frenzy. He then takes the basket of charms and, by throwing them slightly, claims to be able to read from them the past and future and to declare the guilt or innocence of a person. In this way trivial matters, as well as the most weighty, even life and death, are decided. For instance, if while determining whether an accused person is a witch or not, in his shaking and throwing of the charms the little horn with the wax and red seeds should stand upright, that would be taken as evidence of guilt; while if, on the contrary, the little image with the small cowrie shell on the head should stand upright, that is evidence conclusive that the person is innocent. Not only is the question of guilt thus decided, but witch doctors are thought to be able to predict coming events.

An important object in the outfit is a large horn of the roan antelope, containing a smaller antelope horn, medicines, oils, etc., prepared by the ocimbanda. This is known as *ombinga*, or "loaded horn," and is considered efficacious in warding off from its possessor all harm, lightning, disease, witches, spirits, wild animals, etc. Carried upon journeys, it also ensures a prosperous issue to the undertaking and affords protection as well. Somewhat similar in construction, but used for an entirely different purpose, is the *ocifungo*, or rain wand. This is the tail of an ox, into which are inserted two small horns with medicines and oils. By blowing the horns and waving the tail, the ocimbanda is supposed to drive off rains at will.

Of numerous small charms, *umbanda*, in the collection, two are of sufficient interest to merit notice. One consists of two four-inch-long bottle-shaped objects made of woven string, from the mouth of each of which projects a two-inch tuft of very fine feathers. The two objects are joined at the top and bottom, and singly bear a decided resemblance to a Hopi *tiponi*, or religious society's palladium. They contain medicines and are worn from the neck. This is a special war charm and affords protection against bullets and all harm in battle. The other charm is an ox's hoof into which is thrust a small antelope horn and medicines. In times of special danger, it is put up somewhere in the village for protection. Still another form of fetish for protection are two small images also known as ovitekas. They, like the other ovitekas described above, are of wood but are rudely carved from two round pieces of wood about sixteen inches long. No attempt has been made to represent the human form in any detail, only the face, neck, and arms being indicated. The face of both images has been besmeared with some reddish black pigment. These were placed where the path to the village branches off to the caravan road. A small hut before which they stood was built for them, about two feet square, and between two and three feet high, with a thatched grass roof. Within was a shelf on which from time to time was placed food, corn, and a small gourd of beer. This was done to appease certain spirits which were supposed to be angry with the village and were causing sickness.

For the so-called poison test, three medicines are employed. The first and most common is known as the *ombambu*, a drug obtained from the country east of the Quanza River and represented in the collection by a piece of bark. It has the property of a powerful spinal irritant, and it is said that a very small quantity will produce death. There is a current belief among the Ovimbundu that if a bird alights upon the ombambu tree, it will fall down dead. The second drug, or ombambu, employed in the poison test is obtained from the Bihe country and is represented by several roots. It is taken in the form of a decoction. The third test is known as *onsunga*. This is a mixture of powdered herbs and is obtained from the country of the Ganguellas. With these three drugs should be mentioned a small gourd, *okopo*, used by the ocimbanda in mixing the medicines and from which the parties drink during the poison test. The test medicines are stirred with the foot of a small antelope.

Occasion for the administering of the poison may arise in various ways. Frequently one person will accuse another of being a witch. The accused may deny it and appeal to the poison test to prove his innocence. They go to the chief, who calls an ocimbanda, who mixes up a concoction in a gourd, and both the accuser and accused drink. If the drafts make one sick and he vomits, he is acquitted; and if the other one becomes very sick and does not vomit, he is said to be the witch. This same test is often appealed to in other matters where one affirms and another denies. A man may drink by proxy; that is, he may have a friend drink the poison in his stead, or more frequently, a slave drinks for his master.

Finally, it must be noted that the ocimbanda is also a medicine man. He undoubtedly possesses some really valuable remedies, but there is so much of the fetishistic cult bound up in the administering of the remedies that when they do help a person, the credit of the cure is given to the charms and incantations. Of the medicines I shall only mention four: The first is a love medicine, *ekulo*, a powdered mixture of seeds. When a wife becomes jealous of the other wives of her husband, she complains to her mother, who advises her to cook a chicken and in the broth to place some of this medicine, which, when her husband eats thereof, will compel him forever to love her above all the other wives. The second remedy is an emetic *asangu*. This is frequently used, as, for example, when in the poison test a person becomes very sick and the guilt has become fully established, the doctor will administer an emetic to save life. In cases of difficult labor, the woman is given a small piece of the bark of the *oluvanga* to chew. For rheumatism, *ovihata*, a mixed powder called *omatoli* is used.

The Evil Medicine Man
of the Shilluk

(Sudan)

The Shilluk believe that occult power of a malignant nature is possessed by a certain class of men. The man with this power is called *jal yat* (the first *a* as in *lad*, the second *a* as in *father*, and the *t* is a dental). It means the man of the tree, or medicine, as *yat* means either a tree, or the injuring or healing powers of certain compounds, which are usually derived from trees.

The men of this class are all born with the distinguishing mark. Three different marks divide them into three divisions. The first have but one testicle showing in the scrotum; the second have two, but they are very small; and the third have none. The first class is the more numerous and are the dominating class. The members of the first and second classes are supposed to be equal in the manifestation of their powers, but the third are more powerful.

Children born marked as evil medicine men are thrown into the river at birth, which is called sending them to their own country. The father alone has the power to spare his son in such a case.

The young wife always returns to her own home to give birth to her first child. After that she may either remain in the home of her husband or go to her old home, but in either case, a few hours after the child is born, a number of men come to the door of the house and sit down. If the husband is in the village, he is one of the number. If it is the woman's home, her relatives go through this formality. The men say, "What is it?" If the women within reply, "A boy," the men then ask, "It is good?" If the women reply immediately, "It is good," the men go away happy, but if the women hesitate or answer, "It is bad," the men go in to investigate. If they find the child is an evil medicine

From: D. S. Oyler, "The Shilluk's Belief in the Evil Eye: The Evil Medicine Man," *Sudan Notes and Records*, vol. 2 (Cairo: French Institute of Oriental Archaeology, 1919).

man, they immediately begin to go through certain forms. When the child is born in the wife's old home, a messenger must be sent off to the father. Should the messenger merely say that a son has been born and not tell of his deformity, the husband can recover part of the cattle he has paid for his wife, and his relatives-in-law become responsible for any damage the child may do. When the father is told that the child is bad, he usually says it must be killed. He fears to trust his relatives-in-law lest they yield to the pleadings of the mother, and so he sends a messenger to see that the child is killed. Should the father permit the child to live, he is responsible for all the evil done by him. If the father is present, he gives immediate judgment, and if it is for death, the sentence is carried out immediately.

The helpless child is always killed in a certain way. A little basket is woven and the child placed within, and then the top is also woven shut. The basket is then put in a boat and taken to the middle of the river, where it is committed to the water. The basket is a necessity, as they think that the powers of the babe are such that without the basket to restrain him, he would immediately swim ashore and escape.

When the evil medicine man is not killed, his mother loses the power to become a mother again, and when she weeps for the death of the little one, her next child will be deformed in the same way.

If the father spares the child and someone else kills it, the murderer must suffer the usual punishment for murder, which can usually be atoned for by a fine.

After an evil medicine man has reached maturity, he cannot be openly killed except under certain conditions. The people of his village may tire of his evil practices and conspire to kill him accidentally. To accomplish that end, they invite him to join them in the chase, and they manage to get him well to the front. When he is in the right position, they all throw at the animal, but he is their real target. When he falls, the men all cry out, "An accident," and no one is responsible for his death. They do not seek to kill such a person in their local fights lest their own side be thrown into disorder.

This occult power is not hereditary, but many think that the mother of an evil medicine man has some occult power if her husband is not of that class. She does not work as the men do, and the majority seem to think that such a mother is not tainted.

The evil medicine man always works on his own initiative, never at the request of another, and for that reason he never receives fees. He uses as his tools, owls, snakes, eggs, sodom apples, lizards, and crows. The medicine or power in these agents is the same as the power belonging to the man and in action unite with his power to work evil.

As a class they are without mercy and do not intercede for the children who are killed. However, if an evil medicine man has a son afflicted in a like manner, he spares his life. They try to keep people ignorant of the fact that they have the evil power, and when someone mentions the work of the evil medicine man in the presence of one of the class, he usually says, "Why are they so evil?"

They belong to the dark, as they always work at night, and when one is seen casting his charm on the house of another, if he tries to run away he may be killed, and no punishment is inflicted on the murderer; but if he is caught, and held, and then killed, the murderer is fined. If he is caught, he must pay a fine as though he had killed a man. It is very difficult to hold them, as they blind their captors temporarily by throwing some medicine in their eyes.

The statement is made that they usually try to cast their charms on houses where people are sick, and that accounts for some of their apparently wonderful achievements. This statement is also borne out by one case at the mission. The calves had been dying from some disease. One night an evil medicine man came and made a great hole in the mud wall of the barn. Some object, perhaps a snake, had been dragged among the calves, and sticks were placed in a certain manner in front of the opening. The herder was in great distress, as he was sure all of the calves would die, but not another one died from that disease.

The people firmly believe in this black art, and apparently in many cases, at least the victims believe themselves possessed of this power. They go out into a desert place at night and pray thus: "You who are God, give me this person to kill. Why was I created thus if it was not that I was to kill?" If he does not succeed at the first attempt, he tries till he is successful. Their belief in their own powers is also shown by the fact that the little boys of this class work charms on their little playfellows, apparently practicing their powers. Perhaps the child has heard much of his own evil powers, and he desires to learn whether or not he can do the wonderful things attributed to him, and as he tries he becomes convinced of his own power.

To call a man a jal yat_ is a serious matter even though it is a well-known fact that he has the power. The person making the statement must pay a fine unless he has caught the man actually working a charm. The accused says, "Whom have I injured in your house?" He does not try to plead that he is innocent of such work but only that he has not injured his accuser.

The malignant medicine man has many means of bringing disaster to people. If he is able to get a bit of hair, the parings of the nails, spittle, or anything else that has been part of the body, or the clothing of the body, he can work a charm on it, so that the owner will die. If he is ignorant of the identity of the owner, he can do nothing with these things. For that reason, when a man cuts his hair or his nails, he either hides the part removed or else puts it on a public road, so that the identity of the owner cannot be learned.

A case that illustrates their belief in that power occurred here once. One afternoon a man came in great wrath with his daughter. He said someone on the place had killed his daughter that morning. As she seemed to be in good health, his statement seemed to be a little ridiculous. When asked to explain, he said that she had been carrying water and that she had laid off her outer garment, which was of calfskin. When she returned to get her garment, she found that someone had cut a piece out of it. He was sure a man with the occult power to kill had done the deed. When examined, the edge of the marred area was seen to be rough. Others who had been working were called to see if the identity of the person doing the wrong could be ascertained. At last a boy said that he had seen two pups playing with the skin and dragging it about. He had driven them away and returned it to its place. The man was satisfied that harm had not been intended against his daughter, and she returned to work.

Over a bit of mud taken from the wall of a house, or a bit of grass from the roof, a charm can be worked that will kill the owner of the house.

When a man's club falls into the hands of one of these evil men, he buries it, which is symbolic of the burial of the owner which will soon occur, or he may kill the man by cutting the club in two, or a hoe may be given to him by the children while the older people are away. He throws the hoe into the river, and the arm of the owner is destroyed so that he cannot hoe. He may also steal a cow rope or a spear and work a charm on it that will kill the owner.

Many things are done by the evil medicine men. He cuts off a cow's tail, and the cow becomes barren; but if he treats a bull in the same way, it brings disaster on the house of the owner. Any mishap that may come to him is sure to be caused by the fact that his bull was maimed.

He may not be able to get a person in any other way and finally kills his dog. That causes the death of the master. He slips into a house and cuts off a bit of the skin on which the people sleep. The people who sleep in that house all die. He watches a person as he walks and counts his steps. The person dies. He defiles food, and those eating it die that very day. If the food is given to a dog, it coughs and swells, but it does not die. He cuts a bit out of the loincloth of a woman, and she becomes sterile.

For one special device of the evil medicine men, the good medicine men have a special counter. The evil man makes a mud image of the man he expects to kill. He sticks nails in the ears of the effigy and puts it in the fire. The man will either die or go crazy. The good medicine man makes another image of the man when he comes for help, and it is put in water, and then tends to neutralize the heat on the other image.

They have the power to bewitch a herd of cattle so that all the milk is found in the udders of their own cows, so they can injure the grain in the fields. One of the evil medicine men sees the field of a certain man yielding very abundantly, and he becomes envious. He waits till the next crop has been planted and is just coming up. He then goes to the field at night and pulls up a bit of the grain and then throws a dead snake in the field. From that time on, the field will not bear, and the owner takes a new field and leaves the old one. He may hear that a certain person is a very fast hoer. He goes at night and takes a bit of the soil from his field, and in so doing achieves a double victory. The owner of the field loses his power to hoe, and the field loses its fertility.

These men with the occult power are said to be envious of the man with a large family, and for that reason they cast many spells on little children, and they must be guarded so as not to come into the presence of such an evil man. When he spits on a child, it dies. The reason for this envy is that the man cannot have a large family. He may have many children, but as a judgment for the blood on his hands, most of them die in infancy.

The evil medicine man takes advantage of the carelessness of the people. A man may be gathering the old stalks on his field to burn them but fail to burn them that evening. An evil medicine man comes at night and burns them, and then the owner gets the ashes on his hands, and his hands swell. Or the large stick used in planting the grain may be left in the field at night, and the owner of the malignant power enters the field and burns it. The grain will grow well till it gets to be almost ready to yield the harvest, when it is burned by the sun so that it dies. Water that is left in the garden overnight may be defiled, and the people who drink it die.

The evil charmer is envious of the successful fisherman. He gets a bone of a fish that the man has caught. The fish bone is burned in the fire. That works a charm on the fish spear, so that in the future it will not be able to take the fish.

Accidents that terminate in blindness are caused by the evil medicine men.

In the hot season, when the people sleep in their yards, the evil medicine man comes at night and sprinkles blood on the sleepers, and they die.

After a person has been buried, the grave is watched for three or four nights lest the man of evil should take a bit of the earth and, by working a charm on it, kill the whole family of the deceased; but after a short time he cannot work that charm, so at the end of the fourth day the watchmen are dismissed.

When with an evil medicine man, it is well to be on the alert. When a person who is sitting with a man of that class gets up, he should brush the ground where he has been sitting so as not to leave an imprint of his body for the man to use in his witchcraft. When a person sees such a man walking behind him, he should return, and if the man is stepping exactly in his tracks, he should be taken and made to ransom the man as he was killing him. It is not safe to sleep in the same house with them, as they may defile a person in his sleep. In eating with them, it is best to stop before a person is satisfied. To strike an evil medicine man is to invite certain death. The people have the habit of asking a person to wash their backs when they are bathing. Should a person ask an evil medicine man to do that favor for him, he will be very itchy all that night and later have sores all over his back.

All the evil medicine men keep snakes, but usually they have them in a gourd or den in the fields, though a few of the most powerful have kept the snakes in their houses. To deceive the people, they pretend to fear snakes.

A man, who is reliable, tells this story of a transaction he witnessed while he was making a short trip. He came to a village where the people were very much excited. He found that the cause of the trouble was that a sick man said he had been bewitched by an evil medicine man named Akomadul. Poor Akomadul was brought into the center of the village and beaten by all of the people, until at last he cried out, "Do not kill me. I did it, but I will save him. I will remove the charm I have put on him." Akomadul then went into the house of the sick man and took out a bit of hollow *ambach* wood that had been hidden in the grass of the roof. Inside of it were a charm, an egg, and a lizard. The people were not satisfied, and they began to beat him again. He then went to the field of the afflicted man and got a charm that had been buried there. It was a large stick with an iron ring at each end, and stretched between the rings was a lizard. He next went to the doorway of the patient and took up a cooking vessel that had been buried there. The vessel was full of charms, eggs, and lizards. The chief of the village asked him why he wanted to kill the man, and he said, "He cursed me because I killed one of his relatives." Akomadul then took a white sheep and said, "I will save the man." The sheep was cut open while yet alive, and the contents of the stomach were put on the patient and on his house. The blood was put in the hole where the cooking vessel had been buried. He then said, "The man will get well. Even though you kill me, he will recover." The people wanted to kill the witch, but the chief intervened to save his life. It was reported that the man recovered after a long illness.

It can easily be seen that many ills can readily be diagnosed as coming from an evil medicine man. When the good medicine man has found that the malady was caused by an evil medicine man, he proceeds to break the charm. Different methods are used, but one or two will suffice. While the medicine man is working, the parents of the patient pray for him, if they are living. In case they are dead, his male relatives pray for him. The patient sits on the ground while the healer jumps over him in such a way as to encircle him with his legs. The medicine man then spits on his hands, and strikes the patient lightly. He then places his knees in the armpits of the afflicted person and proceeds to knead his whole body, and then concludes by stretching the patient's fingers. A chicken is then killed, put in a cooking vessel, and buried. A burning torch is then passed in circles about the head of the patient. Three *higlig* pegs are then driven in the ground near his door, and the medicine man, taking water in his hands, blesses it and sprinkles it on the ground by the pegs, and as he sprinkles it he prays, "Help my breast that the man may live. I have worked; the matter rests with You. You are God. It was You who created [the patient] and the tree [medicine]."

Others add to the above by grinding up a bit of a certain plant and giving it to the patient in water. Then grass is tied in little knots and scattered on the road, and the patient is then put in a house and a spear stuck up near his head to guard him.

The evil medicine men kill their own relatives first so as to inherit their property.

Sometimes when the evil medicine man is old, he reforms and leaves all his old practices, and hires his powers to help people. When they try to help, they are very powerful. A story was told by different people, but none of them were eyewitnesses of the cure, though they had it from a man who was present.

To begin the cure, two oxen were paid. The patient was tied so he could not move, and laid on the ground. The medicine man then called his two big snakes, and when they came to him, he said, "You see the man and the fee. Shall we help him? If you assent, go to him." The snakes went to the poor victim and, much to his terror, crawled all over him, and they even went so far as to lick his face. The patient called loudly for help and even wept. The medicine man called for water and sprinkled it on the patient, after he had blessed it, and he announced that the patient was cured.

Another reformed malignant medicine man had such power over a certain bit of water that if a person fished in it without permission, some mishap would overtake him. The required permission would be given when the fisherman promised to give as a fee the first fish taken, and another had such power over the animals in a certain district that it was not safe to hunt without his blessing, which was given by spitting on the hunter and his dogs. If that blessing was not obtained, the hunter would be devoured by lions.

As a class they accept the reputation given them and try to live up to it. They are sinned against, and they seek to repay in kind. Shunned as evil, they come to believe in the powers ascribed to them. Many of the miracles accomplished by their power follow so long after the invocation of the power that a less superstitious race would not look upon it as a result of their power.

Through superstition the evil medicine man is a power among the Shilluk. Thoughts of his power may cast a gloom over the most festive occasion, and at night when the world is peopled by the spirits of their fancies, the evil medicine man prowls about. The hooting of an owl or unusual tapping sounds caused by the wind bring a thrill of dread to the heart of the Shilluk, which cannot be dispelled by the bright light of day.

Becoming a Magician

(North Africa)

It is not always easy to become a *boka*. Haj Ali, who is himself one, says that only men who have been through the Fittan Fura and have been initiated into the Bori sect are eligible, and in order to attain to this position, the candidate must take medicines for three months from the other bokas, potions which will increase his capacity for understanding drugs and also teach him how they should be prepared. After that, he offers up a sacrifice of a red cock and a white hen, or more, according to his means, and must then burn incense in the medicine hut (*gidan tsafi*) for five nights running, taking care not to go to sleep. On the last night, his eyes are opened and he sees an *aljan* without a head and then various others, of none of which must he show the slightest sign of fear. Next night he goes into the midst of the forest and meets the dwarf Gajere Mai-Dowa, with his bow and arrow in his hand. This Bori asks what he wants, and he makes his request, and then Gajere will indicate certain roots which will give him special power in particular cases. He returns to the gidan tsafi, offers another sacrifice and incense, and is then a full-fledged Boka. He builds his own gidan tsafi and may be heard inside conversing with the Bori, who appear to him in the shape of frogs, scorpions, snakes, chameleons, etc. If very proud of his Arabic, he may call

From: A. J. N. Tremearne, *The Ban of the Bori: Demons and Demon-Dancing in West and North Africa* (London: Heath, Cranton & Ousely, Ltd., 1914).

himself an *ettabibi,* who is as much like a Boka as is a medical student who has qualified for the M.D. to one content with a mere B.S.

The Boka is a man nowadays, though I fancy at one time women were held to be more powerful in magic, for the Boka may wear a woman's headdress, and the chief *(arifa)* of the temple in North Africa is always a woman. An ordinary female has a harmful effect upon charms, as will be seen. It is said that a proper Boka is too full of medicines ever to wish for intimate relations with a female, and that if he did sleep with one he would be unable to complete the act. In any case, sexual intercourse ruins the power to call up the Bori, as is explained later on.

There was a very celebrated arifa in Tripoli some ten years ago, named Mai-Bille, who had been taken as a slave from Maradi. She had a gidan tsafi of her own, and you could hear the Bori going cheet-cheet-cheet in her house until she stopped them. Her totem was a snake, and she had one in a corner of her room which used to come out, when she would rub its head and promise it eggs and milk. There were scorpions also, and a hare, all being spirits which had taken animal form, the scorpions being some of the Yayan Zanzanna, or smallpox spirits. She kept them so that she might maintain her health and in order to make herself feared. The second reason is easy enough to understand; the other is not. But my informant, Salah, said that had she not lived with them, she would have been ill—she being so full of medicine, apparently, that it had to be given an outlet. Both Haj Ali and Salah had been her assistants, so they knew her well, but I found that her name was a byword to all in Tunis as well as Tripoli, Haja Gogo, the present arifa of Tripoli, being her successor and living in her room. She was better known by her nickname of Giwa Azuza (Old Elephant), which, however, was a compliment! It is not only the Bori which can be brought into a house; the keeper of a tomb will sometimes hear the marabout who has been buried there talking to the ghosts of others of his profession who have come to visit him. This, however, is not surprising, for in time these marabouts will become Bori just as have Mallam Alhaj and others.

Another story of her goes as follows. She would eat no meat except the testicles of rams, and one Tuesday she went to market to buy them as usual. The butcher, an Arab, who did not know her, refused to sell them to her, and she returned home in a rage and, burning incense, told the Bori what had happened. So great was the effect that from early morn till dewy eve the butcher sold none of his meat, and he could not imagine the reason, since it was quite as good—or as bad—as usual. At last, someone told him of what she had done, and he at once brought a whole carcass, testicles and all, to her house, begging her to accept it as a present and to pardon him. She graciously consented and gave him a small drop of scent to rub upon his face, commanding him not to speak a word until he had got back to his stall. He carried out her instructions, and lo! upon his return he sold out his whole stock immediately. Needless to say, she had no more trouble after that, and perhaps it was fortunate for her that she lived in North Africa. In England not so very long ago, she would have been burned as a witch.

Another anecdote is even more interesting. Azuza and another arifa named Jibaliya once had a quarrel, the latter presuming to match herself with her great colleague and saying that she could call up the Bori quite as well as could the Old Elephant. Azuza put medicines and incense into a *malafa* (straw hat) in her room, folded it, and made Salah sew the two sides of the brim together. She then challenged Jibaliya to summon the Bori, but the latter could not do so, because Azuza had imprisoned them all in her hat, and for a whole year there were no dances, since neither woman could give in. At last, however, Sidi Hamura, one of the Karamanli, gave a big performance which was to consist of seven days' Bori dancing, and Jibaliya and her people attended. But they were powerless; the drummers could not even beat the correct rolls, and after three days of failure, Sidi Hamura summoned Azuza. On her arrival she taunted Jibaliya and said, "Now see how *I* shall make you dance." She put a little incense into her mouth and chewed it, and then spat it out upon the drummers' faces, and no sooner did it touch them than they played madly. She then began to undo the hat, and immediately the spirits commenced to roar, and by the time that the hat had been opened fully, every one of the Masu-Bori present had become possessed.

Sometimes an old woman can manage to make a charm by which she sits upon a stool and can reach the sun. She squeezes it (that is the eclipse) and extracts a medicine from it by which she can make other charms. One of these is given to a woman whose rival wife *(kishiya)* has given the husband a drink and made him turn against her (the wife seeking revenge) after having preferred her to the kishiya. By means of the charm made from the sun's juice, the wife will be able to send the kishiya mad if she is able to sprinkle some of it upon the floor of her hut or can get someone else to do so. It is also a boon to a wife who has become unable to bear children. The moon can be milked in the same manner and for a similar purpose.

The moon will give people head colds if exposed to its rays, the cure for which is a bandage and certain lotions. The moon is supposed to die when it disappears, but no means are taken to bring it to life again, for it is well known that it will reappear in a few days. When there is an eclipse, however, drums are taken, and the sun is asked to spare the moon, for the sun has seized it for coming upon its path. The beating of the drums is due to North African influence, no doubt, for the same rites were performed by the followers of Hecate, who has been equated with Artemis.

The rainbow arises from a well of salt and enters an anthill. It drinks up the rain, thus preventing any more from falling. The mirage is a device of the Bori to capture travelers, and the person who is deceived by it is lost, for he gradually goes mad and the Bori drink his blood. The wind is a Bori; in fact, the name Iska is used for both. The rain is Allah's spittle or water.

The thunder is not caused by a Bori; it is a meteorite let fall by Allah. If you see where it has fallen, pour some fresh milk into the hole and you will come upon it, in shape like an iron bar. If this be melted and forged with iron into a sword, whatever you touch with it will drop dead. Abd Allah thought that the sword of Sidi Ali, with which he killed Ghul, was made in this way. Hausas who do not mind swearing falsely upon the Koran will hesitate to do so when they have called upon Aradu (thunder), for when the next storm comes, either a meteorite, lightning, or the rain will find them out and kill them. Haj Ali knows of a case where, during a thunderstorm, a man who was in a café sitting amidst friends suddenly dropped dead though no one else was injured, and it was discovered later that he had sworn by the thunder and had lied. In North Africa there is divination by thunder.

Last, though not least, come the wizard and the witch. People cannot become wizards or be witches; they must be born so. They may marry ordinary persons and have children, some of whom will possess the power of witchcraft, others not, although it is probable that the latter can develop it, for it is a hereditary gift. Office, however, depends upon merit, and a candidate for the rank of Sarikin Maiyu (Chief Wizard) is supposed to take one hundred meals of every kind of food and drink. These people catch the soul of a person they dislike and eat it, but no one can do anything to them, nowadays at any rate, because there is no actual proof which is accepted by a court, although it is well-known who is the culprit. The only thing to do is to go to a boka (who is more powerful still) and get a charm to drink or to wash with, or else to obtain a *laiya* from a *mallam*. Neither a wizard nor a witch can enter fire or deep water in safety, though both the mallam and the boka are protected against the former element.

Testing a Witch Doctor

(South Africa)

A celebrated Fingo doctor was once employed by the chief Kreli to make his army invulnerable before it started for a war. This ceremony is performed by making cuts in every man's forehead and rubbing in a specially prepared medicine. Well, on the return of this contingent, it was found that the chief had lost an uncle and a son, or at any rate they were badly wounded. The doctor was sent for, and the enraged people surrounded him and cut him to pieces before the very eyes of his own sons. His medicine had not been strong enough, they thought.

Perhaps this incident shook the faith of chief Kreli, and he was suspicious of the witch doctors and their methods on other occasions. It happened that a relative of Kreli's was ill, and of course, according to custom, the doctor was sent for to find out the cause. After the usual ceremonies, the latter announced that he had found and extracted from the sick man's body the *ubuti,* or bewitching matter; he at the same time mentioned the name of the person who had done this evil deed.

The accused man was brought and charged with the crime, Kreli saying, "Here is the very matter with which you bewitched this

From: Irene E. Toye Warner, ed., "Black Magic in South Africa," *Occult Review* 20 (1914): 210–17.

person, and which the doctor has taken from his body. *Now put it in again or die!"* The poor man protested his entire innocence and said he had neither inserted it nor could do so then.

Kreli, turning to the witch doctor, said, "Now you say that this man infused the matter and you see he cannot reinfuse it. *You* have extracted it; now *put it in again!"*

"What?" said the alarmed doctor. "This is a new thing. We can only extract ubuti; we cannot reinfuse it."

But the astute Kreli perceived that the doctor was only deceiving him and was an impostor, so he ordered his men to fall upon him, and in a few moments the witch finder was a corpse.

The Making of the Mulombe

(Rhodesia)

The following notes give details of one of the most interesting superstitions that has come to my notice; further, they refer to "that" which is held in the greatest awe by the tribe concerned (the Ba-kaonde, located in the northwest corner of Northern Rhodesia, a tribe of the Luba family). The details, which were acquired with difficulty, were furnished under a pledge of secrecy as to their origin, and I have tested them sufficiently to believe in their authenticity. Hints in court showing knowledge of the nature and habits of the Mulombe have caused something approaching consternation, and references at odd times to certain items recorded here have given rise to genuine fear in the listener.

The Mulombe is also know as Mulolo; an archaic and probably the most correct name is Sung-unyi, but this last is rarely used now. It is

From: Africanus, "'Mulombe': A Kaonde Superstition," *Journal of the African Society* 20 (1920–21): 43–45.

a snake with a man's head, made by certain wizards, that kills the people indicated to it by its owner. This is how it is made: A man wants to own a Mulombe, probably because he wants to be rid of some enemy in a secret manner; he therefore goes to a wizard who has the reputation of being able to make one, and if the wizard agrees to oblige him, he is directed to get five duiker horns. Having returned with these, the client is escorted into the bush by the wizard. The wizard then collects certain medicines, which he places on a piece of bark and mixes with water. He then puts the five duiker horns near the concoction, after which he proceeds to pick some spiky grass (luwamba) and plaits it—the plait is from fifteen to eighteen inches long and from one-half to one inch wide. At one end of this plait he places the five duiker horns. Parings are then taken from the client's fingernails and are placed inside the horns. Incisions are next made on the client's forehead and chest, blood from which is put in the medicine. It is then all mixed together, and a part of it is given to the client to drink. The plaited luwamba is then laid upon the ground, the horns pointing away from the wizard and toward the client. Another plait of luwamba is then made, which is dipped into the remaining medicine, and the medicine is thus sprinkled by means of the second plait upon the first plait, which is lying flat. At the first sprinkling, the prone plait changes into a white substance (the color of white ashes). At the second sprinkling, it becomes a snake. At the third sprinkling, the snake develops the head, shoulders, and arms (in miniature) of the client (later the shoulders and arms disappear), the rest remaining like a snake. It has also, reproduced in miniature, any ornaments that the client may be wearing on the parts reproduced, such as a bangle, necklace, shell, etc. This is the Mulombe. It rears itself upon its tail and addresses the wizard's client.

Mulombe: "You know me and recognize me?"

Client: "Yes."

Mulombe: "You see that your face and mine are the same, and that your necklace and shell [or whatever the ornaments may be] are the same as mine?"

Client: "Yes."

Then the wizard chips in.

Wizard: "There is the Mulombe that you asked me for; take it and tend it carefully. You may keep it where you will—in the reeds by the river [the usual place], in your hut, or wheresoever you wish. It will always be with you now, and so long as you treat it well, so long as it be really well looked after, you will not die—until all your relatives be dead; so tend it carefully. Farewell."

They then separate, the client taking his Mulombe with him and the wizard departing upon his own lawless occasions.

Before long the Mulombe says to his owner, "I want a person to eat." The owner then has to indicate a person whom it may kill. After the kill, the Mulombe comes back very happy and crawls about its owner, licking him all over; which licking makes the body very clean and the owner fat and sleek. It is not long, however, before the Mulombe gets hungry again—hungry for killing, that is, for it does not really eat the victim; in fact it leaves no mark, but the expression "eat" is used—and another victim must be indicated. The owner, if he refuses to indicate a person, becomes ill and will not be cured until he gives way to the importunities of his Mulombe. Provided that he keeps the Mulombe in victims as demanded, he will live and wax fat until all his relatives have died.

But—and here is the fly in the ointment—it probably happens that owing to the numerous deaths that have occurred because of the insatiable appetite of the Mulombe, the people get suspicious and call in a diviner to ascertain the cause of the trouble. The diviner, generally by bone throwing, finds out that someone has a Mulombe and also divines where he keeps it. No hint of this is allowed to reach the man implicated, who—all unsuspecting—remains happily in the village. Then the diviner chooses five strong men and guides them to the Mulombe's lair—which is also invariably near a river. Arrived there he takes some medicine, previously prepared, and sprinkles the adjacent ground with it; rumblings ensue, and water comes out of the river, rising till it reaches the thighs of the men. Then fish come out in large numbers, followed by crabs; and finally the Mulombe itself, rearing itself upon its tail. A poisoned arrow, prepared and brought in readiness for this climax, is fired at it, and the dread thing falls writhing to the ground. Simultaneously the owner, in the village, feels as if he had been shot with an arrow, and he also falls writhing to the ground. Soon the Mulombe dies, and at the same moment the owner dies. Thus are the victims avenged and the deaths in the village cease.

Jinns and the Evil Eye

(Turkey)

Turkish jinns of modern times differ from their cousins, the genies of *Arabian Nights* stories, in that they work only harm to men. Anatolians have no trouble with the belief in a personal devil and his demon legions, which is the background of what we find in the Gospels on this subject. To the ordinary people of the country, earth and air and sky are peopled with spirits malign as well as benign, and to neutralize the one is quite as important as to utilize the other.

An old Hoja, venerable in beard and robe of fur, once informed me that God first created the holy angels, then the devilish jinns of seventy-two classes corresponding to the seventy-two races of men, and finally God created man with character and possibilities partly angelic and partly devilish. The nature of jinns may be understood from the fact that one day after the afternoon call to prayer they destroyed eighty thousand prophets. This was before the creation of man! How there could be eighty thousand prophets before the creation of man is a question that perhaps never occurred to the Hoja, and if one should put it before him, it might seem like needless homiletic nicety. For this offense, Allah wiped the jinns out; that is, he wiped them out of *sight*, and now they are seldom allowed to appear to human eyes. There is also a gruesome fear of ghosts, especially in case of a recent death or in the neighborhood of a cemetery. Jinns are to be expected on moors, by rushing streams or roaring mills, in dark corners and lonely places, where they lurk to work harm to the unwary. They bewitch people and things, and deprive men of their reason; they bind "spells" and pervert the ordinary operation of beneficent natural law; they cause sickness, deformity, lunacy, epilepsy, and even death. Things ought to go well in this world, but they don't because of the activities of these bad jinns.

Fear of the evil eye seems to be a weakened form of the belief in

From: George E. White, "Evil Spirits and the Evil Eye in Turkish Lore," *Moslem World* 9 (1919): 179–86.

hurtful jinns, and both are perhaps a remnant of old-time devil worship. Indeed, the Yezidis of eastern Asia Minor are alleged to be devil worshippers now. Their theory is the negative one of trying to get through life without laying one's self liable to penalty or persecution. God will do men no harm, being of a benevolent disposition, and if they can only "square" Satan, if they can only keep the powers of evil inactive, they will get through the world reasonably well. The chosen people of the old covenant "sacrificed unto demons, which were no God" (DEUT. 32:17), "yea, they sacrificed their sons and their daughters unto demons" (PS. 106:37). In the time of Paul we find him saying: "The things which the Gentiles sacrifice, they sacrifice to demons, and not to God: and I would not that ye should have communion with demons. Ye cannot drink the cup of the Lord, and the cup of demons, ye cannot partake of the table of the Lord, and of the table of demons" (I COR. 10:20, 21). People generally are not Yezidis as we meet them now, but even the intelligent assert and believe that "if we say three-fourths of the dead are in their graves because of the evil eye, we would not be at fault." They are horribly afraid of the "glance" of a person of "short stature, blue eyes, and fair hair." But whether some dreaded "eye" is seen or not, many souls pass their worldly existence in bondage to this fear.

Thus it becomes serious business to break, or better yet to avoid, the wiles of the jinn and the spell of the evil eye. One method, naturally, is to invoke the aid of saints and all good powers. The Muslim teacher Solomon Hoja, after relating that the earth is full of jinns, said that to avoid danger when one goes out at night he should "read" constantly, at any rate he should read (that is, repeat sacred passages from memory) just as he leaves the house door, and particularly as he puts on his shoes. If he does so, he is safe for that walk, especially if he also gently blows in different directions, for blowing the breath is very efficacious in warding off evil spirits, as also is spitting in any direction from which they may be feared. Amulets and charms are very powerful, and their use is all but universal.

Piles of small stones are often seen by the roadside, and passersby heap them higher by adding a stone or two to secure "traveler's luck." One theory is that the pile of stones holds the evil spirits down and prevents their doing harm to people from home. If by casting a small stone on a pile a wagoner may secure protection for a mile, it is a cheap form of insurance, when on any mile of the road a horse may sicken, the wagon break down, or robbers waylay the driver.

Lunacy, epilepsy, and other afflictions are attributed to possession by demons. A man who could not control his mouth properly, probably owing to paralysis, told me that he attributed it to the jinns. If a person is believed to be possessed, one form of treatment is to heat an iron chain red-hot, form it into a ring, and pass the suffering person through the loop, on the theory that evil spirits cannot pass the hot chain, and so they are torn loose from their victim and left behind. Almost every oriental church has its room for the treatment of the insane. They are brought to the sacred building, placed in this room, which is usually very bare and often underground, and allowed to remain overnight. Then the friends earnestly look for signs of returning reason, and if they find them, take the sufferer home with cheer; if they see no sign of improvement, they prolong the detention in hope that the recovery will take place in time.

To continue the Christian parallel, the Armenian monastery near our city has a hand cased in silver alleged to be the hand of Saint Andrew. In one instance, an insane person was locked in the room with this relic overnight and pronounced quite rational in the morning. The office of exorcist has been of much importance in the Eastern churches, and prayers for the banning or exorcism of evil spirits are in constant use. At the baptism of an infant, the priest recites prayers over the water to purge it of such evil presence and blows toward the four points of the compass across the font for the same purpose. Twice a year or more, the priests sprinkle each house of their congregation with holy water to drive away lurking spirits, and that precautions may never be omitted, sacred pictures are hung upon the house walls. These pictures are of saints of the church and are hung first for forty days in the church to hallow them. Then they are put upon the wall of a humble house, and little lamps filled with pure olive oil are often kept alight before them, especially at the sacred seasons in the calendar.

A village woodsman of Muslim faith living not far from my home thought his companions called him to rise and go as usual to the forest. Though it was night, he set out and followed a phantom leader a dozen miles with bare and bleeding feet, until he came to a place known as God's Valley, and there he saw a big meeting of jinns— thousands of them, a veritable pandemonium. A venerable person was at their head as king, a sort of Beelzebub, and the sight finally overcame the woodsman and drove him away. His phantom leader then brought him to a point near his home and left him, but after that experience the man was epileptic and dumb. His friends took him to a famous holy man to "read" over him. This was done, and the dumb man was relieved to such an extent that he spoke and related his story as given here, but he continued to be subject to epileptic attacks about once a month. One of my acquaintances, a Georgian by race, claims to be a successful exorcist and tells me of various cases he has cured. His standard remedy is to write a passage from the Law of Moses, the Psalms, the Gospels, or the Koran and bind it on the neck of the patient.

Dervishes and others are believed to call up familiar spirits. Compare the difficult passage concerning the woman of Endor (I SAM. 28:7–25). A dervish searches his sacred volumes amid the ruins of some deserted village or old castle, and endeavors to learn from familiar spirits where to look for buried treasure. The custom must be very common, for every foreigner is believed to be able to locate hidden treasure in this way. My Georgian friend is a professional *jinnji*, who claims to deal with familiar spirits, to wield occult powers, and to exorcise demons. He has invited me to be present and witness his ceremony of exorcism at some convenient opportunity. But he has even more earnestly proposed that we should join forces, form a partnership, and by combining our skill, endeavor to locate hidden treasure in certain Hittite ruins on a site with which we are both familiar, and with the supposition on his part that there is a good prospect of our locating buried treasure of fabulous value. If a robbery has been committed, a dervish or Hoja may be summoned, who for a small fee will "read" over a cup of water in which some member of the family, preferably a child, may then see black jinns and from them learn such information as whether the thieves were male or female, young or old, tall or short, fair or swarthy, departed to the east or west, and the like. Acting on this information, the parties then endeavor to track the thieves and recover their property. This experiment was tried by a constable, whose young son saw three jinns in the water—but they did not catch the thieves. Gypsies often have recourse to the same means and would hardly continue it if they did not find some satisfactory reward in doing so.

Near us is an important coast and commercial city, and the governor of the district is the absolute ruler of a quarter million people. I once called on the governor in company with the official inspector of agriculture, a Greek gentleman with a European education. As I walked with the inspector through the governor's vineyard, my attention was attracted by a "tink-tink" sound, which I soon found came from a tiny windmill set up on a pole. Each revolution of the wheel raised a little tin rod which dropped and produced the tinking noise. What was the purpose of the windmill and its little noise? To keep the evil eye off the vineyard, by fixing its attention upon the unusual sight and sound of the little mill.

To keep the evil eye from a child, blue beads are put upon it; to avert it from a field, garden, tree, or threshing floor, a skull of some animal is erected on a pole; to counteract its influence on a mill, a great placard with the words WONDER OF GOD is nailed to the roof; to protect a dwelling, a bunch of garlic or a pair of deer's antlers is fixed in a conspicuous place; to prevent milk from souring, bits of charcoal are laid upon it; to protect a camel, its saddle is made of a particular kind of wood; and so forth *ad infinitum*. People's notions and fears of the evil eye vary with their environment and the degree of their intelligence, but there is no marked difference traceable to religious connection.

I was once asked by a villager whom I had never seen before to tie a knot on a string he had wound around his wrist. It seems he had malaria, attributed it to some evil influence, and thought he might use me to bind the spell. His notion was, perhaps, not that I would hold an acceptable brief for him with the superhuman powers, but that I as a Christian would be so *unacceptable* as to attract the evil being and release him. I would thus render a service similar to that performed by a skull planted on a pole in a garden, whose unsightliness transfixes the evil eye and leaves the tender plants to grow without harm.

Just as a bridal couple entered their new home, I once observed an old woman smashing an earthen dish at their feet. Her idea was that as we see human life, we may safely infer that there are superhuman and inhuman forces at work which are likely to smash something. It is better therefore to get the start of them, to keep them quiet by doing their work for them, and lose the value of a cheap dish rather than endanger the health or property of the new household. If such a superstition is not a survival of devil worship, I know not how to account for it.

On the whole, the power most trusted, whether as a prophylactic against or as a remedy for the ill effects of evil spirits or evil eyes, is "reading," that is, reciting from some of the sacred books. If a sheep does not come in from its pasturage at nightfall, read to protect it. Then if a wolf pursues, it cannot catch the sheep; if it catches, cannot bite it; if it bites, cannot pull its teeth out; and the sheep will reach home dragging the wolf as its victim, or rather as the victim of the powerful reading. If the charm does not work—God knows best.

For many people, almost the whole life is passed in bondage to this fear. They are especially anxious for young and tender plants and animals, and tell how often they have seen such an object helpless and beloved overtaken by some "stroke." A foreigner soon learns not to praise children, or even a driver's horses, without adding an expression like "wonder of God" to avert the evil eye which might be attracted by the praise. Some have supposed that Orientals were indifferent to children because they do not express appreciation of them in the presence of strangers and resent such expressions from strangers. Really Orientals love their children exceedingly well, but they dread the awful bewitching. They fear to leave a baby alone in a house, lest jinns get it, but a measure of protection is attributed to the presence of a broom. Native Christians sometimes fix a cross composed of sticks of wood over the chimney of the house to prevent witches from flying down and strangling the little children. A driver on the road is easily troubled about his horses, lest they suffer from some evil glance. If he tells you his trouble, you may recommend him to blow or spit gently toward any person he suspects, and he will probably tell you that he does so every time he sees any reason for suspicion, but the charm doesn't always seem to work perfectly. It is always dangerous to whistle, for you may summon evil spirits by doing so.

Some persons claim to exercise the power of the evil eye. One man, boasting of his accomplishment, called the attention of another to the third camel of a passing caravan, and immediately the beast stumbled and fell. Its saddle, however, was made of the right kind of wood, and the animal rose and went on its way without further harm. Usually one does not like such a reputation and may have his life made miserable by possessing it. People come and cut slivers from the threshold of a person thus feared, to use by way of antidote, and I have heard of old women whose thresholds would be so cut away in consequence that it would be necessary to renew the wood several times a year. If milk from a cow unaccountably sours, the owner will not sell any more, unless perhaps he ventures to do so after tying a powerful writing wrapped up in leather to the horn of his cow. Greek miners, serfs under Turkish feudalism, sometimes quake at a vision of phantom men, tall, large, and hairy. A miner then knows that he has found a rich vein of ore, and further, that he has not long to live. And to pass from things below to things above earth, an eclipse of the sun or moon is habitually attributed to a jinn or dragon trying to swallow the heavenly luminary. The people then get out at once with guns, tin pans, and anything that can make a noise, and try to intimidate and frighten away the awful monster. The sun and moon are always saved, and people rejoice that their efforts have been successful.

People seriously fear to be cursed, and probably at bottom the reason is that they fear curses will release the power of evil spirits or will neutralize all the intercession and influence of beneficient spirits. Evil beings are too many and too strong to be treated with impunity. Life in the Orient is somber. Even its music is in minor keys and mournful. Our fellow human beings pass their days in bondage unto fear.

The Evil Eye

(Sudan)

The Shilluk believe firmly in the power of the evil eye. A few claim that the people who cast the evil eye belong to the evil medicine men and receive their power from them, but the people are almost unanimous in saying that they have their power separately, and they think that it comes from God. The fact that the power is inherited tends to prove that they are really a separate class.

From: D. S. Oyler, "The Shilluk's Belief in the Evil Eye: The Evil Medicine Man," *Sudan Notes and Records*, vol. 2 (Cairo: French Institute of Oriental Archaeology, 1919).

When one person in a family has the evil eye, the house is spoken of as the house or family with the evil eye, though all the members of the family may not have that power. A man may have this power, and his wife be all right, or it may be the wife that is affected, but in every case all their children are affected, though the unaffected husband may have untainted children by another wife. This taint is carried by their descendants, and theoretically at least is supposed to extend to the end of time.

A girl who has the power of the evil eye is not sought in marriage, and while the man afflicted in this manner is not desirable as a husband, yet he does not have so much trouble in getting a wife. This is not because they differentiate between the sexes but because a man pays a heavy dowry for his wife, and he does not want to buy a tainted wife, whose children will also bear the taint of a hidden power. If the afflicted man has the price, the father is very often willing to accept him for a son-in-law, and that is especially true when the daughter is not very desirable. As a class the people with the evil eye try to keep their neighbors ignorant of their powers.

In addition to those who inherit the evil eye, others suddenly receive the power. It suddenly falls upon them or comes on them. They know not how it comes, but suddenly they find themselves with that dread power.

A person possessed of the evil eye cannot always be distinguished. The fact that a certain person has that power is known in his own village, and the stranger coming in soon inquires about it and is told. However, one mark can be relied on to some extent, and that is if a person has eyes in which the whites are small and the iris is large in proportion, and the iris is very dark. This test is not sure, as some people of the class do not have this mark, and others who do not have the power have the mark.

The possessed is conscious of the fact that he has the power and may even mention the fact. The power is made operative by looking fixedly at the person to be made the victim. The person exercising the power is usually in anger when the deed is done. The person who is bewitched says the eye went into him, and if the person who did the deed speaks of it, he will usually say that his eye went into the person.

The evil eye does not always take effect in the same part of the body. If the curse falls on the eye, the person will have sore eyes terminating in blindness. They recognize three causes of blindness, other than accidents. Blindness may follow smallpox or measles, or else it is the result of the evil eye. When the evil eye strikes the ear, deafness is the result, and when it is on the head, sores and swellings appear on the head. When the body is affected, it is covered with sores. The intestines or the liver may be the part afflicted, and they swell to unnatural size, and the worst part about it is that the swelling is permanent. One young man, who was a very fine looking child, was afflicted thus, and ever since he has been out of proportion. The doctors called it enlargement of the spleen. A man who is a very swift runner may have the evil eye take effect in his feet, and in that case the feet swell and the victim has trouble in walking. The curse may fall on the teeth, and they decay. The evil eye may strike the unborn babe, and it disappears. The most dangerous place to have the evil eye take effect is in the heart, and in case it does, the victim cannot live through the day.

The evil eye is not confined to the body, but it may also affect the domestic animals belonging to a person. When a person drinks the milk of a cow that has been touched by the evil eye, it causes his insides to swell. A very fine appearing cow is not permitted to go into the village by herself but is kept with the herd, and she is to be kept in the middle of the herd so that she may not be seen, and the curse come on her. A very fine calf is always kept hidden. Sheep may become the victims of the evil eye.

The power extends beyond animate things to the inanimate. A blacksmith may make a very fine bracelet, and it breaks as he is putting it on the wrist of the owner. The bracelet was bewitched by the evil eye. When a very fine spear breaks when it is being polished just after it is made, it is because of the evil eye.

As can be seen from some of the effects of the evil eye, the Shilluk's idea of sickness has much to do with the increasing of their belief in the evil eye. They do not think of a disease as being contagious so much as they think of it being spread by some hostile agency. Some people carry their views to such lengths that they are inclined to think that every accident and every case of sickness is caused by some occult agency. The power may be exercised by some other agent than the person with the evil eye.

When a person is taken sick, all the symptoms are very thoroughly discussed by the people of the village, and if some mysterious features or circumstances are brought to light, it is immediately looked upon as a visitation from some occult power. Most cases of sickness present some puzzling features, and so it is easy to give credit to the evil eye for much of it. Most accidents occur not because someone was careless but because some hidden power was invoked against the person. The patient is then taken to the good medicine man. He goes through certain forms to determine the source of the evil charm. He may decide it is from the evil eye or from an evil medicine man.

When a medicine man undertakes to cure a case of the evil eye, he aims to do two things. The first is to cure the person suffering, and the second is to put that particular charmer with the evil eye out of business. A sheep is brought, and the medicine man heats a nail red-hot. With the nail he blinds the sheep. He then tells the patient that he is cured, and at the same time the burning out the eyes of the sheep is a type of what will happen to the person who cast the spell. His eyes will waste away. If the eyes of the person who cast the spell do not become inflamed, the cure does not take effect. When the person who casts the charm hears of the cure performed by the medicine man, he hastens to him at night and beseeches him to spare his eyes. The medicine man exacts a good fee from him and then assures him that he will save his eyes, but warns him not to do it again and threatens to kill him if he sees him casting the evil eye on another person.

A person with the evil eye can cure a person who is suffering from the evil eye. Of course he gets a good fee for it. Before he takes the case he gets a small fee, such as a sheep or a hoe, and after the case is cured he demands a large fee, usually a cow. The patient sits down near the person who is to treat him. The latter says, "You have come near me; therefore you will not die." He then grinds up a bit of wood and, putting it in water, makes the patient drink it.

The spell of the evil eye may be cast in the presence of people, and all present even to the victim may be ignorant of what is being done, though it may be known. The man with the evil eye may be seen staring at the victim. For that reason the Shilluk do not like to have a person look them in the eye. When a person stares at a Shilluk, he usually averts his eyes or protests.

When the evil eye has been cast on a person, he very seldom tries to discover the identity of the person who bewitched him. Should the person boast of having done it, he will be fined as though he had killed a man. The victim may have seen the person staring at him and directly accuse him of the act, but that is not always safe, as the case is brought before a medicine man. If the person accused of casting the evil eye shows fear, he is guilty and must pay a fine equal to that paid for killing a man. If he shows no fear, it was a false accusation, and in that case the accuser must pay an equal fine for his false charge.

The motive for using the evil eye is usually envy or jealousy or anger, for the evil eye always picks a shining mark; it does not fall on poor people, nor is a poor thing bewitched. A poor man may occasionally be the victim of the evil eye, but it is always an accident, as he has eaten food that has been bewitched to catch a richer person. They take some precautions to avoid the evil eye.

If a person has some very choice food, it is covered so that the evil eye may not fall on it. Food is very often bewitched, but it is usually meat or fish that is tainted, and it is very seldom that food made from grain is affected. Food that has had the evil eye cast on it can be made fit to eat by giving some of it to a dog. They say that the dog takes off the eye. The milk of a cow that has been affected can be cleansed by taking some of it in a vessel and pouring it on a fire. The fire is put out, and from that time the milk of that cow is safe to use. If these precautions are not taken, the food will cause nausea. After the nausea has passed, evil consequences may remain, or a person may be all right.

The natives weave their hair into fantastic shapes. If a person has very fine hair, he puts a few thorns in it to keep off the evil eye. Should the evil eye fall on his hair, his head would break out in sores.

When a person has his body well oiled or covered with some fine ashes, he is very likely to have the evil eye cast on him. To escape that misfortune, he takes a cucumberlike pod from a wild plant and takes out the seeds. Some of the seeds are put on the temples, and some on the neck, and others on the tip of the shoulder blade, or the entire fruit may be worn suspended from the neck.

When butter is boiled to clarify it, the work is usually done at night so that the evil eye may not be cast on it.

The Shilluk will not say that they are in good circumstances, lest it be heard by some envious person and he should cast the evil eye on their possessions. When a rich man is asked in regard to his property, he usually says, "I have one or two cows, but they are very poor cows."

The parents of a very fine looking child do not like to let people see it for fear someone will cast the evil eye on it, and the parent is very angry when someone comments on the good appearance of the child. Should the child be taken sick, the parents call on the person who made the remark and demand that he pay the fine required when a person is killed. The accused usually holds out, and a compromise is affected. He brings a sheep, and one of its ears is cut off. The sheep then is a witness against the man, and by doing that, he assumes the responsibility for the child. If it dies, he pays the fine as though he had killed it. Even if the child reaches maturity and dies, the man is responsible and must pay the fine.

Frequently people have hard knots in their flesh. These are really stones that have been put there by someone with the evil eye. The swellings do not disappear.

The Shilluk have a custom that when a person is threshing his grain, they go to beg from him. Sometimes they go in such numbers that the man has very little left for himself, but he does not dare to refuse for fear someone in the party may cast the evil eye on him. He gets even by going to beg from some other person.

They give a few warnings as to conduct when with a person who has the evil eye. If you walk with a person who has the evil eye, let him walk in front, for if you go in front you give him a good chance to cast the evil eye on you. When a person with the evil eye begs from you, grant his request, because when he accepts your present his power over you is broken and he cannot injure you. He may regain his power if he comes again and is refused, for if you refuse him, he becomes angry and casts the evil eye on you. When eating, let the oldest of the party take the food first, so that if the evil eye has fallen on the food, he may detect it, and the food can be cleansed. When eating with a man who has the evil eye, do not eat much or he will kill you. When you are angry at a certain village, do not enter that village or you will get the evil eye. Do not speak harshly to a man who has the evil eye, or he will cast the spell on you.

Once a man gave his daughter to the king to be his wife. The girl had the evil eye, and when the king learned that fact, he gave the woman to another man lest she kill his other wives.

At the present time a chief is suffering from the evil eye. The people of another village had stolen his cow. He went to the village in anger and talked harshly. While there he felt a chill run through his body. He went home and took sick. His body has sores on it that have come from the evil eye.

The man with the power to cast the evil eye is feared by the people, but he is not feared as much as the evil medicine man. When he causes death, it is usually sudden, though it may be lingering. When a person with the evil eye dies, the people of the village rejoice, though they do not show their joy openly.

The possessors of the evil eye are deceived even as the people who fear them. They go through life apart from their fellow men in many respects. They believe in their own evil powers, and while their claims sound childish to us, yet we must consider the fact that the history of the English-speaking world reveals the fact that our ancestors were afraid of witches, even after they had reached a much greater development than the Shilluk has attained.

Three-Things Came Back Too Late

(West Africa)

The great-grandfather was a heathen and a polygamist. He had four wives. One of them was a member of an interior tribe, the Boheba, more heathenish and superstitious than his own Batanga coast tribe. Unknown to him, she was a member of the Witchcraft Society, had power with the spirits, and they with her, attended their secret night meetings, and engaged in their unhallowed orgies.

The husband, though not a member of the society, had acquired some knowledge of witchcraft art and, though without the power to transform himself as wizards did, was able to see and know what was being done at distances beyond ordinary human sight.

From: Robert Hamill Nassau, *Fetichism in West Africa* (New York: Charles Scribner's Sons, 1904).

One night she arose from her bed to go and attend a witchcraft play. She left her physical "house," the fleshly body, lying on the bed so that no one not in the secret, seeing that body lying there, would think other than that it was herself nor would know that she was gone out. In her going out she willed to emerge as Three-Things, and this triple unit went off to the witchcraft play. The husband happened to see this and watched her as she disappeared, saw where she went, and though distant and out of sight, knew what she was doing. So he said to himself, "She is off at her play. I also will do some playing here; she shall know what I have done."

Among the several things of which followers of witchcraft are afraid, and which weaken their power, is cayenne pepper. So this man gathered a large quantity of pepper pods from the bushes growing in the *behu* (kitchen garden) and bruised them in a mortar to a fine soft pulp. This he smeared thoroughly all over the woman's unconscious body as it lay in her bedroom. He left not the smallest portion of her skin untouched by the pepper—from her scalp to the interstices of her fingers and toes, minutely over her entire body.

Meanwhile, with the woman at her play, the night was passing. The witches' sacred bird, the owl, began its early morning warning hoot. She prepared to return. As she was returning, the first morning cockcrow also warned her to hasten, lest daybreak should find her triple unit outside of its fleshly "house." So the three came rushing with the speed of wind back to her village. Her husband was on the watch; he heard this panting sound as of a person breathing rapidly and felt the impulse of their wind as she reached her hut and came in to reenter their house.

He saw her approach every possible part of the body, seeking to find even a minute spot that was not barred by the pepper. She searched long and anxiously, but in vain; and in despair they went and hid herself in a woodpile at the back of one of the village huts, waiting in terror for some possible escape.

All this the husband saw silently. When morning light finally came, he knew that this wife was dead, for her life-spirit had not succeeded in returning to its body within the specified time. It was therefore a dead body. But he said nothing about it to anyone and went off fishing.

As the morning hours were passing while he was away and the woman's door of her hut was still closed, his children began to wonder and to say, "What is this? What is the matter? Since morning light our father's wife has not come out into the street." After waiting awhile longer, their anxiety and curiosity overcame them, and they broke in the door. There they saw the woman lying dead. They fled in fear, saying, "What is this that has killed our father's wife?" They went down to the beach to meet him as he returned from fishing and excitedly told him, "Father, we have found your Boheba wife dead!"

The man, to their surprise, did not seem grieved. He simply said, "Let another one of my wives cook for me; I will first eat." Still more to their surprise, he added, "And you, my children, and all people of the village, do not any of you dare even to touch the body. Only at once send word to her Boheba relatives to come."

This warning he gave his people, lest any of them should sicken by coming close to the atmosphere that the witch had possibly brought back with her from her play.

By the time he had finished eating, the woman's relatives had arrived. They were all heavily armed with guns and spears and knives, and were threatening revenge for their sister's death.

The man quietly bade them delay their anger till they had heard what he had to say, and took them to the woman's hut that they themselves might examine the corpse, leaving to them the chance of contamination.

They examined; they lifted up the body of their sister and searched closely for any sign of wound or bruise. Finding none, but still angry, they were mystified and exclaimed, "What then has killed her?" And they seated themselves for a verbal investigation.

But the man said, "We will not talk just yet. First stand up, and you shall see for yourselves." As they arose, the man said, "Remove all those sticks in that woodpile. You will find the woman there."

So they pulled away the sticks and there they found Three-Things.

"There!" said the husband. "See the reason why your sister is dead!"

At that the relatives were ashamed and said, "Brother-in-law! we have nothing to say against you, for our eyes see what our sister has done. She has killed herself, and she is worthy to be punished by fire." (Burning was a common mode of execution for the crime of witch-craft.)

In her terror at being unable to get back into her mortal body, all the while she was hidden in the woodpile, Three-Things had shriveled smaller and smaller until what was left were three deformed crab-shaped beings a few inches long with mouths like frogs. These, paralyzed with fear, could not speak but could only chatter and tremble.

So the relatives seized Three-Things and also carried away the body, and followed by all the people of the village, they burned it and them on a large rock by the sea.

The Jealous Witch-Wife

(West Africa)

A man of the Orungu tribe in the Ogowe region had several wives, of whom the chief, commonly called the "queen" or head wife, had no children. This was a grief to her and a disappointment to the husband. But one of his younger women, who had now become his favorite, had a baby, and the head wife was jealous of her.

The husband still retained the older one as the bearer of the keys and in direction of the other women, though he was beginning to doubt her, as he suspected her of witchcraft. But he said nothing about it, not being sure.

It is believed that witches can enter houses without opening doors or breaking walls, and can do what they please without other people knowing of it at the time. So one night this man and his young wife were sleeping in the same bed with their little babe. Suddenly, after midnight, the mother happened to wake up startled. She missed her baby from the bed. She looked and looked all over the bed from head to foot and did not find it. Then she was frightened, woke up her husband gently, and told him in a whisper, "The child is missing! I don't see the child!"

The husband told her to get up and light a gum torch (for there were coals smoldering on the clay hearth used as a fireplace), that they

From: Robert Hamill Nassau, *Fetichism in West Africa* (New York: Charles Scribner's Sons, 1904).

might look for the child. She did so, and both hunted, looking under the bedstead and elsewhere, but did not find the child. Then they examined the windows and door, for perhaps the child had been taken out by someone. The door and windows were all properly fastened. The mother was very much troubled, but her husband, keeping his own counsel, advised her not to scream or make a noise but said, "Let us go back to bed, but not to go to sleep, and let the room be dark again." So the wife put out the torch, leaving the room in darkness, and they returned to bed. Then the husband said, "Maybe we can prove or see something before morning" (for he suspected), and he added, "Whoever or whatever has taken the child out so secretly will secretly bring it back. So we must not sleep but watch."

So both lay awake in bed for a few hours. Then, just before morning, while it was still dark, they heard a little noise outside near the house, like the rustling of wings and the panting of breath. They were both anxious and had their eyes wide open. Soon they saw the room flashed full of a bright light from the roof. (Witchcraft people are noted for having a light which they can thus flash.) Then the wife, as soon as she saw the light, quietly nudged her husband, and he returned the pressure, to let her know that he was aware and also to intimate that she should continue silent as himself, and they pretended to be sleeping soundly.

Soon they saw the figure of a woman descend from the low roof, but with no hole in the roof. The figure came to the bedside and lifted up the edge of the mosquito net with one hand, in the other holding a child. As soon as she attempted to put the baby back in its place between the father and mother, the father, as he was the stronger and nearer to the figure on the outside of the bed, got up quickly and seized both hands of the woman before she had time to let go of the child and escape from the room. He said aloud to the mother, "Get up! Your baby has been missing. Now light the light, and we will see the person face-to-face who has taken the child out!"

The young mother did so, and they discovered that it was the head wife who had brought in the child.

Then, when the father felt the body of the babe, it was limp—and burning with fever.

As it was so near daylight, the father did not delay but began at once to make a fuss and shouted for the people of the village to gather together. And he began a *palaver* (investigation) immediately. When all the people had assembled to hear the palaver, both the father and the mother related what had passed during the night about their missing the child and its return.

The head wife, being accused, was silent, having nothing to say for herself; for she was both ashamed and afraid to confess that she had been eating the life of the baby. But all the people knew that such things were done, and they believed that this woman had done with the baby whatever she wanted to do while she had it outside that night.

Then the father of the child tied up the head woman, and said to her, "Now I have you in my hands, I will not let you go until you give back the baby's life and make it well again." (The belief is that if the "heart life" has not been eaten, the victim can recover.) This she was not able to do, for she had eaten its "heart." So the next day the baby died. And the husband executed that head woman by cutting her throat.

A Witch-Sweetheart

(West Africa)

A certain man loved a woman whom he expected to marry. He visited her regularly. Whenever he intended to visit her, he always notified her thus: "I will be coming such a day" or "such an hour." Then she would say yes. But it happened on a particular day when he told her, "I'll be coming tonight," she said, "No, not tonight. Wait till next night."

He replied, "No, for I will come tonight."

But she refused, "No, I do not want you to come tonight."

Then he asked, "What is your objection? Hitherto you have let me come when I pleased. What is the matter tonight?"

So she said, "I do not want you to come, because I will be absent tonight."

From: Robert Hamill Nassau, *Fetichism in West Africa* (New York: Charles Scribner's Sons, 1904).

"Where are you going?" he asked.

To this she gave as answer only, "Don't come! I don't want you to come!"

So the man said, "All right! I will not come. If you don't want me, then I'm not coming." So he left her, very much surprised at what she had said, and began to think something was going wrong. He thought he would like to know for himself what it was.

This woman was one of those who belonged to the Witch Society and engaged in its plays. But the man had not suspected this and did not know that she was one of those who played.

The native belief is that when a witch or wizard has seized someone to "eat" his "life" or do him other harm, if there be a nonsociety witness hidden or in the open, the odor of that witness weakens the witch power and the attempt at witchcraft fails.

This man, not suspecting the real state of the case, but in order to know what was going on with the woman, came softly and hid near her house, where he might be able to see whether anyone went in or came out. Soon he heard the door of her house open. He saw her come out of the house without any clothing, and she quietly closed the door after her, and then walked away from the place. All this the man saw, but he said nothing. He stood outside waiting, waiting until she should return. After a long while, as he was tired of standing, he thought he would go into the house and hide himself somewhere. It was not long after this that he heard a little noise outside and, looking through the apertures of the bamboo wall, saw her and others with her, men and women. Some of them were carrying the form of a man on their shoulders. Others spread out on the ground green plantain leaves and stretched the form on the leaves. Each of the party had a knife, and they began their work of cutting the form into pieces. While thus occupied, they saw that their knives would not penetrate. Some of them began to step around, peeping into recesses as if they were looking for something. Still trying to cut, their knives seemed dulled; no one of them could succeed in cutting out a single piece. So they stopped and began to sharpen their knives and again tried to cut, using more force in their efforts. They worked rapidly, for they had to hasten, as there were signs of approaching day.

As they still were unable to make any incisions after the sharpening of the knives, they thought it very strange and began to suspect that someone was near witnessing what they were doing. So some of them began to search in different directions; they sniffed to detect the odor of a person. This they did over and over again and came back and again sharpened their knives, and again they failed. And then they would go around, sniffing for a human being.

At last, as it was near morning, they had to give up their intention of cutting into this form. So they had to take it up again on their shoulders and carry it back to where they had brought it from, and lost their feast.

Then the woman came back to her house, very much disappointed and excited. Though it was still dark, it was so near daybreak that she did not go to bed but took a light and began to hunt all through her house, having at last begun to suspect that perhaps her lover was there. Finally she found him where he was hiding. She was very angry, saying, "Who told you to come here? What brought you? And when did you come? Did I not tell you not to come tonight?"

But he turned on her, saying, "But where have you yourself been? And what have you yourself been doing? I came here expecting to find another man here. But that is not what I saw!"

She trembled, saying, "Have you been here a long time?"

And he significantly said, "Yes, I have!"

Then, furious, she said, "Now you have seen all that we were doing, and you have found me out! And as you have discovered that I am engaged in witchcraft, and lest you tell others about it, you shall see that I will put an end to your life! You shall not go out of this house alive!"

So she pulled out her knife. But the man was quite strong and, though he had no weapon, made a hard fight. He was stronger than the woman, was able to get away from her, and left the house just before daylight.

From that day their friendship was broken; neither cared again to see the face of the other. The man informed on the woman. But she was not prosecuted, for no one was able to make specific complaint that they had lost their "heart life." That form had been restored to its person unrecognized and uninjured. No one out of the society, not even the victim himself, knew of the attempt that had been made on him.

Stories Concerning Wax Figures

(Egypt)

The use of wax figures seems to have been one of the most common methods of causing the removal or death of a victim of the black art. One of the earliest instances of this is recorded in the Westcar Papyrus, where it is narrated how Prince Khāf-Rā told Khufu (Cheops, the builder of the Great Pyramid of Giza) an event that took place in the reign of Neb-ka or Neb-kau-Rā, about 3830 B.C.

According to this story, a married woman fell in love with a soldier in the royal train when the king was visiting a high priestly official called Āba-aner. She sent her tire woman to this soldier with a present, and the latter thereon met her by appointment in a small house on her husband's estate, where they both feasted and made merry for a whole day. When evening came, the soldier went down to the river to bathe. Meanwhile the steward, who had prepared the house for their reception, thought he ought to tell his master (Āba-aner) everything that had happened, and this he accordingly did on the morning following. Āba-aner said nothing, but ordered the steward to bring him certain materials and a special box made of ebony and precious metal. From this box he took some wax and made a model of a crocodile seven spans in length, at the same time reciting over it certain magical words with the final order, "When the man cometh down to bathe in my waters, seize thou him!" He then gave the wax model to the steward saying, "When the man, according to his daily wont, cometh down to wash in the water, thou shalt cast the crocodile in after him."

The man did as he was told, and the next evening, when the lover had entered the water, he threw in the crocodile, which immediately

From: Irene E. Toye Warner, ed., "Black Magic in Ancient and Modern Egypt," *Occult Review* 23 (1916): 138–45.

turned into the living animal about twelve feet long and, seizing the lover, dragged him down into the river. The king stayed with Āba-aner for seven days, during which the soldier lover was under the water. On the seventh day Āba-aner invited his king to go for a walk by the river to see a most wonderful thing which, he said, had happened to a man. When they reached the water Āba-aner abjured the crocodile, saying, "Bring hither the man," and lo! the man was brought to his feet. The king remarked, "What a horrible monster is this?" Whereon, for answer, Āba-aner calmly stooped down and took it up in his hands, when it became the harmless wax figure again.

Then the king was told the whole story of his wife's infidelity, and after hearing it he turned to the crocodile and said, "Take that which is thine and begone!" The monster seized the man, sprang into the water, and disappeared. The guilty wife was burnt, and her ashes cast into the river also. We learn from this remarkable story that a priestly official such as Āba-aner was evidently accustomed to this form of magic, as the tools, wax, etc., were in his possession *before* he heard of his wife's infidelity. This case does not seem to have been regarded as by any means unique.

Wax seems to have been the substance par excellence for all evil magical purposes from time immemorial, as it readily changes its form under heat and pressure and melts away in the fire like the victim was supposed to waste away by disease.

Nectanebus, the last native king of Egypt, about 358 B.C., was a skilled magician. Whenever he was threatened with invasion by sea or by land, he is said to have destroyed the power of the enemy by the following means. On hearing of an enemy coming by sea, instead of sending out his navy as one would naturally suppose, he retired into a private room where he kept all the necessary implements of sorcery, and made wax figures of the enemy's men and ships and also of his own men and ships. These models he put in a bowl of water, and having taken an ebony rod in his hand and "put on the cloak of an Egyptian prophet," he invoked the help of "the gods, the winds, and the subterranean demons, who straightway came to his aid." They caused the waxen models to become living beings who fought against one another until those representing the sailors of Nectanebus vanquished the enemy and sank their ships. And "even as the models sank, so, far away on the sea, sank the actual hostile navy!" By this means, we are informed, Nectanebus maintained his supremacy in peace for many years.

But it happened one day that the king heard that many nations of the East were coming to war against him and were even then on their way. As on former occasions, Nectanebus retired into his secret chamber and performed his magical ceremonies with the usual result, but when he looked at the figures of men and ships, he saw that *"the gods of Egypt were steering the enemies' ships* and leading their soldiers to war against himself." He then perceived that the end of his kingdom had come. So he quitted the chamber, shaved off his hair and beard, put on common dress, and fled to Macedonia, where he practiced as an Egyptian soothsayer and physician.

A Human Sacrifice

(West Africa)

Somewhere in the bush, a poor woman had been done to death in order that her mutilated body might bring prosperity to the farms. It is useless, according to native belief, to employ the necessary part of any corpse that had met its death by accident or from natural causes. The victim must be slain purposely or the rite is of no avail. None of the townspeople had disappeared on this occasion, so that the murdered woman must have been some unfortunate soul brought down from the interior, or one kept prisoner in a lonely bush farm till it was thought that the time had come for her to be sacrificed without the knowledge of the interfering white man.

So jealously was the secret guarded that the most anxious inquiries failed to find actual proof of the murder or bring to justice those responsible. A mass of evidence, however, came to light as to the frequency of such sacrifices in former days.

No one who has attended the festival could fail to be struck by the

From: P. Amaury Talbot, "Through the Land of Witchcraft: Part 3," *Wide World Magazine* 32 (1913): 24–30.

resemblance between the present-day Eja ritual and those descriptions which have come down to us of the old Adonis-Attis-Osiris worship. The ecstatic frenzy of the dancers, the trances into which some of them fall, and the jealousy with which all strangers are excluded show that this ceremony holds a very special significance in the native mind.

On another occasion we entered a town just as a great "war dance" was being given. The men were either masked or wearing upon their heads wooden effigies covered with skin. These are a concession to the prejudices of the white man and take the place of the smoke-dried heads of enemies killed in battle often formerly worn on such occasions.

Once while I was dining in the Ibo shed of a little village reached by a bush track so faint that men with machetes had to go on ahead and clear a way for the carriers, loud cries were heard and people were seen rushing about in a state of great excitement. On sending out to find the cause of this, it was discovered that a "war party" had come in from a neighboring town. When questioned, they quieted down and explained that they had come to inform their friends that "war" had broken out a few miles off. Later, it transpired that they themselves had started the fighting and had been carrying around young palm leaves, on which were hung the jaws of freshly killed men in token of victory. These gruesome trophies were hidden on the first whisper of the arrival of a white man, and information was not brought to me till it was too late to take action.

The inhabitants of this part proved very truculent. What roads there were led through difficult hilly country and over innumerable streams and rivers, and so bad was the reputation of the people that a guide was obtained with difficulty. A picturesque account of their habits had been given to me by a native clerk, who wrote, among other pleasing details, that the houses were all "occupied with skulls." From other sources I learned that the farms were divided off from one another by rows of posts, each bearing a like gruesome trophy. This latter detail was not borne out by fact so far as we could see, but several of the houses had skulls embedded in the sunbaked mud of their thresholds.

At first the people appeared rather timid than otherwise, and in several of the towns white rags were seen fluttering from bamboo poles to act as flags of truce. The juju trees and stones had been freshly smeared with blood, or in some cases red and yellow paint, in order to propitiate the genies and ensure protection from any danger which their white visitors might be bringing upon them. No white man had been through this part of the country before, and everywhere in the bush juju offerings were to be seen—overhead, underfoot, and at each side of the road. The people themselves were away at their bush farms; they only come into the towns during the rainy season or on special occasions, for they have not as yet acquired the habit of living in towns.

Part III

Tales from Asia & the Pacific

The Origin of Evil

(Japan)

I learn from the Ainu that they have a tradition to the effect that the alder, which they call *nitat kene-ni (Alnus japonica),* was the first tree created. And one man told me that it must be, he thought, the same as "the tree of knowledge of good and evil" I had been speaking of a short time before. It is not supposed, however, that this tree was caused to grow or was created in our sense of the word. But it is said to have been sent direct from heaven already grown and planted in a land called Wenpipok, wherever that may be.

This tree is supposed to be the origin of evil, or rather the means by which evil was brought into the world. I speak now not of moral evil but physical evil, in the sense of causing bodily pain and suffering, but not evil in the sense of having brought sin into the world. The bark, not the fruit, is supposed to be the evil-causing agency. Even at the present day some Ainu consider it to be the direct cause of a disease called *shihapapu,* a complaint which is said to consist chiefly in severe internal pains and which most often terminates in death.

Some time after this tree was planted, the bark is said to have fallen off and rotted on the ground, as it does indeed at the present day. But as it decomposed and became a kind of powder, it was blown over the face of the earth by the winds and, in some mysterious way became the cause of many kinds of bodily ailments. But strange as it may appear, the bark of this tree not only is looked upon as the *cause* of illness but also is used as a *means* for its cure. The bark, if taken fresh from the tree and a decoction made by steeping it in hot water, is said

From: John Batchelor, "Items of Ainu Folk-Lore," *Journal of American Folk-Lore* 7 (1894): 15–44.

to work wonders. Not only are there *special* maladies for which it is to be particularly recommended, but it is also supposed to be good for *any kind* of disease.

Evil Spirits

(Philippines)

The Visayans in general believe in three kinds of spirits: the Tamawos, Dwendes, and Asuangs. The first are not especially bad, although sometimes mischievous and accustomed to kidnap children in order to make them like themselves. They live in mounds or elevated places in the fields. Their houses, which are generally on the inside of the mound, although sometimes built outside, are of metal or glass and ordinarily invisible to mortals. Those who have seen them, and in each town there is usually at least one person who claims to have done so, say that the houses have the appearance of those inhabited by men, contain handsome furniture, and usually have in them beautiful young ladies who do their utmost to induce the child whom the Tamawo has captured to partake of their food, since if a mortal once eats of their food he becomes for all time a Tamawo like themselves. If, however, he successfully resists them, the child is, at the end of three or four days, taken back to the spot where he was captured, and released.

The Tamawo can take on any shape he pleases, generally appearing as a man, but sometimes as a dog, carabao, or other animal. The Tamawo, however, can be distinguished from the true animal, because the former has a huge body, big staring eyes, and toes that are much prolonged and end in big claws.

The Duende is a little sprite which lives in men's houses and amuses himself by making noises, throwing sand and stones, and singing. In general, he is good-natured, although if provoked he may take his

From: Berton L. Maxfield and W. H. Millington, "Philippine (Visayan) Superstitions," *Journal of American Folk-Lore* 19 (1906): 205–11.

revenge by making one of the children fall sick and die. At times one can be heard to drop from the ceiling to the floor, and at other times he knocks over kitchen utensils, etc.

Filipino houses swarm with lizards, rats, and bats. One kind of lizard, about three or four inches long, runs over the ceilings and walls, especially at night, and often slips and falls to the floor with a thud. Rats frequently alarmed us by lifting the lids of kettles to get what might be within and letting them down with a bang. They and the bats make noise enough at night to account for almost anything, and it is probable that with the lizards, assisted by the vivid imagination of the people, they are entirely responsible for the belief in the existence of these noisy little imps.

In addition to these, there are the Cama-cama, or little spirits of the well, whose operations are limited to making black-and-blue spots on the bodies of those who come to bathe by pinching them, and ghosts which appear as flaming figures in the graveyards. As the graves are very shallow and bones, coffin boards, etc., are strewn around, it is not improbable that phosphorescent lights may sometimes be seen. A parish priest, in reply to a question once put to him by the writer as to the belief in these ghosts, said, "We do not know. It may be that God permits the souls of men to return to earth as a warning to others, but whether this is so or not I cannot say."

Noxious Spirits and Apparitions

(Bengal)

1. *Ekh*—Nightmare, supposed to be the shadow or apparition of a departed soul which seeks repose.
2. *Barando*—Whirlwind, also a disquieted soul which is seeking rest.
3. Aerolites and meteors are likewise departed spirits who have been disturbed.
4. Evil spirits who cause delirium, epilepsy, fainting fits, and lunacy.
5. Evil spirits who appear as huge giants or without a head.
6. Evil spirits who cause frightful dreams.
7. Evil spirits who haunt ruins or guard hidden treasures.
8. Evil spirits who infest mountains, jungles, and lonely places.

From: F. Hahn, "Some Notes on the Religion and Superstitions of the Orao," *Journal of the Asiatic Society of Bengal* 72 (part 3, nos. 1 and 2) (1903): 12–19.

Of the Ainu Demons

(Japan)

As there are supposed to be gods innumerable, so are there multitudes of demons. Demons too, like the gods, have their chief or king, and they are also called Kamui. In fact, one can only tell whether an Ainu is speaking of a god or demon by the context, or by adjectives prefixed to or nouns following that term.

From: John Batchelor, "Items of Ainu Folk-Lore," *Journal of American Folk-Lore* 7 (1894): 15–44.

The government of the world of devils is conducted in the same way as that of the gods. As the Creator has His angels, so the chief of the devils has his fiends. In His sphere God is supreme and His will must be carried out; likewise the devil is supreme in his sphere, and he too must be obeyed by his angels. Why the devil is allowed to exist and where he came from are questions to which I have as yet received no reply from the Ainu. He is, and that is all about it, and enough too.

Demons on the Earth

(Japan)

As the demons of the air are so near this earth of ours, it is possible for them to pay us frequent visits and even to dwell among us. This accounts for so much that is evil in the world. Only a short time ago I was asking a man whether there were evil dryads in the forests as there are mermaids and water nymphs in the lakes, rivers, and seas. Certainly, he said, great numbers of them. The genies who work evil to men are part of these and, though dwelling in the forests and mountains, have their real home in the air around us. They are servants of the Prince of Devils. He said that he had never seen one, but he firmly believed they existed for all that.

On asking another man what he would do, or what would be the best place to flee to if pursued by an evil genie, he said that the most secure hiding place is close under the bank of a river where the running water has carried the soil away. The devil is certain not to be able to find a person hiding there, providing he did not see in what direction the object of his pursuit ran! However, should he have seen in which direction a person went, the best thing to be done is to climb a tree, for though demons can also climb, yet a person may easily keep him off by hammering away at his claws with a branch!

From: John Batchelor, "Items of Ainu Folk-Lore," *Journal of American Folk-Lore* 7 (1894): 15–44.

The Dark Spirits

(Bengal)

1. Darha, the fiercest of all, lives in the sacred grove of *Sal* or *Bel* trees and is represented by a wooded pole. The Darha is a village *bhut*, but he is not found in all villages. To him human sacrifices must be made, at least once in each generation. The men who are employed to secretly catch a human being, generally a boy or girl, are called *Otamga;* in Kurukh *Ondka,* which means "taken." In defiance of the law prohibiting such sacrifices, and in spite of the vigilance of the police, human sacrifices are still believed to be made secretly.

2. Deswali, another bhut, a female, is found in every village. This too is represented by a block of wood. Every third and tenth year, sacrifices of buffaloes and fowl must be made to her to secure her favor; otherwise she will create mischief like Darha, and fatal diseases will break out among men and cattle.

3. Khunta is the *Nad,* or bhut, of the *Khunt,* or sept. It is represented by a small wooden peg stuck in the field. Every third year when the rice is transplanted, a sheep is immolated to the Khunta, and fowl are sacrificed yearly. Each Khunta Nad has its own name, which is kept secret by the members of the sept. If the name is revealed, mischief will certainly be done by the demon, who appears to be of a very irritable temper, since she is easily disturbed and infuriated through spells or neglect.

4. Erpa-nad, the house demon, is kept in the house in the shape of a wooden peg. Sacrifices of fowl and goats are made in her name when any severe illness occurs.

5. Chalo-Pacho, or Jhakra-Budhi, or Sarna Budhi, is the name of the spirits of the Asur women whose husbands were killed by the son of Dharme, according to the well-known Asur legend. She is especially worshipped at the sacred Sal grove, at the time of the Khadi festival; the sacrifices to her consist of black fowl. Her sisters take up their abode in the *pipal* and *dumbari* (fig) trees.

From: F. Hahn, "Some Notes on the Religion and Superstitions of the Orao," *Journal of the Asiatic Society of Bengal* 72 (part 3, nos. 1 and 2) (1903): 12–19.

6. Chandi is the goddess of hunting. She is worshipped in the form of a stone. Fowl and goats are sacrificed to her to ensure success in hunting.

7. Baranda is supposed to live on the hills. He causes misfortune and poverty by taking up his abode in the dwelling houses, which he is always trying to enter. To prevent him from entering, or to get rid of him, sour or tasteless food is offered to disgust him and so induce him to go elsewhere.

8. Churil or Chordewa is one of the worst bhuts who disturb the quiet life of the Orao peasant. The Churil is the departed spirit of a woman who died during confinement. She appears in the form of a woman, but her feet are turned backward. She also enters the house in the shape of a black cat. She is especially dangerous to newborn children and to women at the time of confinement. Sacrifices must be made to her at the place where her corpse has been deposited, and during his wife's confinement, the husband must guard the house to ward her off.

9. Mua are the spirits of people who have died a violent death, e.g., by strangulation, or accident, or from starvation, or who have been killed by wild beasts or poisonous reptiles.

10. The unknown village bhut is supposed to haunt fields kept fallow at certain places, which must never be brought under cultivation. Only cattle may graze there; otherwise the evil spirit will take offense and give trouble.

An Introduction to Bakemono

(Japan)

The name Bakemono means "transformed thing," from *bakeru,* "to change," and it is the generic name of all the supernatural forms: ghosts, goblins, and other fanciful shapes which prey upon the mind or, as may be, upon the body of man.

The ghost, properly speaking—that is to say, the disembodied ego of a dead person—receives the name Yurei, with the alternatives Nakitama or Onryo more especially applied to the curse of the dead, Bokon, Shoryo, and Enkon, to mention only a few.

The Yurei is a highly developed ghost, although it originates in an almost shapeless form, a mere elongated bubble called s'Hitodama, which leaves the body at death, taking away within its filmy walls all the evil aspirations of the deceased, all his appetites for revenge and destruction. In this connection may be noted a general belief in the fulfillment of the dead man's last wish by his spirit after death. For instance, in a story, the ghost of a painter killed by a rejected pupil came back to finish the picture upon which he was engaged at the time of his death.

The Bakemono, as distinguished from the Yurei, include all the monsters that fancy could create under the influence of Chinese superstition and indigenous tradition. Many are the names used synonymously with Bakemono, such as Henge, Kwaibutsu, and Ayakishi Mono (i.e., wonder thing), but whatever the name used, and however doubtful the existence of the thing itself, it behoves one to be polite when mentioning it, hence, *o bake,* "the honorable changeling."

Finally, there is another name, Oni, or Ki, applied in common parlance to devils, although it appears that Confucius used it with a different connotation, meaning the spirit of the dead, whether good,

From: Henri L. Joly, "Bakemono," *Transactions and Proceedings of the Japan Society* 9 (1909–11): 15–48.

bad, or indifferent in character, for he says explicitly that to speak of those evil spirits (Ki) is to honor them beyond reason. That meaning is still adhered to in Japan when speaking of the revered spirits of such men as Kusunoki Masashige and others who have been semi-deified, but the word Oni is popularly applied to the denizens of the underworld, the servants of the regents of Hades. Confucius, I may add, was of the opinion that well-bred people should not discuss ghosts.

How extensive the list of demoniacal transformations could be made is evident from the following sentences taken from Bakin's *Shichiya no Kura:* "All antique things can assume disguises *(Kobutsu Kwai wo nasu)*, for instance, a stone Fizo appeared as a Bakemono until a traveler cut it down with his sword. All antique things may be taken away by devils *(Kobutsu oni ni taruru)* like the horse in a temple picture *(Ema)* upon which a demon rode away at night." Collectors should perhaps take heed of these warnings. But the best-known story of transformation is that of the lantern Bakemono Toro of Futahara in Nikko, which had been presented to the temple in 1292 by Kanuma Gonsaburo. At night it took the form of a hideous goblin and attacked passersby until a warrior cut it in twain with his sword. A huge gash still remains on the top of the bronze as a proof of the occurrence.

The portion of space especially reserved to ghosts and Bakemono is called Makai or Mado. It extends upward from thirty *ken* (180 feet) above ground level, and we are told that the atmosphere at that height is alive with wicked devils capable of causing untold damage; among them are balls of fire called Tenkwa, Burarihi, etc., which have been known to destroy houses and their contents, leaving hardly any ash behind.

The evening twilight is called Omadoki (this name contains an allusion to that of Wang Mang, who overthrew the Han dynasty in A.D. 8). According to Sekiyen, many ghosts appear at the time of sunset, although spirits seem to suit their own convenience as to time and seem to evince a preference for darkness: one goblin, Ao Ando, appears only when the lamp gutters or goes out for lack of oil; another one, in the shape of a spiteful old woman, blows the light out and then takes the shape of a devil; further, a goblin called Tenjo Kudari drops from the ceiling. (Even now the expression *Tenjo o Miseru* is slang for giving a fright to anyone.) Finally, as a parallel to the European sayings, let us mention *"Koniyami kiwo danzuru koto nakare, Ki wo danzureba kwai ittaru to yeri"* (Do not speak of the devil on dark nights, or he will at once appear).

In Shikoku it was believed that if a man became mad it was because his spirit had been eaten by a ghostly dog, who took its abode in the man's body. One strange creature called Amikiri was supposed to cut holes in nets, especially mosquito nets. A human-headed beast, the Hideri Gami or Kambo, was responsible for periods of drought. Certain large frogs were devils in disguise, particularly the Ogama of Suwo, which fed on snakes and spat out a death-dealing rainbow. Needless to do more than mention the San Sukumi: frog, snake, slug, endowed with magical powers, as set forth in the story of Jiraiya. A wounded snake would come at night and avenge itself upon whomever had struck it unless that person had quite forgotten the deed; absent-minded people apparently possessed a charmed life!

Before leaving the animal ghosts, I must skim over a story told by Ikkiu, showing that brown dogs were enlisted in the service of medicine long before Battersea erected a bronze statue to the memory of a mongrel and caused a policeman to watch it day and night. In a Chinese book the blood of the Aka Inu is indicated as a specific cure for a certain skin disease, but the dog must be tied to the hind leg of a swift horse and made to race behind the galloping steed for fifty *ri*.

In the Tembun period, a man named Saito Kura no Suke Suketomo resorted to this cruel practice to cure his eldest daughter; the dog was duly exhausted, its throat slit, and the blood used. But whether the remedy was a good one or not was never known, for a nurse presented herself to tend the girl, who took a great liking to her. This nurse was the spirit of the dog bent on revenge, and it caused the death of the girl in a few days. A servant found out the true nature of the pretended nurse and drove the Bakemono away. The younger daughter then fell ill, and as she was on the way to recovery, it was found that the Bakemono had returned, and the girl died.

All old trees were haunted by spirits, sometimes benevolent like Fo and Uba in the pine trees of Takasago, but more often malevolent. Even dead timber used for building purposes had to be carefully handled; pillars had to be erected as the tree had grown, with the fibers upright, and if an ignorant or careless carpenter set them upside down, a shrieking host of angry spirits would soon come out of the wood to annoy the inmates. The Hoko is the spirit of a tree a thousand years old. It resembles a black dog without a tail; its face is almost human. It differs from the Yamabiko (echo) and from the dog of Mitsumine.

The Guardian Demons

(India)

I am a pensioned *ressaldar* (troop leader) of the Mysore Horse, and my service took me much into various districts, among others Shivamoogah, where it is a common thing for people to have intercourse with Pisachas. Some possess mantras, or spells, by which they compel them to guard their property. If a thief were to lay his hand upon any article in the house or any fruit in the garden of a man so protected, he would be unable to stir from the spot until the owner returned, and not even then until the spirit was ordered to set him free. A Pisacha so employed is called a *chowdi.* By accepting his help for such a selfish purpose, the sorcerer gives him a stronger hold upon himself, and he has to exercise all the more caution lest he fail for a moment to keep the control and thus lose his life. Sorcerers can transfer the services of their chowdis, and it is a common thing for the purchaser of a garden to take from the seller the mantra by which the guardian chowdi is controlled; otherwise he would not be able to enjoy the fruits of the field or orchard.

Pisachas sometimes take possession of a house, a well, or a tree. They are driven away by a *mantriki* (one possessing knowledge of mantras) by reciting charms, suspending *jantras* (Cabalistic signs inscribed on sheet-copper plaques) on the house walls, side of the well, or tree branches, as the case may be, and other devices. Sometimes, when the Pisacha is expelled from a medium he is obsessing, the mantriki will cut a lock of her hair, wrap it about an iron nail, and drive it into a tree. The Pisacha is then bound to the tree until the nail rusts away.

From: Adolphe d'Assier, *Posthumous Humanity: A Study of Phantoms* (with an appendix of beliefs current in India) (London: George Redway, 1887).

Corpse-Demons

(China)

Celestial roes are not men but belong to the class of Kiang-shi, or corpse-demons. Yunnan province has many mines from which five kinds of metal are extracted. If they collapse, preventing the miners from getting out, then if these men are fed for ten years or even for a hundred by the breath of the earth and of those metals, their bodies do not decay. Though they are not dead, their material substance is dead.

It being underground perpetual night for those who work those mines, these men mostly carry a lamp on their forehead. When, while working their way into the ground, they fall in with a celestial roe, this is entranced with joy. Complaining of cold, it asks them for some tobacco, which it smokes immediately; then it prostrates itself upon the ground, entreating the men to take it out of the mine. In reply the miners say, "We have come here for gold and silver, and we have not yet discovered any veins from which to procure some. Do you know where the gold grows?" And the celestial stag guides them to a mine where they can reap a rich harvest. But on leaving the mine, they delude the specter, saying, "We must get out first, and then we shall take you out of the shaft with the lift." And by the rope fastened to the bamboo lift, they haul the creature up, but halfway they cut the rope, letting the creature fall down and die.

It has occurred that the men in charge of the mine sheds were more benevolent and compassionate, and hauled up some seven or eight of those beings. But as soon as these felt the wind, their clothes, flesh, and bones changed into a liquid giving out a rancid, putrid stench, which smote with contagious disease all those whose olfactory nerves it affected, so that they died. This is the reason why, ever since, those who haul up celestial stags cut the rope, lest they have to endure again that stench and lose their lives. Should they refuse to haul them up, they risk being molested by them incessantly. It is also said that when

From: Jan J. de Groot, *Religious Systems of China*, vol. 5, book 2, parts 2 and 3 (Leide: E. J. Brill, 1907).

a small number of celestial stags are overpowered by a great number of men, tied, placed against an earthen wall, and immured firmly on the four sides with walls of clay, a sort of terrace with a lamp being built overhead, they will do no further harm. But if men are outnumbered by stags, they are tormented to death by these and not allowed to escape."

The Wandering Heads

(Japan)

The Rokurokubi is usually a female goblin, or rather a woman whose head, at the end of a long neck, is addicted to wandering at night, but originally the male sex was also endowed with this peculiarity.

There are a number of ancient books describing these Rokurokubi, sometimes with variants in the spelling and even in the name. For instance, the *Wakan san sai dzue* devotes a long article to these creatures under the name Fei TCheu, men with flying heads called Hitoban in Japan. They live in the southern countries. Their eyes have no pupils; their head leaves the body at night to feed upon reptiles, returning at dawn to its proper place. A thin red line marks the joint of the neck. The commentator says that there are no such creatures in Japan, but we shall see later that there was a certain belief to the contrary, these Hitoban being confused with the true Rokurokubi, whose name is derived from the pulley-and-rope arrangement used for getting water out of wells, called *rokuro*.

Jippensha Ikkiu in his *Bakemono Nenjiu Gyoji*, and Santo Kioden in the *Bakemono Tsure Dzure Gusa*, give a number of male Rokurokubi whose necks extend like a rubber hose to fifteen or twenty feet.

It has been said by various writers that the popular belief in Rokurokubi lasted well into the nineteenth century; at any rate, a

From: Henri L. Joly, "Bakemono," *Transactions and Proceedings of the Japan Society* 9 (1909–11): 15–48.

modern book, the *Yaso Kidan,* seriously relates that during the Horeki period (1751–63) a young girl lived in Hongoku, whose beauty turned the head of every young swain in the city, although she had the reputation of being a Rokurokubi, and people called her by that name. In fact, she was so ashamed of that nickname that she became quite ill, and on her recovery, her father was glad to accept the offer of an early marriage on behalf of a love-smitten youth.

In the night following the wedding, this young man woke up, and watching his wife by the light of the *andon,* he was congratulating himself when, to his astonishment, he noticed that her neck was growing, slowly at first, then more rapidly, until it reached a length of some six feet, when it started whirling around, and the head finally rested itself upon the framework of a screen with a loud laugh. The man fainted with horror, and on the following day divorced his wife without delay. A doctor from Kanda cured her by some unknown process and married her later. This Rokurokubi was comparatively harmless.

Ikkiu, in the *Kwaibutsu Yoron,* gives a much more grisly story, really of Hitoban but under the name of Rokurokubi. A certain samurai named Isogai Heitazayemon Taketsura, of Kikuchi, in Kiushu, became a *ronin* and, to escape impending trouble, passed himself off as a priest under the name Kairyo. Once in the mountains of Kai, he fell asleep upon a flat rock, but a woodcutter woke him up and offered him to sleep in his house, as the forest was full of wild beasts. Kairyo accepted and found that his host was of the same class as himself. After supper he went to the room assigned him, and before laying himself to rest he recited aloud some Buddhist scriptures. Some time later he woke, feeling thirsty, and went to the kitchen for some water. On the way he noticed that there were five headless bodies in the family's room, and he became convinced that he had fallen in a den of monsters, so that he removed the body of the man to a spot in the garden, bearing in mind the Chinese belief that a Rokurokubi's head dies by the morning if it cannot find its body. As he was coming back, he heard the heads of the man and his wife talking: "The priest is very fat and will be good to eat. I wish he had not read his prayers, as that kept me from killing him, but now he must be asleep.—Go and make sure," said the man. The head of the woman disappeared and came back soon after. "He is not there, and your body has been removed from the sleeping apartment."

Then followed wails of dismay and curses against the priest. By now the five heads were together in the garden, and they soon found Kairyo and attacked him, but he fought so strenuously that the four females went away, presumably to rescue their own bodies. The head of the man bit his sleeve, and he could not make it relax its hold, so that he traveled all the way to Suwa in Shinano, people being greatly frightened by his burden on the way. However, he was rewarded for having killed the monster.

The Lustful Pah

(China)

In the twenty-sixth year of the Khien-lung period (1761), when a great drought prevailed in the metropolis, a courier named Chang Kwei had to carry an urgent dispatch from a Banner General to Liang-hiang. He left the city when the water clock was sinking. When he was in a lonely place, a black shower suddenly hurtled around him. It blew out his torch, so that he had to take shelter from the rain in the pavilion of a post house. Here a woman with a lamp joined him. She was about seventeen or eighteen years old and very beautiful. She beckoned him to her house and refreshed him with tea, and he tied his horse to a post, hoping to pass the night with her. The courier's happiness exceeded his wildest expectations. He held her in close embrace until the cock announced the first glimpse of day, causing the woman to throw on her clothes and rise. She could not be prevailed upon to stay. The courier, exhausted, fell again into a sweet doze and became aware in the midst of his dreams that his nose was being cooled by the dew and his mouth tickled by the points of the grass. And when it was a little clearer, he found himself on a tomb in the open plain. Greatly affrighted, he fetched his horse, which he found tied up to a tree.

From: Jan J. de Groot, *Religious Systems of China*, vol. 5, book 2, parts 2 and 3 (Leide: E. J. Brill, 1907).

The dispatch he had to convey to its destination arrived there fifty quarters of an hour too late, and the officer to whom it was addressed sent a message to the general to ask for an explanation and to express his sorrow that matters had been managed in a wrong way by reason of that delay. The general ordered his adjutant to interrogate the courier sharply. The detailed account that this man then gave of the causes induced the general to have that tomb investigated. It was found to be that of a young woman of the Chang family, who had hung herself out of shame at the discovery of the adultery which she had committed in her unmarried state. From time to time her ghost had haunted wayfarers, and some took her for the Pah of the prevailing drought. Whereas specters in the shape of *nao* monkeys, with disheveled hair and on one leg, are animal Pah, while hanged persons whose undecayed corpses appear and bewilder men are spectral Pah. In order to cause rain to fall, it suffices to catch and burn these. The case having been reported to the throne, they opened the coffin, and it contained in fact the undecayed corpse of a woman with features like those of a living person and covered all over with white hair. They burned it, and next day it rained heavily.

The Demon Army

(China)

In the second year of the Kien-chung period of the T'ang dynasty (A.D. 781) false rumors circulated in the regions of the Yangtze and the Hwai about specters coming from Hunan. Some called them hairy demons, while others declared them to be hairy men. It was reported that various tales were told of them, and nothing could be done with success against them in their variable forms. People would have it that they were bent on eating the hearts of men but kidnapped young children of both sexes entire. Frightened out of their wits,

From: Jan J. de Groot, *Religious Systems of China*, vol. 5, book 2, parts 2 and 3 (Leide: E. J. Brill, 1907).

people often crowded together in their houses and kept up flaming fires at night. Lacking courage to sleep, they armed themselves with bows and swords, and each time when the devils entered a house, all other families beat on wooden boards and copper utensils, thus producing a noise which shook heaven and earth. Some died of frantic terror. Such was the state of things everywhere. The mandarins interfered, but they were powerless to put a stop to the matter.

A former Judge of Merit of Yen-cheu, Liu Ts'an by name, had been on duty in Hwai and Szĕ (in Nganhwui province), and therefore dwelt in Kwang-ling with half a dozen sons, fellows all strong and brave. He kept watch with them by night, armed with bows and arrows. For the protection of his many daughters, they barred the hall on the inside. The young men were going their rounds, when after midnight the sky was darkened and alarming cries of "The specters are here!" were heard in the hall. The lads were startled, but the door being barred, they could not enter to run to the rescue, and they had to content themselves with keeping on the alert and peeping into the hall.

They beheld a being like a couch; it had hairs and prickles like a hedgehog, measured from three to four feet in height, and had legs on its four sides, on which it hurried around in the hall. At its side another specter moved, black-haired, naked, and with claws and teeth like swords. It seized the youngest daughter and put her on the hairy couch; then it grasped the other girl, but at this critical moment the brave lads pushed down the wall and entered. They shot their arrows into the couch, and it ran away with the other specter; in a moment the latter vanished, while the couch ran eastward. Then it was hit so truly by a hundred and more arrowshots that it could not fly any further.

One of the men caught it, grasped the bristles, with all his might galloped along with it, and immediately both tumbled from the river bridge. "I have my arms around the specter!" he cried. "It is brought to bay. Be quick; to the rescue with light!" And by the light they found him—with his arms around a pillar of the bridge. Liu and his sons all had nail wounds, and the youngest girl was lying on the road.

The Bijli of the Flaming Torch

(India)

The strange event I am about to relate happened to me some sixteen years ago, when I was out in India. I had started on a shooting expedition with my bearer and *khansamah*, and after having been the greater part of the day in the saddle, I arrived, toward evening, thoroughly fagged out, hungry, and dust-stained, at a little out-of-the-way *busti* in the midst of a wide stretch of cotton fields.

I encamped close to a natural tank on the outskirts of the village, and under the shelter of a wide-spreading, leafy banyan tree, I took up my quarters for the night. There my native servants set about preparing me the evening meal from the inevitable up-country chicken. While these preparations were in progress, I made a tour of inspection of my surroundings, and came across an aged fakir, one of those wandering religious mendicants whom one so frequently meets in all parts of India. With long matted hair, and a dirty loincloth covering his mud-stained emaciated body, he sat absorbed in meditation by the tank. These religious fanatics are held in great veneration and awe by the natives, on account of the occult powers which they possess. So strong is their control of mind over body that they can at will produce in themselves the phenomena of self-hypnotism and catalepsy, and while the body lies cold and inert, the spirit is free to travel into space. As I passed by this old fakir, he looked up from his devotions and, salaaming me, begged of me not to touch or drink the water of that tank lest some evil should befall me.

Imagining some selfish motive behind these words, and being in no frame of mind to be trifled with, I told him to be silent, and informed him that, as for not drinking of the water of that tank, neither he nor anyone else should prevent me from doing so.

From: H. Mayne Young, "The Bijli of the Flaming Torch," *Occult Review* 4 (1906): 269–72.

My servants were terrified at his words, and in fear and trembling my bearer brought me the water from the tank. After a cold bath and a rubdown, I felt considerably refreshed and thought no more of the old man and his warning, until my attention was arrested by the sight of the villagers and my servants, all trooping off to a more distant tank to draw water and to slake their thirst. Inquiring the reason of their aversion for the water of the nearer tank, I then learned that a man who had murdered his wife had drowned himself in it, and it was firmly believed that anyone who drank or bathed in that water would be either killed by this earth-bound spirit or overtaken by some dire misfortune.

About ten o'clock that night, I sent on my two servants with the coolies bearing my tent and next kit to our intended camping ground, while I snatched a few hours' sleep, rolled up in my blanket under the banyan tree.

At 2 A.M., I set out, rifle in hand, to ride across the black loamy fields by a shortcut to my destination, accompanied by a native guide and my boy.

It was now about 3 A.M., and the air was beautifully cool and fresh, and we were able to travel for some time at a good pace; I on horseback, my two attendants running by my side.

By this time we had reached the middle of a wide stretch of cotton fields, when happening to glance ahead, I saw in the far distance a tiny glimmer of light. At first I mistook it for a light in some native hut, but as I looked more intently at it, I noticed that it appeared to be moving rapidly toward us and that in reality it seemed to come from a flaming torch. Turning to the two natives, I asked them what was this moving light? To my great astonishment they uttered cries of terror, and trembling with fear, they gasped out, "It is the Bijli!" (an evil spirit), and the next moment, the two cowards turned tail and fled for their lives in the opposite direction. Cursing them for their cowardly desertion, I spurred up my horse and rode forward to meet the advancing object. I could now see that the torch was apparently held by a native runner, so I called out as loudly as I could in Hindi to him to halt, for I was determined to find out the cause of the baseless fear of my two guides. The figure took no heed of my call but came gliding along toward me with unslackened speed. Enraged at such disobedience, I spurred on my horse to run him down, when suddenly the animal planted his feet, snorted, and nearly unseated me. Trembling in every limb, he refused to advance a foot nearer. There was nothing else to do but to dismount and continue my journey on foot.

Scarcely had I released the reins than the frightened brute bolted back toward the village we had left an hour or so previously.

The situation was now getting exciting. Deprived of my horse and two guides, and in the midst of pathless fields, I felt it would be difficult for me to proceed, so raising the rifle to my shoulder, I cried, "Stand still, or I fire at you!" Hardly had I uttered the words, when I was horrified to see that the figure, which seemed to *fly* along and was now only some few yards distant, was no human being at all. All that was visible was a grinning, bony skull and eye sockets, with long lank hair and a fleshless arm holding a flaming torch; the rest of the figure was a mere trail of gray mist.

As I stood there, unflinching, with my finger on the trigger, the apparition, which was now only ten or fifteen feet distant, suddenly *diverged* from me and rapidly sank into the ground some twenty feet *past* me, so that I had a good view of it. I rushed up to the spot where it had disappeared, but no trace of it was to be found. I stamped upon the ground, but the only proof of the apparition was a sprinkling of red-hot embers, which a moment before had formed the flaming torch. To reassure myself of the reality of what I had just witnessed, I stooped down and picked up some of these embers, which, however, I had hastily to throw down, as I discovered they were too hot to handle. Somewhat startled, I retraced my steps for a short distance, and as good luck would have it, I found my horse quietly grazing some distance away, and so remounting him and, after much hallooing, having got back my guide and boy, I at last reached my destination at daylight.

My guide then spread the news, and the headman of the village, having come to see me, said, "Sahib has seen the face of the Bijli, and evil will overtake him." He and my servants implored me not to go shooting in that neighborhood, "for does not the Sahib remember the Engineer Sahib, who saw the Bijli, and how the next night he was killed by a panther in his tent?"

"Do not go, Sahib," they entreated. "Evil will only come of it." They also told me that a native (who drank of the tank a year before) had been found dead with a *burnt* gash in his head on that plain I had traversed. Laughing at their superstition, I set out for my *shikar* (shooting).

A fortnight after, as we came near one of the hill caves, I heard that a couple of bears had been sighted there the previous night. Sending in the beaters to arouse the animals from their lair, I waited at the mouth of the cave for their approach.

Suddenly the two bears rushed out, and firing at one of them, I mortally wounded him, but as I turned, I found to my astonishment, that I was unexpectedly confronted by a third, too near to fire upon. Stepping back in order to take careful aim and avoid him, I stumbled and fell down a precipitous rock. In my fall, I broke an arm and dislocated my elbow, while a splinter from a fallen tree badly gashed my cheek. Stanching my wound as best I could, and with the help of the natives, I managed to get astride my horse and somehow gained my camp. There I lay for several days in great pain and in high fever, till at last I was strong enough to travel to the nearest station, and put myself into the doctor's hands.

I feel perfectly sure that had I shown any trace of fear, when face to face with the Bijli of the Flaming Torch, or had its eyes looked closely into mine, or had it in any way touched me, death would have been the sequel to this ghostly encounter or contact.

The Demon
of the Monastery

(China)

Ancient tradition having, as we have seen, described the *Siao* as giants of a Chang of ten *ch'ih*, or feet, we see them appear also in modern literature as house disturbers of tremendous stature. "Sun T'ai-poh," P'u Sung-ling recounts, "has told me the following story of his great-grandfather when he was studying for

From: Jan J. de Groot, *Religious Systems of China*, vol. 5, book 2, parts 2 and 3 (Leide: E. J. Brill, 1907).

the [religious] profession in the monastery of the Willow Canal, on the southern mountains." Once after going to his village on account of the wheat harvest, my great-grandfather returned to the monastery after an absence of ten days and, on opening his cell, found the table dusty and the window covered with cobwebs. He told his servant to sweep the apartment clean, and it was evening ere he could sit down refreshed and comfortable. He then dusted his couch and settled his sleeping gear, bolted his door, and went to bed. The moon shone brightly through the window.

Hour after hour passed away, and the music of the countless flutes was hushed, when suddenly a blast of wind began to bellow, and the gate on the hillside creaked. "The monks must have bolted it badly," my great-grandfather said to himself, but no sooner had this thought flashed through his brain than the bellowing wind drew nigh to the dwellings, and the door of his cell flew open. Not knowing in the least what to think of it, he had not yet arranged his ideas when the noise resounded in his cell, and the tramp of boots approaching the inner gate reached his ears. Now he began to feel uneasy, for the inner gate flew open, and turning his eyes, he beheld a large demon pushing through the doorway in stooping attitude. With a bound it stood before his bed. It reached almost to the ridge of the roof; its face had the color of an old pumpkin skin, and with eyes flashing fire it strode around in the room, glancing from side to side. Its gaping large mouth, rather a basin than a mouth, showed teeth wide apart, more than three *ts'un* long; its tongue moved [outside its mouth]; guttural chattering cries echoed along the four walls.

My great-grandsire's terror was extreme. "With a few feet for room," he said to himself, "it is impossible to elude that phantom. The best course to pursue will be to accept the situation and fight it with the edged weapon." Gently he drew forth his sword from underneath his pillow, hastily unsheathed it, and aimed a blow at the specter; he hit its belly, which gave a sound like an earthen pot. The specter flew into a passion. It stretched out its huge claws to grasp my great-grandfather, but as he recoiled a little, it got hold merely of the lapel of his gown. With the folds in its claw it ran away furiously, so that my great-grandfather was dragged forward and fell to the ground, yelling and screaming. The inmates of the building ran together with lights and, finding the door closed, pushed open the window and entered. Their consternation on beholding the scene was great. They placed him on his bed, and on his telling them what had happened, they conjointly examined the spot and found the lapel squeezed into the chink of the inner gate. They opened this and, inspecting it by the light of their torches, found it covered with marks of claws, running over it like the texture of a sieve, and perforated in every spot which the five fingers had touched.

By that time it was daylight and my great-grandfather, not daring to stay any longer in that monastery, shouldered his wallet and went home. Afterward he interrogated the monks, who assured him that nothing peculiar had happened since.

The Rescued Woman

(Philippines)

A man once lived with his wife in a little house in the woods. Their principal crop was maize, and for a long time they prospered. But something began to take the maize. One morning the farmer found that five stalks were gone, and to a Bisayan farmer it is a serious matter to lose a few stalks of maize. Then the next night he lost ten and another night fifty. So he set a watch but saw nothing. He was greatly worried by this, but as he had business in town he went away.

While he was away, a Tik-balan came to the house and took the woman who was left behind and, tying her into a bundle, threw her up on his shoulder and carried her away to a cave in the mountains. There he went down a steep ladder into a large room full of Okos, which, as soon as they smelled a human being, cried aloud in joy, "Here is live human flesh!" They put the woman into a cage to fatten her till she should be ready to eat.

The husband returned, found his wife gone, and being a brave man,

From: Fletcher Gardner, "Philippine (Tagalog) Superstitions," *Journal of American Folk-Lore* 19 (1906): 191–204.

followed the trail of the Tik-balan to his cave. Knowing that he could do nothing without help, he returned to his house and there found two nephews, both brave men, who had just returned from a voyage. These three procured all the *alak* (water) they could, and fastening the bottles around their waists and tying on their bolos, they went to the cave.

Down the ladder they climbed, into the dark. When they reached the bottom, all the Okos set up the shout, "Here is live human flesh!" but these brave men were not at all discomposed and only said, "Very well, but you won't eat us until you have tasted our alak." So the Tik-balan and the Okos tasted the alak and smacked their lips, declaring it was the finest water they ever drank. But soon the alak began to make them drunk, and they sang and talked and finally fell over and went to sleep.

Then the men went to the cage and let the woman out and started up the long ladders. The Okos and the Tik-balan by this time were recovering from their drunkenness and started to follow. But the men and the women reached the top first, and the men cut the ladders loose and threw them with the Okos and the Tik-balan to the bottom, where they were all killed. Then they returned to their homes and were never troubled again.

The Young Man Who Was Not Afraid

(Philippines)

A young man who lived in the country once wished to go to town. He was a brave fellow and started off clapping his hands and shouting to the Tik-balan and the evil spirits that he was not afraid of them. As he went on he felt the touch of invisible hands grasping his clothing. Drawing his bolo, he struck out to the sides and behind him, and although he could see nothing, the steel rang as though striking on a rock. At last he came to a brook, and the invisible hands gripped him closer, tearing his clothes from his back. Looking up, he saw also a gigantic Tik-balan towering above and ready to grasp him. He attempted to cross the brook but could not.

Then he drew his bolo again and struck it on the ground three times, at the same time saying a prayer against the evil spirits, three Hail Marys and three Our Fathers. With that the evil spirits and the Tik-balan gave back a little, but the young man, whether by fear or the power of the evil spirits, was nearly crazed. He went on, but his path, instead of taking him to the village, led into the mountains until he had crossed seven. On and on he went, never daring to stop till midnight, when the Tik-balan drew near to destroy him.

Without knowing what he did, he cut a bamboo and made of it a cross, and carrying it, he went on. The Tik-balan, frightened by the cross, kept at a greater distance but still followed.

After much fatigue and suffering, he came to his mother's house in the country, and she, being skilled in such matters, put crosses about, and put salt on the roof and on her son's body. But though she was a wise woman and knew much of herbs, it was three days before the young man could remember anything or speak.

From: Fletcher Gardner, "Philippine (Tagalog) Superstitions," *Journal of American Folk-Lore* 19 (1906): 191–204.

The Story of a Tengu

(*Japan*)

In the days of the Emperor Go-Reizei, there was a holy priest living in the temple of Saito, on the mountain called Hiyei-Zan, near Kyōto. One summer day this good priest, after a visit to the city, was returning to his temple by way of Kita-no-Ōji when he saw some boys ill-treating a kite. They had caught the bird in a snare and were beating it with sticks. "Oh, the poor creature!" compassionately exclaimed the priest, "why do you torment it so, children?"

One of the boys made answer, "We want to kill it to get the feathers."

Moved by pity, the priest persuaded the boys to let him have the kite in exchange for a fan that he was carrying, and he set the bird free. It had not been seriously hurt and was able to fly away.

Happy at having performed this Buddhist act of merit, the priest then resumed his walk. He had not proceeded very far when he saw a strange monk come out of a bamboo grove by the roadside and hasten toward him.

The monk respectfully saluted him, and said, "Sir, through your compassionate kindness my life has been saved, and I now desire to express my gratitude in a fitting manner."

Astonished at hearing himself thus addressed, the priest replied, "Really, I cannot remember to have ever seen you before. Please tell me who you are."

"It is not wonderful that you cannot recognize me in this form," returned the monk. "I am the kite that those cruel boys were tormenting at Kita-no-Ōji. You saved my life, and there is nothing in this world more precious than life. So I now wish to return your kindness in some way or other. If there be anything that you would like to have, or to know, or to see—anything that I can do for you, in short—please tell me; for as I happen to possess, in a small degree, the Six Supernatural Powers, I am able to gratify almost any wish that you can express."

From: Lafcadio Hearn, "The Story of a Tengu," *In Ghostly Japan* (Boston: Little, Brown & Co., 1899), 215–21.

On hearing these words, the priest knew that he was speaking with a Tengu, and he frankly made answer, "My friend, I have long ceased to care for the things of this world. I am now seventy years of age; neither fame nor pleasure has any attraction for me. I feel anxious only about my future birth; but as that is a matter in which no one can help me, it were useless to ask about it. Really, I can think of but one thing worth wishing for. It has been my lifelong regret that I was not in India in the time of the Lord Buddha and could not attend the great assembly on the holy mountain Gridhrakûta. Never a day passes in which this regret does not come to me, in the hour of morning or of evening prayer. Ah, my friend! if it were possible to conquer time and space, like the Bodhisattvas, so that I could look upon that marvelous assembly, how happy should I be!"

"Why," the Tengu exclaimed, "that pious wish of yours can easily be satisfied. I perfectly well remember the assembly on the Vulture Peak, and I can cause everything that happened there to reappear before you, exactly as it occurred. It is our greatest delight to represent such holy matters. Come this way with me!"

And the priest suffered himself to be led to a place among pines, on the slope of a hill.

"Now," said the Tengu, "you have only to wait here for a while with your eyes shut. Do not open them until you hear the voice of the Buddha preaching the Law. Then you can look. But when you see the appearance of the Buddha, you must not allow your devout feelings to influence you in any way; you must not bow down, nor pray, nor utter any such exclamation as, 'Even so, Lord!' Or 'O thou Blessed One!' You must not speak at all. Should you make even the least sign of reverence, something very unfortunate might happen to me." The priest gladly promised to follow these injunctions; and the Tengu hurried away as if to prepare the spectacle.

The day waned and passed, and the darkness came, but the old priest waited patiently beneath a tree, keeping his eyes closed. At last a voice suddenly resounded above him—a wonderful voice, deep and clear like the pealing of a mighty bell—the voice of the Buddha Sâkyamuni proclaiming the Perfect Way. Then the priest, opening his eyes in a great radiance, perceived that all things had been changed: the place was indeed the Vulture Peak, the holy Indian mountain Gridhrakûta; and the time was the time of the Sûtra of the Lotos of the Good Law. Now there were no pines about him but strange shining trees made of the Seven Precious Substances, with foliage and fruit of gems—and the ground was covered with Mandârava and Man-jûshaka flowers showered from heaven—and the night was filled with fragrance and splendor and the sweetness of the great Voice. And in midair, shining as a moon above the world, the priest beheld the Blessed One seated upon the Lion Throne, with Samanatabhadra at his right hand and Mañjusrî at his left and before them assembled—immeasurably spreading into space like a flood of stars—the hosts of the Mahâsattvas and the Bodhisattvas with their countless following: gods, demons, Nâgas, goblins, men, and beings not human. Sâriputra he saw, and Kâsyapa, and Ânanda, with all the disciples of the Tathâgata—and the Kings of the Devas—and the Kings of the Four Directions, like pillars of fire—and the great Dragon-Kings—and the Gandharvas and Garudas—and the gods of the Sun and the Moon and the Wind—and the shining myriads of Brahma's heaven. And incomparably farther than even the measureless circling of the glory of these, he saw—made visible by a single ray of light that shot from the forehead of the Blessed One to pierce beyond uttermost time—the eighteen hundred thousand Buddha Fields of the Eastern Quarter with all their habitants—and the beings in each of the Six States of Existence—and even the shapes of the Buddhas extinct that had entered into Nirvâna. These, and all the gods, and all the demons, he saw bow down before the Lion-Throne; and he heard that multitude incalculable of beings praising the Sûtra of the Lotos of the Good Law—like the roar of a sea before the Lord. Then forgetting utterly his pledge—foolishly dreaming that he stood in the very presence of the very Buddha—he cast himself down in worship with tears of love and thanksgiving, crying out with a loud voice, "O thou Blessed One!"

Instantly with a shock as of an earthquake, the stupendous spectacle disappeared, and the priest found himself alone in the dark, kneeling upon the grass of the mountainside. Then a sadness unspeakable fell upon him, because of the loss of the vision and because of the thoughtlessness that had caused him to break his word.

As he sorrowfully turned his steps homeward, the goblin-monk once more appeared before him, and said to him in tones of reproach and pain, "Because you did not keep the promise which you made to me, and heedlessly allowed your feelings to overcome you, the Gohōtendo, who is the Guardian of the Doctrine, swooped down suddenly from heaven upon us and smote us in great anger, crying, 'How do ye dare thus to deceive a pious person?' Then the other monks, whom I had assembled, all fled in fear. As for myself, one of my wings has been broken, so that now I cannot fly." And with these words the Tengu vanished forever.

An Unlucky Demon

(China)

There was a fine large temple beside a much traveled road. The idol in this temple received numerous offerings, and had an abundance of food and clothing, with elegant equipage of every sort.

A hill rose behind the temple, and on the hilltop was a little shrine where dwelt the idols called the White Mandarin and his Wife. The goddess found much fault with her spouse because their shrine was neglected. She averred that their ill condition resulted from his stupidity, and she advised him to go to the prosperous god at the foot of the hill and learn from him the art of becoming rich.

Impelled by his wife's discontent, the poor demon went down the hill to learn from his rich neighbor the secret of success. The grand idol received him affably and responded kindly to his inquiries, saying, "I have a lasso which I throw over the heads of people and draw tightly as they pass by. Their heads then ache, they try to remember where they were when their illness began, and they soon return here bringing offerings with which to propitiate me. Thereupon I release them from the lasso, and then they become well, and afterward bring more offerings expressive of their gratitude to me for their recovery. Thus I become famous and have the reputation of being powerful. Now, I will lend you my lasso, and you can so use it as to become as wealthy as I."

From: Adele M. Fielde, "The Character of Chinese Folk-Tales," *Journal of American Folk-Lore* 8 (1895): 185–91.

The poor demon took the lasso with many expressions of gratitude and returned to his abode. A lad who was going out to gather edible snails soon passed the shrine, and the demon lassoed him. His head thereupon began to ache so badly that he turned about and went homeward, and the demon followed him, holding on to the borrowed lasso, of which he dared not lose sight. The lad, having arrived at home, told his mother that his head ached too severely to permit his stooping down to gather snails, and she at once began to berate him for being a lazy, unprofitable child, pretending illness that he might avoid work. Growing angrier while she scolded, she took a stick to beat the boy, and this so frightened the demon for the safety of his lasso that he caught it away and ran home with all speed. As soon as the lasso was removed, the lad's head ceased to ache, and no offerings were brought by either mother or son to the shrine of the White Mandarin.

The poor demon was fearful that some injury to the lasso would oblige him to make recompense for it to his powerful neighbor, so he took it to its owner and told him of the ill success in its use. The great idol called him a dunce for lassoing such poor game as an empty-handed snail gatherer and told him to keep the lasso a while longer and to try it upon someone who had an abundance of goods.

Soon after, the demon saw a man carrying a big load and thinking that he fulfilled the prescribed conditions, lassoed him in haste. He was a bucket mender, carrying an immense bundle of hoops, and could not rightly be termed empty-handed. The man's head began to ache, but being poor, he felt that he could not stop work, and he went on to the next village, where he sat down to ply his trade. The demon drew his lasso tighter, and the mans' head ached harder, till he became angry, and seizing his hatchet, he swung it around his head, exclaiming, "Well, if my plaguey head is going to split, then I'll split it myself." Alarmed for the safety of the lasso, the demon snatched it off and ran away. So the man got better and the shrine got no offering.

Then the demon went again to his friend and was derided for having taken a poor laborer in his toils. He was told that he should snare a rich man, who would be able to nurse his ailment and to make fine compensation for his cure. So the next time the demon threw the lasso, he ensnared a handsomely dressed traveler and followed him to his house, drawing the rope gradually tighter and increasing the resulting headache. If the rich man had consulted a soothsayer or a spirit-medium, as many persons do when ill, he would have been advised to bear propitiatory offerings to the god near whose shrine he was when the headache began. But he did no such thing. He called a physician, who prescribed an infusion of old camphor wood. The rich man said that new camphor wood might easily be obtained, for there were plenty of chips at the idol makers'; but old camphor wood was difficult to get.

"Oh," said one of the farmhands, who stood near, "I know where you can get some that is very old. There is an ancient idol in the little shrine of the White Mandarin on the top of the hill behind the great temple. I will go and get the image to be chopped up and steeped for you."

The poor demon, hearing all this and knowing that the old wood referred to was his own body, loosened the lasso and hurried home. The aching head then got better and the old camphor wood was not sought, but the poor demon returned the lasso to his neighbor, saying, "Here is your lasso. You told me to snare a rich man in it, and I did so. The result was that I came near being myself destroyed."

The Man-Eater

(Philippines)

In a certain village in the kingdom of Y——— there lives a very well-to-do herdsman and his wife and several children. They own the biggest poultry farm and herds of cattle, horses, and flocks of sheep in the kingdom. They are oftentimes so worried by the boundless increase of their animals that they wish they could eat a visible portion of them. One time rinderpest breaks out in the kingdom, and their herds perish in great number. The father becomes more worried, for the perishing cattle cannot all be buried. During this event, so wearisome and dreadful, the wife conceives a child; and as

From: Simon P. Santos, "Notes and Queries: The Man-Eater," *Journal of American Folk-Lore* 34 (1921): 393–95.

a result she manifests a behavior very different from her former life. She now eats very much. Her appetite increases disproportionately as her pregnancy matures. One distinct behavior which she observes during all this time is that, when she takes a light meal, the little seed in the womb moves to her pain, and she can only keep it still when she fills her belly with half a dozen chickens. Time goes on, and soon she gives birth to a baby boy. The boy shows early great insatiability. In the cradle he eats one big chicken at one meal, and when he is as old as to begin to walk, he can consume one big carabao at a meal. The father, who prepares the food of his son, gets more worried because he can do no other work than cook.

The rinderpest ceases. The herds of cattle, horses, and flocks of sheep increase in number indefinitely. One time when the father goes to the pasturelands, he takes his little boy with him, and to his surprise, the boy devours calves and colts as a hungry dog eats chickens. But his father is not discouraged at this; rather, he is proud of his insatiable son. Soon the big flocks of chickens are gone. The herds of cattle and horses are decreasing. The boy's father now sees that the time is coming when he will have no more of his multitudinous wealth. Yes, the time is coming; and what will the boy do after he has consumed all that his father has?

Time goes on, and the boy reduces his father to poverty. He now wanders throughout the country, devouring every animal he meets. Soon the whole village is exhausted of domestic animals, but he must have food. He now eats his brothers, his father, and his mother. Not being satisfied, he again wanders throughout the village, devouring every man, woman, or child he meets. The people in the neighboring villages feel the danger that is approaching them. The news reaches the king, who is also terrified with dread and awe. He makes a public announcement that the man who can kill the terror in his kingdom will win for himself the hand of his daughter and one-half of his kingdom.

In a certain village somewhere in the same kingdom, there lives a very peaceful and loving man by the name of Juan. He finds happiness by living with animals, especially with his pet dog, his horse, and insects. On his farm he spares the praying mantis, and in his house he spares the lizard and all creatures within. His best friends are his dog, about as big as a calf, and his horse. They are his dearest companions. One day he goes to town on horseback. He tells his dog to watch the life-index very carefully while he is gone, and when the dog notices that the leaves begin to wilt, the dog should follow him.

Juan passes through a lonely village which is entirely depopulated. The grass is overgrown, and the houses are like haunted places, very dangerous to enter. In this same place, thirst lays hands on him. Turning his face to the left, he beholds a man sitting on an open porch of a house. He directs his horse to the place. To his surprise, the horse, which has always been very brave and loyal to him, now shows a sort of fear, as if something extraordinary were about to happen. Nevertheless he takes no precautions. As he gets near the house, the Man-Eater yawns, saying as he rubs his hands over his belly, "Thank God!"

But Juan does not hear him. He dismounts from his horse and goes to the house. As he passes the gate in front of the house, he hears the mantis, whose life he has spared, say, "O kind traveler! what are you here for? That man in the house is the Man-Eater. Leave immediately before he eats you up."

Again Juan does not take heed, but this time he begins to ask himself, "What could this mantis mean?" He enters the house; and as he meets the host, Juan asks, "Will you kindly give me a glass of water to drink?"

Man-Eater: "Come in. Take a seat in the house, and I shall get water for you."

Juan enters the *sala*, while the Man-Eater goes to the kitchen. While Juan waits for the water, he suspects that there is something extraordinary about to happen. The lizard on the ceiling says, "O Juan, kind man! the Man-Eater is almost through sharpening his teeth. Leave immediately before he eats you up."

The visitor, taking into consideration the time that has already elapsed, believes the warning of the lizard. He jumps through the window, mounts his horse, and flees away.

Just about this time the dog notices a change in the life-index. He sees that the leaves begin to wilt, and he now remembers his master. He hurries on to the rescue.

The Man-Eater hears the footsteps of the horse and knows that the traveler is gone. He pursues him. Soon Juan comes to a place where seven coconut palms are standing. He looks back, and finding his pursuer about to overtake him, he jumps from his horse to the first coconut palm and climbs quickly up. The horse runs home, and he meets the dog on his way. He tells the dog to speed fast, because their master is in danger. Now the Man-Eater reaches the coconut palms. He bites the trunk, and the tree falls against another tree. The man on the tree jumps to the next one, and so on until the last tree. The Man-Eater looks up the last tree with a pleasing smile, saying to himself as he feels his belly, "Thank heaven! you will give me much satisfaction." And as he bends his head to bite the tree, the dog, which has been traveling for some time, arrives and, seeing the Man-Eater bending, bites him on the neck and kills him.

Juan descends from the treetop to meet his kind and loyal friends, the dog and the horse. He thanks them very much for what they have done for him. He mounts his horse and tells the dog to follow. They all go to the town, the seat of the government. After traveling for some time, they come to the next village. The people of the village are surprised to see a stranger coming from the direction of the haunted region. They ask Juan, "Have you ever met any extraordinary incident in any village through which you passed?"

"Yes," said Juan. "A man almost ate me up, but I am glad he is now dead. I killed him."

The news of the traveler is a relief to them. They shout and laugh and dance, embrace the traveler, and celebrate a feast for him. Juan is surprised by all these festivities, and he asks the people what all these things mean to them and why they honor him too dearly when he has not done anything for them.

"Yes," answer the people. "You have vanquished our most dreaded foe, and we honor you."

After all these festivities, they lead Juan to the palace of the king. Juan tells the king the story of his adventure, and when the king learns that the traveler has killed the Man-Eater, the terror in his kingdom, he jumps in gladness, sends for his daughter, and issues a summons to the effect that every man, woman, and child in the kingdom shall come to witness the marriage ceremony of his daughter with Juan, the hero of the hour, and to celebrate the peace that will forever be enjoyed by the whole people in the kingdom. The marriage is celebrated, and the horse and the dog, the best friends of Juan, become the idols in the palace.

Vampires

(Japan)

The *Hiakku Monogatari* of Tokwa Sanjin describes a strange hairy creature, with lithe body, long limbs, a pointed mouth verging toward a sort of beak, sucking the breath of a sleeping man. This beast is called Yama Chichi, "mountain father." It is described as being a most ancient Nobusuma, that is to say, a bat of enormous age, because the bat changes into a Nobusuma only when a thousand years old. This mountain father sucks the breath of people in the remote province of Oshu, tapping their chest at the same time and causing the death of its victim within a few days, but if there happens to be a human witness of the occurrence, then the victim recovers and lives to a ripe old age.

Sekiyen pictures the Nobusuma as a sort of flying squirrel, and describes it as such under the name Musasabi; it has a brown skin, and resembles a bat in having wings which are part and parcel of four short legs armed with long claws. It feeds on nuts and flaming fire.

Returning to the *Hiakku Monogatari*, we find the Nodeppo, which is a still older bat, having passed through the form Mami. The Nodeppo blows out a batlike creature which covers its victim with its wings and sucks his breath to death, unless the wary traveler carries near his skin for protection a few leaves of a burrweed called *namomi*.

Yet another vampire was believed to exist in the seventh century, the Tsutsuga Mushi, found in the mountains of Yagami. Until a learned man, sent by the Empress Saimei Tenno (655–61), compelled these animals to remain within certain boundaries in the wilderness, they used to enter the houses at night and suck the blood of sleeping folks. Since that time, however, they have ceased to appear, but the expression *tsutsuga nashi* remains in the language to express freedom from illness or disease.

From: Henri L. Joly, "Bakemono," *Transactions and Proceedings of the Japan Society* 9 (1909–11): 15–48.

The Vampire and the Head

(China)

L iu N.N., a literary graduate of the lowest degree in Wu-kiang (in Kiangsu), was in charge of some pupils belonging to the Tsiang family in the Yuen-hwo district. In the season of Pure Brightness he returned home, some holidays being granted him to sweep his ancestral tombs. This duty performed, he would return to his post. He said to his wife, "Tomorrow I must go. Cook some food for me at an early hour." The woman said she would do so, and rose for the purpose at cockcrow. Their village lay on the hill behind their dwelling, facing a brook. The wife washed some rice at that brook, picked some vegetables in the garden, and had everything ready, but when it was light her husband did not rise. She went into his room to wake him up, but however often she called, he gave no answer. So she opened the curtains and found him lying across the bed, headless, and not a trace of blood to be seen.

Terror-stricken she called the neighbors. All of them suspected her of adultery with a lover and murder, and they warned the magistrate. This grandee came and held a preliminary inquest; he ordered the corpse to be coffined for the time being, had the woman put into fetters, and examined her. But this brought no evidence against her, so he put her in gaol, and many months passed away without sentence being pronounced. Then a neighbor going uphill for some fuel saw a neglected grave with a coffin laid bare. It was quite a sound coffin, strong and solid, and yet the lid was raised a little, so he naturally suspected that it had been opened by thieves. He summoned the people. They lifted the lid off and saw a corpse with features like a living person and a body covered with white hair. Between its arms it held the head of a man, which they recognized as that of Liu, the

From: Jan J. de Groot, *Religious Systems of China*, vol. 5, book 2, parts 2 and 3 (Leide: E. J. Brill, 1907).

graduate. They reported the case to the magistrate. The coroners ordered the head to be taken away, but it was so firmly grasped in the arms of the corpse that the combined efforts of a number of men proved insufficient to draw it out. So the mandarin told them to chop off the arms of the Kiang-shi. Fresh blood gushed out of the wounds, but in Liu's head there was not one drop left, it having been sucked dry by the monster. By magisterial order, the corpse was burned, and the case ended with the release of the woman from gaol.

The Corpse-Specter

(China)

When Tsiang, Governor of Ying-cheu, resided in Ngan-cheu, in the province of Pehchihli, he met with a man who nervously moved both his arms continuously as if he swung bells. On being asked why he did so, he told the following tale:

My family lives in the village of ———, which consists of not more than a few dozen houses. There a Kiang-shi came from the hills, soaring through the air, to devour the infants of the people. Though daily at sunset the people exhorted each other to shut their doors and conceal their children, nevertheless it occurred from time to time that some were kidnapped by the monster. The villagers sounded its grave, but they could not find the bottom of it, so that nobody ventured to take any measures against it.

At that time we heard that there was living in the town a Taoist doctor proficient in magic arts. We collected money and presents for him, and went to ask him to arrest that specter. He assented, and appeared in our village on an auspicious day. He put up an altar for the performance of his magic, and said to the people: "My magic enables me to spread a net over the sky and a net over the earth,

From: Jan J. de Groot, *Religious Systems of China,* vol. 5, book 2, parts 2 and 3 (Leide: E. J. Brill, 1907).

preventing that demon from flying away, but you must help me with your weapons. Besides I want a man of much courage to enter that grave."

Nobody in the crowd ventured to present himself for this task, except myself, who stepped to the front and asked for what he would employ me.

"Corpse-specters, " the magician replied, "generally fear very much the sound of jingles and hand gongs. When the night comes, you must watch the moment when the specter flies out, and forthwith enter the grave with two big bells. But do not stop ringing them, for a short pause will suffice for the corpse to enter the grave, and you will then be the sufferer."

The water clock had just begun to sink, when the doctor mounted his altar to perform his magic. And I, with two bells, watched the moment when the corpse flew out. Then with all their might and main my arms waved up and down in a quick succession like raindrops, and I dared not pause for one short moment, as the specter was at the entrance of the grave. Horribly ferocious it looked. Its furious glances never turned away from me while the sound of the bells kept it running about the spot without courage to enter. Beset by the crowd everywhere in front, there was no way of escape for it, so with impetuous movements of its hands and with outstretched arms, it fought the villagers until the first blush of dawn cast it flat on the ground. Our men then took it up and burned it. Meanwhile I remained in the grave, ignorant of the issue, swinging the bells incessantly, as I lacked courage to stop them. It was toward noon when the crowd came and called me out with loud cries. Both my arms then remained in constant motion, and they have been diseased like this to this day.

The Pisacha

(India)

Of all the forms of the real or supposed intercourse between the living and dead, that of the vampire is the most loathsome. The horrid physical effects which follow after the burial of a corpse have no doubt had much to do in creating the sentiment of disgust and terror which associates with the thought of this return of the dead to prey upon the living. And it is another argument in favor of cremation—if any were needed by thoughtful persons—that there are no vampires save in countries where the dead are buried. We do not hear of Hindu vampires, but where such cases occur in India, it turns out that the revenant is a deceased Muslim, Christian, or Jew whose body had been interred.

Some years ago the grandmother of our Mr. Gopalacharlu had a neighbor, a Hindu woman, who was supposed to have been obsessed by a devil (Pisacha). For about a year she would find herself every morning on awakening deprived of all strength, pale and anemic. Twice becoming pregnant, she had miscarriages. Finally, resort was had to a Muslim *mantriki*, or exorcist, who by arts known to himself, discovered that the "control" was a deceased man of his own faith. He went secretly to the country, opened the grave of the suspect, found the corpse fresh and lifelike, made a cut on its hand near the thumb, and found fresh blood flowed spurting out from the wound. He then performed the usual placatory rites, recited his mantras, and drove the phantom away from his victim and back to its grave. The woman recovered, and no fresh victim was visited.

From: Anon., "The Vampire," reprinted from *The Theosophist* 12 (1891).

About the Asuang

(Philippines)

T he Asuang is often confounded by Europeans with ghosts and devils. It is neither devil nor ghost, but human, and is possessed of certain miraculous powers acquired by eating human liver. In certain ways it is a compound of both vampire and ghoul, for it may fly like the vampire and live on human flesh drawn from the living, and on the other hand it may feast on the flesh of those who have died natural deaths, like the ghoul. It has the power to change its corporeal form from human to batlike by a process of division at the waistline, the lower limbs and lower part of the trunk remaining behind while the upper part grows wings and flies away.

It may also take the form of a dog, cat, cayman, or other animal, and in any form possesses the power of causing sickness or death by its spells. In one of the stories of the Asuang of Bacó, the Asuang compels the change of his food into a shape less abhorrent to others.

The defenses against Asuangs are several. Garlic held in the hand is an effectual shield against their malign power. Ashes placed on the divided body prevent the reunion of the upper and lower portions and condemn the Asuang to some dreadful fate which is never more than hinted at in the stories. The most effectual weapon is the tail of the stingray, of which the Asuang is mortally afraid. At the birth of a child, or in sickness, it is customary in some parts of the Philippines to beat the air and the ground with these formidable whips to drive away the Asuangs. La Gironière, writing of a period between 1819 and 1839, says of the Tagalogs of Luzon that a saber is often used in this way, but the natives at the present time usually regard the bolo as useless against the Asuang. La Gironière also defines the Asuang as a malignant divinity, whereas the following detailed stories of Asuangs are sufficient to show that the idea is a very different one.

The Asuang may be cured by binding him hand and foot and placing by him a vessel of water, which must be perfectly clean and

From: Fletcher Gardner, "Philippine (Tagalog) Superstitions," *Journal of American Folk-Lore* 19 (1906): 191–204.

clear. Worms, beetles, lizards, and the like issue from the mouth and nose, and the patient is cured.

The origin of this class of superstitions has been supposed to lie in a former state of cannibalism which, surviving in a certain cult for a long time, has shocked the more advanced portion of the community by its revolting practices. Gradually even this died out, and only traditions survive which have been kept alive by the attacks of animals on bodies buried in shallow graves. It is possible that the last-named factor alone is responsible, but among a people, or rather peoples so diverse in origin as those of the Philippines, it is far from improbable that some at least of the tribes at a remote period may have been anthropophagi, especially as there is much evidence that it has survived in the form of ceremonial cannibalism, almost if not quite to the present time, among the wild tribes of northern Luzon. It is possible too that the superstition itself has given rise to cases of obsession in which some of these acts have been performed. One thing is certain, it is the most universal of all beliefs in the islands. It is believed alike by Christian and non-Christian, by educated and ignorant, almost without exception.

The Asuang is often called Wakwak by Bisayans, and the term is understood by Tagalogs; the converse being also true, that the Bisayans understand the word *asuang*. In Pampangan, the word *asuang* and a variant *ustuang* are used. Padre Bergaño, in his *Pampangan Dictionary*, says: "It is said to be a man who, anointing his body with oil, flies to a pregnant woman and draws her unborn child from the womb." Padre Ortiz speaks of this as being the particular sphere of action of the *Patianak*. Padre Lisboa's *Bicol Dictionary* defines the Asuang simply as a "wizard that eats human flesh."

The Tianak or Patianak is another dreaded and malevolent being cognate to the Asuang, which is said to be the soul of an unbaptized child, living again in a new body in the forest, sucking the blood of any unfortunate woman whom it may find asleep, or who, in compassion, may give it suck. By Padre Ortiz, the Spanish word *duende*, or goblin, is used as a synonym for Patianak. The whole subject is confused and needs further elucidation. It is likely that a more detailed study would find the fundamental idea overlaid with a mass of local tradition.

More about the Asuang

(Philippines)

The belief in Asuangs is too firmly established in the minds of most of the people to be easily shaken, and is sometimes the cause of great mischief, as the Asuang is a mortal, in many respects like themselves—indeed, may be one of their neighbors. The chief characteristic of the Asuang is his liking for human flesh, especially the livers of young children. It is with the greatest difficulty that a teacher can convince his scholars that the cannibals mentioned in the story of Robinson Crusoe were not Asuangs but simply men and women like their own parents. The children believe that the Asuang can catch them and carry them to the tops of high trees in order to eat them. This is one of the reasons why they dislike to be out after dark, and why they will not travel alone at night, or even in the daytime in lonely places, if it can possibly be avoided.

The Asuang is a man or woman who has made a compact with the Evil One. Such a one does not attend the church or enter any other sacred place. He has a hole in the armpit which contains an oil that gives him the power of becoming invisible and flying where he pleases. His nails are very long and his tongue horribly expanded, black, and pliant as silk.

The Asuang, like the Tamawo, can assume the form of an animal at will. The early evening is the time most suitable for him to make a visit of inspection to the houses where, later, when the people are all asleep, he performs his horrible deeds. At midnight he leaves the lower part of his body, from the waist down, and the other half flies off to look for food, especially lonely travelers and babies whose attendants have neglected them. If anyone can manage, during the absence of the Asuang, to cast salt upon the part of his body that he has left behind, it will be impossible for him upon his return to reunite his body.

When a child is sick, the parents go to the house of one who is

From: Berton L. Maxfield and W. H. Millington, "Philippine (Visayan) Superstitions," *Journal of American Folk-Lore* 19 (1906): 205–11.

known to be an Asuang and beg him to come and cure the sick one. If the Asuang can be induced to come and touch the child's hand, immediate recovery is assured and the parents return thanks to the Asuang.

It is a serious matter to be suspected of being an Asuang. Young ladies who belong to the family of an Asuang are not sought in marriage but are condemned to pass their lives in lonely spinsterhood—a fate to be deplored even more in that country than in more civilized regions. Many masters will not engage a servant until after assuring themselves that there is no danger of his being related to an Asuang.

In order to discover whether a person is an Asuang or not, a curious custom is in vogue. The parings of the fingernails are cast into the fire in the presence of the suspect. If the suspicion is correct, the Asuang betrays himself by becoming extremely nervous and restless.

The probable origin of the belief in Asuangs is thus given by a well-educated Visayan:

> Before the Spaniards came to these islands, each datto or rich man had an Asuang, or official who served as counselor in religious and political matters. The Asuangs were the most learned people among them. The Spaniards came and began to preach Christianity, and of course, they had to show the falsehood of the Asuang's doctrine as contrary to morality. Then the neophytes and new Christians looked upon the Asuang as a false teacher, and their hatred of him became so great that they forged and invented many attributes of him.

The Asuang
Who Died of Shame

(Philippines)

There was once a poor widow who had two children. She used always to tell them never to forget to pray for the repose of her soul when she should die. At last she died, and the eldest girl, then verging on womanhood, tried to get the money to bury her, but no one helped her, till a young man came and said that if she would marry him he would bury her mother. She consented to this, and the woman was buried, and although she did not know it, the young man wished the body for himself, for he was an Asuang.

After a suitable time they were married, but the young wife was not happy, however, for her husband was never at home at night. One night she watched him as he flew away. She was greatly frightened and resolved to eat nothing more in the house. When morning came, the young man returned carrying much meat, which he said came from a wild boar he had killed in the woods. This he prepared and told her to eat, but she begged not to be compelled to eat, because she was sick. "You must eat," said the young man, "or I will eat you." So she pretended to eat but dropped the bits of meat through the floor. This the Asuang saw, and threatened again with being eaten herself, through fear she ate the meat. She did not become an Asuang, however, as she did not eat any of the liver.

The next night when the Asuang went away, she went to a chief of the village and begged to be protected from her husband. The chief promised to keep her from harm, and she remained in his house. The next morning her husband came in search of her and found her in the house of the chief, who said to him, "Your wife has left you because

From: Fletcher Gardner, "Philippine (Tagalog) Superstitions," *Journal of American Folk-Lore* 19 (1906): 191–204.

of your wickedness, and will never live with you as long as you continue your evil ways."

The Asuang raised his downcast eyes for a moment, looked at his wife, and fell down dead.

The Woman Who Became an Asuang

(Philippines)

There was once a man who was an Asuang, who married a woman who was not. The two lived in a house with the woman's mother and their own child, a baby girl. The man was absent from home a great deal, and the woman grew jealous lest she had a rival. So one day, leaving the baby with her mother, she went out to the farm in the country to look for the man.

When she came to the house, she could not find the man, but within, swung from the rafters, was a great deal of meat. Being hungry, she was tempted to try the meat and, finding it savory, ate on. After a while she ate a piece of the liver, and her nature changed at once and she became an Asuang. After waiting awhile she returned home, and finding her mother gone about her work, she took her own child and began to eat the flesh of its arm. The grandmother heard the child's cries, and for a while paid no attention to it, but finally returned just in time to see its mother running away and the child with its arm eaten off.

The poor old woman could think of nothing else than that her daughter had gone mad, but she buried the child and went to the chiefs of the village for protection. The Asuang went to the forest and joined her husband, and together they went to another village.

From: Fletcher Gardner, "Philippine (Tagalog) Superstitions," *Journal of American Folk-Lore* 19 (1906): 191–204.

In this village they did very well for a while, till the neighbors began to notice that they never slept, but in and out, up and down, night and day, they were always stirring. So one of the neighbors learned in the ways of the Asuangs went to the house one night and there found the bodies perfect below the waist, but with all above missing, a condition which betokens the Asuang. So he changed the one for the other and placed ashes on the surface where the missing parts should join, and set himself to watch. Soon they returned, but because of what had been done, were not able to resume their normal state. They flew about within and without the house crying, "Woe is me, woe is thee, if the dawn find us thus." Then they flew away again, and as soon as they were gone the man undid his work. Just as dawn was breaking, they came again, and finding all straight and ready, they became human again. But they were so ashamed at being found out that they went away and never again troubled that village.

Nga Chan Kaung and the Ghost

(Burma)

Away back in the year A.D. 1753 there lived a monk named Atula in Ushit village in Tapayin district. He was a man of upright character, steadfast virtue, and religious precept. As the representative of the Buddha, he brought peace and happiness into that small village. Pwès, wrestling matches, gambling, cockfights, drinking, and debauchery were stopped, and everybody became a better Buddhist. Buddhist festivals were religiously held, and five times a year the village of Ushit was as gay as the mansion of the gods, when candles were lit, torches were burnt, offerings were

From: Maung Tin, "Burmese Ghost Stories," *Burma Research Society's Journal* 3 (part 2) (1913): 183–85.

made to monk and layman, and everybody appeared at his or her best.

Two miles away from the village, on the outskirt of a forest was a little hut, the rest house of a cultivator and his wife, Nga Chan Kaung and Mi E Nyo. They were very poor and plowed the field regardless of sun and rain. It was their habit to rest at the hut during the day and return to the village with the last rays of the setting sun. They were the proud owners of two dogs, Táw-lone-hmway and Twáy-ma-shoung, ferocious animals of the hunting breed and plucky enough to fight even tigers and leopards. At that time, the stretch of land between the village and the hut was infested with a band of ghosts which, taking the form of hideous monsters, were wont to frighten wayfarers, seize them, and eat them. Those who managed to escape invariably took ill and died. Such was the terror of these demons that nobody would think of passing by that way after three o'clock in the evening.

It was the eve of Taboung Festival and everyone in Ushit was making preparations against the morrow, which was to be a day of rejoicing when, according to ancient custom, everybody did meritorious acts. Nga Chan Kaung, like a good villager, thought it his duty to be in the village on that day and help in the preparations. So he took his dinner at the hut and went along in the direction of the village in company with his two dogs, not forgetting first to sharpen his trusty *dah*, which he held firmly in his hand. Just as he came near a banyan tree hard by a tank, he heard the trampling of hoofs and presently behold! there came toward him a horse in full gallop. Nga Chan Kaung at once knew that the horse was nothing else but the notorious ghost that had inspired so many with fear and trembling. Being full of courage, he grasped his dah firmly and stood still in self-defense. The ghost disappeared. Instantly, it showed itself in the form of a man hanging on to a branch of the banyan tree. Nga Chan Kaung, letting out an oath as much as to say, "Now I have got you," cut a branch off the tree and threw it at the ghost. The ghost let itself down from the tree and took to its heels.

The two bloodhounds which were used to hunting game needed no encouragement but gave immediate chase. The ghost ran up a *kyun* tree. Nga Chan Kaung, guided by the barking of the hounds, came up and, finding the ghost up in the tree, climbed up and beat every branch of it with his stick. The ghost came down and ran, the dogs chased, the ghost ran up the nearest tree it could find, and Nga Chan

Kaung climbed up and beat the ghost out of the tree. This little scene was acted at every tree on the way until they came close to Ushit, when the ghost entered a tree hollow.

The hounds, unable to enter the hollow, barked from outside and Nga Chan Kaung thrust the end of his stick into the hollow and disturbed the ghost so much that it was obliged to run out. The hounds were again at its heels, and it only escaped by slipping into a prawn hole in a field. Nga Chan Kaung came up and, finding the dogs barking at the prawn hole, uttered an oath, saying, "I won't stop till I kill you." He then blocked up the hole securely, fetched a spade from home, and began digging it up. When he had dug deep enough, he found a lizard inside. He swore that the lizard was the ghost, killed it with the spade, roasted it in the fire, and ate it with some toddy at a toddy seller's shop.

The ghost, finding itself well-nigh annihilated and wishing to continue its existence, took conception in the womb of the toddy seller's wife, Mi Lun Hmway, and in due course was born as her son. When the son was old enough to speak, whenever he saw Nga Chan Kaung, he would scream with fear and fall into strange fits. When the mother asked, he would bawl out, pointing his trembling finger at Nga Chan Kaung, "He ate me up with toddy. I fear him."

Nga Chan Kaung thus found out that the ghost he had molested so much had been born as a human being. And it was his pleasure to entertain people grouped around him on a moonlit verandah by recounting his former experiences and advising them to be always bold in any encounter with ghosts. He lived to a good old age and never more did he hear of any ghost haunting the road which led from the village to his little hut.

Skull-Demons

(China)

In the village of Lai-t'ing in Shang-tu, Mrs. Li was sitting in the hall of her house in broad daylight, when suddenly she beheld her husband's deceased sister in white dress with a linen kerchief over her head. The phantom approached and pursued her and she tried to escape by running around the bed, but the ghost did not give up the chase. She then ran away through the door. At full speed they tore across hills and rocks, and nobody had the courage to help her, but happily some cavalry at the north gate fell upon the ghost with their whips. Under their blows it shrunk away, until nothing remained of it on the ground but the kerchief, covering something which they found to be a skull.

Sun Kiün-sheu of Shang-shuh was an atrociously bad character bent on insulting the *shen* and maltreating the *kwei*. Once he was strolling in the hills with some others and had reason to retire. For fun he squatted over a dry skull by a neglected grave and made it swallow his feces, saying, "Eat this, is it not delicious?" on which the skull, its jaws wide open, spoke, "Yes, it is." Horrified at this, Kiün-sheu ran away as fast as his legs could bear him, with the skull rolling behind him over the ground like a car wheel, till he reached a bridge, up which the skull could not manage to raise itself. From an eminence he saw the skull roll back to its old place. Ashy pale as a corpse, he came home and fell ill. Constantly he brought his excrements to his mouth with his hand, and swallowed them, saying to himself, "Eat this, is it not nice?" Then he voided them anew and devoured them again, going on in this wise for three whole days, when he died."

This story seems an embellished version of another tale which tells that in the year *ping* or *ting* of the Chi-yuen period (1336 or 1337), Yin Kang-lo and some other men of Lü-ling were out in the evening for a stroll to the Sih-kia lake. They were eating salted plums and put the stones into the mouth of a skull lying on the roadside, with the words.

From: Jan J. de Groot, *Religious Systems of China*, vol. 5, book 2, parts 2 and 3 (Leide: E. J. Brill, 1907).

"Do you find them salt?" They then passed on and came to a long trench. Here they saw in the bright moonlight a black ball coming rolling on behind them, crying, "They are salt, salt." In the greatest fright they ran more than ten miles, till they got across some water at the village of Yung and heard the voice no more.

Skulls may haunt even without being so bitterly provoked. The country of Ch'u-cheu (in Chehkiang province) is very mountainous. There, in the district of Li-shui, situated south of the peak of the Residence of the Immortal Genies, farmers plowing and sowing often break up waste ground, even as far as halfway up the mountains. In those mountains specters abound, and people all begin and finish their work early, not venturing abroad in dark. Once in the latter part of autumn, a landowner, Li by name, came to the village to cut his rice, and put up alone in a farmhouse. One night when the moon was shining splendidly, he was taking a stroll on the hill in front, when suddenly he saw a white thing hopping toward him. This strange sight quickly scared him back to his dwelling, which he reached with the thing close on his heels. Happily the entrance of the hut had a kind of railing, which could be slid forward and which the specter could not get over. He succeeded in pushing it to and, regaining his courage, distinctly saw in the bright moonlight through the openings of the railing that a skull was biting the latter and butting against it. The fetid stench was intolerable. After a few moments the cock crew, and he saw the thing drop to the ground as a mere heap of white bone; and when it was light, he saw no more of it.

He asked for information about that apparition, and a husbandman said, "You may congratulate yourself that you have had to do with a white bone ghost. This circumstance has saved you from disaster. Had it been the hoary old wife, feigning to keep a shop, she would of a certainty have offered you some of her tobacco to smoke, and those who smoke it generally lose their vitality. That specter always appears to do its evil work in nights with bright moonshine and a pure breeze, and it can be knocked down with nothing else but a broom."

The Ghost
in the Royal Service

(Burma)

I t was in the year 1762 that King Naungdawgyi sent an army under two of his generals to settle some difference in Zimmè. Udain-kyaw-kaung, one of the officers, happened to die on the way and became a ghost. One night he appeared to the king, who was asleep, shook him by the legs and, having related the circumstances of his death, demanded permission to enter the royal service. The king, who was as fearless as the lion, granted his request and made him Guard of the Palace Verandah.

Hearing that the Siamese had surprised the Burmese Guards at Martaban, the king dispatched two horsemen, Nga Tha and Nga Shoon, by way of Toungoo to report on the matter. The king, being impatient of their return, sent them the man-ghost Udain-kyaw-kaung, who discharged the duty in the course of that very day.

When the king disbelieved that he could have done it so quickly, the ghost reported thus: "May it please Your Majesty. Your most humble servant found on the return journey the two horsemen cooking their food under a tamarind tree at Toungoo at about one o'clock in the evening. To prevent any doubt on the matter, your most humble servant took the precaution to cut down some tamarind leaves and branches and to frighten the horsemen by shaking the whole tree. The horsemen have in their possession a letter from the Governor of Martaban to Your Most Gracious Majesty to the effect that the city, owing to the glory of Your Majesty, is not disturbed by any rebels, *dacoits,* or thieves. These horsemen will arrive in due course at the golden feet of Your Most Gracious Majesty."

When a few days later the horsemen arrived, they confirmed everything the ghost had said. In recognition of this service, the ghost

From: Maung Tin, "Burmese Ghost Stories," *Burma Research Society's Journal* 3 (part 2) (1913): 183–85.

petitioned that he might be honored with a suitable title. The king desired that he should appear bodily in his true colors and take the honor from the royal presence. Thereupon, the ghost pleaded that his true bodily appearance being hideous and awe-inspiring, his presence might be excused, but that the title having been duly conferred would be conveyed by him to his own residence (the Pillar in the Palace Verandah). Accordingly, in the presence of all the ministers, the king had the title of *Javana-yakkha-kyaw-kaung* (the celebrated demon of quick dispatch) inscribed on a gold plate, and everyone present saw the plate being carried by the string and placed at the haunted pillar by the invisible ghost.

The Wandering Corpse

(China)

A certain old man of Yang-sin (in Shantung) lived in Ts'ai-tien, a place in that district. His village lay five or six miles from the walls of the district city. He and his sons kept a roadside inn to lodge traveling traders, and several carters and itinerant peddlers used to put up under their roof. One day as it was getting dark, four men appeared. Perceiving the house, they went thither with the intention of staying, but the sleeping rooms destined for visitors were all occupied. Considering that there was no other place to put up, the four men urgently entreated the landlord to take them in somehow, on which he hemmed and said he thought a place might be found for them, though it would not suit their taste. The strangers replied that all they desired was a single mat to sleep on and a shelter, and that they could not be at all particular.

The fact was that a daughter-in-law of the old man had just died; her body still lay uncoffined in her house, and the son had gone to fetch a coffin and had not yet returned. The old man took the strangers

From: Jan J. de Groot, *Religious Systems of China*, vol. 5, book 2, parts 2 and 3 (Leide: E. J. Brill, 1907).

down the street into the lonely house where the corpse lay. They entered the apartment, where a lamp shed a dim light over a table. Behind this a curtain hung, and the deceased woman lay there under paper shrouds. They saw also a sleeping place in a screened-off section, with four beds placed against each other in a row. Fatigued by their journey, the strangers had no sooner thrown themselves on their pillows than they were snoring loudly.

One of them was not quite off, when suddenly he heard a creaking sound on the couch of the corpse. Immediately he opened his eyes and saw distinctly by the light of the lamp standing before the corpse that it had raised the shroud and risen. In a moment it was on the floor and slowly entered the sleeping room. Her face had a wet-gold hue, and she wiped her forehead with a coarse gauze cloth. In a stooping attitude she approached the beds and blew thrice on three of the sleeping travelers; the fourth, terror-struck, fearing that he too might be hit, gently drew the blanket over his face and held his breath to listen. Forthwith she breathed on him as she had done on the others; then he perceived that she left the room, and hearing the rustling sound of the paper shrouds, he put out his head to take a peep, and saw her lying rigid as before.

The traveler, extremely frightened, lacked courage to raise the alarm. Stealthily stretching forth his foot, he kicked his comrades, but they did not stir in the least, and thus he conceived there was no other alternative for him but to put on his clothes and slink away. No sooner, however, did he rise and move his coat than again there was that creaking noise, which caused him to hide himself anew, terror-stricken, with his head under the blanket. He perceived that the woman came again and breathed over him repeatedly, doing this over and over again before she retried. After a short pause, he knew by the noise on the deathbed that she had lain down as before. Now he put his hand very slowly out of the blanket, seized his trousers, quickly got into them, and ran out of the house, barefooted. The corpse too jumped up as if to give him chase, but by the time it came forth from behind the curtain, the traveler had drawn the bolt and was off.

With the corpse at his heels he rushed forth with loud shrieks, which alarmed everybody in the hamlet. He would have thumped the door of the inn but for his fear that it would make him lose time and bring him within reach of the demon, so seeing the road to the district city before him, he ran up it with all his might, till he reached the eastern suburb. Here he saw a Buddhist convent and, hearing the wooden fish, nervously beat on the outer gate. But the monks, astonished at such an unusual tumult, hesitated to let him in, and as he turned around, he saw the corpse quite near him, hardly one foot off. In these straits he sought shelter behind a white willow four or five feet thick, standing outside the convent gate. When the corpse dodged to the right, he dodged to the left, and so on, which enraged the corpse more and more, and exhausted them both. On a sudden the corpse stood still. The traveler, soaked with perspiration and with panting chest, sheltered himself behind the tree. The corpse raised itself fiercely and threw both its arms around it to grab him. At that moment he sank to the ground in fright, and the corpse, thus missing its victim, remained rigid embracing the tree. For a good while longer the monks stood listening, and hearing nothing more, they came forth circumspectly to find the traveler flat on the ground. By the light of their torches they perceived that, though he was apparently dead, there was still a slight palpitation under his heart. They bore him into the convent, but the night passed away before he came around. Having refreshed him with some broth, they interrogated him, and he related to them the whole story. By that time the morning bell sounded, and in the early dawn still dimmed by mist and fog, the monks examining the tree discovered the woman upon it in a rigid condition.

In great consternation they reported the incident to the magistrate of the district. This grandee appeared in person on the spot to hold an inquest and ordered his men to pull off the arms of the woman, but so firmly were they fixed in the tree that it was impossible to unclasp them. They found, in fact, on a close inspection, that the four fingers of either hand were bent like hooks and sunk into the wood so deeply that the nails were buried in it. A fresh batch of men was set to work to pull with all their might, and as they tore her off, the holes made by the fingers were found to look as if made with a chisel or auger.

Now the mandarin dispatched a messenger to the old man, who gave him a confused mixture of truth and untruth about the disappearance of the corpse and the death of the travelers. The matter being explained to him, he followed the messenger and took the corpse home. The traveler, bursting into tears, said to the magistrate, "I left my home with three men, and now I must return alone. What shall I do to make my fellow villagers believe my words?" So the mandarin gave him a certificate and sent him home with some presents.

The Thieving Corpse

(China)

Corpse-demons do not always content themselves with homicide; many indulge also in theft or robbery. Two men of Kin-ling (Nanking), Chang Yü-kuh, and Li So-and-so, connected by ties of friendship, had a trading business together in Kwangtung. Chang, for some reason returning homeward from the south was entrusted by Li with a letter for his family, which as soon as he came home he went to deliver at its address. On this occasion he saw a coffin in the hall and learned that Li's father had in the meantime died. Wherefore he set out a sacrifice for the soul on the spot and performed the customary worship, which the Li family appreciated highly. The widow appeared, and seeing this charming and elegant youth, not much more than twenty years old, she placed dainties before him and regaled him well, and as it was already dark, she offered him lodgings for the night.

Between his sleeping place and the coffin was nothing but an open courtyard. At the second night drum he saw by the bright moonlight Li's widow come out of the women's apartments and peep through the crevice of his window. He started and, deeming feminine decency inconsistent with such behavior, resolved to repel her forthwith should she open the door and enter. At this juncture it struck him that the woman, with an incense stick in her hand, turned to her husband's soul altar and muttered something there as if she expostulated, upon which she went to the door of Chang's room, put off her waistband, bound the upper iron rings of the door with it, and retired at a slow pace. Chang's fright and suspicion were increased so much by all this that he lacked courage to go to bed. Suddenly he heard a creaking noise from the place where the coffin stood. Off fell the lid, and up sat a man with a pitch-black face. He had sunken eyes with green pupils emitting flashes of light; he was of an extraordinary ferocity and hideousness. With long strides he ran out of the apartment, straight-

From: Jan J. de Groot, *Religious Systems of China*, vol. 5, book 2, parts 2 and 3 (Leide: E. J. Brill, 1907).

way for Chang's room. There he uttered a shrill spectral whistling, on which a cold blast of wind got at the four directions and the waistband on the door snapped into fragments. With all his might Chang pushed back the door, but he was overpowered and the corpse jumped in.

Fortunately there stood beside the door a large wooden cupboard. Chang pushed it against the corpse, so that it overturned and the corpse fell underneath it, but at the same moment Chang swooned away. The incident had not escaped the attention of Li's wife. She and the family ran in with torches and lights and poured some ginger water into Chang's mouth to restore him to his senses, and then she spoke to him: "This is my husband. His life having been far from correct, he has become a corpse-demon, breaking out now to work evil. He was much bent on wealth. Last night he appeared to me in a dream and announced to me the arrival of one Chang with a letter. 'This man,' he said, 'has two hundred coins in his girdle. I will kill him, take half the amount in my coffin, and give you the rest for the household.' I took this all for a bad dream and put no belief in it, but there! you did indeed arrive and put up here for the night. So I burned incense before the corpse, praying, conjuring, and exhorting it not to give rein to its wicked purpose. Yet fearing that it might push open the door and kill you, I tied the rings of the door with my waistband, having no idea that he would exert such tremendous force."

They bore the corpse back into the coffin, and Chang advised the woman to burn it, the sooner the better, so as to cut short its evil works once for all.

"I have long been thinking to do so," the woman replied, "but as he is my husband, I could not find it in my heart. Now, however, I cannot help complying with the prevailing custom."

Chang assisted her in defraying the expenses of an altar, to which they called some Buddhist priests of repute to bring about his transition into a better condition. And they cremated his corpse, and not till then did the family live in peace and quiet.

Javanese Poltergeists

(Java)

In 1837 the Assistant Resident v. Kessinger occupied an official residence, one-storied and standing in its own grounds, with his wife, who was colonial born, and an adopted native child about ten years old. One day when v. Kessinger was absent on an official tour, the child sprang up and ran crying to her adoptive mother, complaining that her *kabaya*, or Indian dress, was stained with *sirih*-colored saliva. A new dress was put on the child, who was playing in Frau v. Kessinger's room, and the same thing occurred again. At the same time, a stone as big as a hen's egg fell at the feet of the lady. After this had occurred several times at short intervals, the native prince, a man of proved uprightness, was appealed to. He posted his retinue about the house and cleared the room, but the phenomena still went on. In the evening the high priest was sent for. He had no sooner opened the Koran than the lamp was sent flying in one direction and the book in another. Thereupon the child and her mother moved out of the house for the night and remained unmolested, a fact which goes some way to prove that the child was not a conscious trickster. On the return of the assistant resident, the phenomena still went on. Only a few stones fell at night, and by day the child alone was molested.

The events came to the ears of the governor general, who sent Major, afterward General, Michiels, an officer renowned for his bravery, to report on them. He posted his soldiers on the roof and in the trees, as well as in the house, and with considerable ingenuity turned the observation room into a tent by spreading linen curtains inside. He then took the child upon his knee, but the dress suffered the same catastrophe as before. The stones flew and were found to be warm in summer weather and wet in rainy. Five or six fell in quick succession, and then a pause intervened. No hole was visible in the linen. They fell vertically and became visible some five or six feet from the

From: Northcote W. Thomas, "A Javanese Poltergeist," *Occult Review* 2 (1905): 223–28.

ground. Once a papaya fruit fell, and the tree was found from which it had been taken. Another time the missile was a piece of lime as big as a fist from the kitchen chimney. The mark of a moist hand was seen on a mirror (fingerprints might have given a clue, but those were early days) and chairs, glasses, and other objects moved.

Two other cases of some interest are reported by the same narrator. In the one a French family named Tesseire suffered from showers of stones when they were at their meals. M. Tesseire was pelted in the fields as he sat in a cart, buffalo bones and a skull fell in the house, and so on. The regent of Sukapore was appealed to and took up his quarters in the house. In the presence of his son, on whose evidence Gerstaecker based his narrative, the regent's bed was raised from the ground several times in a good light. A mountain stream ran about 150 feet almost perpendicularly beneath the house. An ingenious mind suggested that the stones should be marked and thrown over the precipice. The result was surprising. Several were thrown again, sometimes less than a minute after they had found a resting place in the stream. It would of course be interesting to know what precautions were taken to prevent other persons from marking other stones and making use of them for the phenomenon. However that may be, it seems clear that the investigators thought they had secured themselves against deception. Even if they did not, there remains the incident of the bed. Whatever kind of bed it was, it is difficult to see how it could have been raised off the ground by trickery without at the same time exposing the author of the trick to instant detection.

The other case took place near Bandong. The resident ament heard of it, and it was on his evidence that Gerstaecker based his narrative. The phenomena took place in a small native hut inhabited by an old woman, a native. A file of the native militia were marched up and surrounded the scene of the poltergeist's operations. The first thing that occurred was that the old woman was dragged several yards, shouting loudly for help, before she entered the hut. This, however, does not call for any supernormal explanation. She was obviously capable of counterfeiting the games of a tricksy spirit. More important is the fact that the resident, when he approached the hut and opened the door, was met by a volley of gravel full in the chest. As the hut consisted of a single room, was surrounded by soldiers, and was opened by the European observer who was interviewed by Gerstaecker, there does not seem much room for errors of detail. That an old Javanese woman could produce the phenomenon as narrated seems to be stretching the hypothesis of the naughty old girl to the breaking point. At any rate the resident, who was no coward, had no desire to try another experiment, as he assured Gerstaecker. Here too the theory of hallucinatory memory has to be stretched very far to cover the case. No man willingly proclaims himself a coward. If anything, one's recollections are apt to grow in the other direction.

Female Ghosts

(Japan)

kiryo and Shiryo are the spirits of discarded wives or mistresses. The first pursues the deceiver and causes him to become sick if the woman is ill or merely if she bears him spite. It is the evil disposed spirit of the living. Shiryo is the ghost of the woman who dies after desertion or from ill treatment, and it can cause violent illness, even death. Yet the proverb, mindful of the fact that the Ikiryo is the spirit of the living creature, says that it is much more difficult to get rid of the Ikiryo than of the Shiryo.

In some stories of ghostly revenge, the Shiryo of a woman sometimes pursued not only the particular person who had caused her death, but even the whole of the murderer's family; e.g., in the story of O Kiku and her mother, both of whom had been killed by the wife of Obata Magoichi, the Shiryo caused the death by disease of the whole Obata family. So powerful was the ghost that it caused *roasted* poppy seeds to sprout.

Jealousy causes the hair of women to take the form of snakes. Even the Obi of a jealous woman can become a goblin-snake capable of winding itself seven times around the body of a man. The spirit of a woman can also take the form of a serpent to follow her husband about. The most jealous woman was an ugly wench, so ugly that she

From: Henri L. Joly, "Bakemono," *Transactions and Proceedings of the Japan Society* 9 (1909–11): 15–48.

could not secure a husband. The tidings of any wedding made her mad. Finally, her spirit tormented so many newlywed couples that a shrine was built in Yamashiro on the bridge of Uji to appease her anger; she is called Hashihime.

We need not relate the well-known story of Kiyohime, who became a dragon in her anger at being thwarted in her amorous designs upon the priest Anchin.

Callous behavior toward one's relations was punished by the formation of a mouth on the back of the head, or on the knee, the latter being called Ninmen. In either case, the additional mouth cried lustily for food and had a full set of teeth.

In the theatrical version and the Kazane Monogatari, Kazane is described as an ugly woman whose husband Kinugawa Yuyemon loved her so much, in spite of her appearance, that he would not allow her to have a mirror. They were exceedingly poor, and as she thought herself beautiful she resolved to sell herself to a *joroya*, asking the owner whether he would buy a girl as well favored as Hanshiro, then the paragon of beauty. The man came in hot haste, but when he saw Kazane, he thought he had been made a fool of, and finding that she had no idea of her personal appearance he made her see herself in a mirror.

The strange sequel of this adventure was a fit of jealousy on her part, she being mortally afraid of her husband leaving her for some other woman. She consequently made life such a burden to him that he killed her on a riverbank, some say with a mirror, others with a reaping knife, after which he threw the body in the river. She haunted the man forever after, and her ugly face biting a scythe is a well-known subject. Her ghost was exorcised by Yuten Shonin. Tokwa Sanjin gives a very different story. He says that Kazane's proper name was Otsuwa, and her husband was Yoyemon, a peasant of Hanyumura in Shimosa. She was an ugly, rude, ill-tempered female who had been divorced nine times, hence her nickname Kazane, "to pile up." Through jealousy she drowned herself in a well, and her ghost came to worry and bewitch her late husband and his new wife. The true story is said to be given in the *Ingwa Monogatari,* and the theatrical version is garbled to secure sympathy with the wretched woman. The next and perhaps more popular story is that known as *Yotsuya Kwaidan,* or story of Oiwa.

In the Genruku period there lived in Yedo a samurai named Tamiya

Iyemon, whose wife Oiwa was old and ugly. Nearby lived a leech whose daughter was in love with Iyemon and persuaded him to get rid of his wife. The first step in the deed was the administration of a drug which gave Oiwa the appearance of a leper. According to one version, she died and her baby died also. She then appeared to her husband and his mistress, carrying in her arms a stone Fizo. In another version, Iyemon accused his wife of adultery with a young man named Kohei and nailed them both on a door, which he threw in a river. This version is known as *Oiwa no Itagayashi,* and there are souvenir prints showing the two corpses on their respective sides of a door.

In that compilation a further version is given called *Badarai Oiwa.* In it we read that Oiwa was the daughter of Tamiya Matazaemon. Her husband was the son of a *ronin,* Takada Daihachiro, who under the name of Sawada Kichibei kept a private school at Kubotamura in Shimosa, until having killed a beggar, he was beheaded and his head exposed as a *gokumon.* The son, Eikichi, was a bad character. He married Oiwa and became the adopted son of her father under the new name Tamiya Iyemon. When the old Matazaemon died, he quickly squandered all that had been left him, and when destitute he sent Oiwa to work as a seamstress in the household of a *hatamoto* in Rokubancho. After her departure, he gave way to debauchery, and she heard of it through some traveling jeweler. She then went mad, breaking in her anger a large bucket used for washing horses, hence the name Badarai Oiwa. She flew from the house and died of starvation in a field. Her ghost then appeared to Iyemon. Her body was found and buried in the grounds of a temple in the third year of Kioho (1718), but the spirit remained active until a shrine was built upon the place where Iyemen's house had stood. This shrine is called Oiwa no Inari, and it is narrated by a storyteller (Kodanshi) named Shuishinsai Toyo, that unless one pays a visit to the shrine before reciting the story of Oiwa, some trouble will befall the storyteller. Once he forgot to do so, and although his lecture was a successful one, when he returned to his dressing room he knocked his head against a shelf and fainted. That shelf, strange to relate, was placed so high up that he could not reach it without a ladder in ordinary circumstances. As soon as he recovered, he hastened to the shrine to apologize.

Among the innumerable female ghosts are the following:

Yuki Onna—A ghostly woman who appears in snowstorms.

Kejora—A woman with weird eyes whose face is covered with hair.

Ururi Onna, or Nopperabo, or Hagura Bettari—A woman with a mouth the size of a winnowing basket, but without eyes, nose, or eyebrows, who could be seen outside the temple of Suijin.

Ao Niobo—The green court lady appearing with her eyebrows grown (instead of being shaven) in old palaces, her teeth still black with *ohaguro*.

O Shiroi Baba—A servant of the divinity of rouge *(beni)*, makeup, and fards (*oshiroi* is white powder), known as Jifun Senjo, about whom Sekiyen remarks that "there are two dreadful things: moonlight in December and women overpainted."

Botan Toro—The well-known story of a woman who comes back from the grave in search of human intercourse, carrying a lantern in the shape of a peony, from which the name is derived. There are several translations or adaptations of this story. In *Sento Shingwa* the woman appears as a skeleton; Sekiyen calls this specter Hone Onna, i.e., bony woman.

Stories of Haunted Houses

(India)

My first haunted house was in a small hill station, and the haunt consisted in the perambulation of the flagstone verandah by heavy footsteps. I was first introduced to this ghost when nothing was further from my thoughts than the supernatural, as some days had elapsed since I took possession of the house, and the ghost had escaped my memory. I was therefore indignant when I heard someone walking in the verandah at night,

From: S. Eardley-Wilmot, "The Supernatural in India," *Occult Review* 8 (July–December 1908): 151–60.

someone who would not reply to my challenge; and it was not until I was investigating matters with a lantern, thinking chiefly of burglars, that the peculiarities of the house flashed into my mind. I felt certain then that I should meet that ghost. I even hoped that he would not put me to shame by appearing in clothes, for I knew that my future audience might tolerate a spirit body but never a spirit suit of clothes. I spent hours in waylaying the footsteps; I concealed myself in sight of the verandah in and outside the house; I spread flour on the flags to obtain the imprint of his footsteps. But all in vain; I discovered nothing. The walking continued, and my servants would only enter the house after nightfall by the back door. That these footfalls were not caused by human agency both the natives and I were agreed, and no explanation of them has yet been offered.

My second haunted house was in a deserted village in a dense forest. It was a good watertight peasant's house of wood and stone, and I desired to utilize it as a shooting box in the winter or a protection against the heat of the summer months. But I reckoned without my host, for each night was a time of danger and unrest on account of the volleys of stones which descended from all sides. This I was aware was a favorite trick of the Hindustani servant to express disapproval of his master's actions or surroundings, but I took the precaution to have all my servants in the house at night, while I knew that no villagers would dare to cross the forest at that hour to play a trick on an official. Moreover, the uneasiness of my servants acquitted them of all connivance in the matter, and I was compelled to accept the verdict that my presence was distasteful to the shadowy tenant and to leave him in undisturbed enjoyment of his own, lest he should proceed to further violence.

A Death Warning

(China)

I n Tung-lai there was a dwelling where the Ch'en clan lived over a hundred strong. One fine morning the water in the boiler on which the food was being steamed would not bubble. They lifted up the pot containing the food and glanced into the boiler, when lo! a graybeard rose out of it. This event led them to go to a diviner. "This is an important apparition," this man said, "which portends the destruction of a family. Go home, make weapons in great numbers, and have them placed against the walls at the gate, then fasten the gate firmly on the inside, and should horsemen appear with banners and canopies and knock at the door—beware of answering them."

With this advice they went home. All hands armed, and more than a hundred weapons were procured, which they placed against the rooms flanking the gate. Indeed, some men appeared, but however loudly they shouted, no answer was given them. Their leader, enraged by that silence, ordered them to scale the gate. But no sooner had his men cast a glance behind it and seen those hundred weapons of all sizes than they retreated from the gate to report to him. The news threw the leader into great consternation. "Tell our men to come here immediately!" he exclaimed to those that stood by. "If they do not forthwith come, not one will get away from here. How shall I then escape punishment? Some eighty miles hence to the north, one hundred and thirty people live. Let us take them instead." Ten days afterward this whole family had died out. It also belonged to the Ch'en clan.

From: Jan J. de Groot, *Religious Systems of China*, vol. 5, book 2, parts 2 and 3 (Leide: E. J. Brill, 1907).

Two Stories of Werewolves

(China)

At the end of the Yung-t'ai period of the T'ang dynasty (A.D. 765) there lived in the Hung-cheu department, in a village of the Ching-p'ing district, an old man who, having been ailing several months, refused to take any food for more than ten days. He then suddenly disappeared in the evening, and nobody could guess the reason of it. Another evening, a villager who had gone out to gather mulberry leaves was pursued by a he-wolf. He narrowly escaped up a tree, but the tree was not high enough to prevent the wolf from rearing itself up against it and fixing its teeth in the tail of his coat. Under pressure of the danger, the villager hacked at the beast with his mulberry axe, hitting it exactly in its forehead. The wolf then crouched down, but remained on the spot so long that it was broad daylight before our hero could leave the tree. He followed the track of the wolf, which took him to that old man's house. He entered the main apartment, called the sons, and communicated to them the whole affair from beginning to end. And the sons, on inspecting their father's forehead, discovered on it the trace of a wound inflicted with an axe. Lest he might attack people again, they throttled him, and saw him turn into an old wolf. They went to the district magistrate to justify themselves, who let them go unpunished.

In the same year there was in another village of the same department a lad of some twenty years, who after a disease quite lost his vital soul *(tsing shen)*, as he sent it away to change into a wolf. This monster secretly devoured a great number of the village boys. Those who missed their sons did not guess the reason and sought for them in vain.

As a rule the lad was employed by the villagers for sundry jobs. One

From: Jan J. de Groot, *Religious Systems of China*, vol. 5, book 2, parts 2 and 3 (Leide: E. J. Brill, 1907).

day as he was passing the dwelling of a family that also were missing a boy, he heard the bereaved father call him, "Come tomorrow to work with us, and we will prepare a full meal for you."

But he burst into a loud laugh. "What sort of man should I be if I went to your house a second time to work?" he exclaimed. "Do you think that there was the slightest particular flavor about your son?"

This language surprised the father of the lost boy, and he interrogated him.

"Nature orders me to devour men," he answered, "and yesterday I ate a boy of five or six years. His flesh was most delicious."

The father perceived some stale blood in the corners of his mouth, and rained on him a shower of frantic blows, which made him turn into a wolf and expire.

The Origin of Mosquitoes

(Japan)

The following fable explains how the Ainu account for the origin of gnats, mosquitoes, and gadflies. Once upon a time, many years ago, there was a great hobgoblin who had his home far away in the midst of the mountains of Ainu land. In bodily shape he was like a man. His carcass was exceedingly large and was closely covered with hair. In fact, his skin was like that of a bear, so hairy was he. However, he had but one eye, and that was situated in the middle of his forehead and was as large as a common pot lid. This creature was a very great nuisance to the Ainu, for he had such a tremendous appetite that he was actually in the habit of catching, killing, and eating everything and anybody coming in his way. For

From: John Batchelor, "Items of Ainu Folk-Lore," *Journal of American Folk-Lore* 7 (1894): 15–44.

this reason the people were afraid to go far into the mountains to hunt, for though the one-eyed monster had been shot at many times, not an arrow had taken effect upon him.

Now it happened one day that a brave hunter, who was an expert with the bow, unconsciously went near the haunt of this cannibal. While he was in pursuit of game, he was astonished to see something brightly glaring at him through the undergrowth of the forest. Upon drawing near to see what it was, he discovered it to be the big-bodied, hairy, fierce-looking hobgoblin. When he saw what it was, the hunter became so frightened that he knew not what to do; but he soon mustered sufficient courage to draw an arrow from his quiver and, fitting it in his bow, stood on the defensive. As the creature drew nigh, the Ainu took a steady and deadly aim at his solitary eye and, being a good shot, hit it fair in the center. The hobgoblin immediately tumbled down dead, for the eye was the vital—the only vital—part of his body. To make sure that so foul a creature and so deadly an enemy was quite killed and would not come to life again to trouble the people, the brave hunter made a great bonfire over his body and burned it quite up, bones and all. When this was done he took the ashes in his hands and scattered them in the air so as to make doubly certain that the monster was thoroughly destroyed. But lo, the ashes became gnats, mosquitoes, and gadflies as they were tossed upward. However, we must not grumble at these things, for the lesser evil of flies is not so bad as the greater evil of having the one-eyed man-eating monster among us.

Cat Punishment

(Japan)

It is supposed by the Ainu that cats who have died or left this world have the power of bewitching people. I say cats *who* have died advisedly, for the Ainu invest them with personality. But here again allow me to remind you that the individual life or spirit of all the lower animals, as well as that of men, is never supposed to become extinct or lose its own proper personal identity. Each has a distinct separate unit life in another world, with powers to act upon living agents in this. The spirits of cats that have been killed are especially addicted to bewitching people, and those of all animals have the power to do so. But should a person kill a cat, he may prevent himself being bewitched by it by eating part of it. Or should a person be bewitched by any disembodied cat, he may, to cure himself, kill any other cat and eat it. The good effects of this are undoubted.

The way cats bewitch people is to enter their body and cause them to imitate the gestures of a cat, to gradually waste away, and in the end to die a painful death while mewing like a cat. The name of this is called *meko pagoat*, "cat punishment." I find there is also a "dog punishment," "bear punishment," and every other animal punishment. The same principle of the disease or punishment and its cure runs through all alike.

From: John Batchelor, "Items of Ainu Folk-Lore," *Journal of American Folk-Lore* 7 (1894): 15–44.

The Cat-Man

(India)

General Sir Thomas Edward Gordon tells the following story of a modern instance in which a man was said to be transformed into a cat after death.

For twenty-five years an oral addition to the written standing orders of the native guard at Government House near Poona had been communicated regularly from one guard to another on relief, to the effect that any cat passing out of the front door after dark was to be regarded as His Excellency the Governor and to be saluted accordingly. The meaning of this was that Sir Robert Grant, Governor of Bombay, had died there in 1838, and on the evening of the day of his death a cat was seen to leave the house by the front door and walk up and down a particular path, as had been the governor's habit to do after sunset. A Hindu sentry had observed this, and he mentioned it to the others of his faith, who made it a subject of superstitious conjecture, the result being that one of the priestly class explained the mystery of the dogma of the transmigration of the soul from one body to another, and interpreted the circumstance to mean that the spirit of the deceased governor had entered into one of the house pets.

It was difficult to fix on a particular one, and it was therefore decided that every cat passing out of the main entrance after dark was to be regarded as the tabernacle of Governor Grant's soul and to be treated with due respect and the proper honors. This decision was accepted without question by all the native attendants and others belonging to Government House. The whole guard, from sepoy to *sibadar*, fully acquiesced in it, and an oral addition was made to the standing orders that the sentry at the front door would "present arms" to any cat missing out there after dark.

From: Frank Hamel, *Human Animals* (New York: Frederick A. Stokes Co., 1916).

Lecherous Dog-Spirits

(China)

n Poh-p'ing one T'ien Yen was in mourning for his mother, and regularly lived in the mourning shed, but one day about nightfall he entered his wife's private room. She received him with silent astonishment. "Sir," she said, "may you visit me in this place of abstinence?" but he did not listen to this remark, and nature had free course. Afterward the real Yen entered for a moment, but he did not speak one word to his wife, and she, astonished at his silence, reprimanded him for what he had done the other day. This taught the husband that there must have been demonry in play. The evening came. He was not yet asleep, and his mourning clothes hung in the shed, when suddenly he saw a white dog scratch at the shed. Taking the mourning clothes between its jaws, the beast changed into a man, put on the clothes, and entered the women's apartment. Yen hurried after him and found the dog ready to get into his wife's bed. He beat him to death, and his wife died for shame.

In the Hung-chi period (A.D. 1488–1506) there lived in the district of Yü-t'ai, which forms a part of the Yen region (in Shantung), a family of commoners who kept a well-trained white dog, which always followed its master abroad. So also it once accompanied him when he set out to a far region for trading purposes. But unexpectedly it returned after thirteen days, in the shape of its master. The wife asked him what he came back for, and he told her he had fallen in with highwaymen, who had relieved him of everything he had with him, but fortunately he had escaped with his life. The woman did not doubt the veracity of his words. A year later the real husband came home. The two men resembled one another perfectly in shape, and while they were quarreling about the question who was the true husband and who the false one, the wife and the neighbors informed the magistrate, who ordered them to be put in jail. A policeman then related the matter to his wife. "The one that came home first," she

From: Jan J. de Groot, *Religious Systems of China*, vol. 5, book 2, parts 2 and 3 (Leide: E. J. Brill, 1907).

said, "is the spirit of the dog, and this can be proved by discovering whether the breast of the woman bears marks of its paws." The policeman told this to the magistrate. They summoned the woman before him, and on her asking wherefore she was called, he stripped her, thus discovering that there were indeed prints of paws on her breast. He then gave secret orders to suppress that demonry by means of blood, and the pseudohusband changed into a dog, which they instantly beat to death.

The Black Dog

(China)

Under the T'ang dynasty there existed in the Ching-yuen period (A.D. 785–804) one Mr. Han, Secretary to the Court of Revision. He resided temporarily in the south of the Si-ho region and there possessed a horse, a most noble and mettle-some creature.

One fine morning this animal stands in the stable with stooped head, sweating and panting as if exhausted by a long ride. The astonished groom reports the matter to his master, who turns his anger against him, saying, "Whose fault is it that horse thieves ride out in the night on my steed and exhaust it?" He then orders him to be cudgeled, and the groom, having no arguments with which to defend himself, has to submit patiently to this treatment.

Next morning he finds the horse sweating and panting again. The groom stands struck with silent astonishment, and nobody can suggest an explanation of the matter. So he lays himself down that night at the closed stable door to watch the horse through the crevice. Suddenly he sees the black dog which Mr. Han keeps enter the stable, barking and leaping, and it changes into a man wearing a deep black dress and a hat of the same color. That man saddles the horse, mounts

From: Jan J. de Groot, *Religious Systems of China*, vol. 4, book 2, part 2 (Leide: E. J. Brill, 1907).

it, and gallops off. At the gate of the house, which is very high, as is also the surrounding wall, the black man gives the horse the whip, thus making it leap the gate with a bound. Then off he rides; and on coming back he alights, unsaddles the animal, and barking and jumping as before, reassumes his dog's form. Much scared and astonished is the groom at all this, but he lacks the courage to say a word about it.

Thus time goes on, until one evening the dog rides off again and returns at daybreak. Just then the weather clears up after some showers, and the track of the horse being visible on the ground over the whole way it has made, the groom follows it and is thus led in a southern direction to the premises of an old grave over ten miles off. The prints being lost here, the groom builds a small shed of grass on the spot, and next evening conceals himself in it to watch. Toward midnight the black man appears on horseback. He alights, ties the horse to a wild tree, and enters the grave, where he has a most merry conversation with several other individuals. The groom, crouched in the shed, overhears all they say, but he dares not stir ere the man in black announces toward daybreak that he is going, and is seen out of the grave by several persons.

No sooner is that man in the open than a person in a gray hairy dress asks him, "Where is the list of names of the Han family?"

"I have concealed it under the mortar stone," is the answer. "Do not be anxious about it."

He with the hairy coat then replies, "Beware of losing it, lest my relations remain incomplete," upon which the other retorts:

"I will attend to your hint."

"But," thus asks the man with the hairy dress again, "has Han's youngest son been already given a name?"

"Not yet," is the answer, "but as soon as he gets one I will not forget to inscribe it immediately in the list."

"Come back here tomorrow night for a merry chat," adds the hairy-coated man, and on these words the black one spurs his horse and is off.

At sunrise the groom returns home and reveals the matter to his master. Forthwith Han orders some meat to be brought, allures the dog with it, and ties it up; then passing to the other point revealed to him, he examines the mortar stone and discovers an inscribed scroll under it, bearing the names of Han and all his brothers, his wife,

children and servants, not one excepted. It was the list of names of the
Han family, of which Gray Coat had spoken; and the only one not yet
inscribed in it was the son born one month before, who could not be
any other than the said youngest son to whom no name had as yet
been given and whom the two men had been speaking about. Greatly
surprised, Han ordered the dog to be taken to the courtyard. There
they whipped it to death, cooked its flesh, and regaled the servants
with it; then with more than ten strong men of the neighborhood,
armed with bows, arrows, spears, and clubs, they repaired to that old
grave in the south. Opening it, they found it occupied by several
beings with dog's hair. Under general surprise they destroyed them to
the last and returned home.

The Man Who Became a Bird

(China)

I n the first year of the Shao-hing period (A.D. 1131) Honan fell
into the power of rebels. They recognized Liu Yü as their poten-
tate, but our district (Ch'en-cheu) remained a stronghold of the
Throne. Fung Ch'ang-ning, a Hwui-ki man, was its prefect. Liu Yü
attacked him, and finding it impossible to subdue him, sent for Wang
Kwa-kioh, a troublesome insurgent in Shantung. This man having
raised reinforcements among the people in Suh and Poh (the north of
Nganhwui), both generals marched to the attack with combined
forces, and the city surrendered in a year, its provisions being totally
exhausted.

Wang Kwa-kioh then raised three pennons in the center of the town,
where several thoroughfares met, and ordered his men from the two

From: Jan J. de Groot, *Religious Systems of China*, vol. 4, book 2, part 1 (Leide: E. J.
Brill, 1907).

districts aforesaid to arrange themselves under the red one if they were willing to remain in the army; those desirous to become civil mandarins were to place themselves under the yellow pennon, and those who would rather go home he summoned to select the black one. Anxious for their lives, all people flocked to the red colors, and only two gentlemen from Poh, respectively named Wang and Wei, betook themselves to the black standard, reasoning thus: "For a civil office we are too old, and remaining in the army means dying, while placing ourselves under the black colors is certain death too, as we then thwart the will of our chieftain." The whole army stood aghast, but Kwa-kioh, deeming it a grave matter to violate his promise, courteously dismissed them, so that they could return home.

Wang then visited the city of Ch'en to fetch some treasures he had buried there, but he was never seen again, nor was any news of him received from that time or any trace of him found. As to Wei, in some ten years the fortune he made out of his profession became great. Once he had no more than two fowls in his house, when the governor of the town happened to travel through his village. Wei then caught the hen, cooked it, and served it up to the grandee. Next day, when the latter returned home, he was going to kill the cock, but the bird perceived it and sneaked off through the millet. Then he began a chase with a bamboo pole and was on the point of catching the bird, when suddenly it accosted him in a human voice. Raising its head, it exclaimed, "Alas, what cruel evil must befall me here! Is there no longer in you any particle of our old affection?"

Wei started back, with the words: "Who are you?"

"I am Wang," replied the bird. "Do not you remember the incident at Yuen-khiu, when we were in the army? You lodged me then."

Said Wei, "Whither did you go, and where did you die?"

"When we were comrades," was the reply, "I enriched myself with your money, secretly concealing it somewhere till more peaceful times should come. Afterward I entered the city to fetch it, and with two bags on my back put up at a country inn to pass the night, where I opened them before the lamp. But ere I had counted over the contents, the innkeeper espied me. He gave me spirits to drink to make me tipsy, and then I was murdered. Notwithstanding my hidden store of precious metal, my orbate soul was left to its own fate, without any supporters. My thoughts then turned to my fellow villagers and kinsfolk, and finding none of them but you alive, I resolved to join you. When I had settled in your house, four daughters of your neighbor Kia also arrived there, betaking themselves together to the womb of your house hen when it was about to hatch, and thus becoming hens; they are the hens which you killed before. If now you wish to destroy me too, I am ready to submit to my fate."

The Governor had overheard all this discourse. Comprehending the matter at once, he went home and reported it to the prefect. This dignitary summoned Wei and the cock before him. Both appeared, and the crowd behind them gave the streets the aspect of a busy market. The cock repeated its statements before the magistrate, ending with the words: "And now, as I, a domestic bird, have divulged matters of the World of Darkness without authorization, I must die." It stretched out its neck, concealed it under its wings, and breathed its last. The prefect, sighing and astonished, ordered the cock to be committed to the earth behind the temple of Lao-tszě and erected an inscription over the spot, which ran thus: TOMB OF THE MAN-COCK.

Stories of Were-Vixens

(Japan)

In the eighth year of the Kwambei era (A.D. 896) a man called Kaya Yoshifuji resigned the post of a high official in the Bizen province and went to live in Hongo Ashimori. His wife ran away to the capital, and he kept house quite alone. One day he went out of his mind and began to recite love poems to an imaginary woman. After a month passed in this manner, he disappeared and his relatives searched high and low but could find no trace of him, so they concluded that he had committed suicide, and vowed they would make an image of the eleven-faced Kwannon if they found the unhappy man's corpse. They cut down an oak tree and began to carve the life-size image of Yoshifuji, bowing before the unfinished statue to repeat the vow they had taken. This went on for about a fortnight,

From: Frank Hamel, *Human Animals* (New York: Frederick A. Stokes Co., 1916).

when to their intense surprise Yoshifuji crept from under his go-down as thin and pale as though he had passed through a serious illness. The floor of the go-down was only half a dozen inches from the ground, so that it was held to be impossible that a man could have been beneath it. When he had recovered his senses sufficiently to give an account of his adventures, he said that a beautiful girl had come to him, bringing love letters and poems from a princess, and that he had replied to them in the same vein in which they were written.

"At last," he continued, "the girl came with a magnificent carriage and four positions to take me to the princess.

"After a drive of about ten miles we arrived at a splendid palace, where an exquisite meal and a very hearty reception from the princess soon made me feel quite at ease. There I lived with her as inseparably as two branches growing together on the same tree. She gave birth to a son, a very intelligent and beautiful child, whom I loved so much that I thought of degrading my son Jadasada and putting this child in his place as son of my principal wife—this in view of the high rank of the princess. But after three years a Buddhist priest suddenly entered the room of Her Highness, carrying a stick in his hand. The effect of his appearance was astonishing. Chamberlains and court ladies all fled left and right and even the princess hid herself somewhere. The priest pushed me from behind with his stick and made me go out of the house through a very narrow passage. When I looked back I discovered that I had just crept from under my own go-down!"

The curious point of this story is that those who listened to it rushed to the go-down and demolished it without delay. As they did so, twenty or thirty foxes came from beneath it and scattered in all directions, hastening to the mountains. Yoshifuji, bewitched by these wizard-foxes, had been lying under the go-down for a forthnight, believing in his trance that he was spending three years in a palace. The priest who broke the spell was a metamorphosis of Kwannon.

That the were-vixen superstition is deeply ingrained in the minds of travelers is proved by the story of a bishop who once passed the night in a house that was so desolate in appearance that his companions begged him to read a sutra for the purpose of driving away evil influences. Two of them went to a wood close to the house, where they saw a mysterious phantom, large and white, which they took to be a were-vixen. They rushed in to tell the bishop, who, greatly excited, cried, "I have often heard of foxes haunting people, but I have never set eyes on a ghost of this kind," and he hastened to the spot, full of eagerness, only to discover a harmless, ordinary girl—or so he said!

Another were-vixen attempted to steal a child. The nurse was out in the grounds with her charge of two years old when her master, the father of the infant, heard her crying for help. Seizing his sword he ran to the spot, when to his astonishment he found that *two* nurses exactly alike were pulling at his son and heir, one on one side and one on the other. He could not say which was the genuine nurse, and in great terror brandished his sword, making feints at both. Thereupon one of the nurses vanished and the other swooned, the child still in her arms. A priest was sent for and by means of incantations brought the nurse to her senses. She then said that her double had appeared and, laying hold of the babe, had claimed it as her own. Nobody knew whether the phantom was a fox or a spirit.

Here is a story of a vindictive were-fox, taken from the *Uji shui monogatari*:

A samurai was on his way home one evening when he met a fox. Pursuing the animal, he sent an arrow into its loin. The fox howled loudly and limped quickly away through the grass toward the samurai's house. When the man saw the animal was breathing fire, he hastened to overtake him but was too late. The fox, on arriving at the house, assumed human shape and set fire to the building. Then the samurai pursued the culprit, whom he took to be a real man, but resuming vulpine form, the animal disappeared into the thicket.

The house of a Dainagon was haunted by a number of foxes and was so impossible to live in that the owner decided to hold a battue. The very night he gave orders to this effect, he saw a vision of a gray-haired old man, with the figure of a tall boy, wearing a green hunting dress and seated under an orange tree in the garden. The owner asked the apparition's name, and he replied, "I have lived in your house for two generations and have a great number of children and grandchildren. I have always tried to keep them out of mischief, but they never would listen. Now I am sorry because they have made you angry. If you will forgive the things my family have done, I will protect you and let you know whenever good luck is coming your way."

Then the owner of the house awoke from his strange dream, rose, and opened the door of the verandah. There he discovered in the dim morning light an old hairless fox, shyly trying to hide himself behind a bamboo bench.

An unsuccessful transformation into animal shape is the subject of another were-fox story. A man left his house one evening in order to do some business in a neighboring city, but to his wife's surprise he came back accompanied by a servant long before he was due, saying that he had accomplished his business satisfactorily. He was very tired and went to bed at once, but an old woman-servant in the house warned her mistress, saying that she had noticed something odd about the returned traveler, who was blind in the left eye while her master was blind in the right eye. The wife then called to the sleeping man, saying she was ill and asking him to get her some medicine. He did so, grumbling, and to the wife's astonishment, she saw that what the old woman said was true. Then when he lay down to sleep again, she stabbed him to death, and he cried out like a fox, "Kon, kon, kwai—kwai." Then they beat to death the servant the were-fox had brought with him, and found he was also a fox. The one who had taken the shape of the master had not trained himself carefully enough in the art of transformation.

A very uncanny fox and badger story comes from an old Japanese source. Kugano Kendo was a clever doctor who lived in Yeddo. One day he was asked to go and see a patient in the country, and when he reached the house in question, which he had never before visited, he found that the master had gone out and he was asked to wait. A page boy offered him some refreshments after his long journey, and when he was about to thank him for his attentions, the boy turned away and, to the doctor's astonishment, he saw the page's face had utterly changed, becoming enormously long and narrow, with a small nose and big mouth and only one eye in the center of the forehead. Suddenly the apparition vanished. Though he was courageous by nature, this struck the doctor as so extraordinary that he felt inclined to leave the strange house at once. However, he mastered his fears and soon the owner of the house returned. The doctor told him what he had seen, and the master burst out laughing and said, "Oh, that boy has been at it again, has he? He always frightens strangers. Did he pull a face like this?" and suiting his actions to his words, the man imitated the horrible expression, his face taking the same deformity of one eye in the center of his forehead and a foxy snout.

This was too much for the doctor's equanimity. He ran to the front door and called his servants to prepare for the journey home. Then he found that all the servants had run away except one, and outside it was pitch-dark. The remaining servant said he could find a lantern, and presently he appeared out of the darkness with a light in his hand which fell full upon his features. To Kendo's intense horror he noticed the same transformation had taken place in the servant's countenance as had appeared in the faces of the others, and this additional strain being too much for his nerves, he cried out and fell into a swoon.

In the meantime the doctor's friends, growing anxious about his long absence, dispatched a search party to find him, and among those who were sent were some of the servants who had accompanied him earlier in the evening. To their surprise, instead of the fine house they had already visited, they found only an old, dirty, tumbledown cottage, which the neighbors told them was always desolate and only inhabited by foxes and *tanuki*. Nobody dared to pass that way by night. After a long search Dr. Kendo was found lying facedown in a bamboo grove. Weeks passed before he recovered from his adventure. This story seems to throw a light on what may be called "the workings of transformation," as though a partial change were brought about by some hidden occult force glimmering through the human shape.

Fox possession and fox familiars—women, weak men, and even children suffering from the idea of having been transformed into animals—make common beliefs among the Japanese. They are cured by being made to snuff up smoke from a heap of burning refuse, or by drinking weak tea, or swallowing roasted leaves of a certain plant; all these things being detested by foxes, and incidentally no doubt useful in cases of ordinary hysteria. Foxes that take the form of men and women soon resume vulpine shape when fumigated, bathed, or attacked by dogs. Even in the present day, fox possession has as great a hold on the imagination as in earlier centuries, but it is more widely ascribed to human sorcery. Certain sacred temples in Japan still attract crowds of pilgrims who believe that they are possessed by foxes and who come to these holy places to be cured. The bone of a tortoise's foot held in the left hand is prescribed as a talisman against this fearsome spell—probably also many other of the formulas useful in cases of witchcraft would be found efficacious.

The Fox-Temptress

(China)

I n times of yore, the Buddhist monk Chi-hüen, a native of Ho-shoh, led a life of purity and obedience to the Commandments. He wore no silk, but linen; he tramped from town to town, never lodging in convents within the cities, but always in mountain forests abroad.

Once he passes the night in a grave copse, ten miles east of the city of Kiang-cheu (in Shansi). By the light of the moon, which shines as bright as if it were daytime, he sees a wild fox in the copse, which places withered bones and a skull upon its head, and then shakes in such a way that the bones are flung on all sides; and it does this three or four times consecutively, until the movements of the head no longer make them fall. Then the fox accoutres its body with grass and leaves, and walking around the spot, adopts the form of a woman with eyebrows and eyes as lovely as if they were painted; never did this world see her like. Plain and unadorned is her dress. She places herself in the road, behaving as if she feels uneasy, when suddenly the trampling of a horse's hoofs resounds from the northwest. This makes the woman set up a wailing and weeping so piteous that it is impossible to hear it without emotion. A man on horseback appears, and seeing her thus cry and in tears, he alights. "Lady," says he, "what brings you here in the dead of night? What do you want? May I hear it?"

And the woman restrains her tears, and says: "I lived in Yih-cheu. There I was married by my parents, two years ago, to one of the Chang family, living here by the north gate; but my fate as a young wife was by no means happy. My husband died an untimely death last year, and thus ruined, thus left without any support, I set out for the far country of my paternal home. But I do not know the road thither, and this makes me so sad. Indeed, whom shall I ask to tell it me?"

"You want to return to your native place," says the other. "Well,

From: Jan J. de Groot, *Religious Systems of China*, vol. 4, book 2, part 1 (Leide: E. J. Brill, 1907).

there is nothing so simple as that. I am a Yih-cheu official and was dispatched from there the other day with a message. I am now on the road back, and if you do not object against the rather rough work of horse driving, I will give up my horse to you. Be so kind as to mount, and take the road there before us."

The woman withholds her tears and says gratefully, "If I may accept the favor you show me, I shall never forget it."

He invites her to place herself in the saddle, but at that moment Chi-hüen steps forth from the grave copse. "This is no human being," he shouts to the military message bearer. "She is a metamorphosed wicked fox. If you do not believe me, then please stay a little while. I will retransform her before your eyes." He makes a mystic sign (*mudra*) with his fingers, utters a genuine formula (*dhāraṇi*), brandishes his crosier, and exclaims at the top of his voice, "Why do not you forthwith return to your original form?"

The woman faints miserably, falls down, changes into an old vixen, and expires. Her flesh and blood flow away as one fluid, and all that remains on the body of the fox is the dry bones with the skull, the grass, and the leaves. On seeing these things, the military man is no longer skeptical. He salutes the monk several times by kneeling down and knocking his head against the ground, and passes on with sighs of astonishment and admiration.

Fox Sickness

(China)

In the Ching-yuen period of the T'ang dynasty (A.D. 785–805), Mr. P'ei of Kiang-ling (in the south of Hupeh province), a subintendent of the palace whose personal name is lost, had a son over ten years of age, very clever and intelligent, studious, brisk, and accomplished both in manners and appearance, whom he therefore deeply loved. This boy was attacked by a disease, which grew worse and

From: Jan J. de Groot, *Religious Systems of China*, vol. 5, book 2, parts 2 and 3 (Leide: E. J. Brill, 1907).

worse for ten days. Medicines took no effect, and P'ei was on the point of fetching a doctor of Taoist arts who might reprimand and thwart the demon of the disease, in the hope of effecting a cure, when a man knocked at his door, announcing himself as one of the surname Kao whose profession was to work with charms. P'ei forthwith invited him to walk in and look at his son.

"This boy suffers only from a sickness which is caused by a demonish fox," said the doctor. "I possess an art of curing this."

The father thanked him and implored his help; the other set to work to interrogate and call the demon by means of his charms, and in the next moment the boy suddenly rose with the words: "I am cured."

The delighted father called Kao a real and true master of arts, and having regaled him with food and drink, paid him a liberal reward in money and silk, and thankfully saw him off at the door. The doctor departed with the words: "Henceforth I will call every day."

But though the boy was cured of that disease, still he lacked a sufficient quantity of soul (shen-hwun), wherefore he uttered every now and then insane talk and had fits of laughter and wailing, which they could not suppress. At each call of Kao, P'ei requested him to attend to this matter too, but the other said, "This boy's vital spirits are kept bound by a specter, and are as yet not restored to him, but in less than ten days he will become quite calm. There is, I am happy to say, no reason to feel concerned about him." And P'ei believed it.

A few days later, a doctor bearing the surname Wang called on P'ei, announcing himself as an owner of charms with divine power and able to reprimand, thwart, and expel therewith diseases caused by demons. While discoursing with P'ei, he said, "I have been told that your darling son has been rendered ill and is not yet cured. I should much like to see him." P'ei let him see the boy, when the doctor exclaimed with terror, "The young gentleman has a fox disease. If he be not forthwith placed under treatment, his condition will become grave." P'ei then told him of the doctor Kao, on which the other smiled and said, "How do you know this gentleman is no fox?" They sat down, and had just arranged a meal and begun the work of reprimanding and thwarting the demon, when colleague Kao dropped in.

No sooner had he entered than he loudly upbraided P'ei: "How is it that this boy is cured, and you take a fox into his room? It is just this animal that caused his sickness!"

Wang in his turn, on seeing Kao, cried out, "Verily, here we have the wicked fox. Of a surety, here he is. How could his arts serve to reprimand and summon the specter!"

In this way the two men went on reviling each other confusedly, and P'ei's family stood stupefied with fright and amazement, when unexpectedly a Taoist doctor appeared at the gate. "I hear," said he to the domestic, "that Mr. P'ei has a son suffering of fox disease. I am a ghostseer. Tell this to your master, and beg permission for me to enter and interview him." The servant hastened with this message to P'ei, who came forth and told the Taoist what was going on. With the words "This matter is easy to arrange," he entered, in order to see the two.

But at once they cried out against him, "This too is a fox. How has he managed to delude people here under the guise of a Taoist doctor?"

He, however, returned their abuse: "You foxes, go back to the graves in the wilds beyond the town," he shouted. "Why do you harry these people?"

With that he shut the door, and the trio continued for some moments to quarrel and fight, the fright of P'ei still increasing and his servants being too perturbed to devise a good means to get rid of them. But at nightfall all noise ceased. They then opened the door and saw three foxes stretched on the ground, panting and motionless. P'ei scourged them soundly till they were dead, and in the next ten days the boy recovered.

Stories of Rat-Demons

(China)

T he position of the rat in Chinese demon-lore is rather significant. Like the fox and the monkey, it is notorious for assuming
the human shape to commit adultery with men and for
embracing Buddhist religious life with purposes not always
deceitful. Should it wish to bewitch women for immoral purposes, it
may do so without assuming human shape, as the following legend
shows.

In recent times there lived a man, who brought up a girl over ten
years old. One morning she was missed. A year elapsed without any
trace of her being discovered, when they heard from time to time in a
room of the house underground wailing of a baby. They turned up the
ground and discovered a hole, gradually increasing in depth and
width, and more than a *chang* in length and breadth. Here they found
the girl sitting with a baby in her arms and a bald rat as large as a
bushel beside her. She saw them enter without recognizing her
superiors, from which the parents concluded that she was under the
demonish influence of that rat. They slew the beast, whereupon the
girl burst into bitter weeping. "He is my husband!" she cried. "Why
do they murder him!" As they killed the child also, her lamentations
were unceasing, and ere they could cure her she died.

Folklore also allows whole packs of rats, either in other animal
forms or as men, to haunt human dwellings and settlements, or
swarm out of cracks and apertures and withdraw thither; and it
represents such apparitions as omens of evil. Tales on this topic are
numerous, a fact which we may, no doubt, readily assign to the
frequent occurrence of rats in human dwellings, where daily they
disturb the sleep and dreams of man. The following tale may
characterize their position as harbingers or causes of evil.

In the last year of the T'ien pao period (A.D. 755) the Censor Pih
Hang was Governor of Wei-cheu, when this region fell into the power

From: Jan J. de Groot, *Religious Systems of China*, vol. 5, book 2, parts 2 and 3
(Leide: E. J. Brill, 1907).

of the insurgent Ngan Luh-shan. He was just contriving the necessary stratagems to reduce him to submission, and had not yet marched out, when some days later he saw to his surprise several hundred pygmies, five to six inches in size, loiter and gambol in his courtyard. He and his family beat them to death. Next morning quite a troop of such dwarfs, all in white mourning dress, with lamentations took away the corpses in funeral cars and coffins with quite as much care as is observed at funerals of the gentry. They then made a grave in the courtyard, and after the burial, disappeared into a hole in the southern wall. In great fear and wonder, Pih Hang opened the grave and found an old rat in it. He boiled water and poured it into the hole, and on digging it up after a while, found several hundred dead rats. Some ten days afterward his whole family was killed, because he had not been victorious.

Of rats infesting the public roads as well-armed highwaymen, we hear in the following legend. In the first year of the Wan-sui period (A.D. 695) the roads to Ch'ang-ngan were infested by a gang of robbers, who concealed themselves in the daytime and operated during the night. Every now and again itinerant strangers were murdered without a trace of the perpetrators being discovered next day, which disheartened the people so much that they dared not set out in the morning, even though inns might be reached in the evening.

When the matter reached the ears of a certain Taoist doctor who lodged there in an inn, he said to the crowd, "To be sure, these are no men; they must be specters." In the dead of night he provided himself with an antique looking glass, and took his post by the roadside to look out for them.

On a sudden a troop of young men appeared, fully armed and accoutred. "Who stands there by the road?" they shouted with one voice at the Taoist. "Do not you care for your life?"

But the doctor let his mirror shine upon them, with the result that they flung down weapons and shields, and ran off. For some five or seven miles the doctor pursued them with spells and formulas, until they all ran into a big hole. He kept watch over it till the morning came and then, returning to the inn, summoned the people to dig up the hole. It was found to contain over a hundred big rats, which as they swarmed out were slain to the last. The evil was thereby ended.

Rats may also haunt human dwellings in the shape of other animals. Li Lin-fu, a high magnate of the eighth century, was unwell. In the morning he rose, washed, and appareled himself, and intending to repair to the court, ordered his men to bring the letter bag he was wont to use. Feeling it was heavier than usual, he opened it, and out sprang two rats, which on reaching the floor changed immediately into gray dogs. With ferocious eyes and showing their teeth, these beasts regarded him. He seized his bow and shot at them, on which they vanished, but Lin-fu was so deeply impressed with this incident that he died ere a month had passed.

The King of the Rats

(China)

The family of one Chu Jen had lived as farmers at the foot of Mount Sung for a series of generations. Suddenly he missed his first-born boy of five. He sought for him for more than ten years, but he could not find out whether he was alive or dead.

One day, a Buddhist monk wanders past, and stops at his door, accompanied by a disciple whose appearance and features are strikingly like those of the lost child. Jen asks the monk to walk in. He places a meal before him, and after a while he says, "Teacher, both in manners and features your disciple is like my first-born son whom I lost ten years ago."

The monk is amazed and, rising to his feet, says, "Thirty years long I have lived in the wild jungle of Mount Sung, and ten years have gone by since this disciple came to me, weeping and crying. I asked him what was the matter with him, but he showed all the bewilderment of tender youth and could not well explain from where he came. I brought him up, I gave him the tonsure, and he is now so clever and bright that nobody equals him. I have always deemed him to be a sage. If he is your son, then try to find it out by thoroughly examining him yourself."

From: Jan J. de Groot, *Religious Systems of China*, vol. 4, book 2, part 1 (Leide: E. J. Brill, 1907).

Jen and his family now set to work to interrogate and examine their child. "He had a black mark on his back," the mother says, and on searching his body all over, they find that mark, which convinces them that he really is their child. Father, mother, and all the family burst into wailing, and the monk departs, leaving the boy with his parents.

The parents keep him at home, and educate him in the same way as they do their other sons, but whenever the night comes he disappears, to return at daybreak. This having gone on so for two or three years, the parents begin to suspect him of playing the thief. They watch him, and perceive that he changes every night into a rat, which runs away from home and comes back in the morning. Their interrogations do not lead to any confessions, but after a long lapse of time he says, "I am no son of yours. I am a king of the rats under Mount Sung. The rats there, my subjects, have seen me, and so I can come back here no more." His parents think him in a fit of mental derangement, but that same evening he turns into a rat and runs away.

Tiger-Woman

(China)

The most horrid specimens of the tiger-demon class which Chinese fancy has created are those who assume a woman's shape with malicious intent, and then tempting men to marry them, devour them in the end, and all the children in the meantime produced. A victim of such monstrous perfidy was Ts'ui T'ao, a man of P'u-cheu. While traveling to Ch'u-cheu (in Nganhwui) he reached Lih-yang, situated to the south, and started for Ch'u-cheu at daybreak, then halting at an inn for traveling officers, called Benevolence and Rectitude, to pass the night.

"This inn is under evil influence," the innkeeper said. "I pray you, do not lodge here."

From: Jan J. de Groot, *Religious Systems of China*, vol. 5, book 2, parts 2 and 3 (Leide: E. J. Brill, 1907).

But T'ao would not heed this advice and, with his satchel on his back, went up to the main apartment while the innkeeper provided him with a lamp and a candle.

At the second watch T'ao spread out his blankets and was just going to rest, when he saw at the gate a big paw like that of a quadruped. On a sudden the gate was flung open, and he saw a tiger walk in. In his fright he hurried into an obscure corner and, there concealed, observed the beast put off its animal skin in the middle of the courtyard and become a girl of extraordinary beauty, well dressed and ornamented, who walked up the steps into the main apartment and laid herself down on his blankets.

Now T'ao appeared. "Why do you lie down in my blankets?" he asked. "Just now I saw you enter in the guise of a beast. What was that for?"

The girl rose and said, "I hope you will dismiss all your surprise. My father and my elder brother are professional huntsmen, and my family is so poor that all their attempts to find a fashionable match for me have failed. I became aware of this and secretly wrapped myself in a tigerskin at night, for well knowing that there lodge high-class people here, I had resolved to give myself to one of them for sprinkling and sweeping his floor. But all guests and travelers successively have dismissed me for very fear, and this night only I have the good fortune to find a man with intelligence, whom I may hope will pay attention to my feelings."

"If all this is really the truth," T'ao replied, "I desire no better myself than to accept a life with you of joyful concord." Next day he took the girl with him, having first thrown the tigerskin dress into a dry well behind the hall. Afterward he took a degree on account of his studies of the classics and became prefect of Süen-ch'ing. While journeying thither with his wife and boys, they after a month or so again stayed for a night in the inn of Benevolence and Rectitude. "It is here that I met with you for the first time," said T'ao laughingly, and at once he went to the well to look into it. And verily, there the skin-dress still lay. This caused him to burst again into laughter. "The dress you had on at that time is there still," he called to his wife.

"Have it fetched up," she said. And when she saw it in his hands, she continued, still laughing: "Let me try it on again."

He gave his consent. The woman descended from the steps and put on the skin-dress, but no sooner had she done so than she changed into a tiger, which moved up the steps of the main apartment with roars and bounds, devoured the boys and T'ao into the bargain, and ran away.

The Were-Stag

(*China*)

n Mount Sung an aged Buddhist monk had constructed a straw hut, where between shrubs and creepers, he led a life of obedience to the Commandments without ever going out.

Unexpectedly he beholds a young lad, who greets him and entreats him to make him his disciple. But the anchorite goes on reciting his holy books without looking up. So the boy stands there from morn till eve, and then the monk asks him, "My son, what have you come to these high mountains for, where human footprints are scarcely ever seen? Why do you desire to become my disciple?"

"I have been living on this hill" he answers. "My parents are dead, so that I am without any protectors and am so young. I feel sure I deserve this fate for not having cultivated virtue in my previous existences; therefore I have vowed to abjure worldliness and to seek a master. Verily, I long to cultivate the blissful state of the world to come."

"But are you able to do it?" asks the monk.

"Should my words not be consonant with my heart," is the answer, "then may not only you, Master, but also Emperor Heaven and Empress Earth withhold from me their pardon."

The monk finds him clever and intelligent, and sees in him a person with much disposition for good. He gives him the tonsure, and so energetic and industrious does he prove as a disciple that his likes are but seldom found. When he trains other monks in the Law, they are unable to contradict him, and when he asks the brethren for instruc-

From: Jan J. de Groot, *Religious Systems of China*, vol. 4, book 2, part 1 (Leide: E. J. Brill, 1907).

tion in the doctrines, they never checkmate him. No wonder that the old monk appreciates him highly, nay, he regards him as a saint and a sage.

Thus many years go on, till in a frosty autumn the leaves of the trees are falling. A cold breeze is drearily blowing, and in the glens it is all bright freezing weather, when suddenly the young monk scans the four points of the compass and screams out in a distinct voice: "In the depth of the mountains I grew up to old age. Why did I leave them for that one and only Church? I waver as to whether I shall betake myself to my companions of old and give up tormenting my soul any longer from morn till eve." Then again he sends forth a protracted scream, and after a while a troop of stags appears and runs past the spot. Then the young man begins to hop. He throws off his religious garb, changes into a stag, joins the troop with a bound, and is off.

The Snake as the Devil

(Japan)

The Ainu are not different from many other nations in their superstitious fear of snakes. They have a very great dread of every kind of snake. Though the people do not seem to connect them with the entrance of sin into the world, yet many of them certainly believe snakes to be demons both in nature and in deed, and to be at enmity with all mankind; and they think that, having a special spite against women, they will bewitch them and drive them mad if they get the opportunity. To be bewitched by a snake or to be possessed by a devil are the same thing according to Ainu ideas. The men are afraid to kill these reptiles, because they think that the evil spirits which are supposed to dwell in them will, on leaving their former abode, enter the heart of the slayer. It is also said that, if a snake finds any person asleep out of doors, it will immediately enter

From: John Batchelor, "Items of Ainu Folk-Lore," *Journal of American Folk-Lore* 7 (1894): 15–44.

the sleeper's mouth and take up its abode within him, the result being madness. I have never yet heard of the Ainu worshipping snakes.

Some of the Ainu tell of a large serpent which is said to have been the immediate cause of wasps and stinging ants. This monstrous reptile is, curiously enough, said to have been of the feminine gender, of an extraordinary length, and of such a beautiful color as to be quite charming to look upon. She was, however, a very dreadful and dangerous creature, for she used to devour whole villages of people and even to swallow houses. One day this monster met an Ainu who was hunting far away in the forests, and tempted him to sin with her. The Ainu, however, was a God-fearing man, and would not be led into danger but manfully maintained his integrity. Thereupon the serpent, instead of swallowing him up as he expected, told him that as a punishment he should be unable to die for a thousand years. And it came to pass that when this Ainu attained the age of a hundred years he shed his hair, beard, skin, and teeth, and became a child again, subject to all the ills and trials of babyhood, and this took place every time the poor fellow reached the age of one hundred years. He was quite unable to die till he had lived his thousand years and lost his hair and teeth ten times. At length this reptile was slain by the Ainu, but as its carcass became decomposed and fell to pieces, the particles became stinging ants and wasps.

By some Ainu, snakes are supposed to live in large communities in the underworld, and in their real homes assume the bodily forms of men and women. They have houses and gardens just the same as human beings have. Their food, however, consists of dew. They have also a language peculiar to themselves. But their resemblance to men and women extends only to bodily form. Their hearts and natures are decidedly diabolical. They only assume the form of snakes when they come to the upperworld, and they never appear here except with the intention of doing some harm to human beings.

The ancients of the Ainu once met together to pray God to take away these evil-working objects. He heard their prayer and determined to starve them out. But when they were about to leave, a frog stepped forth and told them that, if they would but hold its leg in their mouth, they would not starve to death. One snake tried the remedy, and found the frog's leg so sweet that he swallowed its whole body. From that time to this, frogs have been the staple food among the reptiles of Ainu land.

Serpent Love

(India)

A very intelligent Muhammadan once related to me certain peculiar experiences of a near relation of his, a young woman in sound health and easy circumstances. One unlucky day she was bitten by a snake, and though it was not a deadly serpent, she suffered great pain from the bite, and her health was for a time much impaired. Before she had satisfactorily recovered from this untoward accident, she was again bitten by a snake of the same kind and again went through great suffering. Time after time, at more or less regular intervals, she was bitten by these reptiles although every precaution was taken to guard her from them.

By great vigilance she might escape one or two of the periodical visitations, but complete immunity seemed impossible of attainment. For a period she escaped her serpent enemies by wearing a portion of the skin of the *markhor,* or mountain goat, about her person, as a sort of amulet; but the charm losing its freshness, she was bitten again. Her health eventually failed entirely under the terror of her position and the venom of her tormentors.

When this incident to a well-educated Hindu gentleman—a Master of Arts of the Punjab University—he assured me that stories of serpent love are founded on actual fact. He himself had personal knowledge of one case. His people had a servant who was afflicted in this way. Every six months or so the man used to become subject to a strange morbid restlessness and a mental inquietude which could only be allayed by his being visited and bitten by a serpent. Everyone looked upon him with repulsion as one strangely allied with such a terrible reptile. He also inspired a sort of awe because of this connection. The man himself was generally unhappy, and when the paroxysms were at hand, he was wretched and miserable.

At last the sufferer consulted a wise sadhu, who gave him a *ganda tawiz* (a peculiar malodorous amulet). When he had attached this to

From: John Campbell Oman, *Cults, Customs, and Superstitions of India* (London: T. Fisher Unwin, 1908).

his person, he experienced a sort of nightmare. Serpents seemed to crawl around him, to wind and coil about his limbs, and to hiss and dart at him. Even the ambient air seemed to be peopled with writhing serpent forms. For two hours or so this dreadful vision obsessed him, nearly driving him mad, and then the air cleared, as it were, and the ground at his feet resumed for him its natural appearance. He was cured forever, the mental shadows and the very real serpents passing entirely out of his life.

Both the above cases have peculiarities of their own. In the Muslim family the patient was guarded as much as possible from her serpent visitors, and she died. Whereas the Hindu, laboring periodically under great physical and mental distress, welcomed what may be called the dental attentions of the serpents and was eventually freed by a wise sadhu from his troubles as well as from the visitations of the uncanny reptiles.

A case somewhat similar to the one relating to the Hindu above-mentioned, but without the cure, is described in a book titled *Thirty-five Years in India,* written by Dr. Honigberger, who described himself as physician to the court of Maharaja Ranjit Singh. Dr. Honigberger's is the only book in which I have found any reference to "serpent love." Writing on this subject, he states as follows:

> Speaking of serpents, I may mention here a particular disease which they designate at Lahore, Mar-ashakh (serpent-love), and which, according to their statements, occurs only in the Punjab. I have never heard of it in any other place, and I mention it, hoping that the English physicians, particularly those now living in that country, will take the trouble to investigate the subject and ascertain whether this disease is peculiar to the Punjab, and why it occurs only between the Indus and the Sutlej. . . .
>
> The faqueer, Noor-oo-Din, at Lahore, who at present enjoys great respect from the English for his extended knowledge and eminent merits, was the first who directed my attention to the disease I have mentioned, a short time before my first departure from Lahore in the year 1832, and who introduced to me at that time a patient afflicted with it. It was a laundry man of the age of sixty, although he appeared nearer eighty. He allowed himself to be bitten every month by serpents. He was of short

stature and of a cachectical appearance; his perspiration, which I perceived at some distance, was peculiarly offensive, and was similar to that of serpents. He told me he had been troubled with that malady upwards of thirty years; that at the commencement he permitted himself to be bitten once a year, afterwards twice, but at that time once in every month; and that the serpents followed him even into the water. He stated that only four days previously he had been bitten on the upper part of the hand, on which I could perceive a cicatrix, and he showed me numerous scars on his hands and feet, so that I could not doubt the truth of his statement. . . .

I have seen at least a dozen persons so affected at Lahore, who were all males, and I am told that the number of such patients in the Punjab is very large. The nature of the disease is that the patients at certain periods have an irresistible inclination to be bitten by serpents, which they say does them a great deal of good, as for a few days previously they are troubled with fainting and dizziness, nausea, want of appetite, disinclination to work, and heaviness in the limbs. These are the symptoms of the disease in question, and at these times the serpents are attracted towards them by the scent; the patients looking upon them as their welcome benefactors.

Besides the cases of serpent love mentioned previously, two others were related to me—one by a *kabari* (a seller of old furniture), regarding his son; the other by an Indian gentleman in the Education Department, his sister being the sufferer. From what I have stated it will be seen that there are both Hindus and Muslims in the Punjab who suffer from serpent love, and that the affection is not confined to males only, as Dr. Honigberger seemed to imply.

In native opinion the explanation of the mystery is this. The snake that inflicts the first bite is a female. The poison she communicates ferments in the blood of the victim, and periodically produces in the bitten person the smell of a female snake. The males of the same species are attracted, and as is the nature of the viper tribe, they bite and run away when they are disappointed. So far the explanation is ingenious enough, but why under such conditions should the bite of the male assuage the mental and physical troubles of the victim, as described in the cases given above?

Exorcism of
Wild Animals

(Bengal)

The belief that charms and exorcism are efficacious for the dispersion or destruction of noxious animals has prevailed from a remote period, and it still exists in India. In the Middle Ages, history makes frequent mention of the calamities caused in England and other places by plagues of insects. Few remedies for preventing or mitigating the ravages were known, and recourse was consequently had to the clergy, who heard the complainants, interposed on their behalf with prayers, and declared these scourges of mankind to be the work of the devil.

Between the months of October and May, crowds of woodcutters, come in boats from Barisal, Khulna, Faridpur, Calcutta, and other districts, and enter the forests of the Sundarbans for the purpose of cutting timber. These forests are full of man-eating tigers, and the loss of life that annually occurs from their attacks is so heavy that nothing will persuade woodcutters to proceed to the jungles without their fakir. He is the one person who is believed to possess power to drive away tigers and prevent them from attacking human beings. The belief in the power of the fakir is so great that woodcutters and others declare that even crocodiles, which also cause great loss of life and are frequently met with in the jungles, are under his control. It is said that he can make these great saurians rise or sink in water by his charms, and by his exorcism close their mouths and prevent them from doing any harm.

No work is begun in the forests by woodcutters until the fakir has gone through his charms and incantations, and has performed his *pujas* for the dispersion of all noxious animals.

From: D. Sunder, "Exorcism of Wild Animals in the Sundarbans," *Journal of the Asiatic Society of Bengal* 72 (part 3, Anthropology and Cognate Subjects, no. 2) (1903): 45–52.

For this purpose he has to be provided with a black kid and the following articles: five seers of *batasas* (sweetmeat), two and a half seers of sugar, forty plantains, ten cucumbers, seven muskmelons, two coconuts, five seers of *atap* rice, five yards of white cloth for a dhoti, two yards of red cloth for flags and wicks, two packets of vermilion, one quarter seer of incense, an earthen plate for burning incense, two earthen water pots, seven *cheraghs* (earthen lamps), seven earthen pots for water for the deities, and eleven poles for flags. With these articles the fakir and woodcutters proceed to the block of land selected for the woodcutting operations. On arrival the fakir repeats a charm for the safety of the boat. Translated, it is as follows:

O Kali, thou knot on the head of Shiva, thy name is a sufficient charm over this place, and by it I have made the place as secure as a fort. Keep tigers away. Let them not come anywhere near us. If tigers break into this place and cause any injury, may you, O Kali, eat the head of Kamakhya of Kamarupa.

Having said this, the fakir and his companions go ashore and select a piece of ground on which to propitiate the deities. The jungle is cleared, and the fakir makes a circle on the ground with his right foot and then repeats the incantations, of which a translation is given below:

1. I have made a circle on this ground and it is now like a hive: thirteen thousand evil spirits and Dano, Dudh, Deo, and Pori must keep out of my circle. O tiger, if you injure my enclosure, may you eat the head of Kamakhya of Kamarupa.

2. The clouds in the heavens and the circle of the world are my boundaries. Eighty thousand evil spirits, tigers, and pigs must keep off this boundary. If they dare to put their shoulders within it, may they drink the blood of the goddess.

3. I adore thee, O Kali! Darkness, thou art the hairs of Shiva. I am thy son. I make a circle around the whole world in thy name. I pray thee that thou surround me and all my men with thy darkness and protect us from tigers.

4. Rama's bow is on the other bank of the river and his cottage is on this bank. I make a circle and have taken in the whole world. If this my charm be without effect, may Mahadeva lose his head.

The four words *Dano, Dudh, Deo,* and *Pori* mentioned in the first of the above charms are names for the devil.

After this the fakir builds in his circle seven small huts made of
stakes and leaves. Beginning from the right, the first hut is given to
Jagabandhu and the second to Mahadeva. Four flags hang over them,
one on each side, and a cheragh is kept burning in front of an offering
of batasas, rice, plantains, etc., which is made to the deities. The third
house is assigned to Manasa and the same offering is made to her, but
a pot of water with mango leaves over it is also given to her. A figure
of a deity is made with vermilion on the pot. Next to the third hut a
small platform is erected in honor of Rupapori, and an offering of
plantains, rice, coconut, etc., is made on it on a plantain leaf.

Next to the platform is a hut for Kali-maya and Kali. The hut is
divided into two compartments, in each of which a pot of water,
covered with mango leaves and anointed with vermilion, is placed. A
picture of a diety holding a stick in the right hand is made with
vermilion on the pot which is on Kali-maya's side of the hut. The
offerings to these deities are the same as those made to Mahadeva, but
a larger quantity of batasas is given to Kali. A flag hangs on each side
of the hut, and a cheragh is kept burning in each compartment. The
next is a small platform similar to the one of Rupapori. Offerings of
rice, plantains, coconut, sugar, etc., are made on it to Orpori.

After this is a hut with two compartments, one being for Kamesvari
and the other for Burhi Thakurani. A pot of water covered with mango
leaves is kept in each compartment, and each pot has a picture of a
deity on it, made with vermilion. The offerings are the same as those
made to Manasa and Mahadeva. The next is a tree, the trunk of which
is smeared with vermilion. It is called Raksya Chandi. No offerings
are made to it.

Then come two more huts, with two compartments in each and flags
flying over them. The first hut is given for the Ghazi Sahib and his
brother Kalu, and the next is given for Chawal Pir and Ran Ghazi.
Chawal Pir is said to have been the son of Ghazi Sahib, and Ran Ghazi
is alleged to have been Ghazi's nephew. Five balls of earth are placed
in each compartment, and an offering of sugar, batasas, and coconut
is made to these saints. A cheragh is kept burning in front of the
offering inside each compartment.

The last diety propitiated is Bastu Devata (the earth). The offerings
are the same as those made to Jagabandhu, but they are kept on the
open ground on plantain leaf. There is no hut or platform.

When everything is ready and the offerings have been arranged, the

fakir retires to purify himself. He has a bath and returns, wearing the
dhoti provided for him by the woodcutters and having his hands,
arms, and forehead anointed with vermilion. He then, with hands
folded before his face, goes on his knees and bows his head to the
ground, and remains in this attitude for a few seconds before each of
the deities in turn. His prayers to each of them may be translated thus:

Jagabandhu (Friend of the World)—"I pray to thee. Shield thou
me and keep me under thy care."

Mahadeva (the Destroyer)—"Take me in thy lap and cover
thou me. Keep the tigers of the jungles far off."

Manasa (Goddess of Serpents)—"Hear my prayer. Keep all
serpents and other noxious things very distant."

Rupapori (a spirit of the jungles)—"I beseech thee to hear me.
Keep thy eyes on my companions. Let none of them be
injured."

Kali-maya (said to be the daughter of Kali)—"O my mother,
look thou on me in mercy. Keep far away all injurious things,
tigers and bears, from this place."

Kali—"O Kali of this world! all things are visible to thee. Have
mercy upon us. Hear my cry, and let nothing do us any
harm."

Orpori (a jungle spirit having wings)—"Thou who livest in the
air and dost, fly about, thou also art a tiger of the jungle. I beg
at thy feet. Do us no harm."

Burhi Thakurani (wife of Daksa Raja, the father of Durga)—"I
am at thy feet praying and pleading. Injure me not."

Raksya Chandi (another name for Kali)—"I pray thee, preserve
my life."

Ghazi Sahib—"Thou hast become a fakir. As a fakir I fall at thy
feet and plead. Thou hast come to these jungles with three
hundred tigers. I beg thee to shut the mouths of the tigers."

Kalu—"Thou art brother of Ghazi, and I salute thee in his name
and ask for thy help. If thou shouldst injure me after this
salutation, thou shalt die and burn in hell."

Chawal Pir—"I pray thee to look upon me as thy son. Be a
father to me and protect me from all danger and injury."

Ran Ghazi—"Thou who hast power over them, and dost ride
about on them, I pray thee that thou drive out from these
jungles all tigers and bears."

Bastu Devata—"Thou dost remain on this earth, and all things are under thy control. I pray to thee that thou keep everything peaceful. Let no injury come on us, else thou wilt offend all the other deities."

These prayers have to be offered and the deities propitiated every seven days while woodcutting is going on.

Ghazi Sahib and his brother Kalu are said to have been Muhammadan Pirs, or saints. They are alleged to have had complete power over all living things. It is believed that they possessed the power of bringing to pass whatever they desired, and that tigers would come to them or disperse at their command; also that they used to ride about the jungles on tigers. They are venerated by all Muhammadans and Hindus of these parts, and whenever any person desires to enter any jungle, he first bends to the ground, with hands folded before his face, and says, "In the name of Ghazi Sahib." Having done this, he goes into the jungle, believing that Ghazi Sahib will keep him perfectly safe.

Fakirs and others are unable to say who Ghazi Sahib was, and there is nothing in writing about him. In paragraph 524 of his report on the Bengal Census of 1901, Mr. Gait writes as follows:

Zindah Ghazi, from *Zindik-i-Ghazi*, "conqueror of infidels," rides on a tiger in the Sundarbans and is the patron saint of woodcutters, whom he is supposed to protect from tigers and crocodiles. He is sometimes identified with Ghazi Miyan and sometimes with Ghazi Madar. One Muhammadan gentleman tells me he is Badiruddin Shah Madar, who died in A.D. 840 fighting against the infidels. Songs are sung in his honor and offerings are made after a safe return from a journey. Hindu women often make vows to have songs sung to him if their children reach a certain age. His shrine is believed to be on a mountain called Madaria in the Himalayas.

After finishing his prayers to the several deities, the fakir proceeds to ascertain whether a tiger is present in the locality or not, and he addresses it as follows:

O tiger and tigress! if thou be on my right, roar on the right; if thou be on the left, roar on the left.

Having said this, the fakir blows over his left arm. He then spans the arm from elbow to any finger of the hand. If the span meets the end of any finger exactly, the fakir waits a few minutes and spans a second time. If the span fails to meet the same finger exactly, it is a sign that a tiger is present, and the fakir then has to drive it off. He is said to be able to do this by repeating an incantation, a translation of which is given below:

In the name of my brothers Hingli, Bingli, and Mangala, and the horses of Ghazi Sahib, also in the name of Barkat [God]. O mother Kameshvari, thou art uppermost in my mind. I have put Azrael the Rider on the backs of the tigers and tigresses of this jungle. Go eastward, thou of color of fire; go eastward or westward, go to the right about, I command thee, and feed thyself by killing deer and pig. If this my charm fails, may the topknot of Mahadeva fall at the feet of Kali.

Hingli, Bingli, and Mangala, mentioned in the fakir's charm for driving away a tiger, are said to be deities of the jungles and the fathers of tigers. Azrael the Rider is alleged to be a spirit who is always on the backs of tigers.

The fakir then repeats charms for the protection of the woodcutters and himself. Translated, they run thus:

In the name of Jaya Durga and Shiva, I put this guard over my body (here he blows over the right and then the left side of his chest.) O tiger and tigress! I warn thee that thou leave this place.

The name of my father and mother is Amara [immortal] and that of my companions is Aksaya [indestructible], and my name is also the same. O tiger and tigress! if thou injure any of my men, thou wilt drink the blood of thy mother and brother.

O Muni! I am filled with thee! O Bhagavati! do not fail to aid me, or you will put your foot on the head of Shiva and will eat the heads of Ganesha and Kartika.

After this the eyes of the tiger have to be closed, and the fakir repeats an incantation to effect this. Translated, it reads as follows:

Dust! dust! The finest dust be on thy eyes, O tiger and tigress! I lifted it with my feet and rubbed it on my body. Thou canst not see me now. O mother Nidrapati! grant my prayer and put sleep into the eyes of the tigers. Kali is on my right, and Dudh [the devil] is on my left. O Nidrapati! hear me, I pray thee! I stand here a child of Kali. Be thou watchful over me.

If a tiger is believed to be in the vicinity of the woodcutters, the fakir repeats the following charm to drive it away:

On the north is a stone, the hut of Rama, and with it I have stopped the shedding of blood. If this my charm fails, Mahadeva shall know how the tigers and tigresses were born. If this my charm be without effect, may the headknot of Mahadeva fall at Bhagavati's feet. In the name of Kameshvari I command thee, O tiger and tigress! to either come forward or vanish.

If the growl of a tiger be heard anywhere near the place where the woodcutting is going on, the fakir repeats an incantation to banish it, which may be translated thus:

God is here and God is everywhere. Tiger and tigress! do thou begone! Hark! their roaring has ceased, and they have fled with five spirits mounted on them. In the name of God I have tied the mouths of the tiger and tigress.

If a tiger be seen in the jungle prowling anywhere near the woodcutters, the fakir has to turn toward it at once and show it the palm of his left hand and to exorcise thus:

O thou of fiery eyes! thou are furious for a drop of blood. I command thee that thou stand where thou art. Stand, or turn back, thou bastard! I warn thee to retire, else thou shalt die!

This resembles a charm that was formerly used in Normandy, where during the eight days before Christmas, the people in some of the cantons placed bundles of hay under the fruit trees, and children under twelve years of age were sent with torches to set fire to the hay, which they did, crying out:

> Mice, caterpillars, and moles,
> Get out, get out of my field!
> I will burn your beard and bones,
> Trees and shrubs:
> Give me three bushels of apples.

So much for the fakir and his exorcisms. He believes in prayer and pleads before his gods. Whether his prayers and intercessions are sincere or not is a matter on which we should express no opinion; rather, let us respect him for what he does, even if his methods do not fit in with our own ideas. That he is thoroughly believed in by woodcutters there is no doubt, and it is equally certain that his charms and exorcism give them courage to enter the forests and embolden them to work there, notwithstanding the many dangers by which they are surrounded. Without him they would be utterly helpless. That his incantations have little effect has been proved, for it often happens that the fakir himself, instead of the woodcutters, is carried off by the tiger. This occurred in the cases of two of them, within my knowledge, during the present season, in the Barisal tract of the Sundarbans, where tigers have increased considerably and have caused great loss of life since the people were prohibited from keeping guns. But the people and woodcutters allege that the two fakirs were carried off because the propitiation of the deities of the jungles where the fakirs lost their lives had been neglected a long time, and that the tigers there are consequently very angry.

The Corpse Possessed by a Ghost

(China)

Under the Sung dynasty, there lived to the east of the market-town of Lu-siao, in the Yuen-cheu department, a silversmith, whose clan name was Kwoh. Though upward of thirty years old, he still lived by himself as a bachelor. And to the west of the same place lived an old damsel who, carrying

From: Jan J. de Groot, *Religious Systems of China*, vol. 4, book 2, part 1 (Leide: E. J. Brill, 1907).

on a trade, frequently visited Kwoh to buy or sell hairpins, rings, and other things of this kind. One evening, her daughter, a girl of fifteen or sixteen, fled to Kwoh. "I want to become your wife," she said, and seeing Kwoh startle, she went on to say, "I have yearned for you for a long time, but I have not had a chance till now to elope. Do not waver." And on his asking her for further explanations, she said, "I died yesterday and my mother put me in a coffin, but I opened it, crept out, and shut it again. My mother has thus buried an empty coffin, and no inquiry will be made after me at all." Kwoh now placed her in an unfrequented apartment and kept her there.

Some eight months after that, the mother happened to pay a visit to Kwoh. As he was out, she peeped into the room and perceived the red shoes in which she had encoffined her daughter. She pushed open the door, seized them, and cried out among the neighbors that Kwoh had pilfered her daughter's grave. When Kwoh came home and the neighbors appraised him of it, he was seized with consternation. "My mother came so unawares," said the girl, "that I had to be off in the greatest haste, and thus I forgot to put away my shoes. We must now get out of her reach, but you will never feel sorry for it." With these words she departed, and Kwoh fled also, going in the direction of T'an-cheu.

Ere he had gone some ten miles, the girl overtook him, and together they reached T'an-cheu. Their purses were soon empty, but thus spoke the girl, "I can sing, and among the songs in the *note kung* there must be some that pay." So they opened a music hall at the end of the P'ing-li ward, where her songs brought the clouds to a standstill and attracted the people in crowds packed to the walls. Every day hundreds of notable families vied with each other in engaging her, and on the days they made her come, they threw to her gold hairpins and similar things. Thus in a year they laid by many ten thousand coins.

One day, a Taoist with pointed coiffure, a giant of nine feet, tapped Kwoh on the back and said, "Thousands and ten times thousands of people gaze at that ghost-doll!" These words opened Kwoh's eyes. He drew the man aside and humbly entreated him to help him out of his dilemma. The Taoist advised him to offer up prayers in the temple of the Eastern Mountain. There he went to worship the deity, and in the second watch he saw a yamen runner garrote the girl and take her to the back hall of the temple, where she suddenly sank to the ground and became a corpse. Thus it became quite clear to him it was a *kwei* that took possession of the corpse of the girl. Immediately he offered a sum of money to have the temple repaired in order to atone in this way for the sins the girl might have committed, and he buried her corpse with much ceremony and many burnt offerings. In that same night he dreamed that she came to him to express her thankfulness and bid him farewell, her eyes wet with tears.

Two Stories of Possession by Syads

(India)

There appears to be a kind of possession known amongst the Muhammadans in India. The symptoms are these. Some man, usually one of blameless life and strict habits, is selected by a departed Pir or Syad as the vehicle for conveying his wishes to the living. The entry of the saint's spirit into the body of his chosen vessel is accompanied with violent convulsions. The man possessed of the spirit is thrown into a state of uncontrollable agitation. He foams at the mouth and usually tosses his head from side to side, or up and down, in a frantic manner. At length he speaks, asserting energetically that he is some Pir or other and demanding that a certain offering shall be made at his grave, which seems to be all the Pir cares about. The awe-stricken bystanders promise everything required, and the spirit departs, leaving his medium in a state of much physical prostration. I have had personal knowledge of several cases of this kind.

The 24th of November being a Muhammadan festival, I paid a visit to the shrine of Data Ganj Bakhsh, a saint who settled at Lahore before

From: John Campbell Oman, *Cults, Customs, and Superstitions of India* (London: T. Fisher Unwin, 1908).

the Norman conquest of England. Having lived in Lahore for thirty-four years, he died there in A.D. 1072. I found a large concourse of people seated near the outer wall of the shrine in the open air. Three musicians, two playing on stringed instruments and one on a drum, were singing away lustily a hymn in praise of the saint. Several graybeards sat in a sort of solemn abstraction close to the wall, while a middle-aged man, dressed in green, with a string of beads around his neck, occupied a prominent position a little in front of the elders. The congregation and onlookers, consisting of two or three hundred persons, sat huddled together on dhurries, or cotton carpets, in the foreground. As the music went on with a peculiar sort of throb, one here and another there from the midst of the congregation seemed convulsed, as if by galvanic shocks. Presently their movements became more energetic and violent. In one case a man threw himself forward, resting in a crouching position on his hands and knees. He swayed his head in a frantic manner from side to side, and it was a marvel to me how it escaped collision with the ground. But escape it did. Exhausted at length by the wild energy of his movements, the man fell in a fit upon the ground. One of his companions now came forward and began to press his limbs, in order, I presume, to calm the excitement of his overwrought nerves. Another man, after the usual premonitory convulsions, writhed on the ground in wild contortions. Two men rushed forward apparently to prevent him from hurting himself, and holding him up by the waist, allowed him to fling himself backward and forward in the wildest manner possible. Several other men became excited and convulsed under the influence of the Pir, but all the cases of possession I noticed could be referred to one or other of the types I have just described. None of the *convulsionnaires* uttered a single word throughout the proceedings.

On a previous occasion I had visited one of the favorite places for the exhibition of such manifestations. On reaching the ground, I found several persons congregated around a boy of about ten years of age, who appeared to be in a semiconscious state. This poor little fellow had been hanging, I don't know for how long, suspended head downward from the branch of a tree. In this uncomfortable position he had been swaying himself about in a sort of frenzy, and had almost lost consciousness before he was taken down. His father and other friends who were present on the spot assured me that no harm could come to anyone taken possession of by the spirit of the Pir Sahib.

A tailor in my service, a weakly lad with a very queer look about his eyes, used to be a favorite of some Pir or other. He was fond of attending assemblies such as I have described, would readily fall into the ecstatic state, and died very young. As contributions are expected from those who frequent assemblies of the kind just described, it is evident that the guardians of the shrines where they take place reap a substantial advantage, but it is not easy to see what benefit the poor fellows get who may be called the performers on these occasions. They have themselves told me that in the ecstatic state they are unconscious of the world around them and have the very gates of paradise opened to them.

Curse of the Syad

(India)

Not only have the powerful spells of the wicked to be dreaded; the dead are not less capable of resenting any neglect or affront and, when offended, have to be duly propitiated by gifts and offerings.

A servant of mine at Lahore had been absent from his duties for some days on account of ill health. Inquiring into his condition and the treatment he had been receiving, I learned that he had a few days previously been prostrated by an attack of fever. On the second day of his illness he was, apparently, delirious, and in that state revealed the fact that his fever was due to his having pulled down some branches from a babul tree *(Acacia arabica)* which grew over a Syad's grave just outside my compound. It was a miserable, dilapidated structure, this Syad's grave, but the dead occupant was nonetheless jealous of its honor. According to the sick man, the Syad had taken possession of him and was wreaking his vengeance upon him for having dared to dishonor his shrine: Something had to be done to appease the irate

From: John Campbell Oman, *Cults, Customs, and Superstitions of India* (London: T. Fisher Unwin, 1908).

saint, and so the invalid's afflicted wife caused a *maskh* (leather bag) of water to be poured over the Syad's grave, apparently to cool his temper. At the same time a fellow servant, skilled in such matters, administered a charmed clove to the patient in order to break the spell which had been cast upon him by the indignant saint. But the invalid, instead of improving, became worse, and in his delirium the spirit of the Syad, which had now taken full possession of him, kept uttering through the mouth of the fever-stricken man such contemptuous remarks as these: "Oh, indeed! you have eaten a charmed clove, have you? I will give you a stomach full of charmed cloves!"

The unsuccessful exorcist was called in to try another spell, but as, after the clove episode, the efficacy of his spells appeared somewhat doubtful, the precaution was also taken of endeavoring to pacify the Syad with gifts. He was promised a *cheragh*, or light, upon his tomb, for a certain number of successive Thursday evenings, with an offering of sweetmeats in addition, if he would but forgive the offender. Still the invalid did not mend, and his wife was making up her mind to promise the Syad a more worthy peace offering (a cock or a kid) if he would only restore her husband to health, when I became acquainted with the particulars of the case and recommended her to postpone her vow of a costly offering till she had first tried the effects of sulfate of quinine. I gave her some of the drug with directions how to use it. She followed my instructions and to her great satisfaction found that the bitter white powder had the power either of expelling the spirit or of appeasing it, for her husband quickly rallied and was able to resume work after a few days. I have reason to believe, however, that after all the recovery was attributed more to the spells that had been employed and to the promises made to the saint than to the drug I had administered.

Another interesting case came under my notice at Lahore. A servant, a punkah puller of the *mehtar* caste, was reported dying in an out-office in my compound. The man had been at work only a few hours before. I went down to see him and found him stretched out on a low cot with his eyes shut. His weeping wife and son were endeavoring to rouse him, but he could not or would not move or give any sign of consciousness. A dose of brandy and water put into his mouth by spoonfuls, followed after a little while by a strong cup of tea, brought him round. On questioning him as to the nature and causes of his illness, he asserted that a Syad took possession of him every now and then and was persecuting him on account of the nonfulfillment of certain vows. It appeared that three or four months previously his wife was very ill, and while sitting beside her with some members of the family and a few visitors, the spirit of the Syad took possession of him. He began to be violently agitated, and then spoke, not in his own person but in that of the spirit that possessed him. He talked about many things, and in his discourse predicted that the sick woman, his wife, would die within a week. This prediction uttered in her hearing so alarmed her that she begged piteously for life, promising if she were spared to offer five goats and five cocks on the Syad's grave. She did not die and did not fulfill her vow, so the angry Syad was now victimizing the husband, presumably as the responsible head of the house.

Possession by the Living

(India)

I have a friend at R———, a Parsi, a shopkeeper and a merchant. He has a son, P———, about twenty years old, a nice young man, but physically weak, who was nearly for a year subject to wild ravings and fits, which his father, a man of sound common sense, at first attributed to hysteria. No medicine could cure him, and the boy became more and more violent, and his father assures me that in his fits he would talk in purer Hindustani than in his sober moments; that he was forced to suspect at length, much against his will, that there was something uncanny about it. He took him to his native place, E———, not far from Surat, in Gujarat, and consulted an exorcisist Brahman who was sent for from Surat. It is one of the most interesting features in this remarkable case that on the first occasion after the arrival of the Brahman, P———, or rather his control, in a violent fit eyed a pot of mesmerized water that the Brahman had

From: Adolphe d'Assier, *Posthumous Humanity: A Study of Phantoms* (with an appendix of beliefs current in India) (London: George Redway, 1887).

prepared beforehand, yelled in a highly excited manner, and said that there was fire issuing from the pot and the lambent flames were striking on him with deadly effect. Evidently, he could see the antagonistic aura of the exorcisist issuing from the pot. In accordance with the Brahman's instructions, the father rubbed a small quantity of the water on his chest, and P——— got relief. His father consulted many others known as exorcisist, but P——— failed to get permanent relief from the vampire. At length his father was advised to go to R——— with his son and consult a Sanyasi there. This holy man gave P——— a string, evidently full of his pure magnetism, to be tied around his arm. By all accounts, as far as I know, P——— is quite well now.

The control in this case was very often asked to leave the patient and not to worry him any longer. When matters had grown very serious, his father, being inquisitive and desirous of studying his case thoroughly, induced him to say who he really was. After some trouble a very strange revelation was made. The control said that he was a beggar at M——— and was employed by the wife of a rival shopkeeper to annoy R——— in some way or other by his magical arts, and that he had chosen his favorite son as a victim. On being reminded that P——— had often shown him favors by giving him food and money, and that his conduct toward him was very ungrateful, the controlling sorcerer, evil and mean as he evidently was, did not seem in any way moved by his appeals. He gave further proofs of his identity, and it was found that the sorcerer was then in the land of the living and not dead. The father was advised not to speak to the man "in flesh and blood," and, for all I know, he has never spoken to him about his unwelcome and objectionable visits to his son.

The Monk inside the Nobleman

(China)

A Buddhist monk in Ch'ang-ts'ing (in Shantung), named So-and-so, had reached a high and pure stage in the way to perfection, so that although he was over eighty years old, he had still a strong constitution. One day he sank to the ground. As he did not rise, the monks of the convent ran out to help him up, but he was dead. He remained unconscious of his death, and his soul (*hwun*) soared away toward the Honan frontiers.

Here at that time, there lived a nobleman of old descent. At the head of some ten riders he was hunting for hares with tamed falcons, when his horse stumbled. He fell to the ground and expired. The soul of the monk, happening to be just then on the spot, united itself so firmly to the body of the nobleman that it gradually revived. The servants ran to their master to ask him how he felt, but he gazed at them with staring eyes and asked, "How did I come here?" Then they helped him home. At the gate, the women with powdered faces and eyebrows painted green flocked around to see him and asked how he was. But greatly alarmed, he said, "I am a Buddhist monk. Why do you come here?" The family thought that he was talking nonsense and conjointly grasped his ears to wake him, and the monk, unable to explain the matter even to himself, merely closed his eyes and could not say a word.

They gave him rice to eat, and he took it, but spirits and meat he refused. And at night he slept quite alone, without accepting the services of his wife and concubines. When some days had passed, it occurred to him to take a walk. Everybody was glad of this. He passed through the gate and halted a little while, and there the servants were, rushing forth in a disorderly mass with their cashbooks and grain

From: Jan J. de Groot, *Religious Systems of China*, vol. 4, book 2, part 1 (Leide: E. J. Brill, 1907).

accounts, entreating him all at once to settle their accounts. But the nobleman roundly excused himself because of his illness and fatigue and asked whether they knew the Ch'ang-ts'ing district in Shantung. They conjointly answered they did. "I feel so concerned about those I left there unprotected," he went on to say, "I want to go and see them. Forthwith prepare my luggage." They objected with one voice that newly recovered patients ought not to travel so far, but he did not heed their advice, and next day they set out.

At Ch'ang-ts'ing he found everything as it was before, so he had not to trouble himself with asking the way. They reached the convent. The brethren, seeing so noble a visitor come, came up with humble bows and with marks of great respect. He asked them whether the old monk was gone.

"Our teacher has lately departed this life," they said.

He asked where his tomb was and they all took him to the spot—an insulated tumulus of three feet of earth, which the weeds had not yet had time to overgrow. None of the monks understood what he wanted there.

On ordering his men to bring out the horses to start for home, he spoke to the monks in these terms: "Your teacher was a monk living in accordance with the commandments. You must preserve carefully the wet touches of his hands which he has left behind [his personal effects] and not let them be damaged or lost."

They all exclaimed aye, aye; and he departed.

On coming home, he sat down motionless and as straight as a tree, with a heart of ashes. Not in the least did he care for his domestic concerns. A few months thus passed by, and then he left the house, ran away, and traveled straight to his old convent. "I am your teacher," he said to the brethren, but they thought he was telling stories and looking at one another, burst out into laughter. But as he related to them whence the soul came that reanimated his present body, and also what he did in his life, they believed him, finding everything consonant with the facts. They let him occupy his former bed, and served him as they used to do before. On this, the family of the nobleman frequently came with carriages and horses to implore him wailingly to go with them, but he did not even deign to look at them. And when, after more than a year, his consort dispatched her servants with multifarious presents, he refused to take any metal or silk, accepting nothing but a linen gown. Sometimes his friends visited his residence to pay him their respects, but as soon as he saw them he sank into silence and earnest devotion. He was then just thirty years old, but he could tell of things that had occurred more than eighty years before.

The Curse of the Rejected Lover

(India)

O
n one occasion there came to my knowledge the case of a woman who attributed her illness (a severe hemorrhage) to the magic arts of a fellow servant. According to her story, the man concerned had made improper advances to her, and on her repulsing him, he vowed vengeance against her. A few days after this she got ill and found out that her enemy, as we may now call him, had gone to a well with a male companion; that they had carried with them a lemon, which they cut in half, and repeating some spells, squeezed out the juice of the fruit into the well, accompanying the act with the expression of a wish that the blood of So-and-so (naming her) might pour out as the juice had just oozed out of the lemon under the pressure of their hands. The curse, of course, had its effect, and the unfortunate woman was a miserable sufferer for her virtuous conduct. It only remains to be added that the hapless woman learned these details from the wife of the man who aided her enemy and quondam lover in carrying out the mischievous and wicked rites which cost her so dear.

From: John Campbell Oman, *Cults, Customs, and Superstitions of India* (London: T. Fisher Unwin, 1908).

Ceremony to Drive Away the God of Accidents

(Japan)

*S*arak is a word meaning "accidental death," and Sarak Kamui appears to be a god or demon who presides over accidents. Its evil deeds are not confined exclusively to the fresh waters, but it is also thought to be the cause of all land accidents.

When an accidental death has taken place on shore, either from drowning or otherwise, the Ainu, as soon as they find it out, proceed to perform a certain ceremony frequently called *Sarak Kamui*. The ceremony is as follows: The inevitable sake is of course first procured by the relatives of the victim of Sarak Kamui. Then messengers are sent around to the different villages to invite the men and women to join in the ceremony. The men bring their swords or long knives with them and the women their headgear. On arriving at the appointed hut, the chiefs of the people assembled proceed to chant their dirges and worship the fire god. Then, after eating some cakes made of pounded millet and drinking a good proportion of sake, they all go out of doors in single file, the men leading. The men draw their swords or knives and hold them point upward in the right hand close to the shoulder, and then altogether they take a step with the left foot, at the same time stretching forward to the full extent the right hand with the sword and calling, as if with one voice, "*Wooi.*" Then the right foot is moved forward, the sword at the same time being drawn back and the "*wooi*" repeated. This is continued till the place of accident is reached. The women follow the men, and with disheveled hair and their headgear hanging over the shoulders, they continue to weep and howl during the whole ceremony. Arrived at the place of accident, a continual howling is kept up for some time, and the men strike hither and thither with their swords, thus supposing to drive away the evil

From: John Batchelor, "Items of Ainu Folk-Lore," *Journal of American Folk-Lore* 7 (1894): 15–44.

Sarak Kamui. This finished, the people return to the house of the deceased in the same order as they came forth, and, sad to say, feast, drink sake, and get intoxicated. The ceremony attending Sarak Kamui is properly called *Niwen-horobi*.

Divination of the Past

(Malaysia)

A local chief declared his power to read the past if only he could find the truthful child. In this he appeared to succeed, but when on the following day he came to disclose to me the results of his skill, he said that a difficulty had arisen, because just when the child (a little boy) was beginning to relate what he saw, he suddenly became unconscious, and it took the astrologer two hours to restore him to his normal state. All the mothers of tender-aged and possibly truthful children declined after this to lend their offspring for the ordeal.

My friend was not, however, at the end of his resources, and though only an amateur in divination, he undertook to try by other methods to find the culprit. For this purpose he asked me to give him the names of everyone in the house at the time the robbery was committed. I did so, and the next day he gave me one of those names as that of the thief. I asked how he had arrived at this knowledge. He described the method and consented to repeat the experiment in my presence. That afternoon I went with him to a small house belonging to his sister. Here I found the chief, his sister, and two men whom I did not recognize. We all sat in a very small room, the chief in the center with a copy of the Koran on a reading stand, near to him the two men opposite to each other, the sister against one wall, and I in a corner. A clean, new, unglazed earthenware bowl with a wide rim was produced. This was filled with water and a piece of fair white cotton cloth tied over the top, making a surface like that of a drum.

From: Walter William Skeat, *Malay Magic* (London: Macmillan & Co., 1900).

I was asked to write on a small piece of paper the name of each person present in the house when the robbery was committed and to fold each paper up so that all should be alike, and then to place one of the names on the cover of the vessel. I did so, and the proceedings began by each of the men placing the middle joint of the forefinger of his right hand under the rim of the bowl on opposite sides and so supporting it about six inches above the floor. The vessel being large and full of water was heavy, and the men supported the strain by resting their right elbows on their knees as they sat cross-legged on the floor and face-to-face. It was then that I selected one of the folded papers and placed it on the cover of the vessel. The chief read a page of the Koran and as nothing happened, he said that was not the name of the guilty person, and I changed the paper for another. This occurred four times, but at the fifth the reading had scarcely commenced when the bowl began to slowly turn around from left to right, the supporters letting their hands go around with it, until it twisted itself out of their fingers and fell on the floor with a considerable bang and a great spluttering of water through the thin cover. "That," said the chief, "is the name of the thief."

It was the name of the person already mentioned by him.

I did not, however, impart that piece of information to the company but went on to the end of my papers, nothing more happening.

I said I should like to try the test again, and as the chief at once consented we began afresh, and this time I put the name of the suspected person on first, and once more the vessel turned around and twisted itself out of the hands of the holders till it fell on the floor, and I was surprised it did not break. After trying a few more, I said I was satisfied, and the ordeal of the bowl was over. Then the chief asked me whose name had been on the vessel when it moved, and I told him. It was a curious coincidence certainly. I wrote the names in English, which no one could read; moreover, I was so placed that no one could see what I wrote, and they none of them attempted to do so. Then the papers were folded up so as to be all exactly alike; they were shuffled together, and I did not know one from the other till I myself looked inside. Each time I went from my corner and placed a name on the vessel already held on the fingers of its supporters. No one except I touched the papers, and no one but the chief ever spoke till the séance was over. I asked the men who held the bowl why they made it turn around at that particular moment, but they declared they had nothing to do with it and that the vessel twisted itself off their fingers against their inclination.

The name disclosed by this experiment was certainly that of the person whom there was most reason to suspect, but beyond that I learned nothing.

Exorcism by a Pansu

(Korea)

The performance of exorcism by a Pansu is described in *The Korea Review* as follows:

The Pansu comes into the presence of the afflicted and food is laid out as for a feast. The Pansu invites the various spirits to come and feast, such as the house spirit, the kitchen spirit, and the door spirit. He orders them to go and invite to the feast the evil spirit that has caused the disease, and if he will not come, to call upon the master spirit to compel him to come. When he arrives the Pansu bids him eat and then leave the place and cease to torment the patient. If he consents, the fight is over, but he probably will not submit so easily, in which case the Pansu gets out the book *Thoughts on the works of the Jade Emperor in Heaven* and chants a stave or two. The mystic power of the book paralyzes the imp, and he is seized and imprisoned in a stone bottle and securely corked down. In some cases he is able to burst the bottle, and then he will be invited again to a feast and subdued by the book. He is then put into a bottle, but this time the cork is made of peach wood which has a peculiar power over imps, and the bottle is beaten with peach twigs to reduce the imp to complete helplessness. The bottle is then delivered to a Mutang, and she is told to go in a certain direction, which will prevent the return of the imp, and bury

From: I. M. Casanowicz, *Paraphernalia of a Korean Sorceress in United States National Museum* (Washington, DC: U.S. Government Printing Office, 1916).

the bottle in the ground. The cure is now supposed to be complete.

The instruments of exorcism used by the Pansu are a drum, cymbals, a divination box, and a wand or wands.

Exorcism of Sundry Demons

(Japan)

I t is probable that the wearing of the short sword, *mamori katana*, the scabbard of which was covered with brocade, was considered a protection against evil spirits. Perhaps there is also a similar reason for the leaf coat of the *sennin* being made of leaves. I need not enter into the *oni yarai* ceremony, whereby evil spirits were thrown out of doors, nor into the detail of the *shimenawa*, or of the holly and sardine head charms. I may, however, remark that superstitious people are called to this day *gohei katsugi*, that is to say, "carriers of *gohei*."

When a man meets a s'Hitodama, he must tie a knot in the corner of the lower fold of his kimono (*shitamae*).

If the rice pan makes a noise, due to the presence of an Oni, it is only necessary to call the name of that devil "Renjo" to stop the trouble. Note the belief in the influence of the name.

A certain ghostly fire, called Tengu no Miyakashi, or Rojin no Hi, met with in the mountains of Kiso, between Shinano and Totomi, cannot be extinguished by means of water but with the skins of beasts, or better still, by putting one's *geta* on one's head, when it will disappear without doing any harm.

Kojin, the kitchen divinity, objects to pointed or sharp things being

From: Henri L. Joly, "Bakemono," *Transactions and Proceedings of the Japan Society* 9 (1909–11): 15–48.

put on the hearth, but if by misadventure one does place such a thing as a knife on the hearth, he can be appeased by the guilty party making a sort of trumpet of his hand, bowing to the fire and blowing through the hand.

The goblin of the latrines must be propitiated on New Year's Eve by saying *"Kambari Niudo ototoguisu,"* on entering the privy. This Bakemono is claled Kwatto, or Yuten hiki Taisatsu shogun. But the most usual proceeding to exorcise ghosts was of a religious character, such as the special service called *segaki,* the wearing of a charm, such as the figure of Buddha Tathagata, or of some paper obtained at a temple, suitably inscribed. Such papers were pasted on buildings to ward off the evil spirits. Further, the recital of the *Kyo,* or of the *Tathagata Sutra,* by a priest, or merely a number of invocations, *"Namu Amida Butsu,"* put the ghost to flight. We find, for instance, Genno Hosho exorcising the death stone Sessho Seki, and Yuten Shonin putting to rest the ghost of Kazane, and Mitsakuni Shonin that of O Kiku. The recital of the *Kyo* stops the wailings of the Futon of Tottori and the apparition of the old woman Tofu, seller of Hagi, who had hidden her money in a *kamado.*

The more expensive process of building a temple (*nanzenji*), and installing therein as an abbot the Chinese priest Fumon Mukwan in the thirteenth century, was an imperial way of laying the ghost of Higashiyama.

The *Wa Niudo,* or wheel of Hades, was a dreadful thing to meet, for it made one unconscious, and death followed shortly afterward, but one could ward against this calamity by pasting on one's door the inscription *"Kono Tokoro Shobo no Sato"* ("This is the birthplace of Shobo").

Sheer pluck and a straightforward appeal to the supposed chivalry of the spirit were the only weapons of Iga no Tsubone when she drove away the ghost of Kiyotaka Mitsutsune (another source, but theatrical, makes it the ghost of Fujiwara Nakanari, in the shape of a Tengu). The spirit continuously frightened people in the palace garden, so that she went one night alone on a verandah, carrying fireflies in a lantern, to await the ghost, whom she inquiringly addressed in verse:

> *Suzushi sa o*
> *Matsuki kaze ni,*
> *Wa surarete*

Tamoto ni Yadoru,
Yoha no tsuki kage.

"The pleasant coolness of the evening has vanished, which lent
    charm to the wind blowing in the pine branches.
Wherefore is there only the shadow of my sleeves left in the
    moonlight?"

The ghost explained that it was haunting the palace to obtain the
emperor's pardon for his misdeeds committed in early life, and he
disappeared, never to return.

As a parallel, we may mention the story in Chinese lore of Kikang,
one of the *Shichi ken jin,* in whose room a Bakemono appeared with a
tongue seven ells long. Kikang blew out his candle and merely said,
"Go away. I am not afraid of you, but your ugliness digusts me."

Shamans and Sorcerers

(Korea)

There are two classes of shamans, or sorcerers, in Korea: The
Pansu and the Mutang. They do not constitute an order, nor are
they linked by a common organization, but are nevertheless
practically recognized as a sort of priesthood, inasmuch as they
are the mediators and intercessors between the spirits and the people.
The word *Pansu* is composed of *pan,* "to decide," and *su,* "destiny,"
which designate the bearer of the name as a "fortune-teller." But this
describes the office of the Pansu only in part. *Mutang* is also made up
of two parts, *mu,* "to deceive," and *tang,* "company." The individual is
sometimes called *mu-nyu,* "deceiving woman." So that Mutang may
be rendered "deceiving crowd" or "bad lot." The office of the Pansu
is restricted to blind men, perhaps owing to the common belief among
primitive peoples that those who have been deprived of physical sight

From: I. M. Casanowicz, *Paraphernalia of a Korean Sorceress in United States National
Museum* (Washington, DC: U.S. Government Printing Office, 1916).

have been given an inner spiritual vision. The Mutang is always a woman, generally from the lower classes of bad repute, and her calling is considered the very lowest in the social scale.

While the Pansu is, as it were, born or made by dint of his loss of eyesight, the Mutang enters upon her office in consequence of a "supernatural call," consisting in the assurance of demoniacal possession, the demon being supposed to have become her double and to have superimposed his personality upon hers. The "possession" is often accompanied by hysterical and pathological symptoms. The spirit may seize any woman, maid or wife, rich or poor, plebeian or patrician, and compel her to serve him; and on receiving the "call of the spirit," a woman will break every tie of custom and relationship, leave home and family to become henceforth a social outcast, so that she is not even allowed to live within the city walls. But notwithstanding her low social status, her services are in constant demand. "In traveling through the country, the Mutang or sorceress is constantly to be seen going through the various musical and dancing performances in the midst of a crowd in front of a house where there is sickness." And at the close of the nineteenth century the fees annually paid in Korea to the sorcerers were estimated at $750,000.

The Pansu acts as master of the spirits, having gained by his potent formulas and ritual an ascendancy over them. By his spells he can direct them, drive them out, and even bury them. The Mutang is supposed to be able to influence them through her friendship with them. She has to pray to them and coax them to go. By her performances she puts herself *en rapport* with the spirits and is able to ascertain their will and to name the ransom for which they will release the victim who is under torment.

While in practice the functions of the Pansu and the Mutang largely overlap, so that at times the one may be called to perform the services of the other, theoretically they hold two distinct fields in the domain of the spirits, corresponding to their different attitudes to the spirits.

The services of the Pansu may be comprised under two general heads: (1) divination (*chum*) and (2) exorcism (*kyung*). The former occupies by far the larger part of his energies. In his capacity as fortune-teller and clairvoyant, he is consulted for all imaginable relations of life—whether, for instance, an offender will escape punishment or a deserving man will be rewarded; what will happen during the day, the week, the month, and up to the point of death;

what was one's condition in a former state of existence; how to recover a lost article; what is the condition of a distant friend or relation; whether a tree may be cut down or not (because of the spirit's inhabiting it); whether a dream that one has had augurs good or evil; when one is to marry in order to secure happiness; when a son will be born, whether a woman should give birth to a child in her own house or go to some other place until the child is born, and the like.

For obtaining his answers the Pansu employs three systems of divination: (1) dice boxes (*san-tong*, "number box"); (2) coins (*ton-jun*, "money divination"), and (3) Chinese characters (*chalk-chum*, "book divination").

For the dice-box divination, also called tortoise divination because the box was formerly in the shape of a tortoise box containing eight small metal rods or bamboo splinters must be arranged in order from one to eight notches. The Pansu makes three throws of one rod or splinter each, and from the combination of the notches on them he works out the answer to the question. In the money divination, three coins out of four which he holds in his hand are thrown in the same manner as in the preceeding method, and the combination of the characters on them yields the supposed answer. For the book divination (the highest form), he learns the hour, day, month, and year of the birth of the inquirer, and from the Chinese characters which depict these four dates, he determines the answer. The responses are given in an enigmatic poetical formula which is capable of a double meaning, like the Delphic oracles of yore.

More varied than the functions of the Pansu are the pacifications and propitiations, called *kauts* or *kuts*, performed by the Mutang. The kaut may be carried out either at the house of the patient or at the home of the Mutang, or at some shrine or temple, called *tang*, dedicated to some spirits, which are seen on the hillsides in Korea. If, as is occasionally the case, the Mutang belongs to a noble family, she is allowed by her family to ply her trade only in her own home. Those who require her services send the required fee and necessary offerings, and the ceremony is performed by the Mutang in her own house or at the tang.

Her equipment consists of a number of dresses, some of them very costly; a drum shaped like an hourglass, about four feet high; copper cymbals; a copper gong; a copper rod with small bells or tinklers suspended from it by copper chains; a pair of telescoping baskets;

strips of silk and paper banners which float around her as she dances; fans; umbrellas; wands; and images of men and animals.

The service of the Mutang most in demand is the healing of the sick. If a sick man believes that his distemper has been caused by a spirit, he sends to the Mutang to describe the symptoms and learn what spirit is doing the mischief. The Mutang may declare the name of the spirit without going to the patient's house or may say that she must see the patient first. On retaining her fee she names a "fortunate" day for the ceremony, which will be performed either at her house or shrine or at the patient's house, according to the seriousness of the ailment and the fee he can pay.

A performance of such a kaut at the house of the patient is described by Mrs. Bishop as follows:

In a hovel with an open door a man lay very ill. The space in front was matted and enclosed by low screens, within which were Korean tables loaded with rice cakes, boiled rice, stewed chicken, sprouted beans, and other delicacies. In this open space squatted three old women, two of whom beat large drums shaped like hourglasses, while the third clashed large cymbals. Facing them was the Mutang or sorceress, dressed in rose-pink silk with a buff gauze robe, with its sleeves trailing much on the ground. Over it pieces of paper resembling a shinto *gohei* decorated her hair, and a curious cap of buff gauze with red patches upon it completed the not inelegant costume. She carried a fan, but it was only used in one of the dances. She carried over her left shoulder a stick painted with bands of bright colors from which hung a gong which she beat with a similar stick, executing at the same time a slow rhythmic movement accompanied by a chant. From time to time one of the ancient drummers gathered on one plate pieces from the others and scattered them to the four winds for the spirits to eat, invoking them saying, "Do not trouble this house anymore, and we will again appease you by offerings." The exorcism lasted fourteen hours until four in the next morning, when the patient began to recover. . . . Mrs. Taylor adds:

I have witnessed several of these dances, and it appeared to me that the sorceress produced in herself a sort of ecstasy which increased in force until at length she sank on the ground utterly exhausted. I could not but feel that the banging of drums, and the clashing of cymbals wielded by her attendants together with the whirling motions and violent gestures of the Mutang herself, must at times, themselves, give the *coup de grâce* to the poor patient.

In case of smallpox (*kwe-yuk tasin*), the universal scourge of Korean childhood, the spirit who is supposed to have caused it is treated with the utmost respect. The parents do obeisance to the suffering child, which for the time being is inhabited by the spirit, and address it in honorific terms. On the appearance of the disease the Mutang is called to honor the arrival of the spirit with a feast and fitting ceremonial. Little or no work is done in the house in order not to disturb the "honorable guest." No member of the household may cut the hair, wear new clothes, sweep the house, or bring any goods into the house. No animal must be killed in the house, because if blood flows, it will make the patient scratch and cause his blood to flow. No washing or wallpapering must be undertaken, for this will cause the nose of the patient to be stopped up; and if there are neighbors whose children have not had the malady, they rest likewise lest, displeased with their want of respect, the spirit should deal harshly with them. On the thirteenth day from the appearance of the disease, when danger is supposed to be passed, the Mutang is again summoned, and a farewell banquet is given to the spirit. A miniature wooden horse, loaded with food and some coins and bedecked with a red umbrella and small flags, is placed upon the roof of the house. This outfit is provided for the spirit in taking his departure. The Mutang bids him farewell, asking him to deal kindly with the patient and the family, to let the sick fully recover without being badly marked.

The death of a Korean does not terminate his dependence on the ministrations of the Mutang. The spirit of the departed is believed to hover about the house for some time after leaving the body, having some last words to speak. The Mutang is required to serve as his mouthpiece for his valedictory. Food is set out and the baskets are scraped to summon the spirit, who then enters the Mutang and communicates through her to the family his last wishes, counsels, and exhortations. The members of the family have their cry and say their farewells, after which they fall to consuming the food. A more elaborate ceremony with never-wanting banquet, in connection with death, is performed by the Mutang at a shrine in honor of the judges or rulers of the netherworld to secure their goodwill for the departed.

The surviving members of the family need no less the services of the Mutang. The unclean spirits of death (as also of birth) have for the time being driven out the guardian spirits of the household, and the Mutang has to bring them back. Their whereabouts are found by means of a wand cut from a pine tree to the east of the house, which is set working by the spells of the Mutang, and by prayers and offerings they are induced to return to their place.

As public functionary, the Mutang comes into consideration in the triennial festival lasting three to four days, which is observed to propitiate the tutelary spirit of the locality and to obtain his favor during the coming three years.

Divination is practiced by the Mutang by means of chimes and rice. The latter consists of throwing down some grains of rice on a table and noting the resulting combination. The divining chime is a hazel wand with a circle of tiny bells at one end, which the Mutang shakes violently, and in the din thus created she hears the answer of the spirit.

Fijian Witchcraft

(Fiji)

My brother is not a believer in the supernatural. Only on rare occasions can he be induced to speak of those things which he has seen for himself, and for which he has no reasonable explanation to offer. He has all the Briton's dislike for "tall stories," and he keeps silence rather than permit the average man whom he meets to dub him one of the Munchausen type of travelers. But to me, sometimes, he will speak of Fiji and the natives, for whom he has a genuine affection and admiration, and more rarely he will tell of strange and weird happenings.

From: Loloma (pseud.), "Fijian Witchcraft," *Occult Review* 28 (1918): 213–14.

He has told me of a brilliant, sunny day, when the blue sky was reflected in the bluer sea below, when a little schooner lay tossing at anchor near a great coral reef. Two white men, wearied with the monotony of the schooner's decks, the everlasting smell of coconut oil, and the endless warfare against the giant cockroaches which infest all vessels engaged in carrying coconut and coir, had rowed across to the reef. On the far side they found a small group of Fijians, gathered behind an old, old native, who crooned in a quavering voice a strange haunting tune. He sat at the edge of the water, and his weird song mingled with the lap-lapping of waves against the coral. At a little distance, motionless in the water, were seven huge sharks. For some time he sang, the sharks remaining apparently attentive listeners. Then he finished his song on a long wailing note, and rose. Instantly the monsters swirled through the water and disappeared. Politely, as is their custom, the Fijians bade farewell to the white men and departed in their fishing canoe. Whether the rite had been for the obtaining of good luck in the fishing or was a purely religious rite—some form of ancestor worship—those white men never knew. But they will never forget the eerie feeling which possessed them as those man-eating sharks lay apparently charmed by the thin notes of an old man's voice.

This is another tale of Fiji, but it is not a pretty story. In an inland village there lived a white man—one of those derelicts who drift to the South Seas to hide from all those who once knew them. This man was a university man and had been a doctor. One day, maddened by drink, he shamefully ill-treated the little Samoan girl with whom he lived. My brother noticed that his natives seemed restless and excited, and inquired what was wrong. He was told that early that morning the white man had beaten S——, his native wife. My brother lived three days' journey from the erstwhile doctor, but he knew enough of the strange system of bush telegraphy that exists in Fiji to make no comment on the rapidity with which the news had reached his people.

Late in the afternoon my brother's natives betook themselves to the bush. He heard afterward that with many rites and to the chanting of strange songs they had buried some threads of the white man's clothing in a split bamboo stick. It was perhaps a week afterward that my brother learned that the woman beater had been seized with paralysis at the day and the hour when unseen guardians were called upon to avenge the Samoan girl. That bamboo stick was dug up and turned around and reburied more than once, and on each occasion that it was touched, another stroke of paralysis stole the use from limbs and tongue. The unfortunate man lingered for a few weeks, speechless and helpless, until a final ceremony took place in the mysterious bush and the tortured spirit left the broken body.

It is a beautiful place, is Fiji, but there is something evil, something mysterious and terrifying, hidden beneath the smiling playful exterior.

Makutu, or Witchcraft

(New Zealand)

Makutu, or witchcraft, was a most serious item to the Maori, and indeed it still exists among all the tribes. Their minds were ever saturated with superstition, and many of the *tohunga* (priests) and others were objects of special dread on account of their powers to bewitch and thus cause death.

The most efficacious way in which to slay a person by witchcraft was to take the *hau* of such person. The hau is the very essence of life. It is an essence or ichor, invisible, intangible as ordinary matter, although it can be conveyed by the hand. In fact, it *is* the life of the person; the body is merely an abode for the hau, and should the latter be taken by witchcraft, the body perishes at once or at least very shortly thereafter. It is distinct from the *wairua*, which is the actual body. It is the wairua that leaves the body when a person dreams and goes wandering afield. A Maori will say, "I went to the Reinga [Hades, the spirit land] last night." That is, he dreamed, while his wairua went to Reinga. At death the wairua leaves the body and descends to the Reinga, or underworld, or in some cases it may remain in this world as a *kehua* or *whakahaehae* (ghost), whose pride and pleasure it is to scare travelers by night and utter strange sounds around houses

From: Elsdon Best, "Makutu or Maori Magic," *American Antiquarian and Oriental Journal* 21 (January–November 1899): 41–45.

whose inmates fear these ghostly visitations. The hau is also distinct from the *mauri* of a person, which is the spark or breath of life, or as one authority describes it, "the physical life principle, the hau being the intellecutal spirit." If I startle a man, he will exclaim, *"E tama! ka oho-mauri ahau i a koe"* (You made the breath of life leap up within me). The human mauri must not be confounded with the mauri of a forest or a canoe, this latter being a talisman to protect such forest or canoe from designing enemies.

It will thus be seen that man is possessed of three different and distinct essences or spirits, according to the Maori, besides his earthly body. In this regard he went one better than the ancient Egyptian who had but two such spirits—the *ka,* which much resembled the Maori wairua, and a still more subtle essence which at death went to the gods and was judged by Osiris.

It was the hau which was acted upon in the matter of witchcraft. Any priest or person possessed of this power could destroy life in any other person, could he but obtain a portion of the hair, clothing, or spittle of such person. This object, having been in contact with the body of the doomed man, was used as a medium over which the incantations to destroy life were repeated; such incantations would destroy the hau after which the body naturally perished. This medium taken was termed a *hohona* (*ohonga* among other tribes) and was not the real hau of a person but the *ahua* (semblance) of the hau.

Having become possessed of such a medium, the prist then fashions of loose earth a figure of human form, in which figure he makes a small hole. Here the hohona is deposited and by his potent incantations the priest causes the wairua of the doomed person to enter this hole, in which it is destroyed by *karakia* (incantation) termed *kopani.* The spirit as it enters the hole (*rua-iti*) may be invisible or it may be in the form of a fly (*ugaro*).

Should I have lost a pig by theft, I at once go to the tohunga who, by repeating a certain spell, will cause the wairua of the thief to come and stand before him, but it will be visible to him only. He will then say, "There is the thief. It is such a person." I then go and obtain some article such as the cord by which he led the pig away, and this cord will serve as a destroying medium at the rua-iti of the tohunga. He will hold one end of the cord in his hand and allow the other to hang down into the hole in the dummy figure. He then repeats a spell to cause the wairua of the thief to descend the cord into the pit of death.

It must be borne in mind that every such spell to cause death has its counterspell, and should I become aware that some person was attempting my life by means of the deadly rua-iti, I at once contrive to obtain possession of some article belonging to the man who I know is bewitching me—his *kawe* or swag straps, or his picket rope or a portion thereof. This object I then smear with blood obtained from an incision in my left side or left shoulder, after which I kindle a fire and burn it, repeating at the same time the appropriate *karakia* to nullify or ward off the spell of my enemy. This being a sacred ceremony, I am necessarily *tapu* while performing the same and must therefore obtain the services of a ruwahine (wise woman, or tapu, during ceremony) to take the tapu off (i.e., to *whakanou*, or make common my person, clothing, etc.). The ruwahine employed to take the tapu off a person, war party, or house is an elderly woman either childless or past the age of childbearing. A single potato or *kumara* (sweet potato) is roasted at the sacred fire and eaten by the ruwahine, and the appropriate karakia being repeated, the tapu is lifted and the person or house is *noa* (common or free of tapu). Another way in which to take the tapu off is to place the aforesaid kumara beneath the threshold of my house and get the ruwahine to step over that threshold, which is the most sacred part of a house.

Another mode of makutu is by the sacred fire known as the *ahi-whakaene*. This fire is kindled by the tohunga makuta (wizard-priest) as he repeats the korakia known as *hika ahi* (fire generating). He then recites his spell to slay his adversary, or should he merely wish to reform some person from evil courses, he will repeat the *ka-mahunu*, a spell that will cause the culprit to be utterly ashamed of his sins and desirous of leading a better life.

Or should a man, while traversing some trail, encounter a lizard (a fearful omen), he will first kill it and then get a ruwahine to step over it to avert the evil omen. But as he knows full well that the lizard has been sent by some enemy to work him grievous harm, he proceeds to cut the hapless reptile into diverse pieces, over which the priest performs the *whakautu-utu* ceremony to cause the evil fate to recoil upon the sender of the lizard. Taking up one of the pieces of the lizard, he repeats, "To such and such *hapu* [subtribe]," and reciting a spell, casts the piece into the ahi-whakaene. This is repeated until all the pieces are in the fire, a different subtribe being mentioned each time, after which a lock of hair is cut from the head of the man who encountered the lizard, which hair is also cast into the sacred fire. Yet a little while and the horrors of the ahi-whakaene will descend upon those who sought to slay a distant foe by means of the fearsome lizard, which represents death and ever chills the soul of man.

The *Wero-ugereugere* is an incantation that causes the person against whom it is directed to be assailed by the *ugereugere*, a loathsome disease resembling leprosy and which formerly existed among the Taupo tribes.

Other forms of makutu, such as the *ahi-matiti*, caused a person to become mentally deranged and to go about clutching at the air and committing other foolish actions.

If a man possesses a good reliable Atua (familiar spirit, god), it will not fail to warn him should anyone be working him an injury by makutu. Or his wairua will discover the fact as it wanders forth while the body sleeps and so return and warn him. Thus it is dangerous to suddenly awaken a sleeping person, for his wairua may be out rambling around the world. Still it is a nimble spirit, that wairua, and when the sleeping body awakens, the wairua is back at once. At such a time the sleeper awakens with a start; that is, with *oho mauri*—the startling of the breath of life within the body, the return of the wairua to its earthly body—it is back in an instant.

The rua-iti and other works of makutu are always conducted in the evening or at dawn when it is desired to bring the wairua of a person before the magician, for the reason that the spirit only leaves the body at night; during the daytime the person is naturally presumed to be awake and therefore his wairua is safe within his body.

When a person arises from a seat, he leaves a certain amount of his hau adhering to the seat. He will therefore, as he rises, reach back his left hand and scoop up his hau lest it be taken by some wizard to work him bodily harm. In like manner as a person walks he leaves the *manea*, or hau of his footsteps, adhering to his tracks. This also can be taken by a wizard and used as a means of slaying the witless traveler. Thus in traveling through a hostile country, it is advisable to walk in the water as much as possible, inasmuch as a person's manea does not adhere to water.

The *Matakai* is an incantation to slay a person while he is in the act of eating. Should you meet a wizard (tohunga makutu) in your travels, and should you be carrying food, do not give such food to the wizard or he will use it as ohonga and so take your hau and destroy you.

Such are some of the methods of destroying man by witchcraft, but as remarked, such spells can be warded off if the afflicted person possesses the requisite knowledge, and if his karakia have sufficient *mana* (power). One method of averting the makutu is by tying strips of *harakeke* (*Phormium tenare*) around the limbs and body and then reciting a certain karakia known as the *Matapuru*.

But the most effective way to prevent the spells of sorcerers from having any harmful effect is to ensure the safety of the hau by means of protecting its ahua, or semblance. This is a case of hair splitting in the "black art" with a vengeance inasmuch as the semblance or essence of the hau must necessarily be the semblance (ahua) of an intangible spirit (i.e., the essence of an essence). This points to a high plane of metaphysical reasoning, seldom, I fancy, met with in a neolithic people, but a subject all too long to enter on here.

The *ahurewa* is an emblem of the gods (Atua). It is simply a carved peg stuck in the ground at the village *tuahu*, or sacred place. This ahurewa is a toronga atua (i.e., a medium of divination). Now the ahua, or semblance of a man's hau, may be taken by the priest and conveyed to the ahurewa, where it is planted in the ahurewa, absorbed by that useful article. It is of course the karakia of the priest that causes this ahua to enter the ahurewa, and once established there, the person whose hau it represents is safe from all attacks of witchcraft. The hau cannot now be affected by makutu for the reason that its essence is protected.

Such are some of the leading items concerning witchcraft as practiced and believed in by the ancient Maori of New Zealand, but it would require many pages to thoroughly describe the innumerable customs, ceremonies, and beliefs connected with Polynesian makutu, which in its palmy days rose to the level of a fine art.

An Introduction to Genies

(Malaysia)

The jinns or genies, generally speaking, form a very extensive class of quite subordinate divinities, godlings, or spirits, whose place in Malay mythology is clearly due, whether directly or indirectly, to Muhammadan influences but who may be most conveniently treated here as affording a sort of connecting link between gods and ghosts. There has, it would appear, been a strong tendency on the part of the Malays to identify these imported spirits with the spirits of their older (Hindu) religion, but the only genie who really rises to the level of one of the great Hindu divinities is the Black King of the Genies (Sang Gala Raja, or Sa-Raja Jinn), who appears at times a manifestation of Shiva Batara Guru, who is confounded with the destructive side of Shiva (i.e., Kali). This at least would appear to be the only theory on which we could explain the use of many of the epithets or attributes assigned to the King of the Genies, who is at one time called "the one and only God," at another "Bentara (i.e., Batara) Guru, the genie that was from the beginning," and at another "the Land Demon, the Black Batara Guru," etc.

The following is a description of this, the mightiest of the genies:

> Peace be with you!
> Ho, Black Genie with the black liver,
> Black heart and black lungs,
> Black spleen and tusklike teeth,
> Scarlet breast and body hairs inverted,
> And with only a single bone.

So far as can be made out from the meager evidence obtainable, the spirit thus described is identifiable with the Black King of the Genies, who dwells in the heart of the earth and whose bride, Sang Gadin (or

From: Walter William Skeat, *Malay Magic* (London: Macmillan & Co., 1900).

Gading), presented him with seven strapping black genies as children.

Altogether there are 190 of these (black?) genies—more strictly, perhaps 193, which coincides curiously with the number of "mischiefs" (Badi), which reside in all living things. The resemblance, I may add, does not end here; for though the genies *may* do good and the Badi do not, both are considered able to do infinite harm to mortals, and both make choice of the same kind of dwelling places, such as hollows in the hills, solitary patches of primeval forest, dead parasites on trees, etc.

As to the origin of these genies, one magician told me that all jinns came from the country Ban Ujan, which may possibly be Persia. Other magicians, however, variously derive them from the dissolution of various parts of the anatomy of the great snake Sakatimuna, of the First Great Failure to make man's image (at the creation of man); from the drops of blood which spurted up to heaven when the first twins, Abel and Cain (in the Malay version, Habil and Kabil) bit their thumbs; from the big coconut monkey or baboon *(berok besar)*, and so on.

The theory already mentioned, *viz.* that the Black King of the Genies gradually came to be identified with Kali and later came gradually to be established as a separate personality, appears to be the only one which will satisfactorily explain the relations subsisting between the Black and White Genies who are on the one hand distinctly declared to be brothers, while the White Genie is in another passage declared to be Maharaja Deva or Mahadeva, which latter is, as we have already seen, a special name of Shiva.

This White Genie is said to have sprung, by one account, from the blood drops which fell on the ground when Habil and Kabil bit their thumbs; by another, from the irises of the snake Sakatimuna's eyes *(benih mata Sakatimuna)*, and is sometimes confused with the white divinity *('Toh Mambang Puteh)*, who lives in the sun.

The name of his wife is not mentioned, as it is in the case of the Black Genie, but the names of three of the children have been preserved, and they are Tanjak Malim Kaya, Pari Lang (lit., kitelike, i.e., "winged" skate), and Bintang Sutan (or Star of Sutan).

On the whole, I may say that the White Genie is very seldom mentioned in comparison with the Black Genie, and that whereas absolutely no harm, so far as I can find out, is recorded of him, he is, on the other hand, appealed to for protection by his worshippers.

A very curious subdivision of genies into faithful (Jinn Islam) and infidel (Jinn Kafir) is occasionally met with, and it is said, moreover, that genies (it is to be hoped orthodox ones) may be sometimes *bought* at Mecca from the Sheikh Jinn (headman of genies) at prices varying from $90 to $100 apiece.

Besides these subdivisions, certain genies are sometimes specifically connected with special objects or ideas. Thus there are the Genies of the Royal Musical Instruments (Jinn Nemfiri, or Lempiri, Gendang, and Naubat), who are sometimes identified with the Genies of the State (Jinn Karaja'an), and the Genies of the Royal Weapons (Jinn Sembuana), both of which classes of genie are held able to strike men dead. The only other genie that I would here especially mention is the Jinn 'Afrit (sometimes called Jinn Rafrit), from whom the white man (a designation which is often especially used in the peninsula as a synonym for Englishman) is sometimes said to have sprung, but who belongs in Arabian mythology to a higher class than the mere genies.

Before leaving the subject of genies, I must, however, point out the extremely common juxtaposition of the Arabic word *jinn* and the Malay *jembalang*. From the frequency with which this juxtaposition occurs, and from the fact that the two appear to be used largely as convertible terms, we might expect to find that *jinn* and *jembalang* were mere synonyms, both applicable to similar classes of spirits. The process is not quite complete, however, as although the expression *Jembalang Tunggal* (the only Jembalang) is found as well as *Jinn Tunggal,* the higher honorific Sang Raja or Sa-Raja is never, so far as I am aware, prefixed to the word *jembalang,* though it is frequently prefixed to *jinn*. Of the other members of the Malay hierarchy who owe their introduction to Muhammadan influences, the only ones of importance are angels (Mala'ikat), prophets (Nabi), and headmen (Sheikh).

The Fakir's Personal Jinn

(India)

A holy Muslim fakir who enjoyed a considerable local reputation told me of his own experiences with a jinn. The jinn, in human form, used to visit him but always came with a green shade over his eyes, as if suffering from sore eyes. He represented himself as a devotee who, attracted by the fame of my informant, had come to sit at his feet. He was assiduous in his attentions and one day asked my friend if he knew who he was. On receiving a reply to the effect that the fakir knew nothing about him beyond what he had himself stated, he said he was in reality a jinn. My friend received the statement with incredulity.

Not long after this, being disturbed in his devotions by the noisy chattering of two starlings, my informant asked his disciple, the jinn, to drive them away, when what to his surprise he found the pretended devotee put forth his hand and caught the birds although they were ten or twelve feet above his head. Another time the jinn, to oblige him, caught a young fox by simply putting out his foot and placing it upon its neck. The jinn continued to wear the green shade, because he wished to escape being recognized by that well-known peculiarity of jinns, their inability to wink.

During his sojourn with the fakir, the jinn fell out with one of the persons, a *chaprasi* who was in the habit of visiting the holy man, and having been abused by his adversary, caused the death of his children by literally passing into the poor fellow's house, through closed doors, and strangling his unoffending infants. The mother, in great distress, came and complained to the fakir about the cruel wrong she had suffered. The holy man suggested that she should go for redress to the law courts, but she explained that it was a case of magic and not one

From: John Campbell Oman, *Cults, Customs, and Superstitions of India* (London: T. Fisher Unwin, 1908).

with which the magistrates could deal. On this the fakir reproved the jinn and desired him to discontinue his visits, but the jinn promised better behavior in future and, to make amends for the murder he had committed, promised to give the object of his anger—the father of the strangled babes—whatever he asked for, provided he never told anyone how he came by it.

The aggrieved father looked upon this as *une mauvaise plaisanterie,* but one day being in sore need of four rupees, he held out his cloth and called upon the jinn to fulfill his promise. Immediately four rupees fell into his cloth. After this he asked for several other things and received them, but one of the prying women of his household, having found out how the money came, made a boast of it to some of her friends. The spell was broken. Nothing more was ever received, and the jinn, enraged at his secret having been made public, destroyed two more members of the chaprasi's family. At the fakir's very urgent and positive request, the jinn at length made himself scarce. Every word of this wonderful story the holy fakir assured me was absolutely true.

The Two Wives and the Witch

(Philippines)

There was once a man who had a wife that was not pretty. He became tired of looking at her, and so went away and married another wife.

His first wife was in great sorrow and wept every day. One day as she was crying by the well, where she had gone for water, a woman asked her, "Why are you weeping?"

From: Berton L. Maxfield and W. H. Millington, "Visayan Folk-Tales: 1," *Journal of American Folk-Lore* 19 (1906): 97–112.

The wife answered, "Because my husband has left me and gone to live with another wife."

"Why?" said the witch, for that is what the woman was.

"Because I have not a pretty face," answered the wife.

While she was talking, the witch touched the wife's face, and then she said, "I cannot stay here any longer," and went off.

When the wife reached home, she looked in the glass and saw that her face had been changed until it was the most beautiful in the town. Very soon a rumor spread through the town that in such and such a house there was living a very beautiful woman. Many young men went to see the pretty woman, and all were pleased with her beauty.

The bad husband went also. He was astonished that his wife was not at home and that a pretty woman was living there alone. He bowed to the lady and avowed his love. The lady at first refused to believe him and said, "If you will leave the woman who is now your wife and come to live with me right along, I will take you for my husband." The man agreed and went to live with the pretty woman.

The other woman was very angry when she heard the news, for it was reported that the pretty woman was the man's first wife, who had been changed by a witch. She determined to try what the witch could do for her and went to get water at the same well.

The witch appeared and asked, "Why are you weeping, my good woman?" The woman told her that her husband had gone away to live with the pretty woman. As she was speaking, the witch touched her face and said, "Go home, my good woman, and do not weep, for your husband will come very soon to see you."

When she heard this, she ran home as fast as she could. All the people whom she met on the road were afraid of her, because she was so ugly. Her nose was about two feet long, her ears looked like large handkerchiefs, and her eyes were as big as saucers. Nobody recognized her, not even her mother. All were afraid of such a creature. When she saw in the glass how ugly she was, she refused to eat, and in a few days she died.

The Fakir and the Carpet

(India)

Some years ago, a little pale-faced, blonde-haired, shy-eyed country parson's daughter, whom we will call Lucy Lansbury (as I am not at liberty to mention her real name) married an Indian civilian a good deal older than herself and went straight away with him from her "dead-alive" Devonshire village to the fascinating and mysterious East.

India, that land of strange folk and curious happenings, seemed from the first a more than ordinarily agitating and bewildering kind of place to shy nervous little Lucy, and her ultrasensitiveness, oftentimes degenerating into absolute repugnance toward sights, sounds, and conditions that experienced Anglo-Indians take as a matter of course, irritated her husband not a little, though he hoped in time she would grow more accustomed to her new surroundings.

The following strange occurrence, which happened soon after her marriage, was related word for word by Lucy herself, and even now she can scarcely mention India without a shudder.

Their long sea journey over, the newlywed couple had made their way upward from the plains by a variety of roads and modes of locomotion—train, palanquin, or horseback—to Hugh Lansbury's comfortably furnished bungalow situated at the northern and more civilized end of his large and decidedly scattered "district," having miles of virgin jungle and forest upon the one side and a vast stretch of sandy plain upon the other.

"All the same, my dear, the place isn't quite so drear and desolate as it looks," remarked Hugh to his wife. "Neripur, though that's only a little station, is within driving distance more or less, and there are one or two planters and their wives nearby who are quite pleasant and sociable people. The bungalow likewise isn't half a bad little abode—I've had it redecorated throughout by the best firm in Calcutta," he added wistfully, "while as for the gardens, not even your well-beloved one at the rectory at home can show a finer stock of flowers."

From: Gerda M. Calmady-Hamlyn, "The Fakir and the Carpet: An Indian Story," *Occult Review* 29 (1919): 213–18.

To all of which suggestions Lucy, who was not only a born gardener but a proud and delighted little homemaker as well, most cordially agreed.

Yet, at that very critical moment, when she and her husband drove in through the gates of Bon Repos and caught their first glimpse of its verdant and flowery splendor, Fate held a new and totally unforeseen terror in store for the commissioner's young bride.

Once within the drive, the newly arrived pair dismissed both syce and dogcart, preferring to walk up to the house, when out of the grass at their very feet rose a lean and repulsive figure, stark naked save for a filthy loincloth wrapped around its emaciated thighs, face, and shoulders half shrouded amidst a mass of shaggy matted hair, and nails so long they reminded Lucy of nothing so much as a bird of prey's cruelest talons—while in one bony hand it jingled a brazen bowl, presumably for alms. The entire apparition seemed more like some nightmare figure of dreamland than a sentient human being as it sprang from its lair in the grass and began murmuring and mouthing mysterious prayers or incantations that to the Devonshire rector's scared little daughter appeared wholly unintelligible.

Overcome with terror and surprise, and no longer able to control herself, she gave vent to a wild scream, covering her face with her hands. Hugh Lansbury—cut-and-dried Anglo-Indian as he was—felt seriously annoyed by such behavior, and he jerked Lucy's elbow sharply.

"Really, my dear," he whispered, "you must not give way to such absurd impulses. Try to control yourself, my child, and get over your fear and dislike of these brown people—they are quite harmless, I assure you. As for that ancient fakir there, though I allow that he is neither handsome nor what one would call exactly a 'drawing room ornament,' he won't dream of hurting you, if you on your part leave him and his eccentricities alone."

"Come hither, Rami Bux," cried Hugh in fluent Hindustani. "I and my memsahib here would bestow on you willing baksheesh, and you in turn should invoke the gods for our welfare on this, our homecoming day!" In response to which greeting the ancient mendicant aforesaid, with more strange whines and mutterings, pushed forward his bowl, and a shower of small coins from the commissioner's pocket fell into it.

"I generally give the old fellow a donation of some sort when I pass through the gate and he happens to be seated in his customary place outside that queer little hut he has built for himself under my biggest peepul tree, and no doubt he expresses his gratitude, in true oriental fashion, by calling down blessings on my devoted head. All the same, if you *don't* fancy, and wish to avoid him altogether, my dear," added Hugh Lansbury to his wife as they turned toward the rose-embowered drive, "you must just take exercise in other parts of the grounds, that's all. The old fellow never moves away from that particular pet spot of his, nor would he ever forgive me if I shifted him."

"I see, dear Hugh," replied Lucy penitently. "I'll try not to be so silly another time."

Then, almost immediately, she gripped her husband's arm in a frenzy of silent terror, for the aged fakir, who up to that moment had kept the rheumy eyelids half closed across his bleared eyes, now opened them to their fullest extent and shot a glance toward Lucy, the like of which she will never forget, for it seemed to pierce into her very soul, to hold her in a horrible thrall, dominating all her mentality. So cold, trembling, and overwrought was she, at the mere thought of having to fight such a fearful force with her slender stock of will-power, that she all but fell to the ground in a fit. Her limbs shook; her delicate childish face grew gray and ashen. Even Hugh Lansbury— unimaginative phelgmatic fellow though he might be—felt alarmed by the thought that his wife might be sickening for an attack of fever.

"Come indoors, darling, and rest yourself. No doubt the journey has tired you, and you are so far from strong. Think no more, my dearest Lucy" (drawing her arm affectionately in his own), "of the East with its age-old mysteries and terrors. Think only of those you love and of the new joys that await you!" So saying, he led her gently inside the house, where after a warm bath and excellent dinner Lucy speedily recovered her composure and forgot her woes.

For ten days or more after this she saw and heard nothing of the dreaded fakir chiefly through following her husband's advice to use another, side entrance to the grounds of Bon Repos when going to or returning from outside engagements. At the end of that period, Lansbury himself was called away on business by a quarrel between the headmen of two villages at the most distant end of his district, and though loath enough to leave his newly wedded bride, duty compelled him to go.

"All the same, dear, I shan't be gone long," said he. "Two days and nights at latest, and as you've Tom Rayner and his sister coming tomorrow for 'dine and sleep,' you'll only be one whole evening by yourself!"

Lucy agreed and bade him farewell quite cheerfully. She had letters from home to answer, needlework, and other things to do. Hugh's servants were well trained and attentive, and would provide for her every want. Best of all too she heard it announced form the compound that the aged fakir had been absent from his post some twenty-four hours or more. Please Fate he too had been called off on important business and would stay away for good.

Such wild blissful hopes, however, were foredoomed to disappointment. Toward evening on the second day of her husband's absence, the visitors having departed, Lucy was alone in the dining room, sorting silver and other household treasures that had been brought forth in honor of her guests, when a horrible feeling stole over her that she was *not alone;* another and a sinister presence was in the room likewise. Turning around quickly, she saw to her untold terror and amazement, the old fakir, of all unexpected people, standing there, naked as usual, save for his ragged and filthy loincloth.

And the worst of all was he appeared to be gazing straight at her, just as he had done on that dreadful first occasion when she had met him, in a way that turned the poor girl's blood to veritable ice in her veins!

Whenever she moved, he moved, following her about the room, till at last in a voice almost inaudible with fear, she asked him, "Why do you come here? what do you want?"

There was a pause, pregnant with sinister meaning, then the uncouth, uncanny-looking creature stepped forward into the center of the room and stretched forth one skinny and filth-begrimed finger as though to touch poor Lucy on head and shoulder, and she very nearly fainted away at the thought.

"The memsahib's *hair*—her lovely golden hair, brilliant as the sun's rays, splendid as the moon's finest glory. To the eyes of Rami Bux it is glorious as the gold and gems that gleam on the altar of Shiva, and he would sell his soul to possess one lock of it! Memsahib will give— Memsahib will give!" he broke forth into a monotonous droning kind of chant till poor Lucy's head went around and around like a veritable teetotum, and she thought she should have gone clean out of her mind.

"Give you a lock of my hair, I shouldn't dream of such a thing!" she gasped indignantly, but the hateful eyes held her in their thrall despite all protests.

"If you *must* have it, you *must*, I suppose," she murmured feebly. "Just wait a moment will you, while I go and fetch my scissors."

Then, pulling herself together with a mighty effort, she fled from the room, thankful for even that brief respite from the fakir's evil spell. With heart thumping violently against her ribs and the blood throbbing in her temples, she managed to creep—more dead than alive—to the upper story of the bungalow, and here a sudden brilliant idea struck her.

Inside the little room next to her husband's dressing room—and which she had lately utilized as a boudoir—there stood a wide divan, and on the divan lay a magnificent Persian rug (a wedding gift to Hugh from some raja or other) woven in pale rich colors, chiefly rose, pale green, and straw color. The silken fringe thereof, delicately plaited and of very great width, was strangely like human hair. In fact, Lucy's husband had not infrequently chaffed her on its resemblance to her own pale golden locks, declaring it was difficult, in a dull light, to distinguish one from the other.

Acting on this coincidence, it was but the work of a moment to find a pair of scissors and sever a long and fairly thick tuft of the wide golden border—tying the same together with a twist of pale blue ribbon from her dressing table—then run with tottering footsteps to the floor below and give the shining token to the fakir.

The latter, to Lucy's intense relief, appeared quite unsuspicious and satisfied with his prize—salaamed low and thanked the memsahib for her condescending kindness. Next moment when she glanced over to that corner of the room where the weird and incongruous figure had stood, she was thankful to find it empty.

On her husband's return home, she related to him the entire extraordinary story.

"Well, my dear, how did you and your friend, the old fakir, get on during my absence—all right, I hope?" had been Hugh Lansbury's half-joking inquiry. But he frowned sternly enough and was not in the very least amused when he had listened to his wife's tale, which she told him as they sat together on the verandah, drinking their after-dinner coffee.

"Asked you for a lock of your hair, did he? What an infernal piece of cheek!" Hugh muttered. "I hope you didn't give him any such thing." And when Lucy shook her head sagely, describing her little subterfuge in handing the fakir some fringe from the Persian carpet in lieu of her own hair, Hugh commended his wife for a very wise little woman.

She had scarcely finished her narrative, and they two had stepped down into the garden and were beginning to pace up and down in the pale Indian moonlight, when Lucy held up one hand and cried, shivering from top to toe: "Listen, Hugh! What on earth can it mean, that most extraordinary noise?" A sort of thump-thump-thump bang-bang-bang came from the upper floor of the bungalow, as though some massive and clumsy body were moving about up there.

"It's either in *my* bedroom or *your* boudoir!" exclaimed Hugh, and bold man though he was, as he stood there in the moonlight, his wife—glancing up at him with terrified eyes—saw beads of perspiration upon his forehead.

"How *can* there be anyone in my room except the ayah, and she's as soft-footed as a cat?" cried poor Lucy, but before she could say more, not only had the flapping, banging, and knocking sounds enormously increased in volume, but the weighty body (whatever it might be) that caused them appeared to be hurling itself down the short flight of stairs to the hall below, which the Lansburys used as a sitting room. Through the half-closed *chits* that divided the hall from the outer verandah came loud crashes as of pictures, glass, and china swept from their places upon the walls. The front door suddenly burst open, and (believe me or not, as you choose, kind reader, but the tale is true, and no stranger than many another hailing from the ever-mysterious East) out of it came rolling, over and over and over, like a great yellow-toned Catherine wheel, a vast shapeless, indescribable, yet active and animate mass, hurrying along down the garden path— impelled one knew not how, one could not tell whither!

Across rosebushes, geranium beds, neatly turfed borders, and smooth gravel paths, this extraordinary object made its astounding way, a long trail of destruction left behind it. Lucy and her husband, taking shelter behind a hedge of oleander bushes, watched its progress with amazement.

"It's the carpet—the yellow Persian carpet!" shrieked Lucy, beside herself now with terror, and Lansbury himself, though strong-nerved and not easily upset, could only watch silently and with horrified half-comprehending eyes the destruction of his own and the *mali's* best gardening efforts. Neither one of the pair of watchers felt inclined to follow the carpet in its mad career, or to find out where it went!

Hugh Lansbury first carried his wife indoors and laid her upon a sofa, where mercifully she fell into a heavy sleep, and more mercifully still, on awakening next day appeared inclined to look upon the past night's nerve-racking experience as more or less an evil dream than actual reality. "It couldn't be true; it's too strange to be true!" he heard her murmuring, and she seemed to be very weak and tired.

Chota hazri over, Hugh wandered away by himself, ostensibly to give orders about some chickens that were said to have strayed, but really to follow out the tracks of the missing carpet—these tracks being more visible than ever now in full daylight. On he strode steadily, till he came to the peepul tree beside the gate where the fakir's hut usually stood.

There was not a trace of the old ruffian to be seen, except—"Hullo! What's this?" exclaimed Hugh, picking up a torn golden tuft of some towlike material and holding it aloft upon his cane, then another and another, till finally he reached the rear of the wretched hovel. There on the sunbaked ground outside, an astounding scene of destruction met his gaze.

The magnificent silk-woven Persian carpet, which only twenty-four hours before lay securely in Lucy's boudoir, now showed torn, rent, and scattered into a million shreds. It was just as though some savage and furious creature—bird, beast, or devil (Hugh knew not what to suggest)—had set on the lovely thing with claws, teeth, or talons and destroyed it in a fit of mad ungovernable rage!

What weird inexplicable occult power lay behind such an unusual occurrence, what fierce, malevolent, relentless personality had willed the same for its own purposes (and been cheated of them perhaps, in the end?) was more than Hugh Lansbury, with all his wide knowledge of the strange ways of the Orient, felt able to say. Possibly the reader can give an opinion. I cannot.

Maori Magic

(New Zealand)

In the universal black magic, which relies for its efficacy upon the correspondence between the bodily organs and the orders of demons, the Maori was well versed. His particular feat was the *makutu*. This was a kind of curse operating through the god controlling the viscera. To produce this makutu the *ariki* performed incantations to summon before him the *shadow* of the person he wished to strike. When it appeared before him the ariki would either command or enrage the Atua (familiar) of its shadowy viscera and then dismiss the double back to its physical counterpart. This having been done, terrible pains in the abdomen would rack the object of the curse, and if the spell was not removed he would, in the natural course, die at sunset or sunrise, as the case might be.

Another method of inflicting the makutu was similar to that employed by other savage, and even some civilized, races by means of a waxen image. In this case, however, the image was of clay. It was made to serve as a vehicle for the shadow of the person about to be makutued. When it was fashioned in his likeness, the operator pierced it through the abdomen with a sharp-pointed stick and fastened it to an evil-smelling forest tree, where none could infringe its *tapu*. After reciting *karakia* (incantation) at it, the operator dismissed the shadow back to the victim, and the pain of the sharp stick through the abdomen of the image was transferred to the original. Yet another method was to link the shadow to some green leaves and then bury them so that as they rotted, the body of the one cursed would decay by sympathy.

In regard to these operations, two points may be noted as significant: in the first place the cause of dispute had to be set aside, and in the second it was well understood that if the curse did not strike its mark, it "came home to roost." In setting aside the cause of dispute, the operator would chant at length to the effect that the infringed

From: Reginald Hodder, "Maori Magic," *Occult Review* 4 (1906): 303–8.

tapu, or the stolen ax, was nothing to him. The defaulter could go on infringing tapu or could keep the ax till the Dog Star overtook the sun. And all this in the tone in which we say, "Take it then, and much good may it do you." In regard to the second point—the reversion of the unsuccessful curse upon the sender—it suffices to say that this appears to be the occult law wherever the black magic of cursing is practiced.

The makutu bewitchment could be unconsciously self-inflicted by means of an infringement of tapu. Here the derivation of the word *tapu* helps to an understanding of the particular aspect of Maori magic with which it is connected. According to Tregear, it signifies "real mark" or "real touch." Tapu then is the magnetic touch laid by the Atua upon any object. Thus, if anyone handled an object or trod on ground that was tapu, the essence of the Atua passed into him by contact, with dire results. There are many tales that illustrate the working of this unconscious makutu. An ariki once lost his tinder box, which, of course, was tapu. It was found by several Maori slaves who, not knowing it was tapu, made use of it. The Atua of the chief, of course, immediately began to lay about him, smiting the Atua of the slaves, with the result that they were soon rolling about in agony on the ground. One who had not handled the box hurried off to the nearest *tohunga* (priest), who fortunately arrived before sunset and by means of incantations removed the spell.

A spurious imitation of the makutu is wrought even among the lesser tohunga of the present day. The psychic nature of the Maori renders him very susceptible to suggestion, and the artful tohunga who lives, like so many of our own medicine men, by "suggestion cures" of "suggestion maladies" can do a great deal with him in that way. When the tohunga's shoddy tapu fails of its own strength to smite the unwitting infringer, he takes good care to let him know what is going to happen to him presently. He has broken a tapu and the makutu is about to fall upon him. And sure enough, it does—by suggestion. This gives the wily tohunga a chance to remove the spell by the same trickery, and so increase his prestige.

There are many stories told in which the unfortunate, who has infringed a tapu by mistake, learns what he has done and suffers the penalty of his own fears. But most of them show a balance of priestcraftiness over occult agency, and one is almost tempted to think that the great institution of tapu has degenerated into a mere means of personal advantage. A chief is invited to dine at the house of a European. A fine large joint is on the table. As soon as the chief is served, the whole joint *ipso facto* becomes tapu. Wherefore he considerately takes it away with him lest some misguided one should eat certain death without knowing it. Again, if a chief discovers an island scintillating with diamonds, all he has to do is to lay his tapu on it and none but himself can approach it with safety.

There is a kind of humor in this, and the modern priest no doubt laughs inside his mat. That he is indeed given to humor may be seen by the following anecdote. An Irishman, imagining he was about to be makutued because he had pitched his tent on a Maori burial ground, went to the tohunga and told him his fears. Whereupon the tohunga requested him to open wide his mouth and, when he had done so, spat down his throat and assured him gravely that he need fear nothing now for he had removed the spell.

Magic Made out of Human Organs

(China)

The use of the organs of living persons as medicine is based upon the belief that the vitality of one person can be made to prolong the life of another. This belief has led to other crimes than mutilation. A most revolting case is cited in the Commentary, into the details of which it is not necessary to enter.

From A.D. 1796 to 1810 a certain Chang Liang-pi had followed a practice, well understood among the Chinese, by which he derived, as he believed, the vitality of little girls, bought or otherwise secured by him. Eleven of the children died in that time as the result of these

From: E. T. Williams, "Witchcraft in the Chinese Penal Code," *Journal of the North China Branch of the Royal Asiatic Society* 37 (1906): 61–96.

practices, and one other was in an enfeebled condition when the trial occurred. The criminal paid the full penalty, being executed by the process of *ling-ch'ih*, his head exposed, and his property confiscated and given to the families of the victims. In this case the edict directed that notice of the execution should be circulated to a distance of four hundred *li* from the scene of the crimes and that the families of the children injured should stand around the criminal while he was being slowly cut to pieces.

Another use of the organs taken from the bodies of living persons is that of communicating vitality to an image used for magical purposes. The Commentary says:

> Those who practice witchcraft take the eyes and ears of human beings, cut off their hands and feet, and fasten these members upon the image of a man either carved out of wood, or molded of clay, which image they then by their evil arts cause to do work for them.

This cruel practice finds its origin in that animism which seems to have swayed the minds of all races in their earlier history, the belief that by the observance of a certain ceremony, stones and graven images could be made to be the habitation of spirits and thus to become miracle-working agents. As the blood was commonly held to be the vehicle of life, a part of the ceremony usually consisted in smearing the stone or the image with blood, and to this day in China when the idols in a temple are dedicated, a little blood, or its substitute red paint, is placed in the eyes, ears, nostrils, and mouth of each image, by which it is supposed to be quickened. If the blood of animals can give life to an image made by man, the blood of a human being ought to be much more efficacious. Thus no doubt early men reasoned themselves into the practice of human sacrifice. The attempt to give the image the sense organs and the limbs of a human being is certainly one of which little has been heard, but it is easy to see that those who believe that images can be quickened could persuade themselves without difficulty that the possession of the real organs of sense and not their likenesses would merely make the image still more powerful.

Stories of Soul Taking

(China)

Many illustrations could be given from Chinese literature of the belief in the power of sorcery to call the soul out of the living body as well as to control the spirits of the dead and avail themselves of their service. The use of various organs of the human body in the manufacture of magical remedies for disease is quite in harmony with the orthodox theories of disease and medicine. All residents of China are familiar with attempts of dutiful sons or daughters to prepare a remedy that may save the life of a dying parent by cutting pieces of flesh from their own arms or thighs. One of the most popular stories related of the Goddess of Mercy, Kuan-yin, is that of her sacrifice of a hand and an eye to save her father.

The Commentary cites a case referred to the Board of Punishments in the fourteenth year of Ch'ien-lung (A.D. 1749) in which one Ku Ching-wên of the province of Kiangsu was convicted of boiling the bodies of certain children in order to manufacture medicine of them. In one instance it was the corpse of a child, taken from the grave by a man named P'an Ming-kao, who delivered it to Ku; in another a living child kidnapped by another confederate, Li Yüan-fang, was put alive into the cooling vessel and boiled to death.

Another case was that of a leper, Liu Kung-yo of Hsiang-shan Hsien, Kuangtung, who, having heard that human gall mixed with rice was a cure for his disease, mentioned the matter to Liu Jui-wei, who saw a chance to make a little money. After a few days the latter came to the leper and said that he could get some gall and rice, and asked what price would be paid for it. The leper said he would give a hundred and twenty yuan if a cure were effected. Liu Jui-wei then attempted to secure the gall bladder of Yüan A-chu. He succeeded in cutting open the abdomen of the unfortunate victim, but failed to find the gall bladder, and two days later Yüan died. The criminal Liu Jui-wei

From: E. T. Williams, "Witchcraft in the Chinese Penal Code," *Journal of the North China Branch of the Royal Asiatic Society* 37 (1906): 61–96.

suffered death by *ling-ch'ih*, and the leper was sentenced to one hundred blows with heavy bamboo and three years' exile but, being diseased, was permitted to compound for a money payment. This case occurred in the twelfth year of Ch'ien-lung (A.D. 1747).

Human Sacrifices

(Burma)

The following statement was made to me when on a visit to Kanti state, in the north of the Upper Chindwin district, by a Shan named Ai Kaw. His parents belonged to Kanti. A revolution occurred in the state when he was a baby, and they fled northward and lived for some years under the protection of the Kachins of the Taro Valley. A few years after the annexation, they returned to Kanti. Ai Kaw is a great traveler and has been from Salem near Saramati (12,557 feet) to the head-hunting village of Măkware over the shoulder of the mountain, where he says he camped out four nights in snow a foot deep. Last February the Măkware men attacked the village of Naungmo, in unadministered territory only four miles from the Chindwin, and took away thirteen heads. As Ai Kaw relates:

"When I lived in Kanti I used often to go to Lasa and Lanu, which are both subject to Tăro. I often witnessed human sacrifices at these villages. The victims were brought from another village, never taken in war. The village did not fight with other villages. It is not their custom to break heads. They do their hair in a knot behind without cutting it. Their dress consists of a slip like that worn by Naungmo Nagas, with a strip of cloth hanging loose in front. The women wear a piece of cloth wrapped around the body, about eighteen inches long.

"The victims were always boys or girls. The biggest I have seen was a boy of fifteen. The usual age is six or seven. The price is always one hundred rupees. The sacrifice is always in Wagaung [August], at their

From: G.E.R. Grant Brown, I.C.S., "Human Sacrifices Near the Upper Chindwin," *Burma Research Society's Journal* 1 (part 2) (1911): 35–40.

big festival. I have seen as many as seven victims killed at one sacrifice. They are always brought from villages in unadministered territory, never from those under the Kanti Sawbwa. A rope is put around the victim's neck, and he is taken to the houses of all the relations of his purchaser. At each house a finger joint is cut off, and all the men, women, and children in the house are smeared with the blood. They also lick the joint, and rub it on the cooking tripod. The bone is thrown away. They do all this so as to get good rice crops. [This statement was volunteered.] The child is then taken to a post in the middle of the village, where he is tied. He is then stabbed with a spear several times, with an interval between each time long enough to cook a pot of rice, the spear being driven in only a little way so as not to kill him at first. The blood from each stab is caught in a hollow bamboo, to be used afterward for smearing on the bodies of the purchaser's relations. No one else gets any blood. The object of the repeated stabs is to make the child scream: it is thought not to be good if he does not do so. At length the spear is thrust in and the child killed. Someone then cuts open the body. The entrails are taken out and the flesh cut off the bones, and the whole put in a basket and set on a platform nearby as an offering to the god. It remains there only a short time and is then taken away and throw into the jungle, basket and all. While it is on the platform, the purchaser and his relations smear themselves with the blood while they dance and weep. By 'weep' I mean that they make sounds of lamentation, not that they shed tears. They do so because they are enjoying themselves. That is the way of Nagas: they do not laugh. At the same time the whole village drinks rice beer. None is drunk before the sacrifice or after the flesh is thrown away. The women and children join in the blood smearing and drinking.

"The victim is killed by a *nattein* [custodian of the god], who is always a man without relations, and who holds office for life. When he dies, an orphan without relations is chosen in his place."

I asked Ai Kaw how he knew. He replied that all this is done to get good crops.

"The blood of the victim is taken around to the houses of the purchaser and his relations and poured over the seed paddy, which is kept separately in a shed of its own outside the house. The sowing is in Tagu or Kason [April]."

Like some other great travelers, Ai Kaw is regarded by his fellows as being somewhat of a romancer. The reputation, however, is probably as undeserved as was that of Mendez Pinto, who was described by Colonel Symes in his *Embassy to Ava*, little more than a hundred years ago, as "the Prince of Fiction," but who is now known to have been a truthful and accurate observer. To me his account bears internal evidence of its truth. I have thought it best, however, to obtain confirmation of the fact that the terrible ritual described is really practiced near our borders, and have made a second visit to Kanti before publishing it. The people of Kanti state are somewhat reticent about these customs of their neighbors. The Lasa Nagas have a village within two miles of Kanti, and many of the people who call them-selves Shans are probably of their blood, quite possibly Ai Kaw himself. The statement that the Lasas in unadministered territory practice the right is not confirmed. But the Sawbwa himself says it is practiced by their neighbors of Lanu, and Kyimo of Lasa (near Kanti) has given me an account of sacrifices witnessed by him at Kangzo which fully confirms Ai Kaw's, though it is less detailed. He also says the custom exists at Lyisa and Lanu. The fact that human sacrifices are offered by the Nagas in order to ensure a good harvest is, moreover, mentioned in the *Imperial Gazetteer*, and Mr. Needham, who in 1888 marched from Margherita (now a terminus on the Assam railways) to Hachang, in latitude twenty-seven degrees about half a degree north of the unadministered Lasa, gives a description hardly less gruesome than Ai Kaw's, which I quote below:

"The whole of the Nagas residing on the south of the Patkoi range are designated Rangpang Nagas, and those on the north side Gum-'laus, and the terms are used by the Nagas themselves, as well as by our plains people, when speaking about either tribe.

"The Rangpangs are all human sacrificers, but not so the Gum'laus, and the skulls of their victims may be seen hanging under the eaves in the front verandah of their houses. The custom is not a yearly one, owing chiefly, I suppose, to the difficulty of procuring a sufficient number of victims, and on the score of expense, for the ceremony entails the killing of numerous buffaloes, or cows, pigs, fowls, etc., and the giving of a huge feast, to which many kinsmen and friends, even from a distance, have to be invited, but is performed about every nine or ten years in, I believe, propitiation for health, good weather, good harvests, and victory over enemies. As in addition to the livestock required for the feast given on these occasions, the expenditure of rice, both for food as well as for brewing liquor, is very great, the ceremony is one which is usually performed after a bumper harvest.

"Sometimes enemies taken in battle, but oftener slaves who have to be purchased, are sacrificed.

"The sacrificial *modus operandi* was thus briefly described to me today. The victim, having been tied hands and feet, is made to stand on the edge of the front verandah of the sacrificer's house, and his [or her] hair having been seized, and the head forcibly pulled forward and bent downward, a man, hitherto hidden from view, steps out from one side and severs it from the trunk with one stroke of his Singpho knife, one of which every Naga carries. As soon as the head has been severed, four or five near relations or kinsmen of the sacrificer rush forward, seize the trunk, cut open the chest, and rummage about for the heart, and the one who succeeds in getting hold of it first is looked upon as a very lucky person. After this, the fingers and toes are cut off and stuck on pointed slips of bamboos close to the sacrificer's house, where they remain until they rot away and the body is thrown away uphill to propitiate the hill spirit.

"The head is cleaned of its flesh, and the pieces having been buried close to the sacrificer's house, a stone is placed over the spot, and a piece of a prickly shrub called *Moga phun* (*phun* means a tree in Singpho) by the Singphos, which bears a red berry about the time of the *Bihu,* is planted close to it.

"If the victim has been purchased by a subscription among several relations, and this is apparently a common event, the skull is divided among them, the man giving most money getting the lion's share to decorate his house with. One sex is as good as another for sacrificial purposes, and a child, however small, provided it has cut all its teeth, is as good as an adult. If the victim's hair is long and worth keeping, it is used to ornament hats, etc.; if not, it is thrown away. Women and children are permitted to witness the disgusting ceremony, and at night, singing and dancing, to which all are invited, goes on until a late hour.

"I am told that victims are sometimes given large quantities of *mod* shortly before the time fixed for sacrifice, and if so, this is perhaps the one redeeming point in the disgusting and cruel ordeal, for it shows that a touch of pity exists even in the breast of a Naga savage.

"The Nagas in these parts are apparently almost as fond of fighting as their more westerly neighbors are, as from all I can hear, they are constantly attacking and harassing those whom they consider weaker than themselves. The heads of all victims killed in war are invariably brought home by the conquerors, and a piece of the tongue, nose, and ears having been cut off, they are carried some distance uphill as gift offerings to the spirit supposed to reside there in propitiation of the victory."

Part IV

Tales from the Americas

The Possession of Mercy Short

(United States)

Mercy Short had been taken captive by our cruel and bloody Indians in the east, who at the same time horribly butchered her father, her mother, her brother, her sister, and others of her kindred and then carried her, with three surviving brothers and two sisters, from Nieuchewannic unto Canada, after which our fleet, returning from Quebec to Boston, brought them with other prisoners that were then redeemed. But although she had then already borne the yoke in her youth, yet God Almighty saw it good for her to bear more of that yoke before seventeen years of her life had rolled away.

It was in the summer of the year 1692, when several persons were committed to the gaol in Boston on suspicion of having a hand in that most horrid and hellish witchcraft, which had brought in the devils upon several parts of the country at such a rate as is the just astonishment of the world. Then it was that Mercy Short, being sent by her mistress upon an errand unto the prison, was asked by one of the suspected witches for a little tobacco; and she affronted the hag ('twas one Sarah Good, since executed at Salem) by throwing a handful of shavings at her and saying, "that's tobacco good enough for you." Whereupon that wretched woman bestowed some ill words

From: Cotton Mather, "A Brand Pluck'd Out of the Burning" (1693). In George Lincoln Burr (ed.), *Narratives of the Witchcraft Cases, 1648–1706* (New York: Charles Scribner's Sons, 1914).

upon her, and poor Mercy was taken with just such, or perhaps much worse, fits as those which held the bewitched people then tormented by invisible furies in the county of Essex. A world of misery did she endure for diverse weeks together, and such as could not possibly be inflicted upon her without the immediate efficiency of some agent, whether rational or malicious, until God was pleased at length to hear the multiplied prayers of His people for her deliverance. There were many remarkable things in the molestations then given her, whereof one was that they made her fast for twelve days together.

Being happily delivered, she for several months remained so, even until the following winter. But then she suddenly fell into a swoon, wherein she lay for dead many hours together; and it was not long before the distinct and formal fits of witchcraft returned upon her. She continued variously tortured and harassed by evil spirits and in the same circumstances that had been upon her formerly, until one of the ministers in the town took a little company of his praying neighbors and kept a day of prayer with her and for her. On which day she lay wholly insensible of the people that were thus concerned on her behalf and entertained with none but the cursed specters, whom alone she saw, she heard, she felt; nevertheless while that minister was preaching on March 9, she flew upon him and tore a leaf of his Bible. For some days after this day she continued in her grievous vexations; but then, after what was little short of an entire and a total fast for about nine days together, in those miseries, at length she gained about three days' remission. In this intermission of her anguishes, she did eat a little, and but a very little, victuals; and she was able on the Lord's Day to visit the Lord's House near half a mile from the place of her abode.

While she was in the congregation, she so fell under the arrest of her invisible troublers that she now saw and heard nothing but those horrid fiends, but when the assembly was just broke up, they fell to tormenting her at such a rate that many strong men with a united force could not well carry her any farther than the house of a kind neighbor, who charitably took her in. 'Twas by the singular Providence of God that she was thus cast among a neighborhood whose hearts He stirred up to pity her, to relieve her, to pray for her, and with a most Christian compassion do all that could piously be done for her deliverance. There she lay for several weeks; and you shall now be told in what manner handled! A manner differing little or nothing from that wherein she had been thus long already tortured.

There exhibited himself to her a devil having the figure of a short black man; and it was remarkable that although she had no sort of acquaintance with histories of what has happened elsewhere to make any impressions upon her imagination, yet the devil that visited her was just of the same stature, feature, and complexion with what the histories of the witchcrafts beyond-sea ascribe to him. He was a wretch no taller than an ordinary walking staff; he was not of a Negro but of a tawny or an Indian color; he wore a high-crowned hat, with straight hair, and had one cloven foot. This devil still brought with him to her a considerable number of specters, most exactly resembling the persons of several people in the country, some of whose names were either formerly known or now by their companions told to her. And these wicked specters assisted or obeyed their devilish master, who brought them to infest her with such hideous assaults as were the astonishment of all the bystanders.

When this devil with his confederate and concomitant specters came to this our poor neighbor, it was their custom to cast her into such horrible darkness that she still imagined herself in a desolate cellar, where day or night could not be distinguished. Her eyes were open, moving to and fro after the hellish Harpies that were now fluttering about her, but so little able to see anything else that although we made as if we would strike at her eyes, it would not make her wink. If we laid our hands upon them, it hindered her from a view of those fiends which troubled her; but she gave us afterward to understand that it put her to much pain to be so hindered. Her ears were altogether stopped to all of our noises, being wholly engrossed by the invisible assailants; insomuch that though we sometimes halloed extremely loud in her eyes, yet she heard nothing of it. And it was particularly considerable that although she could be no other than utterly ignorant of what the European books relate concerning such matters, nevertheless the voice of these demons was exactly such as you shall read in Glanvil's collections and elsewhere; 'twas big, low, thick, and such as ordinarily caused her to say Haah! or How! or What do you say? and listen and oblige them to repeat before she could understand. *Note.* That we the bystanders could neither see nor hear the things which thus entertained this young woman, and I hope we never shall; but we were informed partly from the speeches that fell from her in these trances, partly from the accounts by her afterward given unto us, and partly by a multitude of other concurrent circumstances.

The devil and his crew, having thus forced her senses from conversing with their ordinary objects and captivated them to this communion with the powers of darkness, their manner was in the first place to make her a tender of a book, somewhat long and thick (like the wast-books of many traders), but bound and clasped, and filled not only with the names or marks, but also with the explicit (short) covenants of such as had listed themselves in the service of Satan and the design of witchcraft; all written in red characters, many whereof she had opportunity to read when they opened the book before her. This book of death did they tempt her to sign, and condescended so far in their solicitations as to tell her that if she would only touch it with her finger it should be enough. Only the received signification of this little ceremony should be that she now became the devoted vassal of the devil. This was the temptation with which they still persecuted her, and it was the very same that the evil spirits were at the same time using upon far more than a score of miserable people so possessed in several other parts of the country. Whether this book be indeed a real book or not I dispute not. Mercy herself thinks it is, and gives this reason for it, that a touch of it (they told her) would have cured her. Besides they several times made her eyes very sore by thrusting it hard upon them, to make her touch it when she should unawares lift up her hands to save her eyes. And they at last gave her to understand that they thought they should be forced shortly to drop it.

As the bewitched in other parts of the world have commonly had no other style for their tormentors but only *they* and *them*, so had Mercy Short. Wherefore to consult brevity, we shall note the devil and those that accompanied him in this business by that style. And so I go on to say that *they* first used a thousand flatteries and allurements to induce her a compliance with the desire of the devil. They showed her very splendid garments and thence proceeded to greater glories, which they promised her if she would sign their book. They engaged unto her I know not how many more conveniences if she would but so much as touch it. When all these persuasives were ineffectual, they terrified her with horrible threatenings of miseries which they would inflict upon her, and then they as cruelly inflicted a great part of what they threatened.

But that which added to the horror of the matter was that when those tigers were addressing themselves to some of their furious inflictions, they would so clothe themselves in flames of fire (a devilish and most impudent imitation, sure, of something mentioned in the Scripture!) as to render themselves beyond measure formidable; and accordingly, just before they fell upon her with any torments of a more than ordinary account, she would sometimes, by the fright of what she perceived them doing, fall a-trembling so that the very bed would shake under her. *Memorandum.* That one evening I had with me a lantern accommodated with a glass ball, which rendered the light so extremely glaring that one could hardly bear to look upon it, but one might thereby read a very small print a very great way off; and she being then able to see and speak, told us that *he* (meaning the black man) sometimes came to her with eyes flaming like the light of that lantern.

'Twould be a long work to recite all the tortures with which they plagued her. I shall only touch upon the principal. Besides the thousands of cruel pinches given her by those barbarous visitants, they stuck innumerable pins into her. Many of those pins they did themselves pluck out again, and yet they left the bloody marks of them, which would be as 'tis the strange property of most witch wounds to be cured perhaps in less than a minute. But some of the pins they left in her, and those we took out, with wonderment. Yea, sometimes they would force pins into her mouth, for her to swallow them; and though she strove all she was able to keep them out, yet they were too hard for her. Only before they were got into her throat, the bystanders would by some dexterity get hold of them and fetch them away. When this mischief was over, they would then come and sit upon her breast and pull open her jaw, and keep her without fetching one sensible breath, sometimes for half an hour and some-times for several whole hours together. At last, when we came to understand that it was the sitting of the specters upon her which cast her into those doleful postures, we would with main force (and so heavy she was beyond her ordinary weight that the lifting of her called for a more than ordinary force) lift her upright, and the specters would immediately then so fall off that her breath returned to her. At other times there would be heard, it may be by more than seven witnesses at a time, the scratches of the specters on the bed and on the wall.

Another of the miseries whereto they put her was an extreme fasting for many days together. She, having obtained a liberty of eating for three days after a fast of nine days, was immediately compelled unto another fast, which lasted for about fifteen days together. In all this time she was permitted scarce to swallow one bit or drop of any victuals. One raw pear she ate, and now and then an apple, and some hard cider she drank, things that would rather set an edge upon the severity of her fast. Sometimes also a chestnut might go down into her craving stomach and sometimes a little cold water. If anything else were offered her, her teeth would be set and she thrown into hideous torments; and it must be usually for two or three days together that such poor things as these also must be denied her. Briefly, she scarce took any jot of sustenance, but what we supposed would rather increase the tortures and mischiefs of her fast. How she was all this while supported I pretend not now to guess. But the famous Henricus ab Heer, in his observations, affirms unto oath that a bewitched girl, residing in his house kept just such another fast, and that for fifteen days and nights together she took neither meat nor drink. And yet this fast was not so long as that mentioned by Dr. Plott in his *Natural History of Oxford-shire*; who affirms that in the year 1671, one Rebecka Smith, who was thought bewitched, continued without eating or drinking for ten weeks together, and afterward lived only upon warm broths taken in small quantities for a whole twelvemonth. It seems that long fasting is not only tolerable but strangely agreeable to such as have something more than ordinary to do with the invisible world.

But burning seemed the cruelest of all her tortures. They would flash upon her the flames of a fire, that was to us indeed (though not to her) invisible, but to us all, in the mischiefs and effects of it, the most sensible thing that could be. The agonies of one roasting a fagot at the stake were not more exquisite than what she underwent in the scalds which those hellhounds gave her, sometimes for near a quarter of an hour together. We saw not the flames, but once the room smelt of brimstone, and at other, yea, at many times, we saw her made excessively sore by these flames, and we saw blisters thereby raised upon her. To cure the soreness which this fiery trial would give unto her, we were forced sometimes to apply the oil commonly used for the cure of scalds, and yet (like other witch wounds) in a day or two all would be well again, only the marks of some wounds thus given her she will probably carry to her grave. I may add that once they thrust a hot iron down her throat, which though it were to us invisible, yet we saw the skin fetched off her tongue and lips.

Reader, if thou hadst a desire to have seen a picture of hell, it was visible in the doleful circumstances of Mercy Short! Here was one lying in outer darkness, haunted with the devil and his angels, deprived of all common comforts, tortured with most excruciating fires, wounded with a thousand pains all over, and cured immediately, that the pains of those wounds might be repeated. It was of old said, if one went to them from the dead, they will repent. As for us, we have had not only the damned coming to us from the dead, in this witchcraft, but the very state of the damned itself represented most visibly before our eyes. Hard-hearted, we, if we do not repent of the things which may expose us to an eternal durance in such a state!

Possessed by Evil

(United States)

A strange thing occurred when I was in South California ten years ago. When staying at San Diego I used to attend many Spiritualist lectures, meetings, and séances, and had just discovered that I possessed mediumistic powers. One night I had an extraordinary dream, or vision, which seemed very real at the time. I thought I awoke from a deep sleep with a feeling of horror and impending danger, and noticed that the darkness of the room was faintly illuminated by a lurid radiance which was growing gradually stronger, and then several dark forms became visible moving from the other end of the room slowly toward me. Instinctively I tried to jump up and cry out, but found myself incapable of moving or speaking. There were four or five of these figures, all arrayed in long dark cloaks with hoods drawn over their heads, which, however, did not conceal their faces, which were indescribably horrible and malignant. I was

From: Reginald B. Span, "More Glimpses of the Unseen," *Occult Review* 4 (July–December 1906): 145–51.

seized with an agony of fear and prayed with an intensity of feeling I have never before or since experienced, "O Christ save me! Christ save me!" As I did so a brilliant flash of white light shot through the room, and the figures quickly retreated and vanished, while the awful feeling of oppression and paralysis left me also, and I came to my full consciousness, trembling violently and feeling weak and ill, as if I had passed through some great mental and physical strain and spiritual crisis.

The next morning I considered I had had a bad nightmare, and wondered what physical cause could have produced it, as I was in good health when I retired and had not partaken of a heavy supper. I might not have thought much of it again had it not been for what followed.

That afternoon I called to see some friends, a Mr. and Mrs. T———, who were well-known Spiritualists in San Diego. They remarked that I was not looking well, to which I replied that I was all right, only I had been rather upset the previous night by a horrible nightmare, and then proceeded to relate it. We were sitting in their small drawing room, Mr. and Mrs. T——— on one side of the room and I on the other. I was just finishing my short account (we often discussed dreams and kindred subjects together), and Mrs. T——— was laughing and saying that I could not have been very well, when Mr. T———, who had been staring intently at something beyond me and had become very white, suddenly gave a cry of alarm and rose quickly to his feet, at the same time throwing out his arms in front of his head as if to ward off a blow.

The next instant he fell to the floor in what appeared to be a fit of some kind, as he was writhing convulsively and moaning and gibbering like one possessed. We picked him up and placed him on the armchair, and then shrank back in horror, as Mr. T———'s face was quite transfixed, altered beyond recognition into the most repulsive, awful face imaginable. *It was the countenance of a devil.* The features were so strangely contorted, and the half-closed eyes gleamed with a particularly baleful, sinister expression. It would be impossible to describe such a countenance. Mrs. T——— was beside herself with terror and kept calling her husband frantically by name, and then threw her arms around his neck as if to try and drive the evil creature out of him.

I knew it was a case of obsession but did not know how to act beyond praying that he might be delivered from it. Fortunately, the spirit had not gained full possession, and after a short, violent struggle, in which Mr. T—— was thrown foaming on the floor, the spirit came out of him.

Mr. T—— felt very weak and unwell for a time and could hardly speak at first. When he was better, he told us that as I was relating my dream, he suddenly saw clairvoyantly several figures emerge apparently from the wall behind me, and recognized (from my description) that they were the same beings who had appeared to me in my vision of the night before.

They came straight toward him, and he was filled with a great horror, and sensing danger of some kind, he jumped to his feet, instinctively throwing out his hands to ward them off, and then in an instant one of them had gained possession of him. He was particularly liable to anything of that kind, being a good trance medium. It was two weeks before he quite recovered from the shock and strain he then underwent.

Newfoundland Superstitions

(Canada)

The spurious letter of Our Lord to Abzarus, King of Edessa, is used all around the country, and worn especially by women in expectation of motherhood, and with other charms religiously preserved. I have been informed that a thriving business is done in some town printing offices in the sale of these printed spells.

A poor woman at Chance Cove, suffering from toothache, lamented to me that, after she had tried every remedy for this "hell of all

From: "Folk-Lore Scrap-Book: Superstitions in Newfoundland," *Journal of American Folk-Lore* 9 (1896): 222–32.

diseases," she had worn our Lord's letter for a fortnight without avail; and a poor fellow at King's Cove assured me that, as a last resource for the cure of this ugly monster, he had scraped some dust from a tombstone and drunk it in water without effecting a cure.

A man at Change Islands, in the district of Notre Dame Bay, told me he had been ridden to death by an old hag, until a knowledgeable old man advised him to drive nails through a shingle and lash it to his breast when he went to bed, with the nails sticking up. With great solemnity he assured me that, thus fortified, he had just forgotten the world, when down came the old hag all aflop, but with a hideous scream she went "off quicker 'n she come on." His rest has been peaceful ever since.

At Burin a few years ago, a murderer declared he would even touch the murdered man as proof of his innocence, the prevailing belief being that the wound of the murdered man would bleed if he did but touch it.

Fishermen will not proceed to sea if, on heaving anchor, the vessel should wear against the sun. An instance of this occurred a few years ago at Channel. A vessel ready for the seal fishery swung the unlucky way on heaving anchor; the skipper was disturbed; the crew, almost mutinous at his persisting to proceed, declared ill luck would follow them. Within a week the vessel was again in Channel—with the skipper dead and the superstition more deeply rooted than ever.

"I'd as lief cut my right hand off," said a skipper to me, "as cut down a maiden dog-berry tree. A man is sure to die as does it." This same old salt, while we were becalmed, kept throwing coppers overboard, to buy, as he said, "a ha'porth of wind." My remonstrance had only the effect of his assuring me it had often been a potent charm, "only they must be bad ha'pence and I gets 'em from St. Pierre." He also carried money and a candle in the deadwood of his craft—a light to enable him to cross the murky Styx, and a bolus to pay old Palinurus, I suppose.

At Cape La Hune I heard more superstitions than I could tell in an hour. I was assured of dead men's bones bleeding, when taken from a cave, and staining rocks that neither wind nor weather could wash out; of people unable to die lying on pigeons' feathers, and the feathers removed, they die easily; and a host of other superstitions.

The subject may be pursued ad lib. Who has not heard of the belief that the cod and the salmon take in ballast before a storm? And of Mrs.

Stack assuring Bishop Mullock of the fact, when a noble-looking salmon, thus ballasted, had been sold to his lordship? It sounds a joke, but the belief is a reality, as is also another about rats. If your house is infested with the vermin, a notable gentleman informs me, you have only to indite them a letter to quit, place it in the holes they make, and they will go. This he had tried, and the notice was followed by the whole tribe betaking themselves to a neighboring house. This took place in St. John's not six years ago.

Chilean Superstitions

(Chile)

Chile, in spite of its great length extended along the South Pacific seaboard, has today less than four million inhabitants; of these the greater proportion are of Spanish descent, though a mere glance into a crowd of the lower orders suffices to reveal evidences of a considerable admixture of the indigenous races. The population is concentrated in a few large towns and in industrial regions, for example, in the nitrate district of the north. It follows that the vast rural areas, cultivated valleys, and the central plain, flanked by wilderness of mountain and forest, are very thinly peopled, and by reason of their isolation have remained unchanged in essentials for centuries.

Education, despite the good intentions of the government, is not at a high level, the percentage of illiteracy being very high, especially among the women. In the south, the Araucanian Indians still predominate in certain districts, though hard put to it by the continual pressure of encroaching German settlers.

It is no exaggeration to say that the rural population of Chile is saturated with superstitions. At every turn these are encountered, operating as potent influences in the daily life of the people. Sometimes they are merely laughable, occasionally serious enough.

From: Oswald H. Evans, "Witchcraft in Chile," *Chambers's Journal* 11 (1921): 380–83.

An instance of the first kind occurred no longer ago than yesterday, when the writer innocently broke a taboo. It seems that a woman must not gather figs. As a lazy gardener had neglected to collect the fruit which was wanted for the dinner table, I sent a servant-girl up the ladder. There was at once a dismal outcry from the gardener and his wife: "The tree is doomed; it will bear no more fruit. The figs of this season will wither on the branches."

A more malevolent manifestation of superstition was recorded in the newspaper a short time ago. Two women were found in possession of the head of a newly buried child, which they had disinterred from the public cemetery for use in a way of which they could give only a confused account. In some unexplained way the spoils of the burial ground were supposed to confer good luck on the ghouls. The instance is by no means a solitary one.

The belief in buried treasure is very prevalent in Chile, not wholly without justification. The country has suffered so much from "alarums and excursions"—whether from Indians during the Colonial period, from loyalists and patriots during the War of Independence, or from evil contentions that appear inseparable from the best-ordered of Latin-American states—that on many occasions families have buried their most valued possessions and left the locality, sometimes, through accident of fate, never to return. Now, a treasure thus hidden may for one year be taken up by the fortunate finder without let or hindrance, but at the expiration of that time it passed into the custody of the witches, and it is no easy task to obtain possession of it. Even should the deposit be met with by accident, by a blow of the spade or removal of bricks in the course of pulling down a building, it is necessary that special precautions be taken. No word must be spoken, not even an exclamation of surprise and delight is permitted. If the silence is broken even by an ejaculation, the treasure vanishes, to be hidden elsewhere. Keep silence, turn your back toward it and grope for it blindfold, and it is just possible that you may succeed.

The deliberate search for buried treasure is beset with extraordinary difficulties. Times and seasons must be taken into consideration; silence, darkness, and solitude are essential. The searcher must steel his heart against unknown perils; he must be prepared to see and hear terrible things. The determined treasure hunter, however, may avail himself of certain mechanical aids, if we may so call them. These are varied; but the following, I am informed, was tried, without success, in locating a treasure supposed to exist on a hillside within half an hour of Valparaiso. The witches who guard the gold can often be seen at night from the public roadway, in the form of flickering lights known as *candilillos*. The midnight hour approaching, the seeker prepares a hollow gourd. Inside this he fixes a candle and a reel of cotton, so arranged as to unroll easily. Arriving at the spot with his spade and sack to dig up and carry off the gold, he awaits the propitious moment, repeating appropriate formulas and supporting as best he may the molestations of the guardians and their familiars. (It is a characteristic touch that in Valparaiso the witch often takes the shape of a mounted policeman, more often still that of a *perro bravo*—a savage watchdog.) Sometimes he hears people coming. But this is all illusion. At midnight he lights the candle in the gourd, takes hold of the end of the string, and flings the gourd so that it rolls along the ground, leaving him with a clue of thread with which to track it to its resting place. At the spot where the gourd lies, he must dig. The witches redouble their exertions; policemen and dogs converge upon him from all sides. When the treasure is revealed at last, a horrid shape is seated on it, the guardian witch in person, who abuses him with more than the eloquence of a Chilean market woman. It is not surprising that the witches generally manage to retain their hoards.

Witches tell the future by the aid of a shining stone in which they gaze. It is called the *Challanca*, and its use for the same purpose is ancient. Peru shows that "crystal gazing" was not confined to the Old World. Not long since, a woman in one of the small towns in the south was punished for using such a stone for fraudulent purposes, and her apparatus confiscated; but it appears that she had been fortunate in obtaining another one and is carrying on business as usual: "Wise women" are resorted to for medical advice, and for darker purposes that call for police intervention. Of late the spread of education has led them to adopt the technique of the professional medium, and as such they gain credence among classes that have outgrown the native superstitions of the country.

One man I know consults a witch from time to time in reference to a lizard that has taken up its abode in his stomach. The authorities are in continual conflict with a case of unlicensed practitioners, commonly known as "meicos" (*medicos*), who cure or kill by means of potent drugs of the countryside that might, if carefully studied, be found to possess properties of real value in medicine. Charms play no small part in the treatment, and if the account be true that appeared in the press lately, the remedial measures adopted are sometimes of the heroic order. In a house searched by police, an unfortunate old man suffering from rheumatism was found suspended from the roof by his feet, his shoulders only resting on the bed.

In the authoritative work of Señor Cifuentes, we read of a complex organization among Chilean witches that rivals that of Europe in the Middle Ages. There is a central authority, resident in Santiago, and there are three provinces, north, central, and south. Rivalry exists between the practitioners of the country and those of the town, but all receive their education in certain caves, known as *Salamancas*—truly a libel on that ancient university! Their meetings are presided over by Muckle-horned Clootie in person, and a charming assemblage gathers of Calchonas, Chon-chons, and malformed dwarfs—which last are children stolen from their homes and maimed by the witches in such horrible fashion that they cannot leave the caves in which they are secluded and in which they serve as drudges. The traveler "overtaken" by night and strong waters, may awake to find himself a guest and he should take heed of the gifts they give him.

Brazilian Charms and Amulets

(Brazil)

Bentinhos—I suppose there is hardly a Roman Catholic female in Brazil, from the empress to a Negress, who does not guard against invisible foes by wearing, in contact with her person, a couple of these diminutive shields. A friend procured for me a pair from the most esteemed *fabrica*, the convent of Tereza. Two

From: Thomas Ewbank, *Life in Brazil; or, A Journal of a Visit to the Land of the Cocoa and the Palm* (New York: Harper & Brothers, 1856).

embroidered pads, an inch and a half square, are connected by a double silk cord. On one is the Lady of Carmo and Child, on the other a fanciful figure or flower. The Cords pass over the shoulders so that one pad rests on the bosom and the other at the back, thus protecting the wearer before and behind. Large numbers are imported from Rome.

Cavallo marinho—hippocampus—is a favorite with many. This curious-looking little fish, when dried, is worn next to the skin and is powerful in driving off headaches as well as devils. Some have it in gold and silver.

Figa—One day I hinted that Chica, our little old African cook, had no amulet about her, as from her spare dress I could not imagine where it could be. It was said she certainly must wear one. To settle the matter, she was called in and, to my surprise, drew from her bosom a bone figa. She said she wore a tooth the same way in her own country. The first money a slave gets is expended on a figa, which is sometimes carved out of rosemary root.

The Fated Fagot

(*Canada*)

The title seemed very effective then, though now it strikes me as more alliterative than true, as it concerns a single stick and not a fagot at all. It was a round stick about five feet long, probably the trunk of a young ash tree brought home from the woods to serve some purpose as a pole. It lay forgotten in the backyard of a farmhouse close to a little village called L——. It was a fine strong pole about twice as thick as a man's wrist. The sun seasoned it day by day, so that it soon was no longer "green" wood but wood that would have crackled well in the fire. But for whatever purpose it had been brought home, it seemed oddly forgotten. No use was made of it.

From: C. A. Fraser, "Scottish Myths from Ontario," *Journal of American Folk-Lore* 6 (1893): 185–98.

One day one of the young men of the family went to the "bush," spent an hour there, and returned with just such another long, straight sapling. He dragged it into the yard, and his eye fell on the first one. "There," said he, "I've had little to do spending my time seeking a pole, and this one ready to my hand all the while."

"Aye," said Mary his sister, standing in the doorway, "that is what I'm telling them. Since that pole was brought, father has taken a bar from the gateway, and Neil has cut down a young tree in the pasture, and you've been seeking in the bush, all of you wanting this same pole that's only lying in the way."

"Perhaps there'll be something the matter with it, Mary," her brother answered, ever ready to suspect black art. "Anyway, it is dry now, and I'll chop it for you, and it will soon be out of harm's way."

And Mary, bidding him to do it at once—for she was then wanting some firewood—turned into the house.

The young man went, whistling, for his ax, and the pole would have been in half a dozen pieces in a few moments had not a neighbor hailed him from the road. Throwing down the ax, he went to the fence to speak with him, calling meantime to a little brother to gather sticks and chips for Mary. So Mary, or rather *Maari*, for they always pronounced the familiar name just as it is spelled in some of William Black's Scotch novels, cooked the midday meal, but not with the elusive pole of which she had intended to make a speedy end. But she did not forget it; on the contrary, it seemed to prey on her mind. As if fascinated, she would go out and look at it. She dragged it into the woodshed, that its destiny might seem more sure. She recommended it to the men of the family as being small and suited to the stove, but still it remained uncut. Sometimes they said that they could not find it; at other times it was forgotten. If just about to cut it, they were sure to be interrupted. Mary took the ax herself to chop it one day, but a brother laughingly took it from her and sent her back to the house, promising to follow with an armful of sticks in a few minutes; but he failed to keep his word, for a young colt broke loose and needed his immediate attention to prevent its reaching the highway.

One morning a wagon drove up with a family party from a distance, come to spend the day. Mary welcomed them, and the little house was all bustle and noise while the visitors were being made comfortable. A dinner fit for the occasion must be prepared, and Mary sent her brother in haste to the woodshed that the oven might be heated at once. He came back with an armful.

"I would have cut the stick that vexes you so much, Maari," he said, "but it seems gone at last out of our way. Someone has cut it before me."

"No," replied the girl, "here it is." And as she spoke a weight seemed to fall on her spirits, for she did not smile again but moved amongst her guests preoccupied and still. The pole was lying close to the kitchen door, along the path leading from the woodshed. The young man, thinking it in the way and apt to make people stumble, took it to the shed and threw it in.

Dinner was over and all the news discussed, and it was the middle of the afternoon when Mary was observed by someone of the family to be standing in the kitchen doorway alone. I think it was her mother who, wondering at her staying there so long, went to her. She was shivering violently, although it was pleasant weather, and without speaking, she pointed her finger to the pole, which lay at her feet in the pathway again. One of the boys was told to go at once and chop it in pieces, and Mary was kindly chided for her foolish terror. The visitors began to bestir themselves, for they had a lonely drive before them.

"I will leave the cutting of the stick until they are on the road," said Mary's brother; and he went to get out their horses and "speed to the parting guests." Farewells were said in hearty fashion at the gate, and then the family hastened to take up their interrupted tasks, separating, some to one thing and some to another; and yet again the stick was forgotten.

The evening meal was late, and Mary was hurried. A little daughter of one of the neighbors, who was in, bustled about, helping. She flew in and out with chips.

"Shall I drag this pole out of the way, Maari?" asked the child.

"No," said Mary; "*it is too late.*"

And there at the kitchen door it remained, and Mary was pale and silent, her thoughts being elsewhere. That night they were roused from sleep by her cry for help, and when they went to her they found her sick unto death. A doctor was fetched in haste; it was cholera morbus, and hopeless, as he knew at once, and before the sun rose Mary was dead. The stick lay at the door, and one of the kindly neighbors, who were doing what was needful during the following days, lifted it and sawed it carefully in two to serve as rests for the coffin, by means of which the bearers could convey it to the grave; and thus the fated stick fulfilled its mission.

Legend of the Living Specter

(Mexico)

Apparitions of dead people, Señor, of course are numerous and frequent. I myself—as on other occasions I have mentioned to you—have seen several specters, and so have various of my friends. But this specter of which I now am telling you—that appeared on the Plaza Mayor at noonday and was seen by everybody—was altogether out of the ordinary, being not in the least a dead person but a person who wore his own flesh and bones in the usual manner and was alive in them, yet who certainly was walking and talking here on the Plaza Mayor of this City of Mexico in the very selfsame moment that he also was walking and talking in a most remote and wholly different part of the world. Therefore, in spite of his wearing his own flesh and bones in the usual manner and being alive in them, it was certain that he was a specter because it was certain that his journeying could have been made only on devils' wings. The day on which this marvel happened is known most exactly, because it happened on the day after the day that the Governor of the Filipinas, Don Gómez Pérez Dasmariñas, had his head murderously split open and died of it in the Molucca Islands; and that gentleman was killed in that bad manner on the 25th of October in the year 1593. Therefore, since everything concerning this most extraordinary happening is known with so great an accuracy,

From: Thomas A. Janvier, ed., *Legends of the City of Mexico* (New York and London: Harper & Brothers, 1910).

there can be no doubt whatever but that in every particular all that I now am telling you is strictly true.

Because it began in two different places at the same time, it is not easy to say certainly, Señor, which end of this story is the beginning of it; but the beginning of it is this: On a day, being the day that I have just named to you, the sentries on guard at the great doors of the palace—and also the people who at that time happened to be walking nearby on the Plaza Mayor—of a sudden saw an entirely strange sentry pacing his beat before the great doors of the palace quite in the regular manner: marching back and forth with his gun on his shoulder, making his turns with a soldierly propriety, saluting correctly those entitled to salutes who passed him, and in every way conducting himself as though he duly had been posted there—but making his marchings and his turnings and his salutings with a wondering look on the face of him, and having the air of one who is all bedazzled and bemazed.

What made everyone know that he was a stranger in this city was that the uniform which he wore was of a wholly different cut and fabric from that belonging to any regiment at that time quartered here, being in fact, as was perceived by one of the sentries who had served in the Filipinas, the uniform worn in Manila by the palace guard. He was a man of forty or thereabouts, well set up and sturdy, and he had the assured carriage—even in his bedazzlement and bemazement— of an old soldier who had seen much campaigning and who could take care of himself through any adventure in which he might happen to land. Moreover, his talk, when the time came for him to explain himself, went with a devil-may-care touch to it that showed him to be a man who even with witches and demons was quite ready to hold his own.

His explanation of himself, of course, was not long in coming, because the captain of the guard at once was sent for; and when the captain of the guard came, he asked the stranger sentry most sharply what his name was, and where he came from, and what he was doing on a post to which he had not been assigned.

To these questions the stranger sentry made answer—speaking with an easy confidence and not in the least ruffled by the captain's sharpness with him—that his name was Gil Pérez, that he came from the Filipinas, and that what he was doing was his duty as near as he could come to it, because he had been duly detailed to stand sentry that morning before the governor's palace—and although this was not the governor's palace before which he had been posted, it certainly was *a* governor's palace and that he therefore was doing the best that he could do. And to these very curious statements he added—quite casually, as though referring to an ordinary matter of current interest—that the Governor of the Filipinas, Don Gómez Pérez Dasmariñas, had had his head murderously split open and was dead of it in the Molucca Islands the evening before.

Well, Señor, you may fancy what a nest of wasps was let loose when this Gil Pérez gave to the captain of the guard so incredible an account of himself and, on top of it, told that the governor of the Filipinas had been badly killed on the previous evening in islands in the Pacific Ocean thousands and thousands of miles away! It was a matter that the viceroy himself had to look into. Therefore, before the viceroy—who at that time was the good Don Luis de Velasco—Gil Peŕez was brought in a hurry, and to the viceroy he told over again just the same story, in just the same cool manner, and in just the same words.

Very naturally, the viceroy put a great many keen questions to him, and to those questions he gave his answers—or said plainly that he could not give any answers—with the assured air of an old soldier who would not lightly suffer his word to be doubted even by a viceroy, and who was ready, in dealing with persons of less consequence, to make good his sayings with his fists or with his sword.

In part, his explanation of himself was straightforward and satisfactory. What he told about the regiment to which he belonged was known to be true, and equally known to be true was much of what he told, being in accord with the news brought thence by the latest galleon, about affairs in the Filipinas. But when it came to explaining the main matter—how he had been shifted across the ocean and the earth, and all in a single moment, from his guardmount before the governor's palace in Manila to his guardmount before the viceroy's palace in the City of Mexico—Gil Pérez was at a stand. How that strange thing had happened, he said, he knew no more than Don Luis himself knew. All that he could be sure of was that it *had* happened, because certainly, only a half hour earlier he had been in Manila, and now, just as certainly he was in the City of Mexico, as his lordship the viceroy could see plainly with his own eyes. As to the even greater marvel—how he knew that on the previous evening the governor of the Filipinas had had his head murderously split open and was dead of it in the Molucca Islands—he said quite freely that he did not in the least know how he knew it. What alone he could be sure of, he said, was that in his heart he did know that Don Gómez had been killed on the previous evening in that bad manner, and he very stoutly asserted that the truth of what he told would be clear to Don Luis and to everybody when the news of the killing of Don Gómez had had time to get to Mexico in the ordinary way.

And then Gil Pérez, having answered all of the viceroy's questions which he could answer and having said all that he had to say, stood quite at his ease before the viceroy—with his feet firmly planted, and his right hand on his hip, and his right arm akimbo—and so waited for whatever might happen to be the next turn.

Well, Señor, the one thing of which anybody really could be sure in this amazing matter—and of which, of course, everybody was sure—was that the devil was at both the bottom and the top of it, and also there seemed to be very good ground for believing that Gil Pérez was in much closer touch with the devil than any good Christian—even though he were an old soldier and not much in the way of Christianity expected of him—had any right to be. Therefore, the viceroy rid himself of an affair that was much the same to him as a basket of nettles by turning Gil Pérez over to the Holy Office—and off he was carried to Santo Domingo and clapped into one of the strongest cells.

Most men, of course, on finding themselves that way in the clutches of the Inquisition, would have had all the insides of them filled with terror, but Gil Pérez, Señor—being, as I have mentioned, an old campaigner—took it all as it came along to him and was not one bit disturbed. He said cheerfully that many times in the course of his soldiering he had been in much worse places and added that—having a good roof over his head and quite fair rations, and instead of marching and fighting only to sit at his ease and enjoy himself—he really was getting for once in his life as much of clear comfort as any old soldier had a right to expect would come his way. Moreover, in his dealings with the familiars of the Holy Office his conduct was exemplary. He stuck firmly to his assertion that whatever the devil might have had to do with him, he never had had anything to do with the devil; he seemed to take a real pleasure in confessing as many of his sins as he conveniently could remember; and in every way that was open to him his conduct was that of quite as good a Christian as any old soldier reasonably could be expected to be.

Therefore, while he stayed on in his cell very contentedly, the familiars of the Holy Office put their heads together and puzzled and puzzled as to what they should do with him, because it certainly seemed as though the devil, to suit his own devilish purposes, simply had made a convenience of Gil Pérez without getting his consent in the matter; and so it did not seem quite fair, in the face of his protest that he was as much annoyed as anybody was by what the devil had done with him, to put him into a flame-covered sanbenito and to march him off to be burned for a sorcerer at the next auto-da-fé. Therefore, the familiars of the Holy Office kept on putting their heads together and puzzling and puzzling as to what they should do with him, and Gil Pérez kept on enjoying himself in his cell in Santo Domingo—and so the months went on and on.

And then one day, a new turn was given to the whole matter when the galleon from the Filipinas arrived at Acapulco and brought with it the proof that every word that Gil Pérez had spoken was true. Because the galleon brought the news that Don Gómez Pérez Dasmariñas—the crew of the ship that he was on having mutinied— really had had his head murderously split open and was dead of it in the Molucca Islands, and that this bad happening had come to him at the very time that Gil Pérez had named. Moreover, one of the military officers who had come from the Filipinas in the galleon and up from Acapulco to the City of Mexico with the *conducta* recognized Gil Pérez the moment that he laid eyes on him; and this officer said that he had seen him, only a day or two before the galleon's sailing, on duty in Manila with the palace guard. And so the fact was settled beyond all doubt that Gil Pérez had been brought by the devil from Manila to the City of Mexico, and also that the devil—since only the devil could have done it—had put the knowledge of the murderous killing of Don Gómez into his heart. Wherefore the fact that Gil Pérez was in league with the devil was clear to all the world.

Then the familiars of the Holy Office for the last time put their heads together and puzzled and puzzled over the matter, and at the end of their puzzling they decided that Gil Pérez was an innocent person and that he undoubtedly had had criminal relations with the devil and was full of wickedness. Therefore, they ordered that, being innocent, he should be set free from his cell in Santo Domingo and that, being a dangerous character whose influence was corrupting, he should be sent back to Manila in the returning galleon. And that was their decree.

Gil Pérez, Señor, took that disposition of him in the same easygoing way that he had taken all the other dispositions of him, save that he grumbled a little, as was to be expected of an old soldier, over having to leave his comfortably idle life in his snug quarters and to go again to his fightings and his guardmounts and his parades. And so back he went to the Filipinas, only his return journey was made in a slow and natural manner aboard the galleon, not, as his outward journey had been made, all in a moment on devils' wings.

To my mind, Señor, it seems that there is more of this story that ought to be told. For myself, I should like to know why the familiars of the Holy Office did not deal a little more severely with a case that certainly had the devil at both the bottom and the top of it; and also I should like to know what became of Gil Pérez when he got back to Manila in the galleon, and there had to tell over again about his relations with the devil in order to account for his half year's absence from duty without leave. But those are matters which I never have heard mentioned, and what I have told you is all that there is to tell.

The Forked Roads

(United States)

Long ago, in the days of the grandfathers, a man died and was buried by his village. For four nights his ghost had to walk a very dark trail. Then he reached the Milky Way and there was plenty of light. For this reason, people ought to keep the funeral fires lighted for four nights, so the spirit will not walk in the dark trail.

The spirit walked along the Milky Way. At last he came to a point

From: Katharine B. Judson, *Myths and Legends of the Great Plains* (Chicago: A. C. McClurg & Co., 1913).

where the trail forked. There sat an old man. He was dressed in a buffalo robe, with the hair on the outside. He pointed to each ghost the road he was to take. One was short and led to the land of good ghosts. The other was very long; along it the ghosts went wailing.

The spirits of suicide cannot travel either road. They must hover over their graves. For them there is no future life.

A murderer is never happy after he dies. Ghosts surround him and keep up a constant whistling. He is always hungry, though he eats much food. He is never allowed to go where he pleases, lest high winds arise and sweep down upon the others.

The Haunted Grove

(Canada)

A certain man whom it is safe to call Angus, as there was at least one Angus in every household, lived near the stage road that connected two large villages, which were, if I remember right, about fourteen miles apart. His home was situated nearly midway between them and about a mile from the aforementioned hollow. He seems to have taken more interest in the post office than his friends whom I knew, and subscribed for and studied certain Montreal newspapers. For this he was pitied in the parish and called "Poor Angus," for the general sentiment of the place was opposed to literature, and reading was considered a sign of mental weakness. He appears to have adhered, however, to the habit, whether from native independence or native imbecility I cannot say. I have noticed that as a means of separating a man from his fellows, either strength or weakness, if sufficiently pronounced, is equally potent. So this man, following the bent of his nature, went twice or thrice a week to the post office late in the afternoon, when the passing stage threw in a big leather mailbag. The post office was in a farmhouse, and to reach it he

From: C. A. Fraser, "Scottish Myths from Ontario," *Journal of American Folk-Lore* 6 (1893): 185–98.

walked through the hollow with the unwholesome reputation. On the slope of the hill farthest from the post office was a grove, not a dense wood—just about half an acre of thinly wooded land, the trees being so far apart that you could easily get glimpses and peeps of the country beyond. I remember once admiring a pink sunset scantily visible among the dark trunks of those trees.

Well, one autumn afternoon Angus was ascending this hill on his way home with his newspapers, when in the grove on his right suddenly sounded the chopping of a tree. He stopped, interested at once. The grove belonged to a neighbor and cousin of his own, and it had been for very many years left undisturbed. I think it very possible that it was a "sugar bush," that is, a wood reserved for sugar making, but of this I cannot be sure. But if my guess is right, it would account for the surprise he felt at the cutting down of a tree there. He went to the fence, or rather stone dyke, for that is one of the very few parts in which you find fields enclosed by stone dykes in lieu of fences, as in Scotland. The chopping continued, though he saw no one, and he moved along, expecting every moment to see man and ax. Finally he shouted. To his intense astonishment there was no reply, although it was incredible that he was unheard by a person in so near vicinity. As the echo of his shout died away, the chopping, which for a moment or two had been suspended, began again. A curious horror crept over the listener, and he looked no more but made haste up the hill and, turning the corner, was soon at home. He said nothing about the matter on this first occasion, and a few days later was again on the road returning from the same errand, when, lo! on the quiet air came again the same chop, chop, chopping. In telling it afterward, he said that in his heart he made no fight against fate, but he just thought sadly of his worldly affairs and wondered if things were in good shape for him to leave wife and little ones, for from that hour he confidently looked for death before another spring. He stood long listening, and when at last he went home he related the whole circumstance to his wife. Together they recounted it to friends, who went in parties and singly to the place but heard nothing. They also thoroughly searched the little wood, arguing that chopping must leave signs behind in the shape of chips and disfigured trunks. But no, there was no mark of any kind in any part of the grove. Angus was now earnestly counseled to abandon his literary pursuits. He could not but own that he had received a warning, and he did own it but contended that it was undeserved, and refused to be guided, as one might say, by a light that, as all admitted, shone with a lurid glare. He was exhorted to forswear the reading of vain and foolish lies, for with the acumen which surprised and gratified me so much, they even refused to regard our newspapers as mediums of information, recognizing instinctively their right to stand in the ranks of fiction. Their advice was in all points save one unheeded. With one voice they bade him, if he heard the warning again, to pursue his way as if he heard it not, looking neither to the right nor left. This counsel he followed, and the end shows the folly and uselessness of attempting to elude a menace which is—well, which is of this kind.

Angus continued to walk to and from the post office and, when alone, never failed to hear the mysterious ax at work in the wood. He never heard it unless alone, and it was never heard by anyone else. Although the conviction that his death would happen before many months took firm hold of his mind, yet in time he became so accustomed to the thought and its cause as to go about his usual occupations with much of the wonted interest, and even to hear the sound of an ax, wielded by invisible hands, without experiencing agitation.

Weeks sped on and brought winter and an unusual fall of snow. The stage road became blocked, and vehicles left the highway to make a new track through the fields. For several months that winter the real road through the hollow was not used, and the snow, which drifted high in it, covered the dykes on each side. Temporary roads and footpaths made winding lines over the white plains on every hand. Angus now followed one of these roads, which ran parallel to the real highway, just the dyke being between them, until he reached the grove, when he, with extraordinary and fatal hardihood, instead of remaining in it, used to leave it and, striking out at right angles to it, would walk through the grove, aiming directly for his own house and greatly shortening his walk thereby. The trees had of course protected the place from wind; there had been no drifting, and walking was easy. He told it at home, and said with grim humor that the Man in the Bush seemed pleased that he would come that way, for his chopping was louder and gladder than ever before; and his wife repeated her counsel earnestly that he look only straight before him and never stop nor answer any sound, nor take heed in any way of that unholy work. "And," said the Angus who years after related it to me, "the Ax might well be merry when she bade him that way!" But Angus laid the advice to heart and strode steadily through the grove, looking straight before him, and every day the Ax grew gayer and louder. He did not speak of it now. He was getting used to it, and the neighbors had ceased to think of it, the more easily because, as I have told, his literary tastes had separated this Angus from among them. So one day the owner of the grove and his sons went over to chop down one particular tree that, on the day when they had searched the grove in the autumn, had appeared to them to merit destruction. Perhaps it was a beech growing among maples, where it was not wanted, or perhaps it was a dead maple cumbering the ground. They began to chop. It was late in the afternoon. One said with a laugh, "It may be we are taking the tree that Poor Angus's ghost has been working at so long."

Perhaps the invisible man heard them. At any rate he did not chop that evening. It was only his cousin's ax that gave the good strokes that Poor Angus heard as he turned from the track to cross the grove as usual. The tree was swaying and shivering, and all but ready to fall. He had cut trees all his life, and he knew the sound of the stroke when the task was almost done; but no goblin's trick would beguile him into turning his head. He looked neither to right nor left. Then the chopping ceased, and his blood nearly froze as he heard his own name shouted in tones of such horror that a familiar voice was unrecognized. Others caught up the cry. There was a din, the crashing of branches and sound of rushing feet mingled with shouts of warning, and Poor Angus fell with the enormous tree upon him. When at last the burden was removed and the crushed body borne home, there were men there who heard among the trees inhuman laughter and knew that Something had lured Poor Angus to his doom.

Legend of the Callejón del Muerto

(Mexico)

It is an unwise thing, Señor, and there also is wickedness in it, to make a vow to the Blessed Virgin—or for that matter, to the smallest saint in the whole calendar—and not to fulfill that vow when the Blessed Virgin, or the saint, as the case may be, has performed punctually all that the vow was made for. And so this gentleman of whom I now am speaking found out for himself, and most uncomfortably, when he died with an unfulfilled vow on his shoulders and had to take some of the time that he otherwise would have spent pleasantly in heaven among the angels in order to do after he was dead what he had promised to do, and what he most certainly ought to have done, while he still was alive.

The name of this gentleman who so badly neglected his duty, Señor, was Don Tristan de Alculer, and he was a humble but honorable Spanish merchant who came from the Filipinas to live here in the City of Mexico. And he came in the time when the viceroy was the Marqués de Villa Manrique, and most likely as the result of that viceroy's doings and orderings, because the Marqués de Villa Manrique gave great attention to enlarging the trade with the East through the Filipinas—as was found out by the English corsairs, so that Don Francisco Draco, who was the greatest pirate of all of them, was able to capture a galleon laden almost to sinking with nothing but silver and gold.

With Don Tristan, who was of an elderliness, came his son to help him in his merchanting; and this son was named Tristan also and was a most worthy young gentleman, very capable in the management of mercantile affairs. Having in their purses but a light lining, their commerce at its beginning was of a smallness, and they took for their

From: Thomas A. Janvier, ed., *Legends of the City of Mexico* (New York and London: Harper & Brothers, 1910).

home a mean house in a little street so poor and so deserted that nobody had taken the trouble to give a name to it—the very street that ever since their time has been called the Alley of the Dead Man, because of what happened as the result of Don Tristan's unfulfilled vow. That they were most respectable people is made clear by the fact that the archbishop himself, who at that period was the illustrious Don Fray García de Santa María Mendoza, was the friend of them, and especially the friend of Don Tristan the elder, who frequently consulted with him in regard to the state of his soul.

So a number of prospering years passed on, Señor, and then, on a time, Don Tristan the son went down to the coast to make some buyings; and it was in the bad season, and the fever seized him so fiercely that all in a moment the feet and half the legs of him fairly were inside death's door. Then it was that Don Tristan, being in sore trouble because of his son's desperate illness, made the vow that I am telling you about. He made it to the Blessed Virgin of Guadalupe; and he vowed to her that if she would save his son alive to him from the fever, he would walk on his bare feet from his own house to her sanctuary, and that there in her sanctuary he would make his thanks to her from the deep depths of his soul. And the Blessed Virgin, being full of love and of amiability, was pleased to listen to the prayer of Don Tristan and to believe the vow that went along with it, wherefore she caused the fever immediately to leave the sick Don Tristan—and presently home he came to his father alive and well.

But Don Tristan, having got from the Blessed Virgin all that he had asked of her, did not give to her what he had promised to give to her in return. Being by that time an aged gentleman, and also being much afflicted with rheumatism, the thought of taking a walk of near to three miles barefoot was most distasteful to him. And so he put his walk off for a week or two, saying to himself that the Blessed Virgin would not be in any hurry about the matter; and then he put it off for another week or two; and in that way—because each time that he was for keeping his vow, shivers would come in his old feet at dread of being bare and having cold earth under them, and trembles would come in his old thin legs at dread of more rheumatism—the time slipped on and on, and the Blessed Virgin did not get her due.

But his soul was not easy inside of him, Señor—and it could not be, because he was playing fast and loose with it—and so he laid the whole matter before his friend the archbishop, hoping that for friendship's sake the archbishop would be so obliging as to dispense him from his vow. For myself, Señor, I cannot but think that the archbishop, for all that his position put him in close touch with heavenly matters and gave him the right to deal with them, was not well advised in his action. At any rate, what he did was to tranquilize Don Tristan by telling him that the Blessed Virgin was too considerate to hold him to a contract that certainly would lay him up with a bad attack of rheumatism, and that even—so wearied out would he be by forcing his old thin legs to carry him all that distance—might be the death of him. And so the upshot of it was that the archbishop, being an easygoing and a very good-natured gentleman, dispensed Don Tristan from his vow.

But a vow, Señor, is a vow, and even an archbishop cannot cast one loose from it. And so they all found out on this occasion, and in a hurry, because the Blessed Virgin, while never huffed over trifles, does not let the grass grow under her feet when her anger justly is aroused.

Only three days after Don Tristan had received his dispensation—to which, as the event proved, he was not entitled—the archbishop went on the twelfth of the month, in accordance with the custom observed in that matter, to celebrate mass at the Villa de Guadalupe in Our Lady's sanctuary. The mass being ended, he came homeward on his mule by the causeway to the city, and as he rode along easily he was put into a great surprise by seeing Don Tristan walking toward him and by perceiving that he was of a most dismal dead paleness and that his feet were bare. For a moment Don Tristan paused beside the archbishop—whose mule had stopped short, all in a tremble—and clasped his hand with a hand that was of an icy coldness, then he passed onward, saying in a dismal voice, rusty and cavernous, that for his soul's saving he was fulfilling the vow that he had made to Her Ladyship, because the knowledge had come to him that if this vow were not accomplished, he certainly would spend the whole of eternity blistering in hell! Having thus explained matters, not a word more did Don Tristan have to say for himself, nor did he even look backward as he walked away slowly and painfully on his bare old feet toward Our Lady's shrine.

The archbishop trembled as much as his mule did, Señor, being sure that strange and terrible things were about him; and when the mule a little came out of her fright and could march again, but still trembling, he went straight to Don Tristan's house to find out—though in his heart he knew what his finding would be—the full meaning of this awesome prodigy. And he found at Don Tristan's house what he knew in his heart he would find there, and that was Don Tristan, the four lighted death candles around him, lying on his bed death struck, his death-white cold hands clasped on his breast on the black pall covering him, and on his death-white face the very look that was on it as he went to the keeping of his unkept vow! Therefore the archbishop was seized with a hot-and-cold shuddering, and his teeth rattled in the head of him; and straightway he and all who were with him, perceiving that they were in the presence of a divine mystery, fell to their knees in wondering awe of what had happened and together prayed for the peace of Don Tristan's soul.

Very possibly, Señor, the archbishop and the rest of them did not pray hard enough, or perhaps Don Tristan's sin of neglect was so serious a matter that a long spell in purgatory was required of him before he could be suffered to pass on to a more comfortable region and be at ease. At any rate, almost immediately he took to walking at midnight in the little street that for so long he had lived in, always wrapped in a long white shroud that fluttered about him in the night wind loosely and carrying always a yellow-blazing great candle, and so being a most terrifying personage to encounter as he marched slowly up and down. Therefore, everybody who dwelt in that street hurried to move away from it, and Don Tristan had it quite to himself in its desertedness—for which reason, as I have mentioned, the Alley of the Dead Man became its name.

I have been told by my friend the *cargador*, Señor, and also by several other trustworthy persons that Don Tristan, though more than three hundred years have passed since the death of him, has not entirely given up his marchings. Certainly, for myself, I do not think that it would be judicious to walk in the Callejón del Muerto at midnight even now.

The Dead

(Mexico)

There was an old woman who worked much at night, spinning and weaving her cloth. One moonlit night her dog howled much, and the old woman said, "Why does my dog howl so much?" She took it in her arms, took the excretion out of the eyes of the dog and put it in her own eyes, and remained there looking out on the street, and she saw a procession coming—many people with burning candles in their hands. She stood there, and the procession passed the door of her house.

Then one person came out of the procession and gave a candle to the old woman who was standing in the doorway. He said to her, "Take this candle, and tomorrow, when we pass again at the same hour, give it to me."

"Well," said the old woman. She took the candle and put it on her altar. She took the excretion out of her eyes and went to sleep.

The next day, early in the morning, there was no candle but the shinbone of a dead person. The old woman was frightened and went to confession. Then the padre said to her, "Go get a very young infant, and stand in the doorway of your house with the shinbone in one hand and the infant in the other. When the procession passes and the man asks for the candle which he gave you last night, and when you give it to him, pinch the baby so that it cries, and give the man the candle with your other hand."

The old woman did so. She stood in the doorway and pinched the baby while she passed the candle to the man; and the dead said to the old woman, "This protects you, for this was the hour when we were to take you"; and thus the old woman freed herself.

From: Franz Boas, "Notes on Mexican Folk-Lore," *Journal of American Folk-Lore* 25 (1912): 204–60.

Louisiana Ghost Story

(United States)

About two years ago, I reckon, an ole man died in the place whar I useter live. He lef' a heap o' proputty ter his heirs; the' was a right smart head o' chillun, an' he give 'em ev'y one a farm, an' the' was one mo' farm yit lef' over. 'Twas a good farm an' the house all furnished up, but no one didn' keer ter live thar, fer they all said the house was haanted.

But one o' the heirs he said he wan't no way feared but he could lay that ghost ef they 'd give him the farm, 'n' they tole him the farm was his ef he could lay the ghost so 's ter live thar. So he went ter a man o' the name o' Peacock that lived neighbor ter him, an' 'twas a church member, an' offered him a heap o' money ter go an' lay that ghost.

Mr. Peacock, he went that same night ter the house, takin' his Bible along, 'n' he set thar a-readin' it backward and forward; he didn' mind it none whether the ghost came a-nigh or not. Sho' nuff, the ghost came along while he was a-readin', an' it went all about thro' the house, so 's Mr. Peacock could hear it goin' inter the diffunt rooms an' a-movin' things this-a-way an' that-a-way. But he didn' let on to hear the ghost—no indeed—but he kep' a-readin' away ter his Bible.

Arter a while the ghost blowed out his lamp, but he jes' lighted it an' read on, 'n' then he went inter the bedroom an' lay down. That sort o' made the ghost mad, so 's it come inter the bedroom an' he see it, like as ef 'twas an ole woman. Fer the' was an ole woman's ghost that haanted the house anyhow; they said it couldn't rest no way, 'count o' the murder the ole lady done when she was alive. Anyhow Mr. Peacock see her reach out her arm, long an' skinny-like, under the bed, 'n' she jes' turned it over *so*, with him on it. But he on'y crep' out from under it an' went back inter the kitchen 'n' begun to read away in his Bible. An' thar he stayed all night, on'y afore day the ghost came once mo' an' said, "Ef yo' come back 'yer agen, yore a dead man."

Well, nex' night Mr. Peacock came back again, yes indeed, an' he'd

From: Fanny D. Bergen, "Notes and Queries: Louisiana Ghost Story," *Journal of American Folk-Lore* 12 (1899): 146–47.

got two preachers ter come too an' try to lay that ghost. One was a Methodis' 'n the other was a Catholic, an' they both brought their Bibles, 'n' all of 'em kep' readin' forward an' backward. 'Twan't no time at all tell that ghost came agen, an' then it jus' went on mos' outrageous.

The Methodis' he didn't stay ter hear much o' the racket tell out he run an' never come back that night. The Catholic he hel' out a good bit, but 'fore long *he* run an' lef' Peacock ter stay it out by himself.

Well, they say the ghost never spoke ter him no mo', but sho' nuff in the mornin' thar was Peacock a-lyin' dead with his head cut clean off—yes indeed, sir!—an' the' ain't no one ever tried to lay that ghost sence.

The Ghostly Matinta-Pere

(Brazil)

I can learn very little about this mythical being, which seems to be rather a phantom than a definite form. The Indians say that it comes sometimes in the night, walking or flying about the paths and near the villages. Generally it is invisible, and only the rustling of wings is heard or the song *matinta-pere* often repeated. At other times it assumes the shape of an old man, a priest, or any other person or thing. When it is frightened by shouting, it disappears in the air with rustling of wings. The story goes that it is fond of sweets and is often heard at night about the little Indian sugar mills. Probably such accounts are caused by the great moths, which are frequently heard about the mills, flying off rapidly when alarmed but invisible in the darkness.

From: Thomas Ewbank, *Life in Brazil; or, A Journal of a Visit to the Land of the Cocoa and the Palm* (New York: Harper & Brothers, 1856).

The Matinta-Pere is perfectly harmless. Sometimes it calls to a passerby. A Santarem Indian told me of one that accosted an old man who was passing by one of the sugar mills. A voice came from behind a stump: "Where is your molasses?" but when the old man looked, he found nobody.

Another Indian told me that a Matinta-Pere was seen in the streets of Para soon after the rebellion of 1835. The patrol heard one singing. Following the voice, they found an old mulatto woman in an orange tree. As she could not answer their questions, they took her to the guardhouse, and there she was locked in securely, but in the morning she was gone.

The Rich Ghost

(United States)

Once upon a time, in a lonely little house upon a hill, there lived a man and his wife. The husband worked down in the town all day, and the wife worked at home alone. Every day at noon, when the clock was striking twelve, she was startled by the pale, ghostlike figure of a man that stood in the doorway and watched her. She was very much frightened and told her husband that she could not stay in that house any longer. But they were very poor, and the rent was cheaper than they could find elsewhere.

While the husband was looking for another house, the preacher came to see the wife. She told him about the pale-faced ghost that continually watched her. The preacher told her to sit down before her looking glass with her back to the door and read a certain passage from the Bible backward. Then she must turn her chair around, look the ghost in the face, and ask him, "What do you want here?"

The very next day she did as she was told. At first her voice

From: Various, "Folk-Lore Scrap-Book: Ghosts as Guardians of Hidden Treasure," *Journal of American Folk-Lore* 12 (1899): 64–65.

trembled and she did not think that she could finish, but strength came to her and she read it. Then she turned upon the ghost and asked him the question. His face was frightful to look upon, but he told her to take her hoe and follow him. He led her to a lonely spot and rolled away a large stone and commanded her to dig. She dug until she was exhausted and the hoe fell from her hand. He jerked it up and dug until she had regained her strength. Then she commenced to dig again and at last struck something hard. He commanded her to stop, then stooped down and with wonderful strength drew up a large earthen pot. Upon taking off the cover, she saw, by the dim light of the setting sun, gold and silver coins in great abundance.

The ghost told her to go home and tear the plastering from off the western corner of her little one-room house and she would find a package of letters. From these she must get his brother's address and send him half of the hidden treasure. The other half was for herself. She did as she was told. The pale-faced ghost was never seen again, and she was made a rich woman and they lived happily ever afterward.

Newfoundland Ghosts

(Canada)

An old fisherman told me of a locality that was formerly inhabited by Frenchmen. There is a good beach for landing, but no boat will remain tied on it. Fasten the painter as you will, ghostly hands untie the knots again and again. (By the by, most of the ghosts are supposed to be Frenchmen.) That old man has had some other strange experiences. He saw a mermaid sitting on a rock as plainly as he ever saw everything, and he was within a couple of boat's lengths of her when she dived to her crystal caves below and was lost to sight.

From: George Patterson, "Notes on the Folk-Lore of Newfoundland," *Journal of American Folk-Lore* 8 (1895): 285–90.

A headless man is the habitué of one of the stages at ———, and one of the men at the house where I boarded met him one night. His family told me that he got home nearly fainting and that he would not go out after dark for weeks after. This ghost also is a Frenchman.

The old lay reader and former schoolmaster at ——— must be gifted with second sight, for his "manifestations" have been numerous, and he really has had some wonderful experiences, if all he says is true. Once he was walking to ———, and some distance in front of him by the side of the road he saw a pile of firewood with a dog and sled beside it. (I forget whether there was a man too.) As he got near he could not help noticing how beautifully even the wood was arranged, and wondered who had taken so much trouble. Presently the wood, dog, and sled disappeared, and when he reached the spot where they had been, there was not a mark on the snow.

An old Irish woman told me that once on her way to mass she was overtaken by a man who walked some miles with her and entered the chapel. The curious part of the story is that the man was invisible to everyone save herself and the priest. It was only when his reverence told her after service he had seen the ghost beside her that she discovered the nature of her companion.

At Bonavista, somewhere down the Cape Shore, there is an immense treasure, hidden long years ago by pirates. These pirates, after concealing their booty, sailed away in search of further plunder, leaving one of their number to guard the spot, first binding him by a solemn oath to remain till they returned. Years passed away, the unfortunate watchman shuffled off this mortal coil, and nothing but his spirit was left to watch the place. His friends have doubtless long ago departed this life also, and the ghost is so tired of his job that he makes this splendid offer: If anyone will go alone at midnight and shed blood at the spot (any animal will do to kill), that ceremony releases him from his obligation, and the person performing the kindly office can have the treasure. One of the most intelligent men in Bonavista told me that the story was told him by a man to whom the late pirate had volunteered the information. No one has yet been brave enough to venture.

One fact, however, is to be noted, whether for weal or woe, born in the daytime you will never see ghosts.

A Poltergeist in Georgia

(United States)

The astonishing phenomena of the poltergeist variety that disturbed the little village of Llanarthney in South Wales in December of 1909 have been repeated to some extent on this side of the Atlantic in the prosaic little telegraph tower of Dale in Georgia. Totally lacking in all that is romantic or picturesque, the little station of Dale lies seven miles to the south of the city of Savannah, in the county of Chatham, on the main line of the Atlantic Coastline railroad. For nine months of the year Dale is deserted. Being only a telegraph tower in use during the tourist season, when many fast trains whiz past daily with their loads of pleasure-seeking tourists from the North, it is closed and deserted until the season opens again.

Dale tower is the only house of any description there. In fact, the telegraph tower *is* Dale, and the nearest human habitation is a quarter of a mile away. On the borders of an extensive pine forest and so far removed from human activities, Dale is not an inviting-looking place at any time of the year. Each January, as the tourist season opens and the railroad puts the block system of dispatching trains into operation, three telegraph operators take up their residence in the tower of Dale and constitute the sole inhabitants until April, when the tower is again closed and deserted. During the nine months the tower is closed, only the passing of the trains, with the occasional sidetracking of one of them, disturbs the reign of silence.

It is then not strange that rumors of queer happenings should be heard among the trainmen. Few deserted places ever enjoy a very savory reputation, and Dale is no exception. On one occasion, a man was killed by the train hard by the tower, and his body was laid to rest over across the track hardly a stone's throw away and in full view of the tower windows. After that, there were more rumors, and conductors dreaded to have to sidetrack their trains there. The brakemen would report strange noises about the switch where the tragedy had

From: Thomas Hart Raines, "A Poltergeist from Georgia," *Occult Review* 13 (1911): 276–79.

happened, and sometimes on attempting to pull out from the side-track, the engineman would find his train uncoupled in three places, no order having been given to that effect and none of the train crew having put their hands to it. Scarcely a brakeman on the line will enter the tower.

One fine morning when the new telegraphers arrived to open the season, what should they find but the corpse of a man, far advanced in decay, reposing on the floor of the lower chamber of the tower. Poor, old, and neglected, the wanderer had lain down and died far from the sound of all save the chirping of crickets and the rush of the passing trains. With naught to identify him, he was laid away over across the track with the first occupant of the new graveyard. Since that time, Dale has been the bête noire of the trainmen, and many a gruesome tale has emanated therefrom.

The occurrences which I am about to relate have only just ceased. As soon as I heard of them I began an investigation, and while I was so unfortunate as not to witness the phenomena myself, I had the good fortune to interview the three young men who collectively witnessed them, and I personally visited the scene of the disturbance. With these three young men I am personally acquainted and can assure my readers that nothing could be further from their wish than in any way to depart from the strictest truth and accuracy in the details related. They are young men of intelligence whose veracity I cannot question, and so positive are they that they have not been deceived or hallucinated that they have given me a signed statement certifying to the truth of all the facts related.

These three young men, E. A. Bright, R. L. Davis, and J. H. Clark, opened the tower at Dale on January 4, 1911, and since that time have been the sole occupants, working, eating, and sleeping (when possible) within the two rooms that constitute the extent of the tower space, the one above the other, a trapdoor closing the stair leading up to the room above. The first unusual occurrence that attracted the attention of these young men was the difficulty experienced in keeping the door closed in the room below, no matter how securely it was fastened. Apparently securely fastened, no sooner would their backs be turned than the door would fly open with a click. A stout fortypenny nail was then used to fasten the door, with no better result. Then a long iron bar was placed against it. All to no purpose, as the door would fly open again just as soon as their backs were turned.

Then the sound of mysterious footsteps on the stair would be heard, and although the entire tower and premises were carefully searched, no cause for the noises could be found. Then followed the raising and lowering of the window sashes in the upper chamber of the tower in full view of all three of the occupants, no human hand having touched them.

By this time the young men were rather nervous, and to assure themselves against tricksters, the trapdoor leading down to the floor below was closed and securely fastened, and raised only when necessary to descend to the ground. This precaution had no effect whatsoever on the phenomena, and soon various articles began to be levitated about the room in broad open daylight in full view of all three occupants of the tower when there was no possible chance for trickery or fraud. A can of condensed milk was seen to lift itself into the air and pass from one end of the desk to the other without the contact of a visible hand. A large dishpan lying near the stove slowly lifted itself and rolled down the stairs and out of the tower and under it, from whence it had to be fished out with the aid of a long pole. A lantern was levitated onto the desk without having been touched and in full view of all. On another occasion, this lantern made a wild rush across the room and dashed itself into fragments against the wall. An ordinary can opener flew wildly about the room and fastened itself in the center of the ceiling. I saw this can opener, and can assure anyone interested that the most expert could not perform a similar feat once in a hundred efforts. Frequently bolts and taps such as are used in railroad construction work would be hurled into the room, breaking a hole in the glass of the window scarcely large enough to enter through.

On one occasion, when objects were being hurled about the room so persistently that the tower was hastily abandoned by all three occupants, a chair was dashed out of the upper window and fell with such force that one of the rungs was broken, and narrowly missed the head of Mr. Davis—this in broad daylight, with no one in the tower and the only avenue of entrance or of escape guarded by the three occupants of the tower. I saw the chair, and only a terrific blow could have so injured it.

When matters had reached this point, Messrs. Bright, Davis, and Clark were in a state of panic, and Mr. Bright walked the seven miles into Savannah to resign his position. Arriving at Savannah, he was ashamed to relate his experiences and returned to Dale. Twice he has done this, and since the subsidence of the phenomena he has assured me that nothing would induce him again to go through with the eerie experiences that were his for so many days at Dale. The last of these strange occurrences took place a few days before I reached the scene of them and interviewed Messrs. Bright, Davis, and Clark.

A pack of ordinary playing cards having been tossed from the window, in the tentative belief that they were the cause of the supernormal happenings, immediately returned and was found in a bag of rice, while the case that formerly contained them was found in a canister of coffee with the lid tightly closed. The cards were then put back in the case, and as a fast train whizzed past they were tossed beneath the wheels of the engine, only to be found in the bed a moment later. This occurred at ten o'clock in the morning and in full view of the three gentlemen I have named. The day following, a large quantity of sulfur was burned in the tower in the hope of effecting the cessation of the phenomena, since which time, strange to relate, they have ceased altogether.

On looking at the tower of Dale, it would be guessed that a trickster could easily climb the semaphore ladder and produce these phenomena with little trouble. This I deny, as the operator on duty—and there is one always on duty—is always facing the ladder, and any attempt to scale it would instantly be detected. Neither could the stair be the means of entrance, for the trapdoor closes it effectually against all comers. The vibrations of passing trains cannot have caused the phenomena, for I personally tested this point and found that such could not have been the case.

As I cannot question the veracity of Messrs. Bright, Davis, and Clark, who have witnessed all these strange things collectively when there was no chance of deception, are we then to say they were all the victims of a hallucination? This is too absurd to be discussed, and the conclusion is forced upon us that the phenomena really took place, be their cause what it may.

Legend of the Callejón del Padre Lecuona

(Mexico)

Who Padre Lecuona was, Señor, and what he did or had done to him in this street that caused his name to be given to it, I do not know. The padre about whom I now am telling you, who had this strange thing happen to him in this street, was named Lanza, but he was called by everybody Lanchitas, according to our custom of giving such endearing diminutives to the names of those whom we love. He deserved to be loved, this excellent Padre Lanchitas, because he himself loved everybody and freely gave to all in sickness or in trouble his loving aid. Confessing to him was a pleasure, and his absolution was worth having, because it was given always with the approval of the good God. My own grandfather knew him well, Señor, having known a man who had seen him when he was a boy. Therefore, this strange story about him is true.

On a night—and it was a desponding night, because rain was falling and there was a chill wind—Padre Lanchitas was hurrying to the house of a friend of his, where every week he and three other gentlemen of a Friday evening played *malilla* together. It is a very serious game, Señor, and to play it well requires a large mind. He was late, and that was why he was hurrying.

When he was nearly come to the house of his friend—and glad to get there because of the rain and the cold—he was stopped by an old woman plucking at his wet cloak and speaking to him. And the old woman begged him for God's mercy to come quickly and confess a dying man. Now that is a call, Señor, that a priest may not refuse, but because his not joining them would inconvenience his friends, who could not play at their game of malilla without him, he asked the

From: Thomas A. Janvier, ed., *Legends of the City of Mexico* (New York and London: Harper & Brothers, 1910).

woman why she did not go to the parish priest of the parish in which the dying man was. And the woman answered him that only to him would the dying man confess, and she begged him again for God's mercy to hurry with her or the confession would not be made in time—and then the sin of his refusal would be heavy on his own soul when he himself came to die.

So, then, the padre went with her, walking behind her along the cold dark streets in the mud with the rain falling, and at last she brought him to the eastern end of this street that is called the Callejón del Padre Lecuona and to the long old house there that faces toward the church of El Carmen and has a hump in the middle on the top of its front wall. It is a very old house, Señor. It was built in the time when we had viceroys, instead of the President Porfírio; and it has no windows, only a great door for the entering of carriages at one end of it, a small door in the middle of it, and another small door at the other end. A person who sells charcoal, Señor, lives there now.

It was to the middle door that the woman brought Padre Lanchitas. The door was not fastened, and at a touch she pushed it open and in they went together, and the first thing that the padre noticed when he was come through the doorway was a very bad smell. It was the sort of smell, Señor, that is found in very old houses of which all the doors and windows have been shut fast for a very long time. But the padre had matters more important than bad smells to attend to, and all that he did about it was to hold his handkerchief close to his nose. One little poor candle, stuck on a nail in a board, was set in a far corner, and in another corner was a man lying on a mat spread upon the earth floor; and there was nothing else whatever—except cobwebs everywhere, the bad smell, the old woman, and the padre himself—in that room.

That he might see him whom he was to confess, Padre Lanchitas took the candle in his hand and went to the man on the mat and pulled aside the ragged and dirty old blanket that covered him; and then he started back with a very cold qualm in his stomach, saying to the woman, "This man already is dead! He cannot confess! And he has the look of having been dead for a very long while!" And that was true, Señor, for what he saw was a dry and bony head, with yellow skin drawn tight over it, having shut eyes deep sunken. Also, the two hands which rested crossed upon the man's breast were no more than the same dry yellow skin shrunk close over shrunken bones! And seeing such a bad strange sight, the padre was uneasy and alarmed.

But the woman said back to him with assurance, yet also coaxingly, "This man is going to confess, Padrecito," and so speaking, she fetched from its far corner the board with the nail in it and took the candle from him and set it fast again upon the nail. And then the man himself, in the light and in the shadow, sat up on the mat and began to recite in a voice that had a rusty note in it the *Confiteor Deo*—and after that, of course, there was nothing for the padre to do but to listen to him till the end.

What he told, Señor, being told under the seal of confession, of course remained always a secret. But it was known later that he spoke of matters that had happened a good two hundred years back, as the padre knew because he was a great reader of books of history; and that he put himself into the very middle of those matters and made the terrible crime that he had committed a part of them; and that he ended by telling that in that ancient time he had been killed in a brawl suddenly and so had died unconfessed and unshriven, and that ever since his soul had blistered in hell.

Hearing such wild talk from him, the padre was well satisfied that the poor man's wits were wandering in his fever—as happens with many, Señor, in their dying time—and so bade him lie quietly and rest himself, and promised that he would come to him and hear his confession later on.

But the man cried out very urgently that that must not be, declaring that by God's mercy he had been given one single chance to come back again out of eternity to confess his sins and to be shriven of them, and that unless the padre did hearken then and there to the confession of his sins, and did shrive him of them, this one chance that God's mercy had given him would be lost and wasted—and back he would go forever to the hot torments of hell.

Therefore, the padre, being sure by that time that the man was quite crazy in his fever, let him talk on till he had told the whole story of his frightful sinnings, and then did shrive him to quiet him, just as you promise the moon to a sick, fretful child. And the devil must have been very uneasy that night, Señor, because the good nature of that kind-hearted priest lost to him what by rights was his own!

As Padre Lanchitas spoke the last words of the absolution, the man fell back again on his mat with a sharp crackling sound like that of dry bones rattling. The woman had left the room, and the candle was sputtering out its very last sparks. Therefore, the padre went out in a hurry through the still open door into the street, and no sooner had he come there than the door closed behind him sharply, as though someone on the inside had pushed against it strongly to shut it fast.

Out in the street he had expected to find the old woman waiting for him, and he looked about for her everywhere, desiring to tell her that she must send for him when the man's fever left him, that he might return and hear from the man a real confession and really shrive him of his sins. But the old woman was quite gone. Thinking that she must have slipped past him in the darkness into the house, he knocked at the door lightly, and then loudly, but no answer came to his knocking, and when he tried to push the door open, using all his strength, it held fast against his pushing as firmly as though it had been part of the stone wall.

So the padre, having no liking for standing there in the cold and rain uselessly, hurried onward to his friend's house and was glad to get into the room where his friends were waiting for him, where plenty of candles were burning, and where it was dry and warm.

He had walked so fast that his forehead was wet with sweat when he took his hat off, and to dry it he put his hand into his pocket for his handkerchief; but his handkerchief was not in his pocket, and then he knew that he must have dropped it in the house where the dying man lay. It was not just a common handkerchief, Señor, but one very finely embroidered—having the letters standing for his name worked upon it with a wreath around them—that had been made for him by a nun of his acquaintance in a convent of which he was the almoner; and so, as he did not at all like to lose it, he sent his friend's servant to that old house to get it back again. After a good long while, the servant returned, telling that the house was shut fast and that one of the watch, seeing him knocking at the door of it, had told him that to knock there was only to wear out his knuckles, because no one had lived in that house for years and years!

All of this, as well as all that had gone before it, was so strange and so full of mystery that Padre Lanchitas then told to his three friends some part of what that evening had happened to him; and it chanced that one of the three was the notary who had in charge the estate of which that very house was a part. And the notary gave Padre Lanchitas his true word for it that the house, because of some entangling law matters, had stood locked fast and empty for as much as a lifetime; and he declared that Padre Lanchitas must be mixing that house with some other house, which would be easy, since all that had happened had been in the rainy dark. But the padre on his side was sure that he had made no mistake in the matter; and they both got a little warm in their talk over it, and they ended by agreeing—so that they might come to a sure settlement—to meet at that old house and the notary to bring with him the key of it on the morning of the following day.

So they did meet there, Señor, and they went to the middle door, the one that had opened at a touch from the old woman's hand. But all around the door, as the notary bade Padre Lanchitas observe before they opened it, were unbroken cobwebs, and the keyhole was choked with the dust that had blown into it, little by little, in the years that had passed since it had known a key. And the other two doors of the house were just the same. However, Padre Lanchitas would not admit, even with that proof against him, that he was mistaken; and the notary, smiling at him but willing to satisfy him, picked out the dust from the keyhole and got the key into it and forced back hardly the rusty bolt of the lock; and together they went inside.

Coming from the bright sunshine into that dusky place, lighted only from the doorway and the door but partway open because it was loose on its old hinges and stuck fast, they could see at first nothing more than that the room was empty and bare. What they did find, though—and the padre well remembered it—was the bad smell. But the notary said that just such bad smells were in all old shut-up houses and it proved nothing, while the cobwebs and the closed keyhole did prove most certainly that Padre Lanchitas had not entered that house the night before, and that nobody had entered it for years and years. To what the notary said there was nothing to be answered, and the padre—not satisfied, but forced to give in to such strong proof that he was mistaken—was about to come away out of the house and so have done with it. But just then, Señor, he made a very wonderful and horrifying discovery. By that time his eyes had grown accustomed to the shadows, and so he saw over in one corner, lying on the floor close beside where the man had lain whose confession he had taken, a glint of something whitish. And, Señor, it was his very own handkerchief that he had lost!

That was enough to satisfy even the notary; and as nothing more was to be done there, they came out, and gladly, from that bad dark place into the sunshine. As for Padre Lanchitas, Señor, he was all amazed and daunted, knowing then the terrible truth that he had confessed a dead man, and what was worse, that he had given absolution to a sinful soul come hot to him from hell! He held his hat in his hand as he came out from the house, and never did he put it on again; bareheaded he went thenceforward until the end of his days. He was a very good man, and his life had been always a very holy life, but from that time on, till the death of him, he made it still holier by his prayings and his fastings and his endless helpings of the poorest of the poor. At last he died. And it is said, Señor, that in the walls of that old house they found dead men's bones.

Dwarf Lore in New Mexico

(United States)

Duendes (dwarfs) are individuals of small stature who frighten the lazy, the wicked, and in particular, the filthy. The New Mexican idea about Duendes is embraced in the above statement. The people express much uncertainly about the origin, whereabouts, and doings of Duendes. A young lady from Santa Fe, however, seemed to have some definite ideas about their life. She pictured them as living together in a certain lonely place, where they inhabited underground houses, went out secretly to steal provisions and clothing, especially at night, and often even went to the cities to buy provisions. In the caves they prospered and lived with their families. Most of the people, however, profess ignorance about Duendes. They have only the general idea of their being evil spirits that terrorize the wicked, lazy, or filthy, as I have already stated.

From: Aurelio M. Espinosa, "New-Mexico Spanish Folk-Lore," *Journal of American Folk-Lore* 23 (1910): 395–418.

The following story is one well known: A family once moved from one place to another, and on arriving at the new house, the mother was looking for the broom to sweep. Her daughter, a lazy and careless girl, had forgotten it in the old home. Presently a Duende appeared, descending slowly from the roof with the broom in his hand, and presenting it to the lady, he said, "Here it is!"

A confused idea also exists in some localities with respect to the Duende as a wandering soul. I have not been able to obtain any definite information on this point, but the idea of a Duende being a suffering soul from purgatory is found in modern Spanish literature.

How the Elues Punished a Quarrelsome Man

(Mexico)

In former times there was a ranch called La Loma de Bufanda, which I think still exists under that name. The owner had good land, and he had two large barns—one for wheat and the other for hay. Near the barns was a house where the overseer, José Marcía, lived. The household consisted of José, his wife, two sons, and two daughters. One son was a cowherd, the other a shepherd.

Now, this family knew that Duendes inhabited the barn that held hay. They had sometimes caught glimpses of them, and they described them as lightly clad children of diminutive stature. The shepherd was a gentle lad, who had made himself a rude musical instrument like a flute, and on Sundays and holy days he often sat among the haystacks in the barn and played little tunes to the elves. He would hear childish giggles of delight, quickly suppressed, followed by stealthy footsteps toward him, but he rarely saw the little

From: Mary Blake, "Notes and Queries: The Elves of Old Mexico," *Journal of American Folk-Lore* 27 (1914): 237–39.

ones on these occasions. At the close of the concert, a half-eaten fruit or a bright-colored pebble, and sometimes a live frog or a harmless little snake, was dropped at his feet. The elves were like small boys in their tastes and gave the shepherd the things most prized by themselves.

Once there was a dance given at La Loma, and to this there came from a neighboring ranch a man who was most quarrelsome. He began by asking the shepherd's betrothed to dance. When she refused—for of course no respectable girl cares to dance with other than her promised husband—he insisted and tried to pull her from her seat.

Then the cowherd, who stood near, said, "Friend, this maiden is betrothed to my brother. Find thyself another partner."

At that, the quarrelsome fellow, whose head had been heated by drink, answered, "I dance with whom I please," and pushed the cowherd aside so violently that the overseer's son fell against a stone bench and cut his cheek.

The girl screamed and hid her face in her scarf, while all the young men with one accord hustled the brawler from the courtyard, where the dance was going on, to the hay barn, into which they thrust him and locked the door, saying, "There canst thou pass the night, dancing with whichever lady-mouse pleases thee." With much laughter they returned to the dance, leaving the quarrelsome man to kick at the door and shout maledictions.

At last the fellow grew tired of this occupation, and lying down upon the hay, he fell asleep. In a short time he awoke with a scream from a dream of being buried alive, to find himself completely covered with the hay. He shook himself free from it and composed himself to sleep again, but no sooner had he closed his eyes than great bundles of hay fell on him. *There are other prisoners in the barn*, thought the quarrelsome man, and he called in a loud voice, "Who are you, and where are you?"

There was no answer. The man, as was his wont, began to shout insults, which were answered by a perfect shower of hay. He groped around the immense building among the stacks, but he found no one. At last he lay down again and was again nearly smothered.

He knew his tormentors then and began to plead, "Dear Duendes, pretty little Duendes, let me sleep!" He could go no further, for a fistful of hay was suddenly thrust into his mouth. He was half strangled, and each of his painful coughs brought a peal of laughter from the surrounding darkness.

When he had recovered a little, he exclaimed, "Unless you little brutes leave me alone, I shall set fire to the hay, even if I myself perish with you!" Now, this was a threat that the man was powerless to put into effect, as he had nothing with which to make a fire, but the elves were so frightened that they were perfectly quiet after that, and just before dawn the quarrelsome man fell asleep.

The young men came early to release the prisoner, who was mightily shaken by the night he had passed. He related what had happened, and all, narrator as well as listeners, found the account so interesting that they went off to drink coffee together and to astonish the women with the tale.

The Elves and the Holy Father and His Sacristan

(Mexico)

In the ranch of San Jeronimo, jurisdiction of San Francisco del Rincon, many old houses were full of elves. In one house in particular the sprites were riotous from eight at night until dawn. The master of the house went to the priest of the nearest village and begged him to come and exorcise the spirits. The priest willingly consented, and the next night he arrived on horseback, with his sacristan mounted behind him, bearing all the articles necessary for the holy task.

"Now, Father," said the man of the house, as he helped the good man dismount, "my son will unsaddle and feed the horse, while you and the sacristan will have a bite to eat before the service."

From: Mary Blake, "Notes and Queries: The Elves of Old Mexico," *Journal of American Folk-Lore* (1914): 237–39.

The three entered the house and were soon seated upon a bench, while the man's wife placed before them three earthen dishes of pork cooked deliciously with green peppers, herbs, and olives; a pile of fresh tortillas; and three jugs of pulque (the national drink of Mexico, the juice of the maguey plant). Each man rolled a tortilla to use as a spoon, and dipped it into his dish.

Just as the little father had swallowed the first savory mouthful, a clamor of small voices began in the next room. He let his tortilla fall into his dish and asked, "Who is in there?"

"The Duendes, Father," answered the woman. "It is in the hour when they begin their pranks."

Just then there was a sound of metal being drawn back and forth over a stone.

"What are they doing now?" inquired the sacristan.

A shrill voice from within replied, "We are sharpening a knife which we shall use to cut off the priest's head."

"Saddle the horse and follow us with it!" cried the priest to the man of the house, as he started running down the road, dragging the sacristan after him.

They continued to run knee-deep in dust, until they fell upon the moonlit road exhausted. There the man with the horse helped them and assisted them to mount. The priest advised the horse owner to sprinkle the home with the holy water. The man returned to his home and sprinkled the holy water over the floors and walls of his two rooms, but the elves were never so boisterous as that night.

The Duendes never left that house, it is said. They seemed to bring prosperity to a house. It is certain that their hosts never lacked good food and raiment.

Two
Jack-o'-Lantern Tales
(Canada)

About the year 1837 the Lower Canada French were very superstitious, so much so that they believed the devil was about them in different forms. One form was Jack with His Lantern, which would lead travelers into swamps and laugh at them afterward.

Upon one occasion, one Louis LaFontaine was driving home from Alexandria (Glengarry County, Ontario) with his grist, when he was attracted by a light in the road before him. He knew the road well, but as it was dark and the light seemed to make on to his house, he decided to follow it. In the course of about twenty minutes he plunged into a deep swamp, and the light also disappeared and left him in the dark, to get out the best he knew how. Through his excitement he heard the light, or the devil as he called it, laugh at him until morning dawned. So afterward the people would always keep clear of Jack with His Lantern.

One Johnnie Saveau went fishing one dark and foggy night, about one hundred yards from his house, when he saw Jack with His Lantern moving in his direction. He had a torchlight at the bow of the boat, so didn't feel timid until Jack came pretty close to him; and then he became afraid and tied his boat to the shore as quickly as possible and, to make it more secure, pinned the rope to a log with his jackknife and hammered it down as much as he could. Then he ran for the house and closed the door as quickly as possible on arriving there, but the Old Devil (as he called the evil spirit in the light) pulled the knife out of the log and threw it after him, planting it in the door, just as he closed it, with such force that he could not at first pull it away. So to be sure, the devil was working in many a form.

From: W. J. Wintemberg, "French Canadian Folk-Tales," *Journal of American Folk-Lore* 17 (1904): 265–67.

The Devil

(Mexico)

There was a man pursued by the devil, to whom, wherever he went, he appeared in the form of a manikin. Once upon a time the man went to mass, and there was the devil. Whatever the padre did at mass, the devil did too. He alighted on the shoulders of the boys and made them sleep.

The man went and talked with the curate, and the padre said, "I'll take your confession, in order to see why you have these visions. Tomorrow go to early mass, in order to see if you'll again see that manikin."

The man went to mass, and there he was. Then he went to confession, and the demon went there also. Then the padre said, "My son, take this string and follow the demon wherever he goes, catch him with this string, and bring him to me."

Again the man went to church with the string in his hand. The demon left the church, and the man followed behind. He saw how he made some dogs fight; he saw how he made some drunkards fight; and the man followed the demon. He entered a saloon and put himself into a pot of *tepache*.

Then he went to notify the curate that the demon had put himself in a pot of tepache; and the curate said to him, "Go and ask the lady how much she wants to allow you to put your hand in and pull out that beast that is in the pot."

The lady was frightened and said, "You shall pay me nothing; only pull that beast out of there."

Then the man put his hand and the string in and caught him in a noose. It was not a manikin that came out but a person with the feet of a rooster, and he took him to where the padre was, and the padre said to him, "Tie him up here, and give him hay to eat."

Then the padre went to where the beast had been tied up and said to him, "Why are you interfering where it does not behoove you?"

From: Franz Boas, "Notes on Mexican Folk-Lore," *Journal of American Folk-Lore* 25 (1912): 204–60.

The demon said to him, "Let me go! Promise to free me, and I'll tell you why."

"Yes," said the padre, "I promise to free you. But tell me, why do you come to my church?"

Then the demon replied, "Because you owe a vow to Rome, and if you wish to fulfill it, I'll take you there in four and twenty hours."

"Yes," said the padre to him.

"But you know," said the demon, "we shall not travel by land, but by sea."

"All right!" said the padre. "Early tomorrow we will go."

The next day, when daylight broke, a saddled mule was in front of the door of the curate's house. The padre mounted, and they went on the waters. In four and twenty hours they were in Rome.

The padre arrived at a house and tied up his mule. The padre went to church and brought from there many relics, pictures, and rosaries, which he put into a satchel. He did not find the mule tied up, but the people of the house were very much frightened because the mule had turned into a man, and the man said to the landlord, "Would you like to see how I put myself into this bottle of wine here?"

"Yes," said the people, "we should like to see how you do it."

Then he put himself into the bottle.

The padre came, put the string inside the bottle, caught him in the noose, and pulled him out in the shape of a man. "Let us go!" he said, "I am ready." He tied up the man by the nape of his neck, and he turned again into a saddled mule, and the curate mounted her. Then the mule could not walk, on account of the relics which the curate carried. The mule said to him, "Throw away those things which you are carrying, for they burn me much. I promise you that you shall find them on your table."

Then the padre threw his relics into the middle of the sea, and in four and twenty hours he arrived at his house. The padre let him go and said, "Go away, accursed one, and never come again to trouble me." The demon did not come back.

The Demonic Curupira and the Frog

(Brazil)

There was once a man who had a wife and one little child. One day this man went into the woods to hunt, and there he was killed by a Curupira. The Curupira cut out the man's heart and liver, then he took the man's clothes and put them on his own body and, thus disguised, repaired to the house where the woman was waiting for her husband. Imitating the voice of the man, the Curupira called, "Old woman! old woman! where are you?"

"Here I am," said the woman. And the Curupira went into the house.

At first the woman took little notice of him, supposing that it was her husband.

The Curupira said: "Here is some nice meat that I have brought you. Go and cook it for me," and he gave her the heart and liver, which he had cut from her husband's body.

She took them and roasted them over a fire. She brought manioc meal also, and spread the dinner on a mat, and the Curupira sat down with the woman and child, and all ate heartily.

"Now," said the Curupira, "I will go to sleep." And he lay down in a hammock. Presently he called, "Bring the child and lay it with me in the hammock." So the woman brought the child, and laid it in the Curupira's arm, and the Curupira and child went to sleep.

After a while, the woman came to look at him, and then she discovered that it was not her husband but a Curupira. In great alarm, she began to make preparations to leave the house. She put all the clothes and household utensils into a basket; then, softly taking the child from its resting place, she placed a great wooden mortar on the Curupira's arm, and so ran off with the basket on her back and the child astride her hip.

From: Thomas Ewbank, *Life in Brazil; or, A Journal of a Visit to the Land of the Cocoa and the Palm* (New York: Harper & Brothers, 1856).

She had only run a little way down the path, when the Curupira awoke and discovered the trick that had been played on him. Jumping up, he ran down the path after the woman, calling loudly, "Old woman! old woman! where are you?"

The woman saw the Curupira coming, while he was yet a long way off. She ran still faster, but the Curupira gained on her at every step. There was a mundui bush by the path. The woman got under this and lay, trembling, until the Curupira came up, calling, "Old woman! old woman! where are you?"

There was an acurdo bird on a branch overhead, and it called, "Mundui! Mundui!" trying to tell the Curupira where the woman was. But the Curupira did not understand, so after searching for a while, he ran on down the path. Then the woman got up and ran off through the forest by another road, but in the meantime the Curupira had discovered his mistake, and he ran after her, calling, "Old woman! old woman! where are you?"

The woman came to a great hollow tree, with an opening at the base of the branches. On this tree sat a frog, Curucuna, which makes a very thick and strong gum.

"O Curucuna!" cried the woman, "I wish that you were able to save me from this Curupira!"

"I will save you," said the frog. "The Curupira shall not harm you."

Then the frog let down a long rope of gum. The woman climbed up this rope into the tree, and the frog put her into the hollow.

The Curupira came up, calling, "Old woman! old woman! where are you?"

"Here she is," said Curucuna.

Then the woman begged the frog not to let the Curupira come up, but the frog answered, "Never fear. I will kill the Curupira." And he did as he said, for he had covered the tree trunk all over with gum, and when the Curupira tried to climb up, he stuck fast, and there he died. And the woman got away with her child and went home.

The Great Mosquito

(United States)

A great mosquito invaded Fort Onondaga. The mosquito was mischievous to the people; it flew about the fort with a long stinger and sucked the blood of a number of lives. The warriors made several oppositions to expel the monster, but failed. The country was invaded until the Holder of the Heavens was pleased to visit the people. While he was visiting the king at Fort Onondaga, the mosquito made appearance as usual and flew about the fort. The Holder of the Heavens attacked the monster. It flew so rapidly that he could hardly keep in sight of it, but after a few days' chase the monster began to fail. He chased it on the borders of the Great Lakes toward the sunset and around the great country. At last he overtook the monster and killed it near the Salt Lake Onondaga, and the blood became small mosquitoes.

From: W. M. Beauchamp, "The Great Mosquito," *Journal of American Folk-Lore* 2 (1889): 284.

A Black Dog Tale

(Canada)

One harvest time forty or fifty years ago (or perhaps more), in a certain farmhouse not a mile from the grove where Poor Angus met with sudden death, very strange things were observed. Pails left at night in trim rows on benches ready for the morning milking would be found, when required, on the barn floor, or on top of a hayrick, or in some other equally unsuitable

From: C. A. Fraser, "Scottish Myths from Ontario," *Journal of American Folk-Lore* 6 (1893): 185–98.

situation. A spade might be searched for in vain until some member of the family, climbing into bed at night, would find it snugly reposing there before him. Pillows were mysteriously removed, and found sometimes outdoors at a distance from the house. Screws were removed from their places, and harnesses hung up in the stable were taken apart.

The family were rendered materially uncomfortable, and did their best to become also immaterially miserable by searching for proofs of supernatural agency. A great deal of proof was forthcoming. The matter was soon beyond doubt, and nothing else was talked about than the condition of things on this farm. Many speculations were afloat. Every tiny occurrence was examined as possibly affording evidence in the matter.

When a large black dog, evidently without owners, was observed to frequent the vicinity, the eye of the populace was at once upon it. It was shy, hiding and skulking about a good deal, and it was always hard to discover when sought. The owner of the land was strongly advised to shoot it, and the popular distrust was increased when he did one day fire at it without producing any visible results, the dog being seen a few hours later in excellent health.

The interest excited was so great that when a bee was held on this farm for something connected with the harvest, the attendance was immense, quite unusually so, and the neighbor women came in to help in the preparation of supper on an extensive scale. Some of the men made a long table of boards to accommodate the company. The women spread cloths and arranged dishes and viands. When all was ready, they regarded it with approval, pleased especially with the shining of the long rows of plates and the whiteness of the linen. Then some of them took the dinner horn and went out to give the signal to the men, who were at some distance away. The other women went to the cookhouse, where in summer the kitchen stove stood, and the supper table was left alone. A few minutes later, when all gathered around it again, chaos reigned where order had been. The cloth was spotted with symmetrical shapes, a tiny heap of dust and sand was on every plate, and the knives were on the floor. The disorder was of a strangely methodical kind, the same quantity of dust being on every plate, while each knife was placed in the same position as its fellows. The men trooped in while the women were staring aghast, and great was their indignation.

"Give me your gun," cried one, "and I'll put in this silver bit with the charge and see if it will not make an end of such work."

And just then the dog was seen prowling about at the foot of the yard near a thicket of bushes where he probably was often concealed. The gun was fired. It carried a silver bullet, and this time the aim was true, for all saw that the animal was shot. The day had been warm, and they were tired out and did not go to make sure of results at once. They sat around the rearranged board for an hour or more before some of them sauntered down to see the vanquished enemy. They did not wonder at first to find no trace of a dog, as, like any other wounded animal, it was likely to creep into the thicket to die. But the thicket was small and was soon explored on hands and knees. Nothing was there, and the body of that dog was never seen by mortal, although the search grew hourly more diligent and thorough.

And while they searched, there came a boy running from a stone house not far distant, bidding them to come over with him quickly, for grandfather was dead. "He dragged himself into the house," said the child, "as though he were hurt, an hour ago, and lay down on his bed, and now he is dead."

Friends hastened over but were met at the door by the dead man's wife, terrified and weeping, but almost forbidding them to enter. For some unfortunate reason, the poor woman would not let them near the body, little knowing, I suppose, the suspicion in their minds and the construction which must inevitably be put on her demeanor.

The Were-Jaguar

(Guyana)

Many of the Indians in Guyana believe that Kanaima tigers are possessed by human spirits who, as men, devote themselves to deeds of cannibalism. Taking the shape of the jaguar, they approach the lonely sleeping places or waylay Indians in the forests. No superstition causes more terror.

A legend exists among the natives about an old man who lurked in the forest in the shape of a Kanaima tiger. His son, who was hunting, shot the tiger down. His arrow, which was one of the old-fashioned sort, tipped with bone, entered the animal's jaw. The tiger raised its paw, broke off the weapon, and vanished into the forest. The young huntsman picked up the splintered arrowhead and returned home. Next day his guilty father came back groaning, and cried out that his mouth was "all on fire." The son drew from his cheek a bone which, oddly enough, fitted into his splintered arrowhead. Then the son was very sorrowful and said to his father that he must leave him and take his young wife away too, for neither of them would be safe from the dread Kanaima charm. This is a specimen of the "repercussion" stories, in which the wound inflicted on the were-animal appears in the human form.

From: Frank Hamel, *Human Animals* (New York: Frederick A. Stokes Co., 1916).

Transformation into Animals

(Canada)

Once upon a time (about the year 1850) a man refused to pay his church fees, so he was put out of the church by one of the officers. This church officer was taking a load of hay to market next day, when he saw a colt come up and stop the horses, and also bite and annoy them. The man took his whip, and getting down from the load, he tried to drive the animal away, but the colt ran with full force against him and tried to stamp him to the ground. He then thought of his long knife, which he opened and stabbed the colt. As soon as blood appeared the colt turned into a man, and it was the man that had been put out of the church. The officer then tied his horses and led the evil man to a priest, but the priest only banished him to an island to be heard of no more.

Once upon a time, an old woman was so possessed with an evil spirit that she could turn herself into several different animals. She lived on the cream of milk stolen from her neighbors while she was turned into a frog. But one day, after disturbing the pans of milk for days, she was caught hopping around in a neighbor's cellar. Her neighbor took her and put her upon a red-hot iron over the fireplace. She hopped off and out through the door to her home. When she came over the next day to see her neighbor, her hands were seen to be burned and blistered, and she wasn't able to work for days.

From: W. J. Wintemberg, "French Canadian Folk-Tales," *Journal of American Folk-Lore* 17 (1904): 265–67.

The "Little Demons" of Quebec

(Canada)

In the French-speaking parishes of the Province of Quebec, the Lutins are considered as mischievous, fun-loving little spirits, which may be protecting or annoying household gods or demons, according to the treatment that they receive from the inmates of the house where they have chosen to dwell. It generally takes the form of a domestic pet, such as a dog, a cat, a bird, a rabbit, or even a reptile of the inoffensive species, or again, rats and mice that have learned to become familiar with the members of a household.

Black cats have always had a rather suspicious reputation as associates of sorceresses and witches, but it is singular that among our peasants they are regarded as protecting goblins, and that no one would think of parting with them, chasing them away, or ill-treating them in any manner. Lucky is the man whose house, or barn, or stable, has been chosen as a home by a large family of black cats. White cats—they must be of spotless white—are also considered as Lutins, but I do not think that their protective abilities are as highly appreciated as those of their brothers of somber hue. The same may be said of rabbits, birds, or dogs, which have never attained the popularity of the cats but who occupy sometimes the popular position of household spirits but rather in a lesser degree.

I have known an old farmer in the parish where I was born to get in a great excitement and give a good thrashing to a boy who had innocently killed a small yellow snake which he had seen crawling along the grass in front of his house. The old man said that he would have preferred losing his best horse rather than see that snake killed. It had been living in his cellar for some years past, and he considered it as a good Lutin which brought him luck and prosperity.

From: Hon. H. Beauregard, "Folk-Lore Scrap-Book: Lutins in the Province of Quebec," *Journal of American Folk-Lore* 5 (1892): 327–38.

I have said that Lutins could be protective or annoying, according to the treatment that they received. The most fantastic powers are attributed to the good Lutins, and there is hardly any good action or any favorable intervention of which they are not capable. They will procure good weather for the crops, they will watch over favorite animals, they will intercede for the recovery of a sick member of the household, and I have heard of an enterprising Lutin who would, during the night, shave the face of his master and black his boots for Sunday morning.

So much for the good Lutins, who are treated in a proper and affectionate manner; but woe to the wicked or unhappy man who willingly or unluckily offends his household spirit, be it under the form of a black cat, white dog, or yellow snake. Life for him will become a burden, and his days, and especially his nights, will become a pretext for a long series of annoyances and persecutions of all kinds. On rising in the morning, he will find his boots filled with peas or with pebbles; his pantaloons will be sewed up at the knee; he will find salt in his porridge and pepper in his tea, and the meat in the soup kettle will be turned into pieces of stone. If he goes cutting hay or grain, he cannot get his scythe or his sickle to cut properly; in wintertime the water will freeze in his well, and his wife never can cook a good *tourtière* (meat pie) without burning the crust into a crisp.

These are only a few of the ills that await the poor man at his house or in his field; but the stable is the favorite place where the Lutin will make his power felt. He loves to take his revenge on the favorite horse of his offender. He will nightly, during months and months, braid or entangle the hair of the tail or mane of the animal, and when the farmer comes in the morning to groom his roadster, he will find it in a terrible plight, all covered with thistles or burrs. The Lutins will even go farther than that when they have been gravely insulted. They will find their way into the stable during the night, mount the horse, and ride it at the highest speed until the wee hours of morning, returning it to its stall completely tired out, broken down, and all in a lather of sweat.

And what is the farmer to do to cope with its ghostly enemy and to prevent his carrying out his system of persecution? He will sprinkle with salt the path that leads to the stable, and he will place a bag of salt against the door at the interior of the stable, so that the salt will be spilt when the Lutin tries to enter. It would seem that Lutins have a holy horror of salt, and that they cannot pass where that condiment has been strewn in their way. But Lutins will even evade the salt and enter the building to play their ghostly tricks. Then, there is only one way of putting a stop to their annoyances. The peasant will have to kill one black and one white cat, and with the strips of rawhide resulting from that double murder, he will make lattice screen doors and windows for his stable, and the Lutin never was known that could crawl through an aperture so protected against his wiles.

Friendly Lutins will attach themselves to favorite children and guide them safely through the infantine maladies of their tender years. They will befriend sweet and comely maidens, and favor them in the subjugation of a recalcitrant sweetheart, but they must be treated in a just, proper, and affectionate manner, because they seem to ignore the doctrine of forgiveness, and come what may, they are bound to get even with those who have had the bad luck to incur their ill will or their anger.

A Tale of Murder and Witchcraft

(Cuba)

Witchcraft is not yet dead. Fourteen persons were indicted for witchcraft in Havana, Cuba, in 1905 and brought to trial on March 10 of that year. For seven of them the public prosecutor asked the penalty of death. Several were convicted and two were sentenced to death and executed. Others were sentenced to less severe punishment.

A witch doctor in the country had written to another of the profession, stating that in order to effect a cure of a certain colored

From: Albert W. Dennis, "Witchcraft Not Extinct," *Massachusetts Magazine* 9:4 (October 16, 1916), 184–88.

woman, he must have the heart's blood of a white child, that the illness, or affliction, of the patient was the result of ill inflicted by white persons in the old slavery days and could only be cured by the warm lifeblood of a white person. The child was procured in the person of a twenty-month-old babe named Zoila, who was stolen from her parents. Her body, when found, had been dismembered and thrown into a thicket. The sick woman had used upon her abdomen a poultice made of the heart's blood of the child and taken internally a decoction brewed with the heart itself.

Voodoo Worship

(West Indies)

When Haiti was still a French colony, Sir Spenser says, voodoo worship flourished, but there was no distinct mention of human sacrifices in the accounts that have been transmitted. But he gives from the account of a French writer, M. Moreau de St. Méry, a very graphic description of fetishism as it existed in his day (end of eighteenth century). After speaking of the dances which had been brought from Africa to the colony, amongst which was the *vaudoux*, known for a long time principally in the Haitian or western part of the island, he goes on to describe the cult or worship of the Vaudoux, which, according to the Arada Negroes—who are its true sectaries in the colony in the maintenance of its principles and rules—signifies an all-powerful and supernatural being on whom depends all the events which take place in the world. This being is a nonvenomous serpent, who only consents to communicate his powers and to prescribe his will through the organ of a grand priest whom the sectaries select, and still more by that of the Negress whom the love of the latter has raised to the rank of high priestess. These two delegates bear the pompous names of King and Queen (Papa and Maman Roi, corrupted to Papaloi and

From: J. S. Udal, "Obeah in the West Indies," *Folklore* 26 (1915): 255–95.

Mamanloi). They are during their whole life the chiefs of the great family of the Vaudoux, and they have a right to the unlimited obedience of those that compose it. The Papaloi may generally be distinguished by the peculiar knotting of their curly wool, which, like the Fijians', must be a work of considerable labor, and by the profusion of ornaments.

The reunions for the true voodoo worship never take place except secretly, in the dead of night, and in a secure place safe from any profane eye. He then gives an interesting picture of such a "reunion": the adoration of the serpent, which is kept in a box or cage; the installation of the king and queen; the taking of the oath of secrecy before them; their exhortation to the crowd to show their loyalty to them. Afterward the members who desire assistance or favor in their designs approach and implore the aid of the Vaudoux. "Most of them," he says, "ask for the talent to be able to direct the conduct of their masters. But this is not enough. One wants more money; another the gift of being able to please an unfeeling one; another desires to reattach an unfaithful lover; this one wishes for a prompt cure or long life; an elderly female comes to conjure the god to end the disdain with which she is treated by the youth whose affection she would captivate; a young one solicits eternal love, or she repeats the maledictions that hate dictates to her against a preferred rival. There is not a passion which does not give vent to its vow, and crime does not always disguise those which have for object its success."

He then proceeds to describe the manner in which these appeals are made and answered by the queen in the name of the god (the serpent), more or less oracularly, her followers making their offerings to the god. A fresh oath as to secrecy is then taken, and sometimes a vase in which there is the blood of a goat, still warm, puts a seal on their lips to the promise.

After these ceremonies commences the dance of the vaudoux, which is preceded, when necessary, by the ceremony which a candidate for the sect has to go through, and the dance generally ends in scenes of great demoralization.

Voodooism, Fact or Myth?

(Haiti)

T he *New York World* of Sunday, December 5, 1886, for a copy of which I am indebted to the courtesy of the editors, contains an account purporting to come from an eyewitness of the sacrifice of a child at a voodoo ceremony in Haiti, said to have taken place in that year. The want of signature renders it unnecessary to examine the relation, but its publication led to a correspondence in the columns of the same paper (December 6–13), which possesses singular interest as a study in evidence, since the writers, who signed their own names, had lived in the island and had possessed opportunities of judging at firsthand.

A visitor in 1879 thought that the acts alleged would be more likely to occur in San Domingo than in Haiti: "In San Domingo the natives are more lawless than in Haiti. Fetishism and voodooism prevail in all that section."

On the other hand, a lady from San Domingo *knew* that children were unsafe in Haiti:

"I come from San Domingo, and I know that cannibalism existed in Haiti to a fearful extent. The voodoo priests have great knowledge of the power of herbs and do things that would seem to us here impossible. No mother would dare leave her child in the street or out of her sight a moment, knowing what would await it should she do so. . . . I have known instances where a child was fed sweet cakes containing powerful herbs which would make the child appear as if dead. It would be buried, and immediately dug up by the voodoo priests, and kept to offer up as a sacrifice. Its flesh would be cooked and eaten."

Mr. Bassett, Haitian consul-general, wrote:

"I have lived in Haiti as United States minister for nine years, and

From: William W. Newell, "Myths of Voodoo Worship and Child Sacrifice in Hayti," *Journal of American Folk-Lore* 1 (1888): 16–30.

there is just about as much cannibalism there as there is in the city of New Haven."

A well-known author, who considered that he had investigated the stories and ascertained their truth, had seen, in the town of Jacmel, in 1875, eighteen men who had been arrested as members of a band of cannibals, the den where they met being strewn with remnants of their orgies. The foreign residents clamored for the execution of these men, but the authorities reprieved and afterward pardoned them. This lenity was attributed to the political influence of the voodoo priests, an assumption which the writer appears to consider well founded.

A doctor of divinity, a native West Indian, wrote:

"From my own knowledge I can testify that the voodoo worship and the snake dance are practiced in Haiti, but cannibalism, I am sure, is not a custom of the Haitians. . . . I feel quite sure that President Salomon is not a voodoo worshipper."

Some indignant citizens desired that the United States officials be instructed to look into these horrors, with a view to armed intervention if necessary.

Mr. Preston, envoy extraordinaire and minister plenipotentiary of Haiti, denied all the charges.

"I was born in Haiti and spent about half my life in that country, and I never saw any person who had seen anything there in the shape of cannibalism. . . . I have seen persons who were known serpent worshippers, but no such thing exists as voodooism."

The son of the Protestant Episcopal bishop, while not prepared to deny all cases of cannibalism in his country, affirmed that the snake was quite as extensively worshipped in Jamaica, Trinidad, and Dominica.

Consul Bassett, in a second letter, while denying the existence of child sacrifice, declared:

"Voodooism actually exists everywhere in the West Indies, and nowhere more than in the British islands, under the name Obeah."

On the other hand, Mr. Cable (*The Century Magazine*, April 1886) considers the worship of "Obi" as the opposite of that of "voodoo."

It will thus be seen how difficult it is to arrive at any exact information by inquiry on the spot. Is serpent worship or Obeah worship among Negroes as mythical as devil worship? The stories from Trinidad, cited by Charles Kingsley in *At Last*, appear to have come from the same mint as the Haitian tales respecting the horrors of voodooism.

The Voodoo Meeting

(United States)

St. John's Eve is specially devoted to the worship of the voodoos. It is on that night that they congregate at some secret meeting place on Lake Pontchartrain—changed from time to time—and hold their religious dances and impious ceremonies of worshipping the Prince of Evil, for in their theology, the devil is God and it is to him they pray. Voodooism is rapidly dying out, even among the Negroes of Louisiana, but for all that, a Negro is frightened to death if he is "hoodooed," and with reason. The secret magic of the voodoos was nothing more than an acquaintance with a number of subtle vegetable poisons, which they brought with them from Africa, and which caused their victims to fade gradually away and die of exhaustion.

Every St. John's Eve thousands of persons visit the lake ends in the hope of coming upon the voodoos, but few succeed in finding them.

On St. John's Eve last year, the night was dark and on the eastern sky hung a black cloud, from which now and then burst flashes of lightning, which lit up the road, the bayou, and the surrounding swamp with a lurid glow, in fit introduction to what was to follow. The scene on the lake coast from Spanish Fort to Milneburg was one that cannot easily be forgotten. All along the shore, at intervals scarcely more than three hundred yards, groups of men and women could be seen standing around blazing pine knot fires, their dark copper-colored faces weirdly gilded by the red flames and their black forms thus illuminated appearing gigantic and supernatural against the opaque background of the lake and sky on one side and the mystical darkness just tinged with starlight of the seemingly limitless swamps on the other. Some of the men were stripped to the waist, and all were gesticulating with animation or seemed to be in waiting for something. Along the road at various intervals were Negresses standing by small tables where gumbo and coffee were dispensed.

From: Lafcadio Hearn and staff of New Orleans Press, *Historical Sketch Book and Guide to New Orleans and Environs* (New York: Will H. Coleman, 1885).

Between Spanish Fort and Milneburg, the shore was crowded with Negroes, who seemed to be enjoying themselves laughing, talking, and romping like children, but the music that came from the shanty, where a dance had evidently been started, sounded like that of an ordinary Negro ball.

As soon as the purlieus of Milneburg were left, the way down the lake shore toward the now brilliant bonfires was difficult, for in the darkness one had to pick his steps. Between the lake on the one side and the swamp on the other there was a belt of land not more than fifty feet across, and in some places this was diminished by more than half by the encroachment of Pontchartrain's waves. There was no roadway but simply a devious bypath which wended around stumps and mud holes in a most irregular manner.

After some ten minutes' walk there came to the ear the faintest sound as of a drum beaten rhythmically, and on listening a chorus of voices could be heard.

Behind, the hundreds of small watch fires along the shore twinkled like stars in the distance, and where they were built upon little points of land, they were reflected in the water so brightly the duplication added a peculiar weirdness to the scene.

Pursuing the same path was a party of Creole Negroes, the men carrying musical instruments and the women laden with coffeepots and tin buckets of gumbo. They were not inclined to talk, and when asked where the voodoo dance was to take place, answered that they knew nothing about it.

Passing around a little willow copse that grew almost in the lake, there opened to the view a scene Doré would have delighted to paint. The belt of land here was about one hundred feet in width, and in the middle of this little plot was burning a huge fire. Grouped around it were some thirty or forty Negroes, the rising and falling of the firelight giving a grotesqueness to their figures that was as curious as it was entertaining. Their shadows stretched out over the rushes and reeds of the swamp, and their faces brought out in effect looked wild enough to satisfy any lover of the wild and mysterious.

Built half over the swamps and half on the land stood a small hut or, to give it all its pretensions, a house of two rooms. It was like most of the fishermen's cabins seen along the lake, but rather more roomy. Through the open window there came quite a flood of light, and a song was heard chanted, it seemed by some eight or ten voices.

It was about three-quarters of a mile below Milneburg, and the place was appropriately selected, for certainly no more dismal and dreary spot could have been found. Cityward the swamp, with its funereal cypress, stretched in gloomy perspective, while in front, lapping the rushes and stumps, the ripples in the lake came in, the water appearing almost black from the vegetable matter held in suspension.

Near the fire were two or three tables laden with gumbo and dishes of rice, while on the embers hissed pots of coffee. When the group near them was approached, they gave evidence of uneasiness at the appearance of the party, there being no white persons present. A few words in Creole patois made the Negroes feel more at ease, and when a cup of coffee was purchased, they ceased to look suspiciously on the new arrivals.

The music in the house began with renewed vigor at this time, and there was by general consent a movement thither. It was nearly midnight.

The wide gallery on the front was soon thronged, and it was noticed but few were allowed to enter the large room which formed the eastern side of the building. The door was closed, and a stout young Negress guarded it on the inside.

A few words from Chief Bachemin in Creole proved an open sesame, and the door was opened just wide enough to permit the party to enter one at a time. With their entrance, the music ceased and all eyes were turned upon the newcomers.

A bright mulatto man came forward and, in good English, said that if the gentlemen desired to remain they would have to obey the orders that had been given. It would spoil the charm if they did not take off their coats. Accordingly the coats were removed.

Seated on the floor with their legs crossed beneath them were about twenty-five Negro men and women, the men in their shirtsleeves and the women with their heads adorned with the traditional head handkerchief, or *tignon*.

In the center of the floor there was spread a small tablecloth, at the corners of which two tallow candles were placed, being held in position by a bed of their own grease. As a centerpiece on the cloth, there was a shallow Indian basket filled with weeds, or as they call them, *herbes*. Around the basket were diminutive piles of white beans and corn, and just outside of these a number of small bones, whether human or not could not be told. Some curiously wrought bunches of feathers were the next ornamentations near the edge of the cloth, and outside of all, several saucers with small cakes in them.

The only person enjoying the aristocratic privilege of a chair was a bright café au lait woman of about forty-eight, who sat in one corner of the room looking on the scene before her with an air of dignity. She said but little, but beside her two old and wrinkled Negresses whispered to her continually. She was of extremely handsome figure, and her features showed that she was not of the class known in old times as field hands. She was evidently raised about the plantation house. She was neatly attired in a blue calico dotted with white, and on her head a brilliant tignon was gracefully tied. On inquiry it was learned that her name was Malvina Latour and that she was the queen.

As soon as the visitors had squatted down in their places against the wall, an old Negro man, whose wool was white with years, began scraping on a two-stringed sort of a fiddle. The instrument had a long neck, and its body was not more than three inches in diameter, being covered with brightly mottled snakeskin. This was the signal to two young mulattoes beside him, who commenced to beat with their thumbs on little drums made of gourds and covered with sheepskin.

These tom-toms gave forth a short, hollow note of peculiar sound and were fit accompaniments of the primitive fiddle. As if to inspire those present with the earnestness of the occasion, the old Negro rolled his eyes around the room and then, stamping his foot three times, exclaimed, *"A présent commencez!"*

Rising and stepping out toward the middle of the floor, a tall and sinewy Negro called the attention of all to him. He looked a Hercules, and his face was anything but attractive. Nervous with restrained emotion, he commenced at first in a low voice, which gradually became louder and louder, a song, one stanza of which ran as follows:

> *Mallé couri dan déser,*
> *Mallé marché dan savane,*
> *Mallé marché su piquan doré,*
> *Mallé oir ça ya di moin!*
>
> *Sangé moin dan l'abitation ci la la?*
> *Mo gagnain soutchien la Louisiane,*
> *Mallé oir ça ya di moin!*

Which can be translated as follows:

> I will wander into the desert,
> I will march through the prairie,
> I will walk upon the golden thorn—
> Who is there who can stop me?
>
> To change me from this plantation?
> I have the support of Louisiana—
> Who is there who can resist me?

As he sang he seemed to grow in stature and his eyes began to roll in a sort of wild frenzy. There was ferocity in every word, boldness and defiance in every gesture.

Keeping time to his song the tom-toms and fiddle gave a weird and savagely monotonous accompaniment that it was easy to believe was not unlike the savage music of Africa.

When it became time for all to join in the refrain, he waved his arms, and then from every throat went up:

Mallé oir ça ya di moin!

He had hardly ended the fourth stanza before two women, uttering a loud cry, joined their leader on the floor, and these three began a march around the room. As the song progressed, an emaciated young Negro stepped out and, amid the shouts of all, fell in behind the others.

The last addition to the wild dancers was most affected of all, and in a sort of delirium he picked up two of the candles and marched on with them in his hand. When he arrived opposite the queen, she gave him something to drink out of a bottle. After swallowing some, he retained a mouthful which, with a peculiar blowing sound, he spurted in a mist from his lips, holding the candle so as to catch the vapor. As it was alcohol, it blazed up, and this attempt at necromancy was hailed with a shout.

Then commenced the regular voodoo dance with all its twistings and contortions. Two of the women fell exhausted to the floor in a frenzy and frothing at the mouth, and the emaciated young man was carried out of the room unconscious.

Flying Like a Witch

(Chile)

A boy who lived not far from Santiago desired, like many another, to learn to fly. His aunt, fortunately, was a witch, so he pestered her with requests that she should teach him the art, till at last, in weariness, she consented. The preparations consisted in a veritable "tarring and feathering," for she anointed him with certain unguents and scattered feathers all over him. Then, leading him to the brow of a hill at nightfall, she told him to launch out, repeating the phrase *"Sin Dios y sin Santa María"* ("Without God and Mary"). The boy, who began to wish that he had not come, leaped into space and flew for a moment, until, becoming confused with the novelty of his situation, he inverted the formula, saying, *"Con Dios y con Santa María"*—crashing heavily in consequence.

Another form taken by the witches is that of the Calchona. This is a mythical animal, described as a kind of blend between the dog and the goat. It has long silvery hair and is generally inoffensive if left alone, pattering past the affrighted traveler intent upon its own affairs. The witch enters this form by the employment of certain ointments. In the current story, the husband awakes to see his wife rise from the bed, apply the unguents, and glide out in the night in the abhorred form of a Calchona. He takes the ointments and flings them into the *acequia*—the open drain that still traverses some country houses, where the water dissolves and washes away the contents of the pots. At dawn the witch returns and, finding her unguents gone and being unable without their use to return to her human form, dashes frantically about the house, till the growing light drives her forth into the wide world. At night the man hears the pattering footsteps circling the house, and the poor beast rears up against the window to catch a glimpse of the children from whom she is parted forever.

From: Oswald H. Evans, "Witchcraft in Chile," *Chambers's Journal* 11 (1921): 380–83.

Traveling Witches

(United States)

A woman of the neighborhood was at my father's house one evening, when some singular noise turned her attention to the subject of witchcraft and I heard her relate, in substance, the following account: "I was out alone in the dooryard one bright moonlit evening last summer, gathering up some chips to build a fire with the next morning, when I heard several female voices, talking and laughing merrily, apparently coming down the road. They seemed to be rapidly approaching, and I waited to see who they were. When they got near me, I could see no one, but they were heard directly overhead in the air. I looked up and saw nothing but the bright stars. I could hear their talking and laughing as they passed along overhead. Their voices grew fainter and fainter as they passed off in an opposite direction from whence they came, until I could hear them no longer."

This woman was free to state, with perfect confidence, that these voices were a company of witches going through the air to some unoccupied house to hold a frolic and have a dance. She believed they could go invisibly in spirit, separate from the body, and were possessed with muscular power, equal if not superior to that in the body, to perform any diabolical acts they might fancy. And however decrepit they might be in the body, they were as lively and bouyant in the spirit as they ever were in their youthful days.

She believed that witches had the power to disengage the spirit of an individual from the body, when found asleep or unawares, and could take that spirit along with them, when it would be perfectly under their control, and could be made to perform any service they desired; and sometimes such stolen spirits were made the butt of fun at their evening's entertainments at some haunted house. The spirits of those individuals would in all cases be returned to their own bodies before morning, and although the subjects may have slept soundly all

From: John McNab Currier, "Contributions to the Folk-Lore of New England," *Journal of American Folk-Lore* 2 (1889): 291–94.

night, they would be either sick or affected with great lassitude the next day. I have myself heard the question asked, both in sobriety and half in jest, if one "was rode" by witches the night previous.

I have heard related that the witch throws the bridle upon the face of the sleeper and then repeats an incantation before the spirit will disengage and be ready for a journey, and if the sleeper will only awake and throw the bridle upon the witch's face while she is repeating the incantation, her spirit is subdued and must obey the will of the sleeper and continue in that service until the bridle is taken off, or as long as her master or mistress shall remain silent; but if one word should be spoken aloud, the witch is freed from servitude and she is gone.

A Voodoo Curse

(Bolivia/Peru)

In Bolivia and Peru there is a common belief among married women that if they are barren, a curse has been put on them by some voodoo or a dead acquaintance. To counteract this, they retreat into the woods for several days and gather the bark from a certain tree (I could not ascertain the latter's name) and crush it up with large stones. After this the barren woman returns to her village, casts the bark into a pool of water nearby, and plunges into it, remaining there sometimes for hours. The idea is that the strong acids in the bark will purge and cleanse the woman's body from the curse. She returns to her husband, and it frequently happens that she has a child. Very probably—apart from the powerful psychic aid of suggestion—there is really some medicinal value in the bark used in the water, and therefore the subject is worth further research and the attention of the scientist.

From: Irene E. Toye Warner, ed., "Black Magic and Voodooism in America," *Occult Review* 21 (1915): 21–26.

A Spell Cast in Newfoundland

(Canada)

On landing at a cove I met Skipper Kish at his doorstep, with his right hand in a sling. After a cordial greeting, I inquired what ailed his arm. He replied, "Well, sir, last week I bought this 'ere gun from Jan Leck, an gid him varty shilluns for un. Fish was scace, so day afore yisday I thought I'd go over the hills and try un on a hare or partridge. I tooked her and the powder harn and shot bag and starts up yander through the droke. You know the little pond at the top of the hill. When I cumed in sigh' o' un, the first thing I see is a loo' [loon] sitting about the middle uv un. 'A queer place for a loo' to be,' says I, 'for the pond isn't more 'n sixty yards across, and no trouble to get in gunshot o' he.' I drawed down to the tuckamores aside the pond and got twixt thirty and varty yards from un. I lets drive and the loo' dove. The gun kicked pow'ful an' I loads her agen, a light load not more 'n six fingers. The loo' comes up in the same place, and I loaded an fired twenty-eight shots at un, and he dove every time. I hadn't a grain of shot left. At the last shot the loo' disappeared, then I seed I'd been vuled [fooled]."

"What became of the loon?" said I.

"'Twa'n't no loo' at all, sir."

"What was it then?"

"'Twas a spell on me and the gun, and I knowed then that that blankety-blank Jan Baker put it on."

"Nonsense," said I. "You should not believe such things."

"Well, lookee here, sir," opening his shirt, and showing his shoulders as black as my hat, "I've vired too many guns not to know I wouldn't be served like that if there warn't a spell on her."

I replied, "Oh, Kish, you are mistaken. She is an old army musket warranted to kick like a mule."

From: George Patterson, "Notes on the Folk-Lore of Newfoundland," *Journal of American Folk-Lore* 8 (1895): 285–90.

"Mistaken, sir? I got proof, I got proof I'm right. Shortly after I cumed out to the harbor, Jan Baker, he cumed in from vishing, and I says to un, 'Skipper Jan, I thinks there's a spell on my gun.' 'Let me look at her,' says he. I gid her to un, an' he looks along the bar'l. 'Yes,' says he, 'Skipper Kish, there is a spell on her; I can see it. It looks just like a vish's float [fish's air float or air bladder].' I ses, 'Can't take it off, Skipper Jan?' He says, 'No, I can't.' 'Well I can,' says I, 'fur I knows the blankety-blank that put it there.'

"So yistday marnin' when Jan Baker an' the rest went out vishen, I gets a piece of paper and cuts out the shape uv a man's heart, an' I writ Jan Baker's name on it and stuck it up on that picket, six foot in front of the door. I puts a small charge in the gun and cuts off a piece uv silver the size uv a shot, and puts it in with the shot. I stood here in the doorway and vired; and I hope that I may never live another day, sir, if I'm tellen ye a lie—every shot cumed flying back in the house among the crockery on the dresser, and rattlin' on the floor. I looked at the paper heart. Not a shot had passed through it, but I seed a small piece chipped out of the edge, and I knowed the silver had done it, and the spell was off my gun.

"In the evenin' when Jan Baker cumed, he says, 'Skipper Kish, did it take the spell off your gun?' And I says, 'Yes I did, Skipper Jan.' And he says, 'I knowed it, Skipper Kish, fur when I was out on the fishin' ground, I felt a drop of blood leave my heart, an' I says to myself, Skipper Kish is takin' the spell off his gun.'

"Now, sir, didn't I tell that I had proof that 'twa'n't no loo' at all, only a spell on my gun?"

The Haunting of John Bell

(United States)

What I am about to relate should be enough to enable the reader to form some idea of the horrors that our family had to endure during the early settlement of Robertson County, from an unknown enemy and for an unknown cause. Whether it was witchery such as afflicted people in past centuries and the darker ages, whether some gifted fiend of hellish nature practicing sorcery for selfish enjoyment or some more modern science akin to that of mesmerism, or some hobgoblin native to the wilds of the country, or a disembodied soul shut out from heaven, or an evil spirit like those Paul drove out of the man into the swine, getting them mad, or a demon let loose from hell, I am unable to decide. Nor has anyone yet divined its nature or cause for appearing, and I trust this description of the monster, in all forms and shapes and of many tongues, will lead experts who may come with a wiser generation to a correct conclusion and satisfactory explanation.

As I write, a shudder fills my frame with horror, bringing fresh to memory scenes and events that chilled the blood in my young veins, cheating me out of twenty years of life. It hangs over me like the pall of death, and sends weary thoughts like fleeting shadows through my brain, reviving in memory those demoniacal shrieks that came so often from an invisible and mysterious source, rending the air with vile and hideous curses that drove me frantic with fear. It is no ghastly dream of a fevered brain that comes to haunt one's thoughts, but a sad, fearful reality, a tremendous truth that thrills the heart with an unspeakable fear that no word painting can portray on paper. Courageous men in battle line may rush upon bristling bayonets and blazing musketry, and face the roaring cannon's mouth, because they

From: M. V. Ingram, *An Authenticated History of the Famous Bell Witch* (Nashville, TN: William P. Titus, 1894).

can see the enemy and know who and what they are fighting; but when it comes to meeting an unknown enemy of demonstrative power, with gall upon its tongue and venom in its bosom, heaving bitter curses and breathing threatenings of dire consequences, which one knows not of nor can judge in what shape or form the calamity is to come, the stoutest heart will prove a coward, faltering and quivering with painful fear. Why should my father, John Bell, be inflicted with such a terrible curse? Why should such a fate befall a man striving to live uprightly?

I would be untrue to myself and my parentage should I fail to state boldly that John Bell was a man every inch of him and in every sense of the term. No man was ever more faithful and swift in the discharge of every duty, to his family, to the church, to his neighbors, to his fellow man, and to his God, in the fullness of his capacity and that faith which led him to love and accept Christ as a Savior. No moral man ever brought a charge of delinquency or dishonor to his door. Not even the ghastly fiend that haunted him to his death, in all its vile curses and evil threatenings, ever brought an accusation against him or uttered a solitary word that reflected upon his honor, his character, his courage, or his integrity. He lived in peace and in the enjoyment of the full confidence of his neighbors, and lacked not for scores of friends in his severest trials. Then why this infliction? Where the cause, which no man, saint, angel from heaven, or demon from hell has ever assigned?

If there were any hidden or unknown cause why he should have thus suffered, or if it were in the Providence of God a natural consequence, then why should the torments of a demon have been visited upon sister Elizabeth, who was a girl of tender years, brought up under the careful training of a Christian mother, free from guile and the wiles of the wicked world, and innocent of all offense? Yet this vile, heinous, unknown devil, torturer of human flesh, that preyed upon the fears of people like a ravenous vulture, spared not her but rather chose her as a shining mark for an exhibition of its wicked stratagem and devilish tortures. And never did it cease to practice upon her fears, insult her modesty, stick pins in her body, pinching and bruising her flesh, slapping her cheeks, disheveling and tangling her hair; tormenting her in many ways, until she surrendered that most cherished hope which animates every young heart. Was this the stratagem of a human genius skilled in the black art; was it an enchantment, a freak in destiny, or the natural consequence of disobedience to some law in nature? Let a wiser head than mine answer and explain the mystery.

Another problem in the development of these mysterious manifestations that has always puzzled my understanding: Why should the husband and father, the head of the family, and the daughter, the pet and pride of the household, the center of all family affections, be selected to bear the invections of this terrible visitation, while demonstrations of the tenderest love from the same source were bestowed upon the wife and mother? If it were a living, intelligent creature, what could have been the dominating faculty of its nature that made this discrimination? Could it have been an intelligent human devotion springing from an emotional nature that could so love the wife and mother and cherish such bitter enmity for her husband and offspring, both of whom she loved most devotedly? Methinks not; only a fiend of a hellish nature, with poisoned blood and seared conscience, if a conscience at all, could have possessed such attributes. Yet we, who experienced or witnessed the demonstration, know that there was a wonderful power of intelligence possessing knowledge of men and things, a spirit of divination that could read minds, tell men's secrets, quote the Scriptures, repeat sermons, sing hymns and songs, assume bodily forms, and withal exhibit an immense physical force behind the manifestations.

Father suffered with spells, manifesting as a jerking and twitching of his face and a swelling of his tongue that fearfully distorted his whole physiognomy. These spells would last from one to two days, and after passing off, he would be up and about his business, apparently in strong robust health. As time advanced, the spells grew more frequent and severe, and there was no periodical time for their return. Along toward the last, I stayed with him all the time, especially when he left the house, going with him wherever he went. The witch, Kate, also grew more angry and virulent in disposition. Every word uttered to father, "Old Jack," was a blast of curses and heinous threats, while to mother, "Old Luce," it continued most tender, loving, and kind.

About the middle of October father had a very severe attack, which kept him confined to the house six or eight days. The witch cursed and raved like a maniac for several days and ceased not from troubling him. However, he temporarily overcame this attack and was soon able to be out, though he would not venture far from the house. But it was not destined that he should enjoy a long respite.

After a week's recuperation, he felt much stronger and called me very early one morning to go with him to the hog pen, some three hundred yards from the house, for the purpose of giving directions in separating the porkers intended for fattening from the stock hogs. We had not gone far before one of his shoes was jerked off. I replaced it on his foot, drawing the strings tight, tying a double hard knot. After going a few steps farther, the other shoe flew off in the same manner, which was replaced and tied as in the case of the first. In no way that I could tie them would they hold, notwithstanding his shoes fitted close and were a little hard to put on, and we were walking over a smooth, dry road. This worried him prodigiously; nevertheless, he bore up strongly, and after much delay and worry we reached the place and he gave directions, seeing the hogs properly separated as he desired and the hands left for other work, and we started back for the house. We had not gone many steps before his shoes commenced jerking off as before, and presently he complained of a blow on his face which felt like an open hand that almost stunned him, and he sat down on a log that lay by the roadside. Then his face commenced jerking with fearful contortions, soon followed by his whole body, and then his shoes would fly off as fast as I could put them on. The situation was trying and made me shudder. I was terrified by the spectacle of the contortions that seized father, as if to convert him into a very demon to swallow me up. Having finished tying father's shoes, I raised myself up to hear the reviling sound of derisive songs piercing the air with terrorizing force. As the demoniacal shrieks died away in triumphant rejoicing, the spell passed off, and I saw the tears chasing down father's yet quivering cheeks. The trace of faltering courage marked every lineament of his face with a wearied expression of fading hope.

He turned to me with an expression of tender, compassionate, fatherly devotion, exclaiming in a woeful passionate tone, "O my son, my son, not long will you have a father to wait on so patiently. I cannot much longer survive the persecutions of this terrible thing. It is killing me by slow tortures, and I feel that the end is nigh."

This expression sent a pang to my bosom which I had never felt before. Mingled sorrow and terror took possession of me and sent a tremor through my frame that I can never forget. If the earth could have opened and swallowed us up, it would have been a joyful deliverance. My heart bleeds now at every pore as I pen these lines, refreshing my memory with thoughts of the terror that possessed me then in anticipation of a fearful tragedy that might be enacted before father could move from his position.

That moment he turned his eyes upward and lifted his soul to heaven in a burst of fervent passionate prayer such as I had never heard him utter before. He prayed the Lord that if it were possible, to let this terrible affliction pass. He beseeched God to forsake him not in the trying ordeal but to give him courage to meet this unknown devastating enemy in the trying emergency, and faith to lift him to the confidence and love of a blessed Savior, and withal to relieve his family and loved ones from the terrible afflictions of this wicked, unknown, terrifying, blasphemous agency. It was in this strain that father prayed, pouring out his soul in a passionate force that seemed to take hold of Christ by a powerful faith that afforded fresh courage and renewed strength.

After he had finished his prayer, a feeling of calmness and reconciliation seemed to possess him, and he appeared to have recovered from the severe shock. The reviling songster had disappeared, and he rose up remarking that he felt better and believed he could walk to the house, and he did, meeting with no more annoyance as we proceeded on the way. However, he took to his bed immediately on arriving at the house, and though able to be up and down for several weeks, he never left the house again and seemed all the while perfectly reconciled to the terrible fate that awaited him. He gradually declined; nothing that friends could do brought any relief. Mother was almost constantly at his bedside with all the devotion of her nature. Brother John attended closely in the room, ministering to him, and good neighbors were constantly in attendance. The witch was carrying on its deviltry more or less all the while.

The crisis, however, came on the morning of December 19. Father, sick as he was, had not up to this time failed to awake at his regular hour, according to his long custom, and arouse the family. That morning he appeared to be sleeping so soundly, mother quietly slipped out of the room to superintend breakfast, while brothers John and Drew looked after the farmhands and feeding the stock and would not allow him to be disturbed until after breakfast. Noticing then that he was sleeping unnaturally, it was thought best to awaken him, when it was discovered that he was in a deep stupor and could not be aroused to any sensibility. Brother John, who attended to giving him medicine, went immediately to the cupboard where he had carefully put away the medicines prescribed for him, but instead he found a smoky-looking vial, which was about one-third full of dark-colored liquid. He set up an inquiry at once to know who had moved the medicine, and no one had touched it, and neither could anyone on the place give any account of the vial. Dr. George Hopson, of Port Royal, was sent for in great haste and soon arrived; also neighbors John Johnson, Alex Gunn, and Frank Miles arrived early and were there when the vial was found.

Kate, the witch, in the meantime broke out with joyous exultation, exclaiming, "It's useless for you to try to relieve Old Jack. I have got him this time. He will never get up from that bed again." Kate was then asked about the vial of medicine found in the cupboard and replied, "I put it there and gave Old Jack a big dose out of it last night while he was asleep, which fixed him."

This was all the information that could be drawn from the witch or any other source concerning the vial of medicine. Certain it was that no member of the family ever saw it before or could tell anything about it. In fact, no vial and no medicine of any kind had been brought to the house by anyone else except by Dr. Hopson, and then it was handled carefully. Dr. Hopson, on arrival, examined the vial and said he did not leave it and could not tell what it contained. It was then suggested that the contents be tested on something. Alex Gunn caught a cat, and Brother John ran a straw into the vial and drew it through the cat's mouth, wiping the straw on its tongue. The cat jumped and whirled over a few times, stretched out, kicked, and died very quickly.

Father lay all day and night in a deep stupor, as if under the influence of some opiate, and could not be aroused to take any medicine. The doctor said he could detect something on his breath that smelt very much like the contents of the vial which he had examined. How father could have gotten it was a mystery that could not be explained in any other way except that testified by the witch. The vial and contents were thrown into the fire, and instantly a blue blaze shot up the chimney like a flash of powder. Father never revived or returned to consciousness for a single moment. He lingered along through the day and night, gradually wearing away, and on the morning of December 20, 1820, breathed his last.

Kate was around during the time, indulging in wild exultations and derisive songs. After father breathed his last, nothing more was heard from Kate until after the burial was completed. It was a bright December day and a great crowd of people came to attend the funeral. The Rev. Sugg Fort, and the Revs. James and Thomas Gunn conducted the services. After the grave was filled, and the friends turned to leave the sad scene, the witch broke out in a loud voice, singing, "Row me up some brandy O," and continued singing this until the family and friends had all entered the house. And thus ended one chapter in the series of exciting and frightful events that kept the whole neighborhood so long in a frenzy and worked upon our fears from day to day.

After the death of John Bell, Sr., the fury of the witch was greatly abated. There were but two purposes, seemingly, developed in the visitation. One was the persecution of father to the end of his life. The other, the vile purpose of destroying the anticipated happiness that thrilled the heart of Betsy. This latter purpose, however, was not so openly manifested as the first and was of such a delicate nature that it was kept a secret as much as possible in the family and ignored when talked about. But it never ceased its tormenting until her young dream was destroyed. The witch remained with us after father's death through the winter and spring of 1821, all the while diminishing or becoming less demonstrative. Finally it took leave of the family, bidding mother, "Luce," an affectionate farewell, saying that it would be absent seven years but would surely return to see us and would then visit every house in the neighborhood. This promise was fulfilled as regards the old homestead, but I do not know that it visited other homes in the vicinity.

It returned during February 1828. The family was then nearly broken up. Mother, brother Joel, and myself were the only occupants left at the old homestead, the other members of the family having settled off to themselves. The demonstrations announcing its return were precisely the same that characterized its first appearance. Joel occupied a bed in mother's room, and I slept in another apartment alone. After considerable scratching on the weatherboarding on the outside, it appeared in the same way on the inside, scratching on the bedpost and pulling the cover from my bed as fast as I could replace it, keeping me up nearly all night. It went on in this way for several nights, and I spoke not a word about it, lest I should frighten mother. However, one night later, after it had worried me for some time, I heard a noise in mother's room and knew at once what was to pay. Very soon mother and Joel came rushing into my room, much frightened, telling me about the disturbance and something pulling the cover off. We sat up till a late hour discussing the matter, satisfied that it was the same old Kate, and agreed not to talk to the witch and that we would keep the matter a profound secret to ourselves, worrying with it the best we could, hoping that it would soon leave, as it did, after disturbing us in this way some two weeks. This was my last experience with Kate.

The witch came and went. Hundreds of people witnessed its wonderful demonstrations, and many of the best people of Robertson and adjoining counties have testified to these facts, telling the story over and over to the younger generation, and for this and other reasons, I have written this much of the details as correctly as it is possible to state the exciting events. So far no one has ever given any intelligent or comprehensive explanation of the great mystery. Those who came as experts were worse confounded than all others. A few mendacious calumniators were mean enough to charge that it was tricks and inventions of the Bell family to make money, and I write for the purpose of branding this version of an infamous falsehood. It was well known in the vicinity and all over the county that every investigation confirmed the fact that the Bell family were the greatest, if not the only, sufferers from the visitation and that no one, or a dozen persons in collusion, could have so long regularly and persistently practiced such a fraud without detection, nor could they have known the minds and secrets of strangers visiting the place and detailed events that were then occurring or had just transpired in different localities. Moreover, the visitation entailed great sacrifice.

As to how long this palavering phenomenon continued in the vicinity, I am unable to state. It did not disturb the remaining members of the family at the old place anymore. Mother died shortly after this and the house was entirely deserted, the land and other property being divided among the heirs. The old house stood for some years and was used for storing grain and other farm products, and was finally torn down and moved away. Many persons professed to have seen sights and heard strange sounds about the old house and in the vicinity all along up to this day. Several have described to me flitting lights along the old lane and through the farm, while others profess to have heard sounds of wonderfully sweet music and strange voices uttering indistinct words. And it is said that such things have been seen and heard at various places in the neighborhood, but I have no personal knowledge of the facts.

The Evil Eye

(Brazil)

P eople in Brazil still suffer from it. Handsome children have fits and other complaints, induced by earthly and unearthly beings who envy their innocence and beauty. And not hags and ogres only, but spruce ladies possess the unamiable organ. When the hair of a female becomes prematurely gray or drops off by disease, in nine out of ten the look of some envious woman has done it. A young lady in our neighborhood recently had tresses equaling Eve's in length and softness. She has lost them and says she knows too well which of her acquaintances it was whose malicious glances have compelled her to wear a cap.

When a stranger pats a child on the head, calls it pretty and fair, and so forth, both nurse and parents would be troubled if he did not conclude by asking God or one of the saints to bless it, that being the proof that he meant it no harm, that he had not been observing it with the evil eye. It is said that the withering power is allied to that by which serpents draw fluttering birds into their mouths, and that human victims, when once struck, sicken, languish, and if not relieved, must sink into death's jaws.

Among the numerous preventives, horn is not uncommon. I first noticed its use in Barbonnos Street, at a place where fruit, vegetables, and other edibles were exhibited for sale. A loose pair of sheep's horns, painted with alternating bands of blue, red, white, and yellow, hung against the side of the doorpost. Inquiring for what purpose

From: Thomas Ewbank, *Life in Brazil; or, A Journal of a Visit to the Land of the Cocoa and the Palm* (New York: Harper & Brothers, 1856).

they were there displayed, the proprietress laughingly exclaimed, "To keep away the evil eye." H——— asked if she would sell them, to which she gave a decided negative.

There is a cluster of dirty shanties and excuses for tents near the Moura Fountain, in the vicinity of the entrance to Palace Square, at which fowl are always on sale, and often a monkey or two. One of the shanties is kept by Antoine, an active Portuguese in midlife. As I had commissioned him to procure a sloth, I was in the habit of looking into his den. He had two pairs of horns suspended over his coops. For my satisfaction, H——— one day pointed to them and asked what good they did. With animation and immoderate gesticulation, he told us how his neighbors in adjoining shanties used to envy him for doing a greater business than they could get and how they looked on him and his fowl with an evil eye, causing many to pine and die.

"How do they protect me? Why, when anyone now looks in to injure me, he sees them and his envy is quenched. He collects himself and walks off fearful of chastisement; that is, he is afraid of having a fit, of tripping himself up while walking and breaking a leg, of being choked when eating, or of some other misfortune." It need hardly be said that Antoine's neighbors guard themselves and the health of their capons by similar means.

Horn is to be seen in the Vendas. Faith in it seems pretty general except with those who have become disenchanted by contact with foreigners.

The Old Tramp's Evil Eye

(Canada)

My uncle and wife went to Glengarry one day and left their only daughter, about eighteen years of age, to take care of the house. About three o'clock in the afternoon an old tramp passed by the door, then stopped and, seeing the door open, asked for something to eat. The girl, being afraid of the tramp, closed the door on him and told him to go on, for she would not give him anything or let him in. The old tramp became mad, and with oaths and threats he pounded on the door until he became tired; then, seeing the girl through the window, through madness he bewitched her and went away.

When the parents returned, the girl was going through all sorts of maneuvers, such as crawling through the rounds of chairs and trying to climb the walls, so the folks had to tie her. The next day a quack doctor passed up the road and stopped at the house as usual. Upon seeing the girl in such a way, he asked the cause of it. When told, he asked for the petticoat she wore and two packages of new pins. Getting them, he put the girl in bed, sat in the old fireplace, with the door open, and taking the petticoat and pins, he stuck all the pins into the petticoat, then pulled them out and put them in again until the old tramp arrived before the door and asked, "What are you doing there?"

"Go on!" said the doctor. "Why do you want to know?"

"But stop!" said the tramp, "You are doing no good!"

"Oh!" said the doctor, "you are the villain, are you, that put this poor girl in such a state? Now I want you to take that spell off the girl immediately!"

"I can't," said the tramp, "unless I have something to throw it on."

"There's an old hen before the door," said the doctor. "Throw it on her."

The tramp did so, the girl got out of bed sensible, but the hen turned over and died. The doctor took the tramp in charge at once and went away, but the girl was for years silly with spells.

From: W. J. Wintemberg, "French Canadian Folk-Tales," *Journal of American Folk-Lore* 17 (1904): 265–67.

The Bird of the Evil Eye

(Brazil)

Far away in the thickest forest lives the Tucano-yua, Bird of the Evil Eye. It has a nest in a hollow tree, and from a crevice under the branches, it surveys the ground beneath. If any animal passes near, the bird has but to look at it, and the evil eye does its work. All around, the ground is white with bones. The bird feeds on its victims, and not even the strongest can escape it.

Long ago a hunter, straying farther than was his wont, found this tree with the bones lying white about it. As he looked, he saw the Tucano-yua peering out; but the bird did not see him, and ere it could turn its head, the hunter shot it, and it fell to the ground. The man approached the body carefully, walking so he did not pass before its eyes. Then, with his knife, he cut off the bird's head, wrapped it in a cloth, and put it in his hunting pouch. Ever after that, when this man saw a deer or paca or tapir, he held the Tucano-yua's head so that the bill was pointed toward the game, which instantly fell dead. But he took care never to turn the bill toward himself.

The man's wife wondered much at her husband's success at hunting. She questioned him often to discover the reason for this good luck, but he answered always, "This is no business of yours. A woman cannot know of these things." Still she was not satisfied. Day after day, she watched her husband stealthily. And once, when the man and his wife went with a party to the woods, she watched more closely. When a deer or cotia passed by, she saw that her husband took something from his hunting pouch and held it toward the game, which instantly fell dead. The woman's curiosity tempted her to find what his strange weapon could be. It chanced, after dinner, that the man went to sleep on the ground. The woman approached him softly, opened his hunting pouch, and took out the head of the Tucano-yua. Turning it about, she tried to recall her husband's actions.

"He held it so," she said to herself, "with the bill turned toward the

From: Thomas Ewbank, *Life in Brazil; or, A Journal of a Visit to the Land of the Cocoa and the Palm* (New York: Harper & Brothers, 1856).

game." But as she spoke, she had carelessly turned the head against her husband's body, and in an instant she saw that he was dead. Overcome with fear, she started back, but in doing so she turned the deadly beak toward herself, and she also fell dead.

The Witch's Head

(El Salvador)

Wizards come into the houses by night in the shape of dogs, hogs, cats, or owls and entice the women away with them. The women are acquainted with a number of tricks and dodges of which the men have no knowledge. The men are asleep, unaware of everything. Sesimite, or the Giant, was in the habit of coming to a house in the pueblo of Ahuachapan and carrying off the wife of one of the men to enjoy her. The neighbor, the husband's friend, observed it and gave him warning. "Do you not know," said he, "that your wife is a witch, who steals away at night in a disguise to meet her lover? Take care of yourself!" The husband kept watch over his wife and observed her get up in the middle of the night and place a log of wood in his arms instead of herself. Then she swung herself up to the beams of the ceiling, falling straightway to the floor, where she lay headless, her head having vanished through the door.

The husband narrated to his neighbor what had happened. "What am I to do?" he said.

"Let us think out something to do!" said his neighbor. "Let the body lie where it is, but put a heap of hot ashes on the spot where the head belongs. That is the best method of curing women who give themselves up to witchcraft."

The man did as he was told. Later, during the night, the head returned but could not succeed in attaching itself to the trunk. "Where are you, you cruel husband, who have done this thing?" the head exclaimed.

From: C. V. Hartman, "Mythology of the Aztecs of Salvador," *Journal of American Folk-Lore* 20 (1907): 143–47.

The husband, however, who had gone up to the loft, made no reply but sat crouched in a corner perfectly still. Thereupon the head flew up to the loft. When it saw the husband, it settled on his shoulder and stuck fast there. The man being aware of the fact with regard to witches, that you never get rid of them if once they settle on your body in that manner, was grievously distressed at his woeful fate and went to the priest to inquire what he ought to do.

"Take matters quietly and wait!" said the priest. The head, however, remained on the man's shoulder.

The man wept at his misfortune, but that availed nothing. Not until after the lapse of a long time did the man succeed in enticing the head to leave his shoulder. That occurred on one occasion, when the man was out in the woods and at a time of the year when the zapotes were just beginning to ripen. The man, as he was wandering about in the woods, caught sight of a gigantic zapote tree.

"My daughter," said the man to the head, "there are some zapotes already ripe in that tree. Would it not be nice to have some zapotes to eat? I know you are fond of that kind of fruit! Get off my shoulder while I climb up the tree, and do you sit here meanwhile on my serape."

So saying he spread out his garment on the ground, and the head settled itself down upon it. The man then climbed the tree and got hold of a few quite green zapotes, which he hurled with all his force at the head.

It jumped and cried out and called upon the man for mercy. "Have pity, for mercy's sake, have pity upon me. Oh, cruel husband that you are! Do you want to kill me?"

"Oh no," said the man, "why, I was choosing out the fruit that is ripest. Those green zapotes fell off accidentally."

Straightway he began anew to hurl down upon the head the hard green fruit, and the head yelled and uttered lamentations. At that moment a roe happened to be passing quite near to the spot. The head then sprang up into the air and settled on the back of the roe, who in terror made off into the woods. The plaits came undone and the hair was tossed about by the wind. At the first precipice she came to, the roe threw herself over, and nothing remained of them but dust and skulls (*pinole y calaveras*).

A Witch Killer

(United States)

I was well acquainted with a farmer who had a large family of children, all of whom believed in witchcraft. I have heard him relate the following story several times.

One day in March he and his sons went to one of his neighbors with a yoke of oxen, horse, and sled for a load of hay. On their return they came to a bad place in the road, where the horse refused to go farther and lay down in the road. They tried various means to induce the horse to get up, but all in vain. After spending over half the day in the attempt, they suspected her being bewitched by a certain old woman who lived in the neighborhood, and the man seized an ax and attempted to kill the horse by beating out its brains. The skull was broken, and the horse was left upon the roadside till the next morning. Just at that moment the old woman had a bad spell, her head dropped to one side, and a doctor was sent for. She lived only a few days.

In the meantime the family of the old woman sent down to the man's house for some favors, but they were all refused. He believed that if he should accommodate them in the least thing, the old woman would recover, believing that he had struck the deathblow to the witch when he struck the horse. The next morning after, he went down to the horse and was surprised to find it alive. This survival he attributed to blows of the ax falling upon the witch instead of the horse. This man firmly believed that he struck the deathblow to the old woman when he struck the horse and that she would have recovered had he accommodated the family with the least favor. He told this story with evident pride in his skill in gaining advantage over the witch.

From: John McNab Currier, "Contributions to the Folk-Lore of New England," *Journal of American Folk-Lore* 2 (1889): 291–94.

Chon-chon the Witch Carrier

(Chile)

I n certain respects, Chilean witches differ from those of Europe, thanks possibly to their having learned a thing or two from the Araucanian medicine women. The Chon-chon, for instance, seems to be peculiar to the country.

In its least romantic form the Chon-chon is merely a night bird with a harsh and bodeful cry, auguring evil. Some of the nocturnal birds of Chile have lamentable voices, and the popular beliefs concerning them are widely diffused. This bird, however, is no true bird but the vehicle of a witch, and is nothing less than the head of the sorceress, using its ears as wings. At Chillan not long ago, it is recorded, the people turned out nightly to listen to a Chon-chon that flew over the town in the darkness, uttering its doleful cry. The bird is easily brought to earth. A pair of scissors opened till they form an "iron cross" will cause it to fall with a bump when it attempts to fly overhead. A better method still is to trace the figure of the "seal of Solomon," the interlaced triangles, in the dust.

In a very interesting Spanish work on the myths of the Chilean people, published in Santiago by Señor Cifuentes, an excellent story about the Chon-chon is to be found. The scene is laid in Limache, a small town situated about an hour's distance by rail from Valparaiso. The date of the happenings is not given, but a mile or two from the railway it might as well be yesterday as a hundred years ago.

One night some people were gathered together in the room of a farmhouse—one of the low-walled adobe buildings roofed with large red tiles that are still found in country places. The winter nights are long in central Chile, the lighting arrangements in farmhouses of the most primitive kind. The people sit, and often actually squat, Indian

From: Oswald H. Evans, "Witchcraft in Chile," *Chambers's Journal* 11 (1921): 380–83.

fashion, around a *brasero* of glowing charcoal, the noxious fumes of which afflict them with headaches, which they relieve by sticking postage stamps or plaster on each temple. That, to me, "discomfortable drink" maté circulates in a small gourd-shaped vessel, each person taking a pull at the *bombilla*, a kind of spoon-strainer perforated to let the liquid pass, and handing it to his neighbor. The conditions of semidarkness and carbon monoxide fumes would be propitious for the untoward happenings that are to be described.

A Chon-chon passed overhead, giving its melancholy cry, *Tué-tué-tué*. They should have thrown burnt salt in the air and said, "Go thy ways, Chon-chon, and I will go mine." One of the company, however, traced the symbol on the mud floor, and a heavy fall was heard on the tiled roof. All rushed out into the patio, and found a bird the size of a turkey struggling on the ground, from which it was unable to raise itself. They killed it and cut off the head, which was red and naked like that of the vulture. A dog ate the head, and the trunk was flung, in harmony with Chilean ideas of sanitation, on the roof. Shortly afterward a great outcry of mournful sounds told the people that the mates of the dead witch had come for the body. At the same instant, the dog that had eaten the head of the bird suddenly swelled up, and all could see that the appearances warranted the belief that the head had reverted to its human shape.

The following day the grave digger of the place had a tale to tell. At earliest dawn a great company of unknown people, clothed in black, had buried a headless body in the graveyard.

What to Do If a Witch Rides You

(United States)

Take a bottle half full of water and hang it on the outer post of the bed, close to the headboard. Get a new cork, stick into it nine new needles, and hang it over the bottle about an inch above its mouth. Having made these preparations, you may go to sleep prepared to wake and do your part when the hag puts in an appearance. When your mysterious visitor arrives, you must bear her riding patiently, knowing that this ride will be her last. The decisive moment for you is when she at last leaves her seat upon your chest to make her escape before the morning dawns. One of the limitations placed upon this uncanny being is that after her night's fun is over, she must depart over the headboard of the bed, close to the outer post. As her semifluid corporeal substance glides over, she finds the cork hanging, in which the nine new needles are set. Her fatal instinct for counting seizes her; she stops. Now is your time. Rouse yourself, reach quickly up over your head, and cork the bottle by so swift a movement that the hag cannot escape. She cannot, with all her supernatural powers, work her way through the glass or through the new cork defended by the nine new needles. You will not be troubled with that hag again. But someday soon some old woman, faint and weak and nearly dead, will crawl into your house and entreat you to let her spirit out of the bottle or she must die. And if you are obdurate and continue to keep the bottle corked, the poor old thing will gradually waste away and her life is gone.

You may also catch her at the moment of her entrance through your keyhole, by suspending the bottle below and the cork above that orifice. But testimony as to how she is to be taken and forced into the bottle had not yet come in, and we must wait awhile before explaining fully this method of capture.

From: "Folk-Lore Scrap-Book: Beliefs of Southern Negroes Concerning Hags," *Journal of American Folk-Lore* 7 (1894): 66–67.

There is another way by which suspicions of hagcraft may be proved or disproved. A neighbor, whom you suspect, comes to see you. If you are certain in regard to the matter, give your visitor a seat near the fire, and then, when she is not looking, steal quietly up behind her and stick a fork into the foot under her chair. By this means you have pinned her hag-spirit to the floor, and the old woman cannot or will not withdraw her bodily presence until the fork is withdrawn.

How to Cure Bewitchment

(Brazil)

I t is a mercy that old women in compact with the Wicked One are not so numerous in Río as they once were. In the interior they are reported as mischievous as ever. When a person imagines himself possessed, he commonly gets a priest to make the sign of the cross over him with a sprig of rosemary dipped in holy water. Friars are preferred for this business; those of Saint Anthony are reputedly the most successful. If possible, the afflicted must go to the monastery and enter the chapel with two or more monks. After certain rites, they converse with him and judge from his replies respecting the character of the demon and the place of its expulsion. They are careful not to drive it out at the mouth, lest the victim become dumb; nor at the eyes or ears, lest he lose his sight or hearing; nor at an arm, hand, or leg, lest he become disabled; but, if possible, at the soles of the feet.

From: Thomas Ewbank, *Life in Brazil; or, A Journal of a Visit to the Land of the Cocoa and the Palm* (New York: Harper & Brothers, 1856).

Cured by a Conjure Doctor

(United States)

When I was about eight years old, a little girl threw a brick at my head, which cut it very badly, and when I showed the wound to my mother, she became very angry and took the broom, ran out to the girl, and gave her several raps over the head. In about three months I began to have chills, and they lasted eight years. The strange part of my story is how they were cured.

My mother was instructed that the chills were put on me by the hand of the wicked, and she, being anxious about my welfare, employed a conjurer to take them off me. When he came he demanded part pay before entering in business, and that part being settled, he went to work. The first thing he did was to take out of his pocket the "walking boy" which was to assist him in finding the direction of enemies or friends, in this case, the one who put the chills on me. The walking boy is a bottle with a string tied to its neck, deeply colored, that you may not see what the doctor puts in it—something alive, you may know, which enables it to move or even flutter briskly, and this makes you certain of whatever fact the doctor is trying to impress.

The treatment for my chills was a tea and an ointment of his own preparation. The tea was made of roots which looked like potatoes, and silver money. The ointment was made out of herbs fried in hog's lard.

After being thus treated, as I had good faith in the "doctor," the chills vanished.

An old man once was ill with palsy, as they thought, and after spending much money employing medical doctors and getting no

From: "Folk-Lore Scrap-Book: Cures by Conjure Doctors," *Journal of American Folk-Lore* 12 (1899): 288–89.

relief, he was advised to change treatment. He employed a conjurer, who came with his walking boy. The doctor, with boy in hand, ordered a man to bring a hoe and dig where he would order him to, that he might unearth the thing that caused the man's illness.

After he had walked over and around the yard several times with the boy suspended, it was thought by many that he would not be able to find the buried poison, but as they were about to give up their pursuit, the boy fluttered and kicked as though he would come out of the bottle. Then the doctor ordered the man to dig quickly, for the "trick bag" was there. On the order being obeyed, the poison was found. It was rusty nails, finger- and toenails, hair, and pins sewed up in a piece of red flannel.

The doctor carried this to the patient and convinced him that he had found the cause of his illness and that he would surely get well. Not many days elapsed before he was walking as well as ever.

Witches as a Last Resort

(Brazil)

Negro witches cure patients given up by friars. My friend the vicar had a lad troubled with a bruised leg. The sore resisted all attempts to heal it. As a last resource, a "wise woman" was consulted. She raised a smoke of dried herbs, muttered over the wound, made motions as if stitching its lips up, put on a cataplasm of herbs, sent him home, and in a week he was well. Another slave had a diseased foot. Nothing seemed to do it any good, and at length his owner gave him leave to visit a dark sorceress, who talked to it, made signs over it, rubbed it with oil, covered it with a plaster, and in a few days he was sound too.

Ancient cures—worthy of Pliny—are still in vogue. Earthworms fried alive in olive oil and applied as a warm poultice remove whitlows, which are common among whites and blacks.

From: Thomas Ewbank, *Life in Brazil; or, A Journal of a Visit to the Land of the Cocoa and the Palm* (New York: Harper & Brothers, 1856).

Witch Finding in Western Maryland

(United States)

Summer before last there was a great apple crop in Frederick County. Everybody made apple butter. Now, an apple butter boiling, though shorn of much of its former glory as a social event, is yet an important function. I had the pleasure of assisting at more than one. Many a tale of the olden time and many an uncanny experience were exchanged over the "cider and the *schnitts*," and I realized that here, at least, tradition and local influences still held their own against books.

Over the great copper kettle one night an old man remarked, as he stirred its seething wholesome contents, that we didn't hear much of witchcraft nowadays, but when he was young there was a good deal of that business going on. His own father had been changed into a horse and ridden to the witches' ball. All the witches, as they arrived, turned into beautiful ladies, but he remained a horse, and so far and so fast was he ridden, and so sore and bruised was he the next day in his own proper person, that he couldn't do a stroke of work for two weeks.

Aunt Susan remembered well this adventure of her father-in-law. Her own father always kept a big bunch of sweetbriar switches hanging at the head of his bed. And many a night she had heard him "slashing away at the old witches that wouldn't let him sleep."

Progressive farming has about improved the sweetbriar off the face of the earth. But old beliefs are not so easily uprooted, as the stories that followed will testify.

Some of the stories at these gatherings are as follows:

When Grandmother Eiler was young she had a cow of her own raising, of which she was very proud. One evening at milking time, a

From: Elisabeth Cloud Seip, "Witch-Finding in Western Maryland," *Journal of American Folk-Lore* 14 (1901): 39–44.

certain woman passed through the barnyard, stopped, and looked the cow all over. "I was foolish enough to tell her all about the cow, how gentle she was, how much milk she was giving, and all that, and she said I certainly had a fine cow. Well, the next morning that cow wouldn't stand on her feet, and there she lay in the stable till father came home from the mountain, where he was cutting wood. He said it was all plain enough, when I told him everything, but he wondered I hadn't had better sense. However, he knew just what to do. He rubbed the cow all over with asafetida, saying words all the time. And the next day, when I went into the barn, there she stood on her four legs, eating like a hound. Witches can't stand asafetida."

It was this witch-woman who, going to a neighbor's one day on an errand, prolonged her stay without apparent reason, till it was almost night. Though she was very uneasy all the time and kept saying there was sickness at home and she ought to be there, still she didn't go. Finally, it was discovered that the broom had fallen across the door. When it was taken away, she fairly flew. Of course, this looked very suspicious. But not to be rash in their judgment, the people of the house sought further proof. So, the next time she came, salt was thrown under her chair, and there she sat as though bound until it was removed. Then, as her visits were now considered undesirable, nails were driven in her tracks, but the place in the ground marked, in case the footprints became obliterated. It was soon known that she was laid up with sore feet, which refused to heal until the nails were dug up.

Miss K———'s father, when a youth in Germany, had a friend whose rest was disturbed by nightmare. At last he concluded that a witch was troubling him, and he proceeded to entrap her by stopping up every crevice and keyhole in the room (mindful of the fact, of course, that "for witches this is law—where they have entered in, there also they withdraw"). The next morning he found a beautiful girl cowering in the cupboard. He put her to work as a servant about the house. But eventually, thinking her reformation complete, he married her and lived happily for several years. Sometimes, though, she would sigh and say she longed to see beautiful France again. One day she was missing, and her little child, just tall enough to reach the keyhole, told how she had removed the stopping for her. She was never seen again, having of course "taken French leave" through the keyhole. The same story is told of a miller in Frederick County. He too domesticated a witch-maiden, having caught her in the same way. But years after, he incautiously opened the keyhole and found himself a grass widower.

From Miss K——— I have a version of a story told to me as a child by Aunt Sarah, very black and very old. She was fond of her pipe. Yes, she learned to smoke from her mammy, who learned it from her grandmammy, who was a witch. This grandmother was phthisicky, and often called for her pipe at night, as smoking relieved her. It was her granddaughter's duty to fill her pipe just before going to bed, and also to get up and light it if necessary. Some nights, though, the grandmother would say, "Guess you needn't fix my pipe tonight. I don't reckon I'll want it." And on those nights, if the granddaughter woke up, she found herself alone and her mother and grandmother gone.

One night when grandmother had declined her pipe, she only pretended to be asleep and saw the two women get the lump of rabbit's fat off the mantelpiece, rub themselves all over, and say, "Up and out and away we go!" The third time, away they flew up the chimney.

She quickly got up, rubbed herself with rabbit's fat, saying, "Up and about and away we go!" And up and about she went, flying around the room, bumping and thumping herself against wall and rafters until daylight. Her "vaulting ambition" was not repressed, however, by this experience. The next thing she observed more closely and saw that her maternal relatives greased themselves with downward strokes, and said, not "Up and *about*," but "Up and *out* and away we go!" She carefully repeated this procedure and slipped up the chimney after them. Mammy and grandmammy each took a horse out of the field, leaving nothing for her but a yearling. So she took the yearling and rode gloriously till cockcrow.

As Miss K——— told this story, the witches slipped out of their skin after the greasing, and the yearling escaped, since there were horses enough to go around. But the misadventure of the witches' apprentice on the first night was the same.

A woman was suspected of bewitching her husband's horse. The animal refused to eat or drink, flying back from the trough in fright, as if struck by something. A neighbor, who claimed to be able to overcome the power of witches, was called in, and after some mysterious muttering, with pacings around the horse and in and out of the stall, he gave the horse a kick in the side. At this, the woman, who was looking on, walked away, holding her side, as though *she* felt the effects of the kick. As the man was leaving the farm, the woman crossed his path in the form of a snake, but he avoided her and escaped harm. He could have killed the snake but would not, knowing what it was.

This woman's reputation as a witch seems firmly established. I heard many stories of her. She was known as a very industrious, honest woman, not very quarrelsome, but capable of using abusive language when angered. She died but recently.

Miss K——— tells a story of her grandfather, who was a famous witch finder. He was called in once by a farmer who promised him fifty dollars if he could cure a valuable horse that he had reason to think was bewitched. He proceeded to work by taking a hoop off a barrel and passing it over the horse's head, with words known only to himself. He then replaced it and began to hammer it down.

"Shall I drive it hard?" he asked the farmer.

"Yes," was the reply. "I don't care if you kill the witch!"

Just then the farmer's little boy ran out of the house crying, "Little old Stoke" (the witch finder's name was Stokes), "my mother says if you don't stop, you'll kill her!"

At this the owner of the horse (and of the witch too, as it turned out) became very angry with Stokes for harming his wife (he evidently held her a little dearer than his horse) and refused to pay the fifty dollars. Miss K——— says they went to law about the money. It would be interesting to know if such grounds were allowed and the suit actually entered.

Many stories point to a belief in the evil eye. Children fall sick or cry incessantly after having been admired or caressed by some suspicious person.

The hero of the following tale was surely no faintheart.

The pleasure of a young man's visit to a young lady was sadly marred by the ill-timed antics of a black cat, which every night would appear in the room and fly about from floor to ceiling in the most surprising manner. Sometimes a black squirrel would relieve the cat but continue the acrobatic performance. All the time there was a terrific accompaniment, as of droves of rats, scratching and scrambling in the walls and under the floor. At last, being properly advised, he provided himself with a pistol and a silver bullet, stopped up the keyhole, and waited. But that night the cat didn't come back, nor the squirrel, and the powers of darkness no longer interfered with the course of true love. The lady in the case, mindful of her own difficulties, no doubt, now "tries" for witches with great success.

Note that it takes a *silver* bullet to bring down a witch. You have only to aim at her picture and the ball will take effect wherever she may be. And as I was advised, "If you can't get hold of her photograph, just draw off her profile on the end of the barn and shoot at that."

Your silver bullet is easily made by beating up a silver quarter or ten-cent piece. (The molding of the silver bullet in *Der Freischütz* will be recalled.) Witches' bullets are of pith or hair, and are often found in the bodies of animals that have fallen victims to their spells.

While I had not the pleasure of personal acquaintance with a witch or warlock, the promise is mine of introduction to two in good and regular standing.

One, a dweller in the Fox Hills, is the proud possessor of a book nobody can read. But it is chiefly as the "nephew of his uncle" that he is known to fame. This uncle of fearsome memory—among many advantages he possessed over the common run of people was entire independence of police protection or burglar alarms—never turned a key in his house, his barn, or his corncrib. For if any persons came on his premises with evil intentions, they were held there foot-fast until morning or such time as he was pleased to release them. Men have been found standing under his apple trees with open but empty sacks, begging to be freed and sent away.

The other notable, whom I hope to meet next summer, lives on the edge of the Owl Swamp. He was characterized "as about the best man we have left in that line."

But it is a comfort to know that if a witch hath power to charm, there be those also who can "unlock the clasping charm and thaw the spell." And this power does not reside in professionals only; anybody, in fact, who knows how can "try" for a witch. Of course, some people having a natural gift that way are more successful than others. They are possibly more ingenious in devising punishments. But certain conditions must be observed by everybody in all cases. Most important is the time for the trial. This must be within nine days after the spell has been detached.

Persons of small invention had better confine themselves to old reliable methods like the following:

If the cow's milk isn't good, throw the milking into the fire, or heat stones and drop them into the milk, or cut and slash the milk with knives. If this does not bring the witch to terms, she will be obliged to suffer severe pains, as from cutting or bruising.

If your baking fail, burn a loaf. The witch will come to you, seeking to borrow. Give her nothing at all, bite, sup, nor greeting. For if she obtain anything from you, even a word, no counter charm of yours will avail to lift the spell.

I happened to be present when an old lady, who had been away visiting, was asked for news of friends down the country.

"Oh," she said, "I didn't get to see them. I was on my way to their house when someone told me that their cow had died and they were trying for the witch. Of course, I didn't go then."

Aunt Betsy knew well that, had she gone, silence and the cold shoulder would have been her portion, even though she was not among the suspects. For at this critical time, the social amenities are in complete abeyance and hospitality in eclipse.

When Mr. F———'s child was taken with crying spells at night, he stood it as long as he could, but being a workingman, as he said, he couldn't afford to lose his rest. So, when all remedies failed, he decided that the child was tormented and he must try for the witch; especially as his wife admitted having met an old woman some days before who admired and caressed the child. His preparations were elaborate, but neglecting to take his mother-in-law into his confidence, they failed. For when the witch came a-borrowing, she accommodated her. Otherwise, he assured me, the witch's punishment would have been dire: "She would have busted!"

Another man's well-laid scheme went wrong because he couldn't hold his tongue. His cattle had died unaccountably. So he built a pyre of brush and cordwood and began to burn the bodies.

Soon, across the field a woman was seen, circling around in her approach to the fire. At last her clothing nearly touched the flame. "Gad! but that was close!" he exclaimed. Instantly she shot away, released from her punishment.

The year 1899, though a good apple year, was an off one for peaches. But some friends of mine contrived to get a taste at least, which was more than the most of us had. Coming home late one night, these young men passed a place where the only peaches in the neighbor-hood were said to be. They all "felt for peaches," as their peculiar idiom has it, and the coincidence of opportunity with capacity struck them all. But the owner of the peaches was likewise the owner of a savage dog that, howling as he prowled, seemed to realize that eternal vigilance was the price of peaches. But one of the party bethought him how to lay the dog. He took his pocketknife and drove the blade into a stake of the stake-and-rider fence, saying three times, "Dog, keep your mouth shut until I release you."

In the language of an eyewitness, "That dog nearly tore his toenails off getting to the back of the house. And there he stayed, with never a word out of him until we had all the peaches we wanted. Of course, we only took a few to eat. As Jake pulled the knife out, the dog flew around the house again, raging like mad, and we made good time down the road!"

Dr. Troyer, the Witch Trapper

(Canada)

The late E. A. Owen's book was published in 1898. He had been assiduous in gathering traditions of the pioneers, and a whole chapter is devoted to "Doctor Troyer and His Big 'Witch-Trap.'" From this it appears that Troyer was the first white settler to erect a habitation in Norfolk. The date was not long after 1790. His log house was erected on a bar or flat of about fifteen acres running into Long Point Bay, about a mile and a half east of Port Rowan. The earliest apple trees in the settlement were planted by Troyer. Some of these are still productive. He was "Norfolk's first medical practitioner," uncertified, it is true. Owen describes him as "insanely

From: James H. Coyne, "David Ramsay and Long Point in Legend and History," *Proceedings and Transactions of the Royal Society of Canada* (series 3) 13 (May 1919): 111–26.

superstitious, being a hopeless and confirmed believer in witchcraft."
This peculiar mental malady caused him a world of trouble and made
him ridiculously notorious. To prompt the recital of some witch story,
all that is necessary is to mention the name of Dr. Troyer in the
presence of any old settler in the county. The name Dr. Troyer and the
term *witches* are so interwoven in the minds of the old people that they
cannot think of one without being reminded of the other.

The old doctor was terribly persecuted by these witches. All his
troubles of mind and body were attributed to the witches who existed
in human form and possessed miraculous powers for producing evil.
He looked upon certain of his neighbors as witches, one of the most
dreaded being the widow of Captain Edward McMichael. Mrs.
McMichael was a very clever woman, and to be considered a witch by
the superstitious old doctor was highly amusing to her. She was a
woman of strong mind and great courage, and it is said she frequently
visited the lovely ravine and made grimaces at the poor old doctor
from some recess or clump of bushes, just for the pleasure it gave her
to tease and torment him. He was a great stutterer, and her appearance in the ravine would throw him into a fit of wild excitement,
during which he would stutter and gesticulate in a threatening
manner. He was a great deer hunter, but if he chanced to meet Mrs.
McMichael when starting out on a hunting expedition, he would
consider it an omen of ill luck and would turn about and go home. He
kept a number of horseshoes over the door of his house, and at the
foot of his bed a huge trap was bolted to the floor, where it was set
every night to catch witches. The jaws were about three feet long and
when shut were about two and a half feet high. There are people in
Port Rowan today who have a distinct remembrance of having seen
this witch trap in Dr. Troyer's bedroom.

But in spite of this defensive means the witches would occasionally
take him out in the night and transform him into various kinds of
animals and compel him to perform all sorts of antics. Whenever he
met with an experience of this kind, he would suffer from its effects
for some time afterward. One night the witches took him out of a
peaceful slumber, transformed him into a horse, and rode him across
the lake to Dunkirk, where they attended a witch dance. They tied
him to a post, where he could witness the dance through the
windows, and fed him rye straw. The change of diet and the hard
treatment to which he was subjected laid him up for some time. It

required several doses of powerful medicine to counteract the injurious effects of the rye straw and restore his digestive organs to a normal condition.

Strange as it may appear, Dr. Troyer believed all this, yet aside from witchcraft, he was considered a sane man. He is described as wearing a long white flowing beard, and it is said he lived to be ninety-nine years old and that just before his death he shot a hawk offhand from the peak of the barn roof.

Dr. Troyer's only son, Michael, commonly called Deacon Troyer, was highly respected, a pillar of his church, and at his death mourned by the whole community.

It is perhaps not irrelevant to Dr. Troyer's case to mention the fact that his son the deacon is said to have fallen into a trance in the earlier part of his life and to have been "dead to all appearances for three days and nights." Preparations were made for burial, from which he was saved by resuscitation. During the trance he was conscious and believed he was in the realm of eternal happiness. He would fain have remained but was informed that he must first return to earth to do the task assigned him. His restoration to life and health was followed by his conversion.

According to Owen, although Dr. Troyer had no less than four sons and five daughters, the family name has disappeared from Norfolk. Descendants in the male line are however still to be found in Illinois, and a considerable number of persons both in the Long Point region and in the United States claim the famous witch doctor as ancestor through female links in the chain of descent.

Dr. Egerton Ryerson's book on *The Loyalists of America and Their Times* contains a valuable memorandum by his cousin, Mrs. Amelia Harris, on the early days of the Long Point Settlement. Her father, Captain Samuel Ryerse, settled at Long Point in 1794. She describes the arrival of the family at Ryerse Creek, where after a day's rest they reembarked "and went fourteen miles farther up the bay to the house of a German settler who had been there two years, and had a garden well stocked with vegetables. The appearance of the boat was hailed with delight by those solitary beings and my mother and child were soon made welcome and the best that a miserable log house, or rather hut, could afford was at her service. This kind, good family, consisted of father, mother, one son, and one daughter. Mr. Troyer, the father, was a fine-looking old man with a flowing beard and was known for many years throughout the Long Point Settlement as 'Dr. Troyer.'

"He possessed a thorough knowledge of witches, their ways and doings, and the art of expelling them, and also the use of the divining rod, with which he could not only find water but could also tell how far below the surface of the earth precious metals were concealed, but was never fortunate enough to discover any in the neighborhood of Long Point."

Troyer's fame also extended to the remotest parts of Lake Erie and northward to Lake St. Clair. It reached Lord Selkirk's ill-fated Baldoon Settlement, where strange things were happening in 1829 and following years. Witchcraft was at work among the Highland settlers, to their great discomfort and peril. John McDonald's house stood on the banks of the Chenail Écarté. In or about November 1829, his troubles began. Stones and bullets crashed through the windows and onto the floor. Mysterious fires started up in different places in the house; when one was extinguished, another would appear in a different room. No one was hurt, but many were badly frightened. At last his buildings were burned in January 1830. He then removed the family to his father's house. The breaking of windows began afresh, until all were destroyed. From a corner cupboard with glass doors, bullets pierced their way through to the floor. The bullets were gathered up, marked, and put in a leather shot bag. A string was tied around the mouth of the bag, and the bag itself hung up on the chimney. Immediately the same bullets came back through the window.

The balls were then thrown into the deep water of the Chenail Écarté. In a short time the same balls came back through the windows as before. The Black Dog figures prominently in some of the narratives. Certain ludicrous features, in others, are vaguely reminiscent of Mother Goose stories. Many other incidents, as mysterious and startling as those mentioned, are recorded in the pamphlet on "Belledoon Mysteries."

The fame of Belledoon's witchcraft spread throughout the province. People came from far and near, some even from New York, to see for themselves, and went away convinced by the evidence of their own eyes.

Every effort was made to conjure away the evil spirit. Ministers of every known denomination were called to assist. The regular formulas for exorcism were used by the authorized ministers of religion.

Even the priest, with bell, book, and candle, failed to check the manifestations. Happily, the Methodist minister, the Rev. Mr. McDorman, thought of Dr. Troyer of Long Point, more than a hundred miles away, and McDonald and the minister went together to consult him.

Witchcraft accompanied them through the Longwoods, a stretch of about thirty miles of forest north of the Thames without a single dwelling on the road and in which they had to pass the night. McDonald was terrified by the melancholy wind stirring the tree tops, owls hooting, wolves yelping, then the heavy tramp-tramp of a vast multitude, inarticulate voices of men, crashing of boughs and snapping of twigs, and the rush of some great unseen host. Soon there was the sound of combat in the air with an opposing multitude, followed by groans of the wounded and shrieks of the dying.

In three days they arrived at Dr. Troyer's. The various narratives differ greatly in important details. According to one version, it was Troyer's daughter, a sallow fragile girl of fifteen with wild eyes gleaming when excited, who possessed the gift of divination. She used a stone, which she said was "by some called the moonstone," but as its employment was "always attended by great physical prostration and much mental agony," she used it only "under very extraordinary circumstances." Before doing so on this occasion, she had already divined that McDonald had had trouble with neighbors over his refusal to sell them a portion of his land. "I see," she continued, "a long, low, log house." McDonald listened in rapt wonder to the alliterative description of his evil-minded neighbor's dwelling, and minute details of the personal appearance and peculiarities of its inmates.

Promising to look into the stone, she "retired to her chamber, and after three hours returned with a worn look as if suffering from some acute nervous irritability." Then she informed McDonald that his outbuildings had been "burned to the ground just two hours ago." This turned out exactly true.

"Have you ever seen a gray goose in your flock?" she asked. He had; he had shot at it with a leaden ball and the fowl had escaped. She assured him, "No bullet of lead would ever harm a feather of that bird." The bird was merely a shape assumed by his enemy. He must use a silver bullet, and if he hit the mark, his enemy would be wounded in a corresponding part of the body. He and McDorman returned to Belledoon. Next morning, the goose reappeared with the flock in the river. He fired, and the bird, "giving a weird cry like a human being in distress," fluttered into the reeds with a broken wing. Rushing to the long, low, log house, he found "the woman who had injured him, with her broken arm resting on a chair and her withered lips uttering half-ejaculated curses." From that moment the witchcraft ceased. The witch lived for some time but suffered always from racking pains throughout her whole body.

Witchcraft in Alaska

(United States)

A residence of twenty-seven years in Alaska has convinced me that along with the drinking of rum (the invariable effect of which seems to be to incite the natives to murder) witchcraft is the greatest curse of the Alaskan people. I have no doubt that the population along the northwest coast has been kept down to its pitiful proportions of only thirty-five thousand because of the wholesale destruction of life by the consequences of the belief in witchcraft. Why should there not be a teeming population in Alaska as there is in Japan? The Eskimo stock is probably the purest type of the Turanian race in existence; the food supply is sufficient for a populous race. But this devilish system of witchcraft has been a large factor in keeping the population down.

The trouble begins with the Indian doctor or sorcerer. When a child is born into the world with a curly lock of hair on his head, it is taken as a supernatural sign that he is set apart to be an Indian doctor or sorcerer. Herodotus tells us that the Egyptian priests knew that a bull calf born with certain signs was to be a god; they had no doubt about it whatever, and when these signs manifested themselves, the calf was deified. It is in some such spirit that the Indians of Alaska look upon the child born with his curly lock of hair. After being reared with uncut hair and with no taste of beach food—crabs, mussels, clams, or

From: John G. Brady, "Witchcraft in Alaska," *The Independent* 57 (1904): 1498–99.

seaweed—by a final test followed eight days' fast, in which he can drink nothing but salt water, he convinces the people that Yake, the abiding spirit, takes possession of him. After that, whenever he appears with his shaman's paraphernalia of the hideous rattles, the aprons of painted buckskin, the masks, the necklaces and charms, as he dons and doffs these one after another in the symbolic ritual, they have no doubt that in what he does or says he is possessed by Yake. He is now competent to be consulted in all troubles.

They believe that every kind of sickness comes from without. It is the work of evil spirits. Suppose a man has a hemorrhage and is spitting blood. The sorcerer is summoned and he performs his incantations for hours, day after day. When these are of no avail in curing the disease, it is evident to him and the people that a witch is counteracting his influence. The people are all gathered in a circle around the fire, in concern and dread, not knowing upon which one of them the judgment may fall. "O Yake," the Indian doctor cries, "where is the witch?" He passes from one to another around the circle, going around perhaps for several times in vain. Again and again he looks up through the smoke hole, imploring Yake to point out the witch. Then at last he points quickly to a man or a woman: "That is the witch."

Then they seize upon the one indicted. Of course, no punishment is too severe, since they believe him a witch. In the case of a woman, I have known them to tie her hands, and thrust knives through her breasts, through her thighs, and through her lips.

I have had a great deal to do in trying to counteract witchcraft. We have had a hard struggle with it, but we are overcoming it.

Since I became governor I heard of a case of a man with a sore throat. He had consulted an Indian doctor forty miles away, who had said that such and such a man was the witch. They had tied the poor unfortunate to a chair with his hands behind him and had kept him seven days without food or drink when the news reached me. The settlement was Yakutat, 250 miles away to the northwest. We had no telegraph or means of communication, so it seemed that we were obliged to go. I told Captain Sebree of the U.S. gunboat *Wheeling* and he consented to accompany me to the place. We found the story only too true, but its culmination was happier than in most instances. At the end of seven days the man with the sore throat had commenced to get better. They untied the witch, but he was shrewd enough to take advantage of the situation. "I am a witch," he said. "Tie me up again. I bewitched the man. I will make him well." An agreement was struck with him that if he would thus influence for good instead of evil he should have so many blankets, so many camphor wood trunks, and other pieces of property. They tied him again in the chair, the patient continued to recover, and the self-confessed witch was set free with his spoils. They gave him these presents, remember, not because they had wrongly imprisoned him or to recompense him for his tortures, but simply as the price of his ceasing to bewitch the sick man. At this denouncement the witch had a chance to get away on a schooner, and he went at once. He was gone when I arrived there, but George, the Indian chief, told me he was thoroughly convinced the man was a witch.

William Hunter, a Christian native, was sick with consumption. He had a half brother who was a bad boy and half-witted. This boy told William that a woman in the ranch (we call the Indian villages ranches) had made him a medium to make William die with consumption. William and his brother tied the medium, and he could untie himself, whether tied to a chair or to a bed; therefore they believed the boy's story. This was noised about in the village, and there was another boy who conceived the idea that he had been bewitched by a woman, the wife of an old blind man. He had been with them in the woods and was cutting down a tree when he went off into a swoon. As he began to awake, he found this old woman standing over him and grinning. That occurred twice, and he believed that this woman had bewitched him. Gossip repeated the story, and the more they talked about it the more it stirred up the community, until the people in the village were wrought up about it and they came to me.

Then I gathered them all in my office and undertook to teach them the nature of consumption and other diseases. In my office I have a few good physiological charts made in Germany, and I displayed the vital organs of the body, telling them the causes of consumption, from which the white people suffered as well as they. I talked all morning, and in the afternoon we had another session. They had listened all day, but as I ended my talk an Indian chief cried aloud, "Well, that is what the white men say. We are Indians, and we know that there are witches."

The perusal of a few paragraphs from the history of the Salem witchcraft persecutions would show cases parallel to instances which I could relate by the scores. Witchcraft is about the same thing, whether practiced by the Aryan or the Turanian race. There is nothing that will stamp it out but Christian education, just as we ourselves are now kept from superstition by the same means.

Legend of the Mulata de Córdoba

(Mexico)

I t is well known, Señor, that this mulatto of Córdoba, being a very beautiful woman, was in close touch with the devil. She dwelt in Córdoba—the town not far from Vera Cruz, where coffee and very good mangoes are grown—and she was born so long ago that the very oldest man now living was not then alive. No one knew who her father was, or who her mother was, or where she came from. So she was called La Mulata de Córdoba, and that was all. One of the wonders of her was that the years passed without marking her, and she never grew old.

She led a very good life, helping everyone who was in trouble and giving food to the hungry ones; and she dressed simply in modest clothes and was always most neat and clean. She was a very wicked witch, and beyond that nobody really knew anything about her at all. On the same day and at the same hour, she would be seen by different people in different places widely apart—as here in the city, and in Córdoba, and elsewhere variously—all in precisely the same moment of time. She also was seen flying through the air, high above the roofs of the houses, with sparks flashing from her black eyes. Moreover, every night the devil visited her, as was known generally, because at

From: Thomas A. Janvier, ed., *Legends of the City of Mexico* (New York and London: Harper & Brothers, 1910).

night her neighbors observed that through the chinks in the tightly shut doors and windows of her house there shone a bright light, as though all the inside of the house were filled with flames. She went to mass regularly, and at the proper seasons partook of the Sacrament. She disdained everybody, and because of her disdainings it was believed that the master of her beauty was the Lord of Darkness, and that seemed reasonable. Every single one of the young men was mad about her, and she had a train of lovers from which she could pick and choose. All wonders were told of her. She was so powerful and could work such prodigies, that she was spoken about—just as though she had been the blessed Santa Rita de Cascia—as the Advocate of Impossible Things! Old maids who sought for husbands went to her, as did poor ladies who longed for jewels and fine dresses that they might go to the court of the viceroy, miners that they might find silver, and old soldiers set aside for rustiness that they might get new commands—so that the saying "*I* am not the Mulata of Córdoba!" is the answer when anyone asks an impossible favor even now.

How it came about, Señor, no one ever knew. What everyone did know was that one day the Mulata was brought from Córdoba here to the city and was cast into the prison of the Holy Office. That was a piece of news that made a stir! Some said that a disdained lover had denounced her to the Inquisition. Others said that the Holy Office had laid hands on her less because she was a witch than because of her great riches, and it was told that when she had been seized, ten barrels filled with gold dust had been seized with her. So talk about the matter was on every tongue.

Many years went by, Señor, and all of that talk was almost forgotten. Then one morning the city was astonished by hearing, no one knew from where, that at the next auto-da-fé the witch of Córdoba would walk with the unredeemed ones, carrying the flameless green candle and wearing the high bonnet, and would be burned at the burning place of the Holy Office—it was in front of the church of San Diego, Señor, at the western end of what now is the Alameda—and so would have her sins burned out of her. And before that astonishment was ended, there came another and a greater, when it was told that the witch, before the very eyes of her jailers, had escaped from the prison of the Inquisition and was gone free! All sorts of stories flew about the city. One said, crossing himself, that her friend the devil had helped her to her freedom; another said that Inquisitors also were of flesh and blood and that she had been freed by her own beauty. Men talked at random, because neither then nor later did anybody know what really had happened. But what really did happen, Señor, was this:

One day the chief Inquisitor went into the prison of the Mulata that he might reason her to repentance. And being come into her prison—it was a long and lofty chamber that they had put her into, Señor, not one of the bad small cells—he stopped short in amazement, beholding before him, drawn with charcoal on the wall of the chamber, a great ship that lacked not a single rope nor a single sail nor anything whatever that a ship requires! While he stood gazing at that ship, wondering, the Mulata turned to him and looked strangely at him out of her wicked black eyes and said in a tone of railing, "Holy Father, what does this ship need to make it perfect?"

And to that he answered, "Unhappy woman! It is thou who needest much to make thee perfect, that thou mayest be cleansed of thy sins! As for this ship, it is in all other ways so wholly perfect that it needs only to sail."

Then said the Mulata, "That it shall do—and very far!" and there was on her face as she spoke to him a most wicked smile.

With astonishment he looked at her and at the ship. "How can that be possible!" he asked.

"In this manner!" she answered, and as she spoke, she leaped lightly from the floor of the prison to the deck of the ship, up there on the wall, and stood with her hand upon the tiller at the ship's stern.

Then, Señor, a very wonderful marvel happened. Suddenly the sails of the ship filled and bellied out as though a strong wind were blowing, and then before the eyes of the Inquisitor the ship went sailing away along the wall of the chamber, the Mulata laughing wickedly as she swung the tiller and steered it upon its course. Slowly it went at first, and then more and more rapidly, until coming to the wall at the end of the chamber, it sailed right on into and through the solid stone and mortar, the Mulata still laughing wickedly as she stood there steering at the ship's stern. And then the wall closed whole and solid again behind the ship, and only a little echoing sound of that wicked laughter was heard in the chamber. The ship had vanished, and the Mulata was out of her prison and gone.

The Inquisitor, Señor, who had seen this devil's miracle, immediately lost all his senses and became a madman and was put into a madhouse, where till death gave peace to him, he raved always of a beautiful woman in a great ship that sailed through stone walls and across the solid land. As for the Mulata, nothing more was ever heard of her. But it was generally known that her master the devil had claimed her for his own.

This story is entirely true, Señor, as is proved by the fact that the Inquisition building in which all these wonders happened still is standing. It is the Escuela de Medicina now.

The Trial of Bridget Bishop

(United States)

Bridget Bishop was indicted for bewitching several persons in the neighborhood, the indictment being drawn up according to the usual form in such cases. And she pleading not guilty, there were brought in several persons who had long undergone many kinds of miseries which were preternaturally inflicted and generally ascribed to a horrible witchcraft. There was little occasion to prove the witchcraft, it being evident and notorious to all beholders.

Now to fix the witchcraft on the prisoner at the bar, the first thing used was the testimony of the bewitched, whereof several testified that the shape of the prisoner did oftentimes very grievously pinch them, choke them, bite them, and afflict them, urging them to write their names in a book which the said specter called "ours." One of them did further testify that it was the shape of this prisoner, which one day took her with another from her wheel and, carrying her to the riverside, threatened there to drown her if she did not sign the book mentioned, which yet she refused. Others of them did also testify that

From: Cotton Mather, "The Wonders of the Invisible World" (1693). In George Lincoln Burr (ed.), *Narratives of the Witchcraft Cases, 1648–1706* (New York: Charles Scribner's Sons, 1914).

the said shape did in her threats brag to them that she had been the death of sundry persons then by her named, and that she had ridden a man then likewise named. Another testified, ascribing the apparition of ghosts to the specter of Bishop crying out, "You murdered us!" About the truth whereof, there was in the matter of fact but too much suspicion.

It was testified that at the examination of the prisoner before the magistrates, the bewitched were extremely tortured. If she did but cast her eyes on them, they were presently struck down, and this in such a manner as there could be no collusion in the business. But upon the touch of her hand upon them when they lay in their swoons, they would immediately revive, and not upon the touch of anyone else. Moreover, upon some special actions of her body, as the shaking of her head or the turning of her eyes, they presently and painfully fell into like postures. And many like accidents now fell out while she was at the bar, one at the same time testifying that she said she could not be troubled to see the afflicted thus tormented.

There was testimony likewise brought in that a man striking once at the place where a bewitched person said, the shape of this Bishop stood, the bewitched cried out that he had torn her coat in the place then particularly specified; and the woman's coat was found to be torn in that very place.

One Deliverance Hobbs, who had confessed her being a witch, was now tormented by the specters for her confession. And she now testified that this Bishop tempted her to sign the book again and to deny what she had confessed. She affirmed that it was the shape of this prisoner which whipped her with iron rods to compel her thereunto. And she affirmed that this Bishop was at a general meeting of the witches in a field at Salem village and there partook of a diabolical sacrament in bread and wine then administered!

To render it further unquestionable that the prisoner at the bar was the person truly charged in this witchcraft, there were produced many evidences of other witchcrafts by her perpetrated. For instance, John Cook testified that about five or six years ago, one morning about sunrise, he was assaulted in his chamber by the shape of this prisoner, which looked on him, grinned at him, and very much hurt him with a blow on the side of the head, and that on the same day about noon, the same shape walked into the room where he was and an apple strangely flew out of his hand and into the lap of his mother, six or eight feet from him.

Samuel Gray testified that about fourteen years ago, he awoke one night and saw the room where he lay full of light, and that he then saw plainly between the cradle and the bedside a woman who looked upon him. He rose, and it vanished, though he found the doors all fast. Looking out at the entry door, he saw the same woman in the same garb again and said, "In God's name, what do you come for?" He went to bed and had the same woman again assaulting him. The child in the cradle gave a great screech and the woman disappeared. It was long before the child could be quieted, and though it was a very likely thriving child, yet from this time it pined away and, after several months, died in a sad condition. He knew not Bishop nor her name, but when he saw her after this, he knew by her countenance and apparel and all circumstances that it was the apparition of this Bishop which had thus troubled him.

John Bly and his wife testified that he bought a sow of Edward Bishop, the husband of the prisoner, and was to pay another person the price agreed. This prisoner being angry that she was thus hindered from fingering the money, quarreled with Bly, soon after which the sow was taken with strange fits, jumping, leaping, and knocking her head against the fence. She seemed blind and deaf and would neither eat nor be suckled, whereupon a neighbor said she believed the creature was overlooked. And sundry other circumstances concurred which made the deponents believe that Bishop had bewitched it.

Richard Coman testified that eight years ago, as he lay awake in his bed with a light burning in the room, he was annoyed with the apparition of this Bishop and of two more who were strangers to him, who came and oppressed him so that he could neither stir himself nor wake anyone else, and that he was the night after molested again in the like manner, the said Bishop taking him by the throat and pulling him almost out of the bed. His kinsman offered for this cause to lodge with him, and that night as they were awake, discoursing together, this Coman was once more visited by the guests who had formerly been so troublesome, his kinsman being at the same time struck speechless and unable to move hand or foot. He had laid his sword by him, which these unhappy specters did strive much to wrest from him, only he held too fast for them. He then grew able to call the people of his house, but although they heard him, yet they had not power to speak or stir, until at last one of the people cried out, "What's the matter?" and the specters all vanished.

Samuel Shattock testified that in the year 1680, this Bridget Bishop often came to his house upon such frivolous and foolish errands that they suspected she came indeed with a purpose of mischief. Presently whereupon his eldest child, which was of as promising health and sense as any child of its age, began to droop exceedingly, and the oftener Bishop came to the house, the worse the child grew. As the child would be standing at the door, he would be thrown by an invisible hand and bruised against the stones, and in like sort knock his face against the sides of the house and bruise it after a miserable manner. Afterward this Bishop would bring him things to dye, whereof he could not imagine any use, and when she paid him a piece of money, the purse and money were unaccountably conveyed out of a locked box and never seen more. The child was immediately hereupon taken with terrible fits, whereof his friends thought he would have died. Indeed, he did almost nothing but cry and sleep for several months together, and at length his understanding was utterly taken away. Among other symptoms of an enchantment upon him, one was that there was a board in the garden whereon he would walk, and all the invitations in the world could never fetch him off.

About seventeen or eighteen years after, there came a stranger to Shattock's house who, seeing the child, said, "This poor child is bewitched, and you have a neighbor living not far off who is a witch." He added, "Your neighbor has had a falling out with your wife, and she said in her heart your wife is a proud woman and she would bring down her pride in this child." He then remembered that Bishop had parted from his wife in muttering and menacing terms a little before the child was taken ill. The abovesaid stranger would needs carry the bewitched boy with him to Bishop's house, on pretense of buying a pot of cider.

The woman entertained him in furious manner and flew also upon the boy, scratching his face till the blood came and saying, "Thou rogue, why dost thou bring this fellow here to plague me?"

Now it seems the man had said before he went that he would fetch blood of *her*. Ever after the boy was followed with grievous fits, which the doctors themselves generally ascribed to witchcraft and wherein he would be thrown still into the fire or the water if he were not constantly looked after, and it was verily believed that Bishop was the cause of it.

John Louder testified that, going well to bed upon some little controversy with Bishop about her fowl, he did awake in the night by moonlight and did see clearly the likeness of this woman grievously oppressing him, in which miserable condition she held him, unable to help himself, till near day. He told Bishop of this, but she denied it and threatened him very much. Quickly after this, being at home on a Lord's day with the doors shut about him, he saw a black pig approach him, but as he went to kick it, it vanished away. Sitting down immediately after, he saw a black thing jump in at the window and come and stand before him. The body was like that of a monkey, the feet like a cock's, but the face much like a man's. He being so extremely frightened that he could not speak, this monster spoke to him and said, "I am a messenger sent unto you, for I understand that you are in some trouble of mind, and if you will be ruled by me, you shall want for nothing in this world." Whereupon he endeavored to clap his hands upon it, but he could feel no substance, and it jumped out of the window again but immediately came in by the porch, though the doors were shut, and said, "You had better take my counsel!" He then struck at it with a stick but struck only the groundsel and broke the stick. The arm with which he struck was presently disabled, and it vanished away.

He presently went out at the back door and spied this Bishop in her orchard, going toward her house, but he had not power to set one foot toward her. Whereupon returning into the house, he was immediately accosted by the monster he had seen before, which goblin was now going to fly at him. Whereat he cried out, "The whole armor of God be between me and you!" So it sprang back and flew over the apple tree, shaking many apples off the tree in its flying over. At its leap, it flung dirt with its feet against the stomach of the man, whereon he was then struck dumb and so continued for three days together. Upon the producing of this testimony, Bishop denied that she knew this deponent, yet their two orchards joined and they had often had their little quarrels for some years together.

William Stacy testified that, receiving money of this Bishop for work done by him, he was gone but a matter of three rods from her and, looking for his money, found it unaccountably gone from him. Some time after, Bishop asked him whether his father would grind her grist for her. He demanded why, and she replied, "Because folks count me a witch."

He answered, "No question but he will grind it for you." Being then gone about six rods from her, with a small load in his cart, suddenly the off wheel slumped and sank down into a hole upon plain ground, so that the deponent was forced to get help for the recovering of the wheel. But stepping back to look for the hole which might give him this disaster, there was none at all to be found. Some time after, he was awakened in the night, but it seemed as light as day, and he perfectly saw the shape of this Bishop in the room, troubling him; but upon her going out, all was dark again. He charged Bishop afterward with it, and she denied it not; but was very angry. Quickly after, this deponent having been threatened by Bishop, as he was in a dark night going to the barn, he was very suddenly taken or lifted from the ground and thrown against a stone wall. After that, he was again hoisted up and thrown down a bank at the end of his house. After this again, passing by this bishop, his horse striving to draw with a small load, all his gears flew to pieces, and the cart fell down, and this deponent, going then to lift a bag of corn of about two bushels, could not budge it with all his might.

Many other pranks of Bishop's this deponent was ready to testify. He also testified that he verily believed, the said Bishop was the instrument of his daughter Priscilla's death, of which suspicion pregnant reasons were assigned.

To crown all, John Bly and William Bly testified, that being employed by Bridget Bishop to help take down the cellar wall of the old house wherein she formerly lived, they did find in holes of the said old wall several poppets made of rags and hogs' bristles, with headless pins in them, the points being outward. Whereof she could give no account to the court that was reasonable or tolerable.

One thing that was made against the prisoner was her being evidently convicted of gross lying in the court several times while she was making her plea. But besides this, a jury of women found a preternatural teat upon her body, but upon a second search within three or four hours, there was no such thing to be seen. There was also an account of other people whom this woman had afflicted. And there might have been many more if they had been inquired for. But there was no need of them.

There was one very strange thing more, with which the court was newly entertained. As this woman under guard was passing by the great and spacious meeting house of Salem, she gave a look toward the house, and immediately a demon invisibly entered the meeting house and tore down a part of it, so that though there was no person to be seen there, yet the people running in at the noise found a board, which was strongly fastened with several nails, transported to another quarter of the house.

Charles Dolly, Obeah Man

(West Indies)

On the 18th of August, 1904, at the Court House at Plymouth, in the Presidency of Montserrat, Charles Dolly was charged with "practicing Obeah." From the evidence—of which I had obtained a copy through the kind offices of Sergeant-Major W. E. Wilders of Montserrat, now a Superintendent in the Leeward Islands Police Force—it would appear that on the evening of the 12th of August the local sergeant of police, accompanied by other officers and armed with a search warrant, went to Dolly's house and searched the premises.

They found, on entering the living room, a bottle of turpentine, and in a cellar, to which access was afforded by a trapdoor partially under a couch, a cloth hanging from a nail. This was found to be wrapped around a human skull. Some horsehair, together with a tin band, was plaited around the front part of the skull, and inside the cloth was found the sum of four shillings in silver. Upon further search being made in the room above, a piece of skull, with the mark of a cross upon it in chalk, was found concealed underneath the bolster of a bed. Other minor articles were also discovered and were produced before the magistrate.

From: J. S. Udal, "Obeah in the West Indies," *Folklore* 26 (1915): 255–95.

On another visit being paid by the police to the premises subsequent to Dolly's arrest, a small wooden coffin was found in a mango tree near the house, though apparently no steps had been taken to conceal it. The coffin also contained similar cedar leaves to those found in the basin in the house.

The police, several of whom had had previous experience in these cases, stated in their evidence that all these articles were ordinarily used in the practice of Obeah and, further, that the accused man had a notorious reputation for Obeah practices. As to the general characteristics of the "instruments of Obeah," the sergeant-major himself was able to give me some interesting and personal information, for during the few years previously he told me that he had prosecuted some seventeen persons for Obeah practices, of whom sixteen had been convicted. He informed me that the articles seized by the police in these various cases were largely composed of skulls or portions of skulls, human bones, brass chains with pieces of bone attached, silver coins, pieces of chalk, pieces of looking glass, horse-hair, turpentine, vinegar, and asafetida.

It appeared that two other men were charged on the same day as Dolly with similar offenses, the only "instruments of Obeah" being produced in evidence against them being vials containing asafetida and quicksilver. The magistrate, having heard the evidence in all the cases, deferred his decision upon them until the following day.

In the meantime Dolly, fearing, it is presumed, that from the paucity of the evidence against them these two men might be discharged and their evidence utilized against himself, volunteered to give evidence for the prosecution to show that these two articles—asafetida and quicksilver—apparently harmless enough in themselves, were real "instruments of Obeah." It was, of course, however, then too late. The sergeant-major kindly reduced into writing for my benefit the statement which Dolly had made to him. It was to the effect that the skull had been brought to him by another man; that he had dressed it with the horsehair and metal band; that the brass chain and piece of bone attached were intended for a sick girl, who should wear it around her neck as necklaces are worn by women; that turpentine and vinegar form part of the Obeah man's stock-in-trade; that the man who took him the skull also took him the turpentine and vinegar, which were used by the man under his (Dolly's) supervision; that if mixed by any other man than an Obeah man it would be useless; that the mixture was to be applied as a lotion to the sick girl, who was a daughter of the bearer of the skull; that asafetida was a dangerous "instrument of Obeah," it being used as a poison by Obeah men; that if smoked from a pipe by an Obeah man through openings or crevices in a dwelling-house the occupants would be rendered unconscious; that he (Dolly) never used such dangerous things; that he was a firm believer in spirits and could successfully banish them; that the skull with the metal (silver?) band and horsehair, etc., on it was intended to banish spirits from the house of the man who took him the skull; that this man's sick daughter would die if he (Dolly) did not drive away the spirit which was the cause of her illness; that the skull was to be buried outside the entrance door to the house in order to keep off the spirit; that the silver band on it was intended as a bribe to "buy the spirit"; that the spirit would not be kept off unless bought with silver, and that the silver should be given in this manner by the Obeah man—if given by any other person, it would be useless.

"This in brief," said the sergeant-major, "was the information given by one of the most notorious Obeah men in the colony."

In the end Dolly was convicted and was sentenced to twelve months' imprisonment, with the addition in his case, as he had been three times previously convicted of this offense, of a flogging. The government had felt bound to introduce this additional punishment in cases of confirmed practitioners in Obeah and in order to act as a deterrent to would-be participants, for Obeah in many cases wears a much more serious aspect and not all Obeah men carry on their profession in the harmless way that Dolly affected was always his practice.

But this deterrent did not seem to have had the desired effect that it was hoped it would have upon Dolly, for a short time before I left the colony he was again in trouble and for the same offense. The easy prey which the credulous and superstitious native always affords to these unscrupulous impostors, and the large gains they sometimes make (I was told that in this last case considerably over one hundred pounds in silver was found in Dolly's house when it was searched by the police) seem to render it almost impossible for them to give up this practice so long as it is such a lucrative one and carries with it the awe and respect which is so dear to this class of persons.

In some of the milder forms of Obeah I must confess that I can see little difference between those impostures which still in our supposed higher plane of civilization exercise such influence over the credulous and superstitious of all peoples and of all ages. Our old law characterized such poor fortune-tellers as the Gypsy woman as a "rogue and a vagabond," and treated them as such. Those laws still remain in force, and I for one do not see why they should not be applied because the palm now requires to be "crossed" with gold instead of silver.

It may have been with some feeling of this kind in my mind that I first heard of this last lapse of old Dolly as I was returning from holding a circuit court in one of the presidencies not very long before I left the colony, when I happened to hear some of the passengers on the steamer discussing the case of an old and blind man who was on board and who had been convicted of Obeah at Montserrat, and who was being sent up to the prison headquarters at Antigua to undergo his sentence of imprisonment and, once more, a flogging. Upon inquiry I learned that this was Charles Dolly.

It seemed to them, as I must say it did to me, rather an excessive punishment to inflict upon an old man (he was now said to be over seventy years of age), apart from his blindness, even though such a hardened offender as I knew him to be, whose principal, if not sole, motive was greed. I therefore, shortly after my arrival at Antigua, went to the gaol, where I saw Dolly, and after satisfying myself as to the facts, I represented his case to the governor, with the result, I am thankful to say, that the latter part of his punishment was remitted. I trust that this action on my part will not be taken as implying any approval of the practice of even the more harmless phases of Obeah, however much these may have proved interesting to me from a folklore point of view.

A Trial for
Indian Witchcraft

(Canada)

L ouis Gray (the witch doctor) and Dwyer Green, Indians, charged at Port Simpson Police Court with suffering a "tort" or wrong to be inflicted upon one Mary Feak, an Indian woman of the Tsympsean tribe, by circulating charges of witchcraft against her contrary to Section 103, Indian Act.

Both plead not guilty.

Matthew Feak called and sworn:

"My name is Matthew Feak. I am a member of the Port Simpson Band. Some time last March, Louis Gray cut a cedar tree somewhere up in the woods near here and took three men along with him— Dwyer Green, and, I have heard, Hezekiah Wesley; the third I do not know. When the tree was cut down, it happened that one of the Brentzen family died at the same time. Of course I have heard about this Huldagwit a number of times; and this Louis Gray, as a medium, had picked out this tree as being used by one practicing witchcraft and had had the tree cut down. The witchcraft stories were quieted for a time; but in November 1915, a gasoline launch went up from Port Simpson to the Nass to bring the chiefs down for a conference on the Indian land question. The names of those who went up are Dwyer Green, Nathan Lawson, Andrew Wells, Joshua Wells, Celeste Wesley, and Rufus Dudaward. They went up the Nass, and while there, the mention was made of this witchcraft and the cutting down of the tree.

"Joshua Wells turned to Dwyer Green and said, 'You are one of Louis Gray's disciples or followers. Why do you hide the name of the one who is practicing witchcraft?'

"Dwyer Green returned, 'I am a Christian man, and I do not see why

From: "Notes and Queries: Indian Witchcraft," *Journal of American Folk-Lore* 34 (1921): 390–92.

I should hide it. I will name the one who has been using this tree to practice witchcraft.'

"So he named my mother, Mary Feak. Dwyer Green said he was not afraid, so he told the name Matthew Feak."

Celeste Wesley sworn:

"My name is Celeste Wesley. I am a member of the Port Simpson band of Indians. When I was up at Fishery Bay on the Nass River, that is where I heard Dwyer Green say he had cut a tree down where someone had been practicing witchcraft. Dwyer said there was an evil box up in the tree. Joshua Wells is the one who asked him if he knew the owner of the box. Dwyer was quite certain that he knew the party. This is where he mentioned Emma Musgrave [William Musgrave's mother] and Mary Feak [Matthew Feak's mother] as the owners of the evil box found in the tree. Joshua asked Dwyer if he found this when they cut the tree down. 'No,' he said, 'we found it the second day.' Joshua asked what was in it. Dwyer said, 'A dead rat with human hair,' and all sorts of stuff with it. Louis Gray, Dwyer said, had told him to cut the tree down. There were eight of us in the launch who heard the story. This is all I can remember."

Q. Who started the conversation?

A. I am not sure. I was at the stern of the boat when I heard Dwyer Green and Joshua Wells arguing over the question of this witchcraft.

Matthew Lawson (made the same evidence as last witness).

Dwyer Green, wishing to give evidence on his own behalf, was sworn:

"I laid this whole thing before Matthew Feak in his house, and I confessed to what I said on the launch. At the Nass I told Matthew everything of the conversation that was told here today. I didn't mean to say it. I said it as a joke, and I told Matthew Feak this. It was all right then between Matthew Feak and his wife. I shook hands with them and went out. The reason I went to Matthew Feak and his wife, I did not want the story spread around town, so I settled in between them. [Also saw Musgrave's mother and settled it, but William Musgrave told him it would depend on what the law said.]"

Louis Gray (Indian of Port Simpson), wishing to give evidence on his own behalf, was sworn:

"This is my first time in court in the town of Port Simpson. All the time I have been following religion. I did not see any evil box in the tree. I did not see Mary Feak or Emma Musgrave there through my medium while in the trance. You know why I am here. It is about this tree last year. About four weeks before the army came down from the Nass, while in a trance or dream, before the death of Henry Brentzen's son Johnny, I was called up by the Brentzens to their home to test him by the use of my powers as a medium. I placed my hand on his head, and four spirits came to me—two men and two women. I do not know who they were. It was not more than two minutes I saw them. This is where they told me that this tree should be cut down. They told me it was a tree where the trunk had been cut out. The spirits didn't say there was a box in the tree. They did not say that the evil box belonged to Mrs. Feak and Mrs. Musgrave. I did not work this out alone myself. I called Joseph Bradley in council, what was the meaning of this tree. The answer is there. Joseph said there must be a tree. Henry Brentzen called me up four times, and I saw the same thing four times. After the fourth time, the next day I talked it over with the Brentzens. I wanted to know the meaning of it. I asked Henry Brentzen if I could cut a tree down. I did not know if there was a box in the tree or not. All I saw was the tree when I was in my trance, and the names of the two women were never mentioned all the time we were talking of the tree or the evil box.

"We got to the foot of the tree. I asked Henry if it was the kind of tree I mentioned. The tree was leaning downhill. It was chopped out in the trunk. I asked Henry which way the tree was leaning, as twice I had told him in his house. Henry said it was the tree. We didn't see anyone around the tree or any evil box. The size of the tree was not fit for the ax Henry had brought along with him. The alder tree was too big. I mentioned that Dwyer Green had a long saw, so Dan Green and Hezekiah Wesley were called with him, because they were strong men and I wanted that tree to be cut down the same day so I would be in peace. I say again, I never mentioned the women's names or the evil box. Joseph Bradley called the men, and they cut the tree down. After the tree was down, I was out of it. The spirits hadn't given me any more instructions. I had done my duty. When the tree was felled, the men went up to the top of it, and this is where they found some mysterious-looking place where the boughs had been cut off. We thought this was where the witchcraft was practiced."

Cross-questioned by Provincial Constable Deane:

Q. Were you there when the dead rat was found the next day?

A. No. It was brought to me.

Q. Was there anything besides the dead rat?

A. There was something like two or three hairs inside this dead rat.

Q. Where did Hezekiah find the dead rat?

A. He said he found it inside the bark of the tree. He did not tell me if it was near where the boughs were cut.

Q. Have you seen these four spirits before?

A. Yes.

Q. Always the same four spirits?

A. Yes.

Q. Have they never told you what nationality they were?

A. No. It was when I was first sent up as a missionary to Ketseucla that I first saw lights. I prayed for God to open my eyes to show me things I didn't know. They gave me bylaws for Ketseucla, and I didn't know what to say. Mr. Crosby had told me to pray when I wanted to get things straight. It happened in Simpson when I first saw them [spirits]. I saw a kind of light, and before the death of a person I would see the light. Mrs. Welsk is the first person I heard crying before the death of Mrs. Welsk. I saw myself standing in two [duplicate]. I was face-to-face with myself. Then I saw the four spirits. They were singing in the native language. They were standing in the canyon of death. They did not say who was going to die, but the words meant someone was about to die. Two were men, and two were women. The men wore white men's pants and coat. They had a face like a human being, no mustache or whiskers. The two women had long hair hanging down their backs. They were middle-aged.

"I got five dollars from Mr. Brentzen for my services. I did not give Hezekiah a fungus when the tree was cut down. Mr. Brentzen called us into his place after the tree was cut down about dusk. He asked me if I could see or foresee anything in this tree. I said I couldn't say anything myself. Mrs. Brentzen went into another room and came out with a glass in her hand and placed it in front of me, saying she was glad to find out just the reason for the disease of their son. The four spirits came to me again, telling me not to move. I don't go into a kind of fit when I see the spirits. This is when the spirits told me there was a rat in the trunk of the tree. Mary's name, or Emma's, were not mentioned, or a box. I foresaw again a frog. This was not in the looking glass. I did not have hold of anything. I did not even have my eyes shut. Another thing I saw is a broken glass; the other was yellow.

Finally a voice came to me saying this glass was what they used as a dagger, but Emma's or Mary's name were not mentioned.

"I think Johnny Brentzen died of trouble in the throat, not by witchcraft. I have never seen a patient die by witchcraft. They spoke to me up at Nass about witchcraft, but I told them I would have nothing to do with it. I don't know what to call these spirits of mine. Joseph Bradley counsels with me about these spirits. He knows about old customs, not witchcraft. He knows about the old days ever since I was a small boy. I have heard of witchcraft, but I have not known of it being practiced at Port Simpson. Dwyer Green was lying when he said on oath that I told him Mary and Emma were practicing witchcraft. Sam Bennett found the frog I foresaw. It was in the tree above the twelve yards. The glass was never found. I am sure it was not inside Johnny. I could not look into his body."

Both found guilty and each fined ten dollars and costs or thirty days in jail.

A Witch Doctor Captured

(Brazil)

We called at the police office to look over the budget of an African conjurer just arrested. There was enough to load a cart: a large jar, concealed by skirts, constituted the body of the chief idol; two smaller ones were of wood, with jointed arms, their faces smeared with blood and feathers—a fowl being required of every inquirer; iron prongs and stone knives, used as sacrificial implements; goats' horns, ivory tusks, skeleton heads of animals, a string of jawbones, small boxes of colored dust, rattles, a ferule, bundles of herbs (one of rue), the scarlet cap and gown of the enchanter, and the curtain behind which he acted the part

From: Thomas Ewbank, *Life in Brazil; or, A Journal of a Visit to the Land of the Cocoa and the Palm* (New York: Harper & Brothers, 1856).

of a ventriloquist in raising spirits and conversing with them. Being a slave—a shrewd Minas—he is to be flogged. The justice says the apparatus of a wizard's den is known as a *Candomblé*, and that these fellows are successful in plundering slaves of their little savings and stimulating them to rob their owners. Besides furnishing harmless powders as love potions to ensure milder treatment, they sometimes give out ground glass and other noxious matters to be dropped in the master's food.

The Monchy Murder

(West Indies)

Most serious of the cases of Obeah in the British West Indies which have come under my notice is what is known as "The Monchy Murder"—the strangling and mutilation of a boy for purposes of Obeah, of which three men were convicted at St. Lucia, one of the Windward Islands, in 1904. This was indeed a serious relapse from the comparatively innocuous practices of the Obeah man in this part of the world, and may probably be accounted for by the comparatively short time that this French island has been brought under British domination, and by the fact that the crime was committed in a remote rural district and that the natives of the island still speak a French patois—a circumstance already noted by Dr. Earl in its application to the more serious cases of Obeah. Furthermore, the ringleader in the crime was shown to have been a resident in Haiti for some years, where in all probability he had been brought under the influence of voodoo worship, and whence he had brought back with him to St. Lucia the full equipment of an Obeah man.

The particulars of the case I have obtained from a reprint of the evidence at the trial, published at the office of a local newspaper, *The Voice of St. Lucia*, and though somewhat lengthy, are of considerable

From: J. S. Udal, "Obeah in the West Indies," *Folklore* 26 (1915): 255–95.

interest and afford perhaps the first instance of a crime of this nature being tried in an English court of justice and under a form of procedure which gives every assistance to the accused to establish their innocence.

On November 23, 1904, was commenced in the courthouse at Castries, before the chief justice of St. Lucia, the trial of three men named Montoute Edmond, St. Luce Leon, and Edgar St. Hill, all natives of the island, for the murder of a black boy named Rupert Mapp, aged about twelve years, a native of Barbados. The accused were tried separately and were separately defended, the attorney-general of St. Lucia prosecuting in each case. The evidence, as given by numerous witnesses, was much the same in each case. It appeared that the boy Rupert Mapp had been brought to St. Lucia from Barbados on September 28 under the pretense of employment as an errand boy by Montoute. On arrival at Castries he had been taken by Montoute, who was an elderly man, to the house of St. Luce Leon at Monchy, Gros Islet, some twelve miles northwest of Castries, situated in one of the most sparsely populated districts of St. Lucia.

St. Lucia, having only been finally ceded to Great Britain by the Treaty of Paris in 1814, its country inhabitants are mostly ignorant of the English language and only speak a French patois, which the boy Mapp, coming from the English-speaking colony of Barbados, did not understand. Monchy is not far from Dauphin, one of the old French capitals of St. Lucia, where it is said that the French Empress Josephine spent many years of her childhood, for her parents owned an estate at Chaubourg, in the vicinity, at which there is strong evidence to believe that she was born.

St. Luce Leon would appear to be a man of some substance and a typical landowner of his class, owning some five acres of land under cultivation with ordinary tropical produce. The usual practice of men of this class was to hoard their savings and to secrete them in nooks and crannies and in the thatch of their cottages. A fire, however, which had occurred to a neighbor, resulting in his house and all his belongings being totally destroyed, caused Leon to draw all his monies out of their hiding places and to make them up in numerous parcels, which he wrapped in leaves and packed amidst vegetables and fruit and sent in trays to his solicitor in Castries. This subsequently was found to exceed eight hundred pounds in gold and silver coins and colonial banknotes.

It appears that the boy was left by Montoute at Leon's house, but presently, presumably becoming alarmed at being by himself with a person whose language he did not understand, nor did they his, followed the track taken by Montoute and eventually overtook him, and was immediately brought back by him to the house. There, apparently, they all remained for the rest of the day, and being joined by St. Hill, who was considerably younger than the other two, they passed the night together there. The house ordinarily was only occupied by Leon, who also was an elderly man, living apart from his wife who dwelt in a cottage some little distance away with their daughter, which latter gave evidence at the trial as to the movements of the prisoner Montoute and her father on the day in question. This was the last occasion upon which the boy was seen alive.

What gave rise to suspicion of foul play with regard to the boy does not clearly appear from the evidence, but at all events a few days later a sergeant and corporal of police went to the house occupied by Leon, where he was seen with Montoute. The sergeant presently left the house for a few minutes, and on returning, was just in time to see Leon trying to steal out, carrying a tin pan with a lid over it. Upon his taking hold of it and removing the lid, it was found to contain two human hands, cut off at the wrist, and a heart. Upon subsequent search, the body of the boy was discovered in Leon's garden with the stomach cut open and the hands missing. Both men were thereupon arrested and brought into Castries.

Leon affected not to know the contents of what he was carrying and made charges implicating St. Hill, the youngest of the three prisoners. St. Hill was in consequence subsequently arrested upon the same charge, and at the preliminary inquiry before the magistrate he gave the whole thing away by stating how the boy had come by his death at their hands. This statement I give in his own words:

"On Thursday [September 29] about two o'clock [P.M.] I was at my house ready to dig manioc when Montoute arrived with the child. He told me St. Luce asked me to come to him, as he wished to speak with me. I remained talking awhile with Montoute. I reached St. Luce's house at the same time as Montoute did. When I got there St. Luce told me he wanted me to help him dig a hole. We remained there until sunset. After sunset Montoute said to St. Luce to look for a piece of rope for him. St. Luce went to his mill house and brought a long mahaut rope, from which Montoute cut with a knife the length he required. Whilst we were there in the afternoon St. Luce, in going to fetch canes for us to eat, had prepared the place where he wanted the hole dug. When it was time, St. Luce told me to come and dig the hole. We did so.

"When we returned to the house, we found Montoute and the boy asleep. St. Luce awoke Montoute and asked him if it was not yet time. Montoute said it was time—we must wake up the boy. Montoute awoke the boy. St. Luce asked Montoute if he had read the book again. Montoute said, 'Since I read it this morning I do not require to read it again.' Montoute said, 'Let's see what we have to do.' Montoute took the rope and made a knot in it. He said to me, 'Your hand is rougher; tighten it.'

"St. Luce took hold of the boy by both feet. Montoute closed the boy's mouth. We strangled him. We tied him up and took him to the place where we dug the hole. When we got there, Montoute took from his pocket a large knife. He held the knife out to me and asked me to cut the boy open. I refused. He then told St. Luce to open the boy. St. Luce opened him. Montoute gave the knife to St. Luce. The cut was not wide enough. Montoute tried to get his hand in but could not, so he cut the boy's chest further. Montoute was speaking English to the boy when he was closing his mouth at the house, but I do not understand what he said, for I do not understand English. When Montoute could get his hand inside, he felt about till he found the heart. When Montoute had taken out the heart, he cut the boy's two wrists. We buried the boy.

"Montoute said to St. Luce, 'Why did you not take the head, as you said you would, to bury in the mill?

"I said to St. Luce, 'No, you have committed one sin; that is enough.'

"Then St. Luce said, 'There is only a piece of new line wanting.'

"Then we went to the house. Montoute got St. Luce to pound some salt St. Luce had there. Montoute said to St. Luce he would send him some other stuff to sprinkle over it. Montoute told St. Luce he would procure him a new glove, and another for myself also. Montoute said that we should have to procure a piece of coffin pall. I said it would be difficult to do so. Montoute said he had already commissioned someone in Barbados to get a piece for him. While we were digging the hole—St. Luce and I—I asked him if he had known Montoute before he had gone from St. Lucia, and St. Luce replied that they had been comrades from the time they were boys. Up to now Montoute had not told us what he intended doing with the heart and hands. I don't think St. Luce himself knows up to now.

"They say that I alone killed the boy. I am not the only one. They could not have sat down there while I alone did the killing. If I had been the only one to do the killing, I would have carried 'the things' to my house. Up to now not even a crooked pin has been found at my house. The book was found on Montoute; the parts of the boy at St. Luce's house; nothing has been found on me or my place, so I cannot be the only one who killed the boy. St. Luce could not have sat down with Montoute while I alone killed the boy. We all three did it. That's all."

The simple directness of this horrible narrative could scarcely have failed to carry conviction of its truth; but at his trial, however, when he was defended by counsel, St. Hill repudiated what he had said before the magistrate, and stated before the court that Montoute had some time previously come to his house and had told him that he was going to give him something that would make him live more easily, and had said that he wanted him to go to Barbados and get two boys to give to the devil in order to get money from the bank; that he had indeed promised to go, as he was afraid of Montoute, but that he had really no intention of doing so; and that finally Montoute had gone himself. He now gave a very different account as to what had happened to the boy, and explained that on the 29th of September Montoute had come to his house with a little black boy, and had asked him to go with him to St. Luce's to hold a mesmeric séance in connection with St. Luce's hernia, as Montoute had used him as a medium in such séances. He stated that he had then gone to St. Luce's and that there Montoute had put him to sleep, and that on awakening him from his trance Montoute and St. Luce pointed to the ground inside the hut and told him to see what he had done. He was then aghast to see lying before him the body of the boy with his hands cut off and his chest opened, and not knowing what he might have done during his trance, and believing what they said, he carried out the body and buried it. Subsequently he had been seized with terror and, running away to the woods, had been arrested there by the police.

This very ingenious defense, based upon the theory of hypnotism, did not however commend itself to the jury, who had before them the statements made before the magistrate and which were confirmed by the medical evidence given at the trial in the person of the doctor who had been called by the police to examine the contents of a tin pan, which he said contained the two hands of a black child, also a human heart. The hands had been removed at the wrist joint very skillfully, apparently by a practiced hand. He had also examined the body of a black boy, about twelve years old, from which both hands were missing. The body had been laid open from the throat almost to the navel. The breastbone was missing, also the heart and left lung. The doctor also confirmed the statement that the boy had been strangled and stated that a strip of the shirt was wound tightly around the neck of the corpse. He also was of the opinion from their appearance that the hands had been removed before, or immediately after, death.

All three accused, after a short consideration of the verdicts, were found guilty by the respective juries and were executed amid general approval and satisfaction shortly afterward in the gaol at Castries.

The author of a little brochure on *Obeah*, which preceded the reprint of the evidence, in commenting upon the trial makes a distinct and very interesting reference to this book and says that "when Montoute Edmond was arrested at Monchy there was found in a blue bag which he carried about with him a book in which were copied in a good hand a great many formulas for attaining certain advantages or for bringing harm. The recipes, or formulas, were in many instances disgusting, in all ridiculous, but in every instance drawn up in fairly correct French. Among these is the formula of *La Main de Gloire*, which would seem to be the one which the Monchy murderers undertook to work out.

> Take the hand of one who has been hanged [or strangled], dry in the sun in the dog days [August, September, October], or, if the sun should not be hot enough to dry thoroughly and quickly, dry the hand in an oven. When thoroughly dry, sprinkle the hand with salt and a number of other ingredients [which are stated], and wrap it in a piece of coffin pall. Then make a taper of virgin wax, and anoint it with various fantastic oils and fats. Fix the taper between the fingers of the dried hand. The light of the taper will paralyze completely the faculties, both mental and physical, of anybody who comes within its influence.

"This formula," the author, who evidently speaks from firsthand knowledge, goes on to say, "as well as numerous others in the book, in which the grotesque and obscene jests jostle the horrible, is copied from a work titled *Petit Albert*, the pretended author of which is claimed to be a monkish occultist of the Middle Ages. The formulas are followed by prayers in barbarous Latin, which, it is claimed, have the virtue of neutralizing the baneful effects of the sorcery. This *Petit Albert* is a fairly rare and rather expensive book, published at Nantes, in France, and is well known in the French West Indian colonies and in Haiti. In it are contained the child murder formulas and the horrible recipes for hidden treasure, which has such an attraction for that very large class in these countries who wish to get money without working for it. The similarity of the procedure in all the cases which have come to light indicate a common origin in this pernicious volume."

The author then goes on to mention the case of one Adolphe Lacroix, who was executed in St. Lucia in 1876 for the murder of a dumb cripple, a boy of fifteen, whose body he had cruelly mutilated to obtain portions of it for purposes of Obeah. There was also found in the house of Lacroix a notebook belonging to him in which were found recipes for working spells which were known to be used in the practice of Obeah.

Bibliography

Africanus, " 'Mulombe': A Kaonde Superstition," *Journal of the African Society* 20 (1920–21): 43–45.

Anon., "The Vampire," reprinted from *The Theosophist* 12 (1891).

Anon. [des Niau], *Collectanea Adamantaea.—xxi., The History of the Devils of Loudun, the Alleged Possession of the Ursuline Nuns, and Trials and Execution of Urbain Grandier, Told by an Eye-Witness* (trans. and ed. Edmund Goldsmith), 3 vols. (Edinburgh: privately printed, 1887).

Batchelor, John, "Items of Ainu Folk-Lore," *Journal of American Folk-Lore* 7 (1894): 15–44.

Beauchamp, W. M., "The Great Mosquito," *Journal of American Folk-Lore* 2 (1889): 284.

Beauregard, Hon. H., "Folk-Lore Scrap-Book: Lutins in the Province of Quebec," *Journal of American Folk-Lore* 5 (1892): 327–38.

Bergen, Fanny D., "Notes and Queries: Louisiana Ghost Story," *Journal of American Folk-Lore* 12 (1899): 146–47.

Best, Elsdon, "Makutu or Maori Magic," *American Antiquarian and Oriental Journal* 21 (January–November 1899): 41–45.

Blake, Mary, "Notes and Queries: The Elves of Old Mexico," *Journal of American Folk-Lore* 27 (1914): 237–39.

Bleek, W. H. I., and L. C. Lloyd, *Specimens of Bushmen Folklore* (London: George Allen and Co., Ltd., 1911).

Boas, Franz, "Notes on Mexican Folk-Lore," *Journal of American Folk-Lore* 25 (1912): 204–60.

Brady, John G., "Witchcraft in Alaska," *The Independent* 57 (1904): 1498–99.

Brown, G.E.R. Grant, I.C.S., "Human Sacrifices Near the Upper Chindwin," *Burman Research Society's Journal* 1 (parts 1 and 2) (1911): 35–40.

Calmady-Hamlyn, Gerda M., "The Fakir and the Carpet: An Indian Story," *Occult Review* 29 (1919): 213–18.

Casanowicz, I. M., *Paraphernalia of a Korean Sorceress in United States National Museum* (Washington, DC: U.S. Government Printing Office, 1916).

Cox, Katherine, "Wilhelm II and the White Lady of the Hohenzollerns," *Occult Review* 25 (1917): 17–22.

Coyne, James H., "David Ramsay and Long Point in Legend and History," *Proceedings and Transactions of the Royal Society of Canada* (series 3) 13 (May 1919): 111–26.

Currier, John McNab, "Contributions to the Folk-Lore of New England," *Journal of American Folk-Lore* 2 (1889): 291–94.

D. M., *A Full and True Relation of the Tryal, Condemnation and Execution of Ann Foster* (Northampton: Taylor & Sons, 1878, reprint).

d'Assier, Adophe, *Posthumous Humanity: A Study of Phantoms* (with an appendix of beliefs current in India) (London: George Redway, 1887).

de Groot, Jan J., *Religious Systems of China*, vol. 4, book 2, parts 1 and 2 (Leide: E. J. Brill, 1907).

de Groot, Jan J., *Religious Systems of China*, vol. 5, book 2, parts 2 and 3 (Leide: E. J. Brill, 1907).

"Demoniacal Possession in Angola, Africa (attributed to Heli Chatelain)," *Journal of American Folk-Lore* 6 (1893): 258.

Dennis, Albert W., "Witchcraft Not Extinct," *Massachusetts Magazine* 9:4 (October 16, 1916), 184–88.

Dorsey, George A., "The Ocimbanda, or Witch-Doctor of the Ovimbundu of Portuguese Southwest Africa," *Journal of American Folk-Lore* 12 (1899): 183–88.

Eardley-Wilmot, S., "The Supernatural in India," *Occult Review* 8 (July–December 1908): 151–60.

Espinosa, Aurelio M., "New-Mexico Spanish Folk-Lore," *Journal of American Folk-Lore* 23 (1910): 395–418.

Evans, Oswald H., "Witchcraft in Chile," *Chambers's Journal* 11 (1921): 380–83.

Ewbank, Thomas, *Life in Brazil; or, A Journal of a Visit to the Land of the Cocoa and the Palm* (New York: Harper & Brothers, 1856).

Fielde, Adele M., "The Character of Chinese Folk-Tales," *Journal of American Folk-Lore* 8 (1895): 185–91.

"Folk-Lore Scrap-Book: Beliefs of Southern Negroes Concerning Hags," *Journal of American Folk-Lore* 7 (1894): 66–67.

"Folk-Lore Scrap-Book: Cures by Conjure Doctors," *Journal of American Folk-Lore* 12 (1899): 288–89.

"Folk-Lore Scrap-Book: The Devil Bush of West Africa," *Journal of American Folk-Lore* 9 (1896): 220–22.

"Folk-Lore Scrap-Book: Ghosts as Guardians of Hidden Treasure," *Journal of American Folk-Lore* 12 (1899): 64–65.

"Folk-Lore Scrap-Book: Superstitions in Newfoundland," *Journal of American Folk-Lore* 9 (1896): 222–32.

Fox, C. Milligan, "The Haunted Villa: A True Story," *Occult Review* 11 (1910): 158–60.

Fraser, C. A., "Scottish Myths from Ontario," *Journal of American Folk-Lore* 6 (1893): 185–98.

Gardner, Fletcher, "Phillipine (Tagalog) Superstitions," *Journal of American Folk-Lore* 19 (1906): 191–204.

Garnett, Lucy Mary Jane, *The Women of Turkey and Their Folk-Lore: The Jewish Women*, parts 1 and 2 (London: David Nutt, 1891).

Gay, Arthur, "Witches' Unguents," *Occult Review* 15 (1912): 207–9.

Hahn, F., "Some Notes on the Religion and Superstitions of the Orao," *Journal of the Asiatic Society of Bengal* 72 (part 3, nos. 1 and 2) (1903): 12–19.

Hamel, Frank, *Human Animals* (New York: Frederick A. Stokes Co., 1916).

Hartman, C. V., "Mythology of the Aztecs of Salvador," *Journal of American Folk-Lore* 20 (1907): 143–47.

Hartmann, Franz, "Witchcraft in Germany," *Occult Review* 3 (January–June 1906): 237–39.

Hartmann, Franz, M.D., "An Authenticated Vampire Story," *Occult Review* 10 (July–December 1909): 144–49.

Hearn, Lafcadio, "The Story of a Tengu," *In Ghostly Japan* (Boston: Little, Brown & Co., 1899), 215–21.

Hearn, Lafcadio, and staff of New Orleans Press, *Historical Sketch Book and Guide to New Orleans and Environs* (New York: Will H. Coleman, 1885).

Hodder, Reginald, "Maori Magic," *Occult Review* 4 (1906): 303–8.

Hodder, Reginald, "Vampires," *Occult Review* 19 (1914): 223–29.

Ingram, M. V., *An Authenticated History of the Famous Bell Witch* (Nashville, TN: William P. Titus, 1894).

Janvier, Thomas A., ed., *Legends of the City of Mexico* (New York and London: Harper & Brothers, 1910).

Jarvis, A. W., "The Weird-Wailing Banshee," *The English Illustrated Magazine* 35 (1906): 97–102.

Joly, Henri L., "Bakemono," *Transactions and Proceedings of the Japan Society* 9 (1909–11): 15–48.

Jones, Mrs. Frank Currer, "Does Egyptian Magic Still Exist?" *Occult Review* 15 (1912): 270–76.

Judd, A. M., "Curious Forms of Worship: Devil-Worshippers," *Occult Review* 11 (1910): 250–57.

Judson, Katharine B.; *Myths and Legends of the Great Plains* (Chicago: A. C. McClurg & Co., 1913).

Krug, Adolph N., "Bulu Tales from Kamerun, West Africa," *Journal of American Folk-Lore* 25 (1912): 106–24.

Leland, Charles Godfrey, *Etruscan Roman Remains in Popular Tradition*, (New York: Charles Scribner's Sons, 1892).

Leonard, Arthur Glyn, "Southern Nigeria: Religion and Witchcraft," *Imperial and Asiatic Quarterly Review* (series 3) 23 (1907): 279–311.

Lewes, M. L., "Corpse-Candles and the *Teulu*," *Occult Review* 8 (July–December 1908): 75–78.

Loloma (pseud.), "Fijian Witchcraft," *Occult Review* 28 (1918): 213–14.

MacLeod, Philip, "The Fiery Man," *Occult Review* 21 (1915): 286–88.

MacLeod, Philip, "The Precolitsch," *Occult Review* 29 (1919): 156–59.

MacLeod, Philip, "Why the Hunting-Lodge at Griesheim Was Pulled Down: A True Story," *Occult Review* 18 (1913): 86–90.

Mather, Cotton, "A Brand Pluck'd Out of the Burning" (1693). In George Lincoln Burr (ed.), *Narratives of the Witchcraft Cases, 1648–1706* (New York: Charles Scribner's Sons, 1914).

Mather, Cotton, "The Wonders of the Invisible World" (1693). In George Lincoln Burr (ed.), *Narratives of the Witchcraft Cases, 1648–1706* (New York: Charles Scribner's Sons, 1914).

Maxfield, Berton L., and W. H. Millington, "Philippine (Visayan) Superstitions" *Journal of American Folk-Lore* 19 (1906): 205–11.

Maxfield, Berton L., and W. H. Millington, "Visayan Folk-Tales: 1," *Journal of American Folk-Lore* 19 (1906): 97–112.

Millet, John, *The Rest-less Ghost; or, Wonderful News from Northampton-shire and Southwark* (Northampton: Taylor & Son, 1878, reprint).

Milward, Virginia, "The Comte de St. Germain," *Occult Review* 15 (1912): 284–88.

Morrison, David Gordon, "How Warts Were Mysteriously Removed from the Hands," *Occult Review* 15 (1915): 31–34.

Nassau, Robert Hamill, *Fetichism in West Africa* (New York: Charles Scribner's Sons, 1904).

Newell, William W., "Myths of Voodoo Worship and Child Sacrifice in Hayti," *Journal of American Folk-Lore* 1 (1888): 16–30.

"Notes and Queries: Indian Witchcraft," *Journal of American Folk-Lore* 34 (1921): 390–92.

Oman, John Campbell, *Cults, Customs, and Superstitions of India* (London: T. Fisher Unwin, 1908).

O'Leary, Maurice McCarthy, "Notes and Queries: Certain Irish Superstitions," *Journal of American Folk-Lore* 10–11 (1897–98): 234–37.

Oyler, D. S., "The Shilluk's Belief in the Evil Eye: The Evil Medicine Man," *Sudan Notes and Records*, vol. 2 (Cairo: French Institute of Oriental Archaeology, 1919).

Patterson, George, "Notes on the Folk-Lore of Newfoundland," *Journal of American Folk-Lore* 8 (1895): 285–90.

Proudfit, S. V., "Notes and Queries: The Hobyahs—A Scotch Nursery Tale," *Journal of American Folk-Lore* 4 (1891): 173–74.

Raines, Thomas Hart, "A Poltergeist from Georgia," *Occult Review* 13 (1911): 276–79.

Roamer, A. (pseud.), "Spirit Lights and Spirit Voices," *Occult Review* 23 (1918): 136–46.

Rohmer, Sax, *The Romance of Sorcery* (New York: Dutton, 1912).

Santos, Simon P., "Notes and Queries: The Man-Eater," *Journal of American Folk-Lore* 34 (1921): 393–95.

Seip, Elisabeth Cloud, "Witch-Finding in Western Maryland," *Journal of American Folk-Lore* 14 (1901): 39–44.

Seymour, St. John D., *Irish Witchcraft and Demonology* (Dublin: Hodges, Figgis & Co., Ltd.).

Shirley, Ralph, "Count Cagliostro," *Occultists & Mysteries of All Ages* (London: William Rider & Son, Ltd., 1920), 120–44.

Shortt, Vere D., "Two Experiences," *Occult Review* 29 (1919): 214–17.

Skeat, Walter William, *Malay Magic* (London: Macmillan & Co., 1900).

Span, Reginald B., "More Glimpses of the Unseen," *Occult Review* 4 (July–December 1906): 145–51.

Spence, Lewis, "The Familiar: Its Nature and Origin," *Occult Review* 30 (1919): 130–37.

Stuart-Young, John M., "Nigerian Supernaturalism," parts 1 and 2, *Occult Review* 31 (1920): 138–203.

Sunder, D., "Exorcism of Wild Animals in the Sundarbans," *Journal of the Asiatic Society of Bengal* 72 (part 3, Anthropology and Cognate Subjects, no. 2) (1903): 45–52.

Talbot, P. Amaury, "Through the Land of Witchcraft," parts 1–4, *Wide World Magazine* 31 (1913): 134–515.

Theal, George McCall, *The Yellow and Dark-Skinned People of Africa South of the Zambesi* (London: Swan Sonnenschein & Co., Ltd., 1910).

Thomas, Northcote W., "A Javanese Poltergeist," *Occult Review* 2 (1905): 223–28.

Tin, Maung, "Burmese Ghost Stories," *Burma Research Society's Journal* 3 (part 2) (1913): 183–85.

Tremearne, A. J. N., *The Ban of the Bori: Demons and Demon-Dancing in West and North Africa* (London: Heath, Cranton & Ousely Ltd., 1914).

Udal, J. S., "Obeah in the West Indies," *Folklore* 26 (1915): 255–95.

Wall, James Charles, *Devils* (London: Methuen & Co., 1904), 107–18.

Warner, Irene E. Toye, ed., "Black Magic and Voodooism in America," *Occult Review* 21 (1915): 21–26.

Warner, Irene E. Toye, ed., "Black Magic in Ancient and Modern Egypt," *Occult Review* 23 (1916): 138–45.

Warner, Irene E. Toye, ed., "Black Magic in South Africa," *Occult Review* 20 (1914): 210–17.

Warner, Irene E. Toye, ed., "Voodooism on the West Coast of Africa: Narratives by an Eye-Witness," *Occult Review* 20 (1914): 143–50.

White, George E., "Evil Spirits and the Evil Eye in Turkish Lore," *Moselm World* 9 (1919): 179–86.

White, George E., "Saint Worship in Turkey," *Moslem World* 9 (1919): 8–18.

Williams, E. T., "Witchcraft in the Chinese Penal Code," *Journal of the North China Branch of the Royal Asiatic Society* 37 (1906): 61–96.

Wintemberg, W. J., "French Canadian Folk-Tales," *Journal of American Folk-Lore* 17 (1904): 265–67.

Wintemberg, W. J., "German Folk-Tales Collected in Canada," *Journal of American Folk-Lore* 19 (1906): 241–44.

Young, H. Mayne, "The Bijli of the Flaming Torch," *Occult Review* 4 (1906): 269–72.

Zuresta, "A Weird Experience," *Occult Review* 8 (July–December 1908): 103–5.